G

VIETNAM

MICHELIN
Travel Publications

Note to readers

Vietnam is divided into regions. Itineraries, illustrated by maps, will help you plan excursions off the beaten track and the ■ symbol indicates possible overnight stops. The itinerary map on pages 120-121 will help you organise your trip depending on the number of days you have available.

The **Practical Information** section supplies general information you may want to consult when planning your visit. The **Exploring Vietnam** section provides descriptions of each town, site or itinerary, followed by practical details about the place: access, useful addresses, accommodation, restaurants, leisure, shopping, etc. Places to eat, services and shopping ideas are indicated in local currency, while hotels are ranked by price in US dollars. Bear in mind that living costs vary constantly, that opening times are subject to modification, and that the practical information given in the guide may well have changed since publication.

The local names of places or sites of interest are indicated on regional **maps**, but town maps are often also in English to facilitate understanding. The inside rear cover provides a list of local terms commonly found on maps.

Michelin Travel Publications
Published in 2002

◄NE◉S►

N ew – In the NEOS guides emphasis is placed on the discovery and enjoyment of a new destination through meeting the people, tasting the food and absorbing the exotic atmosphere. In addition to recommendations on which sights to see, we give details on the most suitable places to stay and eat, on what to look out for in traditional markets and where to go in search of the hidden character of the region, its crafts and its dancing rhythms. For those keen to explore places on foot, we provide guidelines and useful addresses in order to help organise walks to suit all tastes.

E xpert – The NEOS guides are written by people who have travelled in the country and researched the sites before recommending them by the allocation of stars. Accommodation and restaurants are similarly recommended by a 🏠 on the grounds of quality and value for money. Cartographers have drawn easy-to-use maps with clearly marked itineraries, as well as detailed plans of towns, archaeological sites and large museums.

◉ pen to all cultures, the NEOS guides provide an insight into the daily lives of the local people. In a world that is becoming ever more accessible, it is vital that religious practices, regional etiquette, traditional customs and languages be understood and respected by all travellers. Equipped with this knowledge, visitors can seek to share and enjoy with confidence the best of the local cuisine, musical harmonies and the skills involved in the production of arts and crafts.

S ensitive to the atmosphere and heritage of a foreign land, the NEOS guides encourage travellers to see, hear, smell and feel a country, through words and images. Take inspiration from the enthusiasm of our experienced travel writers and make this a journey full of discovery and enchantment.

Exploring Vietnam

VIETNAM

H Choimet/MICHELIN

Official name: Socialist Republic of Vietnam
Area: 331 000km²
Population: 77 562 000
Capital: Hanoi
Currency: the dong (VND)

Setting the scene

Halong Bay

A TROPICAL EDEN

Located at the crossroads of southern and eastern Asia, on the trade routes between Europe and the Far East, Vietnam hugs the coastline of the South China Sea like a long winding snake. It stretches for 1 650km from north to south while its width varies from 540km at the Red River Delta to just 50km around the town of Da Nang. With a surface area of 331 000km², equivalent to that of Malaysia, Vietnam ranks among the region's middle-weights, compared to heavy-weights such as Thailand, Burma, Indonesia and above all China, a powerful neighbour with whom it shares 1 281km of border. Only its two western neighbours, Laos (1 555km border) and Cambodia (982km border) are smaller in size. Wounded by its recent past and subjected to severe demographic pressure, the country is now facing the new challenge of successfully administering its territory and natural resources.

Recently achieved geographical unity

The creation of the Vietnam we know today was the result of a long historical process which began when the Viet of the Red River Delta broke free of Chinese dominance (*see page 20*). From the 11C, they embarked upon a slow **March southwards** (*Nam Tien*), absorbing the Cham, whose kingdom extended as far as the centre of the country and then the Khmer who controlled the Mekong Delta. The nation's current boundaries date more or less from the 18C, even if some territories continue to be contested. This was the case at the Cambodian frontier, where skirmishes with the Pol Pot regime in the late 1970s were essentially motivated by boundary disagreements. The issue of ownership of Phu Quoc Island and its territorial waters is no longer disputed but a definitive treaty has yet to be signed. The status of the Paracel and Spratly Islands is even more complex.

The Paracels and Spratlys – archipelagos of discord

These two archipelagos in the South China Sea are among the few territories in the world whose sovereignty has yet to be attributed and recognised internationally. Located in the Gulf of Tonkin, 400km from Da Nang and 300km from the Chinese island of Hainan, ownership of the 1 300 islets of the Paracels is hotly disputed by China and Vietnam, both of whom brandish legal and archaeological arguments to support their case. The navies of both countries have already clashed here, but since 1974, only Peking has maintained a military presence. The situation of the 33 Spratly islets (180 000km²) is even more complex. Lying 450km off the Vietnamese coast, 500km from Brunei, the Philippines and Malaysia, 1 100km from China and 1 700 from Taiwan, they are claimed by all these countries. The islands' strategic position on trade routes and, above all, their maritime oil reserves are responsible for the attempts by each nation to retain a foothold, pending a definitive agreement.

An unusual geology

From a geological point of view, the **karstic formations** which occur from one end of the country to the other, are one of Vietnam's distinctive features. They are eroded limestone massifs through which seeping water has, over time, created a network of caves and caverns linked by underground rivers. The most famous is undeniably that of Halong Bay, a former plateau flooded by water from the South China Sea, dotted with a number of small, almost artificial looking, islets. Further north, the Bay of Bai Tu Long reveals the same characteristics, while "Halong Bay without the water" at Tam Coc, has remained above ground. Other similar examples of such karstic formations can be found in the Mekong Delta, near Ha Tien, Chau Doc and Tay Ninh, as well as at Da Nang, where the famous Marble Mountains are located.

However, most of the country along the coast, particularly the Hai Van Pass, is formed of **granite**. In the Central Highlands (near Buon Ma Thuot and Pleiku) and to the north of Ho Chi Minh City (near Dinh Quan), small extinct **volcanoes** can be seen dotted around the countryside to the delight of the peasants who farm the particularly fertile surrounding land. Vietnam is nonetheless a country which is relatively undisturbed by volcanic activity, although minor earthquakes do occasionally occur.

Mountains and water

The country is divided into three distinct geographical zones, **Bac Bo** (north), **Trung Bo** (centre) and **Nam Bo** (south). These zones roughly correspond to the administrative division set up by the French during the colonial period (Tonkin, Annam and Cochinchina) and together make up an extraordinarily varied landscape.

On the shores of the South China Sea
Stretching for over 3 260km, the country's coastline mostly overlooks the **South China Sea**, but the Mekong Delta also drains into the **Gulf of Thailand**. Despite this extensive coast, the country possesses relatively few large islands, with the exception of Phu Quoc, the archipelago of Con Dao, Bamboo (Hon Tre) Island (near Nha Trang) and those of Cat Ba, Van Don and Ban Sen in the area of Halong Bay.

The deltas
The majority of the country's population and wealth is concentrated in two vast and fertile basins. To the north, the **Red River Delta** (15 000km²), the cradle of Vietnamese civilisation, encroaches year by year into the South China Sea thanks to the sediments left by the river's waters. An identical phenomenon occurs to the south in the **Mekong Delta** (60 000km²), parts of which are extending seawards by up to 80m a year. Silt has also raised the level of the two rivers which flow in the neighbouring plains. This led to the canalisation of the Red River by thousands of kilometres of dikes, the target of US bomb attacks during the war. During the monsoon season, torrential rainfall regularly causes flooding and terrible hardship. In November 2000, flooding in the Mekong Delta was responsible for hundreds of deaths and forced several thousand peasants to flee their homes. Such heavily-populated, low-altitude tropical zones are felt to be particularly at risk by the rise in the sea level due to global warming.

On the road to Dien Bien Phu

R. Mattès/MICHELIN

The Mekong, "mother of rivers"

The 4 200km-long Mekong was first explored (1866-68) by a Frenchman, Francis Garnier, who was looking (in vain) for a route into China. In 1995, an Anglo-French expedition discovered its source at the Rup-Sa Pass on the Tibetan plateau. This link between China, Burma, Laos, Thailand, Cambodia and Vietnam was for a long time to exacerbate tensions among them, rather than serve as an axis for development. The river, which can only be navigated as far as the Khone Falls, is essential to the region's ecological and economic balance and at the heart of an immense hydrographical basin. To irrigate, prevent flooding and produce electricity, the Mekong Commission, comprising the four Indochinese nations, has revived the concept of building dams on its lower stretches, despite the fact that their environmental impact is a cause of growing anxiety.

Mountains and rivers

Two-thirds of Vietnam is covered by hills and **mountains**, but its highest peak, **Fan Si Pan**, near Sapa, only rises to 3 143m. It is part of the **Hoang Lien Son Range** of mountains which runs along almost the entire length of the Chinese border. The other major mountain range is the **Truong Son Cordillera** (previously known as the Annamese Cordillera) which stretches for 1 200km from Laos in the north as far as the Central Highlands. It is a medium-altitude range, which begins in fact in the foothills of Tibet and whose highest peak is **Mt Ngoc Linh** (2 598m).

The country is thus heavily partitioned in comparison with its neighbours and split into a multitude of little valleys through which **rivers** run. To the north, the **Song Da** (Black River) and the **Song Bach Dang** (Clear River), which flow into the Red River, open up the way into China, while to the south, the source of the **Song Ma** lies in Laos. Central Vietnam also has its fair share of waterways, including the **Song Ca**, which finishes at Vinh, the **Song Xe Pon** which enters Laos near the Lao Bao Pass and the **Da Rang** which descends from around Pleiku towards Tuy Hoa. Finally, to the south, the **Dong Nai** rises near Da Lat before emptying into the **River Saigon** which supplies the sprawling southern metropolis.

A lavish but capricious climate

Although Mother Nature may have endowed Vietnam with particularly rich alluvial soils and a dense hydrographical network, such generosity is tempered by regular storms and severe flooding.

Vietnam is located in a region with a **tropical** and a **subtropical climate** and is exposed to the monsoons of eastern Asia, which bring with them high rates of rain and sunshine. The country lies between 8° and 23° north of the equator, but is host to a wide variety of climates, further exaggerated by its topography. Nothing could be further from the freezing temperatures some northern mountain villages experience in the winter, than the torrid year-long heat of the Mekong Delta. Although Hanoi enjoys an average yearly temperature of 23°C, summer highs of 35°C and winter lows of 11°C are quite common, while in Ho Chi Minh City, the thermometer only rarely climbs higher than 26°C.

To the **north** of Da Nang there are two quite distinct seasons. From November to April, the northeastern monsoon makes the winters mild (16°C on average), even cold up in the mountains, where daily drizzles are frequent. Sudden bursts of sunshine sometimes light up the monotonous cloudy skies in February and March. After a transition period, summer arrives and lasts from July to November, accompanied by torrential downpours. The average temperature is over 30°C from June to August. Towards late summer, violent typhoons occasionally wreak havoc in the region.

The **centre** of the country enjoys an intermediate climate, with frequent rainfall all year long even during the brief dry season from February to April, particularly around Hue, where the nation's highest rainfall is recorded (3 250mm per annum).

In the **south**, the seasons vary more in terms of rainfall than in temperature. From April-May to October the southwestern monsoon brings winds laden with rain, with maximum monthly rainfall of over 400mm from July to September. The driest season

Landscapes

FLORA

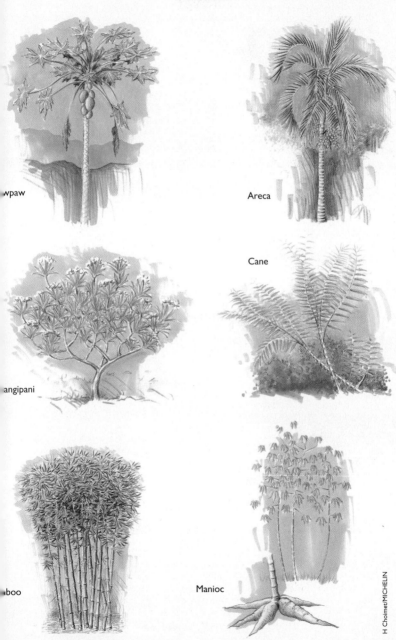

wpaw

Areca

Cane

angipani

boo

Manioc

FRUIT

Mangosteen

Durian

Star fruit

Litchi

Longan

Custard apple

H Choimer/MICHELIN

lasts from December to April. Temperatures range from 27 to 31°C, with peaks of 35°C from March to May. Typhoons sometimes swoop over the coast of the South China Sea in November.

In comparison the Highlands are favoured with a temperate climate and temperatures rarely rise above 26°C, but are much lower in the winter from October to March, when they have been known to drop below 4°C.

A rich but ravaged nature

Despite the ravages of the war and rampant deforestation, Vietnam still has some extraordinary primeval forests which shelter an exceptional wildlife.

Primeval forests the size of a handkerchief

Vietnam was originally almost entirely covered in forests, from the northern temperate mountains to its southern subtropical plains. **Deforestation**, a phenomenon as old as humankind itself, moved into top gear at the time of the colonial period and continued apace after 1945, even increasing after 1975. Heavy **demographic pressure** has led central government to encourage the population to migrate towards the sparsely inhabited regions of the Highlands, where tea, coffee and cocoa plantations are gradually eating away the natural forests. Crops grown on slash-and-burn land and trees felled for fuel further accentuate the phenomenon. A project adopted in April 2000, which is designed to reafforest some 5 million hectares by 2010, should increase the percentage of forest from 30% to 43%, at an estimated cost of US$4.5 billion.

Endangered wildlife

Vietnam nonetheless remains a remarkable sanctuary and possesses a great many species of birds (770), mammals (280), reptiles (130), amphibians (80) and fish (2 500). Even more astounding is the fact that scientists have recently discovered as yet unknown mammals in a region bordering Laos, such as the **saola** (or Vu Quang buffalo) and the **giant muntjac** (a deer of Southeast Asia), together with a number of species of birds.

However, numerous species are threatened with extinction, partly by poachers seeking to supply the traditional pharmacopoeia, but most of them suffer from the disappearance of their natural habitat. Although the tapir would already appear to have become extinct, the rare **Java rhinoceros**, previously only sighted in western Java, has been seen in the National Park of Nam Cat Tien, together with specimens of **kouprey**. In 1994, Vietnam signed an international convention outlawing trade in endangered species, including animals such as the **elephant**, **tiger**, leopard, black bear, stag, rhesus monkey, banteng buffalo, **royal cobra**, tortoises and crocodiles. Birds have suffered less than mammals from war and deforestation, with the notable exception of the **Mekong crane**, which was reintroduced after the war. In all, **87 nature reserves**, covering 3.3% of the country, have been established, many along the frontier with Laos.

The war's ecocide

Invented during the Vietnam War, the term "ecocide" refers to the impact of the American bombing on the environment. In addition to napalm bombs, there was much use of defoliants including the notorious Agent Orange. Between 40 and 100 million litres of this powerful poison, containing dioxin, which remains active for 8 to 10 years, were sprayed over the countryside from 1962 to 1970. Nearly one-quarter of the forests and half the mangrove swamps were destroyed, wreaking irreparable destruction on the flora and fauna. In the south, the deluge of fire resulted in lasting impoverishment of the soil and a fall in productivity. The American army also took the trouble to plant a kind of grass which catches fire very easily. Major work has been carried out to replant the forests, but the effects of the war continue to be felt. One still comes across unexploded bombs and mines. Erosion, landslides and silting up of rivers and streams are also in evidence.

Prior to Dai Viet (2000 BC-939 AD)

10C-2C BC	The Bronze Age and the Dong Son civilisation.
111 BC	Annexed by China up to the Pass of Clouds, Vietnam belonged to the Chinese Empire until 938, under a variety of names.
2C AD	First reference in Chinese documents to an Indianised kingdom, Lin Yi, subsequently the Champa kingdom.
43 AD	The Chinese general, Ma Yuan crushes the revolt of the Trung sisters.
3-6C	Introduction and spread of Buddhism.
380-413	Reign of Bhadravarman I, builder of the first temple at My Son.
875-975	Buddhist interlude in the Champa kingdom.
939	The land of the Viet is freed by Ngo Quyen.

From Hoa Lu to Hue (939-1858)

939-1009	First national Ngo, Dinh and Earlier Le dynasties.
982	The Cham move their capital from Indrapura to Vijaya (Binh Dinh). Now called Dai Viet, the country becomes unified around the Ly dynasty. The capital is established at Thang Long (Hanoi) in 1010.
1069	The Cham lose their northern territories to the Ly.
1123-28	Wars between Champa and Angkor and the Khmer and Dai Viet.
1371-90	Victories of the Cham king, Che Bong Nga, in the Red River Delta.
1413-28	Chinese domination of Dai Viet.
1418-28	Le Loi's guerilla tactics lead to renewed independence.
1428-1527	Golden age of Vietnam.
1471	After their capital is stormed, the Cham lose Amaravati.
1558	The independent Nguyen lords dominate the south.
1687	Phu Xuan (Hue) becomes the capital of the Nguyen lords.
1771-92	Revolt, followed by the reign of the Tay Son brothers.
1802	Advent of Gia Long who founds the Nguyen dynasty and the Vietnamese Empire.

From Indochina to Vietnam (1858 to the present day)

1858	The French seize Da Nang, then Saigon (1859).
1862-69	Cochinchina becomes a French colony, followed by the Protectorates of Tonkin and Annam (1883).
1887	Creation of the Indochinese Union.
1940-45	Indochinese Federation during the Japanese occupation.
1941	Ho Chi Minh founds the Alliance for the Independence of Vietnam (Viet Minh) and establishes his freedom fighters in the province of Cao Bang.
1945	Ho Chi Minh proclaims the Democratic Republic of Vietnam (DRV).
1946-54	Indochina War.
1954	Fall of Dien Bien Phu, Geneva Conference and division into North (DRV) and South (RV) Vietnam on either side of the 17th Parallel.
1959	Establishment of the Ho Chi Minh Trail.
1960	Foundation of National Liberation Front (Viet Cong) in the south.
1961	First military envoys sent by President Kennedy.
1964-75	Vietnam War.
1965	President Johnson bombs North Vietnam.
1968	Giap launches the Tet offensive.
1972	Easter offensive and negotiations between Kissinger and Le Duc Tho.
1975	Fall of Saigon on 30 April. The Americans evacuate 150 000 South Vietnamese. The reunified country becomes the Socialist Republic of Vietnam (SRV). The first boat people flee the country.
1978	Vietnamese troops invade Cambodia.
1979	Chinese troops occupy part of northern Vietnam.
1986	Launch of the economic "Doi Moi" reform programme.
1987	Vietnam begins to receive tourists.
1994	The American embargo is lifted and diplomatic relations re-established with Washington (1995).
1995	Vietnam enters ASEAN.
2000	Official visit of President Bill Clinton.

FOUR THOUSAND YEARS OF MIGRATION

At the crossroads of the Chinese, Malaysian and Indian worlds, Vietnam could only forge its identity by breaking free of its Chinese shackles and nurturing its own heritage. One of the most notable characteristics of Vietnam's history is its constantly evolving geographical boundaries. Born in the north, in the Red River Delta which was the cradle of the Viet, by 1802 the country had gained the shape which it was to reclaim on its reunification in 1975. Like silkworms relentlessly nibbling on their mulberry leaves – in the words of a 19C mandarin – little by little the Vietnamese expanded southwards, inching their way along the mountain ridge of the Annamese Cordillera, swallowing up the rice paddies of the centre in the 15C and the Mekong Delta in the 17C.

On the borders of the Chinese world

Legendary origins
Every year, on the 10th day of the 3rd lunar month, many Vietnamese embark on a pilgrimage to Mt Hung, at Co Tich (80km to the north of Hanoi) in an effort to recapture their long history. Four thousand years ago this mountain was the seat of their very first sovereigns, the **eighteen Hung kings**, descendants of the union of a dragon and an immortal woman (*see page 50*). At the time the country was known as **Van Lang**. Historically and archaeologically speaking, this myth dates back to a Bronze Age beginning in the late 2nd millennium BC and continuing beyond the 7C, in the Dong Son civilisation (Thanh Hoa province). It was this civilisation which, at the same time as the emergence of ironworking, saw the appearance of the bronze drum, an object commonly found up until the mid-20C over an area stretching from southern China as far as eastern Indonesia. The carved scenes on these instruments depict the daily life of rice farmers and part-time fishermen, who lived in stilt-houses.

In 257 BC, a rival kingdom, **Au Lac**, seized the Van Lang Empire. Again according to legend, its capital, Co Loa, was built on the advice of a spirit, the Golden Tortoise, who entrusted the sovereign with the gift of one of its claws to be mounted on a crossbow. Some fifty years later, **Nam Viet**, a kingdom of southern China, only managed to invade Au Lac at the price of the lives of numerous soldiers who were killed by the well-aimed arrows of the enemy archers. Archaeological excavations at the Co Loa site have revealed several thousand arrow tips. However, some 2 000 years ago, the major power of China which had emerged towards the end of the 3C BC had no trouble in gobbling up all these little States. In 111 BC the region was annexed as far as the Pass of Clouds and, for 1 000 years, was to remain a **Protectorate of the Empire**.

The everlasting revenge of water
At the time of the Hung kings, Vietnam's ancestors colonised the Red River Delta and discovered that the river could be as bountiful as it could be merciless. Such was the legend of Son Tinh and Thuy Tin. The 18th Hung king was seeking a worthy suitor for his daughter, but the list was soon reduced to two rivals: Son Tinh, the Mountain Spirit and Thuy Tin, the Water Spirit. The former obtained the king's permission by amassing in a single night a stupendous array of gifts, ranging from nine-tusked elephants, fighting cocks in armour to pitchers overflowing with pearls. These fabulous presents enabled him to whisk the princess away to his mountain retreat, Tan Vien. Blinded by jealousy, Thuy Tin whipped up a tempest of winds, tides and monsters against the mountain. But it was in vain, and so furious, he withdrew vowing to take his revenge. And ever since, once a year the river, swollen with the summer monsoon rains, attempts to destroy all in its course.

A far-flung territory of the Chinese Empire

Although China's presence remained discreet until the 1C, this ceased when the Empire sought to implement the rigid policy it inevitably extended to all its conquered territories. Thousands of Chinese subjects were deported to cultivate these new lands. The descendants of the Hung kings failed to take such intentions kindly. A wave of revolts shook the south of the Empire, from Canton to Vietnam, soon led by two sisters, **Trung Trac** and **Trung Nhi**. China then despatched General Ma Yuan to crush the revolt in 43 AD. From then on, the distant southern protectorate was subjected to a full-scale programme of **Sinicization**. The Empire imposed not only its political system, but also its rites, social order, language and script.

China rubs shoulders with India

While the north of the country entered the orbit of China for a millennium, another page of history was being written to the south of the Pass of Clouds. At the turn of the 4C, the Indian-influenced **Khmer and Champa kingdoms** emerged from the Mekong Delta at the gates of Annam. The history of these nations can be traced through the dates of the envoys they sent to the Chinese court and by the proclamations made in honour of their kings, military campaigns and religious foundations. The Cham used Sanskrit, one of the languages of ancient India, and the royal religion was based on the **cult of the God Shiva**, the kingdom's protector. With the exception of a period from the mid-7C to the mid-8C, during which their reign extended further south as far as the temple of Po Nagar *(see page 288)*, the Cham remained concentrated until the 10C in the regions of Amaravati and My Son *(see page 275)*, the most sacred of their shrines. Although their monarchs and the official religion bore the distinctive stamp of India, the eyes of this nation of skilful mariners were more focused on Java and Sumatra.

A clash of kingdoms

A state is born

In the mid-10C, the north of the country, then called the province of Annam, managed to undermine the dominance of China, which had been weakened by the fragmentation of its Empire. China retained sovereignty but ceased to directly administer the kingdom, which became **Dai Viet**. This led to a direct confrontation between the northern province of Dai Viet and Champa, the Indianised state of the Cham people. These two opposing worlds embarked on a struggle which was to last 900 years, wedging the Champa kingdom in a pincer-grip, between Dai Viet to the north which tightened its clasp, and the Khmer state of Angkor to the west, which was growing in power.

Dai Viet's early steps were uncertain *(see page 162)*. Three rival dynasties, the Ngo, the Dinh and the Earlier Le then succeeded one another in less than a hundred years, but independence was finally achieved in 939. The country enjoyed a period of lasting stability under the **Ly dynasty** in the person of its founder **Ly Thai To** (1009-28). The capital was established at Thang Long, the future Hanoi, and the country was organised on principles bequeathed by a thousand years of Chinese occupation. Power, which was absolute, was clearly in the hands of the sovereign, but military and civil domains were administered by civil servants recruited by public examinations. Eighty percent of the population lived off the land, while the remaining 20 % was composed of trade and craft guilds, an intellectual elite of mandarins and scholars and the royal family and its dignitaries. Until French colonisation, Vietnam was organised traditionally on the basis of two superimposed structures: the **bureaucratic state**, based on the Confucian model , and a **network of village communities**, which remained strongly attached to their local spirits, their ancestors and their tutelary heroes. Indeed it is on these that Vietnam has traditionally relied to rekindle its desire for independence as successive dynasties toppled.

An era of wars

Consolidation by the Ly dynasty enabled the kingdom of Dai Viet to harass and pillage Champa, which relinquished its northern territories in 1069, despite the backing of China. In the 12C, as the royal house of the Ly foundered amid courtly intrigue, the **Khmer Empire of Angkor**, the new great power in Southeast Asia, was to challenge the Cham, setting the stage for nearly a hundred years of war (1145-1220) between the two kingdoms.

In the 13C, Vietnam was the only country in Asia capable of countering the **Mongol invasion** from China (*see page 171*), but as a result the political balance was in turmoil. It signalled the decline of the Indianised kingdoms (Mon, Champa and Khmer) and the rise of new powers (Laos, Siam and Vietnam). The Vietnamese victory was carried off by the Tran, an aristocratic clan which took over the throne in Hanoi. In 1360 at the coronation of **Che Bon Nga**, Champa made one final attempt to reconquer its territories. Encouraged by China's recognition, the Cham king ventured into the Red River Delta and ransacked Hanoi in 1371. He pursued this policy of harassment until he was assassinated in 1390. The pressure was such that the Tran were forced to raise taxes and enlist monks into the army, and the dynasty's popularity, understandably, declined as a result of such authoritarian measures.

Land-eating silk worms

In 1400, General Le Qui Ly, Che Bong Nga's great rival, forced the Tran to abdicate and proclaimed himself emperor with the title of **Ho Qui Ly**. Fearing for his throne, the Cham king **Jaya Simhavarman V** gave up **Amaravati**, the religious heart of Champa since its birth. This sacrifice was immense. Not only had the sovereign handed over the mystic soul of his kingdom, he had lost his most prosperous rice-growing territory. As a result, the Cham began to emigrate massively to the mountainous, poorer region to the south of Quang Ngai. The Vietnamese then embarked on their **March southwards** (Nam Tien), implementing exactly the same policy that China had inflicted previously on the north of the country, whereby colonists were dispatched to manage the new lands with their richly productive rice paddies. Jaya Simhavarman attempted to regain his lost lands by calling on the help of China, which had expelled the Mongols and founded the Ming dynasty. The Chinese responded by sending troops across the frontier, annexing the Vietnamese state and subjecting it to tyrannical rule (1413-28).

In their fight against Chinese oppression, the Viet sharpened a weapon which had already stood them in good stead against the Mongols. Past masters in trapping the enemy rather than facing him head on, they embarked upon a strategy of guerrilla harassment against the Imperial bulldozer rather than attempting an out-and-out war. Two figures dominated the resistance, the soldier, **Le Loi**, a landowner from Thanh Hoa, and **Nguyen Trai**, a strategist and a scholar steeped in Chinese culture. Their alliance was to create a fearsome war machine, which received the backing of the whole nation. Beginning in 1418, by 1426 guerrilla tactics had managed to liberate the Red River Delta and Le Loi was proclaimed emperor in 1428 under the name of **Le Thai To**.

"Harmony returns to the disturbed universe"

This line is from *The Great Proclamation of Peace of the Ngo*, a long poem written by Nguyen Trai to mark the rise to power of the dynasty and the return of peace. Le Thai To negotiated a lasting peace with the Ming, committing his country to uphold a relationship of vassalage with the Chinese Empire which was only broken by the French intervention in the late 19C. For its part, China removed its centre of gravity to the north, to Peking, the capital of the Empire until its fall in 1911, and a full six-week ride away from Tonkin. Le Thai To also managed to establish peaceful relations with Champa, little more than a shadow of its former self. The kingdom now only consisted of the arid lands to the south of Cape Varella, one-fifth of what it had possessed at the time of Che Bong Nga. The rise to power of the Later Le dynasty paved the way for a **century of peace**. The state was rebuilt on the foundations bequeathed by the Ly dynasty in the 11C. Education and agriculture, including the building of dikes and canals and the clearing of land for new crops, became the priorities and were to contribute to shaping Vietnam's awareness of its national identity.

From fragmentation to unity

North against South

From 1527, the authority of the Le was on the wane. The country was the scene of rebellions and uprisings and the feudal lord, **Mac Dang Dung** seized power. Forced to flee Hanoi by the supporters of the Le, he withdrew to Cao Bang and remained under the protection of China until 1677 *(see page 220)*. The Le rulers were at this time little more than puppets in the hands of the **Trinh** and the **Nguyen** families who only restored the dynasty to better fight among themselves. The former had a firm grip on real power in Hanoi and were in reality the actual rulers of the whole of Tonkin due to their control over the army. The latter established their power in the provinces won from the Cham. They also took advantage of the ships and guns brought by newcomers to Asia, the **Portuguese**, who flitted back and forth between their trading posts at Goa and Macao. From 1558, the Nguyen established an **independent feudal domain** and, despite a series of wars against the Trinh (1627-72), built a capital at Hue in 1687 *(see page 235)* and pursued the March southwards, finally absorbing Champa (whose last king was killed in 1692). In the mid-18C, the Nguyen became masters of the **Mekong Delta** and their sovereignty extended over the neighbouring kingdoms of Cambodia and Laos.

Opening to the world

The foundation of the **port of Hoi An** *(see page 264)* on the estuary of the little river of Thu Bon in the first half of the 16C opened up international trading routes to the Nguyen. To a far greater extent than at Hanoi and the mouth of the Red River, tucked away in the Gulf of Tonkin, Hue and its port benefited from their ancient maritime network bridging the Chinese and the Malaysian worlds. Guilds of merchants from southern China settled here in the early 17C, followed by Japanese from Nagasaki. The arrival of the Portuguese opened up the way for firstly Dominican, then Franciscan and Jesuit missionaries, whose presence was further increased when all foreigners were expelled from Japan in 1638. One of them, **Father Alexandre de Rhodes**, bequeathed Vietnam a precious tool for the future, namely a Latin-based script of the Vietnamese language *(quoc-ngu)*. The Dutch attempted to establish trading posts in Vietnam but were forced to withdraw from 1641 as a penalty for having taken sides with the Trinh against the Nguyen. In 1698, the latter erected a fort on a site which had already attracted Chinese tradesmen between 1630-40. This was **Cholon**, the "great market", located on one of the branches of the River Saigon *(see page 344)*.

The peasant uprising

Eighteenth century Vietnam was a divided land, and neither the royal house of the Le, nor the Trinh or the powerful Nguyen families could establish or maintain unity. Moreover, internal tensions among the various communities were growing – the Tonkinese in the north, Annamites of mixed Chinese and Cham blood in the centre and Cochinchinese descendants of the Khmer and Chinese colonialists in the Mekong Delta. Social evolution in the new territories in the south resulted in a peasant uprising at **Tay Son**. Led by three brothers, Nguyen Hue, Nguyen Nhac and Nguyen Lu, their victories were as devastating as they were unexpected, first in 1785 against Siamese troops assembled by Prince Nguyen Anh and then against the Imperial Chinese forces who had stepped in to help out the Le in 1788. **Nguyen Hue** proclaimed himself king at Hanoi in 1788, under the name of Quang Trung, but died four years later leaving only a 10-year old son and heir.

The last empty

Defeated by the peasant uprising, **Nguyen Anh** had fled to Bangkok and found refuge with French missionaries. One of these, Archbishop **Pigneau de Béhaine**, returned to France and succeeded in persuading Louis XVI to give his military support. Bolstered by the evident superiority of his artillery and by his naval strength, Nguyen Anh launched an offensive, capturing the delta, Hue and then Tonkin (1801) thereby unifying for the first time all the northern, central and southern territories. In 1802, he became **Gia Long**, Emperor of Vietnam.

Gia Long built an empire which

The verdict of the Son of Heaven

In 203 BC, a Chinese general founded an independent kingdom in southern China, which he named Nam Viet (Viet of the south). He established his capital at Canton and encroached on Tonkin, but his territories were absorbed by the Chinese Empire in 111 BC. In 1802, Gia Long dispatched a delegation to Peking to request the Son of Heaven's approval of the name of his empire, Nam Viet. Arguing that he had accomplished what neither the Tran nor the Le had done before him, namely the unification of the old land of Annam and the new territories of Viet Thuong, he asked for permission to change the old name of Annam into Nam Viet (a contraction of Annam and Viet Thuong). However the Chinese judged that this name evoked too many unpleasant historic events, in particular the secessionist kingdom of yesteryear. The Son of Heaven gave his verdict: the terms were to be inverted. Thus was born Vietnam.

was marked by its open dialogue with the West, but as soon as his successor **Minh Mang** was invested, the Nguyen returned to the traditional, autocratic Imperial methods of maintaining unity. On the one hand they democratised access to the highest positions in the civil service by opening the mandarin examinations to all, but on the other, they fell back onto the most orthodox of Confucian values. They recognised and rewarded scholars steeped in classical texts rather than pragmatic economists and they rejected modern diplomacy in favour of a view whereby the Chinese world had to defend itself against the invading barbarians. By choosing to reign from Hue, they reawakened the centrifugal forces between north and south which had resulted in the Tay Son uprising. In 1833, the **Saigon uprising** was harshly quashed by Minh Mang.

The universe once again disturbed

The last lands conquered and the first lands lost

By opting for the Chinese practice instead of dialogue with the West, the Nguyen chose unwisely. While the court of Hue withdrew behind a cloak of isolationism, the Middle Empire wavered against the onslaught of European imperialism. From the early 19C, England and France both set about conquering the Chinese market and obtained diplomatic and commercial treaties following the **Opium Wars** (1839-42 and 1856-60). Threatening manoeuvres in Da Nang Harbour in 1858 and the taking of Saigon by the French army in 1859 were symptomatic of this belligerent policy. They were a response to **Emperor Tu Duc's** overtly anti-Western policy and his persecution of Catholics. He was cornered and had no other option than to open his ports to international trade. The whole of the Mekong Delta was the more easily overcome due to the southerners' lasting grudge against the Nguyen regime which had so harshly put down the Saigon uprising. In 1862, the **colony of Cochinchina** was created and **Cambodia** became a French protectorate. By controlling the basins of the two rivers whose sources rise in China, the Red River and the Mekong River, France sought a foothold in Southeast Asia and thereby access to China. However the exploration of the sources of the Mekong, led by Francis Garnier and Doudart de Lagrée, revealed that this was impracticable. To get closer to China, France would have to take Tonkin. The French Third Republic was finally to implement a resolutely imperialistic policy and gain control of the north. Hanoi was taken in 1882. After a short war in 1885, the French obtained China's recognition of the frontier between the two countries and it relinquished its sovereignty over the country (*see page 216*).

The scholars' revolt

The first Vietnamese response to this invasion was legitimist. Known as the **Can Vuong** (1885-95), a body of scholars who supported Emperor Ham Nghi attempted to reinstate the royal authority spurned by the treaties, but this had almost no impact on France. From 1887, the French pursued their construction of the **Indochinese Union**, an administrative conundrum combining a single colony, Cochinchina and four protectorates (Cambodia, Laos, Annam and Tonkin). By abolishing Chinese in favour of a Latin-based script and, above all, by doing away with the mandarin examinations from 1919 to 1925, France little by little stripped the scholars of their prerogative of learning and knowledge. Vietnam's emperors had been reduced to mere figureheads and the new mandarins were obliged to toe the imperialist line.

Schools of nationalism

At the dawn of the 20C, the Japan of Meiji was the only Asian nation which seemed capable of building a modern independent state while maintaining an Imperial system. It provided a model for emerging Asian nationalist movements. In Vietnam, the patriotic scholar, **Phan Boi Chau** masterminded the **Dong Du**, an "Eastbound exodus" of young recruits who were sent to Tokyo for political and military training. The other voice which could be heard was that of **Phan Chau Trinh**, who preached a more radical solution, the establishment of a democracy to be accompanied by widespread education for all. In 1911, the year in which the Chinese Empire collapsed, a young man steeped in Trinh's ideas set sail for Marseilles. His name was Nguyen Tat Thanh, the son of a minor mandarin dismissed for his radical sympathies. In the West, Thanh proved himself to be a jack of all trades. He observed and studied in Paris, London, New York and finally Moscow from 1923. In 1942, he was ready to reclaim his nation's independence and it was now that he assumed his final nom de guerre: Ho the enlightened, **Ho Chi Minh**.

Emperor Khai Dinh

HARLINGUE-VIOLLET

A stateless patriot

In the aftermath of the First World War, it was under the pseudonym of Nguyen Ai Quoc, Nguyen the patriot (one of his fifty aliases), that the future Ho Chi Minh decided that Bolshevism was the way to combat the imperialism of Japan and the West. After spending 18 months in Moscow training as a Comintern agent, he left for Canton and then Hong Kong where he laid the foundations of his national liberation programme. He began by creating the Vietnamese Revolutionary Youth Association, a nursery of future state officials, whose ideas were spread clandestinely in Vietnam from 1925 to 1930 via a newspaper, Thanh Nien ("Youth"). Their thinking was embraced by the nation's new intellectual elite, already open to modern concepts as a result of several years spent in the country's prestigious institutions such as the Lycée Albert Sarraut or the Lycée Chasseloup Laubat at Saigon. They rapidly spread to the working classes, whose living conditions were extremely harsh in what was a prosperous colony. In 1930, the year of the foundation of the Vietnamese Communist Party, renamed the **Indochinese Communist Party** a few months later, the first strikes occurred in factories and plantations and peasant uprisings broke out in protest at the heavy taxes. This social unrest proved to be the main force for action since the demise of the Nationalist Party, founded in 1927 but repressed three years later, after the revolt of the garrison at Yen Bai. Neither was any hope forthcoming from the still occupied Imperial throne, after a thwarted attempt by Emperor Bao Dai to establish a constitutional monarchy.

The colonial regime's counter-attack was merciless. The prisons were crammed, villages were burnt and the leaders executed. Even Nguyen Ai Quoc was arrested in China in 1931 and placed under close surveillance. After taking part in the seventh Congress of the Communist International in 1935 in Moscow, he travelled across central asia to Yanan in China, the headquarters of Mao Zedong and his troops. In 1940, as Vietnam was subjected to the compromise of the **Indochinese Federation**, established by Vichy France and Japan, Nguyen Ai Quoc was knocking at its door, ready to breathe a fresh lease of life into the secret resistance movement with the backing of the Chinese communists.

A cycle of wars

In 1939, even though nationalist aspirations and Japan's imperialistic ambitions seemed to herald great upheavals, the nation was far from imagining that it faced a half century of warfare which would lead it into confrontation with almost all the planet's major military powers: Japan, France, the United States and China. At the end of this period, some historians considered that Vietnam had won its freedom but failed in its revolution.

Second World War (1940-45)

The Japanese interlude – Ever since China had been conquered by Japan in the late 1930s, the French colonial regime had been living in fear of invasion. Anticipating the danger, in June 1940 Governor-General Catroux recognised the pivotal role played by the Japanese in the Far East and granted them a number of military facilities in exchange for the recognition of France's sovereignty over Vietnam. With the exception of a brief Japanese incursion in September 1940, Indochina was to remain the only region of eastern Asia which was not under direct rule from Tokyo between 1940 and 1945. At the same time, the Japanese favoured the emergence of sects in the Mekong Delta and encouraged certain nationalist movements, such as the Dai Viet. The French also tried, in vain, to turn the nationalist sentiment to their own advantage. Back in Vietnam in 1941, Ho Chi Minh created the League for the Independence of Vietnam, the **Viet Minh** and set up a guerrilla unit in the province of Cao Bang. As early as the Spring of 1943, it made contact with the Americans.

The end of compromise – On 9 March 1945, the Japanese, in reaction to an American raid on the Indochinese coasts, decided to oust the French. The garrisons were disarmed, Governor-General Decoux arrested, General Lemonnier and Resident-General Auphelle decapitated and the settlers interned in camps. The effect of the blow suffered by the colonial regime was irremediable. On 11 March, Emperor **Bao Dai** proclaimed independence, but it was little more than a pretence, since the Japanese had requisitioned all the rice and directly controlled all of Cochinchina. The ensuing famine killed over 1.5 million people in the North.

On 10 August, following the announcement of Japan's surrender, the pace speeded up, and the Communist Party was able to assert its position as undisputed spokesman of the independence movement, supported by the majority of the population. Ho Chi Minh seized Hanoi, forced the emperor to abdicate and on 2 September proclaimed the **Democratic Republic of Vietnam** (DRV). In the South, where it had to form alliances with the powerful sects and nationalist movements, the Viet Minh managed to gain control of Saigon on 25 August. Its power was, however, frail and Chinese troops soon took over the North of the country, while the British occupied the area south of the 16th Parallel as decreed at Potsdam by the Allies. The role played by the British in the overthrow of the Viet Minh government received widespread condemnation from figures as diverse as General MacArthur, commander of the American forces in the Pacific, and Pandit Nehru. Armed by the British, French soldiers newly liberated from the Japanese camps, gained the upper hand once again. The Vietnamese retaliated on 25 September by massacring 150 French settlers. By the end of 1945, the British were on their way home, leaving the French in control of the South and Ho Chi Minh in the North.

The First Indochina War (1945-1954)

A missed opportunity – On 5 October 1945, the triumphant entrance of **General Leclerc** into Saigon at the head of an impressive armoured contingent signalled the return of French colonial power in Cochinchina. The general and Jean Sainteny, Commissioner of the Republic of Tonkin, nonetheless set France on the path of compromise. On 6 March 1946, at the same time as the French were replacing the Chinese in Northern Vietnam, an agreement was signed with Ho Chi Minh, recognising the DRV as an autonomous state within the French Union. The fate of Cochinchina was to be decided by a referendum.

However, the French government and **Thierry d'Argenlieu**, High Commissioner for Indochina, were not of the same opinion. Full of nostalgia for the colonial empire and a stalwart anti-Communist, d'Argenlieu intended to re-assert France's authority. He was behind the creation of a provisional government of Cochinchina, which soon gave rise to violent outbursts. The **Fontainebleau Summit** in July failed to settle the issue and by November, the struggle had spread northwards, where the **bombardment of Haiphong** by a French Far-Eastern Expeditionary Force led to the deaths of 6 000 people. The response was not long in coming; on 19 December, Hanoi rose in revolt. The country was well and truly at war.

A pawn on the Cold War chessboard – The ensuing struggle seemed singularly unequal, France's well-equipped troops against the Viet Minh, who were armed only with basic weapons and who decided to opt for guerrilla tactics. Émile Bollaert, who replaced d'Argenlieu in February 1947, decided to negotiate with Bao Dai, in exile in Hong Kong. In December, an initial agreement created the façade of independence for Vietnam under the patronage of **Nguyen Van Xuan**. Paris formed an alliance with Thailand, pursuing its policy of intrigue and negotiation in an effort to counter the "Communist contagion" of Indochina. Encouraged by the United States, France signed another agreement with Bao Dai on 8 March 1949, which granted a limited form of independence to the associated states of Vietnam, Cambodia and Laos.

The eruption of the Cold War in Asia was to wreak havoc with this newly established order and give a serious boost to the Viet Minh. In January 1950, the Communists who had just seized power in **China** recognised the DRV and were soon followed by the USSR. From now on, the resistance movement was to benefit from international sup-

port and substantial military aid. For their part, Britain and the United States recognised the Three Associated States. The outbreak of the **Korean War** (June 1950) further convinced Washington to support the French. The feelings of the United States at this time were in direct opposition to those expressed at the Tehran Conference (1943), when the United States and the Soviet Union had agreed to put an end to France's presence in Indochina. From 1950 on, America was convinced that Vietnam was of vital strategic importance and that the victory of the Communists would lead to the downfall of allied regimes in the region. It was this famous **domino theory** that dominated American foreign policy for decades to come. Inaugurated in 1950, by a US$10 million donation from President Truman to the French, American aid was to represent three-quarters of French military spending by the end of the war.

Despite the support and presence of an expeditionary force of 150 000 men, the French failed to win a decisive victory. On the contrary, at the **battle of the borders** (October 1950), France lost 7 000 soldiers as well as control of the border with China, across which weapons arrived for the Viet Minh armies. In December, the French appointed one of its most prestigious officers, **de Lattre de Tassigny**, Commander in Chief and High Commissioner. He repelled the assault of the North Vietnamese general **Vo Nguyen Giap** against the towns of Tonkin and for the first time, ordered napalm to be used, but the infiltration of the Viet Minh in the delta could not be halted. In addition, the Vietnamese Communist Party, reformed under the name of **Lao Dong**, managed to gain control of its sister parties in Laos and Cambodia. General Salan, who had replaced de Lattre after the latter's death in 1952, was forced to abandon the town of Hoa Binh (February 1952), but in October he repelled an assault by the **Popular Army of Vietnam** (PAV) to the northwest of Tonkin, pushing the attackers back to the frontier with Laos. In March Giap's troops made their first incursion into Laos.

However the political and economic crisis of the French Union, the lack of any prospect of victory and the cost of the war, both in economic and humanitarian terms, led to France's gradual withdrawal from combat in favour of Bao Dai's **Army of the Republic of Vietnam** (ARV). The priority from then on was to negotiate an honourable outcome, and **General Navarre**, Salan's successor, was entrusted with the task of winning a number of victories in order to place France in the best possible position for the negotiations. In October 1953, Paris finally consented to grant the Associated States real independence.

Saigon's Grand Hotel in the 1920s

ND-VIOLLET

A cycle of wars

Dien Bien Phu

In December 1953, when it became apparent that the Viet Minh were collecting their troops around Dien Bien Phu, Navarre refused to evacuate the camp. He was convinced of the effectiveness of his defence system and underestimated the logistical capacity of his enemy. From 27 December, the snare was to be drawn ever tighter. On 13 March 1954, the attack was launched. Giap had an army of 40 000 and some 55 000 reservists, pitched against 15 000 French soldiers. Above all, the Viet Minh commander had had his cannon placed in tunnels dug into the mountains, thus sheltering them from French retaliation. In two days, he had won two outposts and neutralised the aerodrome which supplied the camp. During the final assault on 1 May, Giap's men used the tunnels to get closer to the camp, which finally fell on 7 May. The fighting and 64-day siege resulted in losses of between 20 000 and 30 000 on the Vietnamese side and almost 3 000 on the French (10 000 prisoners were taken).

The turning point of the war – To prevent Giap from reaching Laos and from establishing a link with Annam and Cochinchina, Navarre decided to set up a military base in northwest Tonkin, near the Laotian border. Militarily speaking, **Dien Bien Phu** seemed like a good choice, because its wide basin (6km x 12km) would force the enemy to place its batteries on the steep mountain flanks – within reach of French cannon fire – if it wanted to bombard the base. From November 1953, crack French troops set up camp, while the Viet Minh, encouraged by China, decided to throw their all into the battle in order to carry off a decisive psychological victory. In the event, the repercussions of France's defeat were immense and were to accelerate the conclusion of the nine-year old conflict.

The day after the fall of Dien Bien Phu, the players in the conflict met at the **Geneva Conference** to discuss Korea and Indochina. With the exception of Bao Dai and the United States, all the parties seemed resigned to a division of the country. For their part, the Russians and the Chinese wanted to take advantage of the recent election of Pierre Mendès France, who had promised to settle the conflict within a month and to persuade the Viet Minh to accept a compromise. Peking was in fact very favourable to the curbing of its unruly neighbour's activities. The 20 July treaty, not ratified by Washington, foresaw the neutralisation of Laos and Cambodia and the temporary division of Vietnam along the 17th parallel. Reunification was to take place after elections planned at the latest for July 1956 and organised by the International Armistice Control Commission. The French troops withdrew from the North, which fell under the authority of the DRV, while some 900 000 anti-Communists fled to the South, where the Americans had forced Bao Dai to accept a Roman Catholic and staunch anti-Communist, **Ngo Dinh Diem** at the head of the government.

The Vietnam War

On 26 October 1955, Diem proclaimed the **Republic of Vietnam** (RV) and declared that it was not bound by the Geneva Accords. The stage was set for a new war.

Reunification fails (1954-60) – The Americans decided to make South Vietnam their main base in Southeast Asia, granting Diem their unconditional political and financial support, and they set about creating the **Army**

of the Republic of Vietnam (ARVN). A hermetically-sealed frontier was drawn between the two states, the French being totally ousted. 1956 finally came to a close without any elections having been held, and on 21 May Diem proclaimed the deposition of Bao Dai. Unpopular from the very start, the totalitarian Diem regime instituted a reign of terror, thanks to the Can Lao, the secret police controlled by his brother, Ngo Dinh Nhu. In the countryside, the peasants were forced to pay vast tax arrears to wealthy landowners. In addition, Diem implemented a savage policy of repression against the sects which controlled large portions of the Mekong Delta at the time.

In the North, Ho Chi Minh established a single party authoritarian regime and embarked on an ambitious programme of industrialisation and agricultural reform, which gave rise to violently repressed revolts (15 000 executions). The Communists in the South set up a small army which organised propaganda actions and attacks against the regime. From 1959-60, the armed struggle began again in earnest, soon backed by soldiers sent from Hanoi. On 19 December 1960, the South Vietnamese rebels founded the **National Liberation Front** (NLF) which advocated peaceful reunification and moderate agricultural reform so as not to alienate the peasantry. Dominated by Communists, it was soon to rise to fame under the name of **Viet Cong** (VC).

American involvement (1961-64) – At the beginning of 1961, the different factions of the NLF were reorganised into the **Popular Liberation Army** (PLA) of 15 000 men, with the aim of overthrowing the South Vietnamese regime with the aid of the Communists from the North. Simultaneously, the DRV received the backing of the two rival brothers of the Communist world, the USSR and China. In December 1961, within the context of the Cold War exacerbated by the Berlin and Cuban crises, the recently-elected President Kennedy decided to send in military "advisors", in violation of the 1954 armistice and the Geneva Accords and in response to the growth of the VC. By the end of 1962 their numbers had reached 9 000.

Diem and the Americans attempted to cut off the rural population from VC infiltration, by grouping the peasants into **strategic hamlets** set up in safe zones. Led by Ngo Dinh Nhu, this extremely brutal "relocation" policy was highly unpopular. Moreover, it failed to estrange the peasantry from the guerrilla forces and from 1963, the hamlets were infiltrated. In reaction, the ARVN bombarded the forests with defoliant and spread herbicide in the countryside, but the NLF built a network of efficient underground shelters and pursued its attacks. The lack of results and the negotiations undertaken by Nhu with Hanoi undermined the relations between Diem and the United States. Affairs came to a head with the violent repression of the Buddhists in June 1963, when Nhu's wife joked about the "barbecue", referring to the immolation of a senior Buddhist monk. On 1 November, Diem and his brother were executed during a **coup** that the Americans had allowed to occur. Three weeks later, Kennedy was assassinated and his successor, Johnson, decided to extend the field of operations to Laos, cutting off the Ho Chi Minh Trail. In 1964, Cambodia agreed to allow Chinese arms intended for the NLF a free passage, thereby causing a breakdown in diplomatic relations with Washington. In Saigon, the junta headed by **Duong Van Minh** attempted to form a government of reconciliation in order to negotiate with Hanoi, but it was overthrown by **General Nguyen Khanh** in January 1964. Any chance of a political outcome was at this stage out of the question.

Onset of the war with America – On the ground, the Viet Cong retained its hold over most of the land and the population of South Vietnam, despite America's vast firepower. From 1964, the major part of the NLF was made up of recruits from the South, but the DRV, henceforth directly implicated, was now able to transport entire units through zones controlled by the Laotian Communists. At the other extreme, the American-equipped ARVN suffered from absenteeism and soldiers demotivated and isolated by a hierarchy of corrupt officers. Faced with political instability and the progress of the Viet Cong, Washington decided to increase its financial, material and human aid. The 4 August attack by the North Vietnamese on the American spy vessel

The Ho Chi Minh Trail

The mythical, mysterious Ho Chi Minh Trail proved to be the decisive tool in the North's victory, because it linked, and above all supplied, the various resistance factions in the South. But certain sections which passed through Laos and Cambodia led these two countries to be pulled into the war. Laid out through the jungle from 1959 at the cost of much hardship, the trail was a complex network running more than 15 000km from north to south, complete with hospitals, warehouses and petrol dumps. From 1961, bicycles capable of transporting loads of up to 200kg were using it, shortly followed by night-time convoys of lorries. Neither bombing nor electronic detection devices were able to destroy it, and the Viet Cong even treated itself to the luxury of adding a 200km-long pipeline. It was along this trail that Hanoi's troops embarked on the assault that was to lead them to Saigon in 1975.

Maddox, gave Johnson and his Defence Secretary, **McNamara**, the excuse they wanted to obtain carte blanche from Congress to increase their activity in Vietnam. A subsequent enquiry was to prove that the destroyer was in the territorial waters of the DRV at the time of the first attack and that a second attack never in actual fact took place. On 7 February 1965, the President ordered the bombing of North Vietnam and despatched the first combat units to South Vietnam to protect the air base at Da Nang.

Events escalate – The American commander General **Westmorland**, convinced that the war would be short, obtained an even greater commitment. Already 184 000 in 1965, the US contingent had reached 536 000 by 1968. Search and destroy tactics, although they limited the loss of GIs, required substantial logistical backup. Hanoi and Haiphong were bombed in 1966 in order to destroy petrol reserves and prevent the resupplying of the PLA. Despite massive loss of human life (35 000 / year), their impact was limited, because the DRV carefully camouflaged its factories and warehouses and continued to be resupplied by China and the USSR.

At the beginning of 1967, the Hanoi regime decided to return to guerrilla warfare tactics in order to disperse the enemy forces. It was sure of its decisive numerical advantage and bet on the unpopularity of President **Nguyen Van Thieu**, who was unable to counter corruption within the army and the civil administration. In addition, the American bombing and attacks resulted in large numbers of victims in South Vietnam and gave rise to immense displacements of the population (as many as 4 million people in 1968). Hanoi hoped that in the long run, Washington would finally give in rather than reduce its forces in the rest of the world. The reintroduction of conscription in America in 1967 proved to be very unpopular, while the cost of the involvement continued to escalate, forcing the government to raise taxes and cut back on social programmes.

The Tet Offensive – When it seemed that the opposing forces had stalemated each other, Giap decided to launch a major operation. The PAV led an offensive in the region of the 17th Parallel, where the PLA launched an assault designed to create an uprising. To counter the PAV, Westmorland sent large numbers of reinforcements to the **Khe Sanh** base in the North and entrusted the defence of Saigon to the Vietnamese. On 31 January 1968, during the truce of the Tet festival, 80 000 rebels attacked 105 sites in South Vietnam. However the expected popular uprising did not take place and most of the troops were easily repelled by the Americans. The PLA nonetheless carried off two spectacular and highly symbolic actions. In Saigon, for a few hours it had the run of the gardens of the American embassy in front of the cameras of the world. Further north, Hue, the former imperial capital, was occupied for 25 days and almost 2 500 civil servants accused of collaboration were executed. But the price paid by the PLA, sacrificed by Hanoi, was high indeed. It lost 32 000 men and most of its executive staff, although these were soon replaced by the North Vietnamese. Yet this defeat was to turn to their advantage because it revealed the weakness of the ARVN. The loss of civilians was, however, the cruellest blow (143 000 dead) and it had great repercussions in the United States where public opinion began to judge the cost of the war exorbitant. On 31 March, in a televised speech, Lyndon B Johnson requested the opening of negotiations and limitations on bombing, while indicating that he would not run for a second term as president.

The "Vietnamisation" of the conflict – Negotiations opened in Paris on 13 May 1968 between the United States, the DRV and the RV, as well as a **Provisional Revolutionary Government** (PRG) which represented the NLF. At this point their respective stances seemed irreconcilable and no camp appeared to have a sufficient advantage to impose its will. In addition, talks faltered on the South Vietnamese veto on the presence of the PRG. In October, Johnson agreed to halt the bombing of the DRV. In the field, Washington recalled Westmorland and entrusted the major part of the "pacification" operations to the ARVN, equipped by the United States. At the same time, the CIA organised **Operation Phoenix**, which managed to eliminate nearly 20 000 officials of the NLF. Elected in 1969, the very year when Ho Chi Minh died, **Nixon** increased the American presence, while searching for an honourable outcome to the conflict at the same time. With the help of his advisor, **Kissinger**, he initiated an easing of relations with China and the USSR so that they would also bring pressure on Vietnam. This policy was to prove successful, because, in exchange for its first diplomatic recognition from the United States, China encouraged its ally to find a compromise (1971) and Nixon went on a State visit to Peking in 1972. This visit, together with that of the American president to Moscow the same year, was considered a betrayal by Hanoi. To keep the pacifists quiet on the home front, Nixon began to repatriate GIs in 1969 and replaced conscription by a lottery. Nonetheless the effect on the morale of the young men who hadn't been fortunate enough to avoid their military service was disastrous. Drugs became widespread and cases of indiscipline multiplied, at the same time as relations with the South Vietnamese were deteriorating. It did however seem as if the United States was at last pulling free of the Vietnamese quagmire, but the slow progress of the talks, the massacre at My Lai and the invasion of Cambodia (a neutral country) in April 1970 profoundly shocked American public opinion. As the DRV had still not capitulated, Nixon was forced to abandon military escalation under pressure from the Senate. Hanoi for its part endeavoured to reinforce its military power which had been weakened following the Tet Offensive. On 30 March 1972, Giap despatched a 30 000-strong force to Hue, while the PLA prepared uprisings in the southern towns. In retaliation, Nixon ordered the bombing of the DRV for the first time since 1968 and had the DRV's ports mined. Even if it revealed the weakness of the ARVN, the **Easter Offensive** was a failure and resulted in the deaths of 100 000 Viet Cong. The influence of Giap, deemed responsible, faltered in favour of General **Van Tien Dung** and Hanoi relaunched negotiations between Kissinger and Le Du Tho in August.

Agreement appeared to be within sight, when despite the opposition of Thieu (who was not consulted), Nixon decided to resume the bombing of North Vietnam in order to force it to make further concessions. This decision was not understood and Congress decided to cut off funds to Indochinese operations. Finally a **cease-fire** was signed on 27 January 1973. According to its terms, the US army would withdraw totally, the PLA would remain in the zones it controlled and free elections would be held in South Vietnam. In exchange, Hanoi was to withdraw from Cambodia and Laos and relinquish any claims on the RV. To get Thieu to accept this treaty, Nixon pledged military support if the DRV failed to respect the agreement. Furthermore in a secret letter to Prime Minister **Pham Van Dong**, he agreed to pay the DRV compensation.

The collapse of South Vietnam – In Laos, fighting ceased rapidly, but Cambodia, where the PAV troops held out, was bombed more heavily in six months than Japan was during the whole of the Second World War. The reaction of Congress was to forbid any further American participation in military operations, thereby preventing

30 April 1975, the Fall of Saigon

Nixon from honouring his promise to Thieu. At the same time, the **Watergate** scandal deprived the president of all room for manoeuvre, while the October 1973 petrol crisis forced the United States to reduce aid. Cut off from all popular support and weakened by the economic crisis, the Saigon regime had only a demoralised army of deserters to count on, while negotiations with Hanoi regarding the elections were at a standstill.

In January 1975, encouraged by the resignation of Nixon and from its reinforced position in the Mekong Delta, the Lao Dong (Vietnamese Communist party) decided to launch its first major offensive on the north of Saigon to test its adversary's strength. The success of this operation was such that it then sent its tanks into the Highlands in March. Totally unexpectedly, the ARVN abandoned Buan Ma Thuot almost without a fight. From that point, Saigon was directly threatened. Along the coast, the withdrawal of the ARVN turned into a rout, with almost 15 000 soldiers and 100 000 civilians killed. The capture of the port of Da Nang on 29 March was a decisive victory for the PAV, who were able to regain the weapons left behind by the fleeing ARVN and launch the final assault. The **Fall of Saigon** on 30 April 1975 after only 55 days forced Duong Van Minh, president for only two days, to surrender. The last Americans abandoned their embassy the same day, after having evacuated 150 000 South Vietnamese. The United States, who had failed to save its ally, was totally humiliated.

The disillusion of the day after

The end of the war in Vietnam, far from bringing peace to the peninsula, saw a resurgence of old regional rivalries. Indochina remained a key component of international politics within the Communist world.

Difficult reunification – Officially reunified on 2 July 1976, the country became the **Socialist Republic of Vietnam** (SRV), with Hanoi as capital and **Le Duan** appointed as General Secretary of the Communist Party. Saigon was renamed Ho Chi Minh City. Institutions were based on those of the DRV with a single party system. However, for the previous twenty years, the North and the South had experienced radically different regimes. The population of the North, who had lived with a war economy, were shocked when they discovered the affluence of Saigon's markets overflowing with American consumer goods. The gulf was immense, all the more so as the war had been experienced differently on both sides and suspicions were rife. During the 1975-79 period, 500 000 officials from the North were sent to live in the former southern capital. Over 15 000 "collaborators" were despatched to re-education camps, where living conditions were particularly harsh, and hundreds of thousands of Saigon's inhabitants were forced to move to the border regions of Cambodia and to "Vietnamise" the Highlands close to Laos. The adoption of a socialist economy prompted many peasants and tradespeople to refuse to sell their produce. This policy resulted in a mass flight by sea and the tragedy of the **boat people**.

The country emerged ruined by 30 years of war, as much in the North where the industrial fabric and road network had been completely destroyed by American bombs, as in the South, where the countryside was either ravaged or deserted. In addition, far from keeping the promises made by Nixon, Washington demanded the return of 2 300 GIs reported missing and instituted an economic embargo. This led Vietnam to seek Soviet aid, formalised by a treaty in June 1978.

The Third Indochina War – On the very day after reunification, the peninsula became the scene of diplomatic and ideological confrontation between the USSR and China. China didn't want a Vietnam allied to the Soviets and dominant in Indochina. As the Hanoi-Moscow and Phnom Penh-Peking axes emerged, the scene was set for the first conflict between the Communist states. Regionally, this opposition was further exacerbated by a rivalry between the ASEAN (Association of Southeast Asian Nations), Thailand in particular, and the peninsula dominated by Vietnam. There was no lack of motive for tension between Peking and Hanoi. In addition to disputes regarding maritime borders and the sovereignty of the Spratly and Paracel Islands, Peking was preoccupied by the fate of a significant **Chinese minority** living in the South and who controlled the major part of Cholon's trade. Enjoined to take Vietnamese nationality unless they wished to lose their jobs and suffer food restrictions, 70 000 of them left the country in 1977.

While Laos agreed to sign a treaty of friendship with Vietnam, Cambodia, subjected to the bloodthirsty madness of the Khmer Rouge, refused Hanoi's fraternal offer. Relations soured between the two countries for ideological reasons and because of territorial disagreement in the Mekong Delta. Furthermore, **Pol Pot** held Hanoi responsible for a thwarted plot in 1976. He had no qualms about provoking his powerful neighbour by launching a number of raids on its territory which left several hundred victims. With the firm intention of overthrowing the Khmer Rouge regime, Hanoi set upon the Cholon community in 1978, fearing that it could serve as a fifth column for China, allied to Cambodia. Nearly 250 000 Chinese fled Vietnam. Many Vietnamese took part in this exodus, which further exacerbated tensions between the neighbouring countries.

On 25 December 1978, Le Duc Tho invaded Cambodia and settled former Khmer Rouge forces, exiled in Vietnam, in

The tragedy of the boat people

At the end of the 1970s, the plight of the Vietnamese, heedless of the dangers represented by coastguards, storms, pirates and sharks, was felt deeply by the international community. Almost a third of these boat people died en route, while a million survivors were sent to camps set up in Southeast Asia between 1975 and 1989. Seven hundred thousand obtained the right to emigrate to the West under the safeguard of the UN. At the end of the 1980s a second wave of boat people, fleeing the poverty stricken conditions of the North, aroused less compassion. After years spent in camps, some agreed to return to Vietnam with financial aid and the promise of not being badly treated. Under pressure from China, which wanted to resolve the issue of the 55 000 refugees in Hong Kong before reunification, the British colony repatriated the exiles by force, leading to revolts and the deaths of 200 people in 1995. In February 2000, the few remaining refugees were allowed to stay in Hong Kong.

A cycle of wars

Phnom Penh. In five weeks the country was overrun and Pol Pot's followers were driven back to the frontier with Thailand. However, on 17 February 1979, China retaliated by launching a force of 120 000 men on Tonkin. This occupation, which ceased on 16 March, left over 20 000 dead on both sides but did not result in further outbreaks. Vietnam was, however, increasingly beset by economic problems, resulting from the vast cost of an invasion which dragged on and on. The Khmer Rouge were able to continue guerrilla warfare thanks to Chinese armaments sent via Thailand. Although initially popular because it had put paid to Pol Pot, the PAV was soon as detested as any other occupying army and was also hated due to the fact that it had allowed half a million Vietnamese migrants to settle in the country. The cost of reinforcing the northern frontier and an increasing number of skirmishes with China further emptied the state coffers. Hanoi was forced to cede the base of Cam Ranh to the USSR in order to break its diplomatic isolation and obtain economic aid.

The opening – In 1986, the 6th Communist Party Congress marked a watershed with the adoption of an economic renovation programme entitled **Doi Moi**, intended to introduce a market economy and promote the investment of foreign capital. This transformation had in actual fact already begun in the late 1970s, when collective agriculture was abandoned. Politically, the collegial power created by the 1980 Constitution had favoured a division between the State and the Party. Then, at the 6th Congress, a section of the old guard left the ranks of state (Le Duc Tho and Pham Van Dong) and **Nguyen Van Linh** became General Secretary. The 1992 Constitution further paved the way for the small business sector which had been steadily growing since 1986. From then on, the troika in power at Hanoi appeared to be the product of a triple balancing act between reformers and conservatives, the Party and the army, and the country's three main regions. Democratic reform however progressed far more timidly.

In the same year as *Doi Moi* was adopted, the thawing of Chinese-Soviet relations led Gorbachev to press Vietnam to patch up its differences with Peking. At the beginning of 1988, the PAV began to withdraw its troops stationed in Cambodia, completing the retrenchment in September 1989. China appreciated the gesture and the pressure on Hanoi slackened as did the aid to the Khmer Rouge resistance forces. From then on, the settlement of the Cambodian question was entrusted to the UN and Hanoi could for the first time see an end to its diplomatic isolation. This new situation initially enabled Vietnam to establish relations with China, then with ASEAN, to which it was admitted in 1995. Almost immediately, Vietnam endeavoured to jump on the "Asian Dragon" bandwagon, whose economies nonetheless faltered during the 1997 crisis. Vietnam, however, had to resolve the contradiction between its socialist principles and its economic ambitions. Whatever the case, the move towards normalised relations with the United States gradually progressed, with the lifting of the American embargo (1994), the reestablishment of diplomatic relations (1995) and finally the highly symbolic visit paid by Bill Clinton in November 2000.

ARV	Army of the Republic of Vietnam (founded by Emperor Bao Dai)
ARVN	Army of the Republic of Vietnam (South Vietnamese troops)
ASEAN	Association of Southeast Asian Nations
DRV	Democratic Republic of Vietnam (North Vietnam)
NLF	National Liberation Front (South Vietnamese rebel movement – VC)
PAV	Popular Army of Vietnam (North Vietnamese troops)
PLA	Popular Liberation Army (Viet Cong rebel troops)
RV	Republic of Vietnam (South Vietnam)
SRV	Socialist Republic of Vietnam (official name of Vietnam since 1975)
VC	Viet Cong (South Vietnamese opposing the Diem regime)
VM	Viet Minh (League for Independence founded by Ho Chi Minh)

At the crossroads

The scope of the country's vast human resources initially led economists to predict a brilliant future but such forecasts have yet to be realised. Vietnam has not yet evolved from one of the world's poorest nations into a tiger economy. The burden of an all-pervasive bureaucracy which discourages private initiative and foreign investment is of course a handicap. Yet at a time of globalisation and just after an economic crisis which severely affected the region, the system has paradoxically preserved the country from a slump, at least for the time being. Founded on economic openness but no real democracy, Vietnamese development has however already revealed its limits and at present the country finds itself trapped by what appear to be irreconcilable contradictions.

Political organisation

The regime of the Socialist Republic of Vietnam, developed by Ho Chi Minh between 1946 and 1969, was extended, with a few adaptations, to the whole country after reunification in 1976. Over the years this complex system, which is both rigid and rife with inner conflicts, has nonetheless shown a remarkable ability to survive and adapt.

A two-headed political system

Since the death of its historic leader, a **collegial system**, supposedly representing the main geographical and political interests, runs the country. The **President of the Republic**, Tran Duc Luong, no longer wields any real power. This is shared between the **Communist Party General Secretary**, Le Kha Phieu, a conservative general from the North backed by the army, and the **Prime Minister**, Phan van Khai, of Southern origins and one of the inventors of the *Doi Moi* in the early 1980s. At the heart of the system is the **National Assembly** which in theory controls the State (Presidency, cabinet, justice). The Assembly is made up almost entirely of top officials, but since the declaration of the **1992 Constitution**, private enterprise representation is growing steadily, an indication of how things are changing in the

Ho Chi Minh City

F Soreau/MICHELIN

country. In reality, however, power is firmly in the hands of the government which rules by decree. At provincial, district and communal level, the Assembly is represented by **People's Councils** (legislative bodies) which elect **People's Committees** with a local executive role. Rivalry between these two institutions regularly hinders and blocks the decision-making process.

The role of the Party and the Army

The system's main internal conflict resides in the opposition between the **Communist Party** and the State. In spite of the latter's apparent sovereignty, the all-powerful Party is in fact responsible for all legislative initiative. Vietnam is still under a single-party regime, although only one-quarter of Assembly members are actually Party members. All ministries have a Party section and participate in this way in the election of its leadership. A 1 000-member Congress elects the Central Committee for five years, which in its turn nominates the 19 members of the **Politburo**, who in fact govern the Party and the country. After years of unity, the separation in the early 1990s of the Party and the State has evolved into rivalry. The Party represents knowledge and doctrine, while the State symbolises power and administrative experience. This dichotomy can be found at all levels, from one end of the country to the other and is the cause of endless conflict between the People's Committees and local Party sections.

According to the majority of analysts, the picture is further complicated by the growing influence of the **army**, which took advantage of the Party's weakness in the 1990s and seized a growing share of the country's government. Finally, the role played by numerous popular organisations, such as the Youth Union, Women's Union, Confederation of Trade Unions, Farmers' Association or Veterans' Association, should not be neglected.

Human rights scorned

International organisations regularly spotlight Vietnam's failure to respect human rights, particularly in terms of religious freedom. The Unified Buddhist Church was banned and replaced in 1981 by a state-run body and its respected leader, Thich Huyen Quang, has been under house arrest in the centre of the country since 1982. At the same time, the formerly outlawed Cao Dai movement (see page 363) was legalised and yet the regime represses the Protestant minority of the Highlands. All political prisoners are subjected to the same methods, ranging from summary arrests and searches to harassment and arbitrary trials. In this light, the recent amnesty granted by President Tran Duc Luong to 12 000 prisoners, "among whom were numerous corrupt Party officials, but no political hostages" appears almost farcical.

A fast-growing population

With around 80 million inhabitants, Vietnam now ranks second in the ASEAN (Association of Southeast Asian Nations) in terms of population, but in 1936 it only had 19 million inhabitants and 31.6 million in 1960. The current **demographic growth** rate (2 % / year) is one of Asia's highest. This phenomenon has played a decisive role in the country's recent history and being forced to absorb a growing workforce every year represents a major challenge for its economy. Such growth has also had far-reaching effects on the country's domestic geopolitical situation, with many Viet settling in relatively uninhabited zones where minority populations live. Despite a very **high density** (240 people / km^2), Vietnam's population is in fact highly disparate. The Red River and the Mekong Deltas alone account for some 40 % of the population and 16 % of the territory, with densities in excess of 1 000 inhab / km^2. In contrast, the figures are much lower in the northern foothills (less than 80 inhab / km^2) or the Central Highlands (less than 50 inhab / km^2).

Rural exodus and resettlement

In spite of a substantial **exodus from rural** regions, only 20 % of the total population lives in towns and cities. Apart from Hanoi (3 million) and Ho Chi Minh City (7 million), the country's main towns are Haiphong, Da Nang and Hue. As a result of bombing and domestic policy before 1975, South Vietnamese migrated massively to the towns, now home to 43 % of the population (compared to 26 % in 1964). In the North, where the phenomenon was the opposite because the cities were too easy a target for bombing, the urban population was little more than 12 % in 1975. Between 1975 and 1979, 3 million recently urbanised South Vietnamese were resettled in their former villages. This **resettlement** gave rise to the flight of one million boat people (*see below*). At the same time, 500 000 North Vietnamese moved to Ho Chi Minh City between 1975-79. In an effort to balance the population distribution, migrations were organised from the overpopulated plains to the central and southern mountainous zones. Some analysts and historians consider these far-reaching phenomena to be the last lap of the long "March southwards" of the North Vietnamese.

A significant overseas community

Over 2.5 million Vietnamese or Viet Kieu (expatriate Vietnamese) live abroad. Between the two World Wars, many chose to study in France and stayed on after the Indochina War. The largest exodus took place in 1975 when Saigon fell to North Vietnam. The numbers of South Vietnamese fleeing the new Communist regime were increased by thousands of **boat people**, followed by others between 1979-80, who wanted to join their families abroad. The United States of America is home to the largest foreign community (over 1 million), France comes second with 250 000. In 1981, students and workers were sent on **patriotic missions** to former Eastern-bloc countries and some remained behind after the collapse of the Soviet Union. The increased pace of Vietnam's political openness, clearly a by-product of the demise of Communism, served to heighten the economic importance of its diaspora. Some 250 000 families in Ho Chi Minh City live off their foreign relatives who send bank transfers and parcels, often of medicine, which is then sold. Since the 1990s, the return of Vietnamese refugees who have taken foreign nationality, has enabled **joint ventures** to be mounted with relatives in Vietnam who serve as figureheads.

A convalescent economy

Vietnam's economy still bears the burden of over thirty years of wars and destruction, further exacerbated by the consequences of the Cambodian occupation and the American embargo. Only lifted in 1994, the embargo had prevented the country from trading freely and from acquiring foreign high-tech know-how and equipment. The rigid economy planning applied in the years after 1975 was rife with mistakes and aggravated the situation still further. Since 1986 when the 6th Communist Party Congress opened the door to capitalism, the legendary **Doi Moi** reform programme had been felt to be more an issue of survival than of policy. In the light of this Vietnamese-style *perestroika*, centralisation, planning, industrial voluntarism and nationalisation have been played down in favour of market laws. Monetary reforms have also been implemented.

Vietnam and the Asian crisis

Rampant inflation was the first direct consequence of this turnaround. However, it was accompanied by a high growth rate throughout the 1990s with peaks of 9 %. Other indicators, such as the high investment rate (28 % of the GNP) and the low national debt, seemed to suggest that development would be lasting and solid. But the **financial crisis** of 1997, which originated in Thailand, shook most of the nations in the area. Vietnam's less internationally-open economy was also affected and growth dropped to around 4 %, while exports slowed down and foreign investment fell dramatically.

G Guérard

Despite Vietnam's undeniable progress, it remains one of the poorest countries on the planet, with a GDP per inhabitant of US$370. The **poverty** of part of its large rural population remains one of the government's main preoccupations. Overall living conditions have improved, but at the same time, social services are less freely available and disparities between rich and poor are growing. Endemic unemployment and meagre salaries mean that the majority of Vietnamese either have to have several jobs or grow their own vegetables to survive. This said, Vietnam's relatively well-educated (*see page 72*) and large population is undoubtedly one of the country's major assets.

A growing service industry

Even though **agriculture** continues to employ two-thirds of the population, it only produces up to 26% of the nation's wealth. The staple crop is **rice**, after which come coffee, rubber, corn, soya, tea, potatoes and ba-

Rubber production at Buon Ma Thuot

nanas. Fishing, together with pig and poultry farming, are also significant. **Industry**, which only accounted for 1.5% of the GDP in 1954 when France retreated, now contributes 33%. Sectors include food, clothing, tyres, oil, coal and steel. The most spectacular progress has, however, been that of the **service industries**, which now account for 41% of the GDP. **Tourism** has played a significant role and the state depends on this sector's ability to bring in foreign currency. After a lull in 1998, the number of visitors increased from 60 000 in 1989 to 2 million in 2000.

An uncertain future

Several obstacles continue to hinder the path of progress and deter foreign investment. An excessive and unpredictable bureaucracy and high taxes are the main factors cited by Vietnam's would-be investors. Following the economic crisis, investments dropped spectacularly from US$8.3 billion in 1996 to US$1.6 billion in 1999. Economic reforms are slow to appear and industry is still 50% state-run. At the same time, **private enterprise**, the most dynamic economic sector, employing 80% of the population, is beset with heavy taxes, without the support of bank loans or effective investment grants.

A member of the Asia-Pacific Economic Cooperation (APEC) and ASEAN and a candidate for the World Trade Organisation, Vietnam is under increasing foreign pressure to adapt its economy to market laws and to pay back its foreign debt, which amounts to around 23% of GDP (US$5.7 billion).

ART AND ARCHITECTURE

Three main artistic civilisations have successively flourished in Vietnam with a sin-gular lack of continuity and with gaping chronological interludes. The **Dong Son** bronze civilisation (7C-2C BC), was the first, covering a vast area from southern China to the coasts of Indonesia; the second Cham period (7C-15C AD) produced brick and clay sculptures in honour of the **Champa** gods and kings; the third occurred from the 11C under the impetus of the **Vietnamese kingdoms** and gave rise to the use of carved wood decoration of palaces and temples. Very little remains of any of these civilisations. Ancient, and to an even greater extent, recent, wars have taken their toll. The damage is further aggravated by the fact that up until the mid-20C almost no research into the arts of Vietnam had been undertaken. Now however they are more alive than ever. Whether it be the traditional crafts of the country's various ethnic groups (see page 107) or the work of its contemporary artists, it is as if this nation's tireless will to rebuild its country is constantly rekindling its artistic talent.

Early art in Vietnam

The drum beat

At the end of the Bronze Age and the beginning of the Iron Age, metalworking reached a remarkable level of sophistication in the Dong Son culture (see page 19). In a necrop-olis of 200 burial places near the village of Thanh Hoa, several hundred bronze ob-jects were discovered which had been made using techniques such as **lost-wax metal casting**, planishing, riveting and soldering. The burial places held tools (axes, knives), weapons (swords, lances), a few human and animal statuettes, together with two rit-ual objects, **drums** and **situlae** (bucket-shaped containers), which contained cereals, Chinese coins or shells. The impressive dimensions of these artefacts, some of which are up to 60cm in height and 80cm in diameter, bear witness to their importance even if their decoration is now more subject to conjecture than to certainty. Portraits and scenes of everyday life including figures with feather head-dresses, vividly por-trayed in profile (hunting, farming or soldiering) and animals (deer, aquatic birds, crocodiles) were carved around the lids of the situlae. On the drums, these strip-car-toon-like scenes were laid out in spirals radiating from a central star motif, possibly symbolising the sun. They gradually became simpler, evolving into geometric pat-terns, sometimes accompanied by little frog statuettes in allusion to a water-bound civilisation. Chinese occupa-tion from around the 1C AD si-lenced this art form, but it re-vealed the symbolic significance of these drums. General Ma Yuan, sent to crush uprisings in the south, had the Dong Son leaders' **emblems of power** melted down whenever one of them was captured.

Dong Son drum

Ravaux/RMN

The Dong Son legacy

Despite vigorous attempts to Chris-tianise them, the **Highlanders** today represent a living link with Viet-nam's ancient civilisation. The Austronesians in particular, by virtue of their languages, represent a cultural era which coincides with that of the Dong Son drums, examples of which have been found in the Philippines and in Indonesia. On either side of the South China Sea, ancient architectural traditions have given rise to a **house** similar to that depicted on the drums. The rooftop was the most striking feature of these stilt houses, whether it be the trapezoid E De house, the Gia Rai longhouse or the Ba Nang communal house (*rong*) with its tapered double roof. Ethnographists have yet to agree to what extent the rituals of the Dong Son have been reproduced by the Highlanders, whose communal house contains artefacts held sacred by the community, such as pitchers, gongs and drums. Several groups transmit the myth of a drum-boat which saved humanity from the Flood. **Drums and gongs** continue to summon the community to meet during complex sacrificial funeral rites when the deceased gradually leaves the land of the living for the world of the spirits. Among the Gia Rai, the E De and the Ba Na, the definitive departure of the dead is marked by the building of a **funeral house**, the statues of which represent nature and fertility.

Cham art

The Champa kingdom was heavily influenced by India, the first signs of which had reached the Mekong Delta around the 1C AD. After the fashion of their Khmer neighbours, the Cham sovereigns worshipped the Hindu pantheon of gods, focused around two main divinities, My Son, the "Good Mountain", devoted to Shiva, and Po Nagar, the rock overlooking the sea, devoted to the Goddess Bhagavati. From the 7C, the spoils of war financed large numbers of identical brick spire-shrines and a wide variety of carved sandstone images. Some experts have argued that it is almost as if Vietnam's artistic civilisation had stood still before jumping a few generations, and indeed Cham art only really emerges from the 15C. Such lack of continuity has complicated analyses, already hampered by a clear preference for studies of Khmer art. A few meagre towers scattered along the Mandarin Road, statues in Vietnam and in the Guimet Museum in Paris, old photos of architectural complexes destroyed during the Vietnam War and a few inscriptions are all that remains of this vanished civilisation.

A conservative architecture

The remains of Cham architecture are religious and based almost entirely on a single model, reproduced from the 7C by all the major Indianised kingdoms from the Indochinese peninsula to the Indonesian archipelago, namely that of the *sikhara* or spire-shrine, called **kalan** in Cham. The dwelling-place of the god was designed to be a place of worship and not of assembly. These confined, windowless shrines hold a divine image, either in the shape of a statue or a lingam, as in the case of the cult of Shiva. The image is placed on a pedestal, the *yoni*, sometimes equipped with a drainage system which collects the holy water poured over the statue during ceremonies. The design of the exterior reflects the sacred nature of the edifice, which generally faces east. Each shrine is built on three levels, reflecting the Indian mythological concept of the world, with the foundations, relatively low in the Cham version, representing the world down on earth (*bhurloka*), up to the pyramidal roof depicting the heavenly spheres (*svarloka*). The slenderness of the edifice is enhanced by miniature corner stones, which faithfully reproduce the *kalan's* outline. The shrines at Hoa Lai (late 8C-early 9C) are the oldest examples of this architectural form (*see page 298*). In the 10C, at My Son (*see page 275*), a more complex type of structure emerged. It comprised a perimeter wall within which stood a number of edifices, more or less derived from the *kalan*, such as the **gopura** (tower-porch) which forms the entrance into the holy area, the **mandapa** (four-door pavilion) where the offerings may have been prepared. There were also barlong-type constructions, such as the **koshagraha** (library), covered by a vault, where the sacred objects were kept. Unlike the Khmer, the Cham did not build on a grand scale; the only exception to this rule was the Buddhist complex at Dong Duong (late 9C), which was entirely destroyed during the Vietnam War.

CHAMPA ARCHITECTURE

PEDESTAL ALTAR AT MY SON

arch

recess

pilaster

foliage carving springing from a lion's mouth

riser adorned with entwined dancers

curved step

THE TOWER-SHRINE (KALAN)

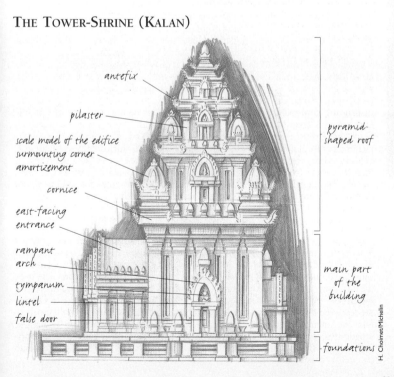

antefix

pilaster

scale model of the edifice surmounting corner amortizement

cornice

east-facing entrance

rampant arch

tympanum

lintel

false door

pyramid-shaped roof

main part of the building

foundations

H. Choimet/Michelin

The materials used by the Cham changed very little over the centuries. Wooden prototypes probably existed, but in the 8C they began to use **brick**, undoubtedly cemented with a resin. Unlike the Khmer, the Cham only used **sandstone** very sparingly, restricting it to a few blocks over or around the doors or in decorative elements, such as tympanums or friezes. The brick was carved to emphasise the building's features, using pilasters around the main entrance doors, recesses and false windows to enliven side walls or moulding on the cornices around the base of the roof. Even if it is true that the basic layout of such buildings underwent few changes over the centuries, their architectural ornamentation reveals a clear evolution in style.

Unique carvings

The few remaining individual pieces or groups of statues which are still in place paint a picture of what is one of the Indochinese peninsula's most unusual types of statuary. The Cham had become master craftsmen in the art of brickwork and some of their buildings still display examples of superb ornamental and figurative sculpture, carved directly into the stone, such as that on the walls of the koshagraha of the B group at My Son (see photo page 274) or the statues which ornament the three façades of the annexe to the temple at Po Nagar. The essentially Shivaist **iconography** of Cham art, with the exception of a Buddhist interlude (late 9C-early 10C) and several rare appearances of the God Vishnu, reveals the undisputed influence of India, although over time it developed its own stylistic forms, enriched by Khmer, Indonesian and sometimes Chinese influences.

The earliest known works, which come from the **E1 tower at My Son** (mid-7C), impress by their sobriety and elegance. The carved altar base, a recurrent element of Cham architecture, features an elaborate blend of divinities with other more everyday motifs. In the late 9C, the **Dong Duong style** reveals a radical change in direction, particularly apparent in its adoption of concepts such as the Buddhist Greater Vehicle. The intricate foliated motifs and thread-like tracery bear witness to the Buddhist abhorrence of empty spaces and the guardian gods (dvarapala) are depicted with exaggerated faces and stances. After a transition phase, My Son returned to its former **classicism**, revealed by the statues of the now-vanished complex at Tra Kieu (10C), such as the pedestal with apsaras or the altar with dancers (see page 258). The style becomes purer and the lines rounder as the Cham also develop a catalogue of naturalistically depicted animals in which the elephant figures prominently. In the mid-12C, the **Thap Mam style** is illustrated by religious furniture and architectural decorative features which echo the exuberant aspects of Dong Duong. Gods, guardians and animals are covered in robes, the details of which are intricately carved. With its garuda (bird-men), begging dragons, lion-elephants and lions balancing on their heads, the Thap Mam style created one of the most fantastic bestiaries of Asian art. But subsequently, Cham art began to repeat itself and entered a long period of decline, reflecting the absorption of the Champa Empire into Vietnam (see page 21).

Art of the Vietnamese kingdoms

To an even greater extent than Champa art, Vietnamese art has suffered from having long been considered little more than a "marginal" Chinese art. Up until the 10C-11C, this epithet was probably justified. At that time, Vietnam was simply a far-flung province of the Chinese Empire and although many religious foundations date back to this era, nothing of them remains today. Archaeological excavations have unearthed only a few artefacts from tombs, which were designed, along the Chinese model, to be dwelling places in the afterlife and accordingly equipped with crockery and tiny ceramic edifices. Vietnamese art only really emerges when the Vietnamese kingdom becomes independent. From this point on, one of its most striking characteristics is an amazing capacity to assimilate other models – mainly Chinese – into its culture, only to break free of them later.

Not built to last

Wood and clay – The oldest remaining architectural traces can be found in the North, though they were sorely damaged by the 20C wars. Destruction by man is not, however, the only reason that so few edifices remain from the Vietnamese kingdoms. Whether built for secular or religious purposes, Vietnamese architecture was never intended to last. Although it won its independence in 1428, Vietnam remained under Chinese influence, which differed immensely from the Indianised traditions favoured by the Champa.

The materials used remained perishable. Buildings were made out of **wood** and not brick and the **structure** was upheld by **columns** instead of walls. The similarity with its Chinese counterparts is however purely superficial. The amplitude and curves of the turned-up roof are in fact more akin to Dong Son constructions (*see above*). Beginning with a primitive farmhouse built around a single, central post, buildings gradually acquired a multitude of supports, thereby offering more scope to the sculptor's chisel. The roofs were covered in flat **tiles**, laid out like overlapping fish scales, or in semicircular tiles in the Chinese tradition. **Pottery** also became a major feature of architectural decoration and appeared on walls, floors and rooftops. **Stone** was used primarily for foundations, bases of columns, balustrades, bridges and staircases. Brick or mud walls served as simple envelopes and were no more structurally load-bearing than were the inner wooden or bamboo partition walls.

Portable buildings – Partition walls were not the only movable features of this foundation-free architecture. The load-bearing columns were erected without mortice and tenon joints, straight onto the stone bases, enabling the structure to be entirely dismantled. Each building could be easily taken down and rebuilt elsewhere in case of war, natural catastrophe or a change in the seat of power. Such **removals** even occurred within the grounds of the Imperial City at Hue. In 1833, Minh Mang had the throne moved to the south in order to build an enormous golden gate in its place, itself built from materials from a former palace at Gia Long. The passing whims of the royal families were not the only motives behind such displacements, which were also dictated by the **logic of geomancy**. This ancestral science of Chinese origin examines the conjunction of a number of phenomena and the disposition of buildings, to determine what is propitious or ill-fated for any given structure. Geomancy was what caused so many buildings to be built with a **southern aspect**.

Official art

Ghost capitals – The inherently temporary nature of Vietnamese architecture explains why the remains of Vietnam's past capitals fit into just a few museum display-cases, and consist of a few forlorn engraved paving stones and ornamental roof features and tiles. Hoa Lu, the first capital of the independent kingdom (*see page 163*) was moved to Hanoi, and, after eight centuries as the seat of power, transferred to Hue. The only notable exception to this rule was the **Temple of Literature** (*see page 140*), founded in the 11C at Hanoi for the cult of Confucius and enlarged by successive dynasties, and which remained in the city.

Power and protocol – The last Imperial capital, Hue was designed on the Chinese model. Three concentric square enclosures define the three areas of the citadel and, by extension, the protocol of the Nguyen court. The **Capital City** (Kinh Thanh), or citadel, marks the separation between the town and the area where the civilian mandarins and soldiers in the emperor's service lived. The immense Southern Gate set in the ramparts leads into the **Imperial City** (Hoang Thanh), which contains the throne room and temples devoted to the worship of the dynasty's ancestors. A third gate leads into the **Forbidden Purple City** (Tu Cam Thanh), the private quarters of the imperial family. The dragons making their way around the rooftops in search of a pearl add a frivolous touch to this otherwise austere edifice.

Eternal palaces – Up until the dynasty of the Later Le in the 15C, Vietnamese monarchs were interred in **simple burial mounds**, marked by a stele. After this they adopted the customs of the Chinese court and had eternal palaces built within concentric enclosures similar to those of their citadels and set in vast grounds. This type of construction is the only departure from the otherwise short-lived, removable qualities so characteristic of Vietnamese architecture. The **tombs** of Hue's emperors are the apotheosis of this style of funerary art *(see page 243)*. Built during the emperor's life, each one is stamped with its future occupant's personality. Tu Duc's tomb illustrates his whimsical, poetic nature, Minh Mang's burial place echoes his austere, rigorous personality and Khai Dinh's symbolises his grandiloquence.

Religious art

The Buddhist pagoda – Introduced between the 3C and 6C, Buddhism, which only prospered from the 11C-14C under the royal patronage of the Ly and then the Tran dynasties, was to bequeath Vietnam a number of masterpieces.

The pagoda *(chua)* is a complex of buildings, whose number varies depending on the importance of the site and its topography. The layout reveals a sense of rhythm and space, characteristic of this modular approach to architecture which alternates courtyards and buildings *(see page 46)*. It is an architectural form which attaches great importance to blending in with its surrounding landscape, as is illustrated by the Thay (Master's) Pagoda, suspended between mountain and water *(see page 159)*, the Keo Pagodas *(see page 166)*, But Thap *(see page 161)* in the flat expanses of the delta or again, the Tay Phuong Pagoda perched on an outcrop *(see page 160)*.

The heart of the pagoda is the **shrine**. It is surrounded by a series of galleries *(hanh)*, which enclose it on three sides and are preceded by a large courtyard, entered through a gate. The rear gallery houses the altars devoted to the patriarchs who lived here. The side galleries provide shelter to the pilgrims and sometimes accommodation for monks. Among the outbuildings, there is often a tower with a bell or a gong, which is rung at prayer times, and stone **reliquary-towers**, which are in fact the real "pagodas", containing the ashes of monks or lay donors.

The shrine is divided up into three successive areas, sometimes all housed under the same roof. An **ante-room** (tien duong), where guardian gods *(ho phap)* protect the faithful come to worship, an **Incense Room** (thieu huong) where the monks read prayers and a **Main Altar Room** (thuong dien) which houses the pantheon's divinities, who stand at the foot of the trinity of Present, Historical and Future Buddhas. Stone carving is rare. Buddhist artists preferred to carve painted, lacquered or natural wood, producing works of immense depth of expression.

A review of Vietnamese Buddhist art would be lacking should it fail to mention one of its most unusual facets, a sort of combined effort of nature and man. These rocky **cave pagodas**, where the blue light of day filters through natural windows, were initially the result of erosion leaving curiously shaped caverns later adopted by worshippers. Among the most famous are the Marble Mountains at Da Nang *(see page 259)*, the caves at Lang Son *(see page 222)* and those on the Mountain of Fragrant Traces *(see page 156)*, not far from Hanoi.

Temples inhabited by spirits – In former times, each northern village had its own **communal house** *(dinh)*, where the wise-men of the village held court, under the aegis of the community's patron spirits – founder, hero or beast. A large courtyard served to welcome the villagers during local festivals. Of a barlong-type construction, each house had altars at either end of its long structure. From the 17C, the *dinh* was to supplant the pagoda in size and in ornamentation. Beams, joists, lintels and façades were smothered in carvings of highly varied themes, ranging from fabulous animals to seasonal flowers and scenes of daily life and fairy-tales and myths. Those communal houses still standing after the ravages of the war have been brought back into service, such as Dong Khang *Dinh* at Dinh Bang *(see page 160)* or Hang Khen *Dinh* at Haiphong *(see page 172)*.

The *den* is a **national or regional temple**, the layout of which varies greatly; built in honour of a king *(such as the den at Hoa Lu page 163)*, a spirit *(see Den Quan Thanh page 141)* or a famous person *(see Den Ngoc Son page 129)*. These cults emerged under the Trinh family (1533-1789) and they contributed to developing a "national" style of architecture which abandoned Chinese themes in favour of a more distinctly Vietnamese style. One of the characteristics of a *den* is that many house a simple **tablet** on which the donor's name or the person's insignia of office (crown, mandarin cap) is inscribed, based on the model of the ancestors' altars. When it contains an effigy, this is placed in the back of the shrine, hidden by a carved wooden screen.

20C hybrid art

Colonial influences

From 1860 to 1945, the whole country was subjected to a new influence introduced by colonial France. This initially gave rise to identical reproductions of styles prevalent in France at the time, but little by little an unusual combination of styles was to emerge. This phenomenon was furthered in the early 19C by the work carried out by French engineers in the building of the Gia Long citadels at Hue, Hanoi and Haiphong.

Cochinchina was the first land conquered and the first to witness Western architecture with the building of the Customs' House in Saigon in 1862. Saigon and Hanoi were to become home to France's administrative and municipal institutions (town hall, law courts, governor's residence, post office and customs house), cultural bodies (theatres) and religious edifices (cathedrals), all of which were built in a style which can only be described as **eclectic neo-Classicism**.

Dating from the late 19C, Phat Diem Cathedral *(see page 165)*, whose construction and decoration are reminiscent of Vietnamese temples, augurs the birth of the hybrid 1920s style, a cross between new international movements and local architectural currents. This **"Indochinese" style** was employed in institutions of a cultural nature, such as the Louis Finot Museum (1925) or the University of Indochina (1926) in Hanoi. Legitimately rejected by the nationalist movement and neglected for a long time by historians, this colonial legacy has recently come back into fashion and is now accepted as an integral aspect of Vietnam's artistic heritage.

From socialist realism to contemporary creations

Contemporary Vietnamese art, released from its ties with religion and royal patronage, took root in the foundation of the **Indochinese School of Fine Arts**, created in 1925 in Hanoi. Trained in the major Western art trends, a generation of painters and sculptors born in the early 20C was, for the first time ever, to acquire the **status of artist** and to discover a **freedom of expression** unhampered by the bonds of patronage.

From 1945, artistic expression was required to reflect daily life and to faithfully reproduce Ho Chi Minh's theories. Vietnam's presence within the sphere of Soviet influence in 1975 effectively ruled out any possibility of individual creativity in favour of a pompous Socialist realism and the glorification of Leninist-Marxist thinkers. Cut off from the rest of the world, Vietnam was to delve into its own past to unearth the foundations of an original art, exhibited in galleries which opened in Ho Chi Minh City, Hanoi and Da Nang, as part of the *Doi Moi* policy. A new artistic language developed, reinforced by a rekindling of **traditional village arts**. This interest in traditional crafts was to revive dormant skills such as **lacquer-work**.

Since the end of the 1990s, the regime has slightly slackened its censorship policy, thus giving rise to the emergence of forms of **contemporary expression**. Exhibitions of the work of Vietnamese artists have been held in London, New York and Paris.

VIETNAMESE RELIGIOUS ARCHITECTURE

PAGODA

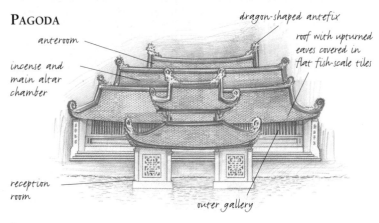

dragon-shaped antefix

roof with upturned eaves covered in flat fish-scale tiles

anteroom

incense and main altar chamber

reception room

outer gallery

LAYOUT OF A PAGODA

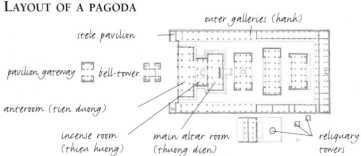

outer galleries (hanh)

stele pavilion

pavilion gateway   bell-tower

anteroom (tien duong)

incense room (thieu huong)

main altar room (thuong dien)

reliquary towers

THE TEMPLE GATE

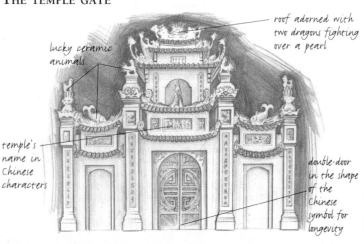

roof adorned with two dragons fighting over a pearl

lucky ceramic animals

temple's name in Chinese characters

double-door in the shape of the Chinese symbol for longevity

H. Choimet/Michelin

VIETNAMESE BUDDHIST GODS

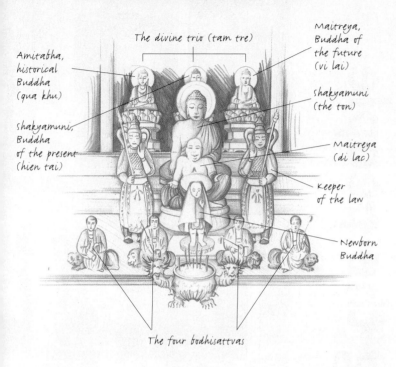

The divine trio (tam tre)

Amitabha, historical Buddha (qua khu)

Maitreya, Buddha of the future (vi lai)

Shakyamuni (the ton)

Shakyamuni, Buddha of the present (hien tai)

Maitreya (di lac)

Keeper of the law

Newborn Buddha

The four bodhisattvas

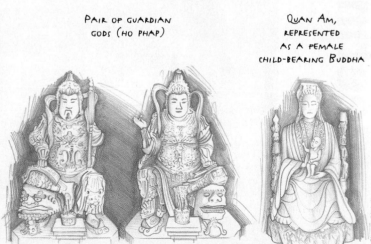

PAIR OF GUARDIAN GODS (HO PHAP)

QUAN AM, REPRESENTED AS A FEMALE CHILD-BEARING BUDDHA

H. Choimet/Michelin

Meeting the people

Newspaper stand

A MICROCOSM OF THE PEOPLE OF ASIA

The ethnic patchwork and linguistic variety of this tiny Asian country are such that it is home to 54 ethnic groups and 5 language families. By comparison, 56 minorities share the immense Chinese territory, but only one single family of languages, Indo-European, is spoken from the western shores of the Bay of Bengal as far as the eastern coasts of the Atlantic. Ethnically, Vietnam reflects the same diversity as its great neighbour. The majority ethnic group (86.7%), the Viet or the Kinh, amount to 56 million, while the smallest, the O Du, number a mere 194 individuals. The roughly 15% of non-Viet occupy two-thirds of the country, most of it consisting of land which is marginal, either because of its harsh climate or difficult topography (or both). Outside the towns and the coastal regions, it is possible to meet tribes who continue to cherish their ancient, cultural identity in an age of globalisation, others who, over time, have created a hybrid identity, and still others who have wholly opted for Vietnamisation or Westernisation (*see costumes in "A festival of colour", page 55*).

Untangling the ethnic web

According to Vietnamese legend

At the dawn of humanity, the **dragon Lac Long Quan** wedded the **immortal Au Co**. Their union produced one hundred identical eggs, each of which contained a boy child. However the different backgrounds of Au Co and Lac Long Quan forced them to part. The immortal mother headed for the high mountains taking with her fifty of their children. The dragon, son of the water, descended underground towards the rivers and seas with the rest of their offspring. His descendants formed the **line of Hung kings**, the country's first sovereigns (*see page 19*). This ancient myth illustrates the divide between the inhabitants of the highlands and the lowlands which still persists today.

According to the map

The homeland of the Viet has spread over time from Tonkin to the centre, the coastal plains of Annam and as far south as the Mekong Delta. They share this southern region with other rice-growers, such as the descendants of the Cham and Khmer kingdoms that have been swallowed up over the centuries. The coastal towns are also home to communities of Hoa, former Chinese nationals, who settled in the region to trade. But it is in the hills and mountains of the Vietnamese Highlands – Au Co's land in fact – that the country's greatest ethnic diversity is found, small but distinctive human groupings which in places straddle the border with the neighbouring states of Cambodia, Laos and China.

According to history

This distribution of populations reflects the "order of arrival" brought about by the migration southwards, which involved not only Vietnam, but the whole of Southeast Asia. The Viet and the Muong are among those that Chinese history books describe as the **Hundred Yue** (Viet being the Vietnamese pronunciation of Yue), who inhabited China to the south of the Yangtse River, well over 2 000 years ago. The **Austronesians** – by which is meant a family of languages spoken from the Philippines to Madagascar and Indonesia – are another very ancient group of settlers. Among these were the Cham who developed the coastal plains of Annam and founded their first kingdom, Champa, at the end of the 2C BC. At around the same period, the **ancestors of the Khmer** had set about draining the marshy lands around the Mekong Delta. All these peoples were to be absorbed by the Viet expansion southwards.

In the mountainous regions of the Tonkin Highlands, similar phenomena have been observed. Around 1000 AD, **Thai speaking peoples** established irrigated rice-growing regions on the borders of China and Southeast Asia, along a strip of land which stretched from Cao Bang to Burma, passing through what is now Thailand. They founded the kingdoms of Siam and Lao, leaving Tonkin to grapple with the vassal rulers of Vietnam and the Middle Empire. Little **colonies of Yao speaking peoples** probably also settled in the same region around the 13C-14C, having reached the end of their march through neighbouring China.

In the 18C, shock-waves from the ethnic uprisings which rocked the Chinese Empire up until the late 19C were to reach as far as the mountains of North Vietnam. **H'mong families**, fleeing the brutal Chinese administration, settled in the northwest of the country. Several **Tibeto-Burmese groups** followed, among which were the Ha Ni, who came from Yunnan through the Red River Valley. All these peoples were already present when the first seeds of the Vietnamese-French Indochinese conflict were sown. The majority rallied to the cause of their adopted nation, but several local chieftains did attempt to back the French.

Contemporary events continue to alter the demographic borders of Vietnam's populations, as is illustrated by the **Highland colonisation** policy begun in the late 1970s. The northern and southern deltas, together with the central coastal region, have always been the dominion of the Viet, but of late, many of them have been resettled in parts of the northern Highlands, formerly the sole domain of the Tai, H'mong-Yao and Tibetan-Burmese, and in the Central Highlands, previously only inhabited by Austronesian and Mon-Khmer peoples.

The five Vietnamese families

The Austro-Asians

The "East Asian" family, numbering some 94% of Vietnam's population, represents a massive majority. They originate from two language groups, Viet-Muong and Mon-Khmer, but this apparent unity hides enormous disparities.

The Viet-Muong – These two peoples were the pioneers of the North.

The **Viet** long confined themselves to the Red River Delta, which they had developed since the Neolithic Period, before embarking on their migration southwards (*see page 21*). Dominated by the Chinese for a millennium, they inherited a culture which caused them to relinquish some of their own customs. Hence, even though they had formerly lived in houses on stilts, as is shown by the architecture of the communal house at Dinh Bang, near Hanoi (*see page 160*), they eventually adopted the Chinese architectural style, building their homes directly onto the ground. The same influence was felt on dress and the women swapped their skirts for trousers.

The **Muong** (915 000 inhabitants), their closest cousins, have for their part remained in the land of Au Co and can still be found in the foothills of Hoa Binh. They have retained ancient traditions which owe nothing to their Chinese neighbour. Their houses are built on low stilts, close to flooded rice paddies. They improvise

G de Benoist/MICHELIN

Brightly-coloured Ha Ni costumes

ingenious hydraulic systems from bamboo to harness and canalise this water power. The women still wear straight skirts, weave brightly-coloured striped cotton fabric on pedal looms and produce the finest woven baskets in the country. They prefer to transport their goods in a basket, strapped across the back or forehead in mountain fashion, unlike their counterparts in the plains who carry their wares in baskets strung on a pole carried over the shoulders.

The Mon-Khmer – Even though this group is made up of 21 different ethnic sub-groups, it represents only 2% of the whole population. The **Khmer** are clearly in the majority (895 300 inhabitants), but not only in numerical terms. They live in the Mekong Delta and are the proud descendants of the Angkor Empire (9C-15C) whose wealth was founded on its intensive crops of rice. These people continue to pass on their know-how by growing 150 species of rice and by their clever craft skills in areas such as weaving, pottery and basket-work. They get about in traditional sampans or what are known as motor-powered "shrimp tails", perfectly at home on the meandering branches of the Mekong. Following in the footsteps of their Cambodian cousins, they practise Theravada Buddhism, unlike the other Vietnamese Buddhists, who follow the Mahayana branch. Their monks wear saffron-coloured habits and withdraw to study in pagodas built by villagers.

The **other Mon-Khmer groups** seem to be centuries apart from the Khmer. They are scattered throughout the Highlands and practise a rudimentary form of dry rice-growing using basic tools such as machetes. In the northwest, the Mon-Khmer and neighbouring Tai groups influenced each other. Most of their craft skills are related to the weaving of baskets which they use to display and carry their wares. Their homes reflect their strong community spirit, whether it be the long house (up to 100m long), where several couples and their children live, or the communal house where the village's teenagers carry out rites of passage into adulthood. The communal house is the pride and joy of stilt architecture and such houses are always larger, higher and finer than any others in the village. In common with their Austronesian neighbours in the Highlands, (the Gia Rai), the largest group, the **Ba Na** from the Buon Ma Thuot region (137 000 inhabitants) also build elaborate tombs, made almost entirely out of plants.

The Tai-Kadai

The Tai – The Tai branch of this family is the one most commonly found in Vietnam. Similar to the Viet, it descends from the Hundred Yue, *(see page 50)* who embarked upon a migratory trail from China's southwest coast westwards. The **Tay** (1.2 million inhabitants) and the **Nung** (705 000 inhabitants), who have settled around Cao Ban and Lang Son on the Chinese borders, probably arrived first. Repeated contacts with China and Vietnam have made deep inroads into their culture and their social organisations, formerly divided into hereditary territories. Such influences can be seen in their dwellings, built generally from a mixture of clay, straw and un-baked bricks, in Chinese fashion. Similarly, their religion is stamped with Taoism and Chinese Buddhism. All the Tai peoples are excellent craftsmen and their family know-how ranges from weaving mats or baskets to wood carving. The **Tai** (1 million inhabitants) developed their rich rice-growing expertise, founded on crop rotation and irrigation, in the fertile valleys of the northwest. Water is

The Tai version of their origins
The birth of the Tai occurred after the Flood, from which only three spirits called "khun" escaped. Together they owned a buffalo, which, on its death, gave birth to little shoots which sprouted from its muzzle, turning into enormous marrow plants. The spirits thought they could hear sounds coming from within the giant plants so they drilled little holes into them with a red-hot poker. One by one, dark-faced highlanders, neighbours of the Tai, emerged from the charred holes. The plants still seemed to be inhabited, so the khun made other holes, this time with a chisel, and out popped the Tai's ancestors.

transported by a wide variety of techniques (canals, dams and channels), including the emblematic bucket wheel. Their irrigation skills led them to plant fruit trees and tea. The Tai continue to practise traditions such as ancestral worship of spirits and use of mediums. The houses, still built on stilts, differ within the various sub-groups. The White Tai add a veranda in front of their houses, while the Black Tai homes feature a rounded roof resembling an upturned tortoise shell.

The Kadai – This family is only represented by tiny groups, such as the **Co Lao** (1 500 inhabitants). They practise slash-and-burn techniques but also manure their fields.

The H'mong-Yao

The H'mong (560 000 inhabitants) and the Yao (480 000 inhabitants) – called Dao (pronounced "Zao" by the Vietnamese), are in fact a sizeable (1.1 %) minority, related to population groups which in China amount to 7.4 million and 2.1 million respectively. They can be found throughout the vast territory extending from southwest China to the borders with Laos and Thailand, in small, scattered hamlets of montagnards or highlanders. They never founded more than what were to be embryonic political organisations. This situation is explained by their way of life, because the H'mong and Yao are traditionally nomadic peasants, who rely solely on the natural resources of the mountains to survive. They are traditionally very attached to their independence and have continued to fight for their autonomy ever since the country's reunification in 1975.

G de Benoist/MICHELIN

The H'mong – They grow crops on the highest lands and live in villages of only a few dozen houses. Their single-storey, often very basic dwellings are made out of planks of wood or woven bamboo. They grow crops, using slash-and-burn techniques, of corn, barley and occasionally rice, as well as flax and fruit trees. They are also distinguished breeders of horses, which are their main means of transport. Their scattered presence and autonomous way of life have enabled them to maintain ancient crafts. Skilled blacksmiths, they make all their own agricultural implements, as well as long barrelled hunting rifles. They still know how to weave bamboo, make silver jewellery, manufacture paper, furniture and harnesses and saddles for their horses. Lineage and ancestor worship continue to play a significant part in the daily life of this scattered people. For the same reasons, fairs remain central to their existence, not only for trading purposes but also so that young people can meet each other.

The Dao – Even more scattered than the H'mong, the Dao speak a variety of languages which are reflected in their different costumes. However this apparent diversity hides a deep-rooted cultural unity, be it just the claim that they all descend from a common ancestor, Pan Hu, a legendary dog married to a Chinese princess. They live in hamlets of less than ten houses, sometimes built on stilts. In the higher regions, they grow corn, but also wet rice crops, fruit trees and medicinal plants. They also breed farmyard animals and draught stock. Chinese practices are strongly reflected in their religion and the Taoist pantheon of gods plays a major role in their exorcism ceremonies.

Soberly-dressed Nung woman

The Sino-Tibetans

The Chinese – Chinese-speakers, among them the **Hoa** (900 000 inhabitants) – ethnic Chinese as strictly defined – the **San Diu** (91 000 inhabitants) and the **Ngai** (1 100 inhabitants), form the great majority of this language family. The Chinese are mostly descended from trading families from southern China, who settled in the ports of Vietnam in the 17C.

The Tibeto-Burmese – A group of half a dozen small tribes, who are highly-skilled and renowned craftsmen, particularly in the area of basket work. They make a whole range of baskets (attached across the forehead or onto the back) used to transport goods. Depending on their ethnic group, they live either in stilt houses or in single-storey homes built on the ground. The **Ha Ni** from the high Song Da (12 500 inhabitants) are the largest of these groups. They carve their terraced and irrigated fields into the mountain flanks, like giant sculptures. Women play a major role in Tibeto-Burman society, which also upholds time-honoured traditions of ancestor and spirit worship.

The Austronesians

The **Cham** (99 000 inhabitants) have bequeathed a great number of inscriptions, both in Sanskrit and in their own language, together with a rich architectural legacy of *kala*, shrine-towers in brick, which can be found dotted along the coast from the Pass of Clouds to Phan Thiet. These monuments show the boundaries of their former kingdom of Champa, subsequently absorbed by Vietnam. In the 15C, the Cham adopted the religion of Islam on contact with Malaysia, whose language is very similar to their own. Still Muslim today, they grow rice and are renowned for their elaborate silk weaving.

The other groups of Austronesians were long confused, under the pejorative term of *Moi* ("savages"), with the Austro-Asians of the Highlands, with whom they share the same rice-growing techniques in either wet or dry paddies. The confusion possibly also stemmed from the fact they share a common construction of longhouses. The most spectacular of these are those of a tribe of elephant tamers, the **E De** (or Rhade) from Buon Ma Thuot (195 000 inhabitants). Built as a ship-like structure, they echo the architecture of the Toraja from Celebes in the Indonesian archipelago. Among the **Gia Rai** of Plei Ku (71 700 inhabitants), the ornamentation of their tombs reveals the influence of their distant Indonesian cousins. The tombs of the chiefs are often decorated by a gallery of wooden sculpture, sometimes elaborate, sometimes quite primitive, depicting men, women and birds.

A microcosm of the people of Asia

The 54 ethnic groups of the five families

Austro-Asians (94%)	
4 Viet-Muong groups	Viet, Muong, Tho, Chut.
21 Mon-Khmer groups	Khmer, Ba Na, Xo Dang (Sedang), Hre, Co Ho, Mnong, Xtieng, Kho Mu, Bru, Co Tu, Gie Treng, Ta Oi, Ma, Co, Cho Ro, Xinh Mun, Khang, Mang, Ro Mam, Brau, O Du.
Tai-Kadai (3.7%)	
8 Tai groups	Tay, Tai, Nung, San Chay, Giay, Lao, Lu, Bo Y.
4 Kadai groups	La Chi, Co Lao, La Ha, Pu Peo.
H'mong-Yao (1.1%)	
1 H'mong group	H'mong.
2 Yao groups	Dao, Pa Then.
Austronesians (0.8%)	
5 Malayo-Polynesian groups	Gia Rai (Jaraï), E De (Rhade), Cham, Ra Glai, Chu Ru.
Sino-Tibetans (0.4%)	
3 Chinese groups	Hoa, San Diu, Ngai.
6 Tibeto-Burmese groups	Ha Ni, Phu La, La Hu, Lolo, Cong, Si La.

A FESTIVAL OF COLOUR

In Vietnam, dress and costume continue to play an important role, not just on festive occasions, but also in everyday life. This diversity is apparent wherever you look, from the young pilgrim women from Tonkin tightly wrapped in black and brown robes to brightly-coloured processions of silk through the rice paddies, clusters of young girls in pastel-coloured tunics or indigo-garbed crowds attending a fair in the Highlands. Whether made from elaborately woven silk, hemp, jute or indigo-dyed cotton, dress remains the visible sign of the multitude of cultures which exists in this nation, even if today's urban population, exposed to Western influence, often sports T-shirts and jeans rather than skirts and shirts. The basic national dress revolves around a button-down or slip-over tunic worn over a long, straight skirt, a pleated skirt over leggings, or trousers. This basic pattern is then adapted and added to with accessories, shapes, colours and techniques which designate individual tribes and peoples.

Ao dai, the most attractive school uniform

From one end of the country to the other, girls can be seen wearing what must be one of the most attractive school uniforms ever invented. The **ao dai**, pronounced "ao zai" in the North and "ao yai" in the South, became the **national costume** in the mid-18C, on the orders of Lord Nguyen. Men and women alike wore a long button-down tunic over trousers. Dressmakers in the 1930s and then again in the 1950s were to transform this costume into the seductive and irresistibly feminine garment worn today. Widened and lengthened to hide the feet, the trousers add allure and grace to all women, their silhouette further enhanced by a zipped side-opening to the tunic and two long fluttering panels which flatter the bust and the waist.

G de Benoist/MICHELIN

Dao woman

Skilled weavers

The Khmer, Cham and Tai tribes are accomplished weavers, but their precious **silk brocaded sarongs**, requiring vastly complex weaving techniques, only come out on the occasion of marriages.

The Tai – The identity of this tribe is displayed by its use of specific colours and patterns. In the past the **Black and White Tai** could be recognised by the former's black skirt and the latter's white tunic. Although such clear distinctions have disappeared today, the Black Tai still have an easily recognisable dress code, particularly at Son La. The women wear a button-down jacket, embellished by silver pieces, and wrap a **dark-indigo scarf** around their head in such a way as to display one of its triangular embroidered edges. Their long hair can sometimes be seen, wound high on top of the head and fastened with a single silver hairpin.

The Nung and the Tay – The rather drab dark- or light-blue cotton tunic, worn over the Sino-Vietnamese-style black trousers of these tribes, who settled along the Chinese border, seems very dull by comparison with their flamboyant neighbours. The Nung women wrap an **indigo turban** around their hair, while the Tay women have adopted the distinctive **conical hat** which can be seen on either side of the border. On feast days, the young Nung women sometimes don **jewellery**, which is made by their own skilled village craftsmen, including necklaces, chains and bands decorated with silver beads.

Textile divides in the North

The H'mong – The H'mong's rich array of textiles contains a wide range of **batik**, **embroidery** and **appliqué** techniques to produce traditional women's costumes of such variety that they have evolved into dozens of sub-groups, each as unique and stunning as the other.

With the exception of the White H'mong (H'mong Trang) from Lai Chau who wear trousers, all the H'mong women wear a skirt. Their hair, always fastened up in a bun, is either hidden under a colourful scarf or increased two-fold, even three-fold, by the addition of a false hairpiece to create an immense turban. The highly distinctive **Red H'mong** (H'mong Do) from Sin Do use scarlet wool in their turbans. They also sport a white-on-indigo batik pleated skirt worn under a tunic, with coins sewn into the collar and sleeves and a little appliqué bag over their shoulder.

The Multicoloured H'mong (H'mong Hoa) wear jackets wtih brightly-coloured sleeves, hems and collars, over elaborately worked skirts, either worn mid-length and made from a pleated fabric which combines batik techniques and printed patterns (at Lai Chau), or fuller, ankle-length and entirely covered in appliqué braid (at Can Cau).

The **Black H'mong** (H'mong Den) from Sapa favour dark indigo fabrics, enhanced solely by silver jewellery. Their dark costume draws the eye to the superb metal-working and jewellery skills of this tribe. Silver necklaces, collar bands (sometimes worn by men), earrings, brooches and buttons abound among this hill tribe.

The Dao – The Dao women are prolific embroiderers. They use almost exclusively **cross-stitch**, worked from the back of the fabric, covering almost every available square inch of fabric. They favour **trousers** over skirts, worn under a long, front-fastening **tunic** split up both sides. Like the H'mong, they embroider from memory, relying on a range of models and patterns passed down from mother to daughter. The variety of models and decorative themes has led to sub-divisions of the Dao into **Red Dao** (Dao Do), who wear a red pom-pom around their necks, hence their name, the **Black Dao** (Dao Den) (*see below*), the "white-trousered" Dao (Dao Quan Trang), the "blue-jacketed" Dao (Dao Thanh Y), the "tunic" Dao (Dao Lan Ten) and the "long jacketed" Dao (Dao Tien). The latter's costume is made up of a long indigo panelled jacket over a batik skirt. Around their necks, they wear a tight necklace of coloured beads, threads of which hang down over their bust and back. They wear a white head-dress, part of which covers the nape of the neck, over their plucked forehead.

The Black Dao from Sin Ho are dubbed *Khau*, which means dressmakers. Their wide, black trousers are entirely covered in colourful embroidered strips. The mid-length tunic, to which embroidered braids are added, is fastened by several layers of fabric; a long indigo apron is sometimes worn over the top. Their hair is tied up in an abundant indigo turban, which reveals the forehead and nape. Around their necks hang heavy silver bands, fastened at the back by long pendants, to which old coins have been added; their arms are encircled in enamelled silver armbands in the shape of double-headed dragons.

Even when not wearing full traditional dress, a distinctive detail often betrays the origins of these women. It might be a long embroidered belt wrapped around a flowered nylon shirt, silver earrings or the custom of plucking the eyebrows and forehead or lacquering their teeth black.

Sober Highland dress

Apart from their use of a **vertical loom** of Indonesian type, the Highland tribes are basket-makers rather than weavers and generally buy or exchange fabric with other tribes. Some tribes however used to practise a technique, now obsolete, called **tapa** or bark fabric, obtained by beating vegetable fibres.

Only a few elderly men and women still wear the traditional dress common to hill Austro-Asian and Austronesian tribes (*see page 51*). For the men, this entails wearing a length of fabric around the hips and passed between the legs, similar to a loin-cloth, and in the case of the women, a straight calf-length skirt. On feast days, a split tunic, sometimes a T-shirt, is worn by both sexes. Jewellery is more discreet here. Some old women still wear "cotton-reels" or **ear-tubes**, made from a variety of materials, often bamboo. Glass necklaces and bracelets, long silver or aluminium hairpins, wooden combs inlaid with metal or feathers comprise all the jewellery worn in the Highlands.

G de Benoist/MICHELIN

Multi-coloured H'mong costume

HYBRID RELIGIONS

The 1976 Constitution provides the Vietnamese with a relative freedom of worship. Most of them are Buddhist, but after a millennium of Chinese occupation (2C BC-10C AD), they have also assimilated Taoism and Confucianism into their own animistic folk religion, leading to a fusion known as the **Triple Religion** or *Tam Giao*. In the 17C, the arrival of Christianity, a monotheistic religion, produced a religious revolution and Vietnam is today the second Catholic Asian country after the Philippines (10% of the population). Small, well-established sections of the community are Muslim and Hindu (0.5%), and in the 20C, Buddhist movements such as Cao Dai and Hoa Hao also emerged in the Mekong Delta.

Animism

Vietnam's various religious cults have always been grafted onto ancient native beliefs, according to which the universe, or rather the heavenly, earthly and human universes are ordered by visible and invisible forces, which must be appeased by way of offerings. The heavens are governed by the Lord of the Sky, helped by the spirits of the Sun, Moon, Wind, Rain and Stars, while the earthly world is governed by the Gods of the Earth and the Hearth, assisted by the Spirits of the Ground, the Rivers and the Mountains. Today many Vietnamese still cherish and maintain a small family **altar** devoted to the domestic triad of the Spirits of the Hearth, the Ground and the Earth Goddess.

A certain number of animals, including mythical divinities, are also worshipped for their supernatural powers. Among them, the dragon which symbolises masculinity (yang), virtue and prosperity, and the phoenix, which symbolises femininity (yin), grace and immortality. The tortoise represents long life, and the unicorn, happiness.

Taoism

Taoism was created in China in the 6C BC by a certain **Lao-tzu**, a mystic, scholar, and contemporary and adversary of Confucius, and this philosophy spread through Chinese-dominated Vietnam some 2000 years ago. In opposition to Confucian doctrine which preaches man's involvement in politics and society, Taoism advocates a more metaphysical view of the world and the search for individual liberty in order to reach the **Tao**, a morally correct "way" or "path". The *Tao* represents a harmonious orderly universe, symbolised by a cosmic force both masculine (the active yang) and feminine (the passive yin) which governs nature and guides humankind by an unspoken, motionless law or moral code. Only a person's inner mystical intuition, as opposed to their intelligence, will enable them to attain the goal of living in perfect harmony with the environment and, by extension, with the cosmos.

A conception of existence such as this, in which contemplation and inner happiness figure so prominently, was only accessible to scholars who had chosen to forgo the earthly world and its trappings. The population at large was content to seize upon the Taoist pantheon and to worship many gods, the statues of whom are invariably placed in Buddhist pagodas or smaller shrines, *den*. Among those worshipped are **Thien Hau Thanh Mau**, Goddess of the Sea and protector of sailors, fishermen and navigators and above all, **Ngoc Hoang** (Jade Emperor), who reigns over the skies in company with his three ministers, **Nam Tao** (Southern Star) who registers births, **Bac Dau** (Polar Star), deaths, and the **Tao Quan** (Spirits of the Hearth) who report on families at each New Year.

Confucianism

Introduced by the Chinese in the 3C, by the 15C Confucianism had become the **state philosophy** in Vietnam, ousting Buddhism which had filled this role up until then. This happened as a result of the victory of King Le Loi, a rich landowner who freed his country from its Chinese yoke thanks to the well-timed advice of his spiritual guide, a highly-astute Confucian scholar and strategist. Freed from the influence of the Buddhist monks, Vietnam became a secular nation. Followers of Confucius, while not refuting the existence of heaven, place more emphasis on human tasks and consequently on education, hard work and duty.

The definition of an honest man

The teachings of **Confucius**, a Chinese humanist who lived in the 6C BC, advocate a social and political morality which can be applied both to the family and the nation. An honest person must, first and foremost, respect two principles of **goodness** and **justice** and **six moral virtues**, namely, filial piety (hence the worship of ancestors), courage, loyalty, keeping one's word, respecting rituals and accepting an order of precedence.

Finally, to maintain harmony and social cohesion, Confucian doctrine defines **five natural relationships** all based on obedience and respect. Subjects must respect their monarch, children their parents, wives their husbands, youth must respect age and there must also be respect between friends. Individuals are conceived essentially as social beings and their own individual freedom comes after their duties to the community.

It was only through **education**, available to all, that humans could acquire these moral values and thus, an honest person was fundamentally an educated person. Pupils had to study classical texts, drawn from Chinese history – very rich in knightly exploits – in which the hero's behaviour illustrates the right attitude to be adopted in all life's circumstances. Nowadays parents instil these precepts of good behaviour into their children, particularly through concepts such as ancestor worship and family solidarity.

Buddhism

The teachings of the Buddha

What is the root of human suffering and how can we break free of it? Such was the vast question Prince **Siddharta Guatama** attempted to answer. After attaining supreme knowledge as a result of meditation and asceticism, he became the **Buddha** – "Enlightened One" or "Awakened One" – and spent the rest of his life teaching a doctrine which opens the way to salvation and thereafter, to supreme bliss (*nirvana*). This is based on the observation that **suffering** is a universal phenomenon. **Desire** binds man to his painful existence and he remains a prisoner of his necessarily transitory passions, leading him to be ceaselessly reborn in this earthly world. According to the doctrine of karma, to put an end to this suffering, desire must be eliminated, thus terminating the cycle of rebirth (*samsara*). This is possible for any human being, providing he or she give up all forms of attachment and endeavour to apply the **eight-fold path**: right understanding, right thought, right speech, right action, right livelihood, right effort, right mindfulness and right concentration.

The life of the Buddha

Siddharta Gautama was born around 550 BC to a noble family near the border of India and Nepal. As a child, he was raised as his rank befitted and enjoyed a happy youth, free from pain and suffering. At the age of 29, however he decided to abandon his palace, his wife and young son and, with nothing but the clothes on his back, embarked upon a long spiritual quest. All his attempts were fruitless and he failed to find the answer to his question about the origins of human suffering and how to end it. Finally, when he was quite alone, deserted even by the handful of followers who had accompanied him up until then, he found his way, after a night of meditation. He proclaimed his thoughts to his followers and he came to be the Buddha, the "Enlightened One".

Key Buddhist concepts

Bodhisattva	"Enlightened" holy being, masculine or feminine, from the Mahayana Buddhist pantheon, who has forgone nirvana to help others find salvation.
Bonze	Buddhist monk or priest.
Hinayana	or Theravada. Name given to early Buddhism. Sometimes called the Lesser Vehicle.
Karma	Group of good or bad acts, the accumulated sum of which determines the conditions of rebirth.
Mahayana	Path of salvation open to all beings, following the virtuous example of the bodhisattvas. Form of Buddhism which appeared around the same time as Christianity, also called the Greater Vehicle.
Nirvana	The "extinction" or cessation of all pain and desire, enabling those who have reached it to live in total serenity.
Parinirvana	The "great extinction" or "total nirvana", at the end of the cycle of rebirth marked by the physical death of the Buddha or the saint.
Samsara	Cycle of rebirths, or reincarnations, which end in salvation.

Buddhism in Vietnam

Towards the late 2C, the **Mahayana** Buddhist school, or path of the Greater Vehicle, spread widely first in North Vietnam, before progressing southwards along the land and sea trading routes from India and China. Buddhism reached its apex in the 11C under the Ly dynasty, which regularly employed bonzes as ministers and advisors. In exchange the monasteries grew rich from the services rendered to the State. Nowadays, the monks live off the land which is allotted to them by the State and charity.

The Buddhist pantheon – The followers of *Mahayana*, breaking away from the austere canons of the school of the Lesser Vehicle (*Hinayana*) which remained faithful to the original teachings of the Buddha, strive to respect the three virtues of goodness, compassion and generosity. They venerate the Three Buddhas of the Past (Amitabha or A Di Da), of the Present (Sakyamuni or Thich Ca) and of the Future (Maitreya or Di Lac), as well as the bodhisattvas, "enlightened beings" who have selflessly chosen to renounce or postpone nirvana in order to help others find salvation. The most popular of these is **Quan Am**, or Avalokiteshvara, the Goddess of Mercy, often represented as a woman in a white tunic seated on a throne in front of pagodas. Two other very popular bodhisattvas are **Van Thu**, or Manjushri, God of Wisdom and Intelligence, and **Dia Tang**, or Kshitigarbha, patron of travellers and saviour of damned souls.

The daily life of Buddhist monks – Monks are recruited by the Buddhist School of Vietnam, a state body which represents two sects. Firstly, the **Dhyana school** (zen or thien), a way of meditation based on asceticism and which is the most widespread in Vietnam, and secondly, the **Pure Land school** (Tinh Do), only found in South Vietnam and based on praying to Amitabha, the Buddha of the Past, symbol of purity. Monasteries are open to monks and nuns alike, who live in separate buildings. They are run by a **Council of Elders**, made up of monks chosen by the oldest members. The latter will have had at least 40 years of monastical existence and fulfil the role of spiritual leaders. Novices are welcomed from the age of 10. Monks or nuns can be ordained as young as 13, but only take their vows at the age of 20. **Ordination** is not however final and it is possible to return to secular life, providing the Council of Elders gives its permission.

Daily visit to the pagoda

Daily life is governed according to a sacrosanct ritual. From 5am to 11pm, the monastery's residents pray and meditate, study or teach holy texts, garden and carry out farm work. Monks and nuns gather together to eat lunch and dinner in a communal dining room, in silence and at separate tables. On the 1st (new moon) and the 15th day (full moon) of the lunar calendar, the community (*sangha*) meets under the auspices of the Council of Elders to examine any breaches in discipline. During the first three months of the Buddhist fasting period, which takes place in the rainy season (July-September), the community lives **in isolation** but prays and studies together. Two or three times a year, the community will embark on a **pilgrimage** to one of the main Buddhist sites in China or India.

Christianity

Although the first Portuguese missionaries spent brief periods in North Vietnam as early as the 16C, full-scale evangelisation of the country only really set in from 1615. Portuguese Dominicans and French Jesuits, sent by the Pope, founded missions in the two rival fiefs of the kingdom of Dai Viet, the Trinh in the North and the Nguyen in the centre and the South. These energetic men and women devised the **quoc-ngu** (*see page 85*) which consisted of a romanised version of Vietnamese script, complete with signs to properly express the language's six tones. Bibles and prayer books were soon printed in this new script, enabling the country's "Sunday School" pupils to quickly assimilate the new religion. By 1685, some 800 000 **Catholics** could be found in Vietnam.

This success distressed the Confucian mandarins and scholars, because the converts were no longer allowed to practise certain customs, such as ancestor worship, as these were considered superstitious. The Trinh, champions of the nation's identity, expelled the Northern Mission in 1630. Over the next two centuries, relations between Vietnam's sovereigns and the Catholic missionaries ranged from poor to bad and some persecution of Christians took place. Eventually, in the 19C, this provided France with an ideal pretext to invade the country. After the Geneva Accords (1954) which ended France's presence and divided the country into two states, 600 000 Christians from the North fled to the South. In 1975, when the nation was reunified, all Christian institutions, such as schools, were nationalised.

The **selection of priests** and bishops remains a subject of controversy with the Communist authorities and, despite a more liberal policy since 1990, diplomatic relations with the Vatican have yet to be restored. The number of candidates allowed to sit entrance exams to seminaries, organised every two years, is subject to a quota (from three to twelve by diocese), and the ordination of priests requires special authorisation from the local People's Committee. Since 1990, a delegation from the Vatican has travelled to Hanoi every year to meet with the Government Department of Religious Affairs in order to negotiate the choice of bishops proposed by the Pope. **Protestants** are a minority (1%). Converted in 1911 by missionaries from the Churches of Good News, the 300 000 followers are mostly Highlanders from central Vietnam.

Islam and Hinduism

Hinduism

Introduced by Indian merchants some 2000 years ago, Hinduism spread for over a millennium along the central coasts bordering the former kingdom of Champa. Today, several thousand Cham, in a minority since the disappearance of their State in the 15C, continue to worship Shiva.

Islam

Islam began to recruit followers among the Cham and also the Khmer living in the Mekong Delta, under the impetus of Malayan and Javanese merchants who landed on the coasts of Champa in the 15C. It failed to gain ground among the rest of the population due to competition from the Europeans who had a monopoly on both sea trade and the promotion of their own faith. Today's several million Vietnamese Muslims have a relatively liberal approach to Islam, particularly as very few of their imams either speak or read Arabic fluently and possess very few copies of the Koran. They pray once a week on Fridays, instead of five times a day and only fast for three days during Ramadan, nor do they go on pilgrimages to Mecca. What is even more striking is that they continue to venerate lingams, phallic symbols of Shiva which are kept in Hindu temples, as well as the traditional spirits of the Ground and the Mountains who protect the Earth.

Other religious movements

Cao Dai

Ngo Van Chieu, a Vietnamese official who claimed to have had "visions" from the beyond, founded this religion which draws upon a variety of Eastern and Western doctrines. A serious student, Chieu was also Taoist, a vegetarian and passionately interested in human beliefs and occult sciences. In 1925 during a séance, a spirit revealed himself to Chieu, claiming to be the Jade Emperor, also called **Cao Dai** ("Supreme Palace or Being"), who had come to show the Way. He was later to reveal himself in the form of an eye, symbolising the Vision of the All.

Founded on Buddhism, the Cao Dai religion describes itself as the "third manifestation of God come to save humanity", after those related by prophets such as Lao-tzu, Confucius, the Buddha, Muhammad and Jesus. The **Cao Dai pantheon** includes personalities chosen for their humanist and moral virtues, such as Joan of Arc, Victor Hugo, Winston Churchill, or the great poet, Nguyen Du.

Although its dogma and rituals are of Buddhist (desire to remove humanity from the cycle of rebirth) and Taoist (use of mediums to communicate with the other world) inspiration, its priesthood is patterned after that of the Roman Catholic Church. At the Holy See at Tay Ninh, a **pontifical sovereign** reigns over a complex religious body, composed of dignitaries, legislators, censors, officials and mediums, all of whom parade with great pomp four times a day *(see page 365)*. The male and female priests all take vows of chastity and poverty and are vegetarian.

Although non-violent, patriotic followers of Cao Dai formed militias which supported the French and then the Americans against the Communists, and their lands were confiscated and churches closed when the country was reunified in 1975. Since 1990, temples have been reopened and the religion now has a reported 2 million followers throughout the world.

Hoa Hao Buddhism

The Hoa Hao sect was founded in 1939 by **Huynh Phu So**, a 20 year-old bonze from a village of the same name. Miraculously cured after a stay on Mt Sam, he returned to his village after studying with the master of the Tra Son Pagoda. One stormy night he fell into a trance and had a revelation of a reformed Buddhism, based on a renewed faith and individual awareness. From then on, Huyn Phu So began to preach a path of abstemious living and renunciation, the **Phat Giao Hoa Hao** ("peace and kindness in the path of the Buddha"), advocating private prayer at home rather than in pagodas, considered to be useless, as were superstitions and other occult rituals. The monk's countless miracle cures attracted many disciples, but his nationalist beliefs led to him to be interned by the French. During the First Indochina War, Huynh Phu So's Japanese-armed militia force gained control of much of the Mekong Delta, until ensuing conflict with the Viet Minh led to his execution in 1947. In the 1960's a faction of his followers, in opposition to the Catholic president, Diem, joined forces with the Viet Cong, but this didn't prevent the latter from outlawing the sect in 1975 after reunification. It has however survived and today numbers some 1.5 million followers.

CEREMONIES AND FESTIVALS

Everyday life in Vietnam is punctuated by countless traditional festivals and local ceremonies, during which each village pays homage to its patron spirit or mythical or historical hero. Most events are based on the lunar-solar calendar and reflect the country's religious diversity. The different religious communities celebrate their own festivals, while the State has imposed a number of national festivals in memory of Communist victories (*see page 67*).

Well-entrenched traditions

Festivals are held according to the **lunar calendar**. This is divided into 12-year cycles, each year corresponding to one of the twelve signs of the Chinese zodiac (Rat, Ox, Tiger, Hare, Dragon, Snake, Horse, Sheep, Monkey, Fowl, Dog, Pig), each of which is divided into twelve months of 29 or 30 days. The Vietnamese thus add an extra month every four years so that their calendar coincides with the Gregorian calendar. All festivals are mobile. In addition to nationwide festivals which are celebrated by the whole population (Tet New Year, Tet Doan Ngo, Trung Nguyen and the mid-Autumn festivals), other local festivals take place in individual villages.

The Tet festival

Of all the festivals in the Vietnamese calendar, New Year is by far the most important. Also called **Tet Nguyen Dan** (Festival of the First Day), it takes place in the first lunar month (late January-early February). It heralds the coming of spring, when the whole countryside is covered in peach and dwarf mandarin (kumquat) trees in full-blossom. In the week prior to the festival, the flower markets of Hanoi and Ho Chi Minh City resemble luxuriant garden festivals such is the profusion of fruit trees in blossom. The trees are also used in all shop window displays. Although the festival in theory lasts a week, only three days are officially national holidays. It is a family festival, often celebrated in one's native village and gives rise to vast migrations from town to country. A strict ritual is respected in order to ensure that the New Year starts under favourable auspices, which involves paying one's debts, carrying out home improvements or repairs, cleaning one's ancestors' tombs, preparing special dishes and buying new clothes.

Preparations – One week before Tet, each home sends its **Spirits of the Hearth** (Tao Quan), often symbolised by a single character, back to the heavens to present the people's wishes to the Jade Emperor (*see page 58*) and to report on the family's behaviour throughout the year. To remain in the God's good books, food, water and betel nuts are offered on the family altar (*see page 58*), and live carp, the spirits' means of transport, are released into the rivers. In some regions, the population also seeks protection from devils, who invade the world of the living when the protective Spirits of the Hearth have their backs turned. A **bamboo pole** is put up in the courtyard, to the top of which is tied a red paper amulet and a mixture of wooden or metal objects, whose cacophony is designed to keep the evil spirits at bay. The house is cleaned from top to bottom and lavishly decorated with peach branches (in the North) and forsythia or kumquat branches (in the South). The walls are also hung with calligraphed verses of wishes and wise proverbs in Chinese characters, painted onto red paper, a symbol of joy. The ancestor's altar is laden with sweet-smelling fruit and fragrant flowers.

Special dishes – All the women of the household take part in the preparations. In addition to crystallised fruit (lotus seeds, coconut), two cakes, which the city-folk now generally buy because they take so long to bake, can be found on every menu. Made out of sticky rice and steamed peas, **banh day** is round "like the sky" and stuffed with bean paste and strips of bacon, symbolising the 10 000 beings of creation; **banh chung** is almost identical but is square "like the Earth".

Wicker masks for Tet

Spring cleaning

During the three days of the Tet festival, it is customary not to clean one's home. Legend relates that a concubine beaten by her merchant husband on New Year's Day fled from her house to find refuge amongst the refuse. She was carelessly swept away with the rubbish, taking with her all the home's luck and causing her husband's business to decline.

Three days of festival – Midnight on New Year's Eve is impatiently awaited. In former times, drums and fire-crackers exploded to welcome the return of the Spirits of the Hearth, whose homecoming put to flight any lingering evil spirits, but nowadays the population has to make do with a tape recording. In front of each family altar piled with food and drink, the master of the house lights joss sticks and kneels down to recite prayers for the New Year. At dawn, the family awakes to prepare offerings for their ancestors before going to the pagoda. The children, decked out in their new clothes, wish their grandparents and their parents happiness, long-life and prosperity. In exchange, they are given "lucky" red envelopes containing crisp, new bank-notes. The first visitor to each house is excitedly awaited, because the home's subsequent good or bad fortune throughout the year will depend on this person, hence a distinct preference for visitors of high moral or social standing. On the first day of the New Year, astrologers are consulted to determine when a variety of events should take place. The second day is devoted to visits to friends and family and the third to visiting the ancestors' tombs.

The unicorn dance – This colourful, boisterous dance starts on New Year's Day in the South, particularly in the Chinese district of Cholon, whose population celebrates New Year on the same day. The mythical, imaginary unicorn, a symbol of **prosperity**, is depicted by a giant papier-maché head which resembles a Pekinese dog and a great length of fabric which looks like a snake covered in fish-scales. Brought to life by martial arts' performers to the frenzied beat of drums, cymbals and gongs, the unicorn parades around the streets, pausing in front of each house or shop for donations. Gifts of money are often attached, together with a head of lettuce, to a bamboo pole which is extended from a first-floor balcony or window; the unicorn's leader is then raised by a human pyramid to reach the prize and devour the lettuce, a sign of good luck. The unicorn is accompanied by another mythical creature, the **Spirit of the Ground**, in the form of a stout man wearing a smiling mask.

Sacred and profane

Buddhist festivals

On the 15th day of the 2nd lunar month (March-April), the **Festival of the Perfume Pagoda** in the province of Ha Son Binh (south of Hanoi) attracts pilgrims from the Red River Delta and the surrounding mountains. They come both to pray to the Buddha and to go on boat trips to the wonderful pagoda-caves and temples on the banks of the River Yen Vi (*see page 156*).

On the 15th day of the 5th lunar month (May-June), the **full moon** is one of the major Buddhist festivals. This day commemorates the birth, enlightenment and death of the Buddha. The faithful go to the pagodas in family groups to pray, listen to the monks and make offerings.

Catholic festivals

Catholics follow the Gregorian calendar and **Christmas**, an official holiday for Catholics, is widely celebrated. Masses are held on 24 and 25 December, particularly in the South and in Ho Chi Minh City, where the illuminated Notre Dame Cathedral is packed to the rafters. Street vendors sell toys and Father Christmas outfits. **Easter** is also an important festival.

January-February	
Tet festival	1st-3rd day of the first lunar month, New Year (Tet Nguyen Dan) heralds the coming of spring (see above).
Firecracker festival	4th day of the New Year. A rocket and fireworks competition on the theme of the animal of the year takes place at Dong Ky (suburbs of Hanoi).
Ha Loi Festival	6th day of the New Year. In memory of the Trung sisters' fight against the Chinese in the 1C, offerings of sticky rice cakes are made in Ha Loi Temple at Me Linh (suburbs of Hanoi) and women parade through the streets.
April-May	
Thanh Minh	5th day of the 3rd lunar month, in honour of the dead, whose tombs are cleaned and to whom offerings of money, food and flowers are made.
Hung king festival	10th day of the 3rd lunar month. A festival held in honour of the founders of Vietnam, including a procession of elephants, offerings of cakes in the Hy Cuong temples (northern Hanoi) and a canoe regatta on the lake.
May-June	
Tet Doan Ngo	5th day of the 5th lunar month. Summer solstice and inevitable coming of winter. It is associated with poor health and bad luck. To ward off such events, paper figures are burnt and offerings are made to the spirits and the God of Death.
August-September	
Trung Nguyen	15th day of the 7th lunar month. Worship of the dead and lost souls. To prevent the latter, liberated from hell, from tormenting the living, families visit their ancestors' tombs and make food offerings to them in the pagodas. Buddhists, however, recite sutras and prayers to ask forgiveness for their sins.
September-October	
Mid-Autumn festival	15th day of the 8th lunar month. The Mid-Autumn Festival (Tet Trung Thu) is in celebration of the full moon of the month. Children parade through the streets, carrying paper lanterns evoking stars and animals. Families tuck into "moon cakes", stuffed with bean paste, and candies. At dusk, candles are burnt in honour of the moon and to seek its protection.
November-December	
Ok Om Bok	14th-15th day of the 10th lunar month. The water festival is when the Khmer of the Mekong Delta celebrate the sticky rice harvest. They offer rice to the Moon Spirit, launch candle-lit banana tree rafts to ward off the darkness and organise canoe regattas.

And yet more festivals...

A number of other national or pagan festivals are also widely celebrated in Vietnam. One is 1 January, the Western **New Year's Day**, which is a nationwide official holiday. On New Year's Eve in Ho Chi Minh City, the whole town goes out partying to restaurants and nightclubs, and the port's boat and ferry sirens blare out at midnight.

On 30 April, the **anniversary of the taking of Saigon** by the North Vietnamese army in 1975 gives rise to popular and military parades in Hanoi and Ho Chi Minh City. Cultural events are also organised in the southern towns which fell before Saigon. Lastly, on 2 September, the **national holiday** commemorates the founding of the Democratic Republic of Vietnam by Ho Chi Minh in 1945 and the declaration of independence; fire-work displays and regattas are organised in Hanoi (*also see page 26*).

DAILY LIFE

It would be untrue to state that Vietnam is now a fundamentally socialist nation. Deep differences divide the North from the South and the cities from the countryside. In the towns, where 20% of the population live, new values introduced by a middle-class grown wealthy through business and trade are creating a conflict within families attached to Confucian ideals. The latter represent a highly hierarchical society in which respect for the aged by the younger generation continues to play a major role. Rural areas continue to maintain time-honoured traditions and beliefs.

Slices of life

The market – Markets are the dominion of women and are open daily from 6am to 6pm. Farm wives come to sell their produce and buy food, clothes, household goods, cosmetics, traditional herbs and Western medicines. Housewives can be seen bargaining doggedly, surrounded on all sides by the shouts and entreaties of the merchants. Chewing on betel nut, old ladies keep a keen eye on their stalls, and young girls count up the morning's takings of dong.

Traditional medicine

The Vietnamese traditionally place great faith in the effectiveness of plants, all the more so as Western medicines are hard to come by. Traditional physicians take the patient's pulse and examine the tongue before making out a prescription of herbs. Liquorice is prescribed for coughs and high temperatures and wild cinnamon for stomach upsets. Headaches and colds are treated by rubbing the head and chest with a mentholated cream resembling tiger balm. Saxifrage is used to cure earaches. Western medicine has adopted over time many drugs of Asian origins, such as rhubarb, iron, castor oil, kaolin and camphor. Spectacular results in the treatment of rheumatism and arthritis are obtained with moxibustion. This consists in burning small moistened cones (moxa) of dried leaves on designated parts of the body, generally the same points as those used in acupuncture, which is also routinely practised. Acupuncture is designed to restore an imbalance of the yin (dark, passive, female forces) and the yang (light, active, male forces) within the body by stimulating the diseased organs and enabling the body's life force or ch'i to flow freely. The physician inserts small, metal needles, generally around 3cm in length, but sometimes up to 25cm, into the skin and underlying tissues at very precise points of the body. Hundreds of points exist, each of which is associated with an organ, gland or joint. The needles are frequently inserted at great distances from the point on which they are to act, such as in the thumb pad for a pain in the abdomen. Acupuncture is widely used as an anaesthetic in Asian medicine and although many theories have been advanced by Western practitioners to explain its effectiveness, none have as yet been proved.

The café – At dawn, before setting off for work, men often buy a black or white coffee and a steaming bowl of Tonkin noodle soup (pho), from the street vendors squatting on the pavements. In the afternoon and evenings however when they have more time, they will sit down with friends or family in a proper café, and drink a cola, listen to music or take part in the general karaoke sing-along.

The park – Many people can be seen going through their tai chi exercises in the parks or other open areas. On Sundays, the strident tape recording of the balloon and ice-cream man can be heard from one end to the other of the parks and squares packed with strollers.

The street – From dawn every morning, the pavements are lined with the vans of the street vendors, who set up stools and tables for breakfast while sandwich ladies heat up the bread and cut slices of cha lua (local salami). Around 8am, these give way to coconut juice, pancakes and ravioli and fresh fruit and vegetable merchants who transport their wares in two baskets hanging from a long

On the way to market

pole slung over the shoulder. They sit side by side with mechanics who repair bicycle brakes and inner tubes until nightfall, hairdressers, barbers and the odd raffle-ticket seller. Hordes of children are always close at hand, attempting to cash in on the activities of the shoe-shine man, pestering his clients with offers of cigarettes, sweets, newspapers, postcards or paper tissues.

At work – Most working days start at 7-7.30am. Everyone stops for lunch around 11-11.30am and families often lunch together at home. After a quick nap, work begins again around 1.30pm and finishes at 4-4.30pm. Wages are so low that many Vietnamese have a second job. The evening meal is also a family dinner and is eaten around 6.30pm.

The pagoda – On the first day of the month, the new moon, whole families go to the temples, laden with offerings. Stalls in front of the temples sell joss sticks and caged birds, which the faithful set free for good luck. Inside the shrine, monks come to meditate. They recite prayers in front of the Buddha, greet him three times with their joss sticks and then leave the sticks in the urns set out for this purpose.

The family

Respecting one's elders

Vietnam is organised on the basis of a highly hierarchical and patriarchal concept of society, deeply influenced by Confucian philosophy. The loyalty and solidarity which bind together members of the same village or community are reflected in the family unit. Just as parents are bound to provide their children with protection and advice, their children owe them **respect** and **obedience** and the same rules apply to relationships between the older and younger generation in general. Language reflects these relationships through the use of honorific personal pronouns, such as *anh* (big brother) or *chi* (big sister) which a young person uses to address his or her elder, referring to him or herself as *em* (little brother or sister).

The first-born male child fulfils an essential role in **ancestor worship**, an expression of filial piety (*see page 59*). This ritual is founded in the belief of the soul's immortality and of the protection granted by each deceased ancestor to his or her

69

descendants. In nuclear families, the eldest son (or eldest daughter and her husband) is required to maintain the family altar which stands in the living room with the wooden tablets bearing the names of five generations of ancestors, or as is more frequent today, the photos of the deceased. In extended families, the oldest member (man or woman) of the oldest branch of the clan is entrusted with this honour. In addition to daily offerings made at daybreak, ancestors are honoured more specifically at New Year and on the anniversary of their death. The family clan prepares a magnificent feast on this day and invites the dead by placing food and drink on the altar and burning incense and fake money to ask for the ancestors' blessing.

Children

In Vietnam it is considered a tragedy not to marry and have children. Large families of 10-15 children used to be common, despite a high mortality rate. Children were regarded as a sort of pension for the parents' old age. Nowadays, the costs of raising and educating children, combined with government's desire to reduce population growth, has affected the birth rate and many urban families only have two children. The birth of a son is still favoured over that of a girl, because sons continue the family line and make offerings to the parents' souls after their death, while daughters get married and leave home. All children are expected to work hard from an early age. Boys and girls look after their younger brothers and sisters, but most household chores are typically done by the girls. All children are also expected to contribute money to their parents to help support them in their old age.

The role of women

Even though Confucian traditions require wives to submit to their husbands and to be content with respecting four virtues – looking after the home and being beautiful, virtuous and softly-spoken – Vietnamese married couples are relatively equal. Without ever appearing to dictate or be authoritative, women are in fact "home ministers" (*noi tuong*) in charge of all aspects of **home management**, from the family budget (mainly daily expenditure) to the children's education. Vietnam has enjoyed only very rare periods of extended peace and with the men away, its women are used to working,

The flower stall

running their homes and bringing up their children. The mother's influence over her children is substantial, partly because the very young remain the exclusive domain of women and partly because the fathers, absent for long periods during wars, have failed to resume their full role as head of the family. Thus a prospective couple will seek the mother's final approval for their marriage. In town and country alike, women are the first up, often before dawn, preparing breakfast and the packed lunch that each family member takes to school or work, then later cooking the evening meal. It is difficult to make ends meet and many wives have to supplement their husband's salary with a job in an office, factory or market or with some small part-time job which has always been the traditional domain of women. In the country, field work requires large numbers of hands and women are often called upon to carry out back-breaking tasks such as rice planting. In addition, the vegetable plot, farm animals and sales of home-grown produce also fall within their realm. Socialism has reinforced their role and it is not unusual to see women in positions of power within the government, but in practice the majority are employed in poorly-paid jobs. Legally men and women have equality in most areas and according to the 1959 Marriage and Family Law Act, sons and daughters must be treated equally.

Vietnamese homes

In the past the Vietnamese lived in stilt-cabins, similar to those which can still be seen in the lakeside villages or hamlets of some ethnic minorities (see page 321), but little by little the influence of China led to the building of homes directly on the ground.
An important part of the process involves calling upon a **geomancer** who will determine the exact position of the main door, which direction the building should face and how the rooms must be laid out, in order to better capture any available positive cosmic energy.

Traditional rural dwellings
The countryside is scattered with circular villages, within which stand clusters of rectangular homes surrounded by bamboo hedges. Made out of packed clay and straw or woven bamboo with thatched roofs of straw or palm leaves, these little huts are set in courtyards around which lie a number of outbuildings for cooking, for grinding the rice and in which to keep pigs. In the gardens, a vegetable plot sometimes coexists with a pond which doubles as a water reservoir and wash-house. Those with the means have whitewashed brick houses with tiled roofs. Tube-houses, similar to those found in towns, can now also be seen along the roadsides, but with the addition of a rear courtyard.

City dwellings
Most city houses have brick walls and tiled roofs, together with a small railed veranda to park the family's two-wheelers. The main door, opposite the family altar, opens into the living room. Then come the kitchen/dining room, the bedrooms, complete with fan and mosquito nets, shower and toilets. Some homes have a first floor for the bedrooms and bathroom.
Overcrowding in towns, linked to pressure from commercial and small-scale industrial activities and the high price of land has led to the emergence of a unique architectural phenomenon, namely the **tube-house** or "bamboo-pipe" house. Two-storey buildings, whose façade is never more than 4m wide, line the main streets, stretching out to the rear, sometimes as much as 60m in depth, in a succession of windowless rooms and open-air courtyards. On the ground floor, the room overlooking the street is either the living-room or the shop, and possibly also the family's bicycle or motorbike garage. In Hanoi, work has recently begun to rehabilitate and preserve some of the oldest houses of this kind and to turn them into museums.

Vietnamese homes

Education

Vietnam is a young country; 40% of its population is under 15 and 60% under 25. The gap between the ruling classes, who spent their youth fighting to achieve power, and today's post-war generation who aspires to more material comforts is steadily widening.

Today's educational system

The prestigious mandarin competitions of yesteryear enabled the state to select the most able elements of its rural society, and any Confucian scholar who successfully sat such exams automatically brought wealth and prestige to his family, however poor. Vietnam's first national university was founded in 1076, two centuries before England's Oxford. Such traditions help explain the importance parents have always placed on their children's education, and, even if nothing today has replaced the former exams, educational aspiration remains high. The literacy level is 82%, which is high considering the country's economic position. Nine years of schooling are mandatory, with five years of primary and four years of lower secondary school. Up until 1989, education was free but this has been cut down to the first three years. School fees now represent a quarter of many city-dwellers' budgets, at least for upper secondary school studies and universities which are both fee-paying. School classes generally run from 7am to 11am and from 1pm to 5pm, but many children only attend part-time, due to shortages in teachers and school space. Confronted with the inability of the national education system to provide schools, city families have set up their own infant schools in each district, where they rent a classroom and hire teachers. In higher education, the emphasis is on science and technology, although poor facilities somewhat hinder the programme.

Discontent among the younger generation

With an uncertain future due to the growing rate of **unemployment** and exposed to the consumer values of the West, today's urban youth is more and more inclined to live life to its full and to let tomorrow take care of itself. However, wearing foreign-branded clothes, drinking Coca-Cola in karaoke cafés or clubbing at the weekends requires money. Increased material needs are no doubt partly behind the increase of female prostitution, although at the time of the Vietnam War there were already some 500 000 prostitutes in the South. Drugs, often fatal night-time motorbike races where the most reckless riders cut their brake cables, together with the growing number of suicides reflect the confused state of this unoccupied youth. The country's economic development has led to a **revolution in moral standards**, particularly among young city dwellers, giving rise to previously unheard of phenomena such as sex before marriage, unmarried couples living together and a growing number of abortions.

The major stages in life

Birth

Although today's city women opt to give birth in hospital, country women still prefer to have their babies at home, helped by experienced female relatives. The birth of a son who will continue the family name, particularly that of the first-born destined to uphold the tradition of ancestor worship, is always welcomed proudly. According to a custom (now dying out in towns), the paternal grandmother is entrusted with the young mother's placenta, which is then placed in an urn and buried in the garden or in a jar full of earth. This gesture symbolises the new-born's future **bond** with his land, the home of his family and ancestors, and with his country.

The fragile new-born baby is considered to be prey to malevolent devils, even more so if the child is handsome and healthy. Thus instead of going into raptures, the first people to see the baby must lament the child's arrival, thus warding off the evil spirits! Relatives carefully note down the child's time and place of birth in order to have his

Primary school

or her **sign of the zodiac** drawn. A first name is chosen for the child, but a nickname is used to send the evil spirits off on a false track. Between seven and nine days after the birth, offerings of betel nuts, cakes and seafood are made to the Heavenly Midwives, in token of thanks. This ceremony is repeated one month after the birth to request their protection of the child, which is finally called by its real name.

Name giving

Most people have three names, very occasionally four. The first designates the father's family name or clan name, the second is a middle name and the third is the Western equivalent of a first name. Although some 300 family names exist, the most common are Nguyen – over half Vietnam's population is called Nguyen in honour of the last Imperial dynasty – Tran, Le, Pham, Ngo, Vu, Do, Duong, Dang, Dinh and Hoang. The most common middle name for women is Thi, while men have a choice between Van, Xuan and Ngoc. The first name frequently gives rise to a whole range of imaginative, meaningful words. Women often have poetic names, meaning flower, bird, beauty or perfume, while men are generally identified with abstract concepts such as bravery, intelligence or strength. When addressing a person, one uses the term *bà* (Mrs) or *ông* (Mr) followed by the first name. Thus a man named Nguyen Van Tuan will often be addressed as Mr Tuan. In families, children are often named according to their order of birth, hence *ba* (third-born), *sau* (sixth-born), sometimes followed by the first name, and always preceded by the personal pronoun which designates the hierarchical relationship *(see page 69)*.

Weddings

In accordance with the Confucian concept of filial piety, whereby the individual is required to carry on his lineage in order to guarantee the tradition of ancestor worship, marriage is a major social event and families often spend vast fortunes, some incurring debts or even bankrupting themselves. The **social prestige** they gain from the occasion is based solely on its cost.

Among traditionalists, mainly in the countryside, marriages are arranged by the families of the future couple who call upon uncles, aunts and close friends to establish contacts. The couple's birth charts are exchanged and, if they are favourable, the

A young farmer

Daily life

young man's family goes to the girl's house to ask for her hand in marriage. An **engagement** renders the negotiations official and stipulates the terms and date of the wedding, after consultation with a seer.

On the wedding day, the groom, dressed in a blue tunic or Western suit and in the company of family and friends, comes to fetch the bride in a rented car. The bride wears a red tunic, a symbol of joy, and a yellow turban or a white Western-style gown complete with diadem and veil. The future parents-in-law place boxes on the family altar containing betel and areca nuts, which symbolise everlasting love and their son's commitment. The young couple kneel in front of the altar and then before the bride's parents. The bride then leaves her home, a few tears in her eyes as a sign of her love for her mother. In her parents-in-law's home, the same **respectful** rituals take place in front of the groom's family altar and his parents. Lucky red threads are then exchanged in honour of the Wedding Spirit and the married couple chew betel nut. Finally a magnificent feast is held, to which both families are invited.

Funeral rites

The responsibility for carrying out funeral rites is entrusted to the eldest son. He is required to lay a piece of silk on his dying father's or mother's chest, intended to capture the dying person's last breath. This "silken soul" is buried with the deceased and materialised on the family altar by a **funeral tablet**. The eldest son must also ensure that the soul leaves the body without straying from the family home, by helping to remind it of all the home's hidden corners. In this way the soul will return to share the family banquet on feast days and in particular at the New Year. White ribbons are tied around the doors and windows of the house as a sign of mourning, and the family members all wear white head-dresses and long tunics.

A **geomancer** is called upon to determine the day, time and place of burial, as well as its exact position. The coffin remains on display for three days, so that the family's cousins, neighbours and friends can pay their last respects, arms laden with flowers and fruit, to the sound of traditional music. On the day of the funeral, Buddhist families call upon bonzes to recite prayers. A hearse transports the coffin to the cemetery, in the company of close family and friends who walk behind. The procession is led by the eldest son, who carries a walking stick as a sign of his position as head of the family. He is followed by the widow, in the case of a married man, then by the oldest grandson, who carries a photo of the deceased, then by the rest of the family. Musicians bring up the rear of the procession, making as much noise as possible in order to ward off evil spirits. A **stele** bearing the deceased's name and his or her date of death marks the burial place.

Seven weeks after the funeral, the head of the family invites the assembly to a banquet for the **ceremony of the 49th day**, in order to free the deceased's soul which leaves its family to be reincarnated. Three years later, the duration of the official mourning period, the bones are exhumed during the **leaving the tomb ceremony** and transferred into a smaller permanent coffin, which is placed in the family tomb. All these rituals are designed to bring the family together and thereby reassert its solidarity and cohesion.

The major stages in life

SOCIAL ETIQUETTE

Vietnam is a very pleasant country to travel in. From north to south a smile will work wonders in breaking the ice and smoothing over any small breaches of social etiquette. Politeness and self-control are paramount and will prevent the unwitting tourist from losing face, an unpardonable sin in Vietnam.

Meeting the people

You will have no trouble at all meeting the Vietnamese, who are naturally outgoing and curious and have no qualms about walking up to strangers with offers of help or simply asking questions. Most questions will revolve around your age and marital status but they are simply a polite way of showing interest. When people get to know you better, they may ask a service of you, which you should politely but firmly refuse, if you are unable to comply.

The market – Every town and village has a market square, which is traditionally where people meet and exchange news. It offers a wonderful opportunity to catch a glimpse of the picturesque bargaining between housewives and merchants. Why not have a go yourself? If nothing else, it will be good fun.

The café – Clearly ideal for a quiet talk over a drink. Many young people won't refuse the offer of a glass of Coke in exchange for a short conversation. Better still, pop into a karaoke bar and sing along in English; you will soon become the star of the bar.

The restaurant – While you explore the wide variety of regional Vietnamese cuisine, your fellow diners will inevitably be curious, even sympathetic, about your dexterity, or lack of, with chopsticks. Your ineptitude (or proficiency) makes a perfect conversation point, which you can prolong by offering your neighbour tea or a cigarette.

The pagoda – Those so inclined can do as the faithful do and purchase three joss sticks in front of the pagoda which are offered to the Buddha by being stuck into the urns inside the shrine. A few banknotes should also be placed in the chests in front of the altar. The monks are more than likely to show their appreciation and will probably be happy to explain their rituals in greater depth.

On public transport – Foreigners are tending to use public transport less and less, in favour of the more comfortable and faster tourist buses. Public transport is nonetheless an excellent way of mixing with local people, who will happily chat with you throughout the trip.

A few basic customs

The Vietnamese are a traditionally hospitable and welcoming nation. However their beliefs relating to good or bad fortune are such that it is best to be forewarned and avoid needlessly upsetting new acquaintances.

Greetings – A person is traditionally greeted by a slight bow of the head. In the country, some people also press their hands together at chest level, in which case you should respond in kind. When meeting someone of the same age or rank, a friendly smile also helps to break the ice. In towns, however, the Western custom of shaking hands has almost totally taken over, particularly among men.

Sociability – Calculate the appropriate degree of familiarity with care. The Vietnamese customarily judge newcomers by asking them apparently guileless questions in order to ascertain the person's educational and cultural standing. Answer good-humouredly.

Beliefs and taboos – If invited to a Vietnamese home on the first day of Tet (New Year), find out exactly what time they want you to arrive. The home's good or bad fortune throughout the rest of the year will depend on the social standing and moral reputation of its first visitor, so make sure you know when you are expected and be

All aboard

punctual. Don't wear white, the colour of mourning and make no reference to death or accidents that day. When greeting children and wishing them a Happy New Year, do not pat them on the head, which represents the spirit, and by extension, their ancestors.

Clothes – Respect the local inhabitants' dress codes. Bare legs, especially in the case of women, can cause offence. In country areas, it's best to wear long trousers. The arms should also be covered when visiting religious sites, such as churches, pagodas, temples and mosques.

Shoes – Remove your shoes before entering a house and some Buddhist temples. When in doubt look around to see if other visitors have left their shoes outside. Sit cross-legged so that the soles of your feet are not directed towards anything sacred (family altars, Buddha) or towards your hosts.

Meals – As a general rule, everyone dips into all the dishes placed on the table. Each person helps him or herself with chopsticks, placing the food in a bowl before eating. If dining with Vietnamese, never stick your chopsticks upright into your bowl of rice, since because of their close resemblance to the joss sticks which are burned for the dead, they are a symbol of death.

Gifts – If you receive an invitation, it is customary to offer your hosts a small gift. Do not however expect them to open it and thank you immediately. The gift will be placed to one side and opened after your departure. Give children pens and pencils rather than sweets.

Photography – It isn't compulsory to ask permission to photograph people, but be discreet and give up gracefully if they refuse. Bear in mind that minority groups, old people, pregnant women and mothers with babies often object to having their photo taken. It is always a good idea to buy something from a merchant or a craftsman if you want to take a photo of their wares or their stall.

Social etiquette

VIETNAMESE COOKING

A steaming saucepan full of soup, as well as some bowls, spoons, chopsticks and a few stools are all it takes to create a pavement snack shop and an ideal opportunity to get a taste of Vietnamese cooking. In Vietnam, snacking is a national pastime and full-blown meals often only take place during festivals or family get-togethers. In towns, street canteens are open from dawn to dusk, and sometimes later. Satisfying a sudden pang of hunger or quenching one's thirst is never a problem.

A savoury blend

The day traditionally begins with savoury rather than sweet foods in the form of noodle soup (*pho*) or a dish made from rice and steamed meat. But many Vietnamese also tuck into improvised sandwiches made with fresh bread from *banh mi* pedlars. Despite the use of chopsticks and countless noodle-based recipes, Vietnamese cuisine is only distantly related to its Chinese neighbour. Sauces are used rarely and oil sparingly. Neither is a Vietnamese meal a succession of starter, main course and dessert. It is rather a combination of **flavours** and **textures** served at the same time, into which everyone dips at will. **Fresh herbs** are used freely, including coriander, ordinary and purple mint (*tia to*), basil, dill and *la lot* (Vietnamese herb) together with more complex flavours such as aniseed, lemon and cumin. Thin slices of cucumber and turnip refresh the palate. Among the variety of textures, crunchy foods are unavoidable, ranging from shallot fritters (*hanh kho phi*), grilled, ground rice and ground peanuts. **Nuoc-mam**, fermented fish sauce, plays the role of salt, spices substitute for pepper, lime juice for vinegar.

A balanced diet

Rice, water spinach, bean sprouts and nuoc-mam make up the basis of a typical Vietnamese menu and are a reflection of its coastal countryside, with its rivers and rice paddies. Dozens of varieties of **rice** exist, ranging from round, ground, perfumed or sticky. Whether steamed (*com*) or fried (*com rang*), it is the staple element of all dishes.

Lunch-time

Xoi is a mixture of sticky rice, beans, fresh peanuts and lean pork, rolled up in a banana leaf and steamed. *Chao* is a dish of ground rice cooked slowly with pieces of meat and served piping hot, strewn with chopped coriander and chives. **Meat, fish** and shrimp often only feature sparingly.

Whether for feasts and banquets or everyday snacks, Vietnamese food reveals a clear culinary divide in the country, even if the dishes remain basically the same. In the North, the population prefers **fresh-water produce** – snails, frogs and eels – while in the South they opt for more Chinese-style meat dishes. In the North, the **soups** are relatively bland, while elsewhere they are more liberal with **spices**, **coconut milk** (*ga cari*, chicken curry in coconut milk), **sweet** flavours (*chao tom*, shrimp paste baked on sugar cane or *heo kho*, pork in caramel) and acidic notes such as tamarind (*canh chua*, acidic fish or shrimp soup). Daring associations which combine land and sea produce are far from uncommon, as in *thap cam nhung dam*, which is an enormous fondue of meat, fish and seafood. *Cha lua*, a pork paste mixed with nuoc-mam and steamed, makes a tasty snack on bread.

Endless ingenuity

Rice is the symbol of life. Called the pearl of the gods, it is also the preserve of specialists. Dried on bamboo racks, translucent moon-shaped **rice paper pancakes**, called *banh da* in the North and *banh trang* in the South, are what gives the food its crunchy or tender texture. Rolled around a stuffing of white meat, vermicelli, bean shoots, black mushrooms and shrimps, they are then sautéed in oil and become crunchy spring rolls (*nem* in the North and *chao gio* in the South). *Cha bap* from the centre is stuffed with pork and corn and *cha gio chay* is a vegetarian version of the same thing. "Fresh" spring rolls (*goi cuon*) are a refreshing mixture of vermicelli, soya beans, shrimps and mint. *Banh cuon*, or Vietnamese ravioli, is a pancake stuffed with minced pork, shrimps and mushrooms and steamed. *Banh da* and lettuce leaves are frequently used to make interesting combinations of flavours. In the *cha ca muong*, pieces of grilled fish are wrapped with vegetables and fruit in a rice pancake. *Bo lui* is a mixture of beef, peanuts and herbs wrapped in a lettuce leaf.

A typical, little restaurant

The ground is littered with paper napkins, chicken and fish bones and other left-overs from the last lot of diners. This is however perfectly admissible and in just one sweep of the broom it all disappears. Follow the owner to the fridge and choose from the available cuts of chicken, duck, beef, pork or dog. Ten minutes later your dish will arrive, served with soup, green vegetables, rice and a herb omelette, all of which are standard additions. Dig in with your chopsticks then wash the whole meal down with a beer ("bia hoi") or a little rice alcohol (called vodka here).

Nuoc-mam, the salt of life

The use of fish (nuoc-mam) and shrimp (mam tom) sauces to season dishes is a widespread tradition in the whole of Southeast Asia. A cocktail of phosphorous and nitrogen, nuoc-mam is the result of a long fermentation process. Alternating layers of fish and salt are left to marinate in concrete tanks with a tap at their base. After a three-month fermentation period, a first liquid is drawn off, while the remaining brine is left for a further three months. The first pressing is greatly sought after by connoisseurs who know that it has the richest flavours and also improves with age. The best sauce comes from Phan Thiet and Phu Quoc. In the North, nuoc-mam is used "neat", but in the South, it is diluted with lime juice, and garlic, spices and a little sugar (nuoc cham) are added.

There are two types of **rice noodles**. Long, white, flat noodles (*banh pho* in the North and *hu tieu* in the South) and clear vermicelli (*banh hoi* or *bun*). The famous Hanoi soup is named after the former. *Pho bo* is a tasty beef noodle soup. A "dry" version exists, *pho xao*, which is a mixture of fried beef and noodles. Vermicelli is served in soups (*bun bo*, beef soup), salads and as a side dish. *Bun cha* is roasted pork and fresh herbs served in an acidic broth with vermicelli.

F Soreau/MICHELIN

Ben Thanh market in Ho Chi Minh City

Soya is a rich vegetable source of protein and understandably figures prominently in a whole variety of forms. Its shoots are used as a vegetable, its salty pods *(tuong hot)* as seasoning, while its seeds *(dau xanh)* are ground into a sweet paste used in cakes and the curd is made into cheese which can be either sweet or savoury.

Fruity desserts

Even though desserts are practically absent from Vietnamese menus, those with a sweet tooth will have no difficulty satisfying their cravings, from the **desserts** sold in the street and the candies which sweeten the bitter green tea to the countless varieties of **fruit** *(see illustrations page 16)*. *Che*, a speciality of Hue, is a creamy dessert which can be served with any variety of flavours, such as *che chuoi* with banana and coconut milk or *che sen* with lotus seeds. *Tau hu* is a jelly of agar-agar with soya seeds and cane sugar syrup. *Banh gan* is a delicious coconut flan and *banh ech tran* are tapioca balls filled with soya paste and coconut milk.

Drinks

Tea is an institution in Vietnam. However the country prefers green tea, an infusion of the leaves roasted just after the harvest, to black fermented tea. A manifestation of hospitality, teatime is an occasion of much to-ing and fro-ing of crockery. The teapot is first stuffed with leaves and filled to the brim with boiling water. The first infusion, too bitter, is thrown away and the pot is filled with water again and this is then poured into cups the size of thimbles.

Draught beer *(bia hoi)* is extremely popular and is served in half-litre glasses in specialised establishments, where the beer, brewed the night before, is delivered every morning. These establishments also serve popular snacks such as peanuts *(dau phong)*, *nems*, fried chicken wings *(canh ga chien)* or octopus *(muc kho)* and thin slices of cold dog meat *(thit cho)*.

The fermentation of sticky rice produces **ruou**, a cloudy wine which tastes somewhat like Japanese saké. Some enthusiasts claim that there is no healthier way to start the day than a glass of **rice alcohol** on an empty stomach.

CRAFTS

Many of the crafts, such as paper, lacquer work, ceramic and engraving, found in Vietnam today were introduced by the Chinese. Blended into the two facets of Vietnamese culture, they have been perpetuated and interpreted in a variety of original forms. On the one hand, the court and its mandarins sponsored a sophisticated culture, heavily influenced by China, while on the other hand, the villagers expressed their know-how and pragmatism through vigorous craft traditions intended to serve the community. At times these two currents ran parallel, at others they fused together, yet in the end, both prevail. The former, which is today controlled by the State and, more recently financed by private enterprise, has endowed Vietnam's craft industry with an international reputation. The latter is more focused on the daily environment, and finds inexhaustible solutions to its needs by recycling, turning the tiniest town or country marketplace into a fascinating showcase of objects which are as pleasing to the eye as they are ingenious.

From everyday objects to works of art

A bamboo civilisation

From chopsticks to hats, bamboo is ever present in Vietnam's daily life. In the flat terrain of the Red River Delta, high hedges of these giant grasses create natural barriers around villages, serving both to signpost the villages and to protect them from prying eyes. People used to say that "the king's authority extended only as far as the village's bamboo hedge". Indoors, bamboo is used everywhere, from the floor to the ceiling, in the form of coat-hangers, storage racks, partition walls, screens and mats on the ground. Its fibres are used as bindings and its flexible, resistant wood serves to make scaffolding. Its hollow, waterproof stems are used to make cooking utensils such as cups and water pipes. The dried roots and leaves are burnt as cooking and heating fuel. It is even used to nourish beasts and humans, who delight in the tender shoots, marinated or fresh.

Specialised centres

Throughout Vietnam, everyday objects, such as baskets or rugs *(see below)*, illustrate a desire to combine the practical with the aesthetic. Furthermore, specific needs have given rise to the specialised manufacture of particular objects. For example, rituals and in particular ancestor worship, encouraged the development of **cabinet-making** and **lacquer-ware** (altars and tablet-stands), **bronze objects** (chandeliers and incense burners) and **paper-making** (coloured paper used at funerals).

The continued existence of Hanoi's guild district bears witness to the high esteem in which the court held its qualified craftsmen. The lords' and mandarins' partiality for furniture and objects made from rare and precious materials guaranteed a constant stream of orders for the workshops, most of which only supplied the court. Those skilled in wood, lacquer, mother-of-pearl, jade, ceramics or silk brocade were never short of work. After

The famous "non"

The continuing use of the conical hat and its association with the national costume (see page 55) have made the "non" a symbol of Vietnam. Particularly suited to the climate, it protects its wearers at work in the rice paddies not only from the pouring rain, but also the harsh midday sun. No one knows when it first appeared, but the current version is a shortened form of the Tonkin "non ba tam", a wide sombrero made from palm leaves. The Hue region and province of Quang Binh have become the undisputed manufacturing centres of this hat, which is also made in the village of Chuong near Hanoi. The palm leaves are whitened and beaten to make them pliable, before being sewn together one by one. Although simple enough to make, a single hat nonetheless requires between 5-6hr of patient labour.

reunification, the Ho Chi Minh City region placed most of the craft manufacturing centres under the control of the State, but in the North the tradition of **specialised villages** continues to operate in the form of cooperatives. Hanoi is still surrounded by a ring, some 20-30km in radius, of these villages, and temples in the region are often devoted to the creator or instigator of a local speciality. The craft industry is only active between the sowing and harvest periods. When entire villages have specialised in the manufacture of a product, the tasks are often broken down, ranging from collecting the raw material to the sale of goods and the development of micro-economies. In this way, one village might supply the fuel, another might produce the clay, while yet another actually produces the earthenware pots.

A selection of Vietnamese crafts

Ceramics

This craft is principally North Vietnamese due to the quality of the clay found in the Red River Delta and its proximity with China, from whom the craft was learnt. Dating from as early as the 11C, objects made from a delicately-coloured ivory or celadon **stoneware**, have been found, which illustrate the craftsmen's skills in both selecting and firing their materials. Several centres developed over the centuries, each with a different specialisation. The kilns of Nghe and Cao produced **non-enamelled pottery**, fired at low temperatures. At Phu Lang, Huong Canh and Tho Ha, stoneware was fired at **high temperatures**. Finally the villages of Bat Trang (*see page 161*) and Bien Hoa specialised in coloured pottery. This speciality enjoyed a boom period in the 14C-15C, producing cobalt **blue and white** enamelled objects heavily influenced at the time by Chinese culture, even if this influence was soon shaken off. In the 17C-18C, a distinctly Rococo-like style was adopted, in particular in **architectural ceramics**, which made full use of fluid colours and contrasting glazes. "Blue and white" pottery in particular frequently borrowed Chinese motifs (ornamental flowers, phoenix and dragons), adapting them, however, to the more spontaneous Vietnamese style and bolder outlines.

Lacquer

This technique was introduced by China a very long time ago and some of the oldest lacquered objects found in the Haiphong region date from the 4C BC. Before developing as an artistic craft, lacquer was used to make porous objects waterproof, or in the case of wood, to protect it from damp and insects. Some of Vietnam's tribes still lacquer their teeth as in days of old.

Lacquer is a natural **resin** which comes from the lacquer tree, (*rhus vernicefera or cay son*), which is boiled for up to four days and mixed with pine resin to give it texture, producing a variety of different qualities. **Several coats** are applied onto a variety of bases, generally bamboo or wood, and each coat is dried and sanded, resulting in polished finishes capable of rivalling those of highly glazed porcelain. The traditional **three-colour range** of lacquers comprises black and brown, which are natural shades, and red which is obtained by adding haematite.

Lacquer work was at its peak in the 17C-18C, as shown by the massive orders of polychrome lacquered Buddhist statues. Lacquer was even used to coat the mummified bodies of certain Buddhist holy men, thereby turning them into statues. The art of lacquering was further enriched by new decorative techniques, such as mother-of-pearl and gold and eggshell inlay used in cabinet-making (*see below*). Vietnamese lacquer-ware is widely regarded as the finest in the world.

Paper and woodcuts

Paper is used in thousands of ways. Even though pedlars selling toys and **paper puppets** made at the time of the mid-Autumn Festival, are rare sights nowadays, all of Vietnam's markets continue to sell **offerings** made out of paper to be burnt during funeral ceremonies. From coins and banknotes (false dollars are more popular than dongs) and ancient and contemporary costumes to means of transport and even household appliances, Vietnam's craftsmen can reproduce anything and everything in paper.

Traditional paper (*do*) is made from the bark of a climbing plant found in the centre of Vietnam. After marinating in a vat of lime, it is baked for several days in enormous cast-iron kilns. After being resoaked in lime, the pulp obtained is crushed and mixed with a vegetable-based glue. This mixture is then dried on bamboo frames, resulting in supple sheets of paper.

Paper is of course the main support for writing and the **woodcut** technique soon emerged to reproduce written texts. A wet sheet of paper was applied to a stele and the inked copy reproduced a negative of the text with the hollow carved letters blank and the surrounding "page" coloured.

Some pagodas still have blocks of carved wood which were used to reproduce works by **xylography** (wooden-block printing). From this technique, the ancestor of printing, was born the **woodcut**, which is the speciality of the village of Dong Ho. An image is made using a series of printing blocks, each intended to be used with a specific colour, all from natural origins. Yellow comes from sophora (in the pagoda tree family), blue from indigo, green from copper, red from sapanwood and black from the ashes of bamboo leaves. Colour by colour, the engraving slowly takes form as each successive block is applied, right down to the last one with the outlines of the drawing. At Dong Ho, the villagers also make a special paper, the surface of which is covered in a mixture of glue and powdered shells called *diep*, giving it a pearly look.

Cabinet-making and carpentry

In former times, **hard** and **precious** woods could be found in all the inland forests. The court, the temples, and also the **performing arts** (musical instruments for the opera and water puppets) required large quantities of furniture, statues and carved objects made from these woods. Cabinet-making is without doubt the domain in which Vietnamese craftsmen have excelled the most, perhaps due to the nation's history of building complex wooden structures and also its ship-building industry. Nowadays, the thrones, altars, decorative panels, screens and tablet-holders visible **inside temples** provide the opportunity to admire some of the masterpieces of yesterday's craftsmen, whose skills are still very much in use today. Although court furniture can now be seen only in museums, today's cabinet-makers continue to use past models to create contemporary objects, such as cribs, tea chests, chairs, coffers, screens, trays and boxes.

The two main techniques used to decorate wood are **lacquer-ware** and **marquetry with mother-of-pearl inlay**. Of two types – *trai*, mother-of-pearl from a variety of mussel, and *xa cu*, iridescent mother-of-pearl from Nha Trang and Hoi An – the mother-of-pearl is first cut into sheets and polished, then inlay motifs (flowers, birds, people and good luck charms) are delicately etched and cut out using a fine saw. The wooden surfaces into which the inlay is to be placed undergo the same careful treatment so that the mother-of-pearl motif fits the intended space perfectly.

A selection of Vietnamese crafts

LANGUAGE AND WRITING

Vietnam's national language is a pure product of the country's history and its faculty of assimilating other races and cultures. Linguists agree that it broadly falls within the Austro-Asian family of languages, but this foundation also features many other influences, borrowed notably from Thai and, to an even greater extent, Chinese. In common with these neighbours, Vietnamese is a **tonal language** whose tiniest vocal unit is a syllable associated with a tone, and a **monosyllabic language**, meaning that each concept can be restricted to a single syllable (as a word can be restricted to a Chinese character). These are however the only common factors between these languages of different families, each of which has its own distinctive syntax.

The other feature of Vietnamese is its relatively recent adoption of a Romanised script, while the other nations of the Southeast Asian peninsula, with the exception of Malaysia, employ alphabets derived from the Indian model. Equally interesting is the fact that the nation's **linguistic diversity** has found almost no outlets in its written literature. Vietnam's many languages are all spoken, but they are not always written. The Khmer, Cham and Tai still sometimes use an Indian-based alphabet, while the Tay, Nung and Dao resort to Chinese ideograms, in particular in their rites, where the Muong and the Pa Then also employ archaic pictograms.

Spoken Vietnamese and written Chinese

Up until the early 20C, literature, governmental and legal bodies used only written Chinese, albeit pronounced with a Vietnamese accent. Vietnam had for centuries fallen under the influence of the Chinese Empire, and like Japan and Korea, had also relied for writing on the bank of thousands of Chinese characters. An embryonic alphabet may have existed in protohistoric (prior to writing) times, but Chinese characters were introduced at such an early stage, even before the Empire began its colonisation, that such a system never had a chance to develop. Even after the nation's emancipation in the 10C, Chinese remained not only the language of diplomacy and government, but also of literature and religion. It thus continued to convey classical Chinese culture, in parallel with a developing Vietnamese which was essentially an oral language. This duality played a significant role in forging Vietnam's rich cultural diversity, based as it was on two different languages whose pronunciation and founding concepts differed so radically. The legacy of this Sino-Vietnamese culture is immense. It is estimated that some 50% of Chinese-based words coexist in today's vocabulary with Vietnamese words meaning the same thing but with a different pronunciation. Thus, "water" is *thuy* in Sino-Vietnamese (*shui* in mandarin), as in *Thuy Tin* (the Water Spirit), and *nuoc* in Vietnamese as in *nuoc mam*. Many northern place names are Sino-Vietnamese. The Song Hong takes its red from the Chinese (*hong*) and not from the Vietnamese (*do*), and Hanoi is the Vietnamese pronunciation of the Chinese *Henei* ("heart of the river"). This borrowing tradition has been pursued in today's speech and many Chinese terms are used to translate concepts such as "customs" (*hai quan* in Vietnamese, *haiguan* in Chinese, which literally means "pushed towards the sea"), or "police" (*cong an* in Vietnamese, *gong'an* in Chinese, which literally means "public safety"). Of late, the country is experiencing a revival of this Sino-Vietnamese tradition, particularly in the religious sphere.

Nom, a demotic but not very democratic system of writing

A brief exception to the use of Chinese in the Imperial administration occurred in the late 18C under the reign of the Tay Son, who imposed the use of Vietnamese, written with a hybrid system of Chinese characters and phonetics, called **chu nom**. Gradually evolved since the 10C, it was a clever composition of Chinese characters with meanings (ideograms and pictograms) and phonetic characters with meaning in the Vietnamese language (*quoc am*, "sounds of the country"). It required a perfect mastery of both classical Chinese and vernacular Vietnamese. *Nom* was a demotic system

F Soreau/MICHELIN

A city billboard

of writing, based on the vernacular language, which was why, despite its complexity, it was always rejected by the country's literary circles as common. Few ever stooped to use it, with the notable exception of one of the nation's heroes, the scholar Nguyen Trai (*see page 86*). The system was never harmonised and it varied considerably over time and from place to place, gradually becoming illegible.

Quoc-ngu, a made-to-measure writing system

In the early 20C, a nationalist and patriotic movement, symbolised by the Free School of Tonkin led by Luong Van Can (1847-1925), rejected Chinese writing in favour of **quoc-ngu**, a Romanised version of vernacular Vietnamese devised by 17C missionaries. The birth of this script can be traced to the publication of a trilingual dictionary (Vietnamese-Latin-Portuguese) by **Father Alexandre de Rhodes** in 1651. The alphabet is made up of 12 vowels and 17 consonants, fashioned after phonetic Portuguese, to which are added diphthongs or double consonants whose sound changes depending on the vowel which precedes them. As this breakdown of syllables was not sufficient to deal with the language's vocal diversity, *quoc-ngu* also has **accents** which indicate the high and low registers of its six tones. These accents take the form of **diacritical marks** which are placed either over or under the vowels to indicate whether they are long or short, open or closed.

Devised for religious purposes, for three centuries *quoc-ngu* remained the exclusive prerogative of Catholicism. In fact, before it became a symbol of nationalism, it was updated by two Catholic Vietnamese, Paulus Cua and Truong Vin Ky, in the second half of the 19C. It was used to translate Western literary and philosophical works, before being declared the official language of the Indochinese government in 1910. *Quoc-ngu* facilitates the assimilation of foreign terms on a purely phonetic basis. During the French occupation, this led to the emergence of terms such as *ca phe* (coffee), *banh mi* (bread, from the French "pain de mie") or *xi mang* (cement) and nowadays, it can be noted that the population wears *quan jeans* (jeans).

85

LITERATURE

It might seem paradoxical in a country which appears to have made so little effort to maintain its architectural heritage over the passing centuries, that such pains have been taken to preserve the written word *(see "Paper and woodcuts" page 82)*. The written word is however felt to be the expression of the national soul and identity, be it in opposition to Chinese or French invaders, an autocratic regime or, as today, censorship. Nonetheless it would be incorrect to place Vietnamese literature under the sole banner of militant patriotism. Although the desire for independence may have inspired many writers, a more in-depth examination reveals a common ancestral attachment to their roots and a subtle approach to emotions, be they individual or collective. Due to the nation's large expatriate population – mainly in the United States and France – many Vietnamese authors have been translated and have enjoyed wide critical acclaim. Of late, Vietnamese literature is increasingly able to express these paradoxes, giving rise to a battle of words between the disillusioned northern victors and the defeated expatriates from the South.

Literary heritage

Vietnam's ancient literature was, with a very few exceptions, written in Chinese. Political works, such as proclamations, archives, edicts (the oldest known of which was that of the transfer of the capital to Thang Long in the 11C), pamphlets and political or moral essays on the exercise of power make up the major part of this heritage. Poetry, particularly from the 14C, has also played a prominent role.

Nguyen Trai (1380-1442) was one of the first major authors to emerge onto the literary scene. The archetypal scholar steeped in Confucian culture (he was made Doctor in 1400), his deep belief in its humanist virtues led him to offer his services to King Le Loi, thereby helping to free the country of Chinese domination *(see page 21)*. In addition to a major work in classical Chinese, Nguyen Trai was one of the first to express himself in *nom* or Vietnamese in his *Collection of poems in the national language* (*Quoc Am Thi Tap*). However the collection's tribute to honesty and the simple way of life was ill-received and the author, who has since become one of the nation's heroes, was tortured to death with his family in 1442. Such an end was perhaps not a surprise to the man who concluded one of his poems with the line: "Only the human heart remains impenetrable".

Nguyen Binh Khiem (1491-1585), a great poet who lived during the time when the Mac dynasty attempted to seize power, extolled the virtues of solitary life in his poems in Chinese and Vietnamese. "I never grow weary of the country pleasures of solitude." His disciple, **Nguyen Du** (16C), expressed similar sentiments in his *Great Collection of Fantastic Tales* (*Truyen Ky Man Luc*), which relates his contemporaries' failings through allegories.

Doan Thi Diem (1705-48), nicknamed the "Red River's woman of letters", was the first

The scholar, a man of character

Until the French put an end to the mandarin examinations, the scholar had been a pivotal figure in Vietnamese society. By scholar, one meant not only a man of letters, but someone who had studied Confucian thought in the Chinese language and script. This involved the study of nine anthologies of texts (Four Books and Five Canons) of philosophy and history. By successfully sitting the entrance exams into the civil service, scholars were able to move up the rungs of mandarin bureaucracy. These exams were intended to verify the scholar's mastery of the major principles of Confucian doctrine rather than his administrative or legal knowledge. Out of the many candidates, only a few successfully passed such exams, especially that of the last rung, the Great Imperial Exam, which was held in the capital's National College. Back in their native villages, those who had failed the exam became schoolteachers and, in turn, prepared a whole new generation of future candidates for the Chinese system.

renowned woman author. She translated into *nom* a long epic, *Grievances of a woman whose husband has left for the war (Chinh phu ngam)* whose painful echo was to resound even in modern Vietnam. Another woman writer, **Ho Xuan Huong** adopted a totally different style which mischievously blended images and sounds into only very thinly veiled erotic poems.

There cannot be a single Vietnamese alive today who has not heard the epic poem *Kim Van Kieu* by **Nguyen Du** (1765-1820). This 3 524-verse story features themes which continue to prevail among contemporary novelists. The hopelessness of fate and the lucidity of the characters endow it with a timeless tragic quality. The beautiful Kieu is in love with the scholar Kim, but must prostitute herself to help her father. Kim marries Van, Kieu's sister and their three entangled fates serve as a pretext for an examination of the inherent contradictions between talent and fate, love and war or virtue and vice.

Contemporary voices

Scholars played a significant role in the anti-French resistance movement, but the colonial government dealt them a decisive blow when it imposed the Latinisation of the Vietnamese language instead of Chinese *(see page 85)*. However *quoc-ngu* was rapidly adopted and gave rise to a literary explosion between 1925 and 1945 which featured all the main currents of Western literature, dominated by a realism which denounced colonial exploitation and the archaism of traditional society. The satirical works of **Nguyen Cong Hoan** (1903-77) and the biting irony of **Nam Cao** (1917-51) mercilessly related the weaknesses of a society whose fall they sought. Some Vietnamese authors even wrote directly in French (**Pham Quynh** and **Pham Duy Khiem**). Many writers joined the revolutionary cause and took to the jungle, in support of Ho Chi Minh.

In the mid-1950s, propaganda began to replace revolutionary ideals and became the only form of expression allowed, provoking nonetheless a few isolated anti-establishment movements, such as **Nhan Van-Giai Pham**. This opposition group was, however, gagged and all artistic creation muzzled, with, as a result, total silence up until the 1980s. In 1989, encouraged by *Doi Moi*, the 4th Congress of the Union of Writers refused to follow party guidelines, thereby indicating the return of individual expression, the spokesman of which is **Nguyen Huy Thiep**. In *A General Retires*, published in 1987, he launched a Kafkaesque debate on the grotesque nature of fate in a world without meaning. In opposition to this cruel, muffled style, the novelist **Duong Thu Huong** proposes a sensual, passionate and only very barely concealed criticism of the absurdity of her nation's government *(Beyond Illusions)*. This rebirth of literature in Vietnam is also echoed in the painful works of those in exile, personified by young writers born out of the boat people generation, such as **Nguyen Khanh Truong** who lives in the United States *(Do you love me?*, 1997), or **Tran Vu**, who has taken refuge in France since 1980 *(Under a Rain of Thorns*, 1989).

Practical information

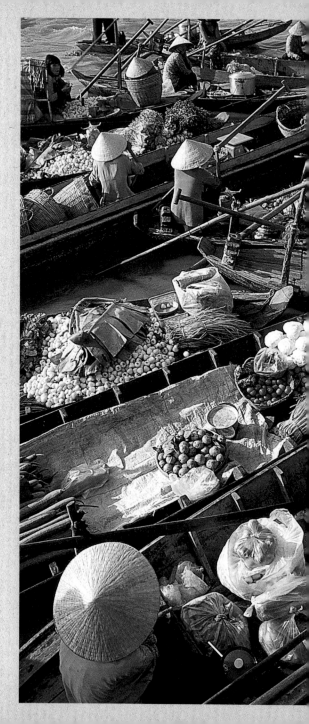

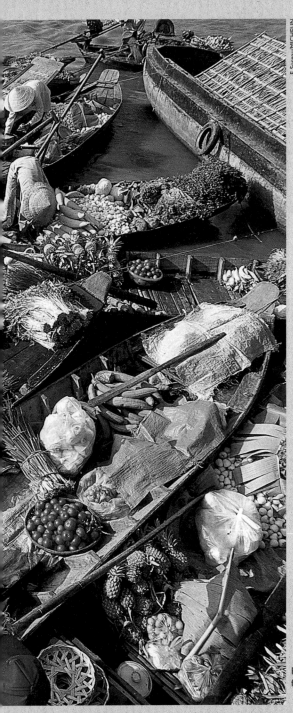

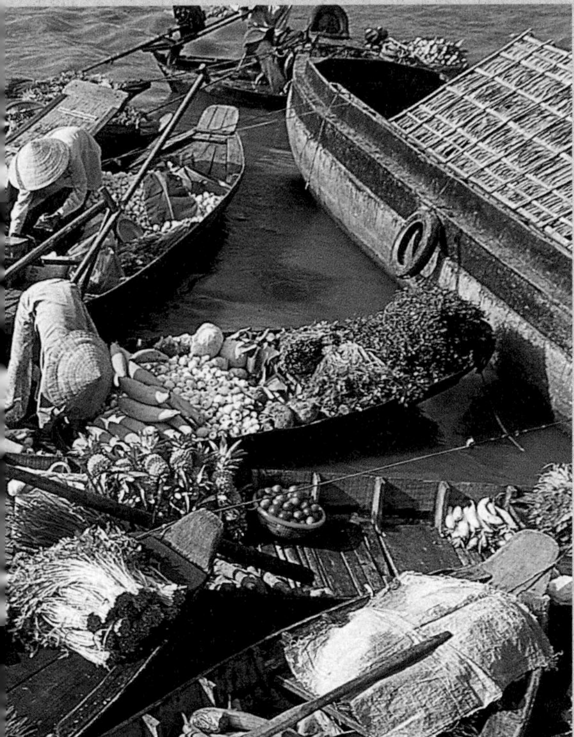
F Soreau/MICHELIN

Phung Hiep
floating market

BEFORE GOING

• Time difference

Vietnam is 7hr ahead of Greenwich Mean Time (GMT), so when it is noon in Hanoi, it is 5am in London, midnight in New York, 9pm the previous day in Los Angeles and 3pm in Sydney.

• When to go

Vietnam has a tropical climate with long hours of sunshine, relatively high temperatures throughout the year and extensive rainfall. As a general rule, there are two distinct seasons, varying from dry and cool from November to April to hot and wet from May to October, but because of its wide range of latitudes, (the country is more than 1 600km in length), there are significant differences between the northern and southern regions. The variations in temperature, much more apparent in the Tonkin region where the climate is more temperate, are hardly noticeable in Ho Chi Minh City and the Mekong Delta *(see page 14)*. In fact, there are no good or bad seasons for visiting Vietnam, although travellers should try to avoid the more marked winters in the North and the monsoon period in the South (September to October). For local weather information prior to your departure, visit www11.cnn.com/WEATHER

	Average annual temperature	Coldest month	Hottest month	Average annual rainfall	Driest month	Wettest month
Hanoi	23.4°C	January 16.5°C	June 28.8°C	1 678mm	December 20mm	August 350mm
Hue	25.1°C	January 19.7°C	July 29.4°C	3 039mm	January 30mm	October 860mm
Ho Chi Minh City	26.9°C	January 25.8°C	April 28.9°C	1 952mm	February 50mm	June 340mm

• Things to take

Clothing

Pack light clothes, preferably cotton, though a pullover is recommended for air-conditioned buildings and in the Central Highlands or the Tonkin Mountains. Day- and night-time temperatures can vary considerably and a jacket or pullover is essential when planning to travel in the winter (September-April). Bring waterproof clothing for the frequent short-lived but often torrential downpours, as well as long-sleeved tops, trousers and socks for protection against mosquitoes. Be sure to always dress appropriately when visiting places of worship including footwear that is easy to slip off, since shoes cannot be worn inside such buildings. Finally, hiking boots are advisable if you plan to go trekking.

Accessories

Certain small items may prove very useful, such as a travel alarm clock if you intend to watch the sunrise, plasters or adhesive tape to repair any holes in mosquito nets, a small padlock for your luggage (especially when planning to use the local transport system), a torch in the event of any power cuts and, depending on your itinerary, a pair of binoculars for a better view of the surroundings, a pocket knife for peeling fruit and a water bottle. A sleeping bag may also be advisable if the bedding provided in local guesthouses should prove to be inadequate (excellent value silk bedding can also be bought locally). Always carry photocopies of your airline ticket, travellers' cheques and the more important pages of your passport, as well as spare passport photographs, which should make eventual replacements much easier if your documents are lost or stolen.

• A trip for everyone

Vietnam poses no particular problems in terms of health or safety, but before leaving home it is nonetheless advisable to take note of your country's official advice for travellers.

Australia: Australian Department of Foreign Affairs and Trade, RG Casey Building, John McEwen Crescent, Barton, ACT, 0221, Australia ☎ (02) 6261 3305 (Consular Duty Officer), www.dfat.gov.au

Canada: Department of Foreign Affairs and International Trade, 125 Sussex Drive, Ottawa, Ontario, K1A 0G2, ☎ Freephone 1 800 267 8376 (or 613 944 4000 in the Ottawa Region), www.dfait-maeci.gc.ca

UK: Foreign and Commonwealth Office, King Charles St, London SW1A 2AH, General enquiries, ☎ (020) 7008 0232 / 0233, Visa enquiries, ☎ (020) 7238 3838, www.fco.gov.uk

US: Department of State, 2201 C Street NW, Washington, DC 20520, ☎ (202) 647 400 – www.state.gov

Travelling with children

The Vietnamese welcome children with open arms, so families should feel quite at home. However, watch their diet while travelling, give them plenty to drink and protect them from the sun and the heat (see "Health"). You will find everything you need in the cities, but check up on transport and lodgings once off the beaten track.

Women travelling alone

A woman travelling on her own should not encounter any particular problems as long as she abides by certain rudimentary rules: avoid plunging necklines and don't visit deserted areas late at night. Vietnamese men may be curious but rarely bothersome.

Elderly people

Elderly people may visit the country in relative comfort, but outside of the typical tourist areas it would be wise to check on available transport and accommodation as well as health services which can still be rather basic.

Disabled travellers

Unfortunately, there are few facilities available for disabled visitors travelling alone. To fully enjoy your holiday, contact a tour operator to help you with the necessary logistical arrangements.

• Address book

Tourist information offices

For tourist information, contact the Vietnamese embassy in your own country.

Australia: Embassy of Vietnam, 6 Timbarra Crescent, O'Malley, Canberra, ACT 2603, ☎ (02) 6286 6059.

Canada: Embassy of Vietnam, 470 Wilbrod St, Ottawa, Ontario, K1N 6M8, ☎ (613) 236 0772, 232 1957, Fax (613) 236 2704, vietem@istar.ca

UK: Embassy of Vietnam, 12-14 Victoria Rd, London W8 5RD, ☎ (020) 7937 1912, Fax (020) 7937 6108, vp@dsqvnlondon.demon.co.uk

US: Embassy of Vietnam, 1233 20th St NW, Suite 400, Washington, DC 20036, ☎ (202) 647 0518, Fax (202) 861 1297.

G de Benoist/MICHELIN

Vietnam Travel Information: asiatravel.com/vietinfo.html
Practical information on Vietnam, ranging from weather conditions to drinking and dining.
An introduction to Vietnam: www.interknowledge.com/vietnam
An illustrated geographical and historical view of Vietnam.
Indochina Services: www.indochina-services.com
Useful travel information including a virtual tour of Vietnam.
Other websites of interest:
www.destinationvietnam.com
dest.travelocity.com
www.casa.umontreal.ca
www.asiasociety.org
www.vietnamonline.com
www.vietnamadventures.com

• Documents required

All formalities are listed for information only and are subject to change. Contact your local embassy at least one month before leaving home for the most up-to-date information.

Identity papers and visas

Residents of Australia, Canada, New Zealand, the UK and the US need a valid **passport** as well as a **visa** to enter Vietnam, obtainable from the Vietnamese embassy or consulate before leaving. Take your passport and two identity photos with you. A tourist visa usually lasts for 30 days and costs US$50. You will be required to fill in two detailed forms which must also include your arrival and departure dates as well as the particulars of your hotel (put the name of the hotel where you will be staying on arrival in Vietnam). It is better to buy flight tickets before going ahead with the necessary formalities, and check the addresses of several hotels in the town you arrive in. A copy of this form must be handed in to customs on arrival in Vietnam.

Customs

On arrival in the country, you will be asked to fill in customs and police papers that you must then keep with you at all times. You will be asked to present the blue police form in all the hotels you stay in, since the hotel proprietors are obliged to declare their clients to the local police.

Vietnamese law allows the **import** of 200 cigarettes, 2 litres of alcohol, perfume and jewellery for personal use, as well as any amount of foreign currency up to US$7 000. The laws are, however, far less lenient regarding literature that may be considered detrimental to the government, pornographic material, video cassettes or firearms. Note that the **export** of antiques is absolutely forbidden, so always ask for a receipt as well as a signed declaration confirming that the article is not an antique and so may be exported.

Health regulations

There are no particular health regulations for entering Vietnam.

Vaccinations

No vaccinations are required except for yellow fever if arriving from an African or Latin American country where it is endemic. It is, however, highly recommended to check the date of your last immunisations against polio, diphtheria, tetanus, typhoid, hepatitis A and B, meningitis A and C, as well as Japanese encephalitis for long stays. Vietnam has cases of malaria and is classified as zone 3. As malaria and its prevention are constantly evolving, discuss details of your planned itinerary with your local doctor before leaving.

British Airways Travel Clinic, 156 Regent St, London W1B 5LB (Monday-Friday 9am-4.15pm, Saturday 10am-4pm); ☎ (020) 7439 9584; branches at 101 Cheapside,

London EC2V 6DT, ☎ (020) 7606 2977 and at the BA terminal in London's Victoria Station ☎ (020) 7233 6661); plus regional clinics (☎ (01276) 685 040 for details).

Hospital for Tropical Diseases, Travel Clinic, Mortimer Market Centre, 2nd Floor, Capper St, London WC1E 6AU, ☎ (020) 7387 4411. Phone the recorded message service on (020) 7388 9600 for information on illness prevention as well as appropriate immunisations.

MASTA (Medical Advisory Service for Travellers Abroad), London School of Hygiene and Tropical Medicine, ☎ (01276) 685 040. Operates a 24hr Travellers' Health Line, supplying written information tailored to your journey by return of post.

Nomad Travellers Store & Medical Centre in London can provide vaccination and health information, plus details on travel kits. They can be contacted on ☎ (020) 8889 7014.

Canadian Society for International Health, 170 Laurier Ave W, Suite 902, Ottawa, ON, K1P 5V5, ☎ (613) 230 2654. Distributes a free pamphlet, "*Health Information for Canadian Travellers*".

International Association for Medical Assistance to Travellers (IAMAT), 417 Center St, Lewiston, NY 14092, USA, ☎ (716) 754 4883 and in Canada, 40 Regal Rd, Guelph Ontario, N1K 1B5, ☎ (519) 836 0102. This non-profit organisation supported by donations can provide a list of English-speaking doctors, climate charts and leaflets on various diseases and inoculations.

Travellers' Medical and Vaccination Centre, Level 7, 428 George St, Sydney, ☎ (02) 9221 7133; Level 3, 393 Little Bourke St, Melbourne, ☎ (03) 9602 5788; Level 6, 29 Gilbert Place, Adelaide, ☎ (08) 8212 7522; Level 6, 247 Adelaide St, Brisbane, ☎ (07) 3221 9066; 1 Mill St, Perth, ☎ (08) 9321 1977.

Health information for travellers to Southeast Asia
www.cdc.gov/travel/seasia.htm

Travelling Doctor: www.traveling-doctor.com
Advice for travellers

Driving licence

An International Driving Licence is required to drive a car in Vietnam, but few tourists are brave enough to hire a car without a driver due to the rather dangerous driving conditions both in towns and in the country.

• Currency

Money

The monetary unit is the **dong** (VND). It comes in notes of 100, 200, 500, 1 000, 2 000, 5 000, 10 000, 20 000 and 50 000VND. At the time of publication, **US$1 = 15 779VND**, **€1 = 13 876VND** and **GB£1 = 22 373VND**. For further details before your departure, visit www.oanda.com/converter/classic

Money exchange

It is advisable to travel with American **dollars**. Avoid worn-out dirty-looking notes as they will not always be accepted. It will be possible to change your money at the Vietcombank and foreign exchange offices as well as in some jewellery shops and hotels. Plan ahead before leaving the larger cities and always ask for smaller notes as changing money elsewhere can prove difficult.

Travellers' cheques

Travellers' cheques are generally accepted in all the large banks as well as some of the more expensive hotels. It is better to use travellers' cheques made out in dollars.

Credit cards

There are very few automatic cash dispensers in Vietnam outside of the larger cities, but in banks money can be withdrawn on a credit card (Visa, MasterCard, American Express). Apart from a limited number of high-class establishments, few hotels or restaurants accept payment by credit card.

• **Spending money**

The cost of living is not high in Vietnam, but do be careful since prices are not marked in the shops and you will invariably be asked to pay more than the real price. Feel free to bargain.

If travelling on a tight budget, count on spending a minimum of **US$20** per day per person, which would include accommodation in cheap hotels (from US$8-10 for a double room), meals in small restaurants (US$3 per meal) and getting around by public transport, motorcycle-taxi, bus or train. When travelling alone, you can spend less by taking dormitory accommodation (around US$5).

A daily budget of **US$50** per person, based on two people sharing, would include accommodation in reasonable hotels (US$30), restaurant meals (US$8), and the hire of a chauffeur-driven car.

Allowing **US$100** per day per person, based on two people sharing, it is possible to stay in luxury hotels (US$70), eat in top-class restaurants (US$15), and travel by plane and hired cars. These figures are an approximate indication and do not include any outings or personal gifts.

• **Booking in advance**

Apart from during the Tet holiday period and other local religious holidays, there should be no problems in finding accommodation and advance booking is not really necessary. However, for domestic flights and sleeper trains it is advisable to buy your ticket several days in advance.

• **Travel insurance**

Consider taking out travel insurance before leaving home as this is the only way to obtain coverage throughout your trip. When purchasing your plane ticket or your holiday from a tour operator, you will generally be offered an optional insurance policy that will reimburse you in case of cancellation, emergency care and repatriation, as well as a lump sum for theft or damage to luggage. Otherwise you can contact companies at home that provide this type of insurance. First contact your credit card company as some will provide coverage abroad. Some insurance companies also offer this service.

• **Gifts**

To thank people for their hospitality, it may be a good idea to bring along some small gifts as a token of your appreciation. Many Vietnamese will want to know about your country and your family and it's a good idea to bring along postcards and photographs. But do try and avoid giving sweets and money to the children.

GETTING THERE

• **By air**

A number of airline companies have daily flights to Vietnam from Europe. Most of them operate flights to Hanoi returning from Ho Chi Minh City or vice versa for no extra cost. A direct flight between London and one of these cities lasts about 15hr and includes at least one stopover.

The price of a return ticket to Vietnam through the different tour operators can vary from between US$650 and US$1 050.

The following is a list of airline companies which operate direct scheduled flights to Vietnam.

Australia: Vietnam Airlines flies directly from Sydney or Melbourne to Hanoi or Saigon. From Melbourne, you can fly into Saigon with **Qantas**, **Lauda Air** or **Malaysian Airlines**.

Canada: Cathay Pacific flies to both Hanoi and Saigon from Vancouver or Toronto via Hong Kong.

New Zealand: From Auckland, **United Airlines**, **Qantas** and **Lauda Air** fly into Sydney and Kuala Lumpur before continuing to Saigon.

UK: From London, there are no direct flights but **Thai Airways** flies to Saigon via a connecting flight in Bangkok. From Paris, both **Air France** and **Vietnam Airlines** fly to Hanoi and Saigon.

US: Cathay Pacific flies to Vietnam via Hong Kong. **Vietnam Airlines** flies to Hanoi and Saigon from Hong Kong, and may soon be flying from Los Angeles to both Hanoi and Saigon. **China Airlines** flies from Los Angeles via Tapei to Saigon. **Thai Airways International** flies from Los Angeles to Saigon via Bangkok.

You can obtain further information from general flight operators:

Thomas Cook Travel, 25 City Rd, Epworth House, London EC1Y 1AS, UK, ☎ (020) 7638 7244, www.thomascook.co.uk

Goway Travel Ltd, 3284 Yonge St, Suite 300, Toronto, Ontario, M4N 3M7, Canada, ☎ (416) 322 1034, Fax (416) 322 1109, res@goway.com, www.goway.com

www.cheapflights.com
www.lastminute.com
www.opodo.com

Flight confirmation
Return flights should be confirmed at least 72hr in advance.

Airport taxes
The airport tax on leaving Vietnam is US$10.

• Package deals
Special interest
Brochures are available in most travel agencies.

Australia:
Orbitours Pty Ltd, 73 Walker St, North Sydney, (PO Box 834), NSW 2059, ☎ (612) 9954 1399, Fax (612) 9954 1655. (For American clients there is a toll-free number in the USA (800) 235 5895).

New Zealand:
Destinations, 2nd Floor, Premier Building, 4 Durham St, Auckland, ☎ (09) 390 4674.

UK:
Asian Journeys, 32 Semilong Rd, Northampton NN2 6BT, ☎ (01604) 234 855, Fax (01604) 234 866.

British Airways Holidays Ltd, Astral Towers, Betts Way, London Rd, Crawley RH10 2XA, ☎ (0870) 24 24 245, www.baholidays.co.uk

Kuoni Worldwide, Kuoni House, Dorking RHY 4AZ, ☎ (01306) 740 888, www.kuoni.co.uk

Progressive Tours, 12 Porchester Place, Marble Arch, London, W2 2BS, ☎ (020) 7262 1676, Fax (020) 7724 6941.

Regent Holidays (UK) Ltd, 15 John St, Bristol, BS1 2HR, ☎ (0117) 921 1711, Fax (0117) 925 4866.

Silk Steps Ltd, PO Box 24, Bristol BS16 6JY, ☎ (0117) 940 2800, Fax (0117) 940 6900, info@silksteps.co.uk, www.silksteps.co.uk

Steppes East, 51 Castle St, Cirencester GL7 1QD, ☎ (01285) 651 010, Fax (01285) 885 888, sales@steppeseast.co.uk, www.steppeseast.co.uk

The Imaginative Traveller, 14 Barley Mow Passage, Chiswick, London W4 4PH, ☎ (020) 8742 8612, Fax (020) 8742 3045, info@imaginative-traveller.com

Tradewinds Worldwide Holidays, ☎ (0870) 751 0003, Fax (0870) 751 0010.

Yorks Travel, Chancery House, 52 Sheep St, Northampton NN1 2LZ, ☎ (01604) 631 535, 622 590, yorkstr@yorks-travel.co.uk, www.yorks-travel.co.uk

USA / Canada:
Indochina Consulting Group, 844 Elda Lane, Westbury, NY 11590, USA, ☎ (516) 333 6662 / 872 3885.
Mekong Travel, 151 First Ave, Suite 172, New York, NY 10003, USA, ☎ (212) 420 1586.
Orbitours, see Australia above.
Saigon Tours, Club Voyages Berri, 1650 Berri, Montreal, Quebec, H2L 4E6, Canada, ☎ (514) 982 6168 / 9, Fax (514) 982 0820.
Trek Holidays, Agents Reservations Canada-wide (toll free), ☎ (1 800) 661 7265.
Wild Card Adventures, 751 Maple Grove Rd, Camano Island, WA 98292, USA, ☎ (800) 590 3776, Fax (360) 387 9816.

Adventure tours
Symbiosis Travel, 205 St John's Hill, London SW11 1TH, UK, ☎ (020) 7924 5906, Mobile (07973) 257 761, Fax (020) 7924 5907, info@symbiosis-travel.com, www.symbiosis-travel.com
Exodus Travel, 9 Weir Rd, London SW12 0LT, UK, ☎ (020) 7675 5550.
Global Spectrum, 1901 Pennsylvania Ave NW, Suite 204, Washington DC, USA, ☎ (202) 293 2065.
The Globetrotters Club, BCM/Roving, London WC1N 3XX, UK. London meetings information line, ☎ (020) 8674 6229, www.globetrotters.co.uk
VeloAsia, 1271 43rd Ave, San Francisco, CA 94122, USA, ☎ (415) 664 6779, veloasia@aol.com

Cultural and ecological holidays
Earthwatch, 57 Woodstock Rd, Oxford OX2 6HJ, UK, ☎ (01865) 311 600.

THE BASICS

• **Address book**

Tourist information
Vietnamese tourist offices are run by provincial administrations. They work in the same way as travel agents, and may charge for their services and basic documentation. In certain regions such as My Tho or Pleiku, they either have a monopoly on local excursions, or else they require privately operated agencies to obtain a permit and even employ a local guide. This is not current practice in the main tourist areas where tourist offices and private agencies generally work together. The two largest agencies in the country are **Saigon Tourist** and **Vietnam Tourism**.

Embassies and consulates
In Hanoi:
American Embassy: 7 Lang Ha, ☎ (04) 843 1500, Fax (04) 843 1510.
Australian Embassy: Van Phuc Diplomatic Quarter, ☎ (04) 831 7755, Fax (04) 831 7711.
British Embassy: 31 Hai Ba Trung, ☎ (04) 825 2510 / 826 7560, Fax (04) 826 5762, behanoi@fpt.vn, www.uk-vietnam.org
Canadian Embassy: 31 Hung Vuong, ☎ (04) 823 5500.
Chinese Embassy: 46 Hoang Dieu, ☎ (04) 845 3736, Fax (04) 823 2826.

In Ho Chi Minh City:
American Consulate: 4 Le Duan, District 1, ☎ (08) 829 9433, Fax (08) 822 9434.
Australian Consulate: Levels 4 & 5 Landmark Building, 5B Ton Duc Thang, District 1, ☎ (08) 829 6035, Fax (08) 829 6031.
British Consulate: 25 Le Duan, District 1, ☎ (08) 829 8433, Fax (08) 822 1971, bcghcmc@hcm.vnn.vn
Canadian Consulate: 41 Dong Khoi, Suite 102, District 1, ☎ (08) 824 2000, Fax (08) 829 4528.
Chinese Consulate: 39 Nguyen Thi Minh Khai, ☎ (08) 829 2457, Fax (08) 829 5009.

• Opening and closing times

Banks
Opening hours are generally Monday-Friday, 7.30-11.30am and 1.30-3.30pm. In certain cities some banks are open at lunch time, and even Saturday mornings.

Post offices
Most post offices open every day between 6-8am and close between 9-10pm.

Shops
They are generally open throughout the day, although some take a short afternoon break. In some large cities they are often open as late as 8pm. Market times are, however, rather more varied: some are open 24hr a day, but most begin trading very early in the morning until around 10pm.

Restaurants
As a general rule, restaurants are open every day. The street vendors serve food throughout the day, although some are only open at lunchtime and close when supplies run out. Most of the higher-class Vietnamese restaurants are only open at meal times (10.30am-2pm and 5-8pm, or 9pm in the South). For more formal establishments in large cities or well-known tourist areas, orders are taken until 10pm. After that, you can always try the typical tourist restaurants which are open until 11pm.

Offices
Monday-Friday, 7.30-11.30am and 1.30-4.30pm. They are sometimes open Saturday mornings.

• Museums, monuments and archaeological sites

Opening and closing times
The closing day is normally Mondays and sometimes weekends in the smaller towns, but some museums are open every day. Usual opening times are 7 or 8am-4 or 5pm, with a break for lunch from 11.30am-1.30pm.

Fees
Entrance fees are very modest, varying between 5 000VND and 10 000VND. When there are no prices indicated, donations are well received. There may be a charge for photos or video films, which can be quite high in some archaeological sites such as at My Son and the royal tombs near Hue.

Religious sites
As a general rule, temples and pagodas are open to visitors throughout the week without a break (except for lunchtimes in some cases), but churches on the other hand are only open during service times. Entrance is free, but donations are appreciated.

Authorised visits
In the Central Highlands, particularly around Buon Ma Thuot and Pleiku, certain villages are only open to those tourists in possession of a special permit issued by the local tourist office (expect to pay about US$10).

Guides
The benefit of a guide is a matter of personal opinion. You won't always have the choice, as in certain villages in the Central Highlands, but it is some consolation to know that their contribution to the visit is often well worth the expense. Their support can also prove to be essential during forest treks.

• Postal services
Vietnam has an excellent postal network (*buu dien*) offering a variety of services including the sending and receiving of faxes, telephone communications and even Internet. Delivery times depend on where you send your mail from, but for a letter to Europe allow between 8 to 10 days from Ho Chi Minh City or Hanoi. Normal rates for a postcard do not exceed half a dollar, slightly more for a letter. Note that an express mail service is available (EMS) which can take as little as four days.

The basics

For **poste restante**, write the name of the receiver in capital letters and underline it, followed by "poste restante" and then the address. Money transfers are possible. The post office will deliver parcels internationally up to 20kg. Over this weight you have to deal with a private company with higher rates.

JVK International Movers, 5A Pho Yet Kieu, Hanoi, ☎ (04) 822 01 43.

Saigon Van, 76 Ngo Duc Ke, Ho Chi Minh City, ☎ (08) 829 3502, Fax (08) 821 3003; 21 Pho Ngo Van So, Hanoi, ☎ mobile (090) 404087, Fax (04) 824 0944.

• Telephone and fax

Unless it is an emergency, avoid making international calls from your hotel as the rates can often be excessive. The post office provides cheaper but still quite high rates (US$3.50 per min). It may be possible to ask the employees to warn you when your call exceeds a certain amount, but they often forget. Local calls, however, are quite cheap. For the operator, dial 101. A useful tip when phoning – dial slowly or else the number often gives out the engaged tone.

International calls

Calling Vietnam from overseas – 00 + 84 + regional code (without the 0) + the number you wish to dial.

Calling overseas from Vietnam – 00 + the country code + regional code (without the 0) + the number you wish to dial.

The **international codes** are 61 for Australia, 644 for New Zealand, 27 for South Africa, 44 for the UK and 1 for the USA and Canada.

Local calls

For a local call within the same area, it is not necessary to dial the local code. When dialling another area, dial 0 before the local code.

Province	Capital	Area code
An Giang	Long Xuyen	76
Bac Can	Bac Can	281
Ba Ria–Vung Tau	Vung Tau	64
Bac Giang	Bac Giang	240
Bac Lieu	Bac Lieu	781
Bac Ninh	Bac Ninh	241
Ben Tre	Ben Tre	75
Binh Dinh	Qui Nhon	56
Binh Duong	Thu Dau Mot	650
Binh Phuoc	Dong Xoai	651
Binh Thuan	Phan Thiet	62
Ca Mau	Ca Mau	780
Can Tho	Can Tho	71
Cao Bang	Cao Bang	26
Da Nang	Da Nang	511
Dac Lac	Buon Ma Thuot	50
Dong Nai	Bien Hoa	61
Dong Thap	Cao Lanh	67
Gia Lai	Pleiku	59
Ha Giang	Ha Giang	19
Ha Nam	Ha Nam	351
Ha Tay	Ha Dong	34
Ha Tinh	Ha Tinh	39
Hai Duong	Hai Duong	320
Haiphong	Haiphong	31
Hanoi	Hanoi	4
Ho Chi Minh City	HCMC	8
Hoa Binh	Hoa Binh	18
Hung Yen	Hung Yen	321
Khanh Hoa	Nha Trang	58
Kien Giang	Rach Gia	77
Kon Tum	Kon Tum	60
Lai Chau	Dien Bien Phu	23
Lam Dong	Dalat	63
Lang Son	Lang Son	25
Lao Cai	Lao Cai	20
Long An	Tan An	72
Nam Dinh	Nam Dinh	350
Nghe An	Vinh	38
Ninh Binh	Ninh Binh	30
Ninh Thuan	Phan Rang	68
Phu Tho	Viet Tri	210
Phu Yen	Tuy Hoa	57
Quang Binh	Dong Hoi	52
Quang Nam	Tam Ky	510
Quang Ngai	Quang Ngai	55
Quang Ninh	Halong	33
Quang Tri	Dong Ha	53
Soc Trang	Soc Trang	79
Son La	Son La	22
Tay Ninh	Tay Ninh	66
Thai Binh	Thai Binh	36
Thai Nguyen	Thai Nguyen	280
Thanh Hoa	Thanh Hoa	37
Thua Tien–Hue	Hue	54
Tien Giang	My Tho	73
Tra Vinh	Tra Vinh	74
Tuyen Quang	Tuyen Quang	27
Vinh Long	Vinh Long	70
Vinh Phuc	Vinh Yen	211
Yen Bai	Yen Bai	29

Charges

Reverse charge calls are the cheapest way to telephone home, but the average price of an international call is about US$3.80 per minute with a 20% reduction on Sundays and public holidays and during the week from 11pm-7am.

Mobile phones

In Vietnam, numbers for mobile phones begin with 090. As for most mobile phone systems, rates are higher than for fixed lines. Check with your service provider that your mobile phone contract covers Vietnam; alternatively most post offices offer the possibility of mobile phone rental.

• Internet

Cyber cafés are very popular in Hanoi, Ho Chi Minh City and in the large tourist centres (between 200 and 400VND per minute). They are also starting up in smaller towns, post offices and big hotels, but rates are slightly higher.

• Public holidays

Fixed public holidays

1 January	New Year.
3 February	Founding of the Vietnamese Communist Party in 1930.
30 April	Liberation of South Vietnam in 1975.
1 May	Labour Day.
19 May	Anniversary of the birth of Ho Chi Minh in 1890.
2 September	A national holiday commemorating the founding of the Democratic Republic of Vietnam by Ho Chi Minh in 1945 in Hanoi.
25 December	Christmas Day. Variable public holidays.
Tet Festival	From the first to the third day of the first lunar month (Mid-January to beginning of February). Many hotels are fully booked at this time, trains and planes are booked several months in advance and most shops are closed.
Birth of Buddha	The eighth day of the fourth lunar month.

For other public holidays, see page 67.

For other public holidays, see page 67.

GETTING AROUND

Transport in Vietnam is an all-important part of the experience of getting to know the country, but you need time and patience to appreciate it fully. For a brief insight into the northern, central and southern regions of the country if travelling by car, bus and train, you will need to set aside a whole month. Three weeks should be enough when travelling by plane.

• By car

Car rentals

If not on a tight budget, sharing a rented car is the best way to visit the country, making touring much more flexible. **Chauffeur-driven cars** are customary in Vietnam and offer the visitor many interesting advantages. It is of course better to hire an English-speaking driver and be sure to check whether his meals and accommodation are included in the price, as is the usual practice. The rental is based on normal working hours, between 8am and 5pm with a lunch break around noon. A number of Vietnamese hotels provide reasonably-priced rooms for the drivers, sometimes even free of charge. Finally, be sure to park the car in a secure area and never leave valuable personal effects inside.

It is difficult to work out a daily rate, since the cost of petrol obviously depends on the actual distance covered in one particular day. Always agree on your itinerary clearly before departure and negotiate accordingly. As a rough guide, allow US$30

Getting around

per day for a tour around the Mekong Delta, US$50 in the Central Highlands leaving from Ho Chi Minh City (or US$40 in the region itself), and US$30 in the north of Vietnam. Rates for hiring a jeep or a 4WD vehicle are of course higher (from US$60 per day).

On Hanoi streets

As a motorcyclist or a pedestrian you should be aware of a certain number of rules to be applied when making your way through the streets of Hanoi. Proceed with caution when approaching a turning in the road, because you may end up face to face with an on-coming vehicle hugging the bend rather too closely. Try and use the brakes as little as possible, and keep up with the other vehicles, whatever their speed. As a pedestrian, trust the drivers' evasion skills: never slow down and don't stop before you get to the footpath on the other side. There are a number of traffic lights and pedestrian crossings, but even if cars come to a halt, allow for the seemingly unstoppable flow of two-wheelers.

Road network

The condition of the roads is very varied. The major roads, particularly Highway 1 which links Hanoi to Ho Chi Minh City, are tarmacked, but after the torrential downpours of the rainy season, road surfaces are soon damaged by heavy vehicles. This problem particularly affects the low-lying parts of Highway 1 to the north of Nha Trang, an area that suffers regular flooding and will need raising in the future.

Most of the roads in the Central Highlands and the Tonkin Mountains are tarmacked, but landslides are frequent due to heavy rain. Certain areas, such as between Dalat and Buon Ma Thuot, Pleiku and Qui Nhon, and Kon Tum and Da Nang are only passable by jeep or motorcycle.

Driving

The highway code seems to have been replaced by the law of the jungle as far as Vietnamese roads are concerned both in town or on major roads. The bullying tactics adopted by the drivers of heavy vehicles are met with indifference and even scorn by pedestrians, cyclists and motorcyclists. So don't be surprised to see a whole family astride a single motorcycle (no helmets of course) refusing to pull over in front of an enormous bus travelling at break-neck speed, hooting furiously. And in other areas, the hard asphalt surfaces double as a perfect play-ground for children or even for drying rice. Unfortunately, such amusing sights can too readily take a more dramatic turn and serious accidents are frequent. The basic rule is give way to bigger vehicles, and in a country where the number of cars on the roads is still rather limited, such a theory is mostly put to the test in the confrontations between public transport vehicles and two-wheelers or cyclos (cycle rickshaws). Another important rule refers to the importance attached to the generous use of the **horn**, far more productive than a glance in the rear-view mirror. Such a technique is hardly likely to lead to any particular change in the behaviour of other drivers, but at least they will find it harder to ignore you. When on two wheels in Vietnam, recognised driving practices can be slightly different: for ex-

G de Benoist/MICHELIN

ample, when turning right at a crossroads, it is customary to ignore a red light. As a general rule, it is advisable to follow the example of other cyclists and motorcyclists and go with the flow... even if this means missing your intended turning.

Fuel

Finding petrol stations along the major roads is easy enough, but they are few and far between along secondary routes in the Central Highlands and the northern mountains. They are usually located just outside built-up areas, but petrol is always available from street vendors on the black market, although it often contains kerosene which is damaging to the engine.

In emergencies

In the case of an accident, you are at a slight disadvantage as a foreigner in that disputes are generally settled by negotiation, and since Westerners are generally considered to have a certain financial status, the onus will be on you to pay for any damage. If the other party's demands seem excessive, or if the situation appears to be getting out of hand, then don't hesitate to call in the police who will probably confiscate both vehicles.

• By bus

Because of the run-down state of the vehicles and the poor driving conditions, travelling by bus can be a rather gruelling not to say alarming experience, especially at night. However, it is certainly the most economic way to see the country and extremely practical. Above all, you are exposed to all sorts of unexpected events which always add a bit of spice to any trip. The old Renault buses of the 1950s have given way to subsequent generations of buses of varying nationalities, from American in the 1970s, Russian in the 1980s, up to the more recent Korean and Japanese of the last decade. Although by far the most comfortable, the Japanese buses are unfortunately equipped with a sound system and karaoke facilities. Otherwise, bus travel involves only basic comfort, and you will more than likely be squashed into narrow, unpadded seats, that is if you don't find yourself travelling standing up.

Bus stations are usually on the outskirts of the towns and the buses leave very early in the morning. There is no booking system, so pay on the bus at the time of departure. To find out the exact price of a ticket it is best to see how much the other passengers are paying. Whatever the case, rates are always very modest. The basic rules of caution also apply to your baggage which must be locked and within sight if possible. If this proves difficult, then keep all your valuables with you in a small travel bag. **Ordinary buses** leave when they are full, with regular stops to pick up other passengers along the way. As a general rule, try not to board an almost empty bus, because there may be quite a wait before departure, although some buses have been known to leave the terminal with very few passengers on board and then, for no apparent reason, to wait for an hour at a petrol station 200m further on!

Sometimes equipped with air-conditioning **express buses** are slightly more expensive and are not supposed to stop en route to pick up other passengers. Don't ever expect average speeds of more than 50kph.

• By minibus

Ordinary minibuses are run by private companies and operate from bus and rail stations and from ferry landings. They are a practical way to cover the busier routes (Hanoi-Haiphong, Ho Chi Minh City-Vung Tau), and they leave when they have a sufficient number of passengers, although they tend to make frequent stops to pick up other travellers, making the trip rather long. Negotiate the price before departure. Some agencies provide comfortable, air-conditioned vehicles and it is often possible to arrange to have one call at your hotel even if there are supposed to be no other stops during the trip. A certain element of exoticism may be lacking with a trip of this sort, but comfort is certainly an added bonus.

• By chartered bus or minibus

This very affordable option is popular with many visitors to Vietnam and offers numerous advantages. One major drawback, however, is the lack of contact with local people. The minibuses provided are comfortable and usually air-conditioned and operate between Hanoi and Ho Chi Minh City (but also between Dalat and Ho Chi Minh City), visiting all the main tourist sites. You have the choice of stopping off in any scheduled town for as long as you like, before taking another "Open Tour" minibus.

• By train

The **Reunification Express** links Hanoi with Ho Chi Minh City. Reservations for soft-class sleepers should be made 2 or 3 days ahead and you should avoid the Tet holiday period. The **S1 express** with air-conditioned berths leaves Hanoi at 9pm calling at Vinh (5hr26min, 319km), Dong Hoi (9hr26min, 522km), Hue (12hr20min, 688km), Da Nang (15hr8min, 791km), Dieu Tri (20hr36min, 1 096km), Nha Trang (24hr37min, 1 315km) and Ho Chi Minh City (32hr, 1 726km). In the other direction, the **S2** from Ho Chi Minh City also leaves at 9pm. The full journey costs 1 million dong for a normal hard-class sleeper, and 1.3 million dong for a soft-class sleeper, but as always with Vietnamese trains, foreigners are supposed to pay a surcharge. The **S3**, **S5** and **S7** trains take longer with three daily departures from Hanoi to Ho Chi Minh City, (a trip of 41hr) and more frequent stops. Departures of the **S4**, **S6** and **S8** trains in the other direction are just as regular. The full trip costs 803 000VND for a normal hard sleeper and 1.2 million dong for a soft air-conditioned sleeper. *For rail links in the north of the country, see the appropriate chapters.*

Travelling in compartment seats is not recommended for long trips, but there is the choice of hard or soft **seats**, with or without air-conditioning. **Sleepers** are either hard or soft, with ventilators or air-conditioning for both types.

The upper berths are cheaper, but climbing up to them is no mean feat since there are no ladders available. Mind your hair doesn't get sucked into the ventilator. The lower berths are generally claimed by early risers.

One of the **golden rules** to adhere to when travelling by train is to always keep your ticket with you until you are out of the station. Some passengers have discarded their tickets in the past and have been forced to buy another one. Petty crime can also be a problem, but this shouldn't affect the enjoyment of your trip if you are careful to lock your baggage and not to leave it unattended on departure. Bulky packages or bicycles can be checked in and carried as unaccompanied luggage. A free **meal** is included as part of the cost for some long distance journeys and you can add to this from the food sold by the vendors that board the train at each stop.

• By air

With such long distances between the north and the south of the country, air travel is faster and less tiring. **Vietnam Airlines**, a state-run company, has a near monopoly on domestic routes, apart from Ho Chi Minh City-Hanoi which is operated by **Pacific Airlines**.

• By boat

Boat travel is limited to the Mekong delta and links with various islands such as Pho Quoc. Boat trips are also organised around Halong Bay, the Mekong Delta and to the islands off the coast near Nha Trang (*refer to the corresponding section*).

• By hydrofoil

The hydrofoil is a convenient way to travel from Haiphong to the island of Cat Ba in Halong Bay, or from Ho Chi Minh City to the Mekong Delta and the port of Vung Tau (*refer to the corresponding section*).

• By motorcycle

An **international driver's licence** is required to hire a vehicle with an engine over 50cc. Rates vary between US$5 and US$12 per day according to the area, and the make and engine size of the vehicle (the word Honda has become a byword for motorcycle). You are liable in case of theft, and you will be required to pay an excess, so check the insurance contract beforehand. Some companies provide the option of hiring a motorcycle in one town and dropping it off in another.

Chauffeur-driven motorcycles are also available in the more remote areas such as the Central Highlands (particularly from Kon Tum to Da Nang or Pleiku to Qui Non) and the Tonkin Highlands. There are certain advantages involved particularly in the case of engine failure, or even a blocked road when the only solution is to carry the motorcycle. On the whole, try and avoid venturing into these areas alone, because they can be quite deserted and help may not always be at hand.

• By bicycle

It is easy enough to rent a bike in most towns, but watch out for the brakes – most of them don't have any! Cycling is a very popular way to get around in true Vietnamese style without the stress of speed to contend with.

• By taxi

More and more taxi companies are beginning to operate in cities and tourist areas. Old French cars are gradually giving way to stylish Japanese taxis with meters. Rates vary according to the different companies but prices are generally worked out according to mileage. Vietnamese taxi-drivers are not likely to overcharge, especially those with radio contact with the main office should they get lost. Drivers usually know the area and are not out to "take you for a ride".

• By motorcycle taxi

This is quite a common form of transport throughout Vietnam and the **xe om** or **honda om** are privately-owned vehicles that pick up passengers in return for a negotiated fee. You'll find plenty of drivers around markets, bus stations or large road intersections. The fare is practically the same as for a cyclo.

• By cyclo

The **xich lo** is the most charming form of city transport in Vietnam, bringing such pleasure to some tourists that it is like watching children on a merry-go-round! Be sure to negotiate the price in dong beforehand (always have some small change), keeping in mind that it is really hard work for the drivers. Most of the time they collect commission on the customers they drop off at different hotels and shops (even if they in no way influenced your choice), and this commission will be passed on to the price of a room or purchase. In the south, cyclo drivers are mostly former soldiers, but the job is attracting more and more young transients from the countryside who rent their vehicles for use in the daytime and then may even sleep in them. The more affluent cyclo drivers have their own vehicles but they need to register them and apply for a residence permit.

• Organised tours

Travel agents offer all-inclusive trips, but if you want a specialised tour, then you can hire a chauffeur-driven car with a guide (*see above*).

Apart from the various travel agencies that organise boat trips on the River Mekong, the Victoria chain of hotels is also planning cruises around the Mekong Delta as far as Cambodia and already offers seats in luxury coaches on trains between Hanoi and Lao Cai (*see page 214*).

BED AND BOARD

• Rates

The addresses given in this guide are listed according to off-season price ranges, on the basis of a **double room** in a middle-range category. Taxes (around 15%) are generally included in the price, except for luxury hotels. Most of the government-owned hotels, however, charge more for foreigners.

It is a good idea to ask to see several rooms, since comfort and price can vary considerably even in the same hotel according to the amenities (air-conditioning, windows, television, hot water), the different floors (rates are lower on the higher floors for hotels with no lift), and the age of the building. As a general rule, it is advisable to negotiate prices, especially when staying off-season or for more than three nights. A double room occupied by a single person should be cheaper. In the larger tourist areas travellers on a tight budget will find accommodation for a minimum of US$5, but there are many other good value-for-money establishments between US$10 and US$20 (satellite TV, air-conditioning).

• Various categories of accommodation

The tourist boom of the 1990s brought exponential growth to the Vietnamese hotel industry, although it still has a long way to go before rivalling the hotels of Thailand or Indonesia in terms of comfort and value for money. However, this basic trend hides an obvious lack of accommodation in the less popular areas where the choice is often limited to one over-priced government-owned hotel or to a handful of equally expensive, but insalubrious, mini-hotels. This situation prevails in certain towns in the Central Highlands, the Mekong Delta (Ben Tre, Soc Trang or Cao Lanh) and the Tonkin Mountains (Cao Bang, Lang Son). Since 1977, however, the decline in tourist numbers has led a number of hotels to reduce their prices, and not a few construction projects have been abandoned in the hope of better days.

It is usual practice to deposit your passport or green entry card (the form you fill in on arrival at the airport) at the hotel reception at the beginning of your stay (in some cases, a photocopy will do). Don't forget to ask for them back on departure. You must be security-conscious and it is, of course, advisable not to leave any valuables in your room, but rather at the reception wherever possible. It is important to note that some unapproved private establishments are not allowed to accept foreign visitors, officially for reasons of safety or hygiene, but unofficially because they represent competition for government-owned hotels.

G de Benoist/MICHELIN

Hotels and mini-hotels

Hotel (*khach san*), mini-hotel or guesthouse (*nha khach*), "room for rent"... the description does not necessarily match the reality. **Government-owned** hotels may be fully or only partly controlled by the state and generally come under the auspices of the local tourist office. Private competition has reduced their former dominance. Comfort varies from neo-colonial elegance to Soviet-style rigour, and categories range from average to super deluxe. The atmosphere is a touch officious and stuffy to say the least (the rooms are rarely aired), and the service leaves much to be desired, but on the whole these hotels provide all the basic comforts.

Private **mini-hotels** are the most common and represent good value for money, providing comfortable accommodation from between US$8 and US$20. Dormitories are starting to catch on in tourist guesthouses, but there are no youth hostels as yet.

Joint-ventures grew in number during the 1990s and represent mostly large hotels established in renovated former palaces, and chains of top international hotels or tourist resorts. Finally, other, more original places to stay do exist, such as former colonial villas (Dalat) or traditional houses (Central Highlands).

Hustlers

Self-proclaimed guides, cyclo or taxi drivers will all bend over backwards to find you a hotel in the hope of gaining some sort of commission (about 10% of the price of the first night), which will be passed onto your own hotel bill. They are also capable of claiming that a particular hotel is closed, since they know they won't earn any commission there.

• Eating out

There is a remarkable choice of restaurants (*nha hang*) in Vietnam, ranging from the most inexpensive to the most exclusive, offering local delicacies, Western cuisine or even other Asian dishes. Off the beaten tourist track it can be difficult finding a restaurant serving meals after 9pm.

In the street

More often than not, the tastiest dishes can be found at street stalls or markets for the bargain price of less than US$1. The food is prepared either at a temporary stall or from a more permanent construction open on to the pavement. Most are limited by the type of ingredients they can prepare and usually close when their supply of fresh food is exhausted. For snacks such as soup, sandwiches or doughnuts, try individual street vendors.

In restaurants

When looking for somewhere quieter and a little more comfortable, opt for a restaurant, air-conditioned or not. The menu generally offers a wider choice of dishes and the prices are higher (careful, they are not always marked). Prices are all-inclusive and the bill will include everything consumed at the table, from the peanuts right down to the table napkins.

There is a large choice of restaurants on offer, ranging from the simplest of styles to the most formal, attracting the new middle classes or a more Western clientele where they serve a less imaginative type of cuisine. The same applies to restaurants with Western-style food, very popular in big cities. From simple tourist fare to exclusive gourmet spreads, prices range from US$2 to US$20 and over, but allow from between US$5 and US$8 for a meal in a respectable restaurant. In the most stylish of establishments, credit cards are usually accepted (sometimes with a commission) and advance booking may be necessary.

In the hotels

With the exception of the luxury hotels at Hanoi and Ho Chi Minh City that sometimes offer true gastronomic restaurants providing a feast of Western or Asian specialities, hotels on the whole serve rather average-quality meals.

SPORT AND LEISURE

• Sports

Whether it be badminton, table tennis, tennis, or hand-ball, the Vietnamese devote a lot of their time to the pursuit of many different sports, including local ones such as body badminton, played without a racket using every part of the body except for the arms, requiring a fair degree of suppleness and rapidity. But the most widespread sport is **tai-chi-chuan**, a type of Chinese gymnastics made up of a sequence of slow movements, performed at any age in parks and gardens at the first light of day.

Golf

Made popular by the French, it disappeared after 1975, a victim of its own aristocratic image and above all its considerable thirst for land and water. Since its legalisation in 1992, new courses have appeared such as those at Dalat or Phan Thiet.

Hiking

This activity is only in its infancy, but certain specialised organisations already offer treks of variable length and difficulty, from between a few hours to several days in the villages of the Central Highlands and the Tonkin Mountains, as well as mountain climbing up the Fan Si Peak near Sapa, and Ciu Mim Ray Mountain near Kon Tum (*refer to specialised sections*).

Mountain biking

Although also considered a sport, mountain biking is above all a means of transport. Apart from the busy major routes such as Highway 1 or the mountain roads in the north and in the Central Highlands, Vietnam is ideal for cycling, and mountain bikes are the best adapted for long trips, but you will have problems finding any equipment outside Ho Chi Minh City or Hanoi.

Water sports

Vietnam boasts some wonderful beaches, but they are relatively few in number considering the length of coastline (3 451km). With the exception of those at Phu Quoc and Hon Chong in the Gulf of Thailand, the most impressive beaches lie along the South China Sea (Vung Tau, Mui Ne, Nha Trang, Da Nang). As for water sports (jet skiing, snorkelling, diving, surfing, wind-surfing), facilities are not likely to be available outside the larger seaside resorts.

• Nightlife

Cinemas and theatres

Almost every town has at least one **cinema** (*rap*), and you'll certainly be spoilt for choice in Ho Chi Minh City or Hanoi. Modern, air-conditioned cinemas are still hard to find and most films showing are Vietnamese productions as well as American or Asian adventure films dubbed with one single voice for all the characters. Well worth viewing!

A trip to the **theatre** or **opera**, both classical and modern, will provide you with an inspiring insight into the imaginative world of the Vietnamese, despite the obvious language barrier in the understanding of the finer points of the dialogue. **Water puppetry** is a regular spectacle for tourists in Hanoi and Ho Chi Minh City, especially during the Tet festival.

Bars, nightclubs and karaokes

The number of local night spots in Hanoi and especially in Ho Chi Minh City has rocketed since the country opened up. Tourists, expatriates and local Vietnamese rub shoulders in the discos and bars, but very few Westerners indulge in the delights of the karaoke bars where the Vietnamese sing their hearts out to the latest local or international hits.

Concerts and shows

The Vietnamese are wild about pop music, and they listen to it all day long. Budding artists regularly head for California or Europe in search of stardom among the expatriate Viet Kiu community, while local stars can be found performing in local concert halls or on open air stages.

SHOPPING

• What's on offer

Lacquered goods

Found all over Vietnam, lacquered wares go back a long way (*see page 82*). Alongside the more traditional naturalistic subjects, more modern images are making a breakthrough in the form of depictions of war, abstract compositions or even portraits of Tintin! Various lacquered items such as boxes or trays are a good buy.

Handicrafts

Popular articles among the vast range of Vietnamese handicrafts include ceramics (plates, bowls, statues, vases), silk-painting, bronze tea pots and embroidery. A wonderful souvenir of your stay would be a reproduction of one of the puppets used in the water puppetry which are found in Hanoi and Ho Chi Minh City.

Often inspired by more traditional work, contemporary handiwork is taking on a more sophisticated aspect, especially for certain decorative items (fabric, mirrors, boxes made from coconut fibre, crockery, vases, furniture).

Ethnic handicrafts

Vietnam's minority groups are exceptionally gifted in all aspects of **basketwork**, particularly in the making of winnowing baskets, baskets used in harvesting, keep nets, hats and mats. The price of each item depends on the intricacy of the work, the thickness of the weave, the pattern and the finish, which is not always natural. Basketry is not difficult to find, especially in Hanoi and Ho Chi Minh City. Colourful **ethnic fabrics** are a speciality of the markets at Sapa and Bac Ha.

Antiques

With the emergence of "antique factories" (bronze items, stone statues, opium pipes), it is better to steer well clear of the antiques market, unless you are an expert. Buy a respectable copy and you'll avoid any complications at customs (always keep the receipt). It is actually forbidden to export antiques and you run the risk of having them confiscated when leaving the country.

War souvenirs

Engraved "Zippo" lighters, military uniforms, binoculars, watches, clocks, stamps, money... a never-ending list of items on sale from street vendors, and in shops and markets. Reproductions are rife, so bargaining is a must.

Fabrics and clothes

T-shirts of Ho Chi Minh or the Vietnamese official colours are ever popular with tourists and very cheap. As a general rule, ready-made clothes can be found at unbeatable prices. **Custom-tailored** articles are also very reasonable due to the low cost of labour and materials, but take a pattern along with you to avoid disappointment. Finally, a silk sleeping bag from Hanoi or Ho Chi Minh City could also prove useful should you ever have to sleep in a train or a poorly maintained hotel.

• Where to shop

Logically, prices increase the further you are from the area of production. However, shops in Hanoi offer a wider range of articles at cheaper prices, especially for ethnic handicraft, than does Ho Chi Minh City.

Local markets

Market stalls are undeniably the ideal place to find the most unexpected souvenirs, whether you're buying handicrafts, children's toys, luminous Buddhas or any other unusual object.

• Bargaining

Whether you loathe it or revel in it, bargaining, with all the techniques of trickery and deception it entails, is a must in many circumstances. The first hurdle is knowing what equation to apply in negotiating the "right" price, even though this might be hard to define. Paying US$6 for a small lacquered box is not really a swindle, and yet it is always annoying when you discover the same article costs a third of the price in the shop next door. The golden rule is first do a tour of the local shops and **compare prices**. This also applies to the street vendors, who, strange as it may seem, always tend to raise their prices two or three times higher than the neighbouring shops. Whatever happens, don't expect to pay the same price as the Vietnamese, since the principle of higher prices for obviously better-off foreigners is such a well-established tradition that it is even applied to plane tickets and hotels. Don't be insulted by this, and, as a general rule, keep all bargaining quite affable. Don't forget, if you don't like the look of the person you're dealing with, or if negotiations take a nasty turn, you can always walk away...

• Mailing things home
See the section on "Postal services" page 97.

HEALTH AND SAFETY

• Illnesses
As in many countries around the world, you will limit your risks of catching a disease by observing some basic rules. *For vaccinations, see page 92.*

Sun
The first rule is to protect yourself from the sun and heat in order to prevent any risk of **sunstroke** or **dehydration**. Expose yourself gradually to the sun's rays and always wear a hat, sunglasses and suntan lotion, even if the sky is cloudy. It is also important to regularly drink plenty of fluids.

Stomach problems
The change in food and climate often causes **intestinal problems** for many travellers. These are more annoying than dangerous. In any case, you can easily cure yourself by eating rice, drinking lots of salty vegetable broth and by taking an anti-diarrhoea pill and upset-stomach medication. As a precaution, never drink tap water that has not been boiled or purified beforehand. Always wash your hands before and after every meal, peel fruit and raw vegetables before eating them and don't eat meat or fish unless it is well-cooked.

Mosquitoes
Vietnam does have cases of malaria and is classified zone 3. The disease is transmitted by a particular sort of mosquito, but the risks of catching the disease vary according to the region and the time of year. The risk is practically nil in the cities and slightly higher near the northern forests and the Central Highlands, especially if you go hiking. In any case, good disease prevention begins with protection against mosquito bites. Use a good dose of repellent, wear trousers, long-sleeved shirts, and closed shoes when evening comes. Check that your mosquito net is in good condition or burn mosquito coils. It is also advisable to avoid wearing dark colours and perfume. For anti-malaria pills, consult a doctor specialising in tropical diseases before leaving home (*see page 93*).

Japanese encephalitis
This viral infection is transmitted by mosquitoes under the same conditions as malaria and can be very dangerous. Symptoms include haemorrhagic fever, which could lead to dehydration. Follow the same preventive measures as for malaria, but with no available preventive treatment, the vaccination (three jabs in the space of a month), is the only effective means to fight off the disease. Unfortunately, the vaccination often provokes an allergic reaction.

AIDS

AIDS is a major problem in Asia, and Vietnam is no exception. Protect yourself by carrying condoms and disposable syringes.

• Medical kit

Don't forget to bring a sufficient supply of medicine if you have a particular prescription. A basic medical kit includes aspirin, antiseptic, antibiotics, anti-diarrhoea pills and upset-stomach medication, antihistamines (for colds, allergies and motion sickness), nasal decongestant, plasters and sterile bandages, an analgesic, water-purifying tablets, mosquito repellent, suntan cream and sunburn lotion, eye drops, and ointment to soothe mosquito bites. More adventurous travellers should also bring sterile syringes for emergency injections, anti-inflammatory lotion, and athlete's foot powder. And finally, don't forget everyday items such as ear plugs, razors, shaving cream, tampons and sanitary towels, contraceptives, condoms, contact lens solution, and spare lenses.

Be sure to get advice from your local doctor before leaving or contact your local international travel medical service for information. Try www.cdc.gov/travel/seasia.htm or www.tripprep.com

• Health services

The quality of medical care depends a great deal on your location. When in need, first call the nearest embassy or consulate, or even one of the big hotels. They usually have a medical service where they can administer first aid before recommending a doctor or a hospital.

Hospitals

Large towns and cities are well-equipped with reliable hospitals and international doctors, but in the provinces English-speaking medical staff are in short supply. For any serious problem, take the first plane to Singapore or Bangkok where you will find far better medical facilities.

Pharmacies

There are pharmacies (*cua hang thuoc*) in every town offering a wide range of medicines, often produced by international laboratories and sold singly. Always check the sell-by date.

• Emergencies

Police, ☎ 113 – **Fire service**, ☎ 114 – **Ambulance**, ☎ 115.

G. de Benoist/MICHELIN

A to Z

• Cigarettes

The Vietnamese are heavy smokers and non-smoking areas are still quite exceptional. You can find most leading American brands at relatively cheap prices.

• Drinking water

Tap water should not be drunk, but bottled mineral water is readily available. The Vietnamese themselves drink boiled water, so there's not much to worry about if you are offered a glass of water. Bring chloride tablets when planning on visiting more isolated areas.

• Drugs

Unless you want your dream holiday to turn into a nightmare, avoid all contact with any drug sellers in the street. They may even be policemen in plain clothes and the possession of any type of drugs can lead to several years in prison.

• Electricity

Although 220 volts is generally used, it is recommended nonetheless to check the voltage before plugging in your appliance.

• Laundry service

All hotels, including even the cheaper ones, offer a laundry service, but avoid entrusting them with your favourite clothes or anything delicate.

• Newspapers

The monthly supplement called **The Guide** from the *Vietnam Economic Times* is full of addresses and articles to do with tourist and cultural events. **Time Out**, the free supplement from the daily *Vietnam Investment Review* also has a selection of useful addresses, and the daily paper the **Vietnam News** reports on Vietnamese and international news. Major international newspapers and magazines are readily available in Ho Chi Minh City and Hanoi a few days after publication.

• Photography

Film can be bought and developed in all tourist areas. Prices are much lower than in Europe, but the choice of film isn't as good. Check expiry dates carefully for film and make sure it hasn't been exposed to the sun for months in a shop window. Black and white and slide film can often be very difficult to find. **Cassettes** for video cameras can be bought in big cities and at major tourist sites.

On the whole the Vietnamese don't mind being photographed and even enjoy posing, but ask for permission. Be sensitive to the situation, and a few kind pleasantries wouldn't go amiss before snapping away. In certain areas, women refuse to be photographed, but often it is out of vanity since they don't like the way they are dressed! In other areas such as Sapa, children have been brought up to ask for money in exchange. Lastly, respect places of worship and don't photograph people washing or bathing when they would prefer their privacy.

• Radio and television

Broadcasting is still totally controlled by the government. The **Voice of Vietnam** is an FM radio station mostly broadcasting music with news programmes in English and in French. National television was set up in 1970 and is made up of three channels. Apart from news reports in English and French, it broadcasts TV films from Hong Kong. Satellite dishes are becoming more and more common in hotels, receiving most international channels including CNN, MTV and cinema channels.

• **Safety**
Apart from cautionary suggestions for tourists travelling by train or bus (*see above*), general safety in Vietnam needs no special comment. Here, as everywhere, pick-pockets are rife, and it is advisable not to display your possessions too openly and keep an eye on your personal belongings in public places. It is a good idea to keep part of your money and valuables in the hotel safe, bring travellers' cheques with you and make photocopies of your passport and personal documents.

• **Tipping**
Most luxury hotels and restaurants include a service charge of between 10 and 15%, but elsewhere you are free to do as you wish and tipping is not obligatory. You are, however, expected to tip guides (about US$1 per day and per person) and drivers (a little less) to show them your appreciation. You are also expected to make a small donation in museums that are free of charge and in religious shrines.

• **Units of measurement**
Vietnam uses the metric system of measuring and weighing.
Distances in this guide are given in kilometres. As a rule of thumb, one kilometre is five-eighths of a mile: 5 miles is therefore about 8 kilometres, 10 miles is about 16 kilometres and 20 miles is about 32 kilometres.
See below for other useful metric equivalents:

Degrees Celsius	35°	30°	25°	20°	15°	10°	5°	0°	-5°	-10°
Degrees Fahrenheit	95°	86°	77°	68°	59°	50°	41°	32°	23°	15°

1 centimetre (cm)	=	0.4 inch
1 metre (m)	=	3.3 feet
1 metre (m)	=	1.09 yards
1 litre	=	1.76 pints
1 litre	=	0.22 gallon
1 kilogram (kg)	=	2.2 pounds

• **Useful documents**
Vaccination papers, an international student card and an international driving licence can all prove useful during your stay, and bring spare passport-size photographs of yourself as well as a photocopy of your passport.

BOOKS

• **History and society**
ARCHIMEDES L Patti, **Why Vietnam?**, University of California Press, Berkeley, Los Angeles & London, 1980.
COLLISON Charles Stuart, **Land to the Tiller in the Mekong Delta**, Lanhami, New York and London, 1983.
DIUKER William, **Since the Fall of Saigon**, Ohio University Press, 1980.
HO Chi Minh, **Prison Diary**, The Gioi, Hanoi, 1998.
HOSKIN John and HOPKINS Allen W, **The Mekong**, Post Publishing Co, 1992.
KARNOW Stanley, **Vietnam: A History**, Viking Press, New York, 1983.
KNOPF Alfred A, **A Biography of Ho Chi Minh**, New York, 1987.
LEMERCINIER Genevieve and VAN Hai, **Life in a Vietnamese Commune**, Zed Books Ltd, 1984.
McNAMARA Robert S, (Preface), **Argument Without End: In Search of Answers to the Vietnam Tragedy**, Public Affairs, 1999.
MANGOLD Tom and PENYCATE John, **The Tunnels of Chu Chi**, Random House, New York, 1987.

MART David, *Vietnamese Anti-Colonialism 1885-1925*, University of California Press, 1970.

MOLE Robert L, *The Montagnards of South Vietnam*, Tuttle, Tokyo, 1970.

NIXON Richard, *Real Peace / No More Vietnams*, Touchstone / Simon & Schuster, 1990.

OSBOURNE Milton, *River Road to China, the Mekong River Expedition*, 1866-1873, London, 1975.

PIKE Douglas, *People's Army of Vietnam*, Presidio Press, Novato, California, 1986.

REID Anthony, *Southeast Asia in the Age of Commerce, 1450-1680, Volume One: The Lands Below the Winds*, Yale University Press, New Haven, London, 1988.

SEWELL WR and WHITE Gilbert F, *The Lower Mekong*, New York, 1966.

TAYLOR Keith Weller, *The Birth of Vietnam*, University of California Press, 1985.

VIEN Khac, *Nguyen, Vietnam: A Long History*, Foreign Languages Publishing House, Hanoi, 1987.

• Present day

BASS Thomas A, *Vietnamerica: The War Comes*, Soho Press, Inc, 1997.

KAMM Henry, *Dragon Ascending: Vietnam and the Vietnamese*, Arcade Publishing, 1996.

JEFFRIES Ian, *Economies in Transition: A Guide to China, Mongolia, North Korea and Vietnam at the turn of the Twenty-First Century* (Routledge Studies in Development Economics), Routledge, 2001.

McKELVEY Robert S, *The Dust of life: America's Children Abandoned in Vietnam*, University of Washington, 1999.

McLEOD Mark and NGUYEN Thi Dieu, *Culture and Customs of Vietnam*, Greenwood Publishing Group, 2001.

PHAM Mai, *Pleasures of the Vietnamese Table*, HarperCollins, 2001.

PRADOS John, *The Ho Chi Minh Trail and the Vietnam War*, John Wiley and Sons, 1998.

SKELTON Olivia, *Vietnam: Still Struggling, Still Spirited (Exploring Cultures of the World)*, Benchmark Books, 1997.

STEINMANN Ron, *Women in Vietnam*, TV Books Inc, 2000.

STUART Anh-Thu, *Vietnamese Cooking*, Angus and Robertson, London, 1986.

TEMPLER Robert, *Shadows and Wind, A View of modern Vietnam*, Penguin USA, 1999.

SCHRAMM-EVANS Zoe, *A Phoenix rising*, Pandora, 1996.

WINTLE Justin, *Romancing Vietnam*, Viking, New York, 1991.

• Religions and traditions

LITTLE Stephen et al, *Taoism and the Arts of China*, University of California Press, 2000.

NGUYEN Tai Thu, *History of Buddhism in Vietnam*, Social Sciences Publishing House, 1992.

QUINCY Keith, *Harvesting Pa Chay's Wheat: The H'mong and America's Secret War in Laos*, EWU Press, 2000.

XIONG Ghia (Contributor), FADERMAN Lillian, *I Begin My Life All Over: The H'mong and the American Immigrant Experience*, Beacon Press, 1999.

• Ethnology

CONDOMINAS George, *We have Eaten the Forest: The Story of a Montagnard Village in the Central Highlands of Vietnam* (Kodansha Globe), Kodansha International, 1994.

KALMAN Bobbie, *Vietnam the People*, Crabtree Pub, 1996.

LIVO Norman J, CHA Dia, *Full Stories of the H'mong: People of Laos, Thailand and Vietnam*, Libraries Unlimited, 1991.

QUINCY Keith, *H'mong: History of a People*, Eastern Washington University Press, 1997.

• Champa

GUILLON Emmanuel, *Hindu – Buddhist of Vietnam: Treasures from Champa*, Weatherhill, 2001.

Museum of Cham sculpture in Danang, Foreign Languages Publishing House, Hanoi, 1987.

SHARMA J-C, *Temples of Champa in Vietnam*, Hanoi, 1992.

BROSSARD de CORBIGNY Pierre, LEMIRE BARRELON Charles, CAHEN Gaston, TIPS Walter EJ (translator), *Cities of Nineteenth Century Colonial Vietnam: Hanoi, Saigon, Hue and the Champa Ruins*, White Lotus, 1999.

TRAN Ky Phuong, *My Son in the history of Cham Art*, Da Nang, 1988.

• Heritage

HALBERSTAM David, *Ho Chi Minh City*, Random House, New York, 1971.

LIPPARD Lucy R, *Different War*, Real Comet Press, 1994.

LOGAN William S, *Hanoi: Biography of a City*, University of Washington Press, 2001.

NGUYEN Phong, *From Rice Paddies and Temple Yards: Traditional Music of Vietnam*, World Music Press, 1990.

NGUYEN Vinh Phuc, *Historical & Cultural sites around Hanoi*, The Gioi, Hanoi, 2000.

SIDEL Mark, *Old Hanoi (Images of Asia)*, Oxford University Press, 1999.

UNGER Ann Helen and UNGER Walter (Editor), *Pagodas, Gods and Spirits of Vietnam*, Thames and Hudson, 1996.

• Literature

Novels

ANDERSON Donald, *Aftermath: An Anthology of Post-Vietnam Fiction*, Henny Holt, 1995.

ATKESON Edward B and SCHWARZKOPF Gen H Norman, *A Tale of Three Wars: A Novel*, US Army War College Foundation Press, 1999.

BUNTING Eve, *The Wall*, Clarion Books, 1990.

CARLSON Bruce E, *Red Bird Down: A Novel about Air Cavalry and Aero-Scouts in Vietnam*, Redbird Publications, 2000.

COONTS Stephen, *Flight of the Intruder*, Pocket Books, 1991.

FORD Daniel, *Incident at Muc Wa*, Universe Publishing Services, 2000.

FRANSCELL Ron, *Angel Fire*, Jove Books, 2000.

GREENE Graham, *The Quiet American*, Heinemann, London, 1955.

McKAY Lawrence, *Journey Home*, Lee & Low Books, 2000.

NAGATA Linda, *Limit of Vision*, Tor Books, 2001.

NINH Bao, *The Sorrow of War: A Novel of North Vietnam*, Riverhead Books, 1996.

NGUYEN Du, *The Tale of Kieu*, Yale University Press, New Haven and London, 1983.

O'BRIEN Tim, *The Things They Carried: A Work of Fiction*, Broadway Books, 1999.

THICH Nhat Hanh, WARREN Mobi (Translator), *A Taste of Earth: And Other Legends of Vietnam*, Parallax Pr, 1993.

WEBB James H, *Fields of Fire* (Bluejacket Books), Naval Institute Press, 2000.

YOUNG Gavin, *A Wavering Grace*, Viking, 1997.

G de Benoist/MICHELIN

Books

113

Travel writing

ALLARD Denise, **Postcards From Vietnam**, Zoe Books, 1996.

COFFEY Maria, **Three Moons in Vietnam: A Haphazard Journey by Boat and Bicycle**, Abacus, 1997.

LEWIS Norman, **A Dragon Apparent**, Eland Books, 1951.

MULLER Karin, **Hitchhiking Vietnam: A Woman's Solo Journey in an Elusive Land**, Globe Pequot Press, 1998.

NOLAND David, **Travels along the Edge: 40 Ultimate Adventures for the Modern Nomad from Crossing the Sahara to Bicycling Through Vietnam**, Vintage Books, 1997.

PHAM Andrew X, **Catfish and Mandala: A Two-Wheeled Voyage through the Landscape and Memory of Vietnam**, Farrar Straus & Giroux, 1999.

SIMPSON Howard R, TURNER Philip (editor) and SALINGER Pierre D (Introduction), **Tiger in the Barbed Wire: An American in Vietnam 1952-1991** (Kodansha Global), Kodansha International, 1994.

SHILLUE Edith, BOWEN Kevin, **Earth and Water: Encounters in Vietnam**, University of Massachusetts Press, 1998.

• **Guides and maps**

NGO, Nh Binh and NGO, Binh Nhu, **Elementary Vietnamese**, Tuttle Publishing, 1999.

Vietnamese: Start Speaking Today, Educational Services Corporation, 1994.

Periplus Travelmaps Vietnam: Vietnam Country Map, Periplus Editions, 2000.

Saigon – Ho Chi Minh City, Jack Joyce (Editor), Treaty Oak, 1996.

Vietnam, 1 / 1 000 000, International Travel Maps, n° 499.

Vietnam-Laos-Cambodia, 1 / 1 500 000, Nelles Maps, Hammond, 1999.

Vietnam Conflict Superior, Hammond Wall Map, Hammond, 1991.

USEFUL WORDS AND EXPRESSIONS

Pronunciation

Vietnamese is a tone language made up of six tones indicated by five diacritical marks (the first tone is left unmarked) giving a different meaning to each word. Incorrect pronunciation of these tones is quite a handicap when trying to make yourself understood, but the following is still useful when reading the names of streets, shops and public buildings.

c	like an unaspirated "k"
-ch	at the end of a word (thich = I like), like a "k"
d (with crossbar)	is pronounced "d"
d (without crossbar)	is pronounced "z" in the North, and "y" in the South
gi-	at the beginning of a word (gio = hour), is pronounced "z" in the North, and "y" in the South
kh-	at the beginning of a word (không = no), is pronounced like an aspirated "k" an exaggeration of the "k" in "key"
ng	at the beginning of a word (ngay = day), like "magnum"
-ng	at the end of a word (thuong = to love), like "thing"
nh-	at the beginning of a word (nha = house), like the "ni" in "onion"
-nh	at the end of a word (anh = sir), like "n" followed by "ng" in "thing"
ph-	is pronounced "f" at the beginning of a word (caphe = café)
r	is pronounced "z" in the North, and like an accentuated "r" in "run" in the South

s	is pronounced "s" in the North, and "sh" in the South		
th-	at the beginning of a word (thich = I like), is pronounced like an aspirated "th" as in "thanks"		
tr-	at the beginning of a word (tra = tea), is pronounced "ch" in the North and "tr" in the South		
x	is pronounced "s"		
â	is pronounced "eung"		
e	is pronounced like the "air" in "hair",		
ê	is pronounced "ay"		
o	like the "o" in "or"		
ô	is pronounced "o"		
o (with hook)	is pronounced "eu"		
u	is pronounced "oo"		
u (with hook)	is pronounced between "eu" and "u", hardly stressed		

Useful phrases

hello (to a man)	thua ông / thua anh "ông" designates an older or senior man; "anh" designates a man of the same age or of equal status	thank you	cam on (o with hook)
		thank you very much	cam on nhieu
		yes	da (d without cross-bar) (in the South) / vâng (in the North)
hello (to a woman)	thua ba / thua cô / thua chi "ba" designates an older or senior woman; "cô" and "chi" designates a young girl of the same age or of equal status	no	không
		perhaps	co thê
		I agree	tôi dông y (d with crossbar)
		excuse me	xin lôi
		I don't speak Vietnamese	tôi không noi tiêng Viêt
goodbye	thua ông (anh / ba / cô / chi) / tôi di	do you speak English?	ông (anh / ba / cô / chi) noi tiêng Anh không?
please	lam on (o with hook)	I don't understand	tôi không hiêu

Conversation

what's your name?	ông (anh / ba / cô / chi) tên gi? (in the South) ông (anh / ba / cô / chi) tên chi? (in the North)	where do you come from?	ông (anh / ba / cô / chi) tu dâu toi? (d with crossbar)
		I come from...	tôi tu
my name is...	tôi tên là	I am a tourist	tôi di du lich (d with ossbar)
how are you?	ông (anh / ba / cô / chi) khoe không? ông (anh / ba / cô / chi) manh gioi không?	how old are you?	ông (anh / ba / cô / chi) mây tuôi?
		I am... years old	tôi duoc... tuôi (d with crossbar)
that's OK	tôi khoe / tôi binh thuong	are you married?	ông (anh / ba / cô / chi) gia-dinh chua?
that's not OK	tôi không khoe		

The time

what time is it?	mây gio rôi?	tomorrow	ngay mai
what day is it?	hôm nay la ngay gi?	morning	buôi sang
now	bây gio	afternoon	buôi trua
today	hôm nay	evening	buôi chiêu
yesterday	hôm qua	night	buôi tôi

year	nam	Thursday	thu nam
month	thang	Friday	thu sau
day	ngay	Saturday	thu bay
Monday	thu hai (u with hook)	Sunday	chua nhât (in the South) /
Tuesday	thu ba		chu nhât (in the North)
Wednesday	thu tu		

Common adjectives

good	ngon	open	mo
bad	do	hot	nong
big	lon	cold	lanh
small	nho	dirty	do (d without crossbar)
closed	dong (d with crossbar)	clean	sach

Colours

white	trang	yellow	vang
black	den (d with crossbar)	red	do (d with crossbar)
blue	xanh	green	xanh la cây

Getting around

where is...?	o dâu? (d with crossbar)	post office	buu diên
next door	kê bên	bank	ngân hang
right	bên mat	pagoda	chua
left	bên trai	temple	dên (d with crossbar)
opposite	truoc mat	church	nha tho
straight on	di thang (d with crossbar)	mosque	thanh duong Hôi Giao
village	lang		(d with crossbar)
town	thanh phô	travel agents	công ty du lich
way	duong (d with crossbar)	paddy field	ruông
road	duong lô	river	sông
street	duong	lake	hô
avenue	dai lô (d with crossbar)	beach	bai biên
square	công truong	mountain	nui
market	cho	forest	rung
museum	viên bao tang		

Transport

plane	may bay	pier	bên tau (in the South) /
airport	sân bay		bên do (in the North)
bus	xe buyt	bicycle	xe may / xe dap (d with
bus station	bên xe		crossbar)
train	xe lua	car	xe hoi
railway station	nhà ga / ga xe lua	motorcycle	xe mô-tô / xe may dâu
boat	tau		

At the hotel

hotel	khach san	bathroom	phong tam
room	phong	hot water / cold	nuoc nong / lanh
single room / double	phong môt / hai nguoi	ventilator fan	quat may
		air-conditioning	may lanh
I want to book a room	tôi muôn muon phong (in the South)	mosquito net	mung
	tôi muôn thuê phong (in the North)		

At the restaurant

restaurant	tiêm an	pepper	tiêu
eat	an com (in the South) / dung com (in the North)	salt	muôi
		sugar	duong (d with cross-bar)
drink	uông nuoc	egg	trung
the menu please	ông (anh / ba / cô / chi) cho xin thuc don	fish	ca
		prawns	tôm
the bill please	ông (anh / ba / cô / chi) lam on tinh tiên	meat	thit
		chicken	thit ga
very good	ngon lam	pork	thit heo
rice	com (o with hook) ò	beef	thit bo
soup	canh	fruit	trai cây
rice soup	chao	banana	chuôi
noodle soup	pho / mi	coconut	dua
water	nuoc	mango	xoai
coffee	ca phê	papaya	du du (d with cross-bar)
tea	tra (in the South) / che (in the North)		
		pineapple	thom
beer	bia	vegetables	rau cai
bread	banh mi		

Shopping

market	cho	it's too expensive	mat qua (in the South) / dat qua (in the North)
shop, boutique	tiêm		
buy	mua		
how much is that?	bao nhiêu	it costs 1 000 VND	mon nay tri gia môt ngan dông

Numbers

1	môt	20	hai muoi
2	hai	50	nam muoi
3	ba	100	môt tram
4	bôn	200	hai tram
5	nam	1 000	môt ngan
6	sau	2 000	hai ngan
7	bay	10 000	muoi ngan
8	tam	20 000	hai muoi ngan
9	chin	50 000	nam muoi ngan
10	muoi	100 000	môt tram ngan

Emergency

I am ill	tôi bênh	hospital	nhà thuong / benh viên
doctor	bac si	chemist	nhà thuôc / hiêu thuôc
dentist	nha si	police	canh sat

Useful words and expressions

Exploring Vietnam

A family outing to
Minh Mang's Tomb

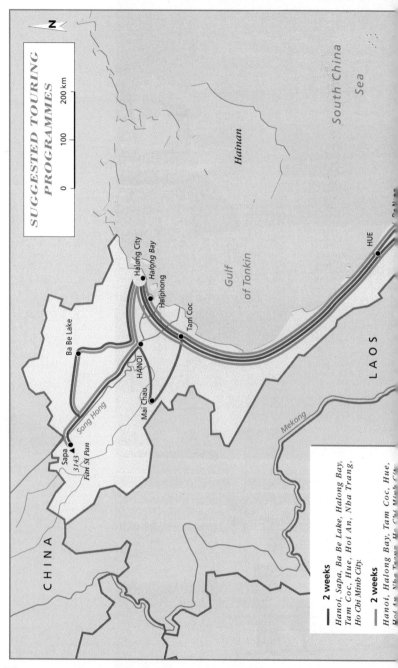

SUGGESTED TOURING PROGRAMMES

0   100   200 km

CHINA

Sapa
3143 ▲
Fan Si Pan

Song Hong

Ba Be Lake

HANOI

Mai Chau

Halong City
Halong Bay

Haiphong

Tam Coc

Gulf
of Tonkin

Hainan

South China
Sea

LAOS

Mekong

HUE

2 weeks

*Hanoi, Sapa, Ba Be Lake, Halong Bay,
Tam Coc, Hue, Hoi An, Nha Trang,
Ho Chi Minh City.*

2 weeks

*Hanoi, Halong Bay, Tam Coc, Hue,
Hoi An, Nha Trang, Ho Chi Minh City,*

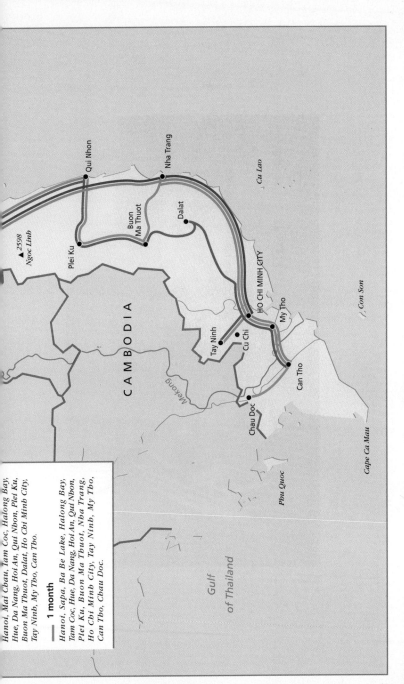

Hanoi, Mai Chau, Tam Coc, Halong Bay,
Hue, Da Nang, Hoi An, Qui Nhon, Plei Ku,
Buon Ma Thuot, Dalat, Ho Chi Minh City,
Tay Ninh, My Tho, Can Tho.

— 1 month

Hanoi, Sapa, Ba Be Lake, Halong Bay,
Tam Coc, Hue, Da Nang, Hoi An, Qui Nhon,
Plei Ku, Buon Ma Thuot, Nha Trang,
Ho Chi Minh City, Tay Ninh, My Tho,
Can Tho, Chau Doc.

Boating in Halong Bay

THE RED RIVER DELTA

"Along the dike-top road, the lush new grass sweeps over yesterday's tufts / A flock of low-flying blackbirds comes to try its luck / A quick flutter of wings as the butterflies drift in the wind / The buffalo slowly lower their heads grazing on the rain-soaked ground.
In the fields, the emerald rice gorges itself in silence / A sudden flight of egrets / Frighten a young girl in a scarlet bodice / Bent over, she dips her hand among the rice-plants full of flowery promises."

Anh Tho (born 1920), *Spring Twilight*

In the Song Hong Delta, the Kinh have managed to reclaim land from the water by building miles and miles of dikes. Outlined against the sky along the dike-top roads and paths is a whole gallery of silhouetted figures, a helmeted *bo doi* on his bicycle and a farmer, hidden by a cone-shaped hat bent under the weight of a yoke, or a buffalo meekly led on a leash like a big dog. A green sea of budding rice plants lies under the low sky and only glimpses of the workers in the fields make it possible to distinguish the hidden channels. The fishermen disappear up to their waists, ladling up crabs and prawns in large scoops made of plaited bamboo. Others move in time to the bailers bringing up water from the canals to the raised ground. Great efforts over many centuries made these flat lands the birthplace of the first kingdoms of Vietnam. First came Co Lao, the shell-shaped citadel. Hoa Lu and its palaces in the middle of stranded reefs were next. Finally there was Hanoi, the city "in the heart of the river".

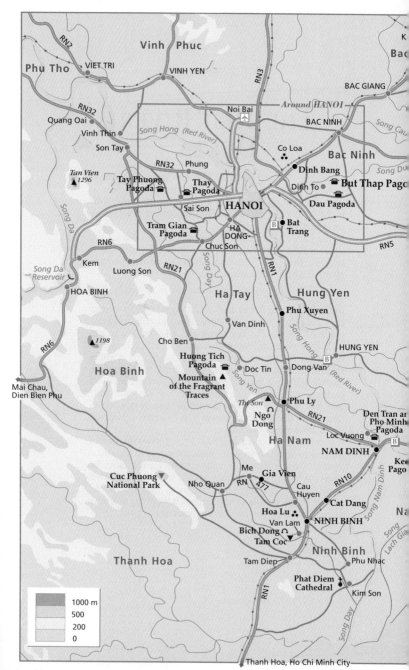

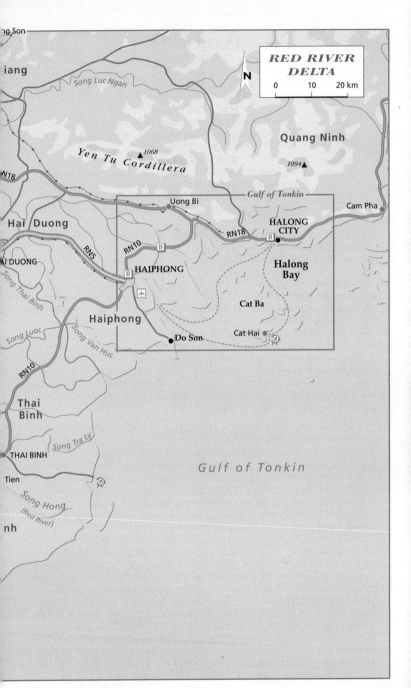

RED RIVER DELTA

0   10   20 km

N

ng Son

iang

Song Luc Ngan

Quang Ninh

1068

1094

Yen Tu Cordillera

N18

Gulf of Tonkin

Uong Bi

Cam Pha

Hai Duong

RN18

HALONG CITY

RN10

AI DUONG

RN5

B

HAIPHONG

Halong Bay

Song Thai Binh

B

Cat Ba

Song Luoc

Song Van Huc

Haiphong

Cat Hai

RN10

Do Son

Thai Binh

Song Tra Ly

THAI BINH

Gulf of Tonkin

Tien

Song Hong
(Red River)

nh

HANOI ★★★

Capital of Vietnam
Pop 3 million
652km from Hue, 1 750km from Ho Chi Minh City
Climate hot and humid. Maps pages 128 and 134-135

Not to be missed
A Sunday trip to see the monuments in Ba Dinh Square.
Take in the atmosphere in the streets of the 36 Guilds.
The Museum of Ethnology.

And remember...
Whether it's breakfast on the pavement, a café den (black coffee), or drinks
in a makeshift pub garden of an old colonial villa,
take it slowly to enjoy Hanoi to the full.
The best times to visit are from October to December and from April to June.

In 2010, Hanoi will celebrate its thousand-year anniversary. For a long time out of the limelight, protected from the Red River by a series of dikes, the capital of the Socialist Republic of Vietnam started to make a gradual comeback at the end of the 1980s.

The guardian gods on the temple façades have been recently painted. Behind the rows of plane trees, the homes left from French colonial times have been renovated and the tube or tunnel houses of the old quarter have been restored to their former beauty, while here and there are miniature concrete tower blocks and glass skyscrapers. Hanoi isn't expanding but only growing like its banyan trees which push through street fronts and take over the pavements. The city is just as lively in the daytime as Saigon is at night, and what was once just a cluster of villages comes to life as regular as clockwork. Inhabitants are awakened by the dawn chorus of cage birds, cries from the street traders liven up the daytime hours, and the evening is invaded by an army of cleaners in their conical hats and masks, sweeping away the traces of the day.

An ancient city

In 1010, the capital of the infant state of Vietnam was moved from Hoa Lu to Hanoi. The latter held a more strategic position over the north of the country, and its location at the head of the delta of the Red River made for better communications. Apart from strategic considerations, geomancy also played a part in the founding of the capital: according to legend, as he approached the river banks, King **Ly Thai To** saw a dragon rising into the air, and as the appearance of such an auspicious animal in Eastern culture consecrates a sovereign's power, the city was consequently named **Thang Long**, "City of the Soaring Dragon".

The Ly (1009-1225) built their capital on the Chinese model. The Imperial City took up the main part of the centre, and was lined with shrines belonging to the state, such as the sacrificial walkway (destroyed in 1937) and the Temple of Literature dedicated to Confucius, the patron saint of the scholars who governed the kingdom. To the east were the commercial and artisan quarters dependent on the wharves handling goods from the To Lich River and the Red River. The entire area was protected from flood waters by a series of dikes erected in 1108. Hanoi remained the capital of the Vietnamese dynasties up until the 19C when all the governing powers were transferred to Phu Xan (Hue). Over this long period, various changes in name were the only noteworthy events in the history of the city. One name in particular, **Dong Kinh**, "Eastern capital", (1427), was for a long time associated with the northern region, and became the Tonkin of French Indochina.

From Dong Kinh to Tonkin

The 19C was a sombre period for Hanoi. In 1802 Emperor **Gia Long** controlled the whole country. Fearing insubordination from the northern tribes, he decided to rule from Hue, the traditional home of the ruling Nguyen families, and in 1805 he ordered the ancient citadel to be reduced so that it would not outshine his palaces at Annam. In 1831, when Minh Mang set up the Empire's administrative divisions, the city became the place of residence for the governor of the province of Hanoi. Under the reign of Tu Duc, the last palaces were demolished and any remaining riches transferred to Hue.

In 1873, during the Opium Wars in China, the French managed to gain possession of a concession of 2.5ha to the south of the city. They then extended their influence with the setting up of the **Annam-Tonkin Protectorate** in 1883, and then the **Indochinese Union** in 1887, with Hanoi, now run by the French, as the capital. The town became an appendage of the republican institutions that had only just been re-established in France, and Gia Long's citadel, considered unnecessary, was destroyed in 1896-97.

Capital of Indochina

From 1888 to 1945, the French in Indochina dominated the fate of their Asian colonies (Vietnam, Laos and Cambodia) from the Governor General's residence in Hanoi. Changes made to the colonial capital at the turn of the 19C, inspired by the eclectic architecture of the Third Republic, had a lasting effect on the appearance of the city. Neo-regionalist or neo-Renaissance villas sprang up in the area of the old concession and on the site of the demolished citadel. **Auguste-Henri Vildieu**, head of Civil Construction in Indochina, housed the colonial administrative bodies in neo-Classical buildings such as the Governor's residence, the Post Office and the Opera. Electricity was gradually brought to the city centre, and the first tramway line was opened in 1917. Summer evenings and Sundays saw the more distinguished classes out in their rickshaws, a means of transport that had been imported from Japan and which was noticeably silent due to the tyres made of rubber from the colonial plantations. Yet this Indochinese capital never achieved the same level of success as the other young Asian cities of Shanghai and Hong Kong. Hanoi was not a port, and although linked to Haiphong by a steamship service, the latter was off the main sea routes.

Wars and peace

Hanoi played a central role in the process of independence started by Ho Chi Minh at the time of the August revolution of 1945 at the end of the Japanese occupation. On 2 September of the same year, he chose Ba Dinh Square, the site of the old citadel and headquarters of the colonial administration, to announce the birth of the **Socialist Republic of Vietnam**. After nine years of war in Indochina, on 9 October 1954, French forces left Hanoi, but the city's rule only extended south as far as the 17th Parallel. The new regime had a brief respite of only ten years in which to industrialise the whole region and modernise the city, relying on voluntary work to implement major building projects. In February 1965, American B52s gathered over the delta, and survival revolved around the sound of sirens and long nights spent in air raid shelters. Under the leadership of the Soviet "Big Brother", Hanoi's trade was limited to countries like Cuba and Albania.

The capital of Vietnam reunified

The old royal capital, cultural centre and historic birthplace of the Vietnamese nation, assumed its position once more as head of the reunited country in 1976. On Ba Dinh Square, the new national institutions took over the former French state buildings, or else settled next to them in buildings constructed during the partnership with the Soviet Union. A good part of the 1980s was taken up with the rebuilding of Hanoi's

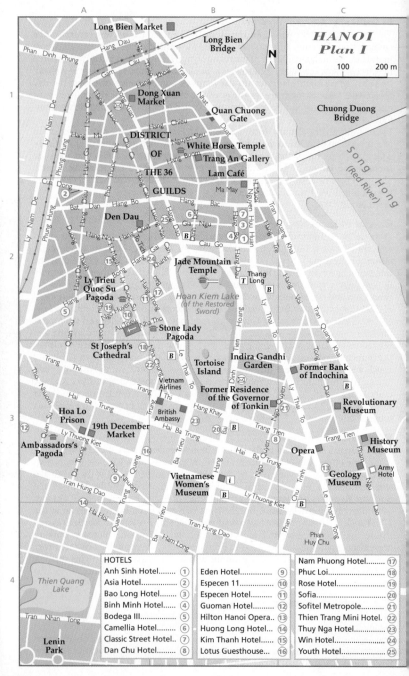

Long Bien Market

Long Bien Bridge

HANOI
Plan I

0   100   200 m

Chuong Duong Bridge

Phan Dinh Phung

Dong Xuan Market

Quan Chuong Gate

DISTRICT

White Horse Temple

OF

Trang An Gallery

THE 36

Lam Café

GUILDS

Den Dau

Ma May

Jade Mountain Temple

Thang Long

Ly Trieu Quoc Su Pagoda

Hoan Kiem Lake
(of the Restored Sword)

Song Hong (Red River)

Stone Lady Pagoda

St Joseph's Cathedral

Indira Gandhi Garden

Tortoise Island

Former Bank of Indochina

Trang Thi

Hai Ba Trung

Vietnam Airlines

Former Residence of the Governor of Tonkin

Revolutionary Museum

Hoa Lo Prison

British Ambassy

19th December Market

History Museum

Ambassadors's Pagoda

Hai Ba Trung

Opera

Army Hotel

Geology Museum

Vietnamese Women's Museum

Ly Thuong Kiet

Thien Quang Lake

Tran Hung Dao

Lenin Park

HOTELS			
Anh Sinh Hotel........	①	Eden Hotel..............	⑨	Nam Phuong Hotel.........	⑰
Asia Hotel..............	②	Especen 11.............	⑩	Phuc Loi......................	⑱
Bao Long Hotel........	③	Especen Hotel..........	⑪	Rose Hotel..................	⑲
Binh Minh Hotel......	④	Guoman Hotel..........	⑫	Sofia..........................	⑳
Bodega III..............	⑤	Hilton Hanoi Opera..	⑬	Sofitel Metropole........	㉑
Camellia Hotel........	⑥	Huong Long Hotel....	⑭	Thien Trang Mini Hotel.	㉒
Classic Street Hotel..	⑦	Kim Thanh Hotel......	⑮	Thuy Nga Hotel..........	㉓
Dan Chu Hotel........	⑧	Lotus Guesthouse.....	⑯	Win Hotel..................	㉔
				Youth Hotel...............	㉕

infrastructure, which had been wiped out during the long war years. The most note-worthy structure was Thang Long Bridge, opening up the northern part of the city and linking it to Noi Bai Airport. The areas of Thanh Xuan and Gia Lam became the site of major industrial facilities. **Doi Moi**, the "open-door economic policy", intro-duced when Soviet aid was ended in 1986, gave the city the appearance it has today. Hanoi is made up of seven districts (Hoan Kiem, Ba Dinh, Dong Da, Hai Ba Trung, Tay Ho, Cau Giay and Thanh Xuan) covering an area of 2 146 km². Visitors with a limited amount of time can hire a motorcycle *(xe om)* or a taxi for a quick trip around the main points of interest. Those with more time should explore the city on foot; everything is within walking distance, and visiting museums and pagodas is a perfect excuse for experiencing all aspects of Hanoi life.

Hoan Kiem Lake (Plan I) is right in the heart of the city, skirted to the north by the **36 Guilds** (Plan I), an area of artisans, craftsmen and small businesses, stretching between the Red River quaysides up to Long Bien Bridge and bordered by the citadel. Hanoi's special brand of warmth and charm radiates from this area, and many of the cheaper hotels are here. To the south of the lake, the **former French concession** (Plan I), characterised by buildings from the early 20C, corresponds to a line drawn at right angles between the Opera and the Cathedral. Still further south, along the Hai Ba Trung and Dong Da quarters, the student quarter around **Lenin Park** (Plan II) is of no special interest apart from its distinctive atmosphere. The northeastern dis-trict includes the area of the citadel. **Ba Dinh Square** (Plan II) is a national symbol surrounded by buildings commemorating Vietnam's independence. Here too are colonial-era villas and the Presidential Palace, once the headquarters of the Governor-General of French Indochina. To the north of the square, around **West Lake** (Plan II), you will find some of the most beautiful temples in Hanoi.

The 36 Guilds (Plan I)
Allow half a day

The old town of Hanoi is a veritable labyrinth where it is easy to lose one's way. There's not a street without its complement of makeshift stalls set up around a flaming brazier, a pan of smoking oil, chunks of bread in a gaudy plastic basket or a few cigarettes sold singly. This district took shape under the Ly dynasty when the first craft guilds became established and were commandeered by the royal power for its own interests and those of the court. In the 15C, their number was fixed at 36. Each guild area *(hang)* brought together craftsmen of the same trade, natives of the same village, who added their own pagodas, their own temples to tutelary heroes *(den)* and their own community houses *(dinh)* to the town of Hanoi. They were laid out in streets *(pho)*, with lines of shops specialising in particular items. The 36 streets, today an area hovering between transformation and renovation, are gradually being abandoned by their inhabitants. Those who can afford to, prefer to live outside this overpopulated architectural museum, where many of the houses still lack the most basic facilities. The older, more nostalgic residents of Hanoi say that money has done more harm to this area than any American bombardment ever did.

Hoan Kiem Lake★ (Lake of the Restored Sword) (B2-3)

This residual lake was once a branch of the Red River and today forms the southern boundary of the old commercial town. Its banks were made into public paths at the beginning of the 1930s; people come here all through the day, though there is a marked preference for the early hours of the morning, when residents of all ages arrive in droves in pursuit of their favourite activities such as jogging, badminton or tai-chi-chuan.

A pretty little wooden bridge straight out of a Japanese engraving leads to the **Jade Mountain Temple**★★ (Den Ngoc Son) *(Open every day 8am-5pm. Entrance fee)*, built in the 19C on an island in the lake on the site of a palace of the Trinh family. It is

B Juge/MICHELIN

The little wooden bridge over Hoan Kiem Lake

dedicated to the scholar **Van Xuong**, to General **Tran Hung Dao**, who defeated the Mongols in the 13C, and to **La To**, the patron saint of physicians. In a side room lies a stuffed giant tortoise, found in the lake in 1968. This is perhaps where history meets legend... In the middle of the lake, **Tortoise Island**, with its seriously dilapidated tower, commemorates this amazing event, as well as the name of the small lake.

Temples and tube houses** (B1-2)

To the north of the lake runs the very busy **Hang Dao** (Peach Flower Street) with its 20C houses and their Westernised fronts. It used to be known as "Silk Street" to the French of Indochina and its Vietnamese name hints at the colour pink, used in the dyeing of silk. This trade has today been passed on to an adjacent street, **Hang Gai** (Hemp Street), where you can find several well-known silk shops.

The legend of the restored sword

In 1427, Emperor Le Loi organised a nautical gala to celebrate the defeat of the Chinese troops sent by the Ming (see page 21). His victory was due in part to a magic sword, which had come into his possession in extraordinary circumstances. When the emperor made his appearance, leaning on his sword at the helm of his ship, an enormous turtle appeared from out of the waves, grabbed the weapon and disappeared into the depths of the lake forever: the magic sword had accomplished its mission, Vietnam had been freed from the shackles of the Chinese.

Parallel to Hang Dao, **Dinh Liet**, the *com pho* (rice noodles) street, is joined by Gia Nu where there is a clothes market (to the west) and stalls selling specially prepared dishes (to the east). Dinh Liet, along with **Hang Bac** (Silversmiths Street) and **Hang Be** (Raft Street) today mark out a new area of budget mini-hotels of the kind that spread like wild-fire throughout the 1990s.

In Hang Bac, the oldest thoroughfare in Hanoi (13C), the silversmiths disappeared when the capital was transferred to Hue in the 19C, and its eastern section is now lined by workshops of monumental masons. Hang Bac leads into Nguyen Huu Huan, an extension of the elegant Ly Thai To Street of quite a different tone, with tradesmen selling *bia hoi*, plywood furniture. It is the haunt of the older beret-clad inhabitants of Hanoi (n°ˢ 20 and 67) and here is the famous **Café Lam** (n° 60), opened by Nguyen Van Lam in 1956. Its walls have been gradually covered in gouaches, water colours and oil paintings, all contributed by local artists by way of thanks for the long hours spent drinking and chatting in the café. Mostly in a realistic style, the pictures recount the history of Hanoi and are examples of the western-influenced art once taught at the Indochina School of Fine Arts, set up by the French in 1925.

Return to Hang Bac.

From Hang Bac, carry on down **Ma May★** (Rattan Street), where the French city of Toulouse has financed the renovation of a splendid house-cum-shop in wood and stone (n° 87). You will reach **Hang Buom** (Sails Street), which still has something of the area's 19C atmosphere, along with touches of Chinese influence here and there. There may be an exhibition in the **Trang An gallery★**, if so, don't miss the opportunity of getting to know contemporary Vietnamese art in a wonderfully-restored traditional house.

Behind a heavy panelled door, the **White Horse Temple★** (Den Bach Ma) (*76 Hang Buom. Open every day 8-11.30am and 2-5.30pm*) is the oldest religious centre in the area (11C), but its modern-day appearance owes a lot to important restoration work of the 19C. It is dedicated to the tutelary spirit **Long Do** who helped King Ly Tjai To in the creation of Thang Long. Considered to be the spiritual guardian of the East, it formed a sacred group along with the temple of Quan Thanh in the north (*see page 141*), the temple of Voi Phuc in the west and Kim Lien in the south.

Markets in the old quarter★ (A-B1)

If you have some more visiting time left for this part of Hanoi, extend your tour further north. Cross over **Hang Chieu** (Mat Street), closed to the north by the **Quan Chuong City Gate** (1749), the only surviving example of the sixteen gates of the fortified enclosure that surrounded the villages of the commercial quarter up until the 19C. Still further north is **Dong Xuan Market★** (Cho Dong Xuan), the biggest in Hanoi. It was constructed by the colonial administration, but then damaged in a fire in 1994 that destroyed all but the original frontage. It is Hanoi's nearest thing to a Western department store, and its three floors sell everything from fabric by the metre, to crockery, clothes, mats and, of course, chopsticks. Keep this shop in mind when looking for traditional reasonably-priced items.

From here rejoin Gam Cau to the north, and head in the direction of the Red River.

Built between 1897-1902, **Long Bien Bridge**, (formerly Paul Doumer Bridge), a long metal skeleton linking the two banks of the river, was for a long time the only crossing-point. **Chuong Duong Bridge**, 650m further downstream, connecting Hanoi to Gia Lam, has since replaced it in importance and it is now only used by trains, bicy-

The street queens

Long Bien Market is the headquarters for Hanoi's women porters. They are natives of the surrounding towns and provinces and represent 90% of the work force of this particular street trade. The women are aged between 30 and 50 years old, and work hard to provide for their families, to care for ailing husbands or to pay for the education of their children. They must work in all kinds of weather, carrying loads of 40 to 50kg, sharing makeshift sleeping quarters in order to save more money and be able to send 300 000 dong back to their family each month. Weighed down by baskets of fruit from the Mekong Delta, or hidden behind armfuls of dahlias and gladioli or kitchen utensils in brightly-coloured plastic, thousands of women trudge the length and breadth of the streets of the capital each day.

cles and pedestrians. Underneath the bridge is a **market*** (Cho Long Bien), one of the most fascinating in the town. It is open 24 hours a day, with two particularly busy periods, firstly between 2am and 5.30am, and then again between 3pm and 6pm when lorries arrive from all over the country to unload their cargoes of fruit, fish and dried prawns.

The old French Quarter* (Plan I)

Allow half or even a whole day if you are planning on visiting the museums.
Remember that most of them are closed on Mondays.

Situated to the southeast of the old town, this was the first area to be taken over by the French. It is easy to trace its very straight avenues on a modern-day map of the town. The area has interesting examples of colonial architecture as well as a much livelier atmosphere than that around the austere embassies of Ba Dinh.

"Little Paris" and the Opera Avenue* (Trang Tien) (B-C3)

The city authorities took over the buildings abandoned by the colonial administration in the area between Dinh Tien Hoang and the stylish cafés of Ly Thai To, to the north of Trang Tien. Recent restoration has made quite an attraction of these typical turn-of-the-century buildings in the vicinity of the Metropole Hotel and the **Indira Gandhi Garden** (Chi Linh). The former Paul Bert Square, built during the development of the lakeside in 1886, has kept its Indochinese-style bandstand. Facing the lake, the post office still occupies the **Post and Communications Building** designed by Vildieu, but a Soviet-style building was erected on the site of the colonial-era town hall, today the headquarters of the People's Committee of Hanoi. At the other end of the square, the Vietcombank has occupied the **Bank of Indochina*** since 2000; one of the most impressive legacies of French rule, this splendid edifice with its combination of Art Deco motifs and quotations from traditional Indochinese architecture dates from 1930 and was built by Georges-André Trouvé. At the entrance to Ngo Quyen (formerly Henri-Rivière Boulevard), the government has commandeered the impressive neo-Classical building of the **Residence of the Governor of Tonkin** for visiting VIPs. Opposite at n° 15, the **Metropole** is the oldest luxury hotel in Hanoi (1901), steeped in contemporary history thanks to the number of celebrities that has passed through its doors.

Between the Red River and the citadel, Opera Avenue (Trang Tien) was the main thoroughfare of the French Quarter. At the beginning of the 20C, all the shops were located along this avenue, together with a French savings bank, the Franco-Chinese bank, the Far East Printing Company and the Veterans' Club. The art galleries, bookshops and shaded walkways leading out onto the restored Opera Square all contribute to the elegant appearance of this avenue, formerly Paul-Bert Street. Its present-day Vietnamese name of Trang Tien is a reminder of the old "sapèquerie" where the royal coins were minted. Garnier's Opera in Paris was the model for the **Opera House** (Nha Hat Lon), which rounds off the area.

It was built between 1901 and 1911, and used to be the only European-style opera house east of Cairo. The scheduled performances (magic shows and military bands) were not always of the best quality, but "a trip to the opera" was really more of an opportunity for the audience to show off its latest European fashions. In August 1945, a revolutionary committee proclaimed the country's independence from one of the balconies of the Opera. Today the building is a venue for frequent concerts and performances.

To the east of the Opera House is the **History Museum*** (Bao Tang Lich Su) (*1 Trang Tien. 8-11.30am / 1.30-4.30pm; closed on Mondays. Entrance fee. Allow 1hr)*. The building was designed by **Ernest Hébrard** and, with its great cupola, draws on traditional Tonkinese architecture. Don't expect to come away with an overall view of

Vietnamese history though, since only the labelling is in three languages (with some rather strange translations), and the descriptive panels and maps are all in Vietnamese. You will learn more at the Fine Arts Museum *(see page 140)*.

The most interesting part of the museum is most definitely the impressive selection of **Cham statuary****, on exhibition in the rotunda: take a clockwise tour of the 50 different sculptures. All the finest pieces of the art of sculpture of the Indianised kingdom are on display, from the very first period (7C-10C), with its strongly Shivaist illustrations, through to the seated Buddhas of Dong Duong (10C), up to the daring combinations of forms at the end of the 11C. It will require a liberal dose of imagination to be able to form a picture of the citadels and capitals of the 15C and 18C by studying the displays such as fragments of bricks and paving with Chinese symbols and tiny metal objects. The **ceramic art** exhibits are far better, enabling you to appreciate the development of ceramics between the 14C and 15C, with pieces from Bat Trang and Chu Dau in the Chinese "blue and white" decorative style, up to the experiments of the 17C and 18C.

The short-lived Tay Son dynasty (1778-1802) is well represented with a fine collection of Buddhist statuary in lacquered wood. The court of the Nguyen family (1802-83) in Hue provides one of the most varied collections (furniture and ceremonial objects, including seats, chests and altars in red and gold lacquered sculpted wood, screens, trays and dark wooden boxes with inlaid mother-of-pearl). Among the various documents, look out for a photograph of the Hue citadel in 1932, with its line of rooftops in the style of the Imperial City of Peking, and a series of **watercolours*** representing the court. The last showcases concern the fate of the country under the colonial administration, and then the revolution.

There are other collections to visit in this area if you have the time and the inclination. The **Geology Museum** (Bao Tang Dia Chat) *(6 Pham Ngu Lao. Open 8-12 noon / 1.30-4.30pm; closed on Sundays)* gives further insight into the karstic formations of Bac Bo.

The **Revolutionary Museum** (Bao Tang Cach Mang Viet Nam) *(25 Tong Dan. Open 8-11.45am / 1.30-4.15pm; closed on Mondays. Entrance fee)* is housed in the old Customs house, the very first public building of the French colonial era, built in 1875. Documents retrace the struggle for independence and the history of the Vietnamese Communist Party.

Along Ly Thuong Kiet Avenue* (A-B3)

The avenues of Hai Ba Trung (formerly Rollandes Boulevard) and Ly Thuong Kiet (formerly Carreau Boulevard) were laid out in 1897 and certain villas can be traced back as far as this date. Some of them have become luxury residences or embassy offices, whereas others are now occupied by families, small restaurants or other makeshift businesses.

Back up Ly Thuong Avenue westwards, at the intersection with Hang Bai, is the **Vietnamese Women's Museum*** (Bao Tang Phu Nu Viet Nam) *(36 Ly Thuong Kiet. Open 8.30-11.30am / 1.30-4pm; closed on Mondays. Entrance fee)*. Hidden behind a (very) ideological message are touching exhibitions about all sorts of different subjects ranging from the worship of the goddess of fertility to the role of women in the Vietnam War and in modern-day life.

At the foot of the ultra-modern skyscrapers of Melia and the Hanoi Tower Center, dive into n° 43, the **19 December Market***, so named to commemorate a victory over France. The stalls of vegetables, meats and spices are spotlessly clean, the dried fish is cellophane-wrapped, and the spices are neatly presented in their brown paper packaging. The squeamish would perhaps do well to avoid the "sides" of dog meat hanging up in the entrance to the market, on Ly Thuong Kiet.

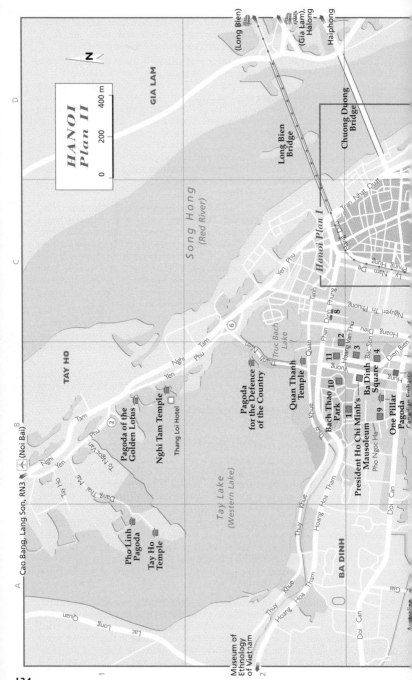

134

HANOI Plan II

0 200 400 m

N

GIA LAM

TAY HO

Song Hong (Red River)

Long Bien Bridge

(Long Bien)

(Gia Lam), Halong

Haiphong

Chuong Duong Bridge

Hanoi Plan I

Cao Bang, Lang Son, RN3

(Noi Bai)

Pho Linh Pagoda

Tay Ho Temple

Pagoda of the Golden Lotus

Nghi Tam Temple

Thang Loi Hotel

Tay Lake (Western Lake)

Museum of Ethnology of Vietnam

Pagoda for the Defence of the Country

Truc Bach Lake

Quan Thanh Temple

Bach Thao Park

President Ho Chi Minh's Mausoleum

Ba Dinh Square

One Pillar Pagoda

Canadian Embassy

BA DINH

1 2 3 4 8 9 10 11

Yen Phu

Yen

Tam

Phu

Nghi

Tam

To Ngoc Van

Dang Thai Mai

Phu

Thanh Nien

Nghi Tam

Yen Phu

Quan

Khue

Buoi

Hoang Hoa Tham

Thuy Khue

Hoang Hoa Tham

Doi Can

Giai

Thuy Khue

Phan Dinh Phung

Hoang Van Thu

Dieu

Hoang Dieu

Bac Son

Dien Bien

Ong Ich Khiem

Nguyen Tri Phuong

Ly Nam De

Phung Hung

Hang Dau

Tran Nhat Duat

Pho Ngoc Ha

Doi Can

Long

Lac

Quan

HOTELS
De Syloia Hotel...... ①
Dragon Hotel........... ②
Phoenix Hotel......... ③
Grand Hotel............ ④
Green Park Hotel..... ⑤
Meritus Westlake.... ⑥
Sunway Hotel......... ⑦

HOAN KIEM

Hoan Kiem Lake

Cathedral

Opera

Thien Quang Lake

Lenin Park

Bay Mau Lake

HAI BA TRUNG

Thanh Nhan Lake

Liên Phái Pagoda

Temple of Literature

Museum

DONG DA

Dong Da Lake

American Embassy

Giang Vo Lake

Kim Lien Temple

Boc Pagoda

Vietnam International Hospital

TU LIEM

1 Ho Chi Minh's Stilt House
2 Ba Dinh Club
3 National Assembly
4 Ministry of Foreign Affairs
5 Army Museum
6 Hexagonal Flag Tower
7 Chi Lang Park
8 Northern Gate
9 Ho Chi Minh Museum
10 Presidential Palace
11 Central Committee

RN 32
Noi Bai

Hoa Binh (express highway)

(Son La)

RN 6

University, RN 6

(Giáp Bát)

(Giáp Bát), RN1

135

At a bend in the road, note the unequivocal inscription "Maison centrale", which means State Penitentiary, over a porch. **The Hoa Lo Prison** (Nha Thu Hoa Lo) *(1 Hoa Lo, at the crossroads of Tho Nuom-Ly Tuong Kiet. Open 8-11am / 1.30-4.30pm; closed on Mondays. Entrance fee)* served as a jail for the colonial administration before taking in American pilots captured by the Vietnamese. It is now a **museum** and relates the ill-treatment suffered by political prisoners at the hands of the French, and the imprisonment of the American soldiers, described in almost idyllic terms, in the place they themselves ironically named the "Hanoi Hilton".

Easily recognisable by its long yellow openwork walls sculpted with stylised lotus flowers, the **Ambassadors' Pagoda** (Chua Quan Su) *(73 Quan Su, between Ly Thuong Kiet and Trang Hung Dao. Open every day from 6am-5pm)* was built in the 15C in an area put aside to accommodate ambassadors visiting Thang Long. In 1822, the temple was restored to house soldiers from a neighbouring garrison, and in 1934 it became the headquarters for the Tonkin Buddhist Association. It was then renovated and given its present-day appearance. The rooms have been decorated with fine pieces of sculpted lacquered wood, such as the enormous panel of writhing dragons holding up the infant Buddha. The pagoda is a favourite with the women of the city and is home to the nation's Institute of Buddhist Studies.

The cathedral area* (A-B2)

Go back up towards Trang Thi avenue as far as Phu Doan Street, then take the little alleyway Au Trieu along the apse of **St Joseph's Cathedral** (Nha Tho Lon) *(Open every day 5-7am / 5-7pm)*. Built between 1883 and 1891 in a neo-Gothic style inspired by Viollet-le-Duc, its two square towers dominate the cathedral square which also doubles as a playground for the neighbouring school. The statue of the Virgin and Child has kept its inscription "Regina Pacis" and the bell chimes every hour from 6 o'clock in the morning. On Sundays, the cathedral teems with young ladies dressed in *ao dai*, clothes usually reserved for very special occasions in Hanoi.

Nha Tho Street is today an area for trendy "expats" who have converted the impressive private residences with their ogival windows into shops and stylish cafés. At n° 3, a porch opens on to the courtyard of the **Stone Lady Pagoda** (Chua Ba Da) *(Open every day 7-11.30am / 1.30-6.30pm)*. It was originally built in the 15C to protect a block of stone that was uncovered during building works on the citadel where workmen had witnessed the appearance of a female Buddha. Renovation work was carried out in the 18C.

A much older building, founded in 1131, and restored in 1855 and 1954 is **Ly Trieu Quoc Su Pagoda*** *(50 Ly Quoc Su. Daily 6am-5pm)* displaying that indefinable style of most Hanoian pagodas with its curved triple porch, its Chinese lettering and its intrusive banyan trees taking over the street.

Around Lenin Park (Plan II C4)
Allow 2hr to wander around this area.

Head south down a little street called Ha Hoi through this quiet residential area near the French Embassy and admire the occasional luxury villa. You will arrive at a quiet little lake called **Thien Quang** busy with fishermen, outdoor hairdressers whose salon consists of a single mirror, karaoke-cafés, and pedalos in the shape of a swan, phoenix or dragon. Next to the lake is **Lenin Park**, the biggest open space in the city *(open daily 5am-10.30pm. Entrance fee)*, where acrobats and bears on bicycles make up part of the traditional Soviet circus delights *(see "Hanoi close up" page 154)*. The gardens were created out of a rubbish dump at the end of the 1950s with the use of "voluntary" labour. Eastwards towards Nguyen Du and Mai Hac De is the students' quarter, alive with cafés and fashionable restaurants.

Allow a full day
and have lunch in a "bun cha" at Tong Duy Tan.

Ba Dinh Square lies northeast of Hoan Kiem Lake. You can get there by taxi or "xe om".
Don't forget that a number of monuments are closed on Mondays and Fridays, and that the
Ho Chi Minh Mausoleum is only open in the mornings.

From the 11C to today, Ba Dinh has been the theatre of power. This overwhelmingly official district has little atmosphere, but its striking collection of buildings is well worth a visit, consisting as it does of an interesting architectural cocktail of classic 11C temples mixed with colonial-era buildings and impressive Soviet-style state monuments. An incongruous mixture to which should be added the old Temple of Literature bordering the former royal city to the south. On Sundays, austerity gives way to bustling warmth when Ba Dinh comes alive with crowds of locals visiting their national monuments.

Monuments of Ba Dinh Square (B2-3)

Development of the site where Ho Chi Minh proclaimed Vietnam's independence began in 1970 with the creation of a vast rectangular esplanade, decorated with 168 grass squares symbolising the intricate patchwork of the rice plantations in the delta. Around it rise the façades of governmental and diplomatic buildings. To the north, the **Presidential Palace** can be found behind the façade designed (1901-06) by Auguste-Henri Vildieu for the Governor General, while the former Lycée Albert-Sarraut (1919), school to many young French students and elite Vietnamese scholars, now houses the headquarters of the **Central Committee**. On the corner of Hoang Van Thu, the solid 1930s style of the former sports club has now become the **Ba Dinh Club** for retired members of the Party. Its neighbour, the **National Assembly**, was built in 1970 in a neo-Classical Soviet style. Opposite, on the west side, are various monuments constructed in memory of the "Father of the Nation".

Ho Chi Minh Mausoleum

B Juge/MICHELIN

The Presidential Palace is not open to the public, but you can visit **Bach Thao Park**, a botanical garden with an area of 20ha developed in 1890 as an arboretum for the different tree species collected in French Indochina *(access via Hoang Hoa Tham or Ngoc Ha. Daily 8am-5pm. Entrance fee)*. An avenue of mango trees leads to **Ho Chi Minh's stilt house★** (Nha San Bac Ho) *(access via Hung Vuong. Entrance fee)*, where Ho Chi Minh lived and worked on and off from 1958 to 1968. Its architectural restraint is in stark contrast to the stuccoed embellishments of the neighbouring palace. On the ground floor, behind simple shuttered windows, Ho Chi Minh used to hold his councils of war around the large conference table. His bedroom and office were on the first floor.

To the south of the Presidential Palace, overshadowing Ba Dinh Square, rises the massive grey marble silhouette of **Ho Chi Minh's Mausoleum** (Chu Tich Ho Chi Minh) *(Open 7.30-10.30am (summer) / 8-11am (winter); closed on Mondays and Fridays and during October and November. No charge. All visitors must register their belongings at 8 Hung Vuong, ☎ (04) 845 51 28 / (04) 845 55 20, as cameras, bags, hats and caps are not allowed. It is forbidden to put your hands in your pockets, to speak or to drive a car or motor vehicle in front of the mausoleum).* The queue of visitors wanting to pay their respects to Uncle Ho every Sunday stretches for several hundred metres. Their patience is rewarded with a brief moment in the dimly-lit room where the embalmed body of the former leader is laid to rest. Like the last resting-places of Lenin and Mao, the mausoleum (built 1973-1978) is the strange product of an ideology which deposed old deities and replaced them with political idols.

A few metres south of the mausoleum is the **One Pillar Pagoda**★ (Chua Mot Cot) *(Ong Ich Kiem. Open every day)*, one of the very few structures remaining from Hanoi's predecessor, Thang Long. The pagoda is made of wood with an elegantly raised roof, positioned on a single stone pillar in the middle of the water. This never-to-be repeated design was created in 1050 by **Ly Thai To** following a dream in which he had a vision of the Lotus Palace of Quan Am. At least that is what the legend says, though some ethnologists believe that it is derived from the tiny shrines once placed on top of posts in homage to the spirits of the rice plantations and the forests. An identical reconstruction of the building was completed in 1249 under the Tran dynasty. The present pagoda was set on its concrete pillar in 1955 following its destruction during the evacuation of Hanoi by the French.

The **Ho Chi Minh Museum**★ (Bao Tang Ho Chi Minh) *(Ngoc La. Open from 8-11am / 1.30-4pm; closed on Mondays and Fridays. Entrance fee. Leave all bags and cameras in the cloakroom)* was built with aid from the USSR between 1985 and 1990. The museum's descriptions can be a little bewildering without prior knowledge of Vietnam's history and details of Ho Chi Minh's life, but you are nonetheless able to browse through a lot of interesting archives and photographs. It is a memorial to a daring conception, combining socialist realism and traditional Vietnamese mythology: an enormous **statue** of Ho Chi Minh impresses each visitor, his hand raised symbolically in a gesture of learning to a backdrop of the sun peeking out from behind the clouds. The dramatically-staged exhibits follow the various periods in the leader's life, from his childhood to his trips to Europe and China. There are faces from Guernica denouncing fascism, flowers with metal petals symbolising the unity of the Communist Party, and rainbows representing reunification. A **funerary altar** positioned in front of a wall of water symbolising the autumn of 1969 represents the leader's death.

The Embassy district (B-C3)

The **Ministry of Foreign Affairs** operates from the former Public Finance building constructed by Hébrard in 1931 in Indochinese style, and which rounds off Ba Dinh Square to the south where Dien Bien Phu Avenue begins. This particular avenue is lined with a succession of French villas now housing embassies. This architectural stroll is made all the more pleasant by the wide shady footpaths.

The **Army Museum**★ (Vien Bao Tang Quan Doi) *(28 Dien Bien Phu. Open from 8-12noon / 1-4.30pm; closed on Mondays and Fridays. Entrance fee. Allow half an hour)* can be found at the foot of the **hexagonal Flag Tower** (Cot Co) constructed during the

Nguyen dynasty *(access possible during museum opening hours)*. In the courtyard, the twisted pile of metal made up of old planes and spoils of war immediately sets the tone of the exhibition which is entirely devoted to the country's lengthy conflicts. One area is given over to the battle of Dien Bien Phu illustrated with a scale model, film footage of that time, and the famous bicycle used by the Viet Minh artillery. Other rooms show campaign maps, war relics, arms and very moving photographs, especially those taken during the war against the Americans.

Further down, **Chi Lang Park** represents a passing reference to Vietnam's former ally. It was laid out between 1985-87 in celebration of the 70th anniversary of the Russian Revolution and to provide a home for a **statue of Lenin** that was imported especially from the Soviet Union.

For the Fine Arts Museum, walk down Tran Phu Street, which is lined with railings to protect the smart villas from prying eyes.

Behind the coffee-coloured façade of a former secondary school for girls, the **Fine Arts Museum**★★ (Vien Bao Tang My Thuat) *(66 Nguyen Thai Hoc, on the corner of Cao Ba Quat. Open from 9.15am-5pm; closed on Mondays. Entrance fee. Allow 1hr)* has three floors devoted to the country's artistic heritage. The rooms on the ground floor begin with the **art of Dong Son**, a rare opportunity to admire the brilliance of the bronze sculptors of this era (1000 BC). A lot of imagination was used in the creation of these magnificent human and animal figures. There are only a few **Cham sculptures** but they are of outstanding quality, including an attractive dancing girl from Tra Kie (9C-10C), a female bust of great classicism, a melancholy flute player and a dancer reminiscent of one of Michelangelo's slaves. It is easy to form a complete picture of 10C-18C Vietnamese sculpture, even though some items are copies that may not be marked as such. The sensitivity of **Ly art** (1009-1225) shows in its architectural sculpture, such as the pedestal showing two playful lions toying with a pearl, and the finely worked dancers and musicians adorning the base of a column. **Tran art** (1225-1413) on the other hand makes vigorous play with more generous forms, with the exception of the figurines decorating the lattice-work of doors or windows. The artistic renaissance under the **Le** and **Mac** dynasties (15C-16C) manifests itself through a Quan Am with forty arms, seated on a lotus flower carried by a giant emerging from the waves, or a through a Western Buddha, his lowered face of great but androgynous beauty (copy of a sculpture from the Phat Tich pagoda at Bac Ninh). **Later Le Art** (1428-1789) shows a less sophisticated type of craftsmanship, nonetheless full of charm in its portrayal of everyday life in the decoration of community houses. The last room is full of old paintings such as the 17C royal couple Ly Nam and his wife painted on wood, the portrait of almost photographic precision of Nguyen Chu Ai in Mandarin costume (early 19C), or the vertical silk ink-painting depicting the triumphant return of the Mandarins.

On the first floor are exhibits of **traditional art** with Dong Ho engravings, Hanoi embroidery, religious paintings on wood by the Tay and the Nung, and funerary sculptures from Gia Lai. The next few rooms mark the start of the collections on the last floor with an important series of **realist paintings** in oil or lacquer by Fine Arts students.

The Temple of Literature is situated opposite the museum, but follow the outer walls to the entrance which opens southwards in accordance with the rules of Far Eastern geomancy standards.

Surprisingly named the "Pagoda of the Crows" by the French, the **Temple of Literature**★★ (Van Mieu) *(Quoc Tu Giam. Open every day 7.30am-6pm (summer) / 8am-5pm (winter). Entrance fee. Dance and classical music performances on request)* is a pleasant step back in time, where the surrounding pavilions and age-old trees are mirrored in the ornamental lakes. It was founded in 1070, 60 years after Hanoi had become the capital and the country had adopted a Chinese-style bureaucracy in line with Confucian ideals. In 1076, the **Quoc Tu Giam**, or National Academy, was added for the well-read elite who were destined to lead the Empire. At the time of the entrance examinations, the candidates were assembled in the **Sage Courtyard** (Trang Thi), to the east of the temple, a name now given to one of the avenues. The temple was restored and extended a number of times and continued to be the most prestigious institution of the whole imperial administration, even after the transfer of power to Hue. The building was severely damaged in the battle of Hanoi in 1947, and since 1990 has been part of an extensive restoration programme which will be concluded with the reconstruction of the National Academy to the north of the complex.

The layout of the **temple** conforms to the Chinese model, notably in terms of a series of divided courtyards with interconnecting gateways. In the second courtyard is the building dedicated to Khue Van Cac, the stellar divinity of Literature. It is a small structure with ornamental moon-shaped apertures (1805). A garden of 82 stelae, each set on top of a stone tortoise, borders the next courtyard. Each stele records the examination date and the names of all those who were awarded doctorates between 1484 and 1779. In the centre, a rectangular lake known as the "Well of Heavenly Clarity" which stretches between two pavilions, was where incense was burned in honour of the graduates during the ceremonies put on to celebrate the anniversary of Confucius. The temple itself is at the end of the last courtyard, flanked by two rooms where the 72 disciples of Confucius were venerated, but which today makes the perfect setting for souvenir shops. Inside the temple, the great Chinese philosopher, along with his four disciples and the ten thinkers who propagated his teaching, are honoured by thrones marked with their names.

The shores of the West Lake★ (Ho Tay) (Plan II)

Allow half a day ending up in one of the cheap eating places of Phu Tay Ho (see page 152). Take several little "xe om" trips, since places are quite far apart and traffic on the dike can be rather daunting.

This former holiday resort for emperors underwent dramatic changes in the second half of the 1990s. What until then had been no more than a collection of villages specialising in flower-growing and paper-making was transformed by virulent property speculation into a motley collection of residences for the local bigwigs and nouveaux riches. Extremely diverse and over-the-top, these dwellings carve up the lakeside into packed lines of "Snow White houses" with little bell towers covered with pink tiles, and Hollywood-style mansions with colonnaded balconies and smoked-glass bay windows. Surprisingly enough, within this complete shambles stand some of the most beautiful temples in Hanoi.

West Lake★ and White Silk Lake (Ho Truc Bach) (B2)

Together they form the largest residual stretch of water left in Hanoi due to the changing moods of the Red River. The name of the second lake conjures up a picture of melancholy royal concubines who were left shut away in the palaces to spin and weave silk all day long. The lake itself is gradually being eaten away by illegal building and could be a mere memory in years to come. On the south side, **Quan Thanh Temple**★★ (Den Quan Thanh) *(Thanh Nien. Open daily 8am-4pm. Entrance fee)* was founded in 1010 in the Earlier Le dynasty in honour of Tran Vu, the Black Warrior and guardian of the north who defeated a fox with nine tails that had been terrorising the local inhabitants. The present building goes back to the 17C-18C; its magnificent woodwork includes superb door panels trimmed with ornate Chinese-style still life, sculpted door frames and ornamental brackets in the shape of dragons. All the structural timber is carefully worked and many delightfully-carved motifs decorate the beams. In the first bay stands a remarkable Cantonese-style sculpted **altar** bordered with royal arms, military standards and cranes perched on top of tortoises. At the rear, **Tran Vu** is leaning on his sword, which has a snake coiled around it and is resting on a tortoise, these two animals being the northern hero's trusty companions. Cast in 1677 using 400kg of black bronze, the 3.72m-high sculpture dominates the entire area.

Youth Road (Duong Thanh Nien) separates the two lakes. It is an old dike, enlarged during the organised work days of the 1960s, its sides converted into landscaped promenades 20 years later. From the **Pagoda for the Defence of the Country**** (Chua Tran Quoc) (*Thanh Nien. Open every day 7-11.30am / 1.30-6.30pm. No charge*), you will first come across the **Monastery Cemetery**, a small forest of tiny brick pagodas with inscriptions in Vietnamese script, set out beneath spindly areca palms. A little dike leads to the islet of Ca Vang ("Golden Fish") with its pagoda which you pass through and then on to bays housing paintings of venerable elders and the altars dedicated to immortals, right up to the main room that still preserves the rustic harmony of the 17C despite restoration work in 1815. Founded in the 6C, this pagoda is one of the oldest in the country. It used to be located on the banks of the Red River, but in 1615 was dismantled following a landslide and moved to its present location.

Along Nghi Tam* (A-B1)

Further to the north, this dike separates West Lake from the Red River. The resplendent **Pagoda of the Golden Lotus**** (Chua Kim Lien) (*Ngo 1, Au Co*) gives the impression of having been washed up at the foot of the unsightly, neglected-looking Sheraton tower. Yet once through the entrance portico, all is magical charm like a cloud of heady perfumed incense. The statues are recent but are set out under a structure which is quite as attractive as the porch, with timbers carved with dragons and ornamented corbels. The wooden columns rest on sculpted flagstones in the shape of blossoming lotus flowers. At the back, plants in blue and white ceramic pots brighten up the modern cloisters. The pagoda was founded in the 12C by King Ly Than's daughter, Princess **Tu Hoa**. She used to teach the art of keeping silk-worms to the village girls living by the riverside, and one of them entered the pantheon of female deities as **Quynh Hoa**, "the silk-worm princess". The main room of the pagoda houses her shrine, along with a statue of Tu Hoa.

Nearby, a small area of nurseries and market-gardens is the only remaining evidence of what used to be, until quite recently, the countryside surrounding the old **village of Nghi Tam**. At the end of the lane bordering the area, behind the Thang Loi Hotel, is a small modern **den** (temple), dedicated to the spirits of the West Lake.

Tay Ho Temple* (Phu Tay Ho) (*open every day 6am-6pm*) stands at the end of a headland surrounded by residences which have sprung up over the last four years. Access is via a little dike lined with small restaurants (*no through road for motor vehicles*) offering lakeside specialities (*see "Hanoi close up" page 152*). The buildings have been restored paying particular attention to detail and the atmosphere is one of respect, especially on busier days (*Sundays, as well as the first and the fifteenth day of each lunar month*). Only the trees in the courtyard can testify to the age of this place of worship; they include an ancient tree creeping along the ground in search of water from the lake and a banyan tree which has already built up its own small forest. This modern-style temple is decorated in red and gold and covered with awnings and lanterns. The **main Chapel** is dedicated to the Holy Mother whose statue is concealed behind a trellised screen guarded by officials in little winged caps. Her powers can be measured by the size of the piles of "Tiger Beer" laid down as offerings. Adjoining the main chapel is a **Buddhist Chapel** containing the large figure of Quan Am with a thousand arms placed in a crib made of pieces of limestone and decorated with flowers and plastic grapes.

A little dike lined with palm trees leads to the **Pho Linh Pagoda**; located amid fisherman's huts, it is a charming little building with its jumble of potted plants and a nun's garden.

Museum of Ethnology of Vietnam***

(Bao Tan Dan Toc Hoc Viet Nam) (Plan II A2, off the map)

Allow 2hr

The museum is on Nguyen Hai Nien in the northwestern outskirts of the city near the Russo-Vietnamese Tropical Institute at the end of a long avenue. Accessible by n° 14 bus, taxi or "xe om". For the return journey go back as far as the busy avenue of Nghia Do to call a taxi. Open daily 8.30am-5.30pm; closed on Mondays. Entrance fee. Photography and video filming permitted. Explanations in Vietnamese, English and French.

A fascinating museum showing ethnic Vietnam in all its multicoloured facets. You will come across objects utterly unknown elsewhere, like the Ba Na scarecrows or the Muong squirrel traps, and you can learn about Vietnam's extraordinary ethnographic wealth via a special pedagogical trail using five distinct linguistic families which lead on to the 54 different ethnic groups in the country *(see page 51)*.

Being in the majority, the **Viet**, or **Kinh**, naturally mark the start of the exhibition, with displays on different cults that continue to bind rural communities in the Red River Delta. The **Holy Trinity Mothers**, rulers of the mountains, the land and the seas, take pride of place on a superb red and gold altar. Water puppetry was developed within this religious background for the entertainment of men and gods alike. Most of the **children's toys** on display, which were made and given as presents during the lunar month festivities, have today disappeared (kites in the autumn and cricket cages for insect fights in the springtime). Traditional craftsmanship figures prominently, an area where the Viet excel, with lacquer ware, sculptures on wood, ceramics from Bat Trang and traditional Dong Ho engravings. The history of the Viet ends with a reconstruction of a **domestic altar** with its ancestral tablets, genealogies and paintings.

The exhibition then turns to the Highlanders or mountain people (muong-viet in Vietnamese), settlers from Than Hoa, west of Nghe An and Quang Binh. The exhibits include hunting nets, cast nets, crossbows and dishes made from bark. The **Muong** society of Hoa Binh appears in connection with the living and the dead around a reconstruction of a typical home, with lengths of material in contrasting colours draped like banners for the ritual wake.

The first floor is devoted to the large **Tai-Kadai** family, with displays on the different **habitats** of these ethnic groups settled in the fertile valleys along the Chinese and Laotian borders, where the Tay, Black Tai and White Tai live in stilt houses and the Nung inhabit ground-level dwellings which are often fortified. A wealth of interesting creations in the **art of textiles** are on show in a Black Tai house reconstructed within the museum, including silk and cotton brocade from Lao Cai, tunics of the Tay Pa Di embroidered with silver pearls, silver-buttoned jackets and pleated skirts of the Nung, and diamond-patterned sarongs of the White Tai. The most elaborate weaving is the work of the Co Lao and the Lu, near the Laos border.

The **Hmong** and the **Dao** stand out due to the variety of their costumes. Admire the tunic with silver discs, the head-dress decorated with Dao coins from Tuyen Quang, or the bright scarlet costume of the Pa Then from Ha Giang.

The section on **Mon-Khmers** represents quite a different world with striking architecture and complex basketwork. The Ba Na make scarecrows in plaited bamboo, or kite-shaped with an animal's head. Like the **Sedang**, they are renowned for their funerary statues, taking inspiration from sexuality and the contemporary environment. These statues are a forerunner to an even more elaborate collection of funerary architecture from the **Gia Rai**, with scale models of a few tombs and statues.

The long sequence of ethnic groups ends with the **Cham**, the **Hoa** and the **Khmers**, presented through symbolic objects from each of their cultures: a cart for transporting earthenware jars, a New Year dragon and silk ikat.

Hanoi

The Red River Delta

COMING AND GOING

By air – The international airport of **Noi Bai** (Plan II B1 or A3, off the map) is 40km from the centre (a journey of 35min to 1hr), ☎ (04) 884 33 89. **On arrival**: "duty free" and a Vietcombank with erratic opening hours. Small denomination dollar bills will get you to Hanoi, either by the Vietnam Airlines airport bus (US$3 to their office in the city, 1A Quang Trung), or by taxi (US$10, including tolls). In both cases, pay at the counters near the exit to the airport where you will be given a sticker. **On departure**: take the Vietnam Airlines bus (US$2, departure every 30min from the Vietnam Airlines office), or book a taxi from Airport Taxi (2 Quang Trung, ☎ (04) 934 40 70) which will pick you up from your hotel. Airport tax is 20 000VND for domestic flights, US$10 for international flights.

By train – Hanoi has one main railway station in the centre and three outside. **Ga Ha Noi** (Plan II C3), the main station, is divided into two. The Reunification Express that goes to Hue and Saigon, leaves from **Ga Hang Co**, with an entrance on Le Duan, at the junction with Tran Hung Dao. Information, ☎ (04) 825 36 97; reservations ☎ (04) 825 39 49. Ticket offices are open every day and for all destinations, 7.30-11.30am / 1.30-3.30pm (special ticket office for foreigners). **Ga Tran Quy Cap** (Ga B), located further north up Nguyen Khuyen, on Tran Quy Cap, operates services to the east, including Haiphong. Trains from **Ga Gia Lam** and **Ga Long Bien**, on the east bank of the Red River (Plan II D2, off the map), ☎ (04) 826 82 80, serve Haiphong and certain areas in the North such as Viet Tri, Yen Bai, Lao Cai and Lang Son.

Trains from **Ga Giap Bat** (Plan II C5, off the map), 7km south of the main railway station, serve the South.

International trains: one train per day at 9.30pm between Hanoi (Ga Hang Co) and Kunming in China (762km, 31hr 30min), via Lao Cai (8hr 30min). Departures from Hanoi (Ga Gia Lam) on Tuesdays and Fridays at 5pm to Ningming (234km) and Nanning (610km).

By bus – Buses are quite chaotic and unreliable, though improvements are being made, including the possibility of buying your ticket at the desk before boarding. But the distribution of the destinations among the various bus stations is still rather difficult to understand. **Ben Xe Gia Lam** (Plan II D2, off the map) (2km northeast of the centre, at the end of Nguyen Van Cu) serves the northeast (Halong Bay, Haiphong, Lang Son), but a lot of buses connect with Kim Ma. A number of minibuses go to Haiphong between 5am and 6pm. **Ben Xe Kim Ma** (Plan II B3) (opposite 166 Nguyen Thai Hoc, on the corner of Giang Vo, ☎ (04) 845 28 46) is the most central bus station. It serves the northwest (Pho Lu, Son La, Dien Bien) and acts as a terminus for the express minibuses from Ha Long. **Ben Xe Son La** (Plan II A5, off the map) (Nguyen Trai, near the University of Hanoi) also serves the northwest (Hoa Binh, Mai Chau, Son La, Tuan Giao, Lai Chau, Dien Bien). **Ben Xe Giap Bat** (Plan II C5, off the map) (Giai Phong, 7km south of the main railway station, ☎ (04) 864 14 67) serves the South. A few buses for Dien Bien Phu.

By "Open Tour" – The Open Tour option from the Toserco-Sinhu café, available from most of the mini-hotels in Hanoi, is still the best value-for-money means of travel to the South. Daily departures around 7pm for Hue (680km, 16hr), via Ninh Binh (90km, 2hr) and Quang Binh (500km, 11hr30min).

Chauffeur-driven car – This service is available from most Hanoi agencies. There are special fares for the most common routes, but you can also hire a car for the day. For Hanoi and the surrounding areas allow 500 000VND per day or 3 000VND per km. For several days, allow US$25 per day for a 4WD Volga (the "Russian Jeep"), US$35 for an air-conditioned car or US$40 for a minibus.

By motorcycle – For hardened motorcyclists only, see below.

GETTING AROUND HANOI

By bus – Hanoians tend to look down on this form of transport, since it is not a very practical way to move around the city centre. Most of the routes link suburbs or more distant built-up areas. Useful bus routes for tourists are the n° 7 Dien-Hang Gai-Bo Ho (Hoan Kiem lake, Hang Gai, Hang Bong, Nguyen Thai Hoc, Kim Ma, Cau Giay) and n° 14 (Hoan Kiem lake, Dong Xuan market, Quan Thanh, Thuy Khe and the Museum of Ethnology).

By taxi – It is very easy to find a taxi in Hanoi, even if you have to phone one of the six taxi companies operating in the city. *Mai Linh Taxi*, ☎ (04) 861 61 61.*Viet Phuong Taxi*, ☎ (04) 828 28 28. *Taxi A*, ☎ (04) 832 73 27. *Taxi Duong Sat*, ☎ (04) 862 62 62. *Taxi Hanoi*, ☎ (04) 853 52 52. *Airport Taxi*, ☎ (04) 934 40 70. The call is free with a maximum wait of 10min. It is more difficult to find one at night, but you can always contact the reception of one of the large hotels. All taxis use a meter. The starting price is 14 000VND which represents about 2km (the average distance covered in the city centre), but be vigilant since the meter tends to run very quickly after that at a rate of about 1 000VND every 200m. A number of taxis wait near the Vietnam Airlines' booking office, on the corner of Quang Trung and Hang Khai.

By motorcycle-taxi – This is the most practical form of transport today and the perfect way to get to know the motorcyclist highway code. Allow 5 000VND for a city centre run and an extra 2 000VND for the surrounding districts.

By cyclo – For short distances or fun trips. You won't have to look for one, they are everywhere. Negotiate the price beforehand, but a trip in the city centre should cost between 8 000VND and 10 000VND, or between 12 000VND and 20 000VND per hour. Cyclo drivers know the city like the back of their hand and can make very good guides.

Bicycle and motorcycle hire – Bicycles and motorcycles can be hired in a number of places in Hanoi. It will cost you US$3-US$7 per day according to the model or US$70 per month. You will normally have to show an international driving licence for engines over 50CC. *Dao*, 42 Hang Bac, ☎ (04) 826 04 93. *Meeting Café*, 59 Ba Trieu,

☎ (04) 825 88 13. *The Red River*, 73 Hang Bo, ☎ (04) 826 84 27. *Garden Café*, 16 Nguyen Gia Thieu, ☎ (04) 822 67 62. *Horizon Café*, 2 Tran Hung Dao, ☎ (04) 933 09 36. *Mai Linh Café*, 22 Cau Go, ☎ (04) 824 45 54. In case of breakdown, call one of the *Piaggio Centres*, 157 Giang Vo, ☎ (04) 514 05 68; 368 Bach Mai, ☎ (04) 863 53 88; 4 Phan Boi Chau, ☎ (04) 826 43 88.

ADDRESS BOOK

Buildings are numbered starting from the river for streets running east-west, and the numbers increase southwards for the streets at right angles.

Tourist information – *Toserco* (Plan II C4), 8 To Hien Thanh, ☎ (04) 826 36 87, Fax (04) 822 60 55. *Vietnam Tourism* (Plan I B3), 30A Ly Thuong Kiet, ☎ (04) 826 41 54, Fax (04) 825 75 83.

Bank / Currency exchange – The Vietcombank and its various branches provide the best rates, but be sure to keep to the following rules: best rates for US$50 and US$100 notes, 1 % commission on travellers cheques in foreign currency and 3 % commission on all credit card transactions (Visa and MasterCard). You can also safely change money in jeweller's shops showing the sign of the Vietcombank on a yellow background. *Vietcombank*, 23 Phan Chu Trinh, Monday to Friday 8-11.30am / 1-3.30pm, Saturdays 9am-12 noon. Cash dispensers are available during opening hours. Branches at 1 Hang Bai; 120 Hang Trong; 36 Hang Bun; 7 Cau Go; 11 Ly Thai To; 198 Tran Quang Khai; 3 Quoc Tu Giam; 39 Ly Thuong Kiet; 250 Minh Khai. Mondays-Fridays 8-11.30am / 1-3.30pm.

ANZ Bank, 14 Le Thai To, ☎ (04) 825 81 90. A 24hr cash dispenser for Visa and MasterCard. Monday-Friday 8am-3.30pm, Saturdays 8.30am-12 noon.

Post office / Telephone – *Buu Dien Trung Uong* (Plan I B3), 75 Dinh Tien Hoang, ☎ (04) 825 27 30. Open daily. Stamps sold from 8am-5.30pm; poste restante closed from 12 noon-1.10pm and all day Saturday. International Telegraph Office on the corner of Dinh Tien Hoang and Dinh Le. Open daily 7.30am-9.30pm. Directory enquiries, ☎1080.

Internet – A number of mini-hotels and agencies in the old quarter provide Internet connections, but there are also many cyber-cafés (300VND-400VND per minute). *Emotion Cybernet Cafe*, 52 Ly Thuong Kiet, near to the Ambassador's Pagoda, ☎ (04) 934 10 66. *Hoan Kiem Internet Café*, 26 Le Thai To, ☎ (04) 828 57 99. *Love Planet Cafe*, 18 Hang Bac, ☎ (04) 828 48 64. *Center Internet Services*, 86 Dinh Liet. *Tin Tin Club*, 2A Bao Khanh, ☎ (04) 928 50 89 (open until midnight).

Medical service – *Vietnam International Hospital* (Plan II C5), Phuong Mai, near Bach Mai hospital, ☎ (04) 574 07 40. Best facilities with a 24hr accident and emergency department, ☎ (04) 574 11 11. *International Clinic*, 31 Hai Ba Trung, ☎ (04) 934 05 05. *Vietnam International Hospital*, Phuong Mai Road, ☎ (04) 8574 0740. *MEDEX*, A1 Van Phuc, 109-112 Kim Ma, ☎ (04) 843 0748. 24hr Emergency, Mobile: 09090 1919. *Hanoi Family Medical Practice*, A-1 Van Phuc, Suite 109-112, Ha Noi, ☎ (04) 843 0748. 24hr Emergency, Mobile: 090 401 99919. *International SOS*, 31 Hai Ba Trung,☎ (04) 934 05 55. Emergency service and dental care. *Pharmacie Nguyen Luan*, 3 Trang Thi, ☎ (04) 826 86 44. Daily 8am-12 noon / 2-6pm; closed Sunday afternoons.

Consulate / Embassies – See "Practical information" page 47.

Useful organisations – *Vietcochamber*, ☎ (04) 825 2961 / 825 3023, Fax (04) 825 6446 and *The Chamber of Commerce & Industry of Vietnam*, ☎ (04) 826 6235, Fax (04) 825 6446, 33 Pho Ba Trieu. *The Vietnam Trade Information Centre* ☎ (04) 826 5476 / 826 2316, 46 Pho Ngo Quyen. *The International Relations Department of the Ministry of Information*, ☎ (04) 825 3152, 58 Pho Quan Su.

Airline companies – *Aeroflot*, 4 Trang Thi, ☎ (04) 825 67 42, Fax (04) 824 94 11. *Air France*, 1 Ba Trieu, ☎ (04) 825 34 84, Fax (04) 826 66 94. *Cathay Pacific*, 49 Hai Ba Trung, ☎ (04) 826 72 98, Fax (04) 826 77 09. *China Airlines*, 18 Tran Hung Dao, ☎ (04) 824 26 88, Fax (04) 824 25 88. *China Southern Airlines*, Binh Minh Hotel, 27 Ly Thai To, ☎ (04) 826 92 33, Fax (04) 826 92 34. *Lao Aviation*, 41 Quang Trung, ☎ (04) 826 65 38, Fax (04) 822 99 51. *Malaysia Airlines*, 15 Ngo Quyen, ☎ (04) 826 88 20, Fax (04) 824 23 88. *Pacific Airlines*, 100 Le Duan, ☎ (04) 851 53 56, Fax (04) 851 53 50. *Singapore Airlines*, 17 Ngo Quyen, ☎ (04) 826 88 88, Fax (04) 826 86 66. *Thai Airways*, 44B Ly Thuong Kiet, ☎ (04) 826 68 93, Fax (04) 826 79 34. *Vietnam Airlines*, 1 Quang Trung, ☎ (04) 825 08 88 / 832 03 20 (reconfirmation), Fax (04) 824 89 89.

Travel agencies – Many mini-hotels represent tour operators and offer the same services. There is strong competition, so shop around (particularly with the Ninh Binh agencies, see page 168), ask which category of hotel they deal with and eliminate agencies offering cars to the northwest.

A II Z Queen Cafe, 50 Hang Be, on the ground floor of the Binh Minh hotel, ☎ (04) 826 08 60, Fax (04) 826 03 00, queenaz@fpt.vn Tight-budget agency.

Buffalo Tours, 11 Hang Muoi, parallel to Tran Quang Khai, to the east of the old quarter, ☎ (04) 828 07 02, Fax (04) 826 93 70, buffalo@netnam.org.vn Top of the range, specialising in ecological tours.

Ecco Voyages, 50A Ba Trieu, ☎ (04) 825 46 15, Fax (04) 826 65 19. Cruises in private junks in Halong Bay. *Especen*, 1 Nha Chung, ☎ (04) 826 68 56, Fax (04) 826 96 12. Low budget.

Exotissimo, 26 Tran Nhat Duat, ☎ (04) 828 21 50, Fax (04) 828 21 46, hansales@exotissimo.com The best top of the range agency.

Dragon Travel, 128 Hang Trong, ☎ (04)928 53 66, Fax (04)928 53 65, dragontravel@fpt.vn. Mid-range, English and French speaking.

Green Bamboo Tours, 49 Nha Chung, junction of Trang Thi and Le Thai To, ☎ (04) 826 87 52. One of the first private agencies, but erratic services.

Le Maquis – Association Bourlingue, 2A Ta Hien, ☎ (04) 828 25 98, Fax (04) 928 17 34, fredo-binh@hn.vnn.vn Specialists in Vietnam by motorcycle.

Red River Tours, 73 Hang Bo, ☎ (04) 826 84 27, Fax (04) 828 71 59, redrivertours@netnam.org.vn Low budget.

Sinh Café, 18 Luong Van Can, ☎ (04) 828 75 52, Fax (04) 822 60 55, hopentour@hn.vnn.vn Low budget.

TF Handspan, 116 Hang Bac, ☎ (04) 828 19 96, Fax (04) 825 71 71, tfhandspn@hn.vnn.vn The most reliable low-budget agency at unbeatable prices.

Visas – Save time for hardly any extra cost by contacting the travel agencies and mini-hotels. Allow US$20 to US$30 according to the length of the visa extension. For neighbouring countries, see "Practical Information" page 97.

Department of Immigration, 40A rue Hang Bai. Mondays-Fridays 8-11am / 2-4pm, Saturdays 8-11am.

Emergency – Police, ☎ 113. **Fire service**, ☎ 114. **Ambulance**, ☎ 115.

Photography – Kodak Express, 2 Le Thai To, to the north of Hoan Kiem. Films and film development, including slides, at unbeatable prices.

WHERE TO STAY
The monopoly of government-run hotels is over: Hanoi is now packed with cheap mini-hotels. Air-conditioning shouldn't be considered a luxury, especially in winter when damp can be a problem. There is also a wide choice in the middle or higher-scale hotels, and the amount of luxury hotels can lead to preferential rates.

• **The 36 Guilds and the Cathedral area** (Plan I)

Under US$10
Anh Sinh Hotel, 49 Hang Be, ☎ (04) 824 22 29, Fax (04) 824 22 29 – 7rm ☏ 🍴 ⤢ The dormitory is more appealing than the single rooms without

bathrooms that are more like run-down, poorly ventilated cubicles. The double rooms are tiled and well maintained.

Bao Long Hotel, 39 Hang Be, ☎ (04) 824 04 34 – 12rm ☏ ⤢ Tourists on tight budgets are made very welcome in this unsophisticated mini-hotel, so cheap it's unbelievable.

Binh Minh Hotel, 50 Hang Be, ☎ (04) 826 08 60, Fax (04)826 03 00 – 30rm ☏ ⤢ Quality and comfort that are hard to beat at cheap rates: some rooms without windows. Look before checking in to your room and go up to the roof terrace for a magnificent view of the tube houses.

Camellia Hotel, 10C Dinh Liet, ☎ (04) 934 37 97 – 5rm ☏ 🍴 ⤢ 📺 Big long rooms, bathrooms the same, with old-fashioned tiling. Not for the claustrophobic and the rooms at the back overlook the fire escape.

Between US$10 and US$15
Youth Hotel (Sinh Café), 33 Luong Van Can (opposite Hang Quat), ☎ (04) 828 58 22, Fax (04) 828 84 55, hopentour@hn.vnn.vn – 17rm ☏ 🍴 ⤢ 📺 ✗ Buzzing with motorcyclists, a friendly welcome. Recently repainted colonial-style rooms, bathrooms could do with the same treatment. Dormitory beds available at US$3 a night. On the ground floor, Internet, a travel agency and a small restaurant serving simple fare.

Between US$15 and US$30
Asia Hotel, 5 Cua Dong, ☎ (04) 826 90 07, Fax (04) 824 51 84 – 10rm ☏ 🍴 ⤢ Has the advantage of being a little out of the way. Very clean and the staff are friendly.

Bodega III, 133 Hang Bong, ☎ (04) 825 75 03, Fax (04) 826 77 87 – 10rm ☏ 🍴 ⤢ ✗ cc Recently repainted functional rooms with high ceilings. A huge room for four featuring pillars and mouldings.

Classic Street Hotel (Kach San Pho Co), 41 Hang Be, ☎ (04) 825 24 21, Fax (04) 934 59 20 – 9rm ☏ 🍴 ⤢ 📺 cc This converted house offers attractive and inviting accommodation. Set in a small courtyard decorated with potted plants, the rooms are perfectly light and airy, with engravings on the walls and well-equipped bathrooms. Breakfast available.

Especen Hotel, 79E Hang Trong, ☎ (04) 825 88 45, Fax (04) 826 96 12 – 12rm ⌂ 🍴 ✗ ♪ TV A spotless mini-hotel in a quiet little courtyard. Internet access.

Especen 11, 28 Tho Xuong by the east end of the cathedral ☎ (04) 824 44 01, Fax (04) 824 59 24, especenhotel11@hn.vnn.vn – 9rm ⌂ 🍴 ✗ ♪ TV Attractive, spacious and airy rooms overlooking the old quarter of Hanoi. Pity the bathrooms aren't quite up to scratch.

Nam Phuong Hotel, 16 Bao Khanh, ☎ (04) 928 50 85, Fax (04) 825 89 64, hiennd@netnam.org.vn – 8rm ⌂ 🍴 ✗ ♪ TV Situated at the start of the busy nightlife area. The cheapest rooms are at the back, which is not really a drawback except on the ground floor where they have no windows. Go for the room overlooking the street on the first floor.

Rose Hotel (Kach San Bong Hong), 56 Ngo Huyen, ☎ (04) 826 04 70, Fax (04) 826 04 71 – 9rm ⌂ 🍴 ✗ ♪ TV A quiet mini-hotel attracting foreign as well as Vietnamese visitors. Very good service. Take the room on the first floor looking out over the little back streets.

Thien Trang Mini Hotel, 24 Nha Chung, ☎ (04) 826 98 23, Fax (04) 828 67 17 – 9rm ⌂ 🍴 ✗ ♪ TV Motorcyclists gather here. The tiled rooms are well-kept, quiet overlooking the courtyard or with balcony overlooking the street. Trips organised by Toserco. Internet access.

Win Hotel, Hang Hanh (a small street between Bao Kanh and Luong Van Can), ☎ (04) 828 73 71, Fax (04) 824 74 48, esm-ntb@hn.vnn.vn – 8rm ⌂ 🍴 ✗ ♪ TV CC Attractive rooms in the area with the most vibrant nightlife. Choose between balcony onto the street or peace and quiet with big windows. The rooms are tiled and fitted out with Chinese furniture. Serves breakfast.

Between US$30 and US$50
Kim Thanh Hotel, 30 Hang Manh, ☎ (04) 825 96 82, Fax (04) 828 69 33, duc-anh@netnam.org.vn – 13rm ⌂ 🍴 ✗ ♪ TV CC Very central and no noise. High-ceilinged rooms with spacious bathrooms with bath. Breakfast is served in the courtyard.

• **Area of the former French concession** (Plan I)
Between US$10 and US$15
Lotus Guesthouse, 42V Ly Thuong Kiet, ☎ (04) 934 41 97, Fax (04) 826 86 42 lotus-travel@hn.vnn.vn – 12rm ⌂ 🍴 ✗ ✗ A steep staircase leads to tastefully furnished rooms with a lot of decorative ideas, such as glass-block walls that let the light through to the back. The bathrooms are respectable.

Sofia, 6 Hang Bai (between Hai Ba Trung and Hang Khay), ☎ (04) 826 68 48, Fax (04) 934 56 71 – 10rm ⌂ 🍴 ✗ ✗ A rather gloomy appearance, but you should be pleasantly surprised. The rooms are set around a small courtyard with a few plants.

Between US$15 and US$30
Huong Long Hotel, 10B Xom Ha Hoi (a small street leading into Quang Trung, behind the Cambodian Embassy), ☎ (04) 826 11 88, Fax (04) 822 67 46 – 9rm ⌂ 🍴 ✗ ♪ TV CC Rather central but quiet. An open staircase leads to large rooms whose balconies look out onto the residential area.

👁**Phuc Loi**, 4 Nha Chung, ☎ (04) 826 73 54, Fax (04) 828 98 97 – 9rm ⌂ 🍴 ✗ ♪ TV CC The hotel overlooks the cathedral courtyard, lively in the daytime, but very quiet at night. Very good value for money with pleasant rooms, and bathrooms (with baths). Laundry service and meals on request.

Between US$30 and US$50
Eden Hotel, 78 Tho Nhuom, ☎ (04) 824 52 73, Fax (04) 824 56 19, eden@hn.vnn.vn – 32rm ⌂ 🍴 ✗ ♪ TV ✗ CC In a colonnaded courtyard behind the lavender-blue façade you will find an Italian restaurant. The adjacent rooms are spotless and the hotel offers a few little extras such as free telephone calls for Hanoi numbers and a free trip to the airport for stays of more than five days. The staff are extremely friendly.

Between US$50 and US$70
Dan Chu Hotel (ex-Hanoi Hotel), 29 Trang Tien, ☎ (04) 825 43 44, Fax (04) 826 67 86 – 41rm ⌂ 🍴 ✗ ♪ TV ✗ CC Massage, sauna, business centre. Don't let the rather austere Soviet-style entrance hall put you off, the

hotel has more to it than meets the eye. The early-19C tiles and solid wood doors add to the overall charm. The cheapest rooms overlook the avenue but are rather old-fashioned. The most expensive are at the back with decorative moulding on the ceiling and fancy fabrics. Each room has its own vast tiled bathroom. A rather stuffy restaurant.

Between US$70 and US$100

Guoman Hotel, 83 Ly Thuong Kiet, ☎ (04) 822 28 00, Fax (04) 822 28 22, guomanhn@hn.vnn.vn – 149rm ⚑ 📺 ✕ ⌁ 🐾 ♨ 🐕 CC A cosy atmosphere in the discreet luxury of neo-colonial comfort. Classically stylish rooms and sizeable bathrooms. A small fitness centre is free of charge for guests. International buffet at lunchtime. An informal bar open from 4pm-midnight. An outside adjoining restaurant lays on barbecues every evening.

Thuy Nga Hotel, 4 Ba Trieu, ☎ (04) 934 12 56, Fax (04) 934 12 52 – 24rm ⚑ 📺 ✕ 🅲🅲 Minibar in each room. A modern hotel on the shores of Lake Hoan Kiem, right between the old quarter and the chic area of Hanoi. Sizeable sound-proofed rooms. Bathrooms with bath.

Over US$100

De Syloia Hotel, 17A Tran Hung Dao, ☎ (04) 824 53 46, Fax (04) 824 10 83, desyloia@hn.vnn.vn htm – 27rm ⚑ 📺 ✕ CC A colonial-era house gives access to the hotel which is located in a ten-storey tower with lift. Emphasis is on restrained elegance throughout the hotel. Excellent service and very warm welcome. Advance booking necessary.

Hilton Hanoi Opera, 1 Le Thanh Tong, ☎ (04)933 05 00, Fax (04) 933 05 30, info_hanoi@hilton.com – 269rm ⚑ 📺 ✕ CC The architecture of the building is on the same lines as the restored Opera House. Comfortable rooms with delicate Vietnamese touches. Bathrooms fitted with Da Nang marble and ceramic sanitary ware from Bat Trang. Every available facility including minibar and satellite TV. We recommend the hotel's Chinese restaurant and its "dim sum" buffet

(steam-cooked specialities) at US$10, its café-cum-patisserie overlooking the Opera and its cosy bar with music every evening from 6.30pm.

Sofitel Metropole, 15 Ngo Quyen, ☎ (04) 826 69 19, Fax (04) 826 69 20 – 244rm ⚑ 📺 ✕ ⌁ CC The oldest hotel in Hanoi has kept all its attractive features despite the addition in 1996 of a more functional extension on Ly Thai To. On the first two floors of the original building, dark atmospheric corridors leading to bedrooms with cream-coloured walls and parquet flooring showing the wear and tear of many generations of travellers. All this with the amenities of a five-star establishment. The restaurants are also well worth a visit. Sunday brunch is a must: for US$25 taste the delights of an inventive buffet using the freshest of ingredients prepared by a French-born chef. Book to avoid disappointment.

• **The Lenin Park Area** (Plan II)

Between US$15 and US$30

Grand Hotel, 71 Trieu Viet Vuong, ☎ (04) 822 77 64, Fax (04) 822 95 67 – 9rm ⚑ 📺 ✕ CC Spotlessly clean, pleasant rooms, particularly the larger ones, with parquet floors, wicker furniture and smart bathrooms.

Phoenix Hotel, 43 Trieu Viet Vuong, ☎ (04) 822 61 51, Fax (04) 822 72 87 – 15rm ⚑ 📺 ✕ CC A modernised version of the mini-hotel with a lift. The most expensive rooms are simply enormous, fully-fitted bathrooms with bath and balconies overlooking a very quiet street. Breakfast available, but any other meals are on request.

Between US$70 and US$100

Green Park Hotel, 48 Tran Nhan Tong, ☎ (04) 822 77 25, Fax (04) 822 59 77 – 40rm ⚑ 📺 ✕ CC Behind its mint-green façade, this hotel boasts all modern facilities and service with a smile. On the 7th floor, the restaurant looks out over Lenin Park.

Sunway Hotel, 19 Pham Dinh Ho, ☎ (04) 971 38 88, Fax (04) 971 35 55, sunway.hanoi@fpt.vn – 143rm ⚑ 📺 ✕ CC A very attractive hotel despite its surroundings. Designed to provide maximum comfort. Emphasis is on personal service. Book in advance.

• **The West Lake Area** (Plan II)

Between US$30 and US$50

Dragon Hotel, 48 Xuan Dieu, ☎ (04) 829 29 54, Fax (04) 829 47 45 – 23rm ▥▤☷ℰ ™ ✗ ℂℂ Avoid the neighbouring Le Tropicana with its exorbitant prices and questionable cleaning service, and beyond the bamboo hedge you'll find roomy accommodation with a view of the West Lake or the little Dinh Lien lake. Try the excellent terrace restaurant on the lakeside with caged songbirds and small pool.

Over US$100

🏊**Meritus Westlake**, 1 Thanh Nien, ☎ (04) 823 88 88, Fax (04) 829 38 88, westlake.mwh@meritushotels.com.vn – 322rm ▥▤☷ℰ ™ ✗ ☄ ℂℂ Fitness Club, massages, beauty salon. A magnificent location with each room enjoying a view over the northern lakes and the Red River. Three bars, including one next to the covered swimming pool and one on the 20th floor with a wonderful view of Hanoi. The three restaurants (brasserie, Chinese and Italian) serve themed buffet meals.

EATING OUT

Years of food shortages have practically been forgotten. From street stalls to top-class restaurants, the delights of Vietnamese and Mediterranean cuisine – now very fashionable – are readily available throughout Hanoi. Seafood restaurants are still rather on the expensive side however. Don't forget to try the buffets in the big hotels (from US$15-25). Apart from the ones already mentioned, check out the **Nikko** brasserie (Plan II C4) (84 Tran Nhan Tong, ☎ (04) 822 35 35) for good value for money. Street vendors and traditional restaurants close at 10pm.

• **The 36 Guilds and the cathedral area** (Plan I)

Under 25 000VND

A street vendor at n° 83 Hang Dieu (A2) is just the place for tasting "hu tieu" Hue-style (from 6pm), such as rice noodles sprinkled with peanuts and minced meat. Try their "banh cuon" as well with a "to phu", chilli pepper and coriander

sauce. Cross the road for dessert and choose from the wide selection of "che". In a small courtyard near the junction with Hang Bong (A2), they serve bowls of "mien luon", grilled eel soup with manioc noodles.

Tong Duy Tan (Plan II C3) is a small street at the end of Hang Bong where you can find a number of restaurants that open late in the evening: the food on offer includes tasty "bun cha" and chicken with medicinal aromatic herbs.

Bia Anh Phuong (B2), 7 Dinh Liet. In a street full of canteens where the locals have lunch you can find "bia hoi" and generous helpings of a number of other dishes.

Bia Hoi (B2), 27 Hang Be. It looks rather like a garage but they serve drinks and snacks.

Kim Dac (A2), 1 Hang Manh. One of the "bun cha" specialists.

Phu Doan (A3), by the Viet Duc hospital. A safe bet, with excellent quality "pho" from as early as 6am.

Between 25 000 and 50 000VND

🏊**Dong Thinh** (A2), 87 Hang Dieu, ☎ (04) 826 79 43. Specialises in eel soup with egg and mushrooms ("sup luon"), salad with manioc noodles ("mien truon luon") and crab pâté ("choc cua").

🏊**Kangaroo Cafe (Con Chuot Tui)** (B2), 18 Bao Khanh, ☎ (04) 828 99 31. An unpretentious English-speaking café in typical Hanoi "bia hoi" tradition (orders are taken next door), where you can treat yourself to international cuisine, vegetarian or otherwise.

Smiling Cafe (B2), 100 Cau Go (on the corner of Dinh Liet), ☎ (04) 825 15 32. Snack time on a terrace overlooking Dinh Liet.

Between 50 000 and 100 000VND

🏊**Cha Ca La Vong** (A1), 14 Cha Ca, ☎ (04) 825 39 29. A family institution where the recipe for the best "cha ca" in Hanoi has been handed down for over one hundred years: a fish dish cooked slowly in a mixture of spices and served with rice noodles and aromatic herbs. If you can't find a seat, try your luck in the neighbouring "cha cas". **Cha Ca 66** (A1), 66 Hang Ga, ☎ (04) 826 78 81, and **Cha Ca** (B2), 66 Hang Tre, ☎ (04) 825 79 24.

Garden (A2), 36 Hang Manh, ☎ (04) 824 34 02. A refreshing water wall and a peaceful courtyard, just 2min from one of the noisiest crossroads in Hanoi. Vietnamese dishes.

Little Hanoi (B2), 21 Hang Gai (on the corner of Luong Van Can), ☎ (04) 928 53.33. Daily 7am-10pm. Cappuccinos, quiches and salads in a colonial-style setting.

Between 100 000 and 200 000VND

Café de Paris (Plan II C3), 10 Tong Duy Tan, ☎ (04) 928 52 27. French brasserie-style cuisine in a former colonial house bang in the middle of the "bun cha" street.

Cyclo (A2), 38 Duong Thanh (near the Hang Bong intersection), ☎ (04) 828 68 44. Their pepper steak and duck fillet are favourites with French expats, but Vietnamese cuisine is also on the menu.

More than 200 000VND

Café des Arts (B2), 11B Bao Khanh, ☎ (04) 828 72 07. Come here just for a drink on the roof-top terrace overlooking the student quarter of Hanoi, or let yourself be tempted by the excellent French menu and come back for lunch or dinner. A jazzy atmosphere with exhibitions of work by local artists. The true French-style tournedos Rossini, leg of lamb, puréed potatoes and crêpes Suzette are too good to be missed. The owners were the founders of an association in support of the farmers around the Red River Delta.

La Salsa (A2), 25 Nha Tho, ☎ (04) 828 90 52. True Spanish tapas served with olive oil, "jamon serrano", and garlic potatoes to die for, all washed down with a pitcher of sangria.

- **The area of the former French concession** (Plan I)

Under 25 000VND

La Ngo 55 (A3), a small back street leading onto Hai Ba Trung, between Tho Nuom and the Hanoi Tower, is the perfect place to try a typical traditional breakfast of manioc rice noodle soup with cubes of duck's blood and/or a bowl of curdled duck's blood ("tiet canh vit"), sprinkled with ground peanuts and chopped basil with a touch of lime juice.

Bia Hoi Tong Dan (C3), next to the Revolutionary Museum. Packed at lunchtimes. Stay for a drink, try well-known Vietnamese dishes or be adventurous and try sow's udders or offal.

Lau De Hong Kong (C4), 9 Tran Hung Dao, near a petrol station. Beer goes down very well here and they serve superb dishes of water spinach and fish.

Bia Hoi (B-C3), 39 Tran Tien. Hidden behind an Art Deco façade, like a stage setting, is a beer hall the size of a hangar. Lunch is also served.

Between 25 000 and 50 000VND

Nang Tam Vegetarian Restaurant (A3-4), 79A Tran Hung Dao, ☎ (04) 826 61 40. Closed on Sundays. Vietnamese cuisine in Buddhist fashion with "to phu" and mushrooms instead of meat. Try the "tuyet hoa" balls, the stuffed cabbage "bap cai nhoi" or even the vegetarian spring rolls. The restaurant also serves chicken and pork dishes.

Between 50 000 and 100 000VND

Hanoi Gourmet (B4), 1 Ham Long, ☎ (04) 943 10 09. A wine bar atmosphere with a choice of quiches, sandwiches and pastries, with a tart or a yoghurt to follow.

Between 100 000 and 200 000VND

A Little Italian (A3), 81 Tho Nhuom, (Eden Hotel), ☎ (04) 825 81 67. International cuisine with an Italian flavour, including scallopine al limone, pizza Margherita, and local variations such as Thai chicken pizza with pieces of chicken marinated in a sweet and sour sauce, pasta à la carbonara and tiramisu.

Cay Cau (Plan II D4), 17A Tran Hung Dao, ☎ (04) 824 53 46. It serves as the restaurant for the hotel De Syloia and is situated in a stylish colonial residence. The menu is a compilation of Vietnamese recipes with a slight leaning towards traditional Hue and southern dishes. Opening hours give mealtimes a certain flexibility: 6-10am / 11.30am-2.30pm / 5.30-10.30pm / 11pm-5am.

Diva Café (C3), 57 Ly Thai To, ☎ (04) 934 40 88. Despite the name, it's more of a restaurant than a café. Mediterranean and Vietnamese cuisine (the first is better), in an attractive decor of warm Italian tones of ochre and green inside, pergola and plants outside. You can expect a pleasant evening in the company of a jazz band in this classy establishment, which is currently in vogue. An impressive wine list of French and Australian vintages.

Emperor (C4), 18B Le Thanh Tong, ☎ (04) 826 88 01. An idyllic setting in a colonial villa with an open courtyard and numerous reception rooms with interconnecting panelled passageways in the style of a former patrician home. An original menu combining Western ingredients with Eastern flavours.

Hoa Sua (A3), 81 Tho Nhuom, ☎ (04) 824 04 48. Delicious main courses and amazing desserts. Enjoy your meal under the shade of a parasol or bougainvillaea in the courtyard, or retire to the airy dining room of this former colonial villa. There is also an in-house bakery that sells the best bread and pastries in Hanoi. Hoa Sua was founded in 1995 to provide catering courses for Vietnamese street children.

Soho Deli (B4), 57 Ba Trieu, ☎ (04) 826 65 55. This elegant establishment offers a Vietnamese cuisine that has been slightly modified for Western tastes, as well as a take-away service. A lively atmosphere in the evenings.

Over 200 000VND

Au Délice (C3), 17 Tong Dan, ☎ (04) 934 53 28. Stock up on your supplies of French wine and cheeses, or even taste traditional French dishes such as kidneys in cream, tournedos or hot goat's cheese. Be sure to book.

Press Club (C3), 59A Ly Thai To, ☎ (04) 934 08 88. Chic lunches and dinners either inside, in a very 1930s atmosphere, or outside, on the terrace looking out over "little Paris" with live music every evening. Their excellent reputation lies with their choice of Mediterranean cuisine prepared by the New Zealand chef, and with their wine list, the best in Hanoi. The wines are cellared, presented and served according to the strictest oenological rules.

Sea Food Market (C3), 77 Doc Bac Co (level with the History Museum, near the riverside), ☎ (04) 825 07 80. Rather surrealist with bears in cages and the little mermaid from Copenhagen all together in an enormous warehouse. Fish tanks full of every possible sea creature are proof of the freshness of their wares. Pay by the kilo (1kg of prawns: 300 000VND).

• **The Lenin Park Area** (Plan II)

Under 25 000VND

Right in the middle of the student quarter, the street Mai Hac De (C4) has a series of stalls selling one single dish up until midnight. N° 47 sets the tone with a scowling cow's head – "pho bo" specialists.

• **The West Lake Area** (Plan II)

Under 25 000VND

Excellent lively little restaurants that serve "oc tom ca" (snails, prawns and fish) in Phu Tay Ho street (B1). For a change from the "banh tom" (prawns in batter) which can be a bit tasteless and disappointing, try the "ca qua nuong", grilled fish southern-style served in a rice pancake with green banana, pineapple, cucumber, aromatic herbs and rice noodles. Try the "oc hap la gung" as well, steamed snails Hanoi-style, stuffed with lemon grass.

Between 100 000 and 200 000VND

Seasons of Hanoi (C2), 95B Quanh Tanh, ☎ (04) 843 54 44. A variety of specialities from Hanoi, Hue, and Saigon, served in an old French villa furnished with colonial antique pieces.

Over 200 000VND

Ho Tay Floating House (B2), Thanh Nien, ☎ (04) 829 04 36. A floating restaurant on the West Lake with a menu specialising in fish and shellfish.

GOING OUT

Cafés

An obvious French legacy, the café is an institution ranging from a "ca phe den" (black coffee – 3 000VND) to a "stylish" coffee (an espresso at 15 000VND). The more traditional Hanoi cafés are open from 6am to 10pm, while the more exclusive are open till later.

• **The 36 Guilds and the Cathedral area** (Plan I)

Café Lam (B2), 60 Nguyen Huu Huan. Open daily 6am-10pm.

Café Nhan (B2), Bao Khanh. The café is always full come the evening, with the locals on the street and the foreigners upstairs.

Café Quynh (A2), 48 Bat Dan (at the end of the street). Photographers tend to hang out here.

Kem Fanny (B3), 48 Le Thai To, ☎ (04) 828 56 56. Situated on the edge of Lake Hoan Kiem, it is the perfect place to taste ice cream made from all the different Vietnamese fruits.

Café Kinh Do (A2), 252 Hang Bong, ☎ (04) 825 02 16. Open from 6am. Try breakfast here "à la française" with croissants served with a smile.

Lac Viet (B3), 46 Le Thai To (on the edge of the lake), ☎ (04) 828 91 55. Stay and browse in this English-speaking café-cum-library that grows with the volume of books donated.

Moca Cafe (A2), 14-16 Nha Tho, ☎ (04) 825 03 43. The most stylish expat café in Hanoi. A cup of coffee will cost you three times as much as anywhere else, but it always comes with a little biscuit. The food is not up to much but no effort is too great in order to be seen here, especially considering the café's own particular cachet of brick walls opening out onto the street.

Thuy Ta Café (B2), 1 Le Thai To, ☎ (04) 828 81 48. Classy, with a terrace overlooking the lake. Vietnamese coffee, espresso or cappuccino, pastries and ice creams.

• **Area of the former French concession** (Plan I)

Au Lac (C3), 57 Ly Thai To, ☎ (04) 825 78 07. A pretty villa serving tea or espressos on the terrace.

Ciao Café (B3), 2 Hang Bai, ☎ (04) 934 14 94. Open daily 7am-11pm. Try the pastries or reasonably-priced main dishes in this very fashionable Italian-style café, with green walls, hanging fuchsias and silver-painted chairs.

Dilmah Quan, 12 Hai Ba Trung. Running the length of the Pacific Airlines offices and shaded by awnings, the terrace is packed every afternoon with young people enjoying the spacey music while sipping Sri Lankan tea.

Café 84 (Plan II C4), 84 Nguyen Du. A student meeting-place.

• **The Lenin Park Area** (Plan II)

Cheer (C4), 69 Mai Hac De, ☎ (04) 978 25 16. A pretty little café with a small courtyard, roof-terrace and wrought-iron furniture in a young quarter.

Bars

The choice is wide, from the "bia hoi", where they serve beer freshly brewed the day before (2 000VND for 50cl), to the Bao Khanh bars that are open throughout the night attracting a particularly young cosmopolitan clientele, and finally, exclusive hotel bars.

Library Park (Plan I C3), 59A Ly Thai To, ☎ (04) 934 08 88. A very select Press Club bar. A prominent English style with wooden panelling and an amazing choice of whiskies. Browse through the newspapers provided, pick out a video and enjoy the happy hour every Friday evening.

GC Bar (Plan I B2), 5 Bao Khanh, ☎ (04) 825 04 99. A staggering choice of cocktails and an amazing variety of deafening music including percussion, house, hip-hop and techno acid jazz.

Polite Club (Plan I B2), 7 Bao Khanh. Competition for the GC above.

Thanh Nien (Plan I B2), Dinh Tien Hoang. Near the Jade Mountain Temple, go past the baggage shop and follow the music to the favourite meeting place of the young people of Hanoi.

Tien Thu Quan (Plan II C4), 55 Trieu Viet Vuong, ☎ (04) 943 16 06. Right in the middle of the student quarter in a beautiful 1900s bistro decor, this is the most surprising café in Hanoi. Displayed on the counter are rows of specimen jars containing spirits made from snakes, toads, lizards, even bears, unless of course they are out of stock.

Z Café (Plan I C3), 17 Tong Dan, ☎ (04) 934 28 98. A large billiard table in a classy jazz-club atmosphere. Occasional live concerts in the evenings.

OTHER THINGS TO DO

Nightclubs – Apocalypse Now, 5C Hoa Ma (Plan II C-D4), ☎ (04) 971 27 83. THE Hanoi disco, packed every evening from 5pm.

Bowling – Cosmos Bowling Centre, 8B Ngoc Khanh, ☎ (04) 831 86 68. **Hanoi Super Bowl**, Fortuna Hotel, 6B Lang Ha, ☎ (04) 831 33 33.

Cinema – Fansland, 84 Ly Thuong Kiet. Vietnamese films, and foreign films dubbed in Vietnamese. **Thang Tam**, 45 Hang Bai. A programme of popular English films.

Karaoke – Enjoy a quick sing-song in Ngo Huyen, near the cathedral. You pay by the hour (from 50 000 to 70 000VND).

Swimming pools – Some hotel pools are open to non-residents. **Army Hotel**, 33A Pham Ngu Lao, ☎ (04) 826 55 40, entrance fee: US$4. **Thang Loi**, Yen Phu

Tay Ho, ☎ (04) 829 42 11, entrance fee: 20 000VND. **Daewoo**, 360 Kim Ma, ☎ (04) 831 50 00, entrance fee: US$15. **Meritus Westlake**, 1 Thanh Nien, ☎ (04) 823 88 88, entrance fee: US$30, including access to the Fitness Club open daily 6.30am-10.30pm.

Tennis – Some hotels have courts to hire, such as the **Daewoo** (US$6 per hour), the **Thang Loi** (55 000VND per hour) and the **Hanoi Horison**, 40 Cat Linh, ☎ (04) 733 08 08 (US$4 per hour).

Jogging – As early as 6am, Hanoians begin their runs through the many parks of Hanoi. They would be happy for you to join them.

Concerts – Hanoi Opera House, 1 Trang Tien, ☎ (04) 993 01 13. Tickets from 80 000 to 120 000VND. **Hanoi National Opera**, 15 Nguyen Dinh Chieu, ☎ (04) 826 73 61. Concerts of traditional music every Monday, Wednesday and Friday at 8pm.

Water puppets – The traditional temple performance has evolved into a show in its own right and the Hanoi troupe has been on several world tours. The puppeteers are hidden behind the stage and move the puppets across the water with the help of long bamboo poles, all to live music provided by an accompanying band. Riveting stuff! **Thang Long Theatre**, 57B Dinh Tien Hoang, ☎ (04) 824 51 11. From Tuesday to Sunday at 8pm, closed on Mondays.

Central Puppet Theatre, 361 Truong Chinh, ☎ (04) 853 45 45. Performances at 7.45pm every Tuesday, Thursday, Saturday and Sunday.

Circus – Central Circus (Rap Xiec Trung Uong), at the northern entrance of the Lenin Park, ☎ (04) 822 02 77. Performances from Tuesday to Sunday at 8pm, Sundays at 9am.

SHOPPING

Shops open from 9am-6pm or 10am-7pm, but some tourist shops at Hang Gai close later.

Markets – The markets have lots of goods on offer: wheat, rice or manioc noodles, spices, crockery, and religious artefacts. There is a good choice at the Dong Xuan market, to the north of the old quarter, as well as the 19 December market.

Antiques – Do Nguyen Khoi, 45B Ly Quoc Su, ☎ (04) 828 55 71. The increasing rarity and price of each item on sale will not cease to amaze as you venture through the shop's various floors.

Crafts and decorative items – There are several very cheap bamboo and wicker shops on the corner of Tran Nhan Tong and Quang Trung, opposite Lenin Park.

Bamboo and Rattan Shop, 2 Ba Trieu, on the corner of lake Hoan Kiem, ☎ (04) 826 91 24. All kinds of wicker and bamboo from a "muong" basket to living-room furniture.

Craft Window, 6 Nha Chung, ☎ (04) 828 94 77. Watercolours and lacquer ware.

Deltadeco, 12 Nha Tho, ☎ (04) 828 96 16. An Italian designer using the experience of local craftsman. Wonderfully-crafted furniture and decorative articles.

Galerie L'Atelier, 6 Nha Tho, ☎ (04) 934 43 29. Ethnic fabrics plus lacquer ware and various other items using H'mong or Dao motifs in the popular surroundings of old-style Hanoi.

Hanoi Art Gallery, 93 Dinh Tien Hoang (entrance through Trang Tien). Sculpted wood and wood engravings.

Indochine House, 13 Nha Tho, ☎ (04) 824 80 71. Antique furniture and exquisite monochromes from Bac Trang displayed in a particularly bright house where the walls have been replaced by glass partitions.

La Boutique and the Silk, 6 Nha Tho, ☎ (04) 928 53 68. Lavish woven fabrics from Vietnam and neighbouring Laos. Everyone's budget is catered for from natural silk scarves at US$4-10 to silk stoles at US$24 and other attractive fabrics from the Thai in Laos at US$45. There is another shop at 10 Dinh Liet.

Lan Vietnamese Handicraft, 26 Au Trieu, ☎ (04) 828 92 78. Dolls, kilts and tablecloths made by young handicapped Vietnamese.

Minh Tam, 2 Hang Bong, ☎ (04) 828 99 07. Lacquered eggshells with original designs and black high-quality lacquer ware decorated with gold leaf, produced outside of Hanoi. From US$2 for coasters to US$30 for large trays.

Pan Flute, 42 Hang Bac, ☎ (04) 826 04 93.

Vietnamese Ethnic Minorities Cultural Products, 40 Hang Be, ☎ (04) 825 19 47. Handicrafts and traditional ethnic costumes.

Silk, embroidery and clothes – Duc Loi Silk Queen, 76 Hang Gai, ☎ (04) 826 87 58. Tablecloths, embroidered handkerchiefs and silk sleeping bags.

Hoa Sua, 63A Trang Thi, ☎ (04) 934 27 92. Attractive embroidered organdie, silk or cotton.

Ipa-Nima, 30B Nguyen Huu Huan, ☎ (04) 934 08 76. Outrageous embroidered or pearly handbags.

Khai Silk, 96 Hang Gai, ☎ (04) 825 42 37. The most exclusive of the silk clothes shops. Some linen and cotton. There is another shop at 121 Nguyen Thai Hoc.

Le Minh, 79-111 Hang Gai. A wide range of articles from simple T-shirts to jacket and trousers in natural silk.

Pinochio, 32 Hang Bong (near the intersection with Ly Quoc Su), ☎ (04) 928 51 85. Interesting variations on flip-flops with wooden soles.

Song, 7 Nha Tho, ☎ (04) 828 96 50. An attractive range of linen and cotton clothing, including delicately-embroidered household linen.

Tan My 109 Hang Gai, ☎ (04) 825 15 79. Just the place to buy tablecloths and embroidered cushions.

Supermarkets – For imported foodstuffs and health products. **Sieu Thi Intimex**, 32 Le Thai To. **Minimart**, 66 Ba Trieu. **Eurofood**, 65 Hang Trong.

Art galleries – From small gouaches, wood engravings and watercolours for next to nothing to contemporary creations at over US$1 000.

Apricot Gallery, 40B Hang Bong (next to Co Do, near the intersection with Tam Thuong), ☎ (04) 828 89 65. A very diverse display of exhibits at all prices.

Co Do Gallery, 46 Hang Bong, ☎ (04) 825 85 73. Work by abstract painters and lacquer artists in a tube house with courtyards recreated by contemporary artists.

Fine Art Association Exhibition House, 16 Ngo Quyen, ☎ (04) 824 18 45. An official gallery.

Mai Gallery, 3B Phan Huy Chu (in the Opera area), ☎ (04) 825 12 25. Opened by an art critic inside his own house.

Nam Son Gallery, 41 Trang Tien, ☎ (04) 826 29 93. This very old gallery is run by artists who organise various exhibitions from the more traditional to the out-of-the-ordinary.

Salon Natasha, 30 Hang Bong (at the intersection with Ly Quoc Su), ☎ (04) 826 13 87. Reputed to be the pioneer of private art galleries, it is also the most daring: art in its raw state, compressed and deformed objects by Vu Dan Tan.

Trang An Gallery, 15 Hang Buom, ☎ (04) 826 94 80. The gallery is located in one of the houses of the 36 Guilds and is managed by the painter Nguyen Xuan Thiep who organises exhibitions.

Bookshops – Photocopied books are very traditional in Hanoi, which means you can buy a large quantity of books quite cheaply. Check the quality of the photocopies nonetheless. They can be found around the Van Mieu area at the kiosk near the One Pillar Pagoda as well as in the small street of second-hand booksellers that starts near 61 Trang Tien.

Thang Long Bookshop, 55 Trang Tien, ☎ (04) 825 70 43. The biggest and the best bookshop in Hanoi.

Hanoi Bookstore, 34 Trang Tien, ☎ (04) 824 16 14. Foreign magazines.

Librairie vietnamienne francophone (Hieu Sach Viet Phap), 64 Trang Tien (close to the junction with Hang Bai) ☎ (04) 825 73 76. As well as French periodicals, this bookshop has a range of books on Vietnam in various languages.

AROUND HANOI★★
Provinces of Ha Tay, Bac Ninh, Hung Yen and Vinh Phuc

Not to be missed
The Perfume Pagoda during the annual pilgrimages.
The Tay Phuong and Tram Gian Pagodas in their rural setting.
The statues in the Thay and But Thap Pagodas.
And remember...
There are no buses, so hire a chauffeur-driven car for the day
or book an organised trip with one of the agencies in Hanoi.
Photographers take note, when the rice harvest takes place (mid-May and again in
mid-November) the Bac Bo plain turns into a vast expanse of bare earth.

The star-shaped pattern of the major roads (Highway 1, 2, 6 etc) leading out of Hanoi covers a vast area of shabby-looking market towns, all with frontages just within the legal length for tax purposes (4.5m). The old pagodas with their dazzling colours of purple and gold are located more on the side roads, to either side of which stretches out the countryside of Bac Do. You travel along the top of dikes built above a sea of rice strewn with washed-up tombstones, turned grey by the beating rain. Here and there, like a piece of stage scenery, the porch of a temple is outlined against the low sky, with its tomcat-like tigers, affable wrinkly-skinned elephants and spindly ridge-top dragons fighting over a pearl. On the river banks, brick kilns huddle together like the naves of ruined churches.

The Mountain of the Fragrant Traces★ (Huong Son)
59km to the southwest of Hanoi. Allow one day there and back.

According to legend, Dieu Tien, a Buddhist princess, chose this mountain retreat to atone for the sins of her cruel father. After a devout and bountiful life, she received spiritual enlightenment and was reincarnated as Quan Am, the compassionate bodhisattva (an individual who renounces nirvana to help humankind). This steep and rocky mountain range became the site of the most famous pilgrimage in the delta when in 1686, under the Le dynasty, the monk Huyen Quang set out to restore and extend the area. Since then, the holy voyage to the Mountain of the Fragrant Traces takes place every year during the first two lunar months (February-March or March-April). Temples, pagodas and chapels have sprung up over the centuries on the surrounding slopes and banks of the River Yen and the faithful pilgrims regard them with as much respect as the Perfume Pagoda, an enormous cavern where stalactites and stalagmites form natural candelabra and altars. Mystery and mysticism pervade this ageless site, home to the melancholy cries of the resident gibbons.

Leave Hanoi on the road to Ha Dong (6km), then turn left towards Van Dinh (25km). After Van Dinh, turn right towards Cho Dau (13km). 2km further on, look out for the sign "Chua Huong 10km" down a little road to the left. On leaving the village of Doc Tin, there will be an entrance fee of 33 000VND, including the boat (but not the boatwomen's tip that they will certainly insist on). The jetty and the car park are 1km away.

Along the River Yen
The 5km trip from the pier to the foot of the mountain involves a one-hour trip aboard a sampan, but according to the rules of the pilgrimage, a stop is scheduled at the **Temple of Presentations** (Den Trinh) to ask permission from the guardian spirit of the site to continue the voyage. Old ladies dressed in a nylon version of imperial dress lead the chanting of the prayers and organise the formalities of the ritual, which include walking up to the three altars, one after the other, and holding up a tray of votive offerings of cakes, fruit and coins. The god is concealed by a screen. At the end of this ritual, it is back into the boat for the prettiest part of the

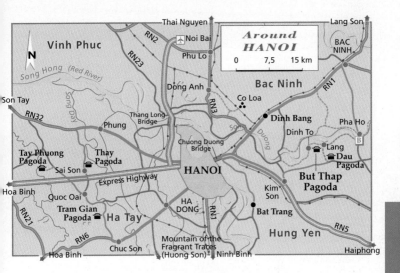

journey which follows the twists and turns of the river, at the foot of limestone peaks standing out against the horizon. The pilgrimage season lasts for two months, and during this period the procession of boats is constant. The passengers are mostly women dressed in black and brown, their hair tied back. Twenty or thirty of them huddle together in a tiny boat singing the praises of Quan Am. On arrival at the foot of the mountain, they make their way up the steep path that leads to the cavern.

The Mountain of the Fragrant Traces

Allow 2hr for the walk up the 2.5km-long path to the grotto. In the pilgrimage season, the route is lined with small stalls selling drinks, snacks and religious souvenirs. The path can get quite crowded during the two official months, and you should keep an eye on your purse, since pickpockets seem undeterred by the holiness of the site. Avoid wet periods when the path becomes muddy and dangerously slippery. You can always follow the locals' example and buy a sugar cane which serves as both a walking stick and source of refreshment.

The **Pagoda Leading to Heaven** (Chua Thien Tru) is one of the first stops. It was destroyed in 1947 and then rebuilt to house a stone **statue**, almost 3m high, of Quan Am. At the entrance, an enormous bronze tripod is set out for incense offerings, while several funerary pagodas stand in an adjacent garden. Every now and then, a little track leads off from the main pathway either to grottoes famous for their limestone concretions, or to small oratories such as **Tien Son Pagoda**, where Quan Am sits enthroned in the company of her sisters, **Giai Oan Pagoda** and **Cua Vong Temple**, a shrine to the goddess of the Mountain.

Pagoda of the Perfumed Vestige (Chua Huong Tich)

Once at the top, go through a **portico** bearing the title of "First Grotto under the Southern Skies", so named by a Trinh nobleman in 1770. One hundred and twenty steps lead into the dark cavern, a petrified refuge of haunting rock formations. One of them, named **Mt Thieu Nhi**, seems to shelter sculptures of children in its stone folds, which are traditionally fondled by women hoping to become pregnant. Each crack and crevice is home to a statue or an altar. A bluish light pervades the whole interior making the smoke from the joss sticks almost tangible.

Allow 1hr for the walk down, then another hour for the boat trip back to the starting point. With motorised transport, you can reach Ninh Binh via Phu Ly (see page 163).

The Pagodas to the West

95km tour leaving from Hanoi. Allow at least half a day.

The following itinerary forms a loop starting from Hanoi. You can also visit the Thay and Tay Phuong Pagodas on the road to Mai Chau (see page 190), taking the new expressway between Highway 32 and Highway 6. The first road is marked off to the right, 25km from Hanoi, and the second one, 27km out of Hanoi, is also to the right.

Leave Hanoi on the Son Tay road (Highway 32). Once past the village of Phung, you will notice a dam on the right built during the colonial period on the Song Day (River Day), an important tributary of the Red River. 36km out of Hanoi, turn left at the sign "Son Tay 15km". A dike track leads to the first pagoda 7km further on in the village of Sai Son.

■ **Thay Pagoda**★★ (The Master's Pagoda) – *Open daily 8am-5pm. Entrance fee.* A craggy mountain reflected in the water, several religious institutions and a cave shrine make up this miniature version of the Mountain of the Fragrant Traces, the only difference being the boat trip. The site is entirely dedicated to the bonze magician **Tu Dao Hanh**, a well-known monk in Ly Nhan Tong's reign (1072-1128). He was born near Hanoi and accepted the faith on this hill. After becoming a monk, he was taken in by a Prince of the Royal Family desperate for a child. He promised the prince a son who would be his "reincarnation". The prophecy came true and the child reigned from 1128 to 1138 under the title of Ly Than Tong.

The Heavenly Blessing Pagoda (Chua Thien Phuc), more commonly known as the Master's Pagoda, is situated at the foot of the mountain. Founded in the 11C and restored in the 15C, the pagoda consists of three long parallel rooms built out of wood, set on a high terrace of blue-coloured schist and surrounded by galleries where pilgrims can rest. The small courtyards decorated with potted plants are swept each day by nuns in brown habits. The visit begins with a shrine to Tu Dao Hanh and his reincarnation. In front of the central altar, where the Buddha Amitabha and two bodhisattva are positioned, sits a statue of the Master, wrapped in yellow monastic robes and wearing a tiara in the shape of the sacred lotus. The supporting stone pedestal is delicately sculpted with a lion carrying a lotus flower. To the right is a second altar devoted to the tablet of Tu Dao Hanh's reincarnation, King Ly Than Tong. The visit continues with rooms devoted to offerings and to the worship of Buddha.

The temple is bordered by **Dragon Lake** (Long Chieu / Tri), with two small covered bridges that shelter incense sellers. The pavilion in the centre of the lake was once used for water puppet shows. A rugged little path leads up the hillside *(the paving is slippery in the wet)*. At the top, 100m above the valley, it emerges into a small naturally-formed rocky opening with a wonderful panoramic view over the Song Day. A pavilion housing a modern statue of Quan Am marks the site of the **Cao Dai Temple**, where Tu Dao Hanh accepted the faith. The path carries on across the hill down to the **Cac Co Cave**, a deep dark hideaway favoured by lovers during the site's festivities on the 7th of the third lunar month. A pathway lined with old trees leads up to the **Upper Temple** and the **Cave of the Wind**, a rocky corridor that attracts all the surrounding air currents. From the Upper Temple, take the west route down towards the **One-roof Pagoda** (Chua Mot Mai), so named, contrary to custom, because the roof has only a single slope backing onto the hill.

Leave the village of Sai Son southwards as far as the intersection with the new expressway from Hao Binh (after 3km). Turn right, then after 2km turn right again in the direction of Son Tay. The entrance to the Tay Phuong Pagoda, hidden from the road, is 4km further on.

Boatwomen on the banks of the Song Yen

C Boisvieux/HOA QUI

■ **The Tay Phuong Pagoda**** – *Entrance fee*. Two hundred and thirty five steps lead up to this architecturally-impressive 18C pagoda. It consists of three massive chambers, their brick walls pierced by bulls-eye windows and supporting boldly curving roof structures surmounted by dragons. The roofing is a clear testimony to the genius of decorative Vietnamese sculpture, but the pagoda is more famous for the lacquered wooden statues*** decorating its altars, each one worked in an expressive realist style. The first room houses an impressive detachment of guardian warriors, brandishing their weapons in a rather suggestive manner. In the centre, Quan Am, complete with her thousand arms, is surrounded by her graceful maids. In the second room, an ascetic Buddha is portrayed as a stooping, middle-aged man in the midst of a group of disciples dressed in brown robes and officials holding their stone tablets. The third room's main display is a group of three Buddhas, preceded by the **Eight Judges of the Underworld**. All around the room stand the **Sixteen Patriarchs***** scratching themselves, laughing and waving their arms about, engrossed in a never-ending conversation. *There is an alternative way back leading down past other newly rebuilt pagodas, then across the village of Yen and back to the starting point round the bottom of the hill.*

Back on the Hoa Binh road, keep on for another 6km before turning left towards Chuc Son and Ha Dong. After 2km, a very poor track goes through the village of Tien Phuong. The pagoda is on a hill 3km further on.

■ **The Tram Gian Pagoda*** (The Pagoda of a 100 Rooms) – *Entrance fee*. Flights of steps wind around this low-lying hill planted with old trees, where the Bell Tower, the Stele Pavilion and the temple itself appear all harmoniously set in their surroundings. Under solid-looking roofs, the large gloomy rooms have been repopulated with a modern pantheon barely visible in the half-light. The Buddhist virtues of asceticism and abnegation are quite evident. Founded at the beginning of the 13C, the group of buildings was altered and restored on several occasions. Its present appearance dates from the end of the 18C.

Go back through Tien Phuong, then return to Hanoi on Highway 6 via Chuc Son and Ha Dong.

Along the Song Duong (Rapids Canal)
99km tour starting from Hanoi. Allow half a day.

Leave Hanoi on the Bac Ninh-Lang road (Highway 1A) crossing the Red River on the Chuong Duong Bridge. Dinh Bang is 18km northwest of Hanoi. The two temples can be reached by a path leading off to the right on the outskirts of the village.

■ **Dinh Bang**** – *Open daily 8am-5pm. Entrance fee*. This village holds a wealth of interest, and as the cradle of the Ly lineage (1009-1225), it is home to the dynastic temple, the Den Do, as well as a *dinh* (Communal House) called the Dong Khang Dinh, financed by the Dinh Bang commune in the mid-18C, and featuring some wonderfully decorative wooden sculptures.

Surrounded by pools, the **Dong Khang Dinh**** shrine stands on a schist terrace. The **roof**** alone is a spectacular piece of carpentry, taking up two thirds of the overall height of the temple and resting on sixty columns of hardwood. The coffered ceiling incorporates traceries of flowers, dragons and other Chinese chimera sculpted in various precious woods. The altars at each end, dedicated to the tutelary deities of Dinh Bang (the spirits of the Earth, Agriculture and Water), are raised up on stilts in contrast to the other *dinh* in the delta, which are built on terraces and columns in Chinese style. This design is clear evidence of the traditional origins behind the inspiration for this 18C building. Before leaving Hanoi in 1954, the French tried to destroy the temple by pulling at the stilts with chains, but the pride and joy of Dinh Bang held fast. The *dinh* festival, which includes performances of traditional opera, is held every year on the 12th day of the second lunar month.

Five hundred metres away is the **Den Do**, which unfortunately did not stand up to the ravages of the Indochina war. It was destroyed in 1950 and then rebuilt in 1990 to perpetuate the cult of the fourth national dynasty. The festivities held every year in its honour on the 15th day of the third lunar month are quite remarkable. Vietnamese from all over the delta gather together to portray society during the period of the royal courts in an enormous procession across the rice fields.

Carry on as far as Bac Ninh (27km from Hanoi), then turn right at the first crossroads to Pha Ho (14km) from where the ferry crosses the Rapids Canal (Song Duong). Once on the other side, follow signs to Dinh To along a dike track and go through the village of Lang.

■ **The But Thap Pagoda***** (The Writing Brush Pagoda) – *Open daily 8am-5pm. Entrance fee.* Access to this 17C pagoda, built on an area of raised ground in the middle of the rice plantations, is through the Bell Tower guarded by enamelled earthenware warriors. The **statues in lacquered wood***** arranged on the altars of the main room are masterpieces of Vietnamese art. To the right of a trinity of Buddhas, **Quan Am, the thousand-armed goddess** emerges from the waves, seated on a lotus flower held by a dragon. This important piece was the work of an artist by the name of Truong in 1656. To the left, an **ascetic Buddha** is meditating, his face leaning on his raised knee.

To the rear, a small stone bridge leads to a many-storeyed pavilion built around a revolving carved wooden **tower**. This is made up of panels illustrating the life of Buddha with scenes of sermons and gatherings of holy people.

In an adjacent courtyard is the structure that gave rise to the popular name for the pagoda. It is a **funerary pagoda**, built in 1646 by order of one of the queens from the Trinh dynasty in honour of the monk Chuyet Chuyet. Its stone pedestal is decorated with sophisticated **bas-reliefs of animals****: there are monkeys trying to dislodge a bird's nest, a couple of lions playing with a ball, and crabs and carp splashing in the waves.

Go back through the village of Lang and look out for "Chua Dau" signposted to the right. The pagoda is located in the village of Thanh Khuong, 54km from Hanoi.

■ **The Dau Pagoda*** – The Dau region was one of the earliest parts of Vietnam to be influenced by Buddhism. Due to its real name of Phap Van ("Dharma Cloud"), the pagoda is thought to have been founded at the beginning of the Christian era and visited by a number of Indian missionaries. In the late 6C, a monk originally from China established the Dhyana sect here. The edifice was entirely rebuilt in the 14C and the main room still displays wooden sculptures from the Tran and Le dynasties. In the courtyard stands an impressive brick **tower** where the bronze gong and bell hang, guarded by four statues of gods from the Orient. The main altar is dedicated to the Lady from the Dharma Cloud, in the company of two other goddesses, the Lady from the Dharma Rain and the Lady from the Dharma Light. These three red lacquer statues date back to the 18C. Young girls in long-tailed tunics and traditional turbans wait on these female Buddhist deities.

Go back towards Hanoi via Kim Son (7km) to pick up Highway 5. Just before reaching the Chuong Duong Bridge, turn off to the left. Bat Trang is about 8km from the centre of Hanoi.

■ **Bat Trang** – This village has specialised in **ceramics**, particularly the "blue and white", for generations *(see page 82)*. The manufacturing techniques in the local workshops make for an interesting visit, and the finished products are on sale in the numerous local shops.

THE DELTA TRIANGLE
TOURS AROUND NINH BINH
Provinces of Ha Tay, Ha Nam, Nam Dinh, Ninh Binh and Thai Binh
Map pages 124-125

Not to be missed
The dynastic temples at Hoa Lu.
Phat Diem Cathedral.
Keo Pagoda.
The little country temples at Tam Coc.

And remember...
Ninh Binh is a perfect stopover for independent travellers.
A word of warning – temperatures in July and August can reach more than 40°C.

The first independent state to free itself of Chinese domination, Dai Co Viet, was born in the delta of the Song Thai Binh and the Song Day, tributaries of the Red River. Surprisingly enough, the capital Hoa Lu was founded amidst a region of limestone hills and peaks with mysteriously disappearing rivers, far from the ordered layout of the future royal towns of Hanoi and Hue. Nothing now remains of the capital's palaces, lined with gold and covered with silver tiles. Everything was moved with great pomp and circumstance to Thang Long, the future Hanoi, at the head of the delta. Nonetheless, for those interested in history or the Viet's long search for independence, the extraordinary landscape of this region, renamed "inland Halong Bay", still retains a definite charm. Around Ninh Binh, which has become the region's central point, you will enjoy visiting the cradle of the great national dynasties near Nam Dinh, tasting the atmosphere of the Vietnamese Rome on the road to Phat Diem, or exploring the hills and caves at Tam Coc and the national park of Cuc Phuong.

The first steps of a new state
The independent kingdom formed by Ngo Quyen after his victory against the Chinese in 938 (*see page 20*) soon collapsed following the rebellions sparked off by the lords of the delta and the Middle Kingdom. One of these lords chose a brave young man by the name of **Bo Linh** to be his successor. One by one, in true warrior fashion, the rebellious lords were brought to heel, and Bo Linh proclaimed himself **Dinh Tien Hoang De**, "First Noble Emperor of the Dinh", and in 968 established the capital of his empire, **Dai Co Viet**, in his native town of Hoa Lu. By recognising Chinese suzerainty, he was able to ensure peaceful relations at the borders, but an unfortunate twist of fate was to lead to the assassination of this instigator of the first Vietnamese state in 979, leaving a successor of only six years of age. His wife, **Duong Van Nga**, acted as regent, backed by Commander **Le Hoan**. The young state was in an extremely unstable condition; it needed to keep its vassals in line, hold the Chinese at bay in its border areas, and ward off the Chams to the south. In 980, growing tension led Duong Van Nga to offer the crown to Le Hoan; with the title of **Le Dai Hanh**, the new ruler went on to triumph on all fronts. The **Early Le** dynasty was born, but it was to be just as short-lived as that of the former Dinh reign. After the death of Le Dai Hanh in 1005, his sons tore each other apart in their fight for power. Intervention from the leading dignitaries put an end to the disputes with the enthroning of one of their men, the mandarin Ly Cong Van. He became King **Ly Thai To** (1009-28) bringing with him a period of stability that would last for almost four hundred years.

From Hanoi to Ninh Binh

95km tour. Allow 2hr30min not including stops.
For buses and trains for Ninh Binh, see page 168

Leave Hanoi on Highway 1. About 15km further on, the first signs for *banh day* start to appear in the shop windows. A speciality of Quan Guanh, these cakes of rice and bean paste wrapped in leaves form piles of little green packets. Christian cemeteries and tombstones, often set around the empty shell of a church in the middle of a rice plantation, are the first indications of the region's evangelisation.

Phu Xuyen *(36 km from Hanoi)* marks the beginning of the entrance to the delta. The whole landscape is divided up by the waters of the Red River and its tributaries, as well as by canals, and fishing goes on everywhere. Consequently, the approach to the area is marked by stalls selling fishing nets and other similar material.

5km beyond the village of Dong Van (45km from Hanoi), there is a sign to the caves of Ngo Dong off to the right, 5km further on.

■ **Ngo Dong** – A series of caverns and sinkholes appears at intervals throughout this limestone area. The "Five Caves" form a 100m-long tunnel down through the Thi Son, a limestone reef forming part of the Mountain of the Fragrant Traces complex, though the mountain itself is a good 7km away as the crow flies, back up the Song Day *(see page 156)*.

Head back to Highway 1 and carry on in the direction of Ninh Binh.

Fifty-six kilometres from Hanoi, **Phu Ly**, the capital of the former province of Ha Nam, was wiped off the map by American bombing, but subsequent years of *Doi Moi* (programme of economic reform) have produced an array of brand new buildings. The Song Day can be crossed here, while far away to the west is the outline of the Trong Son range. Limestone peaks soon close in on the highway.

On reaching Cau Huyen, 89km from Hanoi, turn right in the direction of Trung Yen. 5km further on there is a sign indicating "Co Do Hoa Lu 1 700m".

■ **Hoa Lu★** – *Open daily 8am-5pm. Entrance fee and parking charge. Sale of drinks and souvenirs. Allow 1hr.* Only a few ruins remain of the citadel at Hoa Lu, the centre of power for just 42 years. Yet the memory of these early days of the Dai Co Viet still lingers on in the half-light inside the splendid **dynastic temples**, built in remembrance of these kings. Their sober appearance more disconcerting than any ostentatious quality, these *den* (small places of worship) were constructed after the capital had moved to Hanoi and then restored under the Nguyen. The lane leading off the car park will take you to the first temple, the **Den Dinh★★**, devoted to Emperor **Dinh Tien Hoang**. The temple, with its heavy-looking roof, closes off the third and last courtyard. The wooden columns sit on octagonal stone bases sculpted with flowers and birds in bas-reliefs. Take a giant's stride through the doorway and look up and admire the decorative dragons frolicking in the clouds above. Inside, surrounded by arms and processional banners, the altar of the Royal Bonnet is bathed in a faded purple and gold light. Columns and beams show signs of their former lacquered ornamentation. An intricately decorated latticed screen of birds and dragons soaring through the clouds obscures the back room, which houses a collection of lacquered statues. Dinh Tien Hoang, wearing a crown encrusted with two rows of pearls, is accompanied by his sons in court clothes. Visiting Vietnamese tourists can perhaps be likened to pilgrims, since they never fail to present offerings of incense, biscuits and silver to their very first rulers. A number of photos and items from the site's excavations are displayed in the adjacent pavilions. Enjoy a view of the whole site after a climb up the steps leading to the top of **Mt Ma Yen**. **Dinh Tien Hoang** was laid to rest here in the royal sepulchre, the oldest of its kind in the whole of Vietnam. In complete contrast to Chinese funerary practices adopted for the Imperial tombs at Hue, there is just a simple burial mound with an adjacent altar.

Fifty metres north of Den Dinh, the **Den Le***, dedicated to **Le Danh Hanh**, has a somewhat less formal layout. Every available recess and side path forms part of a kitchen garden, brightened by hibiscus and climbing roses. At the end of a side passage, an unsightly old barn has been built over the pitiful remains of the Dinh **Tien Hoang Palace**, discovered in 1998; it consists of some paving, a section of a wall and a few items of ornamental pottery. The dynastic temple follows the same layout as that of the Dinh except that Duong Van Nga is seated next to Le Danh Hanh in the throne room.

The neighbouring village of Hoa Lu, 100m to the north of the temple of Le Danh Hanh, is bordered by a small brook where a few ducks (and plastic bags) splash about, and over which stands a humpback bridge. The quaint little **Nha Tro Pagoda** features a small protective wall that today screens off an area for a kindergarten.

Images of nautical jousts organised by the Dai Co Viet rulers may come to mind if you take a boat trip along the **River Sao Khe** to the east. Along its banks are a number of attractions such as the Xuyen Thuy Cave, Mt Hom Sach and the Lien Hoa Cave (*make enquiries at the car park*).

Return to Highway 1 and continue to Ninh Binh.

■ **Ninh Binh** – The town's only real attractions are its accommodation and the willingness of its hoteliers to help you organise your trips around the area. There is, however, a large daily riverside **market**, and a small pagoda nestling under the **Ninh Binh rock** also has a certain charm.

From Ninh Binh to Mai Chau
149km tour. Allow half a day not including stops.

Take Highway 1 in the direction of Hanoi. 12km north of Ninh Binh, take Highway 477 to the left leading to the Cuc Phuong park (23km). Gia Vien is 10km further on.

■ **Gia Vien** is a new excursion organised by the Ninh Binh agencies to ease tourist congestion at Tam Coc. The 3hr-trip in little covered boats starts off near Me for a tour of another "inland Halong Bay". The karst landscape is not as impressive as around Tam Coc, but the life of these rural dwellers, like the inhabitants of the village of Ken Ga, is far more lake-orientated.

■ **Cuc Phuong National Park** – *Access to the park via Nho Quan. Entrance fee. Guided hikes can be organised at the entrance to the park. The best period to visit is from October to January.* This protected area of 25 000ha lies in a valley set deep in the karst landscape. Cuc Phuong National Park was created in 1962 and is the last surviving primeval tropical forest, home to 2 000 varieties of plants and 250 species of animals, mammals, birds and reptiles. A number of species that were thought to have disappeared in the region are protected here, such as foxes or langurs that you can even "adopt" for US$250 a year. The enjoyable hike under the cover of the forest is coupled with a visit to the Muong villages in the park.

Carry on down Highway N477 as far as Mai Chau (see page 190).

The Rome of Bac Bo
30km tour leaving from Ninh Binh. Allow 3hr round trip.

Leave Ninh Binh in the direction of Kim Son to the southeast.

There is not one village along this route that cannot boast a neo-Gothic basilica or a red and white colonial-style church. Yet water clearly remains the mainstay of this region so close to the estuary and the coast with its complex network of canals and humpback bridges. Everywhere in this watery landscape there are boats, some fitted with a bamboo pole for plaice fishing, others with oars propelled by the boatman's feet.

■ Fifteen kilometres from Ninh Binh, **Phu Nhac** used to be the headquarters of a junior seminary. It is a rather odd place, and today the site of three large **basilicas**. A positive step towards ecumenicism was the reopening of the old *dinh* on the outskirts of the village.

■ **Phat Diem Cathedral**✶✶ (Nha Tho Phat Diem) − *28km from Ninh Binh, on the edge of the village of Kim Son. Services at 5am and 5pm.* Tonkin's famous cathedral was built between 1875 and 1899 by Father Tran Luoc ("Father Six") who was inspired by the architecture of the pagodas and *dinh* of the Tonkin region. Apart from being a symbol of Christianity, it is also a magisterial example of Vietnamese architecture of the Hue Era. Perfectly intact, this impressive building is more imposing than the remains of the capital of Annam that survived the Tet Offensive. The entrance area, where a gong sounds every hour, is reminiscent of Imperial architecture. The church **doorway** is sculpted with a surprising mixture of Vietnamese symbols of good omen, angels, saints, and scenes from the Life of Christ. Over the porch, mischievous cherubs peek round ornamental flowers. The **nave**, whose timber roof is supported by columns of ironwood *(lim)*, is 80m long. The wooden sculpture is quite remarkable, with dragons wound around the carved beams, and a large red and gold lacquered altarpiece with a Virgin and Child. The wooden partitions of the aisles are quite unique in that they are removable, giving more room at busy times. On the northern side of the basilica, the **Chapel of the Sacred Heart**, which

Phat Diem Cathedral

G de Benoist/MICHELIN

enabled Father Six to test his theories on a smaller scale, features equally impressive wood carvings. Finally, the **Lourdes grotto** was entirely reconstructed in the cathedral chevet. At the time of Mass, women come in pairs to pray, mothers and daughters dressed in their most beautiful *ao dai* (traditional costume).

From Ninh Binh to Haiphong

150km tour. Allow half a day.

Leave Ninh Binh northeastwards on Highway 10, crossing the river on a single-lane bridge with alternating priority.

Three kilometres from Ninh Binh is **Cat Dang**, the first in a series of villages which specialise in the manufacture of wooden temple furniture. Lorry-loads of enormous logs arrive from Nghe Anh or Thanh Hoa.

■ **Nam Dinh** – *On leaving Nam Dinh to the north (31km from Ninh Binh), Thai Binh is signposted to the right, but follow signs to "Den Tran 6km" as far as the village of Loc Vuong.* The area around Nam Dinh was the birthplace of the royal **Tran** family (1226-1400) who had several palaces built here, all of which are now long gone. **Den Tran** stands among rice plantations. This dynastic temple has recently been stylishly refurbished and contains a small **museum** devoted to the victories of Tran Hung Dao against the attempts by the Mongols to invade in the 13C *(see insert page 171)*. **Pho Minh Pagoda***, 300m to the west of the *den*, used to stand within the grounds of one of the Tran palaces. Several of its bricks are marked 1305, obviously the year of its construction. Built on a small embankment decorated with lotus flowers in front of two moon-shaped pools, the same pavilion-like structure with four doors and a canopy is repeated over the thirteen floors. At the back, the rooms of the Buddhist temple have been repainted in red and gold and restocked with statues. Among them, look out for the figures of three Buddhist patriarchs, who were influential members of the Tran Court.

Head back to Nam Dinh and take Highway 10 in the direction of Thai Binh. After 5km, take the Tan De ferry across the Song Hong, quite close to the river mouth. 8km further on, turn off to the right towards Chua Keo, which is very well signposted. The pagoda is another 12km beyond the village of Vu Tien. From Nam Dinh you can also reach Hanoi via Phu Ly (87km).

■ **Keo Pagoda**** (Chua Keo) – Resembling a Japanese temple, this is a simple, substantial, rustic pagoda set in the middle of the countryside. The entrance is reached after a wide detour around a vast, fish-stocked ornamental lake where the women of the village come to do their washing. The generosity of one of the ladies of the court led to the construction of the buildings in the 17C. The main room is T-shaped and its heavy roof structure rests on corbels intertwined with dragons. The whole of the rear of the building forms a cloister off which are a number of quiet rooms. The impressive wooden **bell tower** is another attractive feature. Go up and ring the three bronze bells that hang at three different levels, and at the same time, admire the view over the sea of grey tiles of the pagoda roof tops.

Go back to Highway 10 and head towards Thai Binh (16km from Nam Dinh and 107km from Hanoi). After crossing the rivers Tra Ly, Thai Binh and Van Huc, you reach Haiphong (83km from Nam Dinh). See page 171.

Halong Bay without the water
8km tour. Allow half a day.

Leave Ninh Binh southwards on Highway 1. 3km further on, turn right towards Bich Dong, then carry on for another 5km as far as the quayside at Van Lam.

■ **Tam Coc**★★ – *A boat trip leaving from the quayside at Van Lam. Allow 3hr round trip.* The site at Tam Coc ("Three Caves"), which strangely enough bears a Chinese name, combines peaks, caverns and river formations. As with the well-known Halong Bay, the trip to Tam Coc is by boat. The meanders of the River Ngo Dong flow past vast mounds and various sinkholes for over 3km. The only downside are the tourist detours made by the boatwomen whom the local authorities seem unable to control. This strange, even fantastic landscape can be enjoyed just as much in the course of a walk, made all the more interesting by the presence of a number of temples. **Cac Dinh**★, the communal house in the village of Van Lam, near the landing stage, sets the tone with its imposing roof structure sculpted with dragons. The surroundings of Tam Coc are a delight; pathways run along the embankments between the rice-fields, goats gamble among the rocks, and tiny white-washed houses are tucked away in crevices.

Halong Bay without the water

P de Franqueville/MICHELIN

The Delta triangle

The embroiderers of the delta

In Hoa Lu or Tam Coc, those with a liking for needlework will be in their element, whereas others will probably just be rather annoyed at being harassed by a horde of insistent women. Keep your cool and take a look at their efforts because some are real works of art at very reasonable prices. In Tam Coc, business has unfortunately turned into racketeering, and the money-grabbing boatwomen are quite ruthless. While posing a problem, this nonetheless illustrates a genuine economic quandary. Tourism for the rural Vietnamese is manna from Heaven. But even though there are a lot of visitors, they do not represent enough trade for the tourist administration to be able to employ all the women every day; in fact, no individual is allowed to work for more than two days a month. Hence their relentless determination during the only two days when they can make any money. Should any sticky situation arise, contact the tourist police in the "dinh" at Van Lam.

About 700m along the only path leading to the northwest of Van Lam, you will come to the **Tran Vi Den***, its doors guarded by two stone horses. The temple has been partially rebuilt and its wooden **bell tower** stands out against a fine example of a limestone cirque. Inside, two cranes perched on tortoises keep watch over the **tablet of Tran Vi**, a descendant of King Tran Thai Ton whose statue, along with those of his son and his wife, is displayed in the little room at the back.

Three kilometres to the east of Van Lam, **Bich Dong***, the "Jade Cave", is a temple devoted to a great Buddhist triad, built half above ground, half below (*entrance fee*).

Carry on in a southerly direction to reach Thanh Hoa (57km from Ninh Binh), stretching across the last great plain of Bac Bo. Once past Vinh (138km), Vietnamese territory is reduced to a thin strip as the Hoanh Son mountain range reaches the sea.

Ninh Binh and its surroundings close up

COMING AND GOING

By bus – The **bus station** lies south of Ninh Binh near the junction of the roads from Thanh Hoa and Kim Son. There are regular services to Hanoi-Giap Bat (2hr) and a bus every morning at 5.50am to Haiphong (4hr). For **Open Tour** travellers, the Toserco buses stop off at the Hoa Lu and Thuy Anh Hotels.

By train – Ninh Binh **station** is on the east bank. Trains travelling between Hanoi (3hr) and Hue (15hr) stop here.

ADDRESS BOOK

Bank / Currency exchange – **Vietcombank**, Luong Van Tuy (to the right on the way into Ninh Binh from the north), ☎ (030) 87 26 14.

Post office / Telephone – **Buu Dien Ninh Binh**, in the southern part of the town.

Internet – Internet Access at the **Star Hotel**, opposite Thuy Anh.

Travel agencies – Travellers coming from the South can choose from a number of trips by chauffeur-driven car available from the mini-hotels in Ninh Binh, sometimes at an even better rate than in Hanoi. For example, a 7-day tour of Ninh Binh – Mai Chau – Son La – Dien Bien Phu – Lai Chau – Sa Pa – Hanoi, works out at US$400 for 2 people.

WHERE TO STAY

• **In Ninh Binh**

Under US$10

Thanh Thuy, 128 Le Hong Phong (in the western quarter), ☎ (030) 87 18 11 – 9rm 🛏️📺🌂✕ A little bit noisy during the day and some of the bathrooms are tiny, but the owner deserves the prize for the best hospitality and will bend over backwards to help.

Between US$10 and US$15

Queen Mini Hotel, 21 Hoang Hoa Tham (in the same road as the station),

☎ (030) 87 18 74 – 6rm ⌁ ▤ ⊼ A simple, little hotel with clean, well-kept rooms. The manager is an English teacher and will help organise your trips round the area. There is a lot of useful information in the visitor's book.

Thuy Anh, 55A Truong Han Sieu, ☎ and Fax (030) 87 16 02 – 12rm ⌁ ▤ ⊼ ♪ [TV] ✗

An impeccable place with rooms for all budgets. The better rooms are ideal. Some rooms may have no windows, but the shared bathrooms are kept very clean. It is impossible to fault the level of comfort and value for money, but what a pity the wonderful cuisine should be served in such a smoky restaurant!

Between US$15 and US$30

Hoa Lu Hotel, to the north of Ninh Binh, on Highway 1, ☎ (030) 87 36 84, Fax (030) 87 41 26 – 100rm ⌁ ▤ ⊼ ♪ [TV] ✗ A government-run hotel with very respectable rooms, but the decor is rather dreary. In the modern wing, you can enjoy every available facility at a good price (bath and satellite TV), since only the quality of the furniture affects the rates.

• **In Tam Coc**

Between US$10 and US$15

Tam Coc Hotel, on the riverbank 100m from the landing stage, ☎ (030) 86 10 29, Fax (030) 86 06 26 – 10rm ⌁ ▤ ⊼ ♪ [TV] ✗ The building is quite ordinary, but has nice little touches. Enjoy the atmosphere at first light (a 6am start to the day is guaran-

teed thanks to the piped national radio), or in the evening when the last visitors have left. The rooms are simple and very spacious. The helpfulness of the staff belies the usual reputation of government-owned establishments.

• **In Cuc Phuong**

This is a day trip from Ninh Binh or from Hanoi, but the park administration has rustic accommodation at the entrance (US$10), or, with more amenities, in chalets inside the national park (US$40). Information on site, ☎ (030) 86 60 85, or bookings from Hanoi, 1/13 Tan A, ☎ (04) 86 10 29. The agencies in Hanoi and Ninh Binh can also arrange accommodation in the Muong villages.

Eating out

• **In Ninh Binh**

Under 25 000VND

Hoa Lu Hotel, to the north of Ninh Binh, on Highway 1. The food is decent, but the restaurant is quite uninviting.

Thanh Thuy, 128 Le Hong Phong. A varied menu and several specialities, such as goat meat and snails.

• **In Tam Coc**

Under 25 000VND

The restaurants near the landing stage serve decent meals.

Shopping

The village of **Kim Son** is known for its bamboo basket ware, which is sold near Phat Diem Cathedral.

THE GULF OF TONKIN★★★
HAIPHONG – CAT BA – HALONG
Provinces of Haiphong and Quang Ninh – Map page 173

Not to be missed
A night at sea in Halong Bay.
Trekking in Cat Ba National Park.
And remember...
Stay at Cat Ba rather than Halong City to explore the Bay.
Avoid travelling between February and April, when it is cold (10-15°C), wet and foggy,
as well as during the busy periods, which are July in the Bay,
and the weekend at Cat Ba.

Halong Bay is a traveller's paradise and a tourist eldorado for Vietnam. This is still true if you are willing to turn a blind eye to the transformation of the coastal region into a replica of the Costa Brava. It wasn't that long ago that getting as far as the Bay was an expedition in itself, involving lengthy travel through the water-bound terrain of the Red River basin, passing beneath narrow girder bridges aboard rusty ferry boats. Today, the expressway takes you straight through the rice plantations to the landing place in Halong City in a matter of just three hours. However, there is another

HAIPHONG

0   250   500 m

N

HOTELS
Hoa Binh Hotel..........①
Hôtel du Commerce.②
Huong Sen Hotel......③
Huu Nghi Hotel........④
Navy Guesthouse......⑤
Royal Garden
Harbour View Hotel.⑥
Orient Hotel............⑦
Sunflower................⑧
Thang Nam..............⑨
The Tray Hotel..........⑩

The Red River Delta

Cua Cam

Port Installations

Binh
Landing Stage

Phan Dinh Phung

Hanoi

Bach   Dang

History
Museum

Market

Municipal
Theatre

Sat
Market

Tam Bac

Du Hang
Pagoda

Dinh Hang
Kenh

Station

Mam Tom
Lake

Former Racecourse

Lach Tray

An
Bien
Lake

Dong Khe

Thai Binh, Ninh Binh

Do Son

way of getting to this archipelago of sunken peaks. Make your journey in several stages; stop off in the port of Haiphong, take a walk on Cat Ba Island... and allow the spell of this strange landscape to slowly work its magic on you.

Haiphong*

Capital of the province of Haiphong. Pop 1 580 000 (built-up area).
106km to the east of Hanoi. Allow 1hr 45min.

Haiphong, the main port and industrial centre of Vietnam, was created by the French in 1874. Located on the Cua Cam, the northern branch of the Red River Delta, some 30km from the Gulf of Tonkin, the port was, and still is used by the collieries of the province of Quang Ninh. The city was destroyed beyond recognition by American bombing between 1965 and 1972 and was still something of a ghost town in the early 1990s. But, following Hanoi's example, Haiphong managed to bounce back. Although the city's facelift may have been aimed more at attracting investors rather than tourists, Haiphong nonetheless has style, and you will be able to appreciate the atmosphere of a Bac Bo city other than the metropolis itself.

Victories over the Chinese on the White River

Haiphong signifies "maritime defence" and the area was always a bridgehead of anti-Chinese resistance. The Song Bach Dang, one of the branches of the Red River, was the traditional communication route between the lands of the delta and the Gulf of Tonkin. The Chinese Empire also made full use of this communication route, sending out its junks to curb its unruly neighbours and re-establish order. In 939, Ngo Quyen, at the head of an uprising against the Chinese administration, laid an ingenious trap for the fleet of the Son of the Heavens. Having sent his sampans to entice the adversary upstream, he then had metal stakes positioned at the mouth of the river. When the junks turned back, they were caught in the double trap of the stakes and the ebbing tide. It was the first time that the Chinese had capitulated and Ngo Quyen was able to establish the first, albeit short-lived, national dynasty, the Ngo (939-68). Three centuries later, the same technique was used to thwart the Mongols' attempts to invade.

The built-up area sprawls over mile upon mile of nasty-looking industrial suburbs and apartment buildings, but the city centre itself is somewhat more attractive. The very straight streets of this colonial town grew up on either side of Dien Bien Phu Avenue, still home to a few old hotels, refurbished with varying degrees of success. The collections on display in the **History Museum** (Bao Tang Lich Su) *(66 Dien Bien Phu. Open daily 8-11.30am / 1.30-4.30pm; closed on Mondays. Entrance fee. Allow 30min)* sweep across regional history from the prehistoric period to modern times. There are interesting snippets of information about the wars of anti-Chinese resistance and the difficult conditions in the Quang Ninh coal mines during the colonial period.

On the corner of Dien Bien Phu and Minh Khai, where there are still several buildings worthy of note, an old market hall is now home to a **covered market**. Not far from here, the double boulevard of Tran Hung Dao - Tran Phue borders the area to the south. It extends into a landscaped mall built on a filled-in branch of the river; this leads to the **local theatre** (Nha Hat Lon), whose pink frontage was recently repainted. The square has been taken over by stalls of ornamental flowers and funeral wreaths.

The river reappears to the west, while Cau Dat Street, a busy shopping area, runs off into the southern suburbs. To the east are two remaining relics of the colonial era. The **railway station** has also had a fresh coat of paint in yellow and black, the colours of Hanoi. A little further on, the former **racecourse** has been converted into a football stadium, and there are plans for the regeneration of the neighbouring park and the relocation of the bus station.

Even in colonial times, the southeast part of Haiphong always had a strongly Vietnamese character, and the atmosphere along Hang Kenh can be compared to the 36 guilds area of Hanoi. The first floor of the houses-cum-shops are still in wood. On the ground floor they sell charcoal, basket ware and items to be given as offerings. **Dinh Hang Kenh**, located on Nguyen Cong Tru, a street to the west of Hang Kenh, is a former communal house (*the caretaker will open the door*), amazingly still standing considering its most recent restoration dates from 1767. This rather plain building has clerestory windows and is topped by a magnificent hipped roof. On the inside, the wooden roof structure, resting on cross-beams and corbels in the shape of dragons' heads, contrasts with the recently-restored altars. In front of the tablet of the tutelary spirit, a golden **palanquin** awaits the next procession.

At the end of Chua Hang Street is **Du Hang Pagoda**, also known as **Phuc Lam Pagoda** (Pagoda of the Forest of Happiness) (*Open daily 6am-5pm*). Although founded well before, the pagoda only became important in the 17C, and then again in the 19C, due to the various activities of certain distinguished patriarchs. It owes its present appearance to restoration work in 1905 and 1917. The inside is in stunningly poor taste, but the main altar, devoted to a trinity of Buddhas, is elaborately decorated with Cantonese-style wooden sculptures.

On leaving Haiphong by boat, note the **port installations** at the mouth of the Cua Cam. Most of the facilities are for oil storage and there is constant movement with the comings and goings of barges carrying coal from Quang Ninh.

Cat Ba Island** (Dao Cat Ba)
Pop 12 000.
40km east of Haiphong, 55km southwest of Halong City.

Cat Ba, the largest island in Halong Bay, looks like an impenetrable, barbarian fortress when approached by boat. Then the boat rounds a cliff, and the view opens up of the sheltered cove of **Cat Hai** (Cat Ba Town), over which lingers a strong smell of fish. Suddenly the hustle and bustle of a fishing port becomes apparent, a natural deep-water haven where the fishermen of the bay take shelter from the wrath of the open sea. The children of the sampan owners organise boat trips around this floating village for the modest sum of 15 000VND/hr. The morning sees the return of the fishermen after their night's lamp-fishing, but during the rest of the day, life carries on as in any other village of the Bac Bo. At the stern of the sampans, the women wash and cook, and it is not unusual to see part of the boat taken over by a hen coop, or even a pigsty.

To the northeast of the port are two pretty sandy beaches with equally attractive names, **Cat Co I** and **Cat Co II**. Both offer marvellous views of the mini-bays of Halong. Access to the first beach is via a steep ramp at the end of the seafront at Cat Hai. The second beach leads on from Cat Co I and can be reached by a 700m walkway suspended from the side of the rocks (*entrance fee*).

Lust for life
Cat Ba's popularity with Vietnam's youth is due to its numerous white sandy coves and especially to its electricity supply. Every weekend the whole island is flooded with the sound of motorcycles, karaoke music and discotheques. Hordes of loving couples take romantic strolls on the beach, all to a backdrop of sunsets and love songs blasting out on stereo systems.

The cultivated fields and the buildings of Cat Hai stretch inland in between mangrove swamps. A bumpy road leads to the centre of the island through an unusual landscape in which all thoughts of the nearby sea are forgotten. There are a few mildly interesting caves such as **Quan Y Dong** (8km) and **Trung Trang Dong** (13km. *Entrance fee*), along the road to the **National Park** (Vuon Quoc Gia Cat Ba) (*access to the park is 16km*

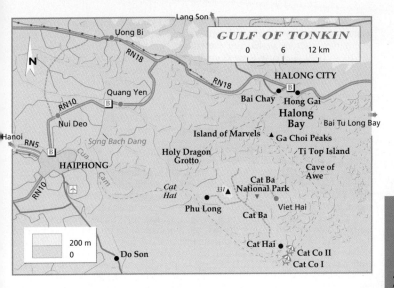

north of Cat Hai. Entrance fee). Although quite steep and slippery in all weather conditions, a clearly-marked and well-maintained route offers a 3hr-round trip hike to the summit, which at 300m has a magnificent view of the island *(sturdy walking boots are essential)*. Note the strange vegetation covering the limestone peaks of the bay, and along the way, look out for the sign pointing to a rare tree specimen, the **Rung Kim Giao**. Otherwise known as the "chopsticks tree", it was so called because the wood, known to react to poisoned food, was used to make chopsticks for the court, where such practices were commonplace. Catching a glimpse of one of the park's dozens of species, including numerous varieties of monkeys, hawks and deer, is not always easy, but the countless butterflies add to the overall charm and the deafening trills rising up from the jungle are proof enough of its hidden inhabitants. The hotels in Cat Hai offer an alternative tour programme with a guide *(see "Cat Ba close up")*.

On the easternmost tip of the island, the market town of **Phu Long** *(32km from Cat Hai)* is bathed in the bright reflection of the surrounding crayfish pools. At the end of a mangrove-covered spit of land, a few fishing boats are moored and can be hired to visit the **Holy Dragon Grotto*** (Dong Thien Long) *(allow 25min one way. Entrance fee)*. The cavern was discovered in 1998 and boasts a wide variety of limestone formations often resembling the silhouettes of real or fictitious animals according to how vivid one's imagination is.

Halong City (Thanh Pho Halong)
Capital of the province of Quang Ninh.
55km from Haiphong by road, 160km from Hanoi and 55km from Cat Ba.

Halong City is made up of the fishing port of **Hon Gai** (to the east) and the seaside resort of **Bai Chay** (to the west). The city may have a fairy-tale name (Halong means "where the dragon descends into the sea"), but it is hardly in keeping with its current appalling state, despite efforts to improve the Bai Chay shoreline. An artificial beach has been created, bordered with a landscaped promenade planted with pines and flame trees, but the jumble of buildings in the background is quite depressing. Furthermore, the horizon is so wide that it is difficult to imagine that the rocky

173

labyrinth of the famous bay is just a few hundred yards from the shore. Hon Gai is interesting at least as a busy port with sampans and coal barges coming and going among the limestone peaks. You can take a short trip in a sampan for less than US$10. In 1999, **St Marie-Rose Church**, a charred ruin since the American air raids of 1967, was restored to its former splendour on the eastern hills. It is worth climbing up to the church for the view of the town against its background of strange rock formations.

Halong Bay★★★ (Vinh Halong)
For access and cruises in the bay, see page 182.

For access and cruises in the bay, see page 182.

There is no doubt that Halong deserved to be designated a World Heritage Site by Unesco in 1994. There are 1 969 islets rising from the surrounding jade-coloured waters, but only 980 have a name. If Hanoi is Thang Long, "Flight of the Dragon", then the bay is Halong, "Descent of the Dragon", because its improbable muddle of rocky peaks look as if they might have been thrown up by the frolics of this mythological beast. Did the cavemen of 6 000 years ago ever meet this monster? Certainly they left a few relics in the form of stone tools and implements. The spectacle is never-ending; outlined against the sky, the limestone rocks have the appearance of rows of blue-coloured teeth or of the summits of submerged mountains; caverns and grottoes swallow up the tides and mists, fog and cloud play strange games. Even more peculiar is the fact that these strange shapes appear to float on top of the water, since each base is so eaten away, while the overall silence of the sluggish sea is broken only by the occasional cry of a sea bird. The French of Indochina drew up very accurate maps of the islets in the bay, giving them names conjured up by their haphazard shapes. There were names such as the Sampan and the Buffalo, the Kepi, Mr Punch or the Phrygian Cap. The Vietnamese did the same, with the Human Head (Hon Dau), the Old Lady (Hon Ba), the Fortress (Dao Phao Dai) or the Perfume Burner (Hon Dinh Huong).

The alchemy of the waters
Cone-shaped formations, fairy chimneys, rocky peaks, solitary pinnacles or groups of hills, all these limestone fantasies were formed by the sea. Millions of years ago, marine sedimentation formed a thick layer of shelly material from Southern China to Vietnam, fractured by movements of the earth's crust. As the sea withdrew, the combined erosive effects of rainwater and underground rivers caused the formation of an extraordinary network of grottoes and caverns. Some of these subsequently collapsed leaving isolated peaks exposed to further forms of erosion. This particular water-formed terrain is known as **karst** topography. Halong is the largest marine karst area in the world, and since ordinary trees cannot survive in such rocky conditions, the area is dominated by **saxifrage**, plants that are well adapted to the sparse soil in this harsh terrain.

Pirate Bay
This rocky coastline riddled with caves was a perfect hideaway for Chinese and Vietnamese pirates. In the late 18C, pirate activities were rife, encouraging fresh upsurges of rebel movements inland. Up until 1810, the pirates held their own against the regular Chinese and Vietnamese armies with an armada of 50 000 sailors aboard hundreds of armed junks. They subsequently moved their operations away from the sea and into estuaries and rivers, when the Royal Navy, based in Singapore and then Hong Kong, drove them away from the coast in order to protect the Empire's trade.

From black gold to blue gold
The archipelago has no reserves of coal, but the region to the north of the bay, which belongs to the same geological period (late Palaeozoic Era) contains the largest deposits of anthracite in the whole of Vietnam. Extracted by open-cast mining

methods, this proved highly lucrative for the French mining companies of the Tonkin region who owned the entire area around Hon Gai and treated the local inhabitants like slaves. Today, the reserves of anthracite and coal are becoming exhausted and have to be extracted at ever deeper levels.

The region has now set its sights on another local treasure, **tourism**. Cruises organised in the bay may appear to be improvised but are in reality designed to take unsuspecting tourists to two particular rock formations, access to which has been specially developed for this purpose. At each stop, tourist vessels are surrounded by hordes of sampans and little round boats made out of plaited bamboo. They are full of fishermen trying to cash in on the tourist business, peddling postcards and shells *(note that the sale of coral is strictly forbidden by the authorities)*. Don't forget to check if the grottoes are included in your boat trip, since each one charges an entrance fee, and a return must be made on the generators needed to light up the otherwise hidden rock formations.

The Island of Marvels, so called by the French of Indochina, is one of the first islands en route from the mainland. It shelters the **Wooden Stakes Cave** (Hang Dau Go) where the sharpened 1.5-3m long poles were discovered which had apparently been used in the defeat of the Mongols *(see page 171)* and which are at the moment on show in the Haiphong Museum. The **Heavenly Palace Grotto** (Dong Thien Cung) suspended 50m above the water, opens onto a small cove. These interconnecting rocky openings are all lit up in Technicolor.

Two peaks facing each other, known as the **Fighting Cockerels** (Hon Ga Choi), mark out the route to another archipelago. Not far from **Cemetery Island** where unnamed sailors are buried, another island is home to the **Cave of Awe** (Hang Sung Sot). Beyond the first chamber, a small passage leads out into an impressive amphitheatre with a candelabra of stalactites. Opposite, a curtain of limestone formations hangs at the entrance to **Pelican Cave** (Hang Bo Nau). In the same area, **Tunnel Cave** (Hang Luon) leads to an inner lake and, a little further on, the beaches of **Ti Top Island** are perfect for swimming.

Strange rock formations in Halong Bay

B Pérousse/MICHELIN

The Red River Delta

COMING AND GOING

By air – The *airport* (Cat Bi) lies 7km to the south. There is one connecting flight a day to Ho Chi Minh City at 10am.

By train – The *station* is located at Luong Khanh Thien Street, southeast of the colonial town. There are nine trains a day in both directions between Haiphong and Hanoi (1hr 50min-2hr 30min per trip).

By bus – 6 buses per day for Hanoi (1hr 45min) and 3 for Ninh Binh (4hr) leave from the bus station **Ben Xe Tam Bac**, near to Cho Sat market, in the western part of the town.

By boat – Boats leave from the landing stage at **Binh**. Tickets for the boat services between Haiphong and Cat Ba (2 departures, 60 000VND) and Haiphong and Hon Gai (4 departures, 50 000VND) can be reserved at the railway station or directly at the quayside (at least one hour in advance). Allow 2-4hr crossing.

There is a **hydrofoil** service between Haiphong and Cat Ba (1hr, 90 000VND), but departures are rather unreliable since it is often chartered by travel agents for luxury trips. Every morning (at 6am, 9am and 1pm) motorboats go from Haiphong-Cat Hai Island-Phu Long (northwest of Cat Ba).

GETTING AROUND HAIPHONG

The "xe om" are the most common form of transport. There are two taxi companies: *VP Taxi*, ☎ (031) 82 82 82 and *Hai Phong Taxi*, ☎ (031) 83 83 83.

ADDRESS BOOK

Bank / Currency exchange – *Indovina Bank*, 30 Tran Phu. Monday-Friday 8-11.30am / 12.30-4.30pm. Change facilities available at the reception of the Huu Nghi Hotel.

Post / Telephone – *Buu Dien Trung Uong*, 3 Nguyen Tri Phuong. Monday-Friday 6am-10pm, Saturdays 6am-12noon

Airline companies – *Vietnam Airlines*, 30 Tran Phu, ☎ (031) 84 71 37, Fax (031) 85 95 09; 60 Dien Bien Phu (Huu Nghi Hotel), ☎ (031) 84 29 89, Fax (031) 85 94 97.

WHERE TO STAY

Accommodation in Haiphong is mostly aimed at businessmen, mass Chinese tourism and local travellers. Since the town has no mini-hotels, it is difficult to find value-for-money establishments at less than US$15, although luxury hotels are open to negotiation.

Under US$10

Thang Nam, 55 Dien Bien Phu, ☎ (031) 84 28 20, Fax (031) 82 34 60 – 18rm ⌂ 🍽 ✕ 📺 Definitely the cheapest hotel in the town. Respectable, although a little dreary, with carpets coming up at the edges while the larger traveller will have trouble squeezing into the bathrooms.

Between US$10 and US$15

Orient Hotel (Khach San Phuong Dong), 73 Luong Khanh Thien, ☎ (031) 85 53 91 – 15rm ⌂ 🍽 ✕ 📺 A very practical location (it gives on to the entrance to the station), this railway-owned hotel is very well maintained, although a little unwelcoming. The staff understand English.

Between US$15 and US$30

Hoa Binh Hotel, 104 Luong Khanh Thien, ☎ (031) 85 90 29, Fax (031) 84 69 07 – 38rm ⌂ 🍽 ✕ 🅿 📺 ✕ Apart from its façade, doorways decorated with the hotel's monogram, and a few beds, there are not many original features remaining of this 1930s establishment. Recent renovation work was to suit the Chinese clientele with soft mattresses and carpets in the more expensive rooms, and Formica and karaoke facilities in the standard rooms. The "Thai massage" salons are aimed at the same clientele. Quite a reasonable hotel on the whole.

Hotel du Commerce, 62 Dien Bien Phu, ☎ (031) 84 27 90, Fax (031) 84 25 60 – 41rm ⌂ 🍽 ✕ 🅿 📺 ✕ 🆑 The colonial style is only apparent from the hotel façade, despite recent refurbishment. The services available are very similar to the neighbouring hotel, the Huu Nghi, but on a much more personal level with a more reasonable range of prices.

Huong Sen Hotel (Nha Khach Huong Sen), 16 Minh Khai, ☎ (031) 82 22 35, Fax (031) 84 29 92 – 24rm ⌂ 🍽 ✕ 📺 A modern building sandwiched between two colonial townhouses offering clean linen despite the flaking wall paint. The bathrooms have seen better days, but the showers work.

Navy Guesthouse (Nha Khach Hai Quan), 5 Tran Hung Dao, ☎ (031) 82 36 72, Fax (031) 84 22 78 – 21rm ⌂ ▤ ✕ ✗ ▣ ✗ Behind a colonial residence from the 1940s (The White Villa), the buildings have been constructed in the same style. Accommodation is available in the old part offering genuine suites, but the plumbing has never really been modernised and harbours a few rats. The modern part of the hotel provides all the necessary facilities (bath, satellite TV and fridge), despite the rather oppressive style of the furniture and carpets. Beware, the hotel has a totally unattractive annexe at 27C Dien Bien Phu.

Between US$30 and US$50

Sunflower, 1 Van Cao, ☎ (031) 89 20 23, Fax (031) 89 20 21, sunflower_marketing@hn.vnn.vn – 110rm ⌂ ▤ ✕ ✗ ▣ ✗ ⟆ ✦ CC This residence, built in a quiet, rural area on the southern edge of the town, offers tastefully-furnished apartments at reasonable daily rates, including a number of attractive services such as breakfast, free local calls, and free access to the fitness centre. Car rental is possible and excursions to Cat Ba or Halong Bay can be organised.

Between US$50 and US$70

Huu Nghi Hotel, 60 Dien Bien Phu, ☎ (031) 82 32 44, Fax (031) 82 35 65 – 126rm ⌂ ▤ ✕ ✗ ▣ ✗ ⟆ ✦ CC Perfect comfort but a very impersonal service in this hotel-cum-factory for Chinese tourists. Three restaurants offer Western, Vietnamese and Chinese cuisine. The swimming pool is situated at the back overlooked by colonial-era buildings.

The Tray Hotel, 47 Lach Tray, ☎ (031) 82 85 55, Fax (031) 82 86 66 – 71rm ⌂ ▤ ✕ ✗ ▣ ✗ ⟆ CC This dis-

creet, elegant-looking international hotel is part of the pleasant surroundings of the future municipal park. The restaurant and the terraced swimming pool are a major feature of the town. Excellent value for money.

Between US$70 and US$100

Royal Garden Harbour View Hotel, 4 Tran Phu, ☎ (031) 82 78 27, Fax (031) 82 78 28, royalgarden@hn. vnn.vn – 127rm ⌂ ▤ ✕ ✗ ▣ ✗ CC Business centre and fitness area. This elegant, neo-colonial building is the best hotel in the town with perfect rooms. The same concern for quality of decor is apparent in the two restaurants, one of which serves excellent Italian meals. Hydrofoil excursions to Cat Ba and Halong Bay are available.

EATING OUT

Good restaurants are few and far between in Haiphong since the majority of visitors are either businessmen who dine in their hotels (the restaurants in the **Tray** and the **Royal Garden Harbour View** hotels are excellent) or Chinese tourists who eat in groups.

Between 25 000 and 50 000VND

Several Vietnamese restaurants on Tran Hung Dao (along the mall, to the east of the municipal theatre) serve decent food.

Le Bar de la Marine, 5 Tran Hung Dao. This open air "bia hoi" (fresh beer) serves inexpensive sea food and snails with lemon grass.

Moka, 115 Cat Dai, ☎ (031) 84 28 20. This tea room is a real godsend. The owner, Mrs Vinh, is over 80 years old and just as sweet as the delicious pastries that her daughter makes. The cream puffs are scrumptious, the cakes melt in your mouth, and the gateaux are truly delectable.

The Red River Delta

COMING AND GOING

Access should soon be much easier, since a road is planned between the port of Haiphong and the island of Dinh Vu. A ferry service will run from Dinh Vu to the island of Cat Hai and from Cat Hai to Phu Long on the island of Cat Ba.

By boat – The island of Cat Ba has two ports, **Cat Hai (Cat Ba Town)** to the south, for the regular sea routes, and **Phu Long** to the north of the island for the little boats from Haiphong. "Xe om" drivers wait for all the arriving passengers to take them to Cat Hai. There are daily crossings between the port of Cat Hai and the Binh jetty at Haiphong (see "Haiphong close up"), and two daily departures for Haiphong (60 000VND). Crossing times vary according to the route which depends on the sailing conditions and the number of passengers (between 2hr 40min and 4hr on average). Links with Hon Gai (3hr 30min-4hr) are much more unpredictable, since the aim of the hotel managers at Cat Ba is to sell as many day trips as possible with the final stopover on the coast. Regular boat services usually leave on even dates at 7am, and "tourist boats" leave every morning at 8.15am (55 000VND).

GETTING AROUND CAT BA

The island's moutainous terrain makes cycling quite an effort. "Xe om" and motorcycles are the best means of transport. Vehicle rental is possible at hotels and restaurants.

ADDRESS BOOK

Bank / Currency exchange – There is no bank, but money can be changed in certain hotels (don't expect the best rates, however).

Post / Telephone – **Buu Dien Cat Ba**, at the bottom of the only road running at right angles to the seafront. Open Monday-Friday 6.30am-9pm.

Internet – Internet access at the Pacific Hotel, opposite the Post Office (2 500VND per min).

Travel agencies – Almost all the hotels double as travel agents. It is not worth booking anything from Hanoi since you can easily arrange motorcycle rental, hikes, boat trips, boat ticket reservations and numerous other services here. As a rough guide, the complete tour of Cat Ba (including a forest trek in the National Park, a picnic in a fishing village and a return boat trip across the Bay of Kan Ha) costs US$15, and a day's boat trip around Halong Bay (including visits to several grottoes, a swim in the sea and a seafood meal on board) comes to US$10. There is a wide range of different services and prices, but avoid any excursion that merely recommends sandals for the hike round the island, since the terrain is very steep and slippery. Check the type of boat allocated for the trip and the nature of the food provided, as some consider a banana to be a full meal.

WHERE TO STAY

Forty or so hotels have sprung up at Cat Hai. They are busy throughout the year with foreigners in the winter and Vietnamese in the summer. Rates vary according to season, doubling in the summer. Prices indicated are for the low season. Most of the mini-hotels can -- arrange breakfast. Mosquito nets are essential, so check they are in good condition.

Under US$10

Giang Son Hotel, on the northwestern edge of the seafront, ☎ (031) 88 82 14 – 20rm 📶 ▤ 🔀 📺 Large, tiled, extremely functional rooms with toilet. The hotel has a pleasant view of the port, but avoid the five rooms overlooking the rocky cliff face. Rates do not vary throughout the year.

Between US$10 and US$15

Cat Co I – 6rm 🍴 Small concrete cubicles with very basic facilities (bed and mosquito net), ideal for those keen to play at Robinson Crusoe on the prettiest beach at Cat Ba. The level of isolation is all very relative, since even after the last evening sunbathers have left for home, the owner likes to swamp the beach with the latest Vietnamese hits.

Far Eastern Hotel (Khach San Vien Dong), on the southeast side of the seafront, directly below the ferry pier, ☎ (031) 88 85 55, Fax (031) 88 83 25 – 25rm 📶 📋 🍽 ℰ TV ✗ A very pleasant hotel with tastefully furnished, bright, spacious rooms each with a private balcony looking out onto the port.

Nam Duong Hotel, on the southeast side of the seafront, next to the government-run hotel, ☎ (031) 88 85 86 – 20rm 📶 📋 🍽 ℰ TV ✗ Immaculate rooms, most with a private balcony overlooking the sea. The other rooms face the mountains at the back. Every facility, quiet area.

Nam Phuong Hotel, one of the last establishments to the northwest of the seafront, ☎ (031) 88 84 73 – 11rm 📶 📋 🍽 TV Built against the cliff face, the inside wall of the stairwell is made out of rock. Every room looks out over the fishing port through a large bow window. The two largest rooms have a balcony facing the sea. The hotel has been recently built, it is very well maintained, and offers the best value for money in Cat Hai.

Sunflower Hotel 2, on the northwest side of the sea front, ☎ (031) 88 82 15, Fax (031) 88 84 51, sunflowerhotel@hn.vnn.vn – 15rm 📶 📋 🍽 TV Most of the rooms have a large bow window and balcony overlooking the port. The toilets are spotless. There is a pleasant roof-top terrace equipped with a billiard table. Don't confuse this hotel with the Sunflower 1 on the other side of the seafront where the rooms are rather poky.

Thao Minh Hotel, on the northwest side of the seafront, ☎ (031) 88 84 08, Fax (031) 88 86 30 – 22rm 📶 📋 🍽 ℰ TV There are eight bedrooms with a view over the port sharing balconies decorated with flowers. The other rooms are to be avoided.

Between US$15 and US$30

Tien Thang Hotel, on the southeast side of the seafront, adjoining the government-run hotel, ☎ (031) 88 85 68 – 26rm 📶 📋 🍽 ℰ TV ✗ Only 6 well-designed rooms have a view, incorporating French windows leading out from the balcony. The rooms at the back are just as spacious and airy. It is most definitely the most expensive hotel, but the amenities justify the price.

EATING OUT

Restaurants in Cat Hai can be found along the seafront. They all offer the same menu at the same price with the emphasis on seafood. The following addresses are provided only as a rough guide, especially since the reputation of certain establishments may vary considerably from one season to another. There is also a floating restaurant accessible by boats laid on by the children of the sampan owners in exchange for a small fee of 10 000VND round trip.

Between 25 000 and 50 000VND

Thang Loi, next to the Quan Duc Hotel, ☎ (031) 88 85 31. Seafood prepared to Vietnamese or international tastes. Tips and advice from the island's young guides.

Nam Phuong, Thang Loi's next door neighbour. A very respectable establishment with more emphasis on Vietnamese tastes with touches of fresh ginger, and crispy, full-flavoured spring rolls.

COMING AND GOING

By bus – A fleet of small boats operates services between the **Hon Gai** bus station and the **Bai Chay** bus station serving Hanoi, Haiphong and Ninh Binh (to the east of the station, next to the Halong Plaza Hotel). 24-seater minibuses depart every 25min, from 5.30am-5.30pm to the Kim Ma station in Hanoi (3hr30min, reckon on 35 000VND). The bus station is well run and there is a ticket counter. Frequent services to Haiphong (2hr, 14 000VND). One bus a day at 6.15am to Ninh Binh (6hr).

By boat – The **pier** for the regular boat services is located at Hon Gai (Ben Tau Hon Gai). 5 daily services to Haiphong from 6am-4pm (50 000 VND). Less regular services to the islands of Cat Ba and Cat Hai. See also "Haiphong and Cat Ba close up".

By helicopter – The company **Northern Service Flight** operates flights combined with boat trips every Saturday from Hanoi. The helicopter takes off at 8am from the Gia Lam Airport (6km northeast of Hanoi) and the flight lasts 50min, including 15min flying over the bay. A 4hr boat trip follows before returning to Hanoi at 3.45pm. The price of a return ticket is US$175. For information and reservations, contact the agency at the Gia Lam Airport, ☎ (04)563 31 10.

Excursions – Unless really pushed for time, all-inclusive package deals for Hanoi – Cat Ba – Halong – Hanoi, available through the capital's travel agents, are not to be recommended. The rates may be attractive at under US$20 for two nights and a day, boat trip included, but even in Vietnam there is never something for nothing, and you face serious disappointment concerning the quality of the hotels, the food and the marathon-like nature of the trip. For those on a tight budget, Cat Ba is an ideal base for visiting the bay. Note that the **TF Handspan** agency has a worthwhile offer involving a night aboard a boat in Halong Bay (116 Hang Bac, ☎ (04)828 19 96, Fax (04)825 71 71, tfhandspn@hn.vnn.vn).

GETTING AROUND HALONG CITY

The "xe om" is the most convenient form of transport, easily found near most railway stations and sea ports. Taxis are readily available at the large hotels (15 000VND for an average trip). Ferries operate between Bai Chay and Hon Gai every five minutes during the day and every 15-30min during the night.

ADDRESS BOOK

Bank / Currency exchange – Vietcombank, Le Thanh Tong, near the Post Office. Monday-Friday 7.30-11am / 1.30-4.30pm, Saturdays 7.30am-12noon. Cheques and cash. There is no bank in Bai Chay, but the large hotels have exchange facilities.

Post / Telephone – Buu Dien Halong, at the end of Vuon Dao Street, at Bai Chay, ☎ (033) 84 62 03. Monday-Friday 6.30am-9pm.

Internet – Emotion Cybernet Café, Bai Chay Road, next to the post office, ☎ (033) 84 73 54, emotioncafe@hn.fpt. vn Internet access at 600VND per min.

WHERE TO STAY

Like Cat Ba, Halong City has two seasons for tourists, summer and winter. In summer, (May to September with peak time in July) hotel rates, already higher than in Cat Ba, are increased two-fold for only mediocre accommodation. Even in the seaside resort of Bai Chay, only two hotels (the Halong Bay and the Halong) have rooms with a view over the sea. The rest of the accommodation is made up of tourist factories and second-rate minihotels. Cat Ba would be a much better base.

• **Bai Chay**

Available accommodation is divided into two different areas. The more pleasant establishments are located to the west, not far from the jetty for tourist boat trips, whereas the others are in the east in a heavily built-up area where views over the sea are scarce.

Between US$10 and US$15

Hoa Binh Hotel, 39 Vuon Dao, ☎ (033) 84 60 09 – 5rm 📶 ▤ ⨯ ✐ 📺 A typical example of one of the dozens of hotels along Vuon Dao, the street where most of the mini-hotels are situated. Small bathrooms but very spacious bedrooms with frilly fabrics and traditional mouldings. By leaning out over the balcony, you can get a view of the sea.

Sao Mai, at the top of Vuon Dao, to the right, ☎ (033) 84 62 56 – 15rm 📶 ▤ ⨯ ✐ 📺 A mini-hotel located high up above the incredible urban sprawl of Vuon Dao, Bai Chay's "town centre". The rooms are quite respectable with large tiled bathrooms.

Vinaly 1 Hotel, 11 Khu 4B, on a hill, behind the Heritage Hotel Tower, ☎ (033) 84 66 94, Fax (033) 84 62 26 – 16rm. 📶 ▤ ⨯ 📺 This mini-hotel stands out from the others thanks to its hilltop location looking down over Bai Chay, possibly even with a glimpse of the sea. The tiled bedrooms and bathrooms are kept very clean.

Between US$15 and US$30

Ha Long 4 Hotel, behind the Halong 1 Hotel, ☎ (033) 84 63 12 – 12rm 📶 ▤ ⨯ 📺 This cheaper version of the Halong Hotels provides basic facilities, but is quite respectable and always a good standby compared to the mini-hotels for those on a tight budget. One important point to note, however, is that the imminent construction of a new highway, doubling the capacity of the coastal road, may disturb the present quiet surroundings.

Between US$30 and US$50

Ha Long 2 Hotel, to the west of the station, above the road leading to the quayside, ☎ (033) 84 63 21, Fax (033) 84 63 20 – 37rm 📶 ▤ ⨯ ✐ 📺 ⨯ ⟨cc⟩ Only two rooms are without balconies overlooking the sea. They would be more attractive without the carpets which are not quite up to scratch. But the bathrooms are spotless. Overall genuine comfort.

Between US$50 and US$70

Ha Long 1 Hotel, beyond Halong Bay, standing alone at the end of a large park, ☎ (033) 84 60 20, Fax (033) 84 63 18 –

22rm 📶 ▤ ⨯ ✐ 📺 ⨯ ⟨cc⟩ Recent restoration work has revived the colonial charm of this hotel, built by the French in 1935. Room 208 is a famous one, since Ho Chi Minh stayed there twice and it became Catherine Deneuve's private residence during the making of the film "Indochina" in 1991. The hotel is spacious, spotless, charming and cosy. It is a pity that the restaurant, located in an older part of the building surrounded by a veranda, is about as welcoming as a railway station. The best position in Bai Chay.

Between US$70 and US$100

Ha Long Bay Hotel, to the west of Ha Long 2, ☎ (033) 84 52 09, Fax (033) 84 68 56 – 42rm 📶 ▤ ⨯ ✐ 📺 ⨯ ⟨⟩ ⟨cc⟩ Half of the rooms overlook the sea, and the others face the rear garden. The hotel is roomy and clean, but sadly uninspiring. The restaurant, on the other hand, boasts a large bow window.

Over US$100

Ha Long Plaza, 8 Halong Rd, near the railway station, Bai Chay, ☎ (033) 84 58 10, Fax (033) 84 68 67 – 200rm 📶 ▤ ⨯ ✐ 📺 ⨯ ⟨⟩ ⟨⟩ ⟨cc⟩ Bar and fitness centre. The most luxurious of the Bai Chay hotels, although not in the best position, since the view offers nothing out of the ordinary. Only for comfort lovers willing to forget they are so close to one of the most beautiful bays in the world.

• **Hon Gai**

Accommodation is not the area's strong point, but two innovative ideas have produced two excellent establishments of contrasting styles.

🏠**Hien Cat Boarding House**, 252 Ben Tau (take the first on the left from the harbour station, and it is at the end of the street, 150m further on), ☎ (033) 82 74 17 – 6rm 📶 ⨯ 📺 The owners are charming and it is a real pleasure to be able to share their home, built over the fishing port. The room on the top floor is ideal with its charming little terrace where you can enjoy breakfast overlooking the activities of the various boats in the bay. The owner is also a cordon bleu cook, and will prepare fresh seafood on request.

@**Nha Nghi Chez Simone**, 10 Cao Xanh, ☎ (033) 82 51 70, vinhth@ho. fpt.vn – 3rm ⚑ 🍴 ☰ ☂ ✎ TV ✗ The appealing Simone Nguyen Thi Than has converted her house into rooms with table d'hôte. Situated in a quiet residential area, the establishment has no view of the sea, but a pleasant garden and attractive rooms. Simone is keen to help both English- and French-speaking tourists enjoy their trip through Vietnam, with valuable advice in avoiding the pitfalls of the often Mafia-like organisation of tourism in Halong Bay. Advance booking is a must. Transport from the station can be provided.

EATING OUT

• **In Bai Chay**

The overall picture is rather bleak, and the choice is limited. Food in the big hotels is dreadful, alternative restaurants are few and far between and ridiculously expensive.

Under 25 000VND

Street stalls serve cheap "com pho" at the foot of the Heritage Hotel tower, and others are located at the bottom of Vuon Dao Street, opposite the Post Office.

Between 25 000 and 50 000VND

Emotion Cybernet Cafe, Bai Chay Rd, near the Post Office, ☎ (033) 84 73 54. A pleasant spot under the pine trees on the edge of the beach. They serve pizzas and other well-known international dishes.

Between 50 000 and 100 000VND

Van Song Restaurant, Bai Chay Rd, at the end of the street leading up to the Heritage Hotel, ☎ (033) 84 60 84. A seafood restaurant with dishes such as mantis shrimp (a hybrid of king prawn and spiny lobster peculiar to the bay), or blue crab (pink when cooked, of course). The owner is a mine of information concerning tourism in Halong.

• **In Hon Gai**

Between 25 000 and 50 000VND

The tables d'hôte at **Chez Simone** and the **Hien Cat** boarding house are probably the best places to eat along the coast.

OTHER THINGS TO DO

Canoeing – Certain agencies in Hanoi organise more adventurous trips of this sort over 2 to 6 days. **Hanoi's Buffalo Tours**, 11 Hang Muoi, ☎ (04) 828 07 02, Fax (04) 826 93 70, buffalo@netnam. org.vn **Ho Guom Tourist Company**, 125 Bui Thi Xuan, ☎ (04) 821 61 99, Fax (04) 976 13 06, inserhan@fpt. vn

Boat trips around the bay – For information and reservations, contact **Bai Chay tourist landing stage** in the western part of Bai Chay, 2.5km from the Post Office, ☎ (033) 84 74 81, Fax (033) 82 13 07. Open daily 5.30am-6.30pm (summer) or 6am-6pm (winter). It is very well organised and serves as a tourist information office with details of the various trips available (weather, routes, caverns and islands to be visited). Boats are available by the hour or on the basis of the proposed routes. The rates are set by the tourist administration and vary according to the size of the boat and the facilities on board. As a rough guide, a traditional wooden boat for 15 passengers on a 4hr cruise costs 280 000VND. Trips in faster 1st class boats with metal hulls (60-80 passengers) cost 30 000VND (4hr), 42 000VND (6hr) and 54 000VND (8hr). The **Mui Ngoc Company** operates a hydrofoil service between the jetty at Bai Chay and the town of Mong Cai (2hr), on the Chinese border. The route crosses Bai Tu Long Bay, an eastern extension of Halong Bay. Two daily departures at 8am and 1.30pm. Allow US$24, with a picnic included. For information and reservations, contact the Bai Chay jetty, ☎ (033) 88 39 88.

Junk cruises – The beautiful junks with their plaited sails have all deserted the bay, but thanks to private initiatives, some have been converted into pleasure boats. Certain agencies in Hanoi specialise in 2 to 3 day trips, accommodation and meals on board included. Allow US$170-860 per person according to the length of the trip and the number of passengers. **Ecco**, 50A Ba Trieu, ☎ (04) 825 46 15, Fax (04) 826 65 19. **Exotissimo**, 26 Tran Nhat Duat, ☎ (04) 828 21 50, Fax (04) 828 21 46, hansales@exotissimo.com **Viet Y**, 18 Hang Chuoi, ☎ (04) 821 32 64.

The H'mong from Son La

THE TONKIN HIGHLANDS

"Youngest daughter of the Black River
With the sweet, fanciful name of Vu Chua Pua,
Nimbly stitching and embroidering,
Ninety-nine silk pouches already completed,
A gift to her loved one of the Red River.
He carries them on his way to bargain for buffalo.
Youngest daughter of the Black River,
With the sweet, fanciful name of Vu Chua Pua,
Nimbly sewing trousers of silk,
A gift to her loved one.
He carries them on his way to bargain for pork..."

Song of the daughter-in-law, H'mong Ethnic Group

In the north, Vietnam branches out in a fanlike fashion
along the borders with Laos and China. Cut into by rivers,
these highlands were like a mirage to the French of
Indochina, who thought they had discovered a secret door
into China. Certain of the outcome of their efforts, they
embarked upon the construction of a railway line along the
Red River heading up into the Yunnan. They had faith that
technology would be able to completely wipe out the
mountainous obstacles. The railway line exists today and
is in good working order, but it was a momentous under-
taking. Roads remain few and far between and are constantly threatened with destruction. Travelling just a few
kilometres along a dirt track is enough to plunge you into
a parallel world shrouded in solitude, deep within the
mountainous expanses. The domain of the blue people of
the Tonkin Highlands starts here with the ethnic groups of
the Tai, Nung, Tay, H'mong and Dao all dressed in indigo,
inhabitants of a remote world where time is measured out
in the days and moons which determine when to sow,
when to go to market, and when to celebrate.

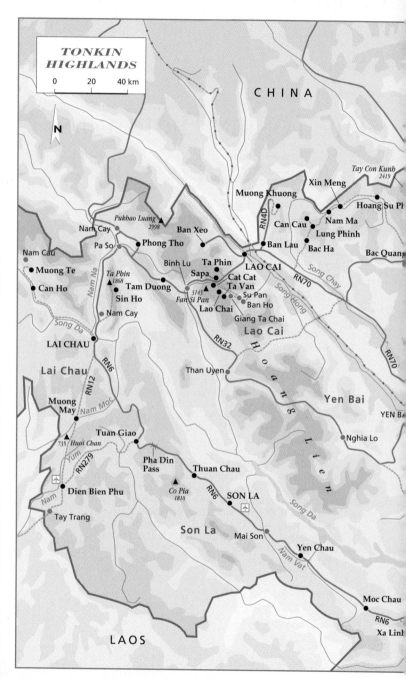

TONKIN HIGHLANDS

0   20   40 km

N

CHINA

Tay Con Kunb
2419

Xin Meng

Muong Khuong

Hoang Su Ph

Can Cau   Nam Ma

Lung Phinh

Ban Lau   Bac Ha

Bac Quang

Pukbao Luang
2998

Ban Xeo

Nam Cay

Phong Tho

Pa So

RN4D

Nam Cau

Binh Lu   Ta Phin

Ta Phin
1868

Sapa   LAO CAI

Muong Te

Can Ho

Tam Duong

Cat Cat

Ta Van

RN70

Song Chay

Song Hong

Sin Ho

3143
Fan Si Pan

Lao Chai   Ban Ho

Su Pan

Nam Cay

Giang Ta Chai

Nam Na

Song Da

LAI CHAU

RN6

RN32

Lao Cai

RN12

H
o
a
n
g

RN70

Lai Chau

Than Uyen

L
i
e
n

Yen Bai

Muong
May

Nam Moc

YEN BA

Tuan Giao

Nghia Lo

735 Huoi Chan

Yum

RN279

Pha Din
Pass

Thuan Chau

Nam

Co Pia
1810

RN6

SON LA

Dien Bien Phu

Song Da

Tay Trang

Son La

Mai Son

Nam Vat

Yen Chau

Moc Chau

RN6

LAOS

Xa Linh

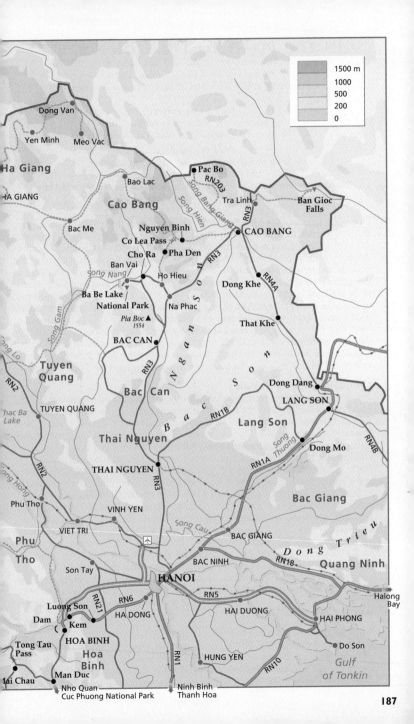

187

ON THE ROAD TO DIEN BIEN PHU ★★

Provinces of Hoa Binh, Son La and Lai Chau – Map pages 186-187
480km tour from Hanoi – Allow 3 days
Accommodation at Hoa Binh, Mai Chau, Son La and Dien Bien Phu

Not to be missed
A peaceful stay in the valley of Mai Chau.
The Black Tai villages of the Nam Vat (River Vat).

And remember...
Bring enough dollars to pay for accommodation
and dongs for everyday expenses.
National radio is broadcast in towns over loudspeakers as early as 5.15am,
so bear this in mind when choosing a hotel.

Fifty years ago, the Dien Bien Phu basin resounded with the noise of bitter fighting that was to mark the end of French Indochina. Fifty years on, the state of Vietnam is still keen to restore and maintain the symbols of victory and its subsequent independence by cementing the bomb craters, renewing the sandbags and reinforcing the bunkers and the tunnels. The town of Dien Bien, however, bears no resemblance to the former battlefield it once was, nor even to a remote town in the countryside hedged in by the Laos frontier. Since Dien Bien was made the capital of Lai Chau province in 1995, the town has developed exactly like all the other provincial capitals with their wide avenues lined with brand new administrative buildings. Flights from Hanoi to Dien Bien Phu now make it possible to take a step back in history on a pilgrimage that is as moving as a visit to the Normandy beaches of the Second World War. But it would be a pity to miss the wonderful sights along the road to Dien Bien, with its valleys and villages, home to the hill tribes of the Muong and the Tai.

Overseeing unruly vassals

The first **Tai** territories were established in the northwest at the same time as the emergence of the Dai Co Viet, the first independent Viet state (*see page 162*). In Hanoi, then in Hue, the supreme rulers of Vietnam modelled their attitude towards these "barbaric" powers on the Chinese system. They supported the customary tribal leaders, provided them with Vietnamese princesses as wives and gave them certain entitlements, in exchange for a levy payable to the court. In 1067, for instance, the Black Tai arrived in Hanoi bearing gold and silver, sandalwood, rhinoceros horns and elephants' tusks. These native lords were able to govern their territories on the basis of a vassal hierarchy in charge of a cultivated area known as *muong* (or *muang*), made up of villages and towns whose boundaries were defined by the surrounding hills and mountains. In the absence of any established alliances, this policy guaranteed relative stability in areas otherwise too difficult to control. Vietnamese expeditions in the highlands were always to quieten any brewing unrest, such as the Le Tai To campaign in the 15C which ended the pirate practices of the White Tai Chief, Deo Cat Han. The advent of the Dai Co Viet in around 1000 was to further contribute to defining the territory of their linguistic cousins, the **Muong**. Today, they are predominant in the Hoa Binh Province, extending southwards on the Nghe Anh and the Thanh Hoa. The Muong were to prove themselves far better neighbours than the Tai however.

Rebellious times

Unlike the Vietnamese rulers, the French were unaware that any attempt at direct administration would end in an uprising. They found this out to their cost when they provoked a series of rebellions at the end of the 1880s on the part of the Muong, the Tai and the Dao. The French riposte was to establish garrisons at Hoa Binh, Son

La, Lai Chau and Lao Cai, but such action failed to pacify the increasing discontent, symbolised by the **Black Flag** gangs, Sino-Vietnamese guerrillas operating along the border. The gravity of the situation forced the French to act with much more restraint, and Son La is today the only remaining evidence of the prisons they built in the highlands.

The 57 days of Dien Bien Phu

After the disastrous evacuation of Cao Bang in 1950, the French gradually lost all control over the highlands. In the northwest, the Viet Minh backed by the activities of the revolutionary Pathet Lao (a Communist organisation based in Laos), forced the French to abandon their airbase at Son La in 1953 and the garrison at Lai Chau later the same year. Certain of his support among the minority groups, the Vietnamese **General Giap** had strengthened his position in the area as early as 1952, even as far as Luang Prabang in Laos. It was in this situation that **Henri Navarre**, the new commander of the French forces in Indochina, launched the operation known as "Castor" with the intention of taking control of Dien Bien Phu by parachuting in six battalions led by **General de Castries**. Navarre underestimated Giap's determination and refused to move the units stationed in central Vietnam, even after the beginning of the battle. He also miscalculated the mobility of the Viet Minh who were able to concentrate their forces with great speed, with the result that there was just one French soldier for every five Viet Minh.

Anticipating a direct attack towards the centre of the valley, the French had set up three main areas of resistance called after girl's Christian names (Gabrielle and Beatrice to the north and Isabelle to the south). The first wave of attack was as they had predicted and Giap suffered severe losses. So severe that he decided to suspend the battle and changed his strategy. The Viet Minh ended direct attacks and initiated a policy of strangulation, substituting spades for guns. In just three months the French were surrounded by a network of tunnels and ditches. On the afternoon of 13 March, Giap ended the siege and attacked. The French sought American assistance, but Eisenhower refused to enter the conflict alone and the British turned a blind eye. On 7 May 1954, the Viet Minh flag flew over Dien Bien Phu and the Geneva Conference began on 8 May.

From Hanoi to Mai Chau★
162km tour. Allow 4hr.

There is a scheduled bus service as far as Dien Bien, but it would be a pity to complete the whole journey by this particular mode of transport, since the sights along the way are far more spectacular and interesting than the actual stop-over towns.

Considering the condition of the roads (especially beyond Mai Chau), it would be better to hire a chauffeur-driven Volga (the "Russian Jeep") to get around, though hardened motorcyclists could hire a bike in Hanoi. Most of the larger built-up areas all have petrol stations. Leave Hanoi on the expressway that crosses 30km of flatlands given over to rice plantations before joining Highway 21. On the way, a pleasant break would be a visit to the pretty West Pagodas (see page 159).

■ **Luong Son**, 60km from Hanoi, is well known for its market stalls (*open on days in the lunar-solar calendar ending in 1, 3, 7 and 9*), selling a wide range of vegetables and bamboo items made by the local Muong.

■ In the village of **Kem**, 24km further on, **green tea** is prepared according to traditional methods. Every house is equipped with a stove where large pots with concave bases are heated to dry the tea leaves as soon as they are picked.

■ **Hoa Binh** – *107km from Hanoi*. The city of Hoa Binh, which means "Peace", is the capital of the province bearing the same name. This lively, modern little city owes a great deal to the close proximity of the hydroelectric dam, the first of its kind to be constructed in Vietnam. In town, anyone with an interest in prehistory will enjoy a look at the **Museum of Hoa Binh** (Bao Tang Hoa Binh) (*Phuong Lam. Open on Sundays and public holidays, 8-10am / 2-4pm / 8-10pm*). Although the building is an ugly Sino-Soviet concrete monstrosity, the collections inside are of great interest, despite being poorly presented. Don't miss the section which extends from the prehistoric period of Hoa Binh to that of the drums of the Bronze Age. Several Tai and Muong costumes and articles round off the visit. Six kilometres to the west of the city, construction of the **dam** on the River Da (Song Da) was started in 1979 with funding and technical assistance from the USSR. As well as preventing flooding further down the Black River in the delta, the dam also supplies electricity to the north of the country, as well as to the Saigon area, thanks to the construction of a power line in 1994. The works are open to visitors and boat trips are organised to the neighbouring **lake** and the hilly countryside, cultivated by the Muong and Dao Tien (*see "Hoa Binh close up" page 195*). The boat trip provides a perfect opportunity to visit their villages, where the streams coming down from the hills are harnessed to mill the paddy. The fertile soils encourage the growth of numerous fruit trees, such as the unusual Meyer lemon. Not all the locals were lucky enough to be resettled around the lakeside, and the number of families forced to move home when the area was submerged has been estimated at 4 000.

Hoa Binh marks the end of the low-lying delta region and the beginning of the highlands. Terraced rice plantations make their first appearance, bordered by banana trees. There is also a noticeable difference in the type of settlements. Houses with thatched roofs are dotted throughout the countryside, including those belonging to the Muong, easily recognisable by their use of low stilts and the traditional cut-off corners of the roof structure. The signposts are written in either Vietnamese or Tai, and the road twists upwards as far as **Man Duc** (Muong Khen in Tai), a little crossroads village on the pass over the mountain where it is possible to get something to eat and drink (*from Man Duc, a road also leads to Nho Quan and to the Cuc Phuong Park, 84km further on. See page 164*). Finally, at the **Tong Dau Pass**, you will be able to appreciate the full beauty of the peaceful Mai Chau Valley (Pho Vang in Tai) below, a delightful plain covered with the rice plantations of the White Tai, whose settlements are scattered around the little town which serves as a market and administrative centre.

Once over the pass, follow signs for Mai Chau, 1km to the west of the road for Son La.

■ **Mai Chau*** – *55km from Hoa Binh. Alt 400m*. This market town was one of the pioneers of the northwestern tourist trade in 1990, and what a difference just ten years can make! The villages of **Van** and **Lac**, nearest to Mai Chau, are now well versed in the art of welcoming tourists (*on leaving Mai Chau, an entrance fee of 600VND is taken at the guesthouse at the start of the access roads leading to the two villages*). The local **houses** are just as attractive as ever and concrete eyesores are few and far between, but the hollows dug out in front of each home, which served as a fire-break and a place for breeding giant catfish, have all been filled in for use as tourist parking areas. The women of Mai Chau are all expert **weavers**, and in the morning, the village echoes with the sound of busy spinning wheels in the upstairs rooms. The heat of the afternoon finds the women working on pedal-operated looms underneath the stilt houses. The entire village of Lac is decorated with their work, all at very affordable prices. Collectors of more authentic items may be disappointed, but the attitudes of those selling the fabrics are a far cry from the hassle or aggressive techniques sometimes found elsewhere.

From Mai Chau to Son La★
170km tour. Allow 6hr.

Once out of Mai Chau, the road heads off with a vengeance towards the cloud-shrouded plateau. Twenty-eight kilometres further on, a track leads off to the left in the direction of **Xa Linh**, one of the rare H'mong settlements in an area dominated by the Muong and the Tai *(see pages 51-52)*. There are no rice plantations on the plateau, but you will find a few manioc and sweet potato fields. Beyond Xa Linh lies the province of Son La, an area of 19 000km² and one of the three largest provinces in the country. The Tai are the largest ethnic minority group in this area, but their settlements are concentrated along the main rivers, making the most of the available water supply for their crops and producing energy with ingenious makeshift hydraulic installations made of bamboo. Beyond the **Moc Chau** plateau *(51km from Mai Chau)*, a large supply centre reaching an altitude of 1 000m, the road follows a 40km-long valley, wide in parts but narrowing elsewhere to slopes which are barren due to slash-and-burn cultivation techniques.

■ Finally, the road leads down alongside the **Nam Vat** (in Tai country, rivers are called *nam* and not *song*). A series of almost identical **Black Tai villages**★ stretches out for a distance of more than 10km. They are built on the opposite bank of the river, and the only sign of their presence is a little **drugstore** selling salt, oil and sweets, as well as a **bamboo bridge**, with no handrail. The village consists of a long line of **stilt houses**, identical to the White Tai dwellings in Mai Chau with the exception of an extra veranda, where the women sew, prepare food, or plait large bamboo baskets carried with the help of a headband. Below, the flow of water is obstructed by pebble weirs where tiny little watermills connected to a network of cables power the electric light bulbs in the village.

Next along the route is **Yen Chau** *(110km from Mai Chau)*, a street-village with a market, a petrol station and a general store. In this upland area, only the valley floors are given over to the cultivation of rice. Everywhere else the serrated frieze of manioc and banana trees dominates the hills left bare by slash-and-burn cultivation.

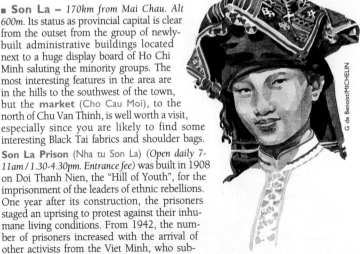

■ **Son La** – *170km from Mai Chau. Alt 600m.* Its status as provincial capital is clear from the outset from the group of newly-built administrative buildings located next to a huge display board of Ho Chi Minh saluting the minority groups. The most interesting features in the area are in the hills to the southwest of the town, but the **market** (Cho Cau Moi), to the north of Chu Van Thinh, is well worth a visit, especially since you are likely to find some interesting Black Tai fabrics and shoulder bags.

Son La Prison (Nha tu Son La) *(Open daily 7-11am / 1.30-4.30pm. Entrance fee)* was built in 1908 on Doi Thanh Nien, the "Hill of Youth", for the imprisonment of the leaders of ethnic rebellions. One year after its construction, the prisoners staged an uprising to protest against their inhumane living conditions. From 1942, the number of prisoners increased with the arrival of other activists from the Viet Minh, who subsequently used Son La as a platform for their

G de Benoist/MICHELIN

A young Tai girl from Son La

ideas. With this in mind, the prison **ruins**, left untouched after the transfer of prisoners to the delta and the French bombings in 1945, were partially rebuilt by the Vietnamese. They are a reminder of the terrible conditions suffered by the prisoners, who at one point numbered more than 600. Access is via the remains of the outbuildings and visitors will see the occasional anonymous joss stick lit in memory of those who died in this sinister jail. A small room houses a moving account of the prison's history, illustrated with photographs of prisoners and documents from the colonial administration.

The former administrative offices for the prison have been converted into a **museum**★ (Bao Tang Son La). The collections on display are far from outstanding, but do provide a perfect opportunity to sort out the differences between the twelve different ethno-linguistic groups resident in the province through their various costumes and traditional articles (functional pottery, ceramic toys and baskets). Pay particular attention to the silver-hook blouse, now worn by only a few Black Tai. The most interesting items are the jewels and wrought ironwork (arms and tools) of the H'mong tribe and the wicker furniture of the Kho Mu (*see "Huoi Chan" page 199*).

From Son La to Dien Bien Phu★
154km tour. Allow 6hr.

The road to Dien Bien Phu leads across the mountains hemming in Son La to the west, then descends into a pleasant valley planted with peach and plum trees among scatterings of limestone rocks. The variety of house types reflects the diversity of the population. The widely scattered dwellings are built of wood or bamboo, covered with tiles or straw, and are erected on ground level or on stilts.

■ Near **Thuan Chau** (*36km from Son La*), the valley widens. Big water-wheels raise water from the river to irrigate the rice plantations and other riverside crops. The town is the main market for this busy farming area and comes to life very early in the morning. Until about 9 or 10am, you will meet the local Tai women in their ceremonial dress, unfortunately just a little weary of being the target for trigger-happy

Tai house on stillts

G de Raz

photographers. Put your camera away and just enjoy a casual wander, a gesture that will be much appreciated. Fabrics and silver jewellery are also on sale, but at somewhat inflated prices.

Highway 6 leads out of Thuan Chau, reaching a height of 1 000m at the **Pha Din Pass**. The Province of Lai Chau starts on the far side, as do plantations of the **tung-trees** which yield the province's famous oil. The first Dao villages also make an appearance in a mountainous terrain completely cleared for the growing of corn.

■ **Tuan Giao** (*39km from Thuan Chau*) is the last stop before Dien Bien Phu, accessible via Highway 279 (*79km away. Allow 3hr 30min*). For those not particularly interested in visiting the famous battle site, Highway 6 goes directly to Lai Chau (*90km further on*). A new rice-growing valley opens up not far from Lai Chau, a Black Tai area, closed off by a wall of limestone peaks.

Dien Bien Phu★
Allow half a day

The road to Tuan Giao leads into the famous plain past a low hill known as **Beatrice** (Him Lam), which was the first French position to fall into the hands of the Viet Minh on 13 March 1954. The setting is lovely with the blue hills of **Phu Xam Xan** dividing Vietnam and Laos, and framing the site of the battlefield to the west and east. In the centre, the **Nam Yum** provides water for this area of land 20km long by 5km wide that used to be known simply as Dien Bien because it was the administrative centre (*phu*) for Dien Bien. With its mini-hotels, karaoke centres, covered market, banks and brand new post office, the town is like a mirage that has just sprung up in the Vietnamese Far West. The *Doi Moi* (programme of economic reforms) has definitely been through here.

To the south of the town, behind a wall resembling the battlements of a Vietnamese citadel, lie some of the 15 000 Viet Minh who died during the battle. The construction of the cemetery (nghia trang liet si doi A1) was financed by the French. The bas-reliefs of the walls recount the events of the assault right up to De Castries' surrender, highlighting the acts of bravery that are mentioned in all Vietnamese history books, such as the attack by **Be Van Dan**, a cannon raised to his shoulder, or the sacrifice by **Phanh Dinh Giet**, who stood up to an enemy battery.

To visit the site, first go to the museum★ (Bao Tang Dien Bien Phu) (*opposite the cemetery. Open Wednes-day-Sunday 7-11am / 1.30-4.30pm; closed Mondays and Tuesdays. Entrance fee*) where the entrance ticket gives access to the reconstructed areas, such as the Eliane hill and De Castries' headquarters. A **scale model** of the battle accompanied by a short film and a series of flashing lights (green for the French and red for the Viet Minh), runs through the chronological events of the 57 days in a similar way to the Army Museum in Hanoi (*see page 138*). The display cases show a slightly less didactic but rather more poignant version of the battle, with black and white photographs and various documents and objects, such as Viet Minh bicycles used to transport the artillery,

The hedgehog becomes a mousetrap

For Brigadier General Christian de Castries and his commanding officer, Henri Navarre, Commander in Chief of the French forces in Indochina, Dien Bien Phu should have played the role of a hedgehog in a strategy designed to impale the poorly equipped Viet Minh army. For the Vietnamese, on the other hand, the plain surrounded by mountains served as a mousetrap. One of the bas-reliefs on the walls of the Vietnamese cemetery of Dien Bien Phu depicts the analogy used by Ho Chi Minh to illustrate this strategy to those at General Giap's staff headquarters; Ho turned his "bo doi" soldier-peasant helmet upside down, showing how the French could be trapped on the valley floor while the Viet Minh were free to manoeuvre around the surrounding heights.

Wanted!

At the entrance to post offices and schools in "Far West" Vietnam, the walls are papered with black and white photographs of various men. These notices bear the descriptions of those wanted in connection with opium trafficking and are a timely reminder of the close proximity of the Golden Triangle and the continuing legacy of the Opium Wars. As the commentaries in the ethnic museums around the country timidly explain, the H'mong were deeply involved in the cultivation of opium poppies, for a long time their main source of income. In 1908, the local H'mong showed their discontent by refusing to pay cash levies and deliver the opium to their backers, the French colonial administration.

tools for digging tunnels and ditches, cotton jackets that served as uniforms, and the flagpole that flew over De Castries' bunker.

The neighbouring hill known as **Eliane** (A1 to the Vietnamese) barely dominates the adjacent crossroads. This hill was at the centre of the hedgehog operation and was the last position to fall to the Vietnamese on 6 May 1954, after 36 days of fighting. On top of the hill, near the "mechanical buffalo" (an abandoned French tank christened the *Gazelle*), is a reconstructed anti-aircraft shelter. Nearby, an enormous crater scars the ground, next to the opening of a series of tunnels which is just a small part of the underground operations used by General Giap during the siege. One thousand kilogrammes of explosives were detonated at 11pm on 6 May 1954, marking the end of the final assault.

The headquarters of General de Castries (Ham Kien co cua Tuong De Castries) are on the opposite bank of the river (*leave Dien Bien Phu in the direction of Lai Chau and turn left after the bridge*). A large rose garden, the work of a local horticulturist, marks the site. The shelter, protected by a few sandbags, is only half underground and several tanks and artillery guns rust nearby. A little further on, a tiny enclosure houses the **Memorial to the French Soldiers**, erected on the initiative of Rolf Rodel (ex-sergeant and chief of the commando unit of the 10th company of the Foreign Legion during fighting at the Isabelle position) and inaugurated on 7 May 1994 on the occasion of the 40th anniversary of the battle. The French have since classified it a National Monument.

The Nam Yum, providing a source of water for the Dien Bien Plain, flows into the Mekong with Laos only 38km further on. The border is closed to foreigners here, so you can either head back or continue your journey towards Lai Chau (*see page 199*).

Mai Chau close up

COMING AND GOING
By bus – See "Hoa Binh close up".

WHERE TO STAY, EATING OUT
Under US$10

The villages mentioned below are those that are used to tourists, but there is no reason why you shouldn't try your luck further down the valley. Normal rates are set at 80 000VND for bed, breakfast and dinner. The quality of accommodation is practically the same wherever you stay, with a mattress on the floor, rooms separated only by a see-through

mosquito net and shared bathrooms and toilets. Some owners have built separate sanitary blocks with showers and hot water.

Single travellers may prefer the peace and quiet of **Van**, with not a fabric stall in sight and no organised tourist shows. Contact Miss Trung in the large house at the entrance to the village.

Lac, however, is far more popular with organised groups. The houses are very attractive and the residents know how to look after foreigners unused to living close to the ground.

OTHER THINGS TO DO

Shows – In *Lac*, dinner/dances can be organised to the sound of the khene (a reed musical instrument), with plentiful supplies of local sake and regional specialities (catfish, sticky rice, young shoots of fern), all for 400 000VND

SHOPPING

Weaving – In *Mai Chau*, the expert fingers of the White Tai women produce all sorts of woven articles. They specialise in diamond-shaped patterns woven in natural silk. Their skills are endless and they collect fabrics from other ethnic minority groups. It is no wonder then, that the village of Lac is decorated with H'mong batiks, ikat silk from the Tai in Laos, and Dao embroidery, with prices a tenth of those of the shops in Hanoi.

Hoa Binh close up

COMING AND GOING

By bus – The **bus station** is located at the entrance to the town when arriving from Hanoi. There are 2 buses daily, at 5am and at noon, to Mai Chau (90min) and one bus in the morning to the Kim Ma station in Hanoi (4hr).

By chauffeur-driven 4WD vehicle – Usual fixed rates to Hanoi (1 to 3 people, 6 days and 5 nights, from Hanoi to Sapa) can vary from between US$100-US$165 per person, based on an established route (watch out for the so-called unlimited mileage deals, there is no such thing, and once off the set route those extra miles soon add up). The price includes petrol as well as food and lodgings for the driver. Allow between US$15-US$20 per day for a guide and US$25 for each extra day's vehicle rental for a 4WD Volga. The typical schedule would be Hanoi – Mai Chau (1 night) – Son La (1 night) – Dien Bien Phu (1 night) – Lai Chau (1 night) – Sapa (2 nights) – Hanoi.

By motorcycle – Allow US$6 rental per day from Hanoi.

WHERE TO STAY

Since Hoa Binh is only a 2hr 30min drive from Hanoi and has very little to offer, an overnight stay is not essential. Here are some addresses to fall back on.

Between US$10 and US$15
Phuong Lam Hotel, 186 Cu Chinh Lan (on arrival at Hoa Binh from Hanoi), ☎ (018) 85 32 08, Fax (018) 85 38 78 – 40rm ♦ ▤ ⊁ ✆ TV ✗ To avoid disappointment, choose the spotless, tiled rooms with air-conditioning rather than risk those with a fan. The rooms the furthest away from the busy Highway 6 are preferable. The staff speak a little English and chauffeur-driven cars are available for rent for the excursion to Mai Chau, 400 000VND round trip.

Between US$30 and US$50
Hoa Binh 1, 54 Phuong Lam (on the way out of Hoa Binh on the road to Mai Chau), ☎ (018) 85 29 38, Fax (018) 85 43 72 – 27rm ♦ ▤ ⊁ ✆ ✗ CC An excellent idea that hopefully will be repeated in the area is the availability of very comfortable rooms in large wooden Tai stilt houses looking out onto the countryside. The only downside is the size of the bathrooms. The hotel generally operates with groups, and so the restaurant service can be rather unpredictable for single travellers. On the other side of the road, **Hoa Binh 2** offers the same level of service with 19 rooms available.

OTHER THINGS TO DO

Excursions – Hoa Binh Tourist Corporation, located in the hotel of the same name, organises boat trips on the lake at the Song Da Dam. Allow US$25 per boat for a 3hr trip, which includes a visit to a Muong and Dao Tien village.

COMING AND GOING

By bus – The **bus station** is located at the entrance to the town on Chu Van Trinh. Quite respectable minibuses provide a service between the capital's Kim Ma station and Son La. Watch out when leaving Son La; if the driver doesn't think his bus is full enough he is quite capable of making you transfer to an already overcrowded vehicle just as its leaving. There is an hourly bus service to Hanoi (12hr) from 4am-noon, twice a day to Dien Bien (10hr) from 4am-noon, and once a day to Moc Chau (9hr).

By plane – The **aerodrome** for Son La is at Na San, 20km eastwards on Highway 6. **Vietnam Airlines** operate a return flight to Hanoi every Tuesday and Friday (Allow US$50).

GETTING AROUND

The two avenues running either side of Nam La (Chu Van Trinh on the east bank and To Hieu on the west bank) make up the centre of Son La. To the south, at the entrance to the town, are the Son La Hotel, several small restaurants and the railway station. The Post Office is on To Hieu, at the bottom of the hills where August 26 Avenue (Duong 26-8) forms a loop.

ADDRESS BOOK

Post office / Telephone – **Buu Dien Son La**, 168 To Hieu, ☎ (022) 85 24 21. Monday-Friday 6.30am-9pm. All the necessary facilities including telephone and fax.

Airline companies – **Vietnam Airlines**, Son La Hotel, Nguyen Luong, ☎ (022) 85 39 27.

WHERE TO STAY

Between US$10 and US$15
Hoa Ban Hotel 1, 4 Quyet Thang, ☎ (022) 85 46 00, Fax (022) 85 27 12 – 14rm 🛏 📧 🍴 Reminiscent of a run-down brothel, with singularly unappealing green walls, but the hotel is quite clean.

Phong Lan, Chu Van Thinh, ☎ (022) 85 35 16, Fax (022) 85 23 18 – 10rm 🛏 📧 🍴 📺 The floors are a bit lop-sided, but the rooms are quite inviting with a balcony or a veranda. The staff speak English.

Trade Union Hotel (Kach San Cong Doan), Duong 26-8 (high up to the southwest of the town), ☎ (022) 85 22 44, Fax (022) 85 53 12 – 50rm 🛏 📧 🍴 🅿 📺 🍴 A large hotel belonging to the Communist Party, with an appropriately "comradely" atmosphere. But the pleasant attitude of the staff (they speak English) helps to compensate for the coldness of the concrete, and the rooms are very welcoming. Tiles, TV and mouldings in the larger bedrooms, baths and running hot water in the bathrooms. The food, a choice of international or Vietnamese cuisine, is of a high standard.

EATING OUT

Between 25 000 and 50 000VND
The meals are quite decent in the **Trade Union**, but you can also try the small restaurants along Nguyen Luong, opposite the Son La Hotel, such as at number 10D (no name), a respectable little eating place, and its neighbour, the **Luong Phuong**, serving "bun" in an immaculate dining room. Otherwise try the **Truong Anh**, 158 To Hieu, ☎ (022) 85 25 66, a more tourist-orientated restaurant with English-speaking staff and Vietnamese cuisine with a hint of Chinese.

COMING AND GOING

By air – The *airport* is 1km away, on the road to Lai Chau. A daily flight operates between Hanoi and Dien Bien Phu (1hr) every Thursday, Saturday and Sunday from March to April, or every Tuesday, Thursday and Sunday from April to October. Contact the booking office at the *Airport Hotel*, ☎ (023) 82 46 92.

By bus – The *bus station* is in the town centre on the road to Lai Chau. A daily morning service to Ninh Binh (17hr), Lao Cai (15hr), via Lai Chau (5hr), and Son La (8hr). Three buses per day for Hanoi-Giap Bat (16hr).

GETTING AROUND

Dien Bien Phu stretches out down a long avenue which forms the continuation of Highway 279 from Son La to Laos, and which runs parallel to Nam Yum. North of the market, the avenue is called Him Lam, then Be Van Dan, and southwards, May 7 Avenue (Duong 7-5). The bridge across the Nam Yum marks the centre of the town, the Thanh Binh quarter. The main battlefield (A1) is located 2km further south, near the museum and the military cemetery.

ADDRESS BOOK

Bank / Currency exchange – *Lai Chau State Bank*, Duong 7-5. Monday-Friday 8-11.30am / 1-3.30pm.

Post office / Telephone – *Buu Dien Dien Bien*, Duong 7-5. Monday-Friday 6.30am-9pm.

WHERE TO STAY

Between US$10 and US$15
May Hong Hotel, Thanh Binh, ☎ (023) 82 63 00 – 13rm ⌂ 🍴 ✕ ✕ Rather surrealist with Corinthian columns in gold-coloured plaster, a murky green aquarium and a roof-top hen coop, but the rooms, somewhere in between these two extremes, are quite decent.
Phong Huyen Mini Hotel, Thanh Binh, ☎ (023) 82 44 60, Fax (023) 82 47 08 – 5rm ⌂ 🍴 ✕ ▣ A family atmosphere in line with the mini-hotels

in Hanoi. A clean and cosy atmosphere. The owners only speak Vietnamese, but their hospitality more than compensates for any problems in communication. Breakfast on request.

Between US$15 and US$30
Airport Guesthouse (Nha Khach San Bay), Thanh Binh, ☎ (023) 82 50 52, Fax (023) 82 49 08 – 17rm ⌂ 🍴 ▣ ✕ Respectable rooms with parquet flooring, mosquito nets, mini-fridges and a balcony. The double rooms are fitted with a bath.
Muong Thanh Hotel, 25 Him Lam, ☎ (023) 82 67 19, Fax (023) 82 67 20 – 37rm ⌂ 🍴 ✕ ▣ ✕ 🏊 Karaoke and Thai massage. Every taste is catered for with the choice of accommodation in a reconstructed Tai house or a more modern concrete equivalent, with a view over the countryside. There are even "VIP" rooms with whirlpool baths! A rockery and a few bonsai brighten up the swimming pool, complete with nearby caged animals pacing up and down. The food is decent, although the service is rather unpredictable.

EATING OUT

There are a number of small restaurants serving breakfast from 7am, but no orders after 9pm.

Between 25 000 and 50 000VND
Lien Tuoi, at the foot of Eliane, near the cemetery, ☎ (023) 82 49 19. Good food and an ideal position, although the owners still think they hold a monopoly in Dien Bien. Much more expensive than the other restaurants in town.
Luan Nga, 415 Be Van Dan, access via a small alleyway to the north of the market, ☎ (023) 82 56 04. A varied menu served in a pleasant little courtyard with a rockery and wicker furniture.
Ngoc Mai, Trau Cau, set back from the May 7 Avenue, to the north of Eliane, ☎ (023) 82 63 22. Noodles and goat meat are the restaurant's specialities.

OTHER THINGS TO DO

Swimming pool – The open-air pool at the **Muong Thanh Hotel** is open to non-residents for a fee of 10 000VND.

THE SOURCE OF THE BLACK RIVER★★
FROM DIEN BIEN PHU TO SAPA
Provinces of Lai Chau and Lao Cai – Map pages 186-187
290km tour – Allow 2 to 3 days
Accommodation in Lai Chau, Muong Te, Sin Ho and Tam Duong

Not to be missed
The Tai, H'mong and Kho Mu villages.
Crossing the Nam Da canyon on a suspension bridge.
The weekly markets at Muong Te, Sin Ho, Tam Duong and Binh Lu.
A stroll in the tea plantation at Tam Duong.

And remember...
Whatever the season, the rain can make the tracks around Lai Chau
scarcely passable, even dangerous.
Always take a few biscuits and enough drinking water,
since there are very few places along the way for general supplies.

More unruly than the Red River, the Black River (Song Da) has nonetheless been brought under control by the construction of the Hoa Binh Dam. The river flows down from the Yunnan Mountains in China, creating a deep canyon breaking through the natural barrier formed by the northwestern corner of Vietnam. Mountain peaks of over 2 000m dominate the region, which is only traversed by the river. At Lai Chau, the river is joined by the Nam Na and, in 1996, the waters of the two rivers, swollen by the summer rains, engulfed the valley, leaving 4 000 people homeless. The unrelenting nature of the region's watercourses has seriously compromised the future of Lai Chau, and the inevitable construction of the River Na Dam will one day mean flooding the surrounding area. But for the moment, this region is undeniably one of the most spectacular of the Tonkin Highlands, the home to members of Vietnam's five linguistic families.

Between Vietnam and Laos
Once known as Muong Le, Lai Chau was a former stronghold of the **White Tai**, who shared control of the northwest with the **nine Muong**, the nine Black Tai lords in the Son La region. In 1923, the ruler of the region received a golden seal from the Chinese Empire and the hereditary title of Prefect of Ninguyan. The line of descent, the **Deo**, still exists today. In the 15C, they tried to form an alliance with the Lan Xang kingdom (formerly of Laos), their border with Vietnam being situated to the south of Lai Chau. But at the beginning of the 19C, the aggressive attitude of the Siamese in Laos drove several Tai powers back into Vietnam, and the whole region, from Sam Nua to Savannakhet, came under the control of the Minh Mang.

The tiger of Lai Chau
The Deo line of descent from Lai Chau were at first hostile to the advance of the French, attempting to form an alliance with the Black Tai, but they finally surrendered in 1890. **Deo Van Long** was appointed Governor of Lai Chau by the colonial administration in 1940, which meant that not only was he the ruler of the White Tai of Muong Te and Phong Te, but also of the Black Tai of Son La. In 1945, when the Viet Minh began to spread beyond their base in northern Vietnam (*see page 26*), Deo Van Long left the country for France, where he took part in the Fontainebleau Conference in July 1946. On his return, he was appointed king of the new Tai independent zone (1946-54). When the Lai Chau garrison was evacuated by the French on the eve of the Dien Bien Phu battle, their ally was forced to flee. He made Laos his first place of safety before finally reaching France, where he died during the

1970s. His memory lives on today, a legend from another time, half king, half warlord, and inhabitants of the valley still recount many terrible stories about his life. You will hear tales about Deo Van Long's morning ritual of drinking milk from a woman's breast, his habit of sleeping with nine women every night, or the fact that during his escape, he pushed half of his entourage into the Black River Canyon, impaling the rest on bamboo stakes in the mountains.

From Dien Bien Phu to Lai Chau★★
102km tour. Allow at least 4hr.

When visiting the region, either travel by car, stopping whenever you like, or, if you have more time on your hands, use the local bus services and go hiking.

The road crosses an invisible boundary between two contrasting worlds. To the south lies the pleasant plain of Dien Bien, home to the Black Tai and orientated towards Laos, while to the north lies a mountainous terrain of canyons, home to the White Tai. It is here too that an important watershed is crossed, as the rivers in the north flow towards the delta of the Red River, while in the south they feed the Mekong. Few areas of this rather wild countryside are used for cultivation, but groves of wild *ban* (orange) trees give off a delightful jasmine aroma. Unsurfaced and badly rutted by the buses and lorries, the road was built with the help of the Chinese in 1970 in connection with the **Friendship Route** project linking Dien Bien with Nam Cay on the border *(the road is impassable without a 4WD vehicle during the rainy season).*

Twenty-two kilometres from Dien Bien lies **Huoi Chan**, a small area which is home to the **Kho Mu** (or Xa). Originally from Laos, these descendants of the Mon-Khmer adopted the Black Tai culture, but now live in a rather precarious situation, since each year the unpredictable nature of the neighbouring river forces them to abandon their lands. Their dwellings resemble those of the Tai, although the stilts used are generally a little lower, providing room for a poultry yard and pigsties. The walls and floors are made of bamboo and the roof is covered with straw. The women are dressed according to Black Tai traditions, with a three-quarter length sarong and a sequinned jacket worn over a T-shirt or often on its own.

About 15km further on, **Muong May★** is one of the last remaining Black Tai villages. It is located on the bank of a river that provides water for domestic purposes as well as power to drive a number of miniature hydro-electric plants. Water is also drawn from the mountains via a series of channels. The large houses, made of either wood or bamboo, often have attractively carved wooden **windows**. The terrace gives an insight into the daily activities with different sorts of fishing nets, cages of songbirds or chicken coops, and large pots of aromatic herbs and onions. Inside, the home is divided into two. On one side, all the family activities take place around a table and fireside, and on the other side is a series of small rooms used as bedrooms. A large selection of **woven baskets** for every possible use are a reminder of the wealth of Tai crafts.

Red H'mong

G de Benoist/MICHELIN

Red H'mong settlements appear further along the road to Lai Chau, (*28km from Muong May*), easily recognisable when travelling through on washday, when large pleated skirts in blue and white batik trimmed with embroidered coral decorate the village walls, or the period between two harvests, when local women of all ages, either alone or in groups, sit sewing on the steps. **Hair** is all important to the Red H'mong, especially since dietary deficiencies in this remote area can greatly affect hair and teeth (the latter are usually replaced by gold fillings). The women put their hair up using enormous hairpieces made of real hair, plaited into fine braids and then rolled up inside a turban. Indoors, their humble abodes include a brazier set up near a low table on the earth floor, and a shelf fixed to the wall to honour the household god, cluttered with bowls of alcohol, incense sticks and cockerel's feathers as offerings. The H'mong's prized possessions hang from the walls, among them trophies such as hand-forged muzzle-loading hunting rifles.

■ **Lai Chau** – The town nestles on the floor of a valley to the south of the confluence of the Song Da and the Nam Na. There is a rather temporary feel to the area after the disaster that befell this former provincial capital in 1996. Disturbing scars mar the view, such as the Cultural Centre, marooned like a concrete ship in the middle of a wasteland, or the hollowed-out track which was once the main street in the town, and which begins at the Lan Anh Inn and runs up the valley to the post office area. A **memorial** has been erected at the entrance to the town to appease the distressed souls of those who perished in the disaster. The early morning **market** (Cho Xa) is busy with White H'mong who come down from the villages along the Tuan Giao road. The women are identifiable by their striped sleeves following the Ha Ni fashions from Muong Te, and by their Viet-style black trousers, most unusual among women who so love to dance in their pleated skirts.

From Lai Chau to Muong Te★
A tour of 92km. Allow 3hr 30min.

Before venturing further on the journey towards Sin Ho and Tam Duong, the upper valley of the River Da as far as Muong Te is well worth a visit. Muong Te lies in a genuine cul-de-sac, for although China is only 30km away as the crow flies, it is in fact seven gruelling days away on horseback.

Leaving Lai Chau, the road continues across the Song Da on the **Hang Tom Bridge**, an amazing structure suspended above the canyon. Two kilometres further on, the road forks off to the left and crosses the Nam Na on a breathtaking bridge whose slats rest on chains pulled taut between the two river banks.

Eight kilometres from Lai Chau, the **house of Deo Van Long**, located next to a primary school, is nothing more than a burnt, but still standing ruin. On the spur that dominates the opposite bank, several yellow buildings are all that is left of a barracks from the colonial era (*access from Lai Chau is along the track that leads off from the bridge and runs along the valley to the west*).

Six kilometres further on, a sign points to an **inscription** below the level of the road. It was engraved in 1432 and commemorates a peace campaign led by Le Thai To against the Tai leaders of the region (*see page 21*). From here, the road climbs dangerously steeply in twists and turns, and a small shrine has been constructed around one of the sharp bends in memory of the souls of those who perished here in a tragic accident. The countryside opens up to almost frightening proportions. The vegetation is dense and tropical, in places almost smothered in the tendrils of dark blue morning glory, home to many birds and butterflies.

Next on the tour is the **Can Ho** area (*74km from Lai Chau*) where the Tibeto-Burmese group of the Ha Ni have become established. Worn over long dark tunics and black trousers, female dress is a whirl of colour. The ladies' narrow sleeves are bright with multi-coloured stripes, and their hair is tied up under vividly-coloured, decorative tasselled bonnets. Rows of coins adorn the front of the tunics, and glint here and there on the head-dress.

The last section of the road is tarmacked, and after several bends, leads to a third suspension bridge. At the entrance to Muong Te, a path off to the left will take you to the village of the La Hu in **Nam Cau** *(3km)*. The traditional costume of this Tibeto-Burmese group is very similar to that of the Ha Ni, along with their houses which are grouped together into tiny villages. The tour ends in **Muong Te**, a better-kept town than Lai Chau, with a permanent market, which is particularly busy on Sunday.

From Lai Chau to Sapa★★
188km tour. Allow one day not including the detour to Sin Ho.
If you want to visit Sin Ho, stop off at Tam Duong.

The road follows the valley of the River Na northwards and after 21km passes through a Black Tai village on the riverside. 4km further on, a track off to the right leads up to the plateau of Sin Ho. If you want to make this side trip, be prepared for an early start (7am) to be able to take in some of the most spectacular sights in the area. A return trip is also possible with an extra night at Lai Chau. The stay in Sin Ho is subject to authorisation from the local police, but the accommodation provided is far from welcoming.

On leaving the River Na, the earth track defiantly winds its way up to the top of the plateau for a distance of 20km, including numerous hairpin bends. The only sign of human existence across this sweeping panorama is the occasional terrace carved out of the mountainside. The first **Red H'mong villages** can be found at the top of the ascent. Wood is a rare commodity on the plateau, as can be seen by the fact that the houses are not made out of planks, but use the old wattle and daub technique.

G de Benoist/MICHELIN

Dao Khau from Sin Ho

■ **Sin Ho**★★ – *63km from Lai Chau. Allow 3hr. Alt 1 700m.* The town itself is a ghastly place, but its setting, a series of limestone peaks around the foot of Ta Phin (1 868m), is magnificent. Even outside the **market** days *(Thursdays and Sundays)*, many villagers come to stock up on supplies. The women of the Red H'mong and the Black Dao are particularly noticeable because of their colourful outfits *(see page 56)*.

Go back to the road to Tam Duong which follows the Nam Na valley. Care is needed here, since the lorries and jeeps have made the dusty track a corrugated nightmare.

A lot less imposing than the Song Da gorges, the Nam Na flows through a world of dense tropical vegetation. Past the **Pa So** crossroads *(from here you can reach Nam Cay on the Chinese border)*, the last few kilometres of the trip are some of the most beautiful. The route leads through the middle of a splendid forest of tung trees, before emerging into an area of limestone hillocks surrounding Tam Duong.

An early morning start along this road will give you the option of a small detour via the market of **Phong Tho**, where the Tai, Dao and H'mong are regular visitors *(turn left 10km after Pa So)*. This very old White Tai centre was completely destroyed during the Sino-Vietnamese war in 1979. It has been rebuilt since, but the administrative authorities have been moved to Tam Duong.

■ **Tam Duong*** – *112km from Lai Chau. Allow 4hr 30min.* This large street-village has prospered since it became the regional centre. It has, nevertheless, retained a certain country atmosphere and constitutes a pleasant stop on the road to Sapa. The **market** (Cho Phong Tho), which has inherited the name of Phong Tho, is particularly lively on market days (*Mondays, Thursdays and Sundays*), attracting villagers from the neighbouring areas, including the Red H'mong and Dao Khau from Sin Ho, the Black Dao from Binh Lu, and the Nhang, ethnic cousins of the Giay from the Lao Cai province.

Various paths will lead you through the enormous **tea plantation** running along the northern edge of the town and the small H'mong, Dao and Kinh villages whose inhabitants pick the tea every four days (*the path starts at the western entrance to the town, opposite the post office. Be sure to bring a stick or a handful of stones to ward off the dogs*). The adjacent factory produces black tea, but you can buy good-quality green tea dried in the traditional way from the tea-picking families or at the market.

The **Tam Duong Dat** fair ("Tam Duong of the Earth") is open on the same days as that of Tam Duong, 3km away. The tea plantation extends for another 5km beyond the village, and is then replaced by terraced crops as far as Binh Lu.

The Sunday fair at **Binh Lu** (*25 km from Tam Duong*) is a regular meeting place for the women of the Black Dao. Their hair-styles are even more eye-catching than their clothes, and they strive to emphasise the curve of their foreheads, holding their hair back with a silver headband, attached with fine twisted plaits covered with a head-scarf decorated with small coins. The Dao have realised the interest shown in their head-dresses and wait in ambush to sell them to unsuspecting groups of tourists.

Beyond Binh Lu, the road begins the climb up to Sapa, running alongside a river that originates in the **Fan Si Pan Mountain Range**, and flows around its northern flank. The deforestation of the foothills is not due to cultivation techniques, but to the rigours of the winter climate, which forces the local inhabitants to get firewood however they can.

Fifteen kilometres from Sapa, the **Tram Ton Pass** opens on to the western slopes of Fan Si Pan, and 3km further on, the **Silver Waterfall** only lives up to its name outside of the dry season, when it is little more than a meagre trickle.

Lai Chau close up

COMING AND GOING

By bus – Buses leave from the market crossroads and from Main Street. There is an early morning service every other day for Hanoi (21hr) and daily morning services for Lao Cai (12hr) and Dien Bien Phu (5hr). Other random services for Tam Duong, Sin Ho and Muong Te.

ADDRESS BOOK

Post office / Telephone – *Buu Dien Lai Chau*, at the crossroads where Main Street and the Tuan Giao road meet. Monday-Friday 6.30am-9pm.

WHERE TO STAY

Under US$10

Song Da, Main Street (at the entrance to Lai Chau coming from Dien Bien Phu), ☎ (023) 85 25 27 – 9rm 📶 ⛝ 📺 Basic comfort, lacking in charm, but well-kept. The bathrooms are clean.

Between US$15 and US$30

Lan Anh Hotel, 200m west of the market, beyond the bridge, ☎ (023) 85 23 70, Fax (023) 85 23 41 – 31rm 📶 ⛝ ✕ Accommodation is available in brick-built structures or wooden Tai houses that afford little privacy. Mosquito nets are a must. Small, tiled bathrooms with hot running water.

EATING OUT

Under 25 000VND

Apart from the appalling **Lan Anh**, there is practically no other choice available. The restaurant, near the entrance to the market serves decent "bun" and "pho" for breakfast, but for other meals of the day, try the small "com pho" opposite the bus stop.

Muong Te close up

WHERE TO STAY, EATING OUT

Under 25 000VND

Kim Oanh, Khu Pho 2 (opposite the Post office), ☎ (023) 88 12 13 – 2rm ✗ Despite its being a little off the beaten track, you can expect a really good meal. Mats are available for hire on the mezzanine, or you can take one of the basic bedrooms. No running water.

Sin Ho close up

ADDRESS BOOK

Post office / Telephone – Buu Dien Sin Ho, at the start of the road leading down to the market. Monday-Friday 6-11am / 2-5pm.

WHERE TO STAY

Under US$10

People's Committee Guesthouse (Nha Nghi Uy Ban), at the entrance to the town, ☎ (023) 87 01 68 – 13rm ⚐ ⚒ Extremely basic, filthy and depressing, but this is all there is in Sin Ho.

EATING OUT

Under 25 000VND

The only "com pho" situated at the entrance to the market serves varying quantities of food depending on the day.

Tam Duong close up

COMING AND GOING

By bus – The **bus station** is opposite the Tam Duong Hotel and next to the Phong Tho market. Daily services to Dien Bien (9hr), Lao Cai (6hr 30min), Lai Chau (6hr) and Sa Pa (4hr 30min).

ADDRESS BOOK

Post office / Telephone – Buu Dien Tam Duong, at the entrance to the town coming from Lai Chau. Monday-Friday 6.30am-9pm.

WHERE TO STAY, EATING OUT

Between US$10 and US$15

Phuong Thanh Hotel, 118 Phong Chau (just after the market as you come from Lai Chau), ☎ (023) 87 52 35, Fax (023) 87 52 42 – 24rm ⚐ ⚒ TV ✗ Quite respectable, despite its rather rustic atmosphere and saggy mattresses. Stay in the wing to the right of the road. The country location provides a certain charm. Good, traditional Vietnamese cuisine (25 000-50 000VND).

Tam Duong Hotel, opposite the bus station, ☎ (023) 87 52 88 – 8rm ⚐ ⚒ TV Huge, tiled, functional rooms with bathrooms in similar style. It is a government-owned hotel, and so is "lucky" enough to be close to the loudspeakers broadcasting the national radio as early as 5.30am.

OTHER THINGS TO DO

Trekking – The **Phuong Thanh Hotel** organises local treks (including trips to Sin Ho), and also provides camping gear. Allow 150 000VND per person for two days, with an overnight stay in a local village.

THE FOOTHILLS OF FAN SI PAN
AROUND SAPA
Province of Lao Cai – Map pages 186-187
Cold and wet climate (2 778mm of rainfall per year)
Allow 3 days for the complete tour

Not to be missed
Trekking across terraced rice paddies around Sapa,
or in the hills around Bac Ha.
The weekly markets at Sapa and the neighbouring villages.
The amazing gardens of the Dang Trung guesthouse in Sapa.

And remember...
The best months for visiting Sapa are February, March and September.
Knock back a few glasses of "rouo" (pronounced "zio"),
a local drink that the inhabitants will be keen to share in most of the villages.
Thank you is "o tcho" in H'mong country.

During the French Protectorate, the colonial elite built their holiday homes at Sapa, part of the high plateau facing Vietnam's highest summit, **Fan Si Pan** (3 143m). This hill-station vanished from the map during the 10 years between the Sino-Vietnamese war in 1979, the cause of much destruction, and the rediscovery of the area, nicknamed the "Tonkinese Alps", by daring travellers in the early 1990s. Rumours of a new locality "up for grabs" first spread among backpacking circles, and it has now become a must for scheduled tours, with visitors attracted by catchy advertising such as "Head for Sapa for that perfect rest, the people are friendly and the cool climate is ideal". Over the years, the attraction of tourists to this miniature paradise has become a godsend for the local inhabitants, especially since this northern equivalent of Dalat also attracts just as many Vietnamese tourists on weekend breaks. The residents of Sapa have converted their houses into shops, restaurants or guesthouses, and the Dao and H'mong mountain tribes earn a fair share of the takings by selling their needlework products. Sapa is a fine destination in its own right, but it is above all a starting point for wonderful walks among the cultivation terraces or treks venturing further afield into remote valleys.

A train bound for hell
The railway engineers encountered few difficulties between Haiphong and Lao Cai and the first stage of the works was completed over three years between 1903 and 1906.

But once past the confluence of the River Ti and the River Hong, they were faced with an impassable change of level (1 600m in 90km), forcing them to abandon the Red River valley and opt for the River Ti, which involved far more civil engineering structures (107 viaducts and 155 tunnels). A new base was set up at the French Consulate at Mengzi in China. Provisions for the workers and construction equipment at first had to be transported via traditional methods, which in those days meant 30 days aboard junks on the Red River, then cross country with the aid of horses as far as Mengzi via "The route of Ten Thousand Steps". Out of the 60 000 men and women who were involved in the construction, 12 000 lost their lives.

By French train to China
After setting up garrisons at various points around the Tonkin Highlands, the French opened up a new railway in 1910 linking the port of Haiphong with Kunming in China. This was one of the most reckless undertakings ever attempted during the colonial period. The heavy investments were never redeemed and work on the railway was to cost the lives of 12 000 of the 60 000 people involved. The dream of mineral wealth in Yunnan had encouraged Paul Doumer, Governor General of Indochina, to create the **French Railway Company of Indochina and Yunnan**

(CIY) on August 10 1901. But the little ore available proved to be of such poor quality that only the trade in opium was able to secure a return on the investment, despite the League of Nations' ban on all such crops in 1920. From the beginning of the 1930s, competition from the Trans-Indochina railway serving the mountain resort of Dalat *(see page 306)* forced the CIY to turn towards tourism with the launch of the sleeper between Hanoi and Kunming (a 21hr 30min trip which has hardly changed today) and the construction of a luxury international hotel. Despite numerous flyers describing Yunnan as "one of the most picturesque regions in the world", very few European tourists took the plunge. Most of the tickets sold were 3rd and 4th class for short trips by the locals. A virtual monopoly in the transport of supplies to Free China, the government of which was based in Chongqing during the Japanese occupation, increased CIY profits considerably, but in 1940, the Chinese chose to protect themselves from the Japanese by blowing up the border bridge at Lao Cai. It was rebuilt between 1955 and 1957, only to be sabotaged once more in 1979 during the Sino-Vietnamese War. The bridge is back in service today, opening up the border between the two countries.

Fan Si Pan Mountain

E Raz/HOA QUI

The foothills of Fan Si Pan

On the way to the fair

Between 7 and 9am, local roads and mountain tracks become very busy. One farmer can be seen tugging at his stubborn mule, while another is pulling a small piglet on the end of a lead, egging him on with a bamboo whip. Others, more sensibly, prefer to transport their prize pigs by yoke, thus avoiding any weight loss on the way. Elsewhere, farming couples head towards the fair together, with the wife carrying the pile of baskets that she has woven, and the husband cradling the jerrycan of alcohol he has distilled. But more often than not, men and women form separate little groups, with the women and girls sporting their Sunday best, while the men and boys appear more soberly dressed.

Market day

Tourist descriptions of the markets of Sapa and the surrounding area such as "picturesque", "traditional", and "colourful" can be their making or breaking. Visitors are spoilt for choice and most of the weekly markets are held on Saturdays and Sundays. A market is a social event in itself, always interesting, a faithful reflection of the quality of its wares. At the **permanent markets** (in Sapa for example), the stallholders sell essential goods (groceries, books and school stationery, toiletries, and haberdashery supplies), with a rota system of farmers selling fresh produce (vegetables, meat and dairy products, and arts and crafts).

The **weekly markets**, on the other hand, are completely empty the rest of the week, with deserted wooden and bamboo stalls. Before all thoughts of capturing that perfect holiday photo of "colourful minorities", visitors should first consider the market as an ideal place to rub shoulders with the local inhabitants, without disturbing them with surprised or admiring looks. Take the time to observe women calculating the day's profits or comparing the different produce, the young girls smartening themselves up for a quick pose in front of a passing photographer, and the men sharing a glass of the local *sake*, deep in discussion about horses and land. In a world where everyone goes about their daily business, the inconspicuous outsider can learn a lot.

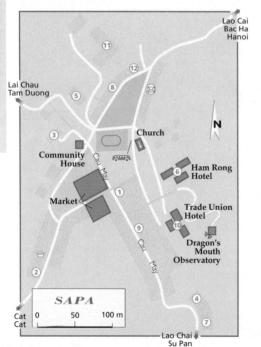

Sapa

Pop 67 000. Alt 1 630m. 380km from Hanoi.

The clouds around Sapa scurry by at an incredible pace, enveloping the old hill-station in a real pea-souper in next to no time. There is no need to go looking for the highlanders (also known as **montagnards**), they will come to you. Representatives of both groups of the region, the **Red Dao** and the **Black H'mong**, will certainly be easy to spot. Their comings and goings are a daily occurrence, their billhook in hand and their baskets filled with fodder, vegetables, wood or fabrics to sell. The ladies of the Red Dao are formidable saleswomen and the little old ladies from the H'mong tribe are even worse, using strong-arm sales tactics and reeling out a few words of French or English to compliment tourists on the stunning effect of the new hat they have just plonked on their heads. The costumes of the Black H'mong are surprisingly plain. Locally, they are called the "Indigo H'mong", not only because of the varying shades of blue of their clothes, but also because of the bluish tinge to their hands from the dyeing and handling of the fabrics. The Red Dao women stand out with their black lacquered teeth and their hair pulled off their faces with an enormous scarlet-coloured turban. Look out for the intricate embroidery on their trouser-legs and the tails of the tunic down the back.

The market is a hive of activity all through the week. Villagers come to sell an abundance of fresh vegetables, including leaf broccoli, commonly grown in the area. Hardware, stationery and haberdashery supplies are piled high under the awnings, as well as **medicinal herbs**, a speciality of Sapa, for flavouring the local *sake*. Whatever their medicinal properties, they do make ideal pot-pourri.

In town, some of the few remaining colonial buildings are situated at the bottom of the hill, including the **Dragon's Mouth Observatory** (Ham Rong) *(access via steps as far as the television relay station)*, the **Community House** with its belfry, the 1940s villas of the **Trade Union Hotel**, the canopy roofs of the **Ham Rong Hotel** and the **church**, ransacked in 1954 and recently rebuilt as a symbol of Sapa.

Treks from Sapa★★

Trekking is one of the main attractions when considering a trip to Sapa. The region's charm has a lot to do with the terraced rice paddies set out in giant steps mirroring the sky across their flooded expanse. You can stroll at will along the tracks used by the H'mong and the Dao, but you would definitely gain by turning to the services of the local agencies for logistical support *(see "Sapa close up")*. Their experienced guides will help you choose a tour well within your abilities, and their knowledge of the H'mong and Dao languages will be invaluable in venturing further into the world of the highlanders. Finally, they can also arrange transport for the return journey, which is an obvious advantage considering the Sapa terrain. In most cases, tours tend to begin with a descent towards the surrounding valleys, followed by a stiff climb back. The fee of 5 000VND at the entrance to the villages goes towards financing schools and health centres.

The valley of Cat Cat★

2.5km from Sapa on the road leading on from the market. Be careful of the very steep slope.
A classic route that is also possible by motorcycle. The road winds downwards in a series of bends across land given over to market garden cultivation. **Cat Cat**, a H'mong village made up of about twenty houses, owes its name to a nearby waterfall. A small hydroelectric station was built on the River Muong Hoa by the French in 1925.

The valley of Lao Chai★★

6km from Sapa down the road leading on from Cau May Street. During the dry season, cars can continue right up to the caves.

The track crosses the Muong Hoa River and then back up across the rice plantations to the Black H'mong village of **Lao Chai**. Continuing across the fields on the same side of the river, you will reach the Giay village of **Ta Van** (*2km on, opposite a fast-moving stretch of water*). Back down to the Muong Hoa River, across a small suspension bridge (*2km from the village*) and you will arrive at the site of the **cave drawings** (*2km from the bridge, southeastwards along the valley*). From here, you have the option of taking the steep climb in the direction of Sapa (*10 km*) or continuing towards the H'mong and Dao villages further south. (*The Sapa agencies organise an interesting 3-day trek, staying overnight with the local people and avoiding the climb back up the valley. After Ta Van, the tour takes you along the Muong Hao River towards the Dao village of Giang Ta Chai, then as far as Ban Ho, a Tay village at the bottom of the valley, 26km from Sapa. At the H'mong village of Su Pan, 5km upstream, motorcycle-taxis will be waiting to help with the return journey to Sapa.*)

Ta Phin*

9km from Sapa. Take the Lao Cai road for 6km, and then a path leading off to the left for a further 3km. After going through the ruins of a seminary, destroyed in 1952, the path then leads downwards for 4km to the Red Dao village of **Ta Phin**.

Along the Chinese border

The road linking Sapa and Lao Cai is one of the prettiest routes in the area, winding in a series of hairpin bends between terraced mountainsides and rushing torrents deep in gorges.

The Chinese origin of the name **Lao Cai**, the "Old Street", underlines its role as a border market, since this is how some market towns are designated in China. Apart from its flattering place name, Lai Cai has little else to offer, except for a few onlookers from Yunnan, all wearing red caps, travelling in groups behind their guide's megaphone.

Ban Xeo*

71km from Sapa via Lao Cai. A trip suitable only for motorcycles or 4WD vehicles due to the poor condition of the last part of the road. Allow one day there and back and take a picnic.
Beyond Lao Cai the road is well maintained, running alongside the Chinese border. The long stretch of tarmac does, however, come to a halt 90km from Lao Cai at a little market just 1km from China as the crow flies. A track then leads up the mountainside next to a torrent of water cascading down between the rocks. The path comes out over a vast basin divided up into rice paddies, then follows a zigzag course past a monument to soldiers killed during the Sino-Vietnamese War. The track finally arrives in Ban Xeo, the main **market town** of the Bat Xat canton.

The region's country folk, all members of particularly colourful ethnic groups, can be seen here regularly, even in the week. The local **Red Dao**, in contrast to those in Sapa, cover their heads with a cylinder-like turban in Chinese fabric printed with large peonies. The **Black H'mong**, dressed in indigo, rub shoulders with the **Multi-coloured H'mong**, their outfits decorated with yellow, orange and fuchsia braid with a square of checked material covering their heads. The **Giay** (or Nhang) have the largest population in the region and are recognisable in their blue or light green smocks buttoned down the side, worn over trousers.

Brightly dressed H'mong

Muong Khuong*

89km from Sapa via Lao Cai. When travelling by car, you will be able to find accommodation at Bac Ha rather than returning to Sapa.

Twenty kilometres from Lao Cai, you will go through the village of **Ban Lau**. The market stalls are empty during the week, but the Sunday fair sees the arrival of the neighbouring clans of H'mong, Dao, Giay and Nung. The village marks the start of a two-hour climb up a stony track (in quite good condition since it is hardly used) towards Muong Khuong passing a series of **tea plantations** and cultivation terraces.

Nestling on a mountainside surrounded by jagged peaks lies the town of **Muong Khuong**, the centre of a large covered **Sunday market**. Beyond, Highway 4D enters a prohibited area under military control, where tourists are not allowed.

Bac Ha*

100km from Sapa via Lao Cai. Beyond Lao Cai, the first two thirds of the tour are along Highway 70, a very good road leading to Hanoi lined mostly with Kinh villages. Seventy three kilometres from Lao Cai, it climbs steeply up towards Bac Ha, with panoramic views over the patchwork patterns of the paddy fields. The area is planted with cassia, a type of cinnamon, and you may even come across convoys of cassia bark. In **Bac Ha**, the bright costumes of the Multicoloured H'mong who gather here for the **Sunday market** even overshadow those of the Indigo H'mong and the Red Dao at the Sapa market.

The hamlets around Bac Ha, known poetically as **Ban Pho I** and **Ban Pho II**, are mostly inhabited by **Multicoloured H'mong**, who are a lot better organised than their Black H'mong cousins. Their large houses are built on an earth floor, but the inside is partitioned off providing privacy for each member of the family. They distil a rich amber-coloured liquid from corn.

Within easy walking distance is the **abandoned residence** of Huang A Tuong, a former H'mong king. The building's terraced roofing, labyrinthine stairs and balconies provide an almost theatre-like setting, strangely incongruous in this rustic environment, which is used by the children of the village as a playground.

Can Cau

21km from Bac Ha via a spectacular road, but in an appalling condition. Allow 1hr. The Can Cau **fair**, that every Saturday brings together all the neighbouring Multicoloured H'mong, is one of the most picturesque in the area. Three different worlds converge, the H'mong, the Chinese and the Vietnamese, without ever really mixing. The H'mong, dressed in their elaborate costumes, come to exchange their produce and livestock. Outside the market area there are horses, pigs and dogs for sale, while inside the hard peddling of goods continues as usual, carried out by stallholders most of whom are of Yunnan origin. They come from a small Chinese town called Xiaobazi, a 6hr walk just the other side of the border. They sell the usual Chinese hardware, but also everything that the locals need in the making of their traditional costumes. All their goods are definitely "Made in China", including embroidered braid (applied generously to the jackets and skirts), lengths of indigo, and bands of imitation batik used for skirts and shoulder bags. The food stalls serve mostly local dishes and the "bar", with its lines of jerrycans full of amber-coloured liquid, is the meeting place for all the married members of the group.

The track to Bac Quang

149km tour from Bac Ha. Allow 9hr.

In clement weather, with a 4WD and an experienced driver, the track from Bac Quang is a spectacular way to reach the neighbouring province of Ha Giang or Hanoi, although it is best avoided by those nervous of heights. Before leaving Bac Ha, check that the police will let you through this border area. You are not advised to travel alone, since there is very little traffic and a breakdown could very well become a nightmare. Sunday, in the right conditions, is the ideal day to set out along this route lined with several weekly markets, and processions of locals in their elaborate costumes seem to appear from nowhere.

■ Leave Bac Ha northwards in the direction of **Lung Phinh**, the site of a small Sunday fair. For 35km the track crosses a vast and barren limestone plateau, then comes to an abrupt end and is replaced by a steep mule track which climbs up in a series of frightening bends over a surface of extremely slippery blocks of stone. It finally emerges at **Nam Ma**, a Multicoloured H'mong village, at an altitude of 1 000m above the valley of Xin Meng.

■ The track then sweeps downwards, twisting and turning in the direction of **Xin Meng** (*48km from Bac Ha. Allow 3hr*), a small and charmless town that marks the border between the settlement areas of the H'mong and the Dao and the great arc of land inhabited by the **Tai-Kadai** from the northeast. A few Multi-coloured H'mong from Nam Ma still come to the Sunday fair, but the hints of coral-pink and fuchsia in their costumes are overshadowed by the combinations of indigo sported by the **Tay** and the **Nung**. The Tay wear a discreet, light-coloured smock over black trousers, while the Nung's costume stands out with its pleated indigo skirt tucked under the bottom in the shape of a fan. Others in the group, particularly the girls, wear attractive silver hairpins.

■ Further on, the road looks down over the deeply incised valley of the Chay River, a rocky landscape dotted with waterfalls, where people nevertheless manage to cultivate a few tiny fields. You then reach **Hoang Su Phi** (*37km from Xin Meng*), which is also a Sunday market centre for the Nung and the Tay. The road then changes, no longer suspended between Heaven and Earth, winding down towards **Bac Quang** (*64km from Hoang Su Phi*), the gateway to the highlands of **Ha Giang** (*47km from Bac Quang via Highway 2*) or to the Middle Region around **Tuyen Quang** (*106km via Highway 2*).

A permit is required to visit the region of Ha Giang, and it is often difficult to obtain, which is why the area has not been mentioned in this guide. However, included below are details of several places to stay in Ha Giang and Tuyen Quang.

Sapa close up

COMING AND GOING

By train – Tickets can be purchased in agencies and hotels in Sapa. The **Victoria Hotels & Resorts** chain (see details below) offer special fully-equipped carriages on trains between Hanoi and Lao Cai.

By bus – The church square doubles as the bus station. Minibuses, 4WD vehicles and motorcycles operate a shuttle service to the Lao Cai station and are available here between 6am and 3pm (45 000VND).

By minibus – This is an option available from agencies in Hanoi with various different schedules ("Saturday fair in Sapa" and "Sunday fair in Bac Ha"). The minibuses pick up passengers from their hotels in Hanoi and leave about 9pm (11hr trip).

By chauffeur-driven 4WD – This option enables tourists to undertake a journey of several days across the Northwest (see details in "Hoa Binh close up" page 195).

By motorcycle – For the more experienced driver, this is the best way to explore the market towns of Sapa. The roads may not be in good condition, but at least they are not busy. But watch out for oncoming jeeps, lorries and buses around the bends, since they all seem to have the nasty habit of cutting corners and hooting at the last minute. Refuelling is possible at Petrolimex stations in every built-up area. Contact the agencies and mini-hotels for rental details and allow 6 000VND per day. The less adventurous may consider riding pillion and arrangements can be made with the "xe om" drivers parked opposite the church.

ADDRESS BOOK

Bank / Currency exchange – There is no bank, but certain boarding houses may be able to change some money (at poor rates, however).

Post office / Telephone – *Buu Dien Sapa*, the church square. Monday-Friday 7.30am-9.30pm

Internet – *Viet Hung*, not far from the post office. The bill can be quite steep since the connection through Hanoi is very slow. Allow 2 500VND / min.

WHERE TO STAY

In Sapa, fans and air-conditioning are not necessary, but heating can be a welcome facility in winter. Check that the heating system is not too old (coal braziers that give out toxic fumes are definitely out). Prices are much higher, even double, in summer due to the large number of Vietnamese tourists. Prices listed below apply to the rest of the year.

Under US$10

Binh Minh Guesthouse, 20 Cau May (opposite the entrance to the market), ☎ (020) 87 17 09 – 4rm ✴] At the back of a fabric shop, stairs lead to rooms straight out of a gypsy caravan with their red curtains and cushions decorated with peonies. Mosquito nets and very small bathrooms.

Cat Cat Guesthouse, past Sapa on the road to Cat Cat, ☎ (020) 87 13 87 – 9rm ✴] It overlooks the Cat Cat valley and is very good value for money. The room on the top floor has a magnificent view and is fitted out with a fireplace and a bath. Attractive fabrics make for pleasant surroundings. The very athletic lady owner is charming and will obligingly serve breakfast in the lounge.

Queen Hotel, Cau May, ☎ (020) 87 13 01, Fax (020) 87 12 82 – 16rm ✴] ⟰ TV ✗ The best room on the top floor has a fireplace and offers a unique panoramic view through the wide bay window. Each room is tastefully decorated and has a fully equipped bathroom. The only downside is the stuffy ground floor where meals are served in the middle of all the cooking smells. Treks and excursions can be organised in partnership with the Viet Hung Hotel.

The La Rose Guesthouse, Cau May, ☎ (020) 87 12 63 – 8rm ✴] A little over-elaborate but quite adequate, especially the four rooms with balconies. The English-speaking staff will be able to provide you with tips on the region.

Viet Hung Hotel, on the church square, ☎ (020) 87 13 13, Fax (020) 87 12 82, HungNV@fpt.vn – 20rm ✴] ✗ Rooms for every budget, and six rooms with a fireplace. The rooms all have spotless bathrooms, and electric heaters are available in winter.

Between US$10 and US$15

Cau May Hotel, ☎ (020) 87 12 93 – 11rm ✴] A little out of the way, this peaceful establishment offers spacious tiled and wood-panelled rooms.

☺Dang Trung Auberge, Cau May, ☎ (020) 87 12 43, Fax (020) 87 16 66 – 12rm ✴] ✗ Perhaps the most charming accommodation in Sapa. The rooms are ideal, with open fires in the winter. Three of the rooms have a television and a bathroom with bath, but the two most attractive rooms are the ones overlooking the wonderful terraced garden. Admire the abundance of wallflowers, hollyhocks, nasturtiums, tulips and strawberries, and as many bulbs as the owner's friends around the world have been able to bring him. The delightful food includes a number of vegetarian dishes, and is served inside or on the terrace.

Forestry Guesthouse (Nha Nghi Lam Nghiep), ☎ (020) 87 12 30, Fax (020) 82 00 80 – 9rm ✴] An attractive Sino-Colonial building above the road to Lai Chau and at the foot of the pine-covered hill overlooked by the Victoria Hotel (see below). The rooms are functional and clean, with old-fashioned tiling.

Thanh Sonh Hotel, at the foot of the stairs to the Victoria Hotel. ☎ (020) 87 12 85, Fax (020) 87 12 82 – 18rm ✴] TV Modest and unpretentious. A pleasant stay is guaranteed by the friendliness of the owners and their family.

There are rooms to suit a variety of tastes and budgets. The most expensive, with a balcony overlooking the square, are roomy, bright and welcoming.

Trade Union Hotel (Kach San Cong Doan), Xuan Vien, ☎ (020) 87 12 12, Fax (020) 87 16 02 – 54rm ⌐| A group of French villas from the 1940s spread out over a hill overlooking the Cat Cat valley. The quality of the rooms probably doesn't match the architecture, but they are still quite respectable with wood-panelling and mosquito nets.

Between US$15 and US$30

Ham Rong Hotel, in the colonial quarter of Sapa at the foot of the Ham Rong hill, ☎ (020) 87 12 51, Fax (020) 87 13 03 – 32rm ⌐| ♪ 📺 ✕ |CC| A large building in the French style of Hanoi with yellow walls, cornerstones, windows with wooden shutters and awnings. The high-ceilinged rooms are very spacious. Electric heaters are available in winter on request.

Between US$70 and US$100

🐼**Victoria Sapa Hotel**, ☎ (020) 87 15 22, Fax (020) 87 15 39, for information and reservations, contact Victoria Hotels & Resorts, 70 Nguyen Trong Tuyen, Phu Nuan, Ho Chi Minh City, ☎ (08) 990 13 50, Fax (08) 990 02 29, or 33A Pham Ngu Lao, Hanoi, ☎ (04) 933 03 18, Fax (04) 933 03 19, www.victoriahotel-vietnam. com – 77rm ⌐| 🍴 ♪ 📺 ✕ 🛁 |CC| A safe and mini-bar in every room. A successful architectural combination of the colonial and the traditional. Luxury bathrooms and comfortable rooms with parquet flooring, tastefully designed wooden furniture and walls with that "colonial yellow" patina. Electric heating. Dinner can be served in the huge dining room or, for a more intimate meal, in the bar next to the fireplace. The French cuisine is quite outstanding, and the cheese fondue is totally mouthwatering. 50m away in another building, with glass panelling on one side overlooking the neighbouring pine forest, is a heated swimming pool, bar, sauna and billiard table. Weekend deals available (return train from Hanoi over 3 nights).

EATING OUT
Unfortunately, some establishments may only last a season. The food on offer in Sapa is just like its own development, spontaneous and diversified. Glancing through the menu look out for "doufu chasseur", (tofu braised with mushrooms and seasonal fruits), pâté-mayonnaise-gherkin sandwiches, cheese fondue and pizza with king prawns and Chinese red pepper. There are other specialities to try such as perfumed alcoholic drinks, game and wild mushrooms.

Under 25 000VND
The little "com pho" opposite the post office serves excellent soups.
Observatory, next to the post office. The whole backpacker range of food from 300VND (banana fritters) to 15 000VND (sautéed Chinese-style dishes).

Between 25 000 and 50 000VND
Camellia, alongside the market steps, ☎ (020) 87 14 55. Full breakfasts, "pho" and several specialities, such as wild boar and frogs' legs at very reasonable prices.

Between 50 000 and 100 000VND
Delta, Cau May, ☎ (020) 87 17 99, tungsapa@hotmail.com Mouthwatering Italian food prepared with olive oil and other imported ingredients from Italy. Carrying on the traditional art of pasta plus sauces.

Hoang Hon Restaurant, Cau May, next to the market entrance, ☎ (020) 87 18 12. Breakfast through to dinner, non-stop service. The menu includes a surprising mixture of surrealist items and culinary challenges, but with excellent results and careful preparation. The pizzas are cooked in a special oven, and the yoghurts are home-made, as is the local apple-flavoured *sake*.

OTHER THINGS TO DO
Swimming pool – The covered, heated pool at the **Victoria Sapa** is open to non-residents for a small charge.

Trekking – All the agencies in Sapa operate on the basis of "satisfaction guaranteed or your money back", and your 50% deposit will be reimbursed.
Cha Pa Café, 29 Cau May, ☎ and Fax (020) 87 12 45. An excellent range

of activities for all levels, from a day's trekking with picnic (US$12 per person) to a tour of 3 days and 2 nights covering the main sites of interest (US$14).
Dang Trung Auberge, Cau May, ☎ (020) 87 12 43. A team of 5 guides in charge of trekking trips.

Viet Hung Hotel, on the church square, ☎ (020) 87 13 13. In close liaison with the Sinh Café in Hanoi, they offer varied activities and information on the surrounding markets, and take responsibility for all the necessary formalities for crossing the Chinese border.

SHOPPING

Local specialities – "Ethnic" fabrics and clothing are readily available, but prices are not necessarily lower than in Hanoi. Don't hesitate to barter with the Dao and H'mong women, keeping in mind that profits from their sales make up a large part of their income.

Lao Cai close up

COMING AND GOING

By train – The **railway station** is in the southern part of the town, on the left bank of the River Hong, ☎ (020) 83 00 93. There are two daily trains to Hanoi-Gia Lam (10hr), leaving at 10.10am and 6.45pm and from Hanoi to Lao Cai leaving at 6am and 9pm. The Victoria Hotel in Sapa can offer a comfortable air-conditioned sleeping car on the 9pm train leaving Hanoi every Thursday and Friday. For further information and reservations contact the Victoria Hotel offices (see below). The international train for **Kunming** stops at Lao Cai (see "Hanoi close up" page 144) but the border controls in both Vietnam and China can be rather lengthy (90min in Lao Cai and 90min in Hekou). It is much simpler to cross the border on foot and then catch another train (departure at 2.45pm) or a bus in Hekou for Kunming (14hr).

By bus – The large **bus station** located on the right bank of the River Hong provides no bus link with China. Buses leave every morning for Sapa (2hr), Bac Ha (2hr 30min), Muong Khuong (4hr), Tam Duong (6hr 30min), Lai Chau (12hr) and Hanoi (10hr), via Tay Binh.

GETTING AROUND

Lao Cai spans the two banks of the River Hong to the south of its confluence with the River Ti, which marks the border with China. The bus station is situated on the right bank near the bridge. On the left bank is the railway station (2km further south) and the main hotels.

ADDRESS BOOK

Post office / Telephone – Buu Dien Cuc Cua Khau, Nguyen Hue (near the Hanoi Hotel). Monday-Friday 6.30am-9.30pm.

Visa – Visas for China are only available from Hanoi (see page 97).

Border post – The bridge over the River Ti, 3km north of the railway station, serves as the border with China. The police and customs offices are open every day from 7am-4pm. Allow 90min for all the paperwork. The customs office is just before the bridge over the Ti. Dongs and dollars can be exchanged for yuan.

WHERE TO STAY

Staying in Lao Cai is not much fun, but the following addresses will be useful to those tourists arriving too late to cross the border. That said, accommodation is no better in Hekou, on the Chinese side.

Between US$10 and US$15

Hanoi Hotel, 19 Nguyen Hue (700m from the border), ☎ (020) 83 24 86, Fax (020) 83 24 88 – 9rm 🚻 ▤ 🎤 TV Respectable, functional and clean, but the bathrooms are a little run down.

Song Hong Hotel, 50m from the border bridge, ☎ (020) 83 00 04 – 14rm 🚻 ▤ 🎤 TV The only reasonably inviting hotel in the whole of Lao Cai. It is very clean and the rooms, fitted with mosquito nets, look out onto the Chinese bank of the River Tam. The management speak English, which is quite rare in Lao Cai.

Bac Ha close up

COMING AND GOING

By bus – The only bus services leave from Lao Cai (see above).

By minibus – Agencies and mini-hotels in Sapa organise minibus trips during the Sunday fairs. Allow 3hr.

GETTING AROUND

The road from Lao Cai to Can Cau serves as the town's main street. At the first crossroads, the road to the right leads down to the bus stop, the post office and the market, while the road to the left goes to the health centre and the group of tracks leading to the H'mong villages. Heading straight on, the next street off to the right leads to the former residence of the chief of the H'mong.

WHERE TO STAY

Credit must be given to those responsible for making this tiny little village a worthwhile place to stay. Hot running water is readily available despite a rather unpredictable electricity supply. Such shortcomings can have their advantages, since the inhabitants have been able to have the loudspeakers turned off, putting a stop to the national radio broadcast right from the early morning.

Between US$10 and US$15

Dang Khoa Hotel, at the crossroads opposite the road leading to the market, ☎ (020) 88 02 90 – 18rm ⚐ 🗶 A simple hotel with clean, tiled rooms fitted with mosquito nets. The beds are covered with big Chinese-style eiderdowns. A word of caution: no-one speaks English and the manager drives a hard bargain.

Sao Mai, 127 Hoang Lien (leaving the village to the northeast), ☎ (020) 88 02 88, Fax (020) 88 02 85 – 30rm ⚐ 🗶 ✗ There is a choice of accommodation in a large wooden house with pine-scented rooms fitted with mosquito nets, or in a concrete building with wooden-panelled rooms. The bathrooms are all quite decent.

Tuan Anh, on the way to Ban Pho, ☎ (020) 88 02 64 – 8rm ⚐ 🗶 Outstanding accommodation, with tiled bedrooms and bathrooms equipped with mosquito nets. The roof terrace looks down over the village.

EATING OUT

Between 25 000 and 50 000VND

Cong Phu, at the start of the road leading to the market. Open every day from 6am-8pm. Simple, decent food.

Ha Giang close up

WHERE TO STAY

Between US$10 and US$15

Huong Giang, 18 Nguyen Trai, ☎ (019) 86 64 13, Fax (019) 86 60 15 – 6rm ⚐ 🗏 ♪ 📺 A mini-hotel decorated with all the ends of lines of the local Focus store and flowery Chinese bed-covers. Respectable bathrooms.

Between US$15 and US$30

Phong Duong, 19 Nguyen Trai, ☎ (019) 86 79 79 – 17rm ⚐ 🗏 📺 A rather tacky mini-hotel with carpeted, functional bedrooms. Mosquito nets are provided, but the bathrooms are rather run down.

Tuyen Quang close up

WHERE TO STAY

Between US$15 and US$30

Lo Giang, 219C Duong 17/8, looks out onto the River Lo, ☎ (027) 82 14 52 – 52rm ⚐ 🗏 ♪ 📺 An enormous government-run hotel from another era, with dusty corridors and a rather gloomy atmosphere. The rooms, although dull and depressing, are quite acceptable. The staff do not speak English, and a room here should only be as a last resort if it is too late to carry on to Hanoi.

THE FRIENDSHIP GATE
(VIETNAM – CHINA)★★
BA BE LAKE – CAO BANG – LANG SON
Provinces of Thai Nguyen, Bac Can, Cao Bang and Lang Son
684km tour from Hanoi – Allow 5 days
Accommodation in Ba Be, Cao Bang and Lang Son – Map pages 186-187

Not to be missed
The little roadside markets.
Travelling up the Song Nang as far as Ba Be Lake.
The atmosphere of the old market at Cao Bang.

And remember...
October to April is the best time to visit the area.
Work out your itinerary from Hanoi.
Except at the frontier post at Dong Dang, changing money is difficult,
so be sure to take enough dongs and dollars.

In the northeast of Vietnam, the hills and mountains which extend into the Chinese province of Guangxi make for a rather indefinite and permeable border between the two countries. Here and there in this jumbled landscape there occur little areas of flat country; one such area around the town of Lang Son, known as the **Friendship Gate**, has been both an invasion route and a commercial highway. You will not find the harrowing brutality of the upper valleys of the Red River and the Black River in this stretch of land, but rather a poetic collection of the strange limestone formations that geographers call karsts, scenery worthy of any landscape print. For 2 000 years, the region has been the territory of the Tay who, along with the Nung, followed by the Dao and then the H'mong, took over this area, which now buzzes with activity every five days on the lunar-solar calendar during the numerous fairs and markets.

A frontier is born
These divided lands were difficult to control for both the Chinese Empire and for the state of Vietnam. The latter practised the same **protectorate** system towards the leaders of the Tay and the Nung as for the Tai of the northwest (see page 211). Up until modern times, relations between these tribes and the Chinese and the Vietnamese were fairly volatile, alternating between military support and outright rebellion. In the late 19C, the Chinese mandarins tried to repress certain French expansion in the Tonkin region by secretly backing the guerrilla groups of the **Black Flags**, Sino-Vietnamese bandits operating in the mountainous regions along the frontier. At the end of a short war in 1885, the French colonial army finally crushed the rebels at the same time as they won their victory over the regular Chinese army. Following the signing of the **Treaty of Tianjin**, Chinese troops became committed to observing the Tonkin borders, while the French gained permission for the construction of a railway link to the southern provinces. After the battle, General de Négrier, commander of the French army, even had a sign fixed to the Friendship Gate written in Chinese with the words, "Borders are not protected by stonewalls, but by the enforcement of treaties". The boundaries agreed on in the Treaty of Tianjin are still the same today and were not challenged either during the creation of the Republic of China in 1911 or when Vietnam gained its independence.

A land of resistance
In February 1941, a learned Vietnamese scholar moved into the **Coc Bo Grotto**, not far from Cao Bang, with his typewriter. He was then known as Father Thu, later to become Ho Chi Minh. Two months afterwards, in this remote area, he organised

The Tonkin Highlands

the **VIII Session of the Communist Party**, which marked the beginning of a series of measures leading to the independence of Vietnam. The region served as a base for the **Viet Minh** during the war against the French from 1946 to 1954. The artillery that sealed the fate of the camp at Dien Bien Phu in 1954 was also stationed here *(see page 193)*.

War and peace

In 1979, the Chinese army occupied the border towns of Lao Cai, Cao Bang and Lang Son, launching a 16-day lightning war during which their troops destroyed everything in their path. Economic aid to Vietnam was suspended, the Vietnamese consulates were closed, and road and railway links with Hanoi were blocked. This particular incident gave both countries the ideal opportunity to call into question the definition of land and sea boundaries such as they had been decided during the Treaty of Tianjin. The beginnings of a reconciliation between these two socialist regimes came only after ten years of "cold war" *(see page 33)*.

From Hanoi to Ba Be Lake
295km tour. Allow 6hr by road.

Highway 3, leading to Thai Nguyen, follows the valley of Song Cau. The landscape has nothing more to offer than views of the chaotic urban sprawl that has grown up around Hanoi since the end of the 1990s.

■ **Thai Nguyen** – *134km from Hanoi.* Anyone who has not visited the Museum of Ethnology in Hanoi should not miss the chance to visit the **Cultural Museum for Ethnic Minority Groups in Vietnam** (Bao Tang Van Hoa Cac Dang Toc Viet Nam) *(359 Tu Minh, northeast of the town on the road to Bac Son. Open every day from 7.30am-12noon / 1.30-5pm. Entrance fee).* Set aside at least one hour for the visit if only to enjoy the quality of the fabrics on display as well as the reconstructions of domestic interiors and workshops. The building's strange architecture is a mixture of traditional Vietnamese and pompous Stalinist. The layout of the museum with texts in Vietnamese, English and French is based on the major ethno-linguistic families. The section devoted to the Viet-Muong shows all sorts of fishing instruments used in the southern part of the delta (shrimp spoons, landing nets, keep nets) and the ingenious Muong traps. A display, including a Shamanic embroidered Tay dress and a Nung religious attendant wearing a bonnet inlaid with mirrors, highlights the importance of spiritualist cults among these ethnic minorities. A mezzanine is entirely given over to the complicated weaving of the Tai, while the Mon-Khmers and the Austronesians are represented by their indigo weaving and their basketwork. The H'mong and Dao fabrics are also of equally good quality.

Continue along Highway 3 and you will enter the **Middle Kingdom**. Small valleys appear between the hills planted either with Thai Nguyen **tea**, the most

G de Benoist/MICHELIN

A Tay stall-holder at Cho Ra Market

acclaimed blend in the country, or staked out with clumps of bamboo and banana groves. The first Tay villages also come into view, with their stilt houses topped with enormous thatched roofs.

■ The town of **Bac Can** (*101km from Thai Nguyen*) served as a retreat for Ho Chi Minh when, in 1946, the French forces in Indochina were deployed in the Red River Delta using numerous small forts and blockhouses. In 1947, the French closed in, forcing the Viet Minh to go further into the mountainous area along the Chinese border. Confronted with the Vietnamese military force (60 000 soldiers spread over an area of 20 000km²), General Etienne Valluy chose to stay along a fortified line following Highway 4 (RC4) between Cao Bang and Lang Son (*see insert page 221*).

Eighteen kilometres further on, a road leads off to the left up towards Bac Be Lake above a cultivated valley, while the mountainous wall of the **Pia Boc** spreads out to the west, reaching a high point of 1 554m. The road is narrow but not as bumpy as Highway 3 and wends its way up through wild mountain country as well as through valleys cultivated by the Tay.

■ **Cho Ra**, the "market of Ra", 60km from Bac Can, is a modest street-village with low houses made of primitive bricks and covered with grey tiles and sometimes white-washed. The market is held on days ending in 0 or 5 of the lunar-solar calendar, and it is regularly attended by the Tay and the Nung people wearing conical hats, black trousers and a short blue- or violet-coloured tunic, by the Black H'mong in their pleated indigo skirts, and by the Red Dao, who have exchanged their traditional costumes for off-the-peg shirts and trousers. Market stalls sell all sorts of items associated with fabrics (hanks of cotton, looms and weaving combs) as well as material, woven and dyed the traditional way by the Tay and the Nung. It is either sold by the metre, cut into frogged jackets or made into the popular "progressive" bags, which are worn over the shoulder or across the back. The locals still deal in rice and fresh fish from the lake, cans of rice beer and sugar cane.

The Ba Be National Park** (Vuon Quoc Gia Ba Be)
Allow one day for the boat trip on the lake

The park is 17km from Cho Ra, beyond the Ba Be guesthouse. It is also possible to reach the lake from the river. The landing stage is 2km from the Cho Ra market. Entrance fee. Take your swimming clothes in case you feel like a dip.

The area was renowned for its landscapes during the colonial period, but was only designated as a National Park in 1992. The park protects 23 000ha of rivers and waterfalls around the Ba Be, the "Three Ornamental Pools". This huge 8km-long lake is accessible by road, but the trip up the Song Nang is much more interesting.

Along the Song Nang**
The river threads its way through various cultivated areas before reaching a landscape of **limestone cliffs**. Tiny patches of wild vegetation cling to the rock face, creepers and roots hanging down in search of nourishment. Here and there, muddy hillocks are swallowed up by the jungle, dotted with blood-red canna lilies, and mottled with spindly, silver tree trunks, while the twisted trunks of ancient trees lean out over the water. The activities of the local **fishermen** are another interesting attraction along this stretch of the water. Keep nets line the riverbank, and men can be seen casting other nets as well as banging away at the rocky water's edge to dislodge the tiny shrimps. The river then flows into one side of the **Tunnel Cave of Puong** (Hang Puong), leaving a convenient bank where you can admire the stalactites of this sinkhole on foot. Beyond the cave, the countryside turns wild, filled with over a hundred species of butterflies and birds and 23 different sorts of reptiles and amphibious creatures, including certain species of water snake. One hour further on is the Trading

Across the rice field

Post at **Ban Vai**, offering light lunches. It serves as a drugstore and café for the H'mong at Ban Tuo, a village 2km further up. The women of the village come to chat and sew, while their menfolk prefer the hookah. Flat-bottomed craft returning from the market bring back bundles of rice that are transported on horseback after being weighed. A path leads down towards the **Dau Dang Waterfall** (Thac Dau Dang), which gushes out with a crashing roar between two rock faces and never runs dry.

The Ba Be Lake★★ (Ho Ba Be)
This small sea of sluggish water is set in a landscape of limestone cliffs, mottled with traces of water and signs of gardens. Erosion has gouged out several caves in these rock faces, all with poetic names such as **Dong Ba Cua**, the cave "with three windows" that faces towards the lake. The little islands are even more interesting, and you can either moor alongside or dive in nearby for a better look. On **An Ma Island**, "the Horse's Saddle", a small temple is dedicated to the Spirit of the Waters.

The riverbanks to the south and west are inhabited by the Tay. In the village of **Pac Ngoi** (*accessible by boat in the southern part of the lake*), their houses are raised up on stilts, whereas in the numerous villages that line the road from the lake to Cho Ra, the houses are on ground level.

From Ba Be to Cao Bang through the Co Lea Pass★★
115km tour. Allow 7hr.

Leave Cho Ra on the road to Ho Hieu. 17km further on, go past the turning on your right that leads to Na Phac and Highway 3 (Cao Bang is 128km from Ba Be along this road).

The rutted and stony surface of this rambling road makes progress a little slow, even arduous at times, but the route is breathtaking and the different worlds of the Tay, Nung, H'mong and Dao gradually unfold as the road leads upwards. The highly organised environment of the big Tay villages is soon left behind and replaced by the scattered, isolated houses of the H'mong and Dao. They dominate the area as far as the town of **Pha Den** (*47km from Cho Ra, the market is held on the days ending in 1 or 6*), more than 1 000m up. Their ground level houses are built close to the slopes

219

which they cultivate using slash-and-burn techniques. As in Cho Ra, the Dao women have abandoned their traditional costumes, though the Dao "with coins" (Dao Tien) still decorate their clothing (*see page 56*).

Beyond Pha Den, the road climbs for 7km to the **Co Lea Pass** through the remains of the **extensive forest** that used to cover the entire highland region. Clumps of tree ferns can be seen growing among the surprisingly large variety of tree species. Once at the pass, the **panorama** over the mountains is spectacular. The road then winds down towards the blind valley of **Nguyen Binh** (*27km from Pha Den, the market is held on the days ending in 3 or 8*), through reddish hills planted with sparse pine forests, then climbs up again, leaving behind the fields of maize for cleared mountain sides.

Cao Bang and surrounding area★
Allow one day for the surrounding area

The town is small and ordinary but enjoys a wonderful setting at the foot of a long line of white cliffs at the confluence of the River Hien and Song Bang Giang. In the 17C, the area became a refuge for the **Mac Family** (1527-1677), usurpers and secessionists driven out of Hanoi. The town's large **covered market★** along Kim Dong Avenue is probably the most interesting feature of the town and well worth a visit. From daybreak to the end of the afternoon, stalls spill out onto the neighbouring avenue with groups of women and their baskets selling vegetables in a sea of clothing of every possible shade of indigo. At the end of the day, cooks take over from the growers. Inviting aromas waft from the large cooking pots and braziers where rice cakes, Peking duck and different sorts of offal simmer in large cauldrons. Inside, in the market hall, Chinese odds and ends take pride of place. There are a few old ladies selling religious items for the people of the Delta, such as coins for offerings, incense sticks and paper objects to burn during funeral ceremonies.

On the road to Pac Bo
56km northwest of Cao Bang. Take Highway 203 and allow 2hr for the journey. If you are short of time, continue the tour as far as Cao Binh.
A visit to the cave where Ho Chi Minh stayed for four years and founded the Viet Minh is an important experience for the Vietnamese (*see page 25*). For the visitor from abroad, it is the ideal opportunity to explore the picturesque countryside of the Cao Bang plain.

G de Benoist/MICHELIN

Dao woman

■ The **Ky Sam Den** is perched on top of a low hill 5km from Cao Bang. This temple was erected in homage to the Tay chief Nung Tri Cao, who had tried to create an independent kingdom for the Dai Co Viet in the middle of the 11C. His rebellion troubled the region for more than ten years, extending even as far as the Chinese provinces of Guangxi and Guangdong. The uprising was only crushed with the support of the Chinese army. The structure has been entirely rebuilt, but the galloping red and white horses painted on the walls contribute to maintaining its naïve charm as a small country temple.

Follow the road for 10km, then turn left along a path leading to Cao Binh, 2km further on.

■ **Cao Binh**, "Superior peace", is now just a modest little village despite its previous status as the administrative centre of the region from the time of the Mac dynasty until the colonial administration transferred its functions to Cao Bang in 1884. A few colonial houses and a church are the only remaining evidence of these former times.

Go back to Highway 203 and carry on to Pac Bo.

■ At **Pac Bo**, a small museum *(open daily from 8am-5pm. Entrance fee)* gives an account of the events associated with Ho Chi Minh's stay. His retreat, the **Coc Bo Cave**, is open to the public, and is situated at the foot of Cac Mac (Karl Marx) mountain and bordered by the River Le Nin (Lenin).

From Cao Bang to Lang Son
123km tour. Allow 4hr.
Bus between Cao Bang and Lang Son, or between Hanoi and Lang Son, see page 225.

Highway 4 is narrow and in poor condition. There is nothing of particular interest before Dong Khe, apart from a few Tay houses with large verandas on stilts, and the market held in **Nam Nang** *(18km from Cao Bang)* on days ending in 2 and 7.

■ On entering **Dong Khe** *(24km from Nam Nang)*, you will notice a whole group of houses miraculously preserved after the evacuation by the French in 1951. The town's war memorial is dedicated to all those Vietnamese soldiers who died in the storming of the town, an event that marked the first important French defeat in the Indochina War.

■ The road runs through a picturesque landscape of craggy peaks and cliff faces dotted with caves as far as **That Khe** *(22km from Dong Khe)*, a town with mint-green coloured houses whose market *(days ending in 2 and 7)* is popular with the Tay, the Nung and the Dao. Beyond the town is a patchwork of rice paddies, a rare sight in an area mainly given over to the cultivation of maize.

The bloody route
In 1950, the liberation army, led by General Giap, had regrouped in the protection of the mountains, and was supported by rear bases in Yunnan and Guangxi in China. The French army had formed a fortified line along Highway 4 between Cao Bang and Lang Son. In May 1950, Giap launched his first attack on Dong Khe, splitting the French defence system in two and isolating Cao Bang which fell a few months later. The evacuation of Cao Bang ended in one of the bloodiest episodes of the Indochina War, with the only avenue of retreat left open to the French being Highway 4 and the trap set by Giap. The French lost 6 000 soldiers who were either killed or taken prisoner.

The Friendship Gate

■ Forty-eight kilometres from That Khe, the road becomes a dual-carriageway on the approach to **Dong Dang**, an unwelcoming sort of town of low apartment blocks faced with tiles or smoked glass. The big Chinese brother and the socialist market economy is not far from here – the border is just 5km away. The historical routeway linking China and Vietnam starts here, and the **China Gateway**, renamed the **Friendship Gate** (Cua Khau Huu Nghi) by the Chinese, has been used time and again by the armies of the Empire. A ceremony held on 1 April 1992 heralded the reopening of the crossing. To mark the occasion, the Chinese rebuilt the gateway of the citadel *(only visible from the Chinese side of the border)* that used to guard the pass, *(for details on crossing the border, see page 225)*. *Head back to Highway 14 in the direction of Lang Son, 11km further on.*

Lang Son
Allow half a day

The town was almost totally destroyed during the war in February 1979, but smuggling and the reopening of the border have brought about an economic boom period. The town has unfortunately developed on similar lines to Cao Bang and is rather unattractive, but it is set in beautiful countryside of limestone peaks.

The markets of Lang Son are well worth a detour. **Cho Ky Lua** (*to the north of the town on Tran Dang Ninh*) and especially **Cho Dong Kinh** are perfect illustrations of the close economic relations between Lang Son and its Chinese neighbours. The stalls at Cho Dong Kinh are almost like a shrine to Chinese hardware with a deluge of incredible gadgets.

A few houses on the southern outskirts of the town still remain from French garrison days, near the most revered shrine in Lang Son, the **Pagoda of the Immortals** (Chua Tien) (*Open daily 7am-5pm. Entrance fee*). Go down a flight of steps to get to the pagoda, situated in the recess of an enormous cave. The pyramids of cans of Coca-Cola and other fizzy drinks respectfully placed at the altars bear witness to the powers attributed to the pagoda's various divinities. At the back of a room dedicated to Quan Am, the Holy Mother is paid her respects, surrounded by a forest of incense sticks in their blue and white perfume-burners. A tunnel leads to naturally-formed windows opening out onto the picturesque countryside bordering Lang Son.

At the foot of the hill, another path climbs up towards the site of **Gieng Tien**, a little shrine with a superb view over Lang Son and the surrounding area.

On the northwest edge of Lang Son, in a small market garden district, the caves have become popular destinations for people on Buddhist pilgrimages.

The cave of the Three Pure Precepts* (Dong Tam Tanh) (*access is signposted from the crossroads between Tran Dang Ninh and Le Loi. Open daily 7am-5pm. Entrance fee*) closely resembles a pagoda. At the entrance, statues of the Buddhist pantheon grace an altar by a rock face carved with stelae from the 16C to the 18C which record donations made to the shrine. But further on, in the numerous nooks and crannies, Holy Mothers and deified local heroines also receive their fair share of worship. Water dripping down from the stalactites has healing properties, which explains the presence of the plastic cups near the pools of water. In the half-light of the cave, visitors grope their way over steps hacked out in the limestone, intermittently lit by "windows" or wells of natural light. The hill adjacent to the Tam Tanh Cave has become the emblem of Lang Son. It is called **Nui Vong Phu** (Mountain of the Waiting Lady), because its rocky outline resembles that of a lady holding a child. The rock features in one of those tragic love stories that are so popular in the country's literary works.

Further to the west, the **Cave of the Two Pure Precepts*** (Dong Nhi Thanh) (*Open daily 7am-5pm. Entrance fee*) was made a shrine in the 18C and also shelters a Buddhist chapel. A maze of alcoves, bends and fissures ascend in a spiral across the rock, forming numerous chapels and shrines dedicated to Buddha and his peers.

Forbidden love

An astrologer once predicted that a twin brother and sister would eventually marry. In order to avoid such a prediction coming true, the brother seized the opportunity during a trip to the forest to hack his sister to death. He left the region, changed his name and settled in Lang Son where, a few years later, he married the daughter of a local merchant. While his wife was combing her hair one day, he noticed a deep scar around her neck. He quizzed her about it, and the young woman declared that she had been injured and left to die by her brother before being taken in and cared for by bandits who then sold her to her "father". Deeply disturbed by these revelations, the man left home. From that moment, his wife climbed the hill every day, waiting for her husband's return. One day, no longer able to bear her grief, she turned to stone, committing herself to an eternity of waiting.

From Lang Son to Hanoi
151km tour. Allow 4hr.
Buses and trains between Hanoi and Lang Son, see page 25.

Leave Lang Son on Highway 1, which takes you past a picturesque patchwork countryside of red soil and green crops. Beyond, the road follows the mountainous corridor of the Song Thuong Valley, the site of a number of battles in attempts to take control of this thoroughfare. **Dong Mo** is a small village nestling at the foot of a natural amphitheatre of limestone 35km from Lang Son. Eastwards and southwards there are gorges and more natural amphitheatres, which the Sino-Vietnamese pirates from Bac Son used as a hideout in the 1890s. In 1884, the Chinese army, based in Lang Son, laid ambush to a detachment of 350 French soldiers. The French subsequently pushed the Chinese forces back to the far side of the China Gateway.

Beyond Met *(33km from Dong Mo),* the cliffs and peaks are replaced by the flat lands of the delta. Eastwards, the curved line of hills of Dong Trieu extends southwards to form the famous Halong Bay *(see page 174).*

Cho Ra close up

COMING AND GOING

By bus – There is no bus station in Cho Ra and using the regular bus service can be rather hazardous. There is a daily bus service from Cao Bang, but from Hanoi you must get off at Bac Can and rent a motorcycle-taxi.

Excursions – Agencies in Hanoi offer 3-day round trips in small groups from between US$35 and US$60 per person.

Chauffeur-driven 4WD vehicles – This is really the only sensible option if you want to see all the above places in reasonable comfort. Trips from Hanoi (1 to 3 people, 5 days and 4 nights) vary from US$80 to US$150 per person, based on a standard tour and including petrol as well as board and lodgings for the driver. A typical schedule would be Hanoi – Ba Be (1 night) – Cao Bang (1 night) – Lang Son (1 night) – Ha Long (1 night) – Hanoi.

ADDRESS BOOK

Post office / Telephone – *Buu Dien Cho Ra* is situated in the middle of the only street in the village. Open Monday-Friday, 6.30am-8pm.

WHERE TO STAY

Between US$10 and US$15
Ba Be Guesthouse (Nha Khach Ba Be), 2km from the lake's west shore and 15km from Cho Ra, ☎ (0281) 87 61 27 – 22rm ⚑ ⤬ ✗ A standby if you fail to find lodgings with the local inhabitants. This unattractive state-run hotel is in the country, but not beside the lake. It offers a choice between a dirty and dilapidated concrete building or a decrepit wooden bungalow. It is also the administrative centre for the park.

Between US$15 and US$30
Ba Be Hotel (Khach San Ba Be), at the entrance to Cho Ra, ☎ (0281) 87 61 15 – 8rm ⚑ ⤬ A simple, comfortable little hotel. The back rooms look out onto the rice plantations bordering the village. A boat trip on the lake can be arranged from here. No restaurant, but breakfast is available.

EATING OUT

Between 25 000 and 50 000VND
Nha Hang Thanh Dung, next to the Ba Be Hotel. The restaurant serves simple fare.

OTHER THINGS TO DO

Excursions – For further information concerning cruises, contact the Ba Be Hotel or the guesthouse. Motorised punts travel up the Song Nang as far as Ba Be Lake. You sit on garden furniture and are protected from the sun by a plastic tarpaulin. Allow US$20 for the day. You can return by boat or along the road from the landing-stage on the east bank of Lake Ba Be.

Cho Ra close up

Nguyen Binh close up

EATING OUT

Between 25 000 and 50 000VND
Nha Hang Thui Hong, ☎ (026)
87 21 77. A "com pho" that stands out
from the rest, offering delicious, nour-
ishing meals, which is just what the doctor ordered along this rather arduous
route. Try the soya cheese stuffed with
meat balls ("dau phu nhoi chit") or the
sautéed pork with perfumed mushrooms ("thut lon xao nam huong"), all
washed down with local spirits.

Cao Bang close up

COMING AND GOING

By bus – The **bus station** is on the outskirts of the town on the road to Lang
Son. Service buses leave early in the
morning for Bac Can (5hr), Thai Nguyen
(7hr), Nguyen Binh (3hr), Lang Son
(6hr) and Cho Ra (4hr). More comfortable minibuses leave for Hanoi at
2.30pm (10hr).

GETTING AROUND

Kim Dong Avenue forms the centre of
Cao Bang. It is overlooked to the west by
Ba Dinh Square and continues north-
ward over the bridge across the Bang Giang, close to which is the old market.

ADDRESS BOOK

Post office / Telephone – **Buu Dien
Pho Tau**, Kim Dong, ☎ (026) 85 38 52.
Open daily 7-11.30am. **Buu Dien Cao
Bang**, Ba Dinh Square. Open daily 6am-
9pm.

WHERE TO STAY

Between US$10 and US$15
Duo Trung, Be Van Dan (near the central post office), ☎ (026) 85 34 24 –
36rm ⌂ ▤ ✕ TV Chinese businessmen are regular customers, and the
rooms are pleasant and spacious, with a
balcony looking out over a quiet street.
Clean carpets and spotless linen.

Between US$15 and US$20
Khach San Bang Giang, Kim Dong
(near the bridge, opposite the old market), ☎ (026) 85 34 31, Fax (026)
85 59 84 – 66rm ⌂ ▤ ✕ ✍ TV ✕
An ugly building, but an ideal location
on the edge of the River Bang Giang. The
well-ventilated, spacious rooms are
quite functional, and those with a balcony over the river are very quiet. The
bathrooms could do with a lick of paint,
but the hotel provides the best value for
money in Cao Bang with English-speaking staff. Rates vary according to the
quality of the mattress.
Huong Thom, 46 Kim Dong, ☎ (026)
85 58 88 – 8rm ⌂ ▤ ✕ TV ✕ Although quite comfortable, the rooms are
small and stuffy, but the bathrooms are
very clean. The view of the river is somewhat spoilt by the noisy generator.

EATING OUT

Under 25 000VND
The stalls in the **covered market** provide the ideal opportunity to try the local fare in an informal setting. Settle
down on one of the benches side by
side with a Kinh lorry driver and a Tay
grandmother and dig into the soup, a
bowl of noodles or some other local
speciality. Other stalls outside the market offer take-away or sit down meals
(from 5-7pm). Food in the market is
available from 6am until 8pm.

COMING AND GOING

By train – The *Ga Lang Son* can be found at the end of Le Loi Avenue. There are four daily trains in both directions between Lang Son and Hanoi-Gia Lam (5hr 30min). Departures at 6.30am, 10.10am, 2.04pm and 6.05pm. Caution: foreign visitors will only be allowed entry into China by train from Hanoi (see "Hanoi close up", page 144).

By bus – The *bus station* is in the same area as the railway station. Air-conditioned minibuses with video screens operate two daily services, at 6.30am and 1.30pm, from Hanoi-Gia Lam (5hr 30min) and Haiphong, via Bac Giang, Bac Ninh and Gia Lam (9hr). Two daily bus services, at 9am and 3pm, operate between Lang Son and Pingxiang, the first Chinese town on the other side of the border. Local morning bus for Cao Bang (6hr).

GETTING AROUND

Tran Dang Ninh Avenue goes through Lang Son as an extension of Highway 1. The old Ky Lua market is on the northern side. To the south, the avenue forms an intersection with Le Loi leading to the bus and railway stations. Another road leads off this same intersection towards Nhi Thanh and Tam Thanh (2km). The River Ky Cung is situated on the southern outskirts of the town. The Dong Kinh market extends as far as the northern bank.

ADDRESS BOOK

Post office / Telephone – *Buu Dien Lang Son*, Le Loi, ☎ (026) 85 38 52. Open daily 7am-9pm.

Visas – Visas for China can only be obtained in Hanoi (see page 96).

Border post – The Chinese border is 11km from Lang Son, near Dong Dang. There is a regular bus service from Lang Son. A number of buses travel directly to Pingxiang, 20km from the Chinese border post, where buses and trains serve Ningming and Nanning. The 800m of no man's land between the Vietnamese and Chinese border posts must be crossed on foot.

WHERE TO STAY

It can prove difficult to find accommodation in Lang Son, since the best rooms are taken up most of the year by Chinese businessmen involved in border trading. In any case, the quality of the rooms will not encourage long stays.

Under US$10
Huu Nghi Hotel (Khach San Huu Nghi), 68 Ngo Quyen (near the bus station), ☎ (025) 87 11 20, Fax (025) 87 66 23 – 24rm ⚐ 🍴 ✕ TV This stopover for Lang Son lorry drivers is perfectly respectable and the courtyard building is even quite appealing. The mattresses are on the thin side, but the bathrooms are serviceable.

Between US$10 and US$15
Hoang Nguyen Hotel, 84 Tran Dang Ninh, ☎ (025) 87 45 75 / 87 03 49 – 12rm ⚐ 🍴 ✕ TV A clean and decent mini-hotel, although most of the rooms are windowless.

Hoang Gia Hotel (Khach San Hoang Gia), 67 Le Loi (near the post office), ☎ (025) 87 17 31 – 10rm ⚐ 🍴 ✕ TV A mini-hotel with a somewhat tasteless decor. The rooms are adequate, but the bathrooms are tiny.

Between US$15 and US$20
Dong Kinh Hotel (Khach San Dong Kinh), 25 Nguyen Du, ☎ (025) 87 01 66, Fax (025) 87 54 61 – 21rm ⚐ 🍴 ✕ TV Located on the River Ky Cung, this is a very peaceful government-run hotel, despite the nearby market. Wonderful views of Lang Son from the upper floors. Adequate accommodation.

EATING OUT

Between 25 000 and 50 000VND
Nha Hang Minh Quang, 44 Ngo Quyen, next to Huu Nghi, ☎ (025) 87 04 17. Share a drink with the local lorry drivers in this lively bar serving good Vietnamese cuisine.

Cham tower at Po Nagar

THE CENTRE

Wedged in between the Truong Son Cordillera to the west and the South China Sea to the east, the Annamite Coast forms a curve, often likened to a yoke from which hang the two baskets of rice of the deltas of the Red River and the Mekong. The western mountains on the border with Laos occasionally encroach as far as the dunes, creating a string of tiny coastal plains dotted with lagoons. The deep blue sea contrasts with the lush green forests and rice paddies in this region where time often seems to have stood still. Farmers and buffaloes continue to plough the land just as in ancestral times and the women can be seen sowing rice by hand, while on the roadsides, the seeds and stems are dried, beaten and sorted. To the north of Da Nang, the Pass of Clouds (496m) separates two distinct geographical zones. The Hue region is exposed to the winds and rains while to the south, the climate is milder and the sun shines all year round. The magnificent beaches stretching from Da Nang to Mui Ne have long been favourites with leisure-seekers. Colourful fishing boats bob up and down on the turquoise waters of the coast's countless creeks and bays, while sleepy villages doze in the shade of coconut trees.

What used to be known as Annam is now called Trung Bo (Central Vietnam), but the Mandarin Road down the coast, used by the Viet in their March southwards, has kept many reminders of the glories of the kingdoms which succeeded one another along its course. Among them are the citadel, palaces and Royal Tombs of Hue, the fine houses of Chinese merchants in the old port city of Hoi An, the Cham ruins at My Son and the tower-shrines which line the road as far as Phan Thiet, all of them demanding attention in the course of your journey through Vietnam.

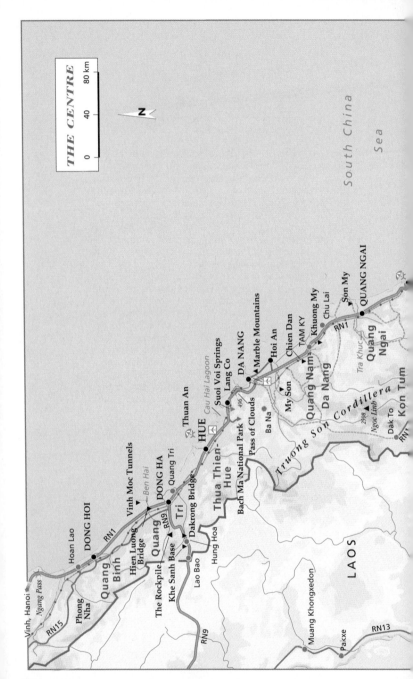

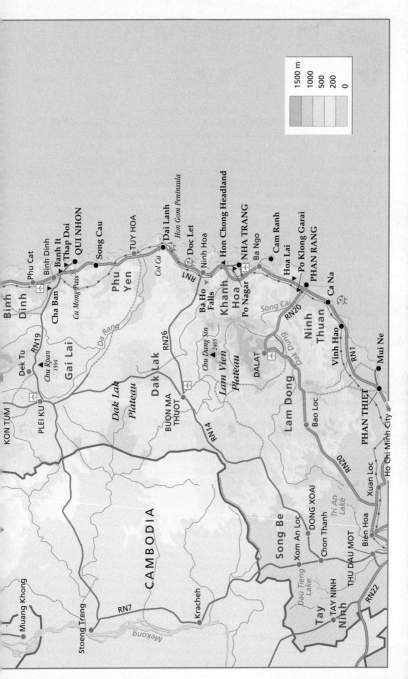

1500 m
1000
500
200
0

Binh
Dinh

Phu Cat
Binh Dinh
Cha Ban
Banh It
Thap Doi
QUI NHON
Song Cau
TUY HOA
Dai Lanh
Doc Let
Hon Gom Peninsula
Ninh Hoa
Hon Chong Headland
NHA TRANG
Ba Ngo
Cam Ranh
Po Klong Garai
PHAN RANG
Hoa Lai
Ca Na

Dek Tu
Chu Rpan
1504
RN19
Gai Lai

Cu Mong Pass
Col Ca

Phu
Yen

Da Rang

RN1

Ba Ho
Falls
Po Nagar

Khanh
Hoa

Song Cai

RN26

RN20

Ninh
Thuan

Vinh Hao

RN1

Mui Ne

KON TUM
PLEI KU

Dak Lak
Plateau

Dak Lak

Chu Dang Sin
2405

Lam Vien
Plateau

DALAT

Dak Dung

Lam Dong

Bao Loc

PHAN THIET

RN14

BUON MA
THUOT

Ho Chi Minh City

CAMBODIA

DONG XOAI
Xom An Loc
Chon Thanh

Song Be

Tri An
Lake

Bao Loc

Xuan Loc

Bien Hoa

RN20

THU DAU MOT

RN22

Muang Khong

Stoeng Treng

RN7

Kracheh

Pau Tieng
Lake

Tay
Ninh

TAY NINH

Mekong

229

AROUND THE 17TH PARALLEL
Provinces of Quang Binh and Quang Tri – Map pages 228-229

Not to be missed
Phong Nha Cave.
The Vinh Moc tunnels.
And remember...
It is preferable to hire a guide to visit the Demilitarised Zone (DMZ),
and not to stray from the way-marked paths.

Once over the border into Annam, the Trans-Vietnamese railway weaves its way between the coast and the Truong Son range, crossing the most impoverished provinces of the country, Quang Binh and Quang Tri. The deep scars left by the bloody fighting that went on around the 17th Parallel during the Vietnam War have yet to heal and a pilgrimage to the sites where so many thousands of men and women were sacrificed on the altar of war remains deeply moving.

18km north of Dong Hoi, leave the RN1 at the village of Hoan Lao and take a turning to the right opposite the post office. The landing stage for Phong Nha Cave is 30km further on, at the village of Son Trach.

■ **Phong Nha Cave*** – *Entrance fee: 100 000 VND. Allow 2hr.* This vast complex of caves is located in a 10 000km^2 park of limestone mountains covered in a rich carpet of 41 000ha of primeval forest, home to a very varied flora and fauna. The region has some fifteen or so caves in all, of which Phong Nha is the most beautiful. It was first explored in the 19C by a Frenchman, who did not however go further than 600m into them. It wasn't until 1990-92 that a British team managed to explore all 7 729m of the underground galleries. Five kilometres from the landing stage, the cave is reached after a pleasant boat trip down the River Son of Son. The heart of the cave consists of a succession of sandy beaches and grottoes, where stalactites and stalagmites sculpted over the centuries provide a wonderful pageant of colourful scenes.

Return onto the RN1 and head for Dong Hoi.

■ **Dong Hoi** – *488km from Hanoi and 166km from Hue.* Its status as capital of Quanh Binh province has attracted large numbers of government officials and businesses to the peaceful and somewhat charmless country town. Tourists are few and far between, except for the few on excursions to Phong Nha. If you absolutely have to spend time in Dong Hoi, the **market** *(to the south of Nhat Le Hotel)* and the **beach** stretching alongside River Nhat Le are both quite pleasant.

Continue on towards Dong Ha.

The Demilitarised Zone (DMZ)
Allow 1 day

The Geneva Accords signed on July 20 1954 between the French and the Vietnamese drew a provisional demarcation line along the 17th Parallel through the centre of Vietnam, dividing North from South and effectively sharing out the country between Ho Chi Minh's "Democratic Republic of Vietnam" and the "State of Vietnam", led by Bao Dai and subsequently by President Ngo Dinh Diem *(see page 28)*. The agreement also provided for a 10km-wide demilitarised zone (DMZ) and it was to the south of this band that in 1967, the Americans established a highly sophisticated electronic defence line intended to halt the Viet Minh forces. Dubbed the **McNamara Line**, it was in fact a barricade of mines and toxic booby traps, strung together with barbed wire fences equipped with infrared and acoustic devices. Although nothing now remains of these fortifications, the surrounding area is still deeply pockmarked by bombshells and the region's impoverished inhabitants, who dig up the leftover half-buried scrap metal in the hope of selling it, continue to fall victim to unexploded bombs.

North of Dong Ha

■ Some 20km to the north of Dong Ha, the line of the 17th Parallel is more or less followed by the **River Ben Hai** which flows from the Truong Son Mountains down to the estuary of Cua Tung and into the South China Sea. For twenty years the river separated North and South, flowing through a 10km-wide no-man's-land. The 178m-long steel **Hien Luong Bridge** spanning the river, served as a frontier post between the zones. On the north bank stands a very Stalinist-looking monument erected on the ruins of the former customs post.

500m north of the bridge, before the station, take a little turning to the right off the RN1 which will take you through rice paddies (signposted). The Vinh Moc tunnels are 18km away.

■ The **Vinh Moc tunnels**⋆ are one of the most striking examples of Vietnamese tenacity and courage in the fight against the Americans. It is difficult to imagine how 400 people managed to live for almost two years in the 1 700m of underground passages, none of which were over 1.8m high or 2m wide. Located close to the village of Vinh Linh, reputed for its iron ore, and the archipelago of Can Co, which was a vital source of fresh supplies, Vinh Moc's strategic importance resulted in practically non-stop bombing throughout the war. The villagers finally got together and dug themselves an underground village where they lived from 1966-68. There were three levels of galleries, 12, 15 and 23m deep. Each consisted of tiny cells, kitchens, toilets, wells, a hospital, where 17 children were born and a communal room large enough for 50 to 60 people. Near the tunnels, an on-site **museum** has photos of this period illustrating what life was like underground.

Return onto the RN1 and go back to Dong Ha.

On the road to Khe Sanh

■ At the junction of the RN1 and the RN9, the ugly town of **Dong Ha** *(92km from Dong Hoi and 74km from Hue)* is of little interest, except as a stopping point on the road to Lao Bao. The RN9 was initially the work of the French who built it to reach the border with Laos and, in so doing, cleared a large part of the jungle which formerly covered the region. The intensive bombing and the defoliants used by the Americans during the Vietnam War transformed the landscape even more drastically. As the effects of Agent Orange last for over a hundred years, only a few rare species, such as rubber trees or coffee bushes, are able to survive on this almost barren soil.

The Rockpile stands some thirty kilometres to the west of Dong Ha, on the outskirts of Hak Lam village. It is a rocky outcrop which served as an American lookout during the war. Its caves were occupied by relays of GIs, totally cut off from the rest of the world and supplied only by helicopter.

On the way to Khe Sanh, **stilt houses** made of woven bamboo and with thatched roofs can be seen on either side of the RN9. They are the homes of the **Bru**, an ethnic minority which played a significant role in the war against the Americans. They chose to support Ho Chi Minh and showed themselves to be highly efficient jungle fighters, operating in an environment in which they were totally at home. They numbered some 80 000 before the war, but only 20 000 still remain today.

A few kilometres further on, to the left, is a new bridge over the River Dakrong, built to replace the old **Dakrong Bridge** which finally crumbled away in the autumn of 1999. Built in 1972 with Cuban funds, it was at the time a key component of the Ho Chi Minh Trail *(see page 30)*.

In the village of Hung Hoa, take the track to the right of the monument at the entrance into the village (before the station). 3km further on, a narrow dirt track on the right (signposted) leads to the Khe Sanh Base.

■ Just like Dien Bien Phu, the American military base of **Khe Sanh** was supposed to have been impregnable. Today, it is a desolate, wind-battered place, whose meagre vegetation seems incapable of thriving in the barren, ruddy soil, as if soaked in the blood of all those who died here. A modest **museum** has a map of the region which outlines the numerous battles that raged here, together with a few period photos and objects found on the site, such as baskets, weapons and a radio. Outside the museum, little remains of the base, except for a tank (the latest model at the time), a propeller, a machine gun and a monument to the Liberation.

Black market dealers
The sight of particularly voluptuous women waddling along the edge of the RN9 often intrigues visitors to the region. They are in fact black market dealers on their way back from the Laotian border, their jackets stuffed with cut-price cigarettes. To avoid the police barricades, they walk down through the hills before catching a bus down on the coast.

From Huong Hoa, you can either push on as far as Laos or return to Dong Ha. From here, the RN1 borders the coast as far as Hue, passing through Quang Tri, former home to a major citadel.

Dong Hoi close up

The Centre

COMING AND GOING

By train – The *railway station* is on the west side of Dong Hoi, at the end of Tran Hung Dao. Four trains daily to Hanoi and Ho Chi Minh City.

By bus – There is no *bus station*, but you can always flag down one of the many buses on the RN1 between Hanoi and Ho Chi Minh City. Be patient however as they are often full and don't stop.

ADDRESS BOOK

Post office / Telephone – *Buu Dien Dong Hoi*, on the corner of Ly Thuong Kiet and Tran Hung Dao, opposite the My Ngoc Hotel. Daily 6.30am-10pm (summer) / 7am-9.30pm (winter).

WHERE TO STAY

Avoid the Nhat Le, Phuong Dong and Huu Nghi Hotels, which are neglected, dirty, thoroughly depressing and over-priced, particularly those on the river bank. It should also be noted that English is not commonly spoken in Dong Hoi.

Between US$10 and US$15
My Ngoc Hotel, 5 Ly Thuong Kiet, ☎ (052) 82 20 74 – 12rm 🛏 🖥 ♪ Λ

well-kept little hotel. The rooms are clean and light and the staff is very pleasant. It is well-located on the edge of the RN1 and most probably the best place to stay in Dong Hoi. Ask for a room which doesn't overlook the main road.

Dong Hoi Hotel, 50 Quang Trung, ☎ (052) 82 26 69, Fax (052) 82 21 60 – 30rm 🛏 🖥 ♪ 📺 ✕ The Dong Hoi is totally devoid of charm, but the rooms are clean and have a balcony. Cars or minibuses can be hired. Bus tickets can also be booked and excursions organised to Phong Nha.

Between US$15 and US$30
Phong Nha Hotel, 5 Truong Phap, on the river bank, to the north of the town, ☎ (052) 82 49 71, Fax (052) 82 25 36 – 37rm 🛏 🖥 ♪ 📺 ✕ One of last "grand" hotels of Dong Hoi. The establishment is a little cold and impersonal, but it has a pleasant view of the beach and is very quiet. The rooms are acceptable and clean. The hotel organises excursions in the region and can reserve a car or book a bus ticket. The receptionist speaks English.

Hoa Hong Guesthouse, 34 Truong Phap, on the river bank, ☎ (052)

82 20 42 – 15rm 🍴 📺 📶 📺 ✕ Similar to the above establishment. The blue tiles and smoked glass façade may not inspire you, but the hotel has yet to suffer from old age.

Under 25 000VND

Nam Long, 22 Ho Xuan Huong. A modest establishment with no character, but the food is excellent and the helpings are generous. Menu in English and pleasant staff.

EXCURSIONS

To visit Phong Nha Cave, which is 48km northwest of the town, you can ask at the **Phong Nha** and **Dong Hoi Hotels**, but it is much cheaper to go there under your own steam, by renting a motorcycle taxi (200 000VND round trip), a car (350 000VND for 4 people) or a minibus (450 000VND for 12 people).

Dong Ha close up

COMING AND GOING

By train – The **railway station** is on the right as you head south out of the town.

By bus – The **bus station** is at 122 Le Duan, on the corner of the RN1 and the RN9. Several buses leave daily for Hanoi (580km) and Hue (74km, 90min). Numerous services to Lao Bao (80km, 2hr) and one daily bus, at midnight, to Savannakhet (330km), in Laos. For this destination, the bus comes from Da Nang; tickets from the Dong Ha Hotel.

ADDRESS BOOK

Post office / Telephone – **Buu Dien Dong Ha**, Le Duan. Daily, 6.30am-10pm.

Travel agencies – **DMZ Open Tour / Sinh Café**, 94 Le Duan, ☎ (053) 85 32 56. **Quang Tri Tourist Information Office**, Dong Ha Hotel, ☎ (053) 85 29 27 / 85 30 47.

WHERE TO STAY, EATING OUT

Between US$10 and US$15

Dong Ha Hotel, 66 Le Duan, next to the bus station, ☎ (053) 85 52 34, Fax (053) 85 16 17 – 26rm 🍴 📺 📶 📺 ✕ This hotel uses its location to full advantage, but its rooms are shabby and far from clean. To be avoided, together with its restaurant and awful food. You can however book bus tickets and excursions from the agency near the restaurant.

Phung Hoang 2, 146 Le Duan, to the south of the bus station, ☎ (053) 85 45 67, Fax (053) 85 54 41 – 15rm 🍴 📺 ✕ 📶 📺 ✕ A modern, comfortable hotel. The rooms are decent and clean, but the cheapest ones (US$10) have neither windows nor air-conditioning. The manager speaks a little English. Avoid the dreadful Phung Hoang 1, at 295 Le Duan.

Mini Hotel Thanh Tinh, 220 Le Duan, ☎ (053) 85 22 36, Fax (053) 85 28 50. 🍴 📺 Decent establishment. Only if the Phung Hoang 2 is full.

Between US$15 and US$30

Buu Dien Hotel, Le Duan, to the south of the bus station, ☎ (053) 85 44 18, Fax (053) 85 28 50 🍴 📺 ✕ 📶 📺 ✕ This hotel is laid out around a vast courtyard where cars can be parked. The rooms are comfortable and clean and the staff friendly.

EXCURSIONS

The "DMZ Tour" leaves from Hue or Dong Ha. By booking in Dong Ha (US$15), it is more than likely that you will join a group from Hue, with whom you can return to the Imperial city in the evening. Two tours of one or two days are available, but unless you are particularly interested in this tragic page of history, a one-day tour will probably be sufficient.

HUE ★★★

Capital of the province of Thua Thien Hue
654km from Hanoi, 1 071km from Ho Chi Minh City
Pop 280 000 – Humid climate

Not to be missed
The Imperial City.
The Royal Tombs.
The road between Hue and Da Nang.

And remember...
A bicycle is the best way to explore the town and its outskirts.
Showers are frequent, so always take an umbrella.

The former Imperial capital nestles in a bend of the Song Huong, the Perfume River, which gently flows past green hills into the estuary at Thuan An, passing on its way many remains of a glorious past. Even though the nation's administrative and economic authorities traditionally neglected Hue in favour of strait-laced Hanoi or hot-headed Saigon, the city remains the intellectual and cultural heart and soul of the country. It is the traditional muse of artists, who are attracted by its poetic landscapes, the indefinable charm of its palaces, pagodas and tombs, its sophisticated way of life and the graceful elegance of its women, many of whom continue to wear the *ao dai* and the conical hat.

Bicycles rule the city. The citadel and old shopping districts on the west bank and the modern town stretched along the east bank, together with the surrounding countryside, are all ideally suited to leisurely bicycle rides. Losing oneself in the wide

Down the Song Huong

B Juge/MICHELIN

The Centre

shady avenues or the stony narrow lanes is an ideal pretext for asking directions from the friendly inhabitants. Many will spontaneously come up and talk to you and are genuinely interested in who you are and where you come from. Despite the extent of the ravages of the Vietnam War, Hue remains an essential part of any trip and ranks among the most appealing and likeable cities in Vietnam.

A bitterly disputed territory

Although the foundation of present-day Hue only dates back to the 19C, the region was already inhabited some 4000 years ago, as is illustrated by the stone carvings found in the area. After a period of rule by China, it fell under the influence of Champa from the 3C-14C, until King Che Man was forced to relinquish the region to Dai Viet *(see page 20)*. Thus, in 1466 the region of **Thuan Hoa** was born, although it remained a subject of dispute between the two kingdoms for a century. After the fall of the Cham, the country was once again divided in two, under the Le dynasty, with the Trinh in the north and the Nguyen in the south. In 1636, the latter established their residence and administrative headquarters at **Kim Long**, but moved their capital in 1687 to **Phu Xuan** (5km to the north of present-day Hue) where they built an immense citadel. From 1778 the south was troubled by new conflicts between the Nguyen lords and the Tay Son brothers. The latter seized the region of Thuan Hoa and Phu Xuan and held them from 1786 until 1802. Nguyen Anh then recaptured the citadel of Phu Xuan, after having put down the rebellion and united the northern, central and southern territories. Now Emperor **Gia Long**, he decided to build a new citadel on the banks of the Song Huong at Hue to replace that of Phu Xuan. It was to become the political and cultural centre of the new empire of Annam.

The last Imperial capital

Under the French Protectorate, Hue for a time remained Vietnam's official capital, but was in fact only the seat of puppet emperors. In the pay of France, the Nguyen emperors were reduced to symbols until the abdication of **Bao Dai** in 1945. The Geneva Accords in 1954 ratified the end of Vietnam's monarchy and the supremacy of Hue. The country was divided into two zones. To the north, Ho Chi Minh's Democratic Republic of Vietnam chose Hanoi as capital, while to the south, Ngo Dinh Diem's Republic of Vietnam ruled from Saigon. Over the ensuing dark years, particularly during the Tet Offensive, Hue suffered terrible bombing and the greater part of the city had to be rebuilt. If the former Imperial capital has lost much of its former grandeur, it still retains a distinctive charm which leaves no visitor indifferent.

The citadel★★ (Kinh Thanh)
Allow half a day

The bustle of the city almost vanishes once inside the citadel's walls. Deeply scarred by successive wars, it is still nursing its wounds and this is reflected in its melancholy, muted atmosphere. Nonetheless the wrinkles and bruises of the passing of time have not totally erased all glimpses of its former sparkling grandeur. Take the time to listen to this grand old lady as she nostalgically relates her life of

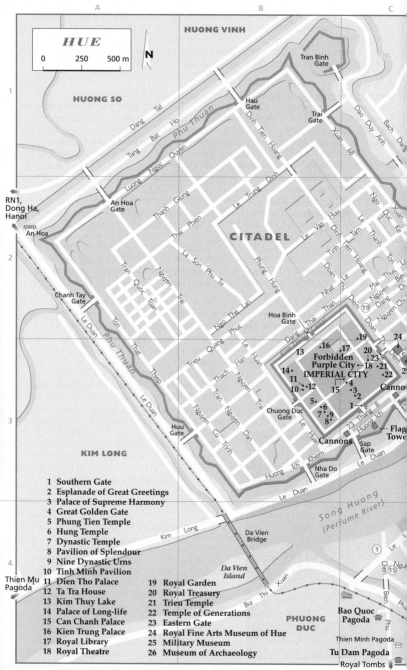

HUE

0   250   500 m

N

HUONG VINH

HUONG SO

Tran Binh Gate

Hau Gate

Trai Gate

Phu Thuan

Dang Tat

Bat Ho

Tang

Luong

Ngoc Quyen

Dinh Tien Hoang

Dao Duy Anh

Bach

RN1, Dong Ha, Hanoi

An Hoa

An Hoa Gate

Thanh Giong

Thai Phien

Le Trung Dinh

C I T A D E L

Le Van

Huu

Dinh Tien Hoang

Tam Thanh

Xuan 68

Ngo Duc Ke

Xuan

Chanh Tay Gate

Tran Quoc Toan

Nguyen Trai

La Son Phu Tu

Ngo The Lan

Phung Hung

Tinh

Doan

Nhat

Mai Thuc

Nguyen Dang

Biet

Nguyen Chi

Le Duan

Phu Thuan

Ton That Thiep

Trieu Quang Phuc

Le Huan

Thach Han

Tran Nguyen Trai

Nguyen Dan

Hoa Binh Gate

Dang Dung Kim Long Canal

Thai Thuong Dien

Doan

19

13   •16   •17
•14   •11   Forbidden Purple City   •20   •23   •24
•10   •12   IMPERIAL CITY   •18   •21
5   •3   •22
•6   •4   Canno
7   •9   15   1   •2
8   •5

•19

Chuong Duc Gate

23 Thang 8

Huong Ich

Cannons

Flag Towe

Huu Gate

Nguyen Cu Trinh

Huong Ich

Khiem

Nha Do Gate

Sap Gate

Le Duan

KIM LONG

Huong

Le Duan

Kim Long

Da Vien Bridge

Da Vien Island

Song Huong (Perfume River)

Bui Thi Xuan

Dien

Ngu

1

15

PHUONG DUC

Bien

Phu

Bao Quoc Pagoda

Thien Minh Pagoda

Tu Dam Pagoda

Royal Tombs

Thien Mu Pagoda

1 Southern Gate
2 Esplanade of Great Greetings
3 Palace of Supreme Harmony
4 Great Golden Gate
5 Phung Tien Temple
6 Hung Temple
7 Dynastic Temple
8 Pavilion of Splendour
9 Nine Dynastic Urns
10 Tinh Minh Pavilion
11 Dien Tho Palace
12 Ta Tra House
13 Kim Thuy Lake
14 Palace of Long-life
15 Can Chanh Palace
16 Kien Trung Palace
17 Royal Library
18 Royal Theatre
19 Royal Garden
20 Royal Treasury
21 Trieu Temple
22 Temple of Generations
23 Eastern Gate
24 Royal Fine Arts Museum of Hue
25 Military Museum
26 Museum of Archaeology

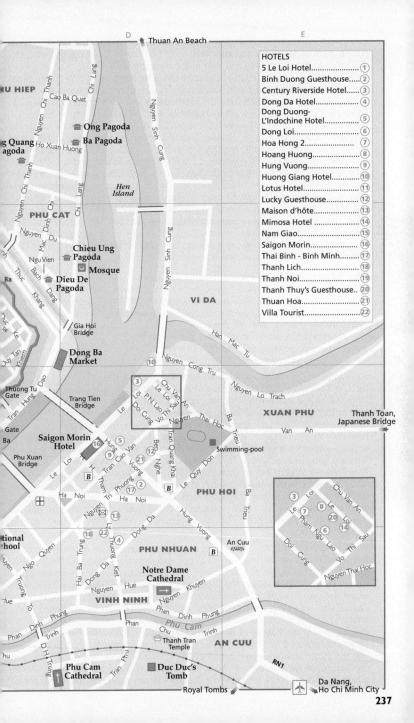

Thuan An Beach

D · E

HU HIEP

Cao Ba Quat

Chi Lang

Ong Pagoda
Ba Pagoda

g Quang
agoda

Ho Xuan Huong

Hen Island

PHU CAT

Nguyen Sinh Cung

Chieu Ung Pagoda
Mosque
Ngu Vien
Dieu De Pagoda

Bach Dang

Khang

VI DA

Gia Hoi Bridge

Dong Ba Market

Thuong Tu Gate
Trang Tien Bridge

Han Mac Tu

Nguyen Cong Tru

Nguyen Lo Trach

Le Loi

P.N Lao

Vo Thi Sau

Chu Van An

Doi Cung

Nguyen Thai Hoc

Ba Trieu

XUAN PHU

Van An

Thanh Toan, Japanese Bridge

Saigon Morin Hotel

Phu Xuan Bridge

Hung Vuong

Tran Cao Van

Ben Nghe

Tran Quang Khai

Le Quy Don

Swimming-pool

Gate
Ba

Ha Noi

Phuong

Ha Noi

PHU HOI

Ba Trieu

tional hool

Ngo Quyen

Nguyen

Dong Da

Hai Ba Trung

Thuong Kiet

PHU NHUAN

Hung Vuong

An Cuu

Le Loi

Chu Van An

Pham Ngu Lao

Vo Thi Sau

Doi Cung

Nguyen Thai Hoc

Notre Dame Cathedral

Nguyen Hue

Khuyen

VINH NINH

Phan Dinh Phung

Phu Cam

Phan Chu Trinh

AN CUU

Thanh Tran Temple

Phu Cam Cathedral

Tran Phu

Duc Duc's Tomb

RN1

Da Nang, Ho Chi Minh City

Royal Tombs

courtly majesty and tragedy. Follow the joyfully chattering schoolgirls as they pedal past in their white *ao dai* uniforms, their long silk scarves fluttering behind them. Surrender to the gentle pace and style of these ancient walls.

Built in 1805 during the reign of Emperor Gia Long on the model of fortifications by the French military engineer, Vauban, the citadel comprises a series of concentric enclosures, within which stand the Imperial City and the Forbidden Purple City. Surrounded by a moat and a 10km-long brick wall, it covers an area of 520ha.

Built in 1807, the **Flag Tower** (Cot Co) (C3) rises above the outer ramparts. Originally made out of wood, it was knocked down by a typhoon in 1904 and replaced by an iron column, but this too was destroyed in 1947 and the tower is now made out of reinforced concrete. It has three pyramidal tiers and is 17.5m high. Whether entering by the Ngan or the Sap (Quang Duc) Gates, two of the ten gates into the citadel, visitors are struck by the nine intricately carved **dynastic cannons** (Cuu Vi Than Cong) (C3), cast by order of Emperor Gia Long from bronze weapons and objects belonging to the Tay Son brothers *(see page 22)*. The four cannons near Ngan Gate symbolise the **four seasons**, while those near Sap Gate represent the **five elements** (metal, wood, water, fire and earth). They were never intended to be fired, but were venerated and each one was given the honorific title of "Than Oai Vo Dich Thuong Tuong Quan" (Champion All-powerful General).

The Imperial City✶✶ (Hoang Thanh) (B-C3)

Daily 6.30am-5.30pm (summer) / 7am-5pm (winter). Entrance charge: 5 5000VND. Ask at the entrance if you would like a guide. Allow 50 000VND for a 1hr tour, which will generally only take you as far as the dynastic urns. If you want to see the whole of the citadel, make sure this is agreed upon in advance.

The Imperial City and its shady paths, flower gardens, ruined palaces and canals dotted with overgrown islands are ideal for a pleasant stroll. The entire area is traffic-free and seems miles away from the turmoil outside.

Surrounded by the **Kim Thuy Canal** (Golden River), four fortified gates are set in the City's wall. The largest and most beautiful is the **Southern Gate✶** (Cua Ngo Mon), which was built in 1833 during the reign of Minh Mang and restored in 1990 with funds from Unesco and Japan. It was reserved for the sole use of the king and only opened for important ceremonies. It consists of five archways: a central archway used only by the monarch, the left and right-hand ones for use by the mandarins, civilians and army dignitaries and the side arches for elephants, horses and soldiers. The Southern Gate is topped by a splendid lacquered-teak watchtower called the **Five Phoenix Watch Tower** (Ngu Phung). The watchtower rests on a hundred beautifully painted columns and is covered in yellow (the colour of the king) and green (for the mandarins) enamel porcelain tiles. The king came here to make Imperial proclamations before the court's mandarins. It was from this balcony that Bao Dai abdicated on 30 August 1945. The only women allowed here were the king's mother and grandmother.

Walking in the footsteps of the Nguyen emperors, go through the archway decorated with bronze carvings of dragons and clouds and over the Trung Dao Bridge spanning Thai Dich Lake, which is filled with lotus flowers and bordered with frangipani trees. This will take you into the **Esplanade of Great Greetings** (Dai Trieu Nghi) where the mandarins would have witnessed ceremonies. Depending on their mandarinal rank, of which there were nine, each would have sat in an allotted place, indicated by the stones you can see round the courtyard.

In front stands the **Palace of Supreme Harmony✶✶** (Dien Thai Hoa), one of the Imperial City's most remarkable edifices. It was in this sumptuously decorated hall that the emperor would have presided over ceremonies and received officials and dignitaries. On the teak walls and columns, lacquered in red and inlaid in gold, are poems in Chinese script telling of the country's beauty as well as traditional carved

The Palace of Supreme Harmony

motifs, such as the dragon, the symbol of royal power. Many of the 80 columns were eaten by termites and have had to be replaced or are currently being replaced with wood which has to be imported from Laos and Cambodia, now that the Vietnamese government exercises strict control over forestry practices. The gilt-lacquered wooden **throne** of the thirteen emperors of the Nguyen dynasty stands under an ornately carved canopy. In a rear room, a **scale model** gives an idea of what the Imperial City looked like before it was partially destroyed by the French in 1947 and by the Americans in 1968.

Behind the Palace of Supreme Harmony is a courtyard where the **Great Golden Gate** (Dai Cung Mon) formerly stood. It was reputed to be the most beautiful in the City but was sadly entirely burnt down in 1947. It was through this gate that the emperor and his family would have passed to enter the **Forbidden Purple City** (Tu Cam Thanh), where they resided in forty or so buildings. It was totally off-bounds to anyone outside the royal family, with the exception of mandarin-eunuchs.

Go along the avenue to the left towards the Chuong Duc Gate.

At the end of the avenue, on the right, a porch is all that remains of **Phung Tien Temple** (Dien Phung Tien). The temple was dedicated to the memory of the Nguyen emperors and empresses, whose births and deaths would have been commemorated. As women were not allowed into the dynastic temple, this one was built for them so that they too could worship their ancestors. On the porch it is possible to distinguish fragments of enamel on bronze, a very hard-wearing technique imported from China.

A little further on, go through the small gate on the left into an enormous garden. Within stands **Hung Temple** (Hung Mieu), devoted to the worship of Gia Long's parents. Originally built in 1821, it was rebuilt in 1951 and restored in 1997.

Next door is the **Dynastic Temple★★★** (The Mieu), erected in 1821-22 during Minh Mang's reign, given over to the **worship of the Nguyen kings**. Inside, each of the ten wooden altars, lacquered in red and gold is devoted to a king and queen. Those

239

of Duc Duc and Hiep Hoa, both of whom were deposed for having falsified their father's wills, are missing, as is that of Bao Dai, exiled to France. It was only after 1954 that three other altars were added, dedicated to the Kings Ham Nghi, Thanh Thai and Duy Tan, who were exiled to Réunion and Algeria by the French because of their anti-colonialist sentiments. Numerous descendants of the Nguyen dynasty still living in Hue come here to honour the memory of their ancestors.

Opposite, the **Pavilion of Splendour** (Hien Lam Cac) was built in 1821-22 in memory of the mandarins who served the Nguyen dynasty. This 13m-high edifice is the tallest in the citadel.

In front of the pavilion are **Nine Dynastic Urns***** (Cuu Dinh), cast in 1835-37, each of which weighs between 2 and 2.5t. These gigantic three-footed urns are ornately carved with designs intended to represent the qualities of each of the various Nguyen sovereigns. Although at first glance they seem identical, a closer look will reveal that they all have different feet and handles and that no two carved designs are alike. Each urn features 17 motifs which represent the country's flowers, trees, rivers, mountains, animals and spices. All are works of art and bear witness to the mastery of Hue's craftsmen in the art of casting.

From here, return to the path which skirts the Imperial City and head for the much-damaged Western Gate (Cua Chuong Duc). The path opposite the gate leads to a colourful porch which gives access into buildings undergoing renovation at the time of writing.

On the left-hand side of the courtyard, **Tinh Minh Pavilion** (Lau Tinh Minh) was built in 1927 for the first wife of Emperor Dong Khanh, Empress Thanh Cung, in place of a former wooden 19C edifice. It was subsequently renovated and became the private residence of Emperor Bao Dai in 1950.

The central pavilion is **Dien Tho Palace** (Dien Tho Chinh Dien). Built in 1804 and renovated in 1916, it was the private residence and audience hall of the queen-mothers. A covered alleyway leads to **Ta Tra House** (Nha Ta Tra), now in ruins, which served as a waiting room.

Leave by the gate to the right of Ta Tra House and turn left to **Kim Thuy Lake**. You will go past the **Palace of Long-life** (Cung Truong Sinh) which formerly served as the king's recreation hall *(undergoing reconstruction)*.

After skirting the lake for a few metres, enter the Forbidden Purple City through one of the gates on your right. This will take you into a vast overgrown, somewhat neglected plot of land, whose former splendour can only be guessed at. Nothing remains of **Can Chanh Palace** (Dien Can Chanh) where the king worked, or of the queen's and the concubines' living quarters.

A flight of stairs leads to an esplanade, site of the former **Kien Trung Palace** (Kien Trung Lau). Built in a hybrid European-Asian style, it was the private apartment of King Khai Dinh and then the residence of Emperor Bao Dai until 1947. Unfortunately, it was totally destroyed in the bombings of 1947 and 1968.

The absolute number

The bronze urn with three feet ("dinh") is an ancient emblem of royal power in China. One of China's mythical sovereigns is said to have had nine of them cast representing the territory he controlled, depicted by carvings of mountains and rivers. The number 9 is an odd and a yang number and is considered to be the absolute number, representative of the All. The "dinh" of Hue echo the same symbolism. Indeed it is not a coincidence that each of the nine dynastic urns of the Imperial City has 17 drawings. 9 multiplied by 17 makes 153 and the sum of 1 + 5 + 3 = 9.

Returning down towards the Palace of Supreme Harmony, you will go past the **Royal Library*** (Thai Binh Lau) where the king came to read and relax. Just in front is a pretty shaded garden and pool, in the centre of which stands a small artificial mountain. This is the only building of the Forbidden Purple City which was not destroyed during the war.

On the way to school

Once in the courtyard to the rear of the Palace of Supreme Harmony, take the avenue on the left towards the Eastern Gate.

A path on your left leads to the **Royal Theatre** (Duyet Thi Duong) (*undergoing renovation*) and the **Royal Garden** (Vuon Thuong Uyen), now a thriving wilderness. Before reaching the Eastern Gate, you will skirt a handsome European-style 19C building which is now home to Hue's Fine Arts School. It occupies the site of the **Royal Treasury** (Phu Noi Vu) which produced and stocked the court's valuables.

On the right, hidden behind a high wall, **Trieu Temple** (Trieu Mieu) was built in 1804 and devoted to the worship of the parents of Nguyen Hoang. It was restored between 1983 and 1985 but once again seems to have fallen into neglect. Further south, the **Temple of Generations** (Thai Mieu), now in a very sorry state, was devoted to the nine generations of the Nguyen dynasty.

You can leave the Imperial City by the **Eastern Gate** (Cua Hien Nhon), or Gate of Humanity, which has some very fine mosaics.

Once through the gate, turn left into Doan Thi Diem, then left again into Le Truc.

Beyond the Imperial City

Founded in 1923 under Khai Dinh's reign, the **Royal Fine Arts Museum of Hue**★ (C3) (*3 Le Truc. Daily 7am-6pm. Entrance charge*) contains a splendid collection of some 500 priceless artefacts bequeathed by the Nguyen dynasty, including crockery, furniture, embroidered clothes, ritual bronze objects, household pottery and Japanese and "Blue Hue" porcelain vases. Just as interesting as the museum itself is the building in which it is housed, the superb Long An Palace, built in 1845 at the time of Emperor Thieu Tri. Its teak walls and rafters are inscribed with poems in Chinese script inlaid with gold and pearl, in celebration of the country's glory and the beauty of its landscapes.

241

The **Military Museum** (Bao Tang Tong Hop) (C3) *(main entrance at 23 Thang 8. Daily 7.30am-5pm. No charge)*, just across the street, contains photographs, weapons, press cuttings and a variety of objects documenting the role played by the inhabitants of Hue in the Vietnam War. The building opposite houses the **Museum of Archaeology** (C3) with exhibits of remains found in Hue which date back to the Palaeolithic and Neolithic Ages.

The west bank of the Perfume River

Outside the citadel's walls, life seems to return to normal. The streets are liveliest around **Dong Ba Market** (D2) *(Tran Hung Dao, near the Trang Tien Bridge)*, which is the real heart of Hue. Take the time to stroll around the multicoloured stalls, overflowing with fabric, conical hats, fresh produce and the usual jumble of ironmongery. Large numbers of boats can be seen around the landing stages near the central covered hall, from which fresh fruit, vegetables, fish and spices are unloaded from the neighbouring villages. Notice the women going from sampan to sampan selling bowls of soup, which they prepare in the tiny floating kitchens.

> **The Perfume River**
>
> The Perfume River, which winds its way down the Truong Son Mountains into the Thuan An estuary, is the very soul of the city and has determined its layout and structure. Its evocative name has of course given rise to countless legends and artists, painters and poets have gone to great pains to vaunt its beauty, comparing it to a young girl or a silk ribbon fluttering in the wind. Nowadays the majority of Hue's business is centred around the Song Huong. Sampans transporting sand or fresh produce to Dong Ba Market float alongside boats full of tourists on outings to the Royal Tombs.

Cross the Gia Hoi Bridge to the Phu Cat district and take a sharp left turning into Bach Dang which runs alongside the river.

By n° 100, before Ngu Vien, a stone portal with three doors indicates the entrance to **Dieu De Pagoda** (C2) which stands at the end of a tree-lined avenue. Built in 1842 during the reign of King Thieu Tri, it was one of the largest and most beautiful pagodas of the town. In the past, it housed the national mint and was also the setting for meetings of students and Buddhists opposed to the regime of Ngo Dinh Diem. It has lost much of its former lustre, but is still very busy during services.

Continue along Bach Dang and take the dirt track to the right of the bridge which leads into Nguyen Chi Thanh. Three hundred metres further on, a little off the street to the left is **Tang Quang Pagoda** (C1), which is often very busy come the 14th of each month. The interior can be visited *(ask for the key)* but is of very little interest.

Continue on Nguyen Chi Thanh, then turn right into Ho Xuan Huong. This will take you to Chi Lang, on the corner of which are the **Ong** and **Ba Pagodas** (D1). As you return towards the citadel, you will also go past a communal house, **Chieu Ung Pagoda** and the old **mosque** (D2).

The modern town
Allow half a day

The east bank of the Perfume River is where Hue's modern districts are located. In striking contrast to the citadel whose charm they lack, these recent neighbourhoods and some of the peaceful streets and lanes are nonetheless very pleasant to wander about in. There is however not a lot to see apart from a few pagodas and churches, but most of the town's hotels, restaurants and shops are to be found here, along Hung Vuong and Le Loi.

As you go over Trang Tien Bridge to the east bank, you will be met with the impressive outline of **Saigon Morin Hotel** (D3), a superb example of French colonial architecture, now a hundred years old.

Go down Le Loi towards the station. On your left you will see the pink buildings of the **National School** (C4). If in the area in the early evening at the end of classes, you may be lucky enough to see one of the open-air martial arts classes.

Turn left into Dien Bien Phu Street by the 5 Le Loi Hotel, and go under the railway line. Take the first turning on the right, then the next left.

A flight of steps leads up to **Bao Quoc Pagoda** (C4) and its impressive stone door decorated with inlaid blue and white porcelain. Built in the late 17C by the bonze Giac Phong, it was only later raised to the rank of State Pagoda. Its appeal however lies in the peaceful atmosphere within. In a nearby building, monks attend classes while in a shady garden to the rear of the sanctuary, among the tombs of bonzes who worked in the pagoda, students can be seen revising in this peaceful, quiet setting.

Back on Dien Bien Phu, you will go past the pretty Thien Minh Pagoda next to n° 45. A few metres beyond, take the first turning on the left to Tu Dam Pagoda.

Built in 1695 by the bonze Minh Hoang Tu Dung, **Tu Dam Pagoda** (C4) has an immense courtyard capable of holding thousands of worshippers. In a corner an enormous fig tree planted in 1936 continues to thrive. The pagoda owes its fame to its role in the foundation and development of Buddhism in Vietnam. Over time, it has been home to the Association of Buddhist Studies of Annam (1936), anticolonialist Buddhist activities (1945), as well as to the Buddhist movement against President Ngo Dinh Diem's regime (1960-63).

Turn left into Phan Boi Chau and go down to the river bank, then turn right before the bridge into Phan Chu Trinh. When you come to the next bridge, bear right into Doan Huu Trung.

Phu Cam Cathedral (C-D4) and its two tall grey towers is singularly lacking in charm. It is the work of the Vietnamese architect, Ngo Viet Thu, who won the Prix de Rome, and who was also responsible for the Presidential Palace in Ho Chi Minh City. Begun in 1961, the cathedral has yet to be completed.

Go back down to the river, and take the first turning on the right, past the bridge, then the next left into Nguyen Khuyen.

Dominated by its unusual three-storey bell-tower, **Notre Dame Cathedral** (D4), is an interesting example of ecclesiastical architecture, built by the Vietnamese architect, Nguyen My Loc between 1959 and 1962 .

The Royal Tombs★★

Allow a day if you want to visit them all.

There are two ways to visit the Royal Tombs. The first is a boat excursion, which can be organised by all the travel agencies in town (see page 251), which takes in Thien Mu Pagoda and the tombs of Tu Duc, Khai Dinh and Minh Mang. Alternatively, you can rent a bicycle or motorcycle in Hue and devise your own tour. The surrounding countryside is full of hidden rice paddies and remote hamlets and is well-worth exploring if you have time to venture down the narrow bumpy lanes.

The Nguyen emperors did not differ from other dynasties, in that they were preoccupied with their life in the hereafter and supervised the building of their mausoleum-cum-palaces very closely. In fact during their lifetime these grandiose works of art doubled as secondary residences, as the emperors stayed in them to better oversee their construction. The tombs represented years of back-breaking labour for thousands of craftsmen and soldiers, who were enlisted against their will and many of whom lost their lives in the process. These architectural gems set against a lush, green landscape continue to bear witness to the past splendour of the Nguyen dynasty and the skills of its craftsmen, justly making them one of Hue's main tourist attractions.

Respecting the rules of geomancy

Although each mausoleum has its own quite distinctive charm and character, all are a simplified replica of the citadel and are built according to a precise blueprint, modelled after that of the Chinese sovereigns' tombs. The planned site of the mausoleum was studied in depth by the king's geomancers (see page 43) and the building itself was always set within an immense landscaped garden of ponds and streams.

Among the architectural features common to all the Nguyen tombs is an **outer wall**, within which lies a spacious paved **Courtyard of Honour**, with statues of civil and military mandarins, intended to represent the mandarins who waited on the monarch in front of the throne room, and horses and elephants. At the far end of the courtyard is a tower which houses a marble **stele**, on which are engraved all the exploits and merits of the deceased king, usually written by his successor. On either side of this pavilion stand two obelisks, symbolising the king's power. A **temple**, in honour of the monarch and his queens and concubines, houses the funerary tablets and the altar. Last of all is the **tomb**, often inside a low-walled enclosure.

Duc Duc's tomb

Go down Tran Phu, then right into Duy Tan. The tomb is a little further on, to the right.
Duc Duc only reigned for three days before being deposed and imprisoned for having falsified part of the will of his uncle and adoptive father, King Tu Duc. He died shortly after and it was only seven years later, when his son, Thanh Thai, was crowned, that this mausoleum was built in his honour. Duc Duc's tomb is one of the simplest of those around Hue. It is little visited and you will have to ask for the key to see the temple and its somewhat battered tombs.

Around HUE

0   2,5   5 km

N

Tu Duc's tomb**

6km from Hue. Go along Bui Thi Xuan to the right of the railway station for 3km, then turn left towards the arenas. Continue for 2km until you reach Tu Duc's tomb on the left. Daily 7am-6pm. Entrance charge: 55 000VND. If coming by boat, plan on a 20min walk or paying 10 000VND for a motorcycle taxi. Allow 1hr.
The second son of King Thieu Tri, Tu Duc loved poetry and conceived his mausoleum as a kind of pleasure park for his afterlife. His tomb thus stands in a particularly attractive setting; surrounded by a perimeter wall more than 1 500m long, the enclosure covers an area of around 12ha and contains some 50 or so edifices. Tu Duc reigned for 35 years from 1848 to 1883. He super-

vised the works himself, regularly escaping here to get away from the oppressive court atmosphere. Construction took three years (1864-67) and occupied a work-force of 6 000 soldiers and labourers.

On entering the park, one first walks round the shores of **Luu Khiem Lake**, where the king used to relax and read or write poems. **Xung Khiem Pavilion**, which stands on one of the shores, continues to offer a lovely view of this magnificent landscape. A flight of steps takes you up to **Khiem Cung Gate** which leads into the temple devoted to the worship of Tu Duc. The first courtyard is flanked by Phap Khiem and Le Khiem Pavilions, intended for the mandarins. Ahead stands **Hoa Khiem Palace** where the monarch used to come and work when staying here. After his death, it was dedicated to him and his queen and some of their personal belongings are exhibited, including a clock, a vase and a casket. Behind this pavilion is the grey-brick **Luong Khiem Palace** which housed the private apartments of Tu Duc. On his death, it was given to his mother. On the right, **Minh Khiem Pavilion** houses the old classical theatre. It was built in 1866 and the stage and balcony where the monarch

F Soreau/MICHELIN

Guardian of the Royal Tombs

Hue

would have sat can still be seen. *Go down the path which winds down to the tomb.*

You now enter the **Court of Honour**, lined with frangipani trees and statues of mandarins. The nearby massive stone **stele** is one of the largest in Vietnam, weighing nearly 20t. It is engraved with the "Khiem Cung Ky", a eulogy to the deceased which, exceptionally, was drafted by Tu Duc himself. Beyond is his granite **tomb**.

Not far away is the tomb of Emperor **Kien Phuc** (1883-84), Tu Duc's adopted son, but it is in bad condition and most of the ceramic tiles have disappeared. His temple, however, has been restored and contains a number of fine ceramics and paintings.

Dong Khanh's tomb

Not far from Tu Duc's tomb. Take the path on the left, to the south of the entrance of Tu Duc's tomb. Entrance charge: 22 000VND. A guide with faltering English will take you round. Keep an eye out for snakes.

Tu Duc's son only reigned for three years, from 1885-88. He died young at the age of 25 and didn't have time to supervise the building of his own tomb. This took place in two stages. He was first worshipped in an existing temple, Trung Tu Palace, now Ngung Hy Temple, where later on (1917), a tomb was built for him by his son, Khai Dinh. This explains the two different architectural styles of the mausoleum.

Inside the **temple**, a number of objects which once belonged to the emperor and his wives are exhibited, including crockery, shoes, a pillow, a painting given by Napoleon and Vietnamese and French vases. In a rear room is an altar for his concubines. On leaving the temple, take the path leading down to the **tomb** some 100m further on.

Thieu Tri's tomb

8km from Hue. If approaching from Hue, continue past the burial mound of Nam Giao and down Minh Mang. If approaching from Tu Duc's tomb, continue along the road towards Minh Mang's tomb. Thieu Tri's tomb is at the crossroads with the road from Hue. Daily 7am-6pm. Entrance charge: 22 000VND.

Thieu Tri, son of Minh Mang, died at the age of 41, leaving his son, Tu Duc, the task of building his tomb. It stands in a peaceful rural setting of gardens and rice fields, where the peace and quiet are interrupted only by the cheerful singing and chattering of the children in the nearby school. The tombs of Thieu Tri's family, his mother, wife and children have been placed around the mausoleum. The Court of Honour, the stele tower and tomb can all be visited independently of the temple. It is not however possible to actually go inside the tomb itself, which stands on a hill surrounded by a high wall. The much-damaged temple is of very little interest.

Khai Dinh's tomb★

10km from Hue. Once past the burial mound of Nam Giao, continue down Minh Mang until you reach a junction where the tomb is signposted. If coming by boat, plan on a 20min walk to the tomb or 10 000VND for a motorcycle taxi. Daily 7am-6pm. Entrance charge: 55 000VND. Allow 30min.

This mausoleum is nothing short of an architectural folly, blending as it does traditional Vietnamese style with that of Western influences ranging from classical to modern art. Mirrors, ceramic tiles and colourful mosaics are combined in ornate bas-reliefs, masterpieces of Vietnam's 20C craftsmen. Undeniably impressive, though not in the best possible taste, the mausoleum is in complete contrast to the harmonious character of the other tombs and in no way attempts to blend in with the surrounding landscape. Its construction lasted eleven years (1920-31) and it was also one of the most expensive, requiring materials to be imported from France, China and Japan.

The first courtyard is entered by a long flight of stairs. Beyond is the **Court of Honour**, complete with rows of civil and military mandarins and servants, all in finely embroidered robes. Notice the intricate carving of the pillars around the octagonal **Stele Tower**. **Thien Dinh Palace** ("Fate") which houses the tomb is up two more flights of stairs. In the centre of the temple stands the **altar** devoted to Khai Dinh and a heavy bronze **statue**, cast in France in 1922 and protected by an impressive reinforced-concrete canopy. The sovereign's body lies under this.

Minh Mang's tomb★★

12km from Hue, on the west bank of the Perfume River. If coming by car or motorcycle, you will have to catch a ferry across the river (10 000VND round trip). Daily 7am-6pm. Entrance charge: 55 000VND. Allow 30min.

Minh Mang's tomb is entirely devoted to its founder's love of painting, poetry and philosophy and, together with Tu Duc's mausoleum, is one of the most impressive of Hue's royal tombs. Minh Mang reigned from 1820-41 and although he had the plans of the tomb drawn during his lifetime, it was only built after his death by his successor. Construction lasted from 1841-43.

The complex is laid out around a 700m-long axis, and consists of some 35 monuments, palaces, pavilions, bridges, canals and ponds. **Dai Hong Gate**, the main entrance to the mausoleum, was only used once when the monarch was laid to rest. The entrance is now through a side gate. The **Court of Honour** leads up to the somewhat damaged **Stele Tower**, on which is engraved the "Thanh Duc Than Cong", written by Thieu Tri in honour of his father's exploits.

Beyond, **Hien Duc Gate** opens into an area devoted to ritual ceremonies, in the centre of which are three terraces, on the top of the highest of which stands **Sung An Palace** devoted to the monarch and his queen. After crossing **Trung Minh Lake** ("Pure Clarity"), you will reach the handsome grey-brick and red-lacquered **Minh Lau Pavilion** ("Light"), which symbolises the three powers of the heavens, the earth and mankind. A terraced garden leads down to **Tan Nguyet Lake** ("New Moon"), but no further, because the tomb stands on a hillside covered in thick undergrowth.

Minh Mang's Tomb

Gia Long's tomb*

18km south of Hue. Once past the landing stage which leads to Minh Mang's tomb, continue southwards as far as a hamlet, from where you can cross the river to reach Gia Long's tomb (allow 10 000VND round trip). Once on the other bank, the site is a further 3-4km away. No entrance charge.

Gia Long (1762-1819), the first king of the Nguyen dynasty, was crowned in 1802. He chose the site of his mausoleum himself on a peninsula in the Perfume River and its construction lasted six years, from 1814-20. Other tombs were built nearby to house his family. In a green landscape of wooded hills, the tomb stands in a quite enchanting spot where only the sounds of nature interrupt the site's peace and quiet. Very few visitors ever come this far.

Other sights around Hue

Thien Mu Pagoda** (Pagoda of the Heavenly Lady)

4km from Hue, on the west bank of the Perfume River. Go down Le Duan, then Kim Long. A visit to the pagoda is included in most of the tours organised by the town's travel agencies. On your own, it is best to go in the late morning or in the afternoon, because from 9am the pagoda is invariably swamped with guided tours. No entrance charge. Allow 1hr, which includes time to stroll around the gardens.

Lord Nguyen Hoang had the original pagoda built in 1601, but the emblematic red-brick **octagonal tower** (Phuoc Duyen) was only put up in 1844, on the orders of King Thieu Tri. Each of its seven storeys represents one of the Buddha's reincarnations. Four smaller hexagonal towers stand nearby. One of these houses a 2.5m-high **bell**, weighing over 2t, which was cast in 1710 on the orders of Nguyen Phuc Chu. The latter was also responsible for the immense marble **stele**, held up by a stone tortoise, which tells the story of the pagoda.

Go through an **arch** with three gates, guarded by brightly coloured figures of important personages, and into a courtyard and a charming flowered garden. Within stands the **pagoda** and enthroned in front of it a magnificent smiling copper

The legend of the Heavenly Lady

Legend relates the story of an old woman who appeared to Nguyen Hoang as he was out walking on a hill near present-day Hue. She predicted that a noble lord would build a pagoda on the site which would ensure the country's prosperity. In 1601, he accordingly had the said pagoda built, naming it Thien Mu (Heavenly Lady) in honour of the divine apparition.

Buddha. Behind the altar are three other copper Buddhas: Amitabha, the Buddha of the Past, Sakyamuni, the Historical Buddha and, Maitreya, the Buddha of the Future. To the left is an altar devoted to the bodhisattva Pho Dien and to the right, another dedicated to the bodhisattva Van Thu.

Behind the pagoda stretches a spacious garden with bonsai trees, at the rear of which rests a bonze who laboured hard to further Buddhism. To the left is a building which houses the blue Austin motorcar of the monk **Thich Quang Duc** who set fire to himself in Saigon on 11 June 1963, in protest at President Ngo Dinh Diem's policies and his discrimination against Buddhists.

The Royal Arenas (Ho Quyen)

5km outside Hue. Leave town on Bui Thi Xuan to the right of the railway station and go through the Phuong Duc district. 3km further on a signpost on your left indicates "Ho Quyen, Den Voi Re". The arenas are 200m further on.

The Nguyen monarchs were very fond of staging tiger and elephant fights for the amusement of their court and subjects. During the reign of Minh Mang, the Royal Arenas were built in the vicinity of the citadel. Symbols of royal power, the elephants always emerged victorious from these contests because the organisers took good care to cut the tigers' teeth and claws, even going so far as tying them up. All that remains today of the arenas are the high brick walls and gates through which the animals entered the pit. A short distance away, along the same path, is a pond near to which are the remains of **Voi Re Temple** (Den Voi Re).

The burial mound of Nam Giao

At the end of Dien Bien Phu, which begins opposite 5 Le Loi Hotel. No entrance charge.
On the occasion of a great yearly ceremony, the Nguyen sovereigns made sacrifices here intended to guarantee their kingdom's safety and the dynasty's stability. Built in 1806 under the reign of Gia Long, the burial mound is laid out on the Chinese model. Made up of three superimposed circular terraces, it echoes the altar of the Heavens, whose son is the emperor. The circular shape is that of the celestial vault in Chinese cosmology, while the figure 3, both odd and yang, represents heaven.

Tu Hieu Pagoda

5km to the southwest of Hue. Beyond the Nam Gia mound, head for the tomb of Tu Duc, then take a right turn into Le Ngo Cat at the crossroads. The pagoda is a short distance away on your right, at the end of the red dirt track. It is also possible to get to the pagoda from the Royal Arenas (see map page 244).

This peaceful pagoda stands in an immense pine forest. It was built in 1843 by the bonze Nhat Dinh and enlarged in 1848 on request of the mandarin-eunuchs. The main temple is devoted to the Buddha and the founding bonzes. The courtyard in front has been turned into a splendid garden with potted plants and trees. The pagoda is also home to a community of monks who live in the surrounding buildings. In the garden it is possible to see the tombs of some of the Nguyen dynasty's mandarins.

Japanese bridge

7km east of Hue. Go down Le Quy Don near the Vietcombank and cross over Bat Trieu into Van An. Afterwards, continue straight on until you reach the hamlet and bridge of Thanh Toan.

Those unable to visit the famous Japanese bridge in Hoi An can always console themselves with the more modest 200-year old construction at Thanh Toan. The road leading to the bridge is well worth the trip in its own right. The delightful red dirt track winds its way through green rice paddies, occasional colourful tombs and waddling ducks and ducklings.

Thuan An Beach

12km northeast of Hue. First take Le Loi then Nguyen Sinh Cung. The beach is located at the mouth of the Perfume River. It is however dirty and not really worth a trip.

On the road to Da Nang★

The most picturesque section of the **Mandarin Road**, the country's main thoroughfare, lies between Hue and Da Nang. Running alongside the Truong Son Mountains on the border with Laos, its highest point (1 450m) is the Pass of Clouds, which affords a wonderful panorama of the coast from Hue in the north as far as Da Nang Bay in the south.

Leave town on Hung Vuong and get onto the RN1. 40km south of Hue, at the village of Cau Hai, turn right towards Bach Ma. The park's reception area is 4km away, but the summit is a further 13km. Vehicles must be left at the reception car park because only forest rangers are authorised to drive inside the park. Allow 250 000VND for a group of 4, 300 000VND for 6, 400 000VND for a 14-person minibus and an extra 50 000VND if you want to stop overnight in the park (bookings advisable).

■ **Bach Ma National Park** – *Daily 7.30am-4.30pm,* ☎ *(054) 87 13 30, Fax (054) 87 13 29, bachma@dng.vnn.vn Entrance charge: 10 000VND per day.*
Backing onto the Truong Son range which extends as far as the coast nearby, Bach Ma was discovered by the French during the colonial period. In 1936, they set up a mountain resort whose mild climate was greatly appreciated, and built a road linking the peak of Bach Ma with the RN1. The site was declared a nature reserve in 1987 by the government in an effort to protect the country's forest resources. It officially became a National Park on 15 July 1991 and today covers some 22 000ha. This semi-tropical humid forest is home to an exceptionally rich variety of plants and animals, which visitors are introduced to in a little **museum**. The park contains 1 280 species of plants, 124 species of mammal, 330 birds, 31 amphibians and 218 butterflies. A network of **trails** around the park makes it relatively easy to bird-watch and examine the plant life, taking visitors from waterfall to pool and up to the summit for a magnificent view overlooking the whole Da Nang region. At the time of writing, a two-day boat-trip-cum-trekking excursion from Tri Sao to Cau Hai Lagoon was in preparation.

Return to the RN1 and continue for 10km. At the village of Thua Luu, at kilometre marker 879, a signpost on the left-hand side of the road indicates "Suoi Voi Summer Resort". Turn right and go over the railway line then turn right onto a dirt track.

■ **Suoi Voi Springs** – *Entrance charge. Beyond the ticket office, the path winds for 2km through the hills and down to the river.* The waterfall itself is not very impressive but the setting is pleasant, peaceful and shady and it is possible to swim in the little pools dug out by erosion. The water is crystal-clear and enormous rubber rings can be rented from the little eateries around the site. It is worth stopping here if on the way to Da Nang, but not worth going out of your way specially.

Beyond Thua Luu, the RN1 climbs up through the hills before dropping down to the sea. The landscape changes quite dramatically as the vegetation becomes more parched and sparse and dunes appear along the coastline.

■ **Lang Co** – *15km from Suoi Voi Springs. Accommodation possible, see "Lang Co close up".* The village of Lang Co is set on a narrow strip of land with the sea on one side and a lagoon on the other. Dotted with tiny stalls selling potted shrimps and bottles of nuoc-mam, the road meanders through a coconut grove where a few shops and houses cluster together. Although it may be appealing at first glance, the beach is dirty and disappointing and the only two hotels in the village are devoid of charm and amenities.

■ On the way out of Lang Co, the road begins to climb up towards the Truong Son Mountains as far as the **Pass of Clouds**★ (Hai Van), the country's longest and highest pass. At an altitude of 496m, it clearly divides North from South. As its name suggests, it is frequently engulfed in cloud, but on a clear day, it is possible to see the turquoise waters of the South China Sea and the miles and miles of immaculate sandy beaches along the coast. Da Nang is 26km away.

COMING AND GOING

By air – Phu Bai **airport** lies 14km to the south of Hue. Vietnam Airlines operate 1-2 flights daily to Hanoi (90min) and Ho Chi Minh City (1hr 20min). Airport tax: 10 000VND. Taxi service (15min) available from the airport, allow US$5.

By train – The **railway station** is at the southwesternmost end of Le Loi Street, at n° 2 Phan Chu Trinh (C4), ☎ (054) 82 21 75, Fax (054) 84 59 20. Reservations open daily, 7.30-11am / 1.30-4pm. Left luggage, post office and shops. 8 trains daily to Ho Chi Minh City (19hr journey), via Da Nang (2hr 45min), Quang Nai (6hr), Tam Ky (8hr), Dieu Tri (9hr), Thuy Hoa (11hr), Nha Trang (13hr 30min) and Thap Cham (16hr). 7 trains daily to Hanoi (15hr), Dong Ha (95min), Dong Hoi (3hr), Vinh (7hr 30min), Thanh Hoa (11hr) Ninh Binh (12hr), Nam Dinh (13hr) and Phu Ly (13hr 30min).

By bus – Hue has three bus stations. **An Cuu** bus station, on Hung Vuong (E4), opposite the Vietcombank, operates services to the South. **Dong Ba**, on Le Duan (C3), near the Phu Xuan Bridge, operates northbound services, as does **An Hoa**, on RN1, to the northwest of the citadel (A2).

GETTING AROUND HUE

By taxi – **ATC**, ☎ (054)83 33 33; **Gili**, ☎ (054)830 830.

By rental car – Vehicles can be rented from all the travel agencies and from many hotels.

By rental bicycle and motorcycle – Most hotels have a number of bicycles and motorcycles which they rent out by the hour or day (allow US$1 / day and US$6 / day respectively). The **Cafe On Thu Wheels**, 10/2 Nguyen Tri Phuong (D3), in a cul-de-sac two minutes from Hung Vuong, is a tiny family enterprise run by a bouncy, cheerful young woman. Her two brothers, Minh and Toan, also organise motorcycle rides around the Hue area.

ADDRESS BOOK

Bank / Currency exchange – **Vietcombank**, 46 Hung Vuong (D4), ☎ (054) 82 46 29 / 84 60 55, Fax (054) 82 46 31. Monday-Friday 7-11.30am / 1.30-4.30pm, Saturday 7-11.30am. Withdrawals and currency exchange. Accepts travellers' cheques and Visa, MasterCard, American Express and JCB credit cards. **Vietindebank**, 41 Hung Vuong (D3), ☎ (054) 82 60 07 / 82 50 68, Fax (054) 82 35 61. Monday-Saturday 7-11.15am / 1.30-4pm. Accepts travellers' cheques and Visa and MasterCard. **Agribank**, 10 Hoang Hoa Tham (D3), ☎ (054) 82 32 60, Fax (054) 82 28 83. Monday-Saturday 7-11.30am / 1.30-5pm. Visa and MasterCard.

Post office / Telephone – **Buu Dien Hue**, Ly Thuong Kiet (D3). Daily 6.30am-9pm. Little branches offering just postal services are dotted around the whole town.

Internet – Getting online in Hue is no problem. Countless cafés and travel agencies around town offer Internet connections for around 400VND / hr. Two among many are: **Hi.Net**, 14 Hung Vuong, and **Napeco Computer**, 6 Tran Cao Van.

Medical service – **General Hospital**, 16 Le Loi (C3), ☎ (054) 82 23 25.

Airline companies – **Vietnam Airlines**, 12 Ha Noi (D3), ☎ (054) 82 32 49, Fax (054) 86 11 31. Daily 7-11am / 1.30-4.30pm.

Travel agencies – You will be spoilt for choice such is the variety of agencies in town, most of which are located around Le Loi and Hung Vuong.

All offer the same excursions at the same prices. One in particular which stands out by virtue of its clear, well-documented information (timetables and prices of flights, trains and buses to Hue) is **Queen Café / Kim Travel**, 29 Nguyen Tri Phuong and 38D Le Loi (D3), ☎ (054) 83 38 97 / 84 71 25.

WHERE TO STAY

Under US$10

Binh Duong Guesthouse, 10/4 Nguyen Tri Phuong, ☎ (054) 83 32 98, Fax (054) 83 32 98, binhduong@dng.vnn.vn – 14rm 🛏 🍴 ✕ Ideal for shoestring budgets. This friendly guesthouse, located at the end of a peaceful lane, has a dormitory (US$3) and cheap, cheerful, clean rooms. The staff and atmosphere are friendly.

Hoang Huong, 46/2 Le Loi, ☎ (054) 82 85 09 – 10rm 🛏 🍴 ✕ If the Mimosa is full, you can always fall back on one of the basic, but spacious and clean rooms of its neighbour.

Maison d'hôte, 9 Ly Thuong Kiet, ☎ (054) 82 37 53, Fax (054) 82 58 14 – 10rm 🛏 🍴 This elegant French colonial villa and charming garden are perfect for a peaceful stay. The four rooms in the main house are more expensive (US$15-20) but those on tighter budgets can ask for one of the rooms in the nearby building (US$7) which are a little decrepit but perfectly acceptable.

Mimosa Hotel, 46/6 Le Loi, ☎ (054) 82 80 68, Fax (054) 82 38 58 – 6rm 🛏 🍴 ✕ This little family guesthouse, run by a French teacher from Hue, is ideally situated at the end of a tranquil lane. The rooms are rather basic, but the atmosphere is pleasant and there is a terrace.

Thanh Thuy's Guesthouse, 46/4 Le Loi, ☎ (054) 82 45 85 – 4rm 🛏 🍴 ✕ Located in the same quiet back-street as the Mimosa, this guesthouse has four basic, but spotlessly clean and pleasant rooms.

Between US$10 and US$15

Dong Loi, 11A Pham Ngu Lao, ☎ (054) 82 22 96 / 82 62 34, Fax (054) 82 62 34, interser@dng.vnn.vn – 34rm 🛏 🍴 ✕ 🛏 📺 ✕ A tranquil hotel located in a quiet street in the centre of town. Tasteful contemporary paintings adorn the walls and corridors, giving the whole place a touch of class. Rooms for all budgets from US$6-US$20. Excellent restaurant (see "Eating out").

Lucky Guesthouse, 4 Ben Nghe, ☎ (054) 88 91 06 – 27rm 🛏 🍴 📺 ✕ Tucked away in a peaceful street, this

pretty blue establishment has basic, but decent rooms. Popular among travellers on mini budgets, it is friendly and cheerful.

Nam Giao, 3B Dien Bien Phu, ☎ (054) 82 57 36 / 82 21 40, Fax (054) 82 57 35 – 15rm 🛏 🍴 ✕ Not far from the station, this establishment provides reasonable rooms and an average level of comfort.

Thai Binh – Binh Minh, 10/9 Nguyen Tri Phuong, ☎ (054) 82 80 58, Fax (054) 83 28 67 – 35rm 🛏 🍴 📺 ✕ Hidden away in a quiet side street opposite the Binh Duong, this hotel offers very good value for money. Major renovation works were underway at the time of writing and new, more expensive rooms should soon be available.

Villa Tourist, 14 Ly Thuong Kiet, next to the post office, ☎ (054) 82 54 61 – 3rm 🛏 ✕ Three relatively basic, but clean, pleasant rooms can be found in this attractive villa. Its old-fashioned charm is most appealing and the owners are very welcoming.

Between US$15 and US$30

Dong Da Hotel, 15 Ly Thuong Kiet, ☎ (054) 82 38 84 / 82 82 54, Fax (054) 82 32 04, dongda.h@dng. vnn.vn – 40rm 🛏 🍴 📺 ✕ Karaoke, nightclub and shops. Breakfast included. The spacious rooms of this fine 2-star international establishment are very pleasant and some have a sitting-room. Two rooms at US$35 which sleep four.

Dong Duong – L'Indochine Hotel, 3 Hung Vuong, ☎ (054) 82 60 70 / 82 60 71, Fax (054) 82 60 74 – 12rm 🛏 🍴 📺 ✕ This hotel is located in a magnificent French colonial villa right in the heart of town. The rooms upstairs which are bigger and lighter are the most pleasant. Good restaurant (see "Eating out").

Hung Vuong, 2 Hung Vuong, ☎ (054) 82 38 66 / 82 37 97, Fax (054) 83 36 06 – 70rm 🛏 🍴 📺 ✕ A recently renovated, attractive hotel right in the centre of town. The rooms are comfortable and quiet. A dozen or so cheaper rooms are also available in the annexe. Friendly staff.

Lotus Hotel, 33 Dinh Cong Trang, ☎ (054) 52 59 97, Fax (054) 52 59 96 – 9rm 🛏 📺 ✕ This is one of the rare hotels located within the citadel, which makes it peaceful. The rooms are reasonable and some have a small sitting-room.

Thanh Lich, 33 Hai Ba Trung, ☎ (054) 82 59 73 / 82 59 74, Fax (054) 82 59 72 – 36rm 🛏 📺 ✕ Breakfast included. A relatively modern establishment compared to the others in town. Comfortable, spotless rooms.

Thanh Noi, 3 Dang Dung, ☎ (054) 52 24 78 / 52 72 09, Fax (054) 52 72 11, thanhnoi@dng.vnn.vn – 50rm 🛏 📺 ✕ This attractive hotel, situated in the citadel, is both quiet and shady. The rooms are spacious, well fitted out, attractive and clean. The staff are pleasant and eager to help. Bicycles, motorcycles and cars for rent and excursions in the area. A pity the restaurant is rather gloomy.

Between US$30 and US$50

Hoa Hong 2, 1 Pham Ngu Lao, ☎ (054) 82 43 77, Fax (054) 82 69 49 – 52rm 🛏 📺 ✕ 💳 Lift. This international hotel caters mostly for groups. Its only appeal is its spacious rooms overlooking the town or river.

Thuan Hoa, 7 Nguyen Tri Phuong, ☎ (054) 82 25 53 / 82 33 40, Fax (054) 82 24 70 – 70rm 🛏 📺 ✕ Shop, nightclub, sauna, massages. This international establishment caters mainly to groups. The cane-furnished rooms are pleasant, but the overall atmosphere is cold and impersonal.

Between US$50 and US$70

5 Le Loi Hotel, 5 Le Loi, ☎ (054) 82 21 55 / 82 21 61, Fax (054) 82 88 16 – 24rm 🛏 📺 ✕ This handsome, recently renovated establishment on the river-bank has very pleasant rooms with period furniture. Attentive staff.

Huong Giang Hotel, 51 Le Loi, ☎ (054) 82 21 22 / 82 39 58, Fax (054) 82 31 02 – 150rm 🛏 📺 ✕ 💳 Conference room, art gallery, fitness centre, sauna, lift. Breakfast included. It is a pity that this riverside hotel caters mainly to groups, but it remains a very attractive 3-star establishment. Tasteful, distinctive decoration.

Saigon Morin, 30 Le Loi, ☎ (054) 82 35 26, Fax (054) 82 51 55, sgmorin@dng.vnn.vn – 127rm 🛏 📺 ✕ 💳 Conference room, nursery, gallery, shop, fitness centre, sauna, massages, lift. This splendid 100-year old colonial-style establishment is reputed to be the most luxurious hotel in Hue. The spacious, tasteful rooms are in a number of villas along the riverbank. Excellent service. Most attractive garden and swimming pool with bar.

Between US$70 and US$100

Century Riverside Hotel, 49 Le Loi, ☎ (054) 82 33 90 / 82 33 91, Fax (054) 82 33 94 – 155rm 🛏 📺 ✕ 💳 Lift. It is impossible to miss this vast concrete block on the river-bank. Although it might offer all the comfort of a standard international hotel, this tourist factory lacks charm and is vastly overpriced. Those in the previous category are much better value.

EATING OUT

Hue is renowned for its sophisticated cooking. Among the town's specialities are "banh cuon", steamed rice pancakes stuffed with beef and lettuce, and "banh khoai", pancakes stuffed with vegetables, shrimp and meat, both served with a peanut sauce.

Under 25 000VND

Café 3, 3 Le Loi (C3). This unpretentious establishment serves good, cheap food. Vietnamese, Chinese and Western dishes, together with breakfasts and snacks. Also organises excursions.

Mandarin Cafeteria, 12 Hung Vuong (D3), ☎ (054) 82 12 81. This establishment's Western and Asian cuisine is not very original, but it is a good place to meet other travellers. More suited to breakfast, a snack or a drink rather than dinner. Doubles up as a travel agency.

Dong Tam, 48/7 Le Loi (D3), ☎ (054) 82 84 03 🍴 This restaurant is located in a peaceful, shady courtyard at the end of a lane and is ideal for lunch or dinner far from the bustle of the town. Simple, low-price Asian and vegetarian dishes.

Between 25 000 and 50 000VND

Paradise Garden Restaurant, 17 Le Loi (D3), ☎ (054) 83 22 20. Dining by the flickering candle-light of the lanterns hanging from the trees of this open-air restaurant by the riverside is particularly pleasant. Very popular with Vietnamese.

Tay Nguyen Restaurant, 49 Le Loi (D3), next door to the Century Riverside, ☎ (054) 84 56 80. On the water's edge, this tranquil establishment affords a particularly good view of the Perfume River. It also serves good traditional dishes – made before your very eyes – and the staff are very friendly.

Between 50 000 and 100 000VND

L'Indochine Restaurant, 3 Hung Vuong (D3), ☎ (054) 82 60 70. Daily 6am-10pm. This restaurant in the hotel of the same name serves good Vietnamese cooking at reasonable prices in an attractive setting of potted plants, paintings and nicely-laid tables.

La Carambole, 11A Pham Ngu Lao (D3). If looking for somewhere to have a quiet dinner, you will appreciate this tastefully decorated establishment. The mouth-watering menu features a wide choice of reasonably priced Vietnamese and Western dishes. The duck and stuffed squid are particularly delicious.

Between 100 000 and 200 000VND

Tropical Garden, 5 Chu Van An (D3), ☎ (054) 84 71 43, Fax (054) 82 80 74 🍴 This tiny oasis of greenery is a lovely spot to stop for a refreshing drink during the day. In addition to the dining room, the little wooden tables under parasols of palm leaves dotted around the garden are most appealing. Good traditional à la carte and set menus from US$7-US$25. Caters mainly to tourists and the price is in dollars.

Club Garden, 12 Vo Thi Sau (D3), ☎ (054) 82 63 27, Fax (054) 82 80 74 🍴 This establishment was designed along the same lines as its twin, the Tropical Garden, but the dining room is larger and noisier. Try here if the first is full.

GOING OUT

Tea rooms – Dilmah, 7 Doi Cung (D3), ☎ (054) 84 51 03. Daily 6am-midnight. Music and attractive wooden furniture set the scene for this tea room. 25 different teas (banana, mango, strawberry, peach and rum) and pastries. Attentive staff.

Mai Huong Cake Shop, 14 Nguyen Tri Phuong (D3). Daily 7am-10pm, next door to the Binh Minh Hotel. Those with a sweet tooth will adore the wide choice of cakes, including grape, hazelnut, banana, strawberry, mango and coconut, to name but a few, all equally appetising. Take away or eat in.

Cafés and bars – In the evening, countless little cafés and bars come to life throughout the town particularly on the west bank by the river. Their strings of fairy lights and blaring music make them impossible to miss. A perfect opportunity to meet Hue's youth.

Apocalypse Now, 7 Nguyen Tri Phuong (D3), next door to the Thuan Hoa Hotel.

DMZ Bar, 44 Le Loi (D3). THE trendy bar of the town and haunt of night-owls.

Nightclubs – Ngoc Anh Club, 7 Nguyen Tri Phuong (D3). The nightclub-bar-karaoke of the Thuan Hoa Hotel.

OTHER THINGS TO DO

Excursions – All Hue's agencies offer the classic boat-trip down the Perfume River with lunch on board and a visit to Thien Mu Pagoda and the tombs of Tu Duc, Khai Dinh and Minh Mang (allow US$2). Take a sweater or windcheater because the weather can turn cold. Excursions also available to the Thermal Springs of My An, Bach Ma National Park, Suoi Voi Springs, and to Hoi An and Da Nang, the DMZ zone and to Phong Na Cave.

Sports – Swimming pool, 2 Le Quy Don (D3), near the stadium, ☎ (054) 81 00 22. Daily 6am-midday / 1-7pm. Entrance charge (US$2). The Saigon Morin's swimming pool is also open to non-residents (US$2).

Tennis, 11 Le Loi (D3), and at the Huong Giang and Century Riverside Hotels.

SHOPPING

Market – From a conical hat and Vietnamese nougat to fabric woven by ethnic minorities and nuoc-mam, **Dong Ba Market** (D2), open daily from 7am to 7pm, is sure to have what you want.

Art galleries – Boi Tran, 30 Le Loi (D3), ☎ (054) 84 67 98, Fax (054) 82 51 55, boitranart@dng.vnn.vn Saigon Morin Hotel art gallery.

Duy Tan Gallery, 12 Hung Vuong (D3), ☎ (054) 83 45 56. Contemporary Vietnamese art.

Gallery Newspace, 7 Pham Ngu Lao (D3), ☎ (054) 53 44 53, thanhhaiart@dng.vnn.vn Contemporary Vietnamese art.

Local specialities – Hue is famous for its conical hats which are covered in dec-orative transparent designs. Most shops sell them but those from Dong Ba Market are reputed to be the best.

Shops – Vina Silk, 38D Le Loi (D3), ☎ (054) 82 84 04. Silk fabric and clothes made to measure.

Hai Quang, 1 Pham Ngu Lao (D3), ☎ (054) 82 20 64. Small antiques shop.

Nhu Y, 10 Hung Vuong (D3), ☎ (054) 83 29 16. Lacquered objects.

Bookshops – Van Hoa Bookshop (D3), 18b Hung Vuong, ☎ (054) 83 26 37, sells works in foreign languages.

Bach Ma close up

WHERE TO STAY, EATING OUT

Under US$10

Bach Ma Guest House, Bach Ma, ☎ (054) 87 13 30 – 22rm ⁀] 天 ✕ It is possible to stay either outside the park, near the reception, or in the park, in one of the old renovated French villas (allow US$15-US$20). Camping is also authorised (50 000VND per tent).

Lang Co close up

WHERE TO STAY, EATING OUT

Under US$10

Lang Co Tourist Hotel, Lang Co Beach, ☎ (054) 87 44 26 – 30rm ⁀] 天 ✕ The spot is grim, the beach, complete with overhead electricity wires, is filthy and the restaurant is disappointing. Only as a last resort.

Between US$10 and US$15

Thanh Tam Seaside Resort, Lang Co Beach, ☎ (054) 87 44 56 – 11rm ⁀] 📇 天 ✕ ☆ The rooms are relatively basic and the walls could definitely do with a lick of paint, but this hotel is a whole sight better than its neighbour, above.

DA NANG★

Capital of the province of Da Nang – Pop 680 000
105km from Hue, 759km from Hanoi, 960km from Ho Chi Minh City

Not to be missed
The Cham Museum's superb collection.
A stroll along Bach Dang Avenue.
The Marble Mountains.

And remember...
Save a visit to the museum for the hottest part of the day.

On a vast bay at the mouth of the Song Han, Da Nang is dominated by the Son Tra Peninsula which forms a natural barrier sheltering the city from the ocean. The port of Tien Sa to the northwest of the town is the third largest in Vietnam, after those of Ho Chi Minh City and Haiphong. Despite this, Da Nang does not look to the sea to revive its flagging economy, but to the skies. An international airport, opened in autumn 1999, has unveiled new horizons which, it is hoped, will drag the town out of its current lethargy. Half-way between Hanoi and the former Saigon and within easy reach of the Imperial City of Hue, the ancient port-city of Hoi An, the sacred site of My Son and the Highlands, Da Nang has ambitions of becoming the "gateway to Indochina" and of exploiting its tourist potential. The climate is pleasant all year round and there is mile upon mile of white sandy beaches, much appreciated by GIs during the Vietnam War. However Da Nang is still not really on the tourist trail and most visitors only come to see the famous Cham Museum or the Marble Mountains. It is true that this sprawling modern city – the fourth largest in Vietnam – is not particularly appealing as such, yet a number of pleasant surprises await the curious visitor. Take the time to wander through the town, avoiding the noisy, crowded main streets in favour of the quieter lanes and quaysides.

The gateway to Indochina

Even though mentions of the town of Da Nang are relatively recent (17C), the region was in fact occupied from the 15C and many colonists from the north settled here in the territories ceded by the Champa kingdom to Dai Viet (*see page 20*). As early as the following century, Da Nang had become a major port and a serious rival of the old trading city of Hoi An. The first Spanish and French settlers landed in Da Nang in 1858. Thirty years later, the latter had made it one of their concessions and given it the name of **Tourane**. During the colonial period, the town was one of the most important in Indochina. The French were expelled in 1945, but in March 1965 it was the turn of the Americans, who turned Da Nang into their most important naval- and air-base in Southeast Asia. The town's fall in 1975 coincided with the beginning of the collapse of the South Vietnamese regime. After reunification, Da Nang was made part of the province of Da Nang-Quang Nam though in 1997 it was given administrative independence.

The town
Allow half a day

Although the town may at first seem rather dreary, a stroll down Bach Dang Avenue reveals a series of superb French colonial residences, which now house State ministries. This riverside promenade is particularly pleasant in the evening, when it is lit by thousands of lights and makeshift little cafés start to do business beneath the tall trees facing the port.

Opened on 29 March 2000, a resolutely modern bridge now links the town with the Son Tra Peninsula.

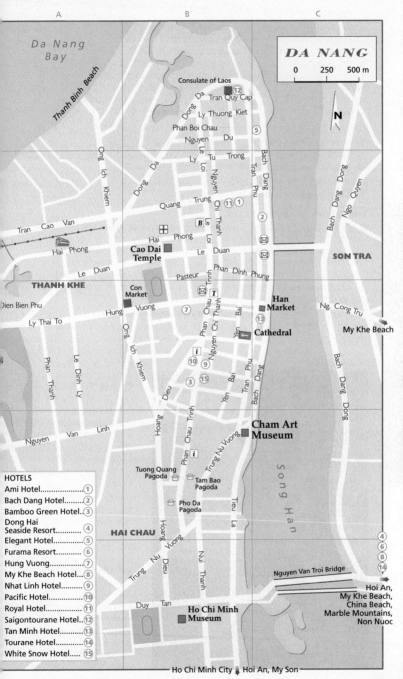

DA NANG

0   250   500 m

N

Da Nang Bay

Thanh Binh Beach

Consulate of Laos

Da Dong

Tran Quy Cap ⑫

Ly Thuong Kiet

Phan Boi Chau

Nguyen   Du

Bach Dang

Tran Phu

⑤

Ly   Le   Tu   Trong

Loi

Nguyen Chi Thanh

Quang   Trung   ⑪ ①

B

②

Hai   Phong

Le Loi

Le   Duan

Phong

Cao Dai Temple

✉

✉

Bach Dang Dong

Ngo Quyen

SON TRA

Tran Cao Van

Hai   Phong

Le   Duan

THANH KHE

Dong Da

Ong Ich Khiem

Pasteur

Phan Dinh Phung

Con Market

Han Market

Ng. Cong Tru

My Khe Beach

Hung   Vuong

✉

⑦

T

Phan Chau Trinh

Yen Bai

⑬

Cathedral

Dien Bien Phu

Ly Thai To

Phan Thanh

Le Dinh Ly

Ong Ich Khiem

Nguyen Chi Thanh

i

⑩   ⑨

⑮

③

Dieu

Tran Phu

Bach Dang

Yen Bai

Cham Art Museum

Bach Dang Dong

Nguyen   Van   Linh

Hoang

Phan Chau Trinh

Trung Nu Vuong

i

Song Han

Tuong Quang Pagoda

⛩

Tam Bao Pagoda

⛩ Pho Da Pagoda

HAI CHAU

Tieu La

HOTELS	
Ami Hotel	①
Bach Dang Hotel	②
Bamboo Green Hotel	③
Dong Hai Seaside Resort	④
Elegant Hotel	⑤
Furama Resort	⑥
Hung Vuong	⑦
My Khe Beach Hotel	⑧
Nhat Linh Hotel	⑨
Pacific Hotel	⑩
Royal Hotel	⑪
Saigontourane Hotel	⑫
Tan Minh Hotel	⑬
Tourane Hotel	⑭
White Snow Hotel	⑮

Hoang Dieu

Trung Nu Vuong

Nui Thanh

Duy   Tan

Ho Chi Minh Museum

Nguyen Van Troi Bridge

④
⑥
⑧
⑭

Hoi An, My Khe Beach, China Beach, Marble Mountains, Non Nuoc

Ho Chi Minh City   Hoi An, My Son

257

Further south, beyond Hung Vuong, is **Han Market** (Cho Han), the liveliest in town. Market gardeners and housewives crowd around the colourful, attractively-arranged stalls, whose products, spices and aromatic plants fill the air with a thousand scents. Squatting behind their over-laden baskets or by their stalls, women can be seen beating large strips of rice noodles with extraordinary dexterity. The regular hammering nearly drowns out the sound of the live fish thrashing about in large steel basins or the squawking poultry in cages. The market continues inside the vast covered hall, with two storeys of textiles and other household wares.

Leave the market on Tran Phu and head left, southwards.

On your right, you will see **Da Nang Cathedral** (*158 Tran Phu, but the entrance is on 47A Yen Bai. Services at 5pm*), an elegant pink-coloured edifice built in 1923 by the French. Inside are some attractive stained-glass windows.

Go all the way down Tran Phu to the crossroads between Trung Nu Vuong and Bach Dang. The Cham Museum is straight ahead.

The Cham Museum*** (B3)

☎ (0511) 82 19 51. Daily 7.30am-6pm. Entrance charge. Allow 1hr.

Founded in 1915 by the French School of the Far East, this museum now holds one of the most extensive collections of Cham sculpture, including 300 original sandstone and terracotta works covering the evolution of Cham art from the 7C-15C. Designed by the architects Delaval, Auclair and Henri Parmentier, the architecture of this charming building is roughly based on a Cham temple, complete with courtyard and frangipani trees.

Begin your tour of the museum in the **My Son Room*** in the centre of which stands part of the **altar*** found in the E1 tower at My Son (mid-7C), with bas-reliefs featuring hermits praying, meditating or playing music. Opposite the entrance, another

Graceful apsara

bas-relief depicts Vishnu in repose between two cosmic orders. In the next-door **Quang Tri Room**, admire the 8C **statue of Shiva**, complete with moustache and rather unusual attire, as well as an amazing **bas-relief** of a polo game (10C), a sport of Persian origin which was all the rage in medieval China.

Continue into the **Quang Nam Gallery** which houses two particularly fine 9C and 10C statues of Shiva, then on into the **Tra Kieu Room***, home to the museum's finest artefacts by far. In the northwestern corner of the room a 10C pedestal is carved into a stunningly beautiful **apsara***, noted for her serene expression and gracefully carved sensual forms. On the wall opposite is a superb 9C statue of the

J Siepinski/DIAF

Goddess Laksmi★ above an amusing frieze of elephants, horses and lions. In the centre of the room the **pedestal of Tra Kieu★★★** is without a doubt one of the masterpieces of Cham art. It relates the miraculous events which gave birth to the God Krishna. Take a careful look at the frieze of graceful and extremely sensual celestial dancers on the north side. Although they all look alike, each adopts a different pose and wears a distinctive flimsy garment.

Beyond the **Quang Ngai** and **Kontum Rooms** is the **Dong Duong Room** devoted to the site of the old Buddhist Champa capital (9C). During this period, Cham architecture and sculpture adopted a more original, dynamic style, quite unique in Southeast Asian art. Among the remains found are a bronze statue of the bodhisattva Tara together with the **altar** from the main temple, with carvings depicting the life of the Buddha. In the next room, photographs of a variety of Cham temples illustrate what they looked like before being damaged or destroyed during the Vietnam War.

Beyond the **Quang Binh** and **Binh Dinh Rooms**, the tour ends in the **Thap Mam Room** which reveals the emergence of a new style featuring carvings of strange and fabulous animals, their workmanship of a far less refined kind than previously. The exhibits here come from the group of Vijaya towers built in the 10C near the citadel at Do Ban.

Leave the museum and turn left into Trung Nu Vuong continuing as far as the junction with Nui Thanh. Take the latter and turn right into Duy Tan. The Ho Chi Minh Museum is 250m further on to the left.

The Ho Chi Minh Museum (B5) *(daily 7-11.30am / 1.30-4.30pm. Entrance charge. Visitors are sometimes refused admittance from 4pm)*, which is somewhat decrepit and unattractive, relates the nation's struggle for independence against the French and Americans. It is illustrated by photos, the personal belongings of war heroes and a variety of weapons and scale models. In the courtyard outside the museum stand aeroplanes, tanks, cannons and lorries, together with a faithful reproduction of Ho Chi Minh's stilt-house, which may be of interest to those unable to see the original in Hanoi.

To get to the town centre, turn left into Hoang Dieu on leaving the museum and then Phan Chau Trinh where you will be able to admire the Tam Bao (n° 323), Pho Da (n° 340) and Tuong Quang (n° 316) Pagodas. Continuing further north, you pass the town theatre (on the corner of Hung Vuong) and then turn left into Hai Phong.

At n° 63 Hai Phong stands the second largest **Cao Dai Temple** in the country. This handsome colonial-style building was built in 1906. Inside the temple, the altar is surmounted by the divine eye, the symbol of Cao Dai, together with the five founders of the world's main religions, namely Muhammad, Lao-tzu, Jesus Christ, the Buddha and Confucius *(see page 63)*. You can attend one of the four daily prayer services held at 5.30am, 11.30am, 5.30pm and 11.30pm.

Around Da Nang★

The Marble Mountains★★

8km to the southeast of Da Nang. Entrance charge. Allow 90min. A plan is on sale at the entrance. A torch is useful when exploring the caves.

The **Ngu Hanh Son** (Mountains of the Five Elements), better known as the Marble Mountains, consist of five limestone hills sculpted by rainwater. Each is named after one of the five elements: Thuy Son (water), Tho Son (earth), Hoa Son (fire), Kim Son (metal) and Moc Son (wood). Once inhabited by the Cham who built holy shrines here, the mountains are strewn with pagodas and caves with fantastic rock formations where Buddhist, Confucian and Taoist divinities are worshipped.

Thuy Son, the highest and largest of the five, is also the most popular. Access is down a steep staircase whose pink, blue, grey and red marble steps were carved out of the mountain itself. It leads into **Tam Thai Pagoda** built in 1825 under the reign of Emperor Minh Mang. Inside stands a statue of the Buddha in the company of Quan Am (Goddess of Mercy), Van Phu (Goddess of Wisdom and Intelligence) and Pho Hien (Goddess of Generosity and Forgiveness).

Behind the pagoda, take the path on the left to the **Hoa Nghiem** and **Huyen Khong★★** Caves. The latter, 30m-high, is particularly magical, bathed in a few rays of light which stream in from tiny overhead openings in the vault. The air is heavy with incense and the atmosphere could not be more mystical. During the war, this former Cham shrine served as a refuge and a hospital to the Viet Cong and has now become a major Buddhist pilgrimage site. Hosts of followers come here to worship in front of the statues of the Buddha, Van Phu and Pho Hien.

Behind Tam Thai Pagoda, **Linh Nham Cave** houses a number of garish statues of the Buddha and two guardians, protected under a glass dome. Continue along the path and under a porch which leads into a narrow passage flanked by two steep mountain faces. On your right is **Van Thong Cave** (*now is your chance to use your pocket torch!*) within which stands a Buddha. Behind the statue is a narrow, winding passage leading to the peak's summit. The **view★** over Da Nang, the sea and the four other Marble Mountains is superb.

The **Vong Hai Pavilion**, a short distance away, also affords a pretty view of the sea and the village of Non Nuoc.

The path finally ends at **Linh Ung Pagoda**, built by Emperor Minh Mang and renovated in 1970 thanks to Buddhist donations. Behind the pagoda, **Tang Chon Cave** is a rocky labyrinth sheltering sitting and reclining Buddhas and a few Cham remains over 900 years old.

A staircase leads down to the village of Non Nuoc.

The marble extracted from the hills has been sculpted by generations of artists from the hamlet of Non Nuoc which lies at the foot of Thuy Son. Along the roadside you will see them carving statues of animals, the Buddha and Ho Chi Minh, together with a variety of objects and jewellery, all in the ear-splitting din of lathes and hammers.

The dragon's sons

According to legend, the Ngu Hanh Son Mountains were the offspring of a sea dragon. The dragon left an egg on the beach and one thousand days and nights later, it hatched a beautiful young girl who flew off into the heavens. The legend doesn't say what became of the maid, but the fragments of egg-shell grew in size until they became the Marble Mountains.

My Khe and China Beach★

Not far from Da Nang, My Khe and China Beach stretch out as far as the eye can see. These immense white sandy beaches were as popular with war-weary GIs, as they are with today's tourists. A few hotels have been opened here, but most of the beach is deserted and it is easy to find a quiet, tranquil spot to relax in the sun and enjoy the sea.

It is also possible to combine this stay with a visit to the Cham sites at My Son, 50km to the south of Da Nang (see page 275).

Da Nang close up

COMING AND GOING

By air – The *international airport* is 2km to the west of Da Nang, on Dien Bien Phu Road, the continuation of Hung Vuong. Vietnam Airlines operate two flights daily to Hanoi (90min) and Ho Chi Minh City (90min), one daily flight to Bangkok (4hr 30min), three weekly flights to Ban Me Thuot (90min) and four weekly flights to Nha Trang (1hr 20min). Pacific Airlines operate 3-4 flights daily to Ho Chi Minh City, Hanoi and Taiwan, and Thai Airlines fly to Bangkok three times a week.

By train – The *railway station* (Ga Da Nang) is in the western part of town, at 122 Hai Phong, ☎ (0511) 82 38 10. The ticket office is open daily 6am to 5pm. Some 9 trains daily to Hanoi (18hr 30min journey), Hue (3hr), Nha Trang (11hr) and to Ho Chi Minh City (16hr30min-21hr).

By bus – The intercity *bus station* is at n° 31 Dien Bien Phu, 1km west of the town centre. 10 buses daily to Hue (3hr), 5 to Ho Chi Minh City (24hr) and Nha Trang (12hr), 4 to Qui Nhon (10hr) and Dalat (16hr) and 3 to Hanoi (20hr).

GETTING AROUND DA NANG

By taxi – *Dana Taxi*, ☎ (0511) 815 815. *Tra Taxi*, ☎ (0511) 655 655. *Huong Lua*, ☎ (0511) 82 82 82.

By rental vehicle – Bicycles and motorcycles can be rented from *Lien Coffee*, 20 Dong Da, ☎ (0511) 89 54 22. See "Excursions".

ADDRESS BOOK

Tourist information – *Vietnam Tourism*, 92A Phan Chau Trinh, ☎ (0511) 82 36 60, Fax (0511) 82 15 60. Daily 7.30-11.30am / 1.30-5.30pm. The excursions organised by the agency cater mainly to groups, but they also rent cars and you can buy an Open Tour or air ticket.
Saigon Tourist, 357 Phan Chau Trinh, ☎ (0511) 82 70 84, Fax (0511) 82 71 58. Daily 7.30-11.30am / 1.30-4.30pm. Air and train tickets sold.

Guides can also be hired but most of the excursions are for groups.

Bank / Currency exchange – *Vietcombank*, 140 Le Loi, ☎ (0511) 82 35 03, Fax (0511) 82 60 62. Monday-Friday 7.30-11am / 1-4pm. Travellers' cheques and Visa, MasterCard and American Express accepted.

Post office / Telephone – *Buu Dien Da Nang*, 60B Bach Dang. Daily 6am-10pm (summer) or 6.30am-9.30pm (winter). Express mail by DHL or Fedex. Another DHL branch is open at 37 Tran Phu, next-door to Vietnam Airlines, ☎ (0511) 83 45 18, Fax (0511) 83 45 17.

Internet – Internet connections at *Christie's Cool Spot*, 112 Tran Phu, for 1 000VND / min.

Medical service – *General Hospital*, 74 Hai Phong, opposite the Cao Dai Temple, ☎ (0511) 82 14 80. Health service for foreigners.

Consulate, embassy – *Consulate of Laos*, 16 Tran Quy Cap, ☎ (0511) 82 12 08. Monday-Friday 8-11.30am / 2-4.30pm.

Airline companies – *Vietnam Airlines*, 35 Tran Phu, ☎ (0511) 82 11 30 / 82 64 65, Fax (0511) 83 27 59. Monday-Friday 7-11am / 1.30-5.30pm, Saturday and Sunday 7.30-11am / 1.30-4.30pm. Accepts payments by Visa and MasterCard. *Pacific Airlines*, 52 Hai Phong, ☎ and Fax (0511) 83 09 99. Daily 7.30am-5.30pm.

WHERE TO STAY

Under US$10
Hung Vuong Mini Hotel, 95 Hung Vuong, ☎ (0511) 82 39 67 / 89 27 59, Fax (0511) 82 19 94 – 9rm ⚒ ⌀ Located in a colonial-style villa, the rooms are very basic, but spacious and clean. The manager doesn't speak English.
Pacific Hotel, 92 Phan Chau Trinh, ☎ (0511) 82 21 37, Fax (0511) 82 29 21 – 39rm ⚒ 🍽 🖧 📺 ✕ Lift. Only the cheapest, very ordinary but clean rooms are worth a mention.

Between US$10 and US$15

Ami Hotel, 7 Quang Trung, ☎ (0511) 82 44 94 / 82 44 07, Fax (0511) 82 55 32 – 18rm ⌂ 🗒 ♋ 📺 Set in a quiet street near the port, this pleasant hotel offers a variety of room categories. However only the least expensive, which are clean and face two directions, are good value for money.

Nhat Linh Hotel, 194 Nguyen Chi Thanh, ☎ and Fax (0511) 82 56 26 – 12rm ⌂ 🗒 ♋ 📺 This attractive three-storey building has clean, pleasant rooms and friendly staff.

Tan Minh Hotel, 142 Bach Dang, ☎ (0511) 82 74 56, Fax (0511) 83 01 72 – 10rm ⌂ 🗒 ♋ 📺 Pleasantly located on the waterfront, the rooms are spacious and clean. Guests can breakfast or read and relax on the pleasant roof-top terrace with a superb view of the town and river.

Between US$15 and US$30

🐚**White Snow Hotel – Tuyet Trang Hotel**, 177 Phan Chau Trinh, ☎ (0511) 83 43 33 / 82 34 76, Fax (0511) 83 43 32 – 12rm ⌂ 🗒 ♋ 📺 ✗ Mini-bar. Located in a quiet city centre street, this hotel offers excellent value for money. The tastefully decorated rooms are spacious, airy and clean.

Between US$30 and US$50

Bach Dang Hotel, 50 Bach Dang, ☎ (0511) 82 36 49 / 82 30 34, Fax (0511) 82 16 59 – 91rm ⌂ 🗒 📺 ✗ There is no point in hoping for the charm of a picturesque hotel, because this establishment caters essentially to groups. The oldest section is located in an attractive colonial building but the rooms are on the decrepit side. Only if all else fails!

Between US$50 and US$70

Bamboo Green Hotel, 158 Phan Chau Trinh, ☎ (0511) 82 29 96 / 82 29 97, Fax (0511) 82 29 98, bamboogreen@dng.vnn.vn – 46rm ⌂ 🗒 ♋ 📺 ✗ ⒸⒸ Mini-bar, conference room, fitness centre, sauna, massages, karaoke, shop, lift. This three-star establishment offers all the amenities of a standard international hotel. The rooms are pleasant and have a fine view of the town, but the overall atmosphere is rather impersonal.

🐚**Royal Hotel**, 17 Quang Trung, ☎ (0511) 82 32 95, Fax (0511) 82 72 79, royalhotel@dng.vnn.vn – 28rm ⌂ 🗒 ♋ 📺 ✗ ⒸⒸ Mini-bar and private safe, lift. A cosy English pub-style atmosphere reigns in what is one of the town's most attractive hotels. Attentive staff.

Elegant Hotel, 22A Bach Dang, ☎ (0511) 89 28 93, Fax (0511) 83 51 79, elegant@dng.vnn.vn – 32rm ⌂ 🗒 ♋ 📺 ✗ ⒸⒸ Lift. A comfortable hotel overlooking the port with tastefully decorated, spacious rooms. Friendly staff.

Between US$70 and US$100

Saigontourane Hotel, 14A Tran Quy Cap / 5 Dong Da, ☎ (0511) 82 10 21, Fax (0511) 89 52 85, sgtouran@dng.vnn.vn – 82rm ⌂ 🗒 ♋ 📺 ✗ ⒸⒸ Shop, karaoke, sauna, massages, lift. This three-star establishment in the north of town is relatively remote but offers excellent rooms and is most pleasant.

● **My Khe Beach**

Between US$15 and US$30

My Khe Beach Hotel, 142 Nguyen Van Thoai, Son Tra District, ☎ (0511) 83 61 25 / 83 66 62, Fax (0511) 83 61 23 – 40rm ⌂ 🗒 ♋ 📺 ✗ 🛏 🍽 Ideal if you want to stay on the beach on a shoestring budget. The clean, pleasant rooms are in different buildings depending on their category. Some have a balcony and a sea view. Four basic rooms from US$10.

Between US$30 and US$50

🐚**Tourane Hotel**, Phuoc My Ward, Son Tra District, next-door to the above, ☎ (0511) 93 26 66 / 93 22 22, Fax (0511) 84 43 28, tourinco@dng.vnn.vn – 30rm ⌂ 🗒 ♋ 📺 ✗ 🍽 ⒸⒸ Breakfast included. The tastefully decorated, attractive rooms are located in handsome colonial-style villas on the edge of the beach.

● **China Beach**

The abysmal Non Nuoc Beach Resort is to be avoided at all costs.

Under US$10

Dong Hai Seaside Resort, 251 Huyen Tran Princess, Hoa Hai Ward, Ngu Hanh Son District, ☎ (0511) 96 10 09 –

7rm ⚑ 🗲 ✕ ⚑ Those lacking the funds to stay in the Furama will appreciate the little brick bungalows with thatched roofs hidden in this shady pine grove. The rooms are basic but clean and very near the beach.

Over US$100

⚑**Furama Resort**, 68 Ho Xuan Huong, ☎ (0511) 84 73 33 / 84 78 88, Fax (0511) 84 72 20 / 84 76 66, furamadn@hn.vnn.vn – 186rm ⚑ 🖃 ✒ 📺 ✕ ⚒ ⚑ ♨ ✂ **cc** Mini-bar, business centre, fitness room, beauty parlour and hairdresser's, sauna, massages, shops, lift. This is by far one of Vietnam's most luxurious and exquisitely decorated resorts. The stylish rooms feature polished parquet floors, elegant period furniture, marble bathrooms and a balcony overlooking the sea or the swimming pool. Delicious Asian and Western cuisine is served in one of the hotels four restaurant-bars. Muted ambience in the cosy lounge with jazz pianist. Excellent, high-quality service.

EATING OUT

Under 25 000VND

Lien Coffee, 20 Dong Da, ☎ (0511) 89 54 22. This little café has seen better days, but continues to attract travellers in search of information. Bus reservations and bicycles and motorcycles for rent. Simple but cheap fare. Friendly, helpful staff.

Christie's and Cool Spot Restaurant, 112 Tran Phu, ☎ and Fax (0511) 82 66 45, christies_danang@hotmail.com Daily 10am-11pm. Also very popular with tourists who appreciate its information and helpful staff. Low-price Vietnamese and Western cooking.

Between 25 000 and 50 000VND

Phi Lu, 225 Nguyen Chi Thanh, ☎ (0511) 82 37 72. Daily, lunch-time and evening. This establishment is very popular among large Vietnamese families. Moderately-priced, generous helpings of Chinese cuisine. Somewhat noisy.

Ngoc Anh Restaurant, 30 Tran Phu, ☎ (0511) 82 27 78 🏠 A quiet, pleasant restaurant serving good Vietnamese and Chinese fare. Dinner is served on a tiny patio full of potted plants.

Vietnam, 53 Ly Tu Trong, ☎ (0511) 82 38 45. A friendly local restaurant if staying in the neighbourhood.

Between 50 000 and 100 000VND

⚑**Hana Kim Dinh**, 15 Bach Dang, ☎ (0511) 83 00 24 / 83 00 14, Fax (0511) 82 82 67 🏠 **cc** Daily 10.30am-11pm. This floating restaurant is one of the most attractive restaurants in Da Nang. Tasty Vietnamese, Chinese, Japanese and European cuisine is served on two terraces, with a fine view of the boats of the port. Attentive, elegant service.

Kim Do Restaurant, 180 Tran Phu, ☎ (0511) 82 18 46, Fax (0511) 89 10 29, k.co@dng.vnn.vn Daily, lunch-time and evening. The smartest restaurant in Da Nang. Although the setting is attractive and the food good, it is often full of groups and the service suffers accordingly. The staff could be more welcoming.

GOING OUT

Cafés and bars – Christie's and Cool Spot Bar, 112 Tran Phu, ☎ and Fax (0511) 82 66 45, christies_danang@hotmail.com. Daily 10am-11pm.

Bamboo, 5 Bach Dang, ☎ (0511) 83 71 75, bamboo_dn@dng.vnn.vn Exotic, musical ambience for a relaxed drink or game of billiards. Also provides tourist information and organises excursions.

Shows – Town Theatre, corner of Phan Chau Trinh and Hung Vuong.

Nightclubs – Night-owls can try the following two clubs, high in "local colour": **Royal Hotel**, 17 Quang Trung and **DTC Dancing**, 8 Le Loi.

OTHER THINGS TO DO

Excursions – If you are interested in going to My Son by car, enquire at the **Bamboo Bar**, the **Lien Coffee** or **Christie's and Cool Spot Bar** (allow US$30). **Danatours** (130 Dien Bien Phu, ☎ (0511) 74 64 47) also organises 1-2-day excursions to Ba Na, a mountain resort (1 482m) 40km from Da Nang.

HOI AN ★★

Province of Quang Nam – Pop 75 000
30km from Da Nang, 130km from Hue, 510km from Nha Trang

Not to be missed
The old Chinese houses.
An early morning stroll in the market.
And remember...
Take the time to wander about and enjoy the architecture and atmosphere.
Plan your visits to get the most out of your pass.

On the banks of the calm waters of the River Thu Bon, sleepy Hoi An seems to be under a magic spell that has suspended it in time. Its colourful houses and worn and somewhat decrepit façades exude an old-fashioned charm untarnished by the passing centuries. All around, craftsmen can be glimpsed in their workshops, hard at work pursuing time-honoured skills and traditions. The lanes abound with lanterns, paintings and brightly-coloured silk fabrics and resound to the beating of hammers and the whirring of sewing machines. The town is becoming more and more popular with tourists, many of whom decide to extend their stay and enjoy the peace and quiet of the town and of nearby Cua Dai Beach. Hoi An is now wholly devoted to tourism and countless restaurants, bars, Internet cafés and travel agencies have sprung up together with a multitude of places offering tailor-made garments in record time.

Declared a World Heritage Site in December 1999 by Unesco, Hoi An is a genuine living museum, with 844 sites of historic interest, including bridges, wells, pagodas and private houses. It is the city's unique historic atmosphere, tinged with a hint of nostalgia, that enchants so many tourists as they explore the streets of this seaport from a bygone era.

A thriving city

The Hoi An of today may strike visitors as a peaceful market place, but two centuries ago, what was then called **Faifo** was an important link in the chain of Southeast Asian trading posts and the country's largest international port. As early as the 15C, it was a major maritime crossroads and port of call for vessels from all over Asia and even further afield. In the 16C, Chinese-Japanese trade increased in the province of Quang Nam, following the ban on Japanese vessels putting into Chinese ports. Officially founded between 1602 and 1613 by Governor **Nguyen Phuoc Nguyen** (1563-1635), Hoi An was to experience two hundred years of intense trading, involving Dutch, English, French and Portuguese merchants. Silk, tea, spices, porcelain and lacquer-ware were all handled here. Early trading took the form of simple exchanges which followed the seasons and the monsoon periods, but the volume of trade was such that many merchants finally set up shop in the city, building rich residences which were living quarters, shop and warehouse all rolled into one. Little by little the city was divided up into Japanese, Chinese and French districts, each with its own community and customs. The first missionaries landed here, among them **Father Alexandre de Rhodes** who arrived in 1625 and spent three years in Hoi An. It is to this Catholic priest that we owe the Romanisation of the Vietnamese language (*see page 85*).

In the late 18C, the war between the Nguyen and the Trinh, followed by the Tay Son uprising, were to seriously damage the town, and from then on the port of Hoi An declined in favour of Da Nang. The silting up of the river, which prevented all navigation other than that of sampans and other small craft, was the final straw.

An open-air museum

Hoi An is an unparalleled example of architectural diversity. The coexistence of Chinese, Japanese and Western communities over the last few centuries gave rise to the development of an extraordinarily fertile culture expressed in a wide variety of architectural styles.

The old **Chinese houses**, the city's pride and joy, should on no account be missed. These elongated merchant residences open both ways, onto the street and the river. They are divided into three parts, with the shop at the front, a living-room, inner courtyard and well in the middle, and a warehouse to the rear.

A walk through the town will reveal many other unusual architectural sights, such as the **wooden shop fronts**, closed at night by long horizontal planks slipped into grooves cut into the pillars supporting the roof. Notice also the **roofs** covered in curved yin (concave) and yang (convex) tiles to better drain the rainwater, or the **eye motifs over the doors**, intended to ward off evil spirits. Since 1991, important renovation work has been undertaken with the help of Japanese teams to preserve this priceless cultural legacy.

The town

Allow a day on foot

The town of Hoi An has created a compulsory pass (50 000VND) giving access to one museum, one old house, the Japanese bridge or the Quan Cong Pagoda and one other site of your choice. All other visits require the purchase of another pass. Passes can be bought from the tourist information offices (see the "Close up" section).

Hidden from prying eyes by a high Chinese-Japanese-style wall, the **Tran Family House**** was built in 1802 by a civil mandarin, Tran Tu Nhac, and consecrated to the worship of his ancestors (*21 Le Loi, corner of Phan Chu Trinh. Daily 7.30am-6pm. Entrance charge*). A tour is all the more interesting because visitors are shown round by Mr Tran's daughters. The entrance leads into a pretty flowered garden, called the West Garden, which symbolises the future and paradise, while to the rear, the East

Nguyen Thai Hoc Street

B Brillion/MICHELIN

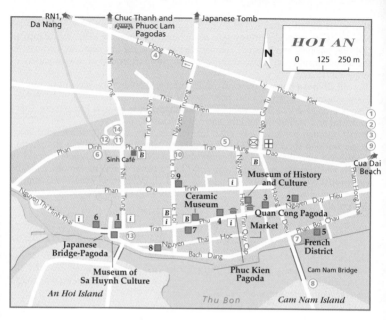

1 Cantonese Chinese Congregation Hall
2 Chaozhou Congregation Hall
3 Hainan Congregation Hall
4 Five Congregation Community Hall
5 Tran Duong House
6 Phung Hung House
7 Quan Thang House
8 Tan Ky House
9 Tran House

HOTELS			
Cua Dai	①	Pho Hoi 2	⑧
Dong Xanh Hotel	②	Sao Bien	⑨
Hai Yen	③	Thanh Binh	⑩
Hoai Thanh	④	Thanh Binh 2	⑪
Hoi An Hotel	⑤	Thien Trung	⑫
Hoi An Trade Union	⑥	Vinh Hung 1	⑬
Huy Hoang	⑦	Vinh Hung 2	⑭

Garden, where the family's umbilical cords are buried, represents the past. The chapel itself symbolises the present and is divided into two parts, the first devoted to the worship of the family's ancestors, while the second part is the family's living quarters. The **chapel's** three rooms represent happiness, prosperity and longevity. Visitors are welcomed into the antechamber, an intimate family museum with lovely dark wooden furniture. Responsibility for the upkeep of the **ancestors' altar** is passed down from father to eldest son. Watch out for the step, the sill between the two rooms has been raised deliberately in order to make visitors bend their heads to the altar! Each of the wooden boxes on the altar contains the relics of an ancestor. In a third room, admire the family collection of **ceramics**.

Congregation Halls

Over the centuries a large Chinese community from all over China settled in Hoi An. The immigrants built congregation halls in Hoi An to worship their ancestors. These halls are sometimes called pagodas, but they are only devoted to the worship of divinities which the Chinese community wished to thank for their help.

Return onto Le Loi and turn left into Tran Phu to the **Quan Thang House**, at n° 77 (*daily 6am-6pm. Entrance charge. The owner doesn't speak English*). Built over 200 years ago by a Chinese merchant, this chapel is very similar to the Tan Ky house. The latter is however in much better condition.

On the other side of the street, at n° 80, the **Ceramic Museum*** *(daily 7am-6pm. Entrance charge)* is located in an elegant early 20C Chinese wooden house. Originally used as living quarters and shop, it was restored between 1993 and 1995 with Japanese funds. Today it houses exhibits of Chinese, Japanese and Vietnamese pottery found in the region, together with some drawings of the town's different architectural styles.

Beyond the **Five Congregation Community Hall** *(64 Tran Phu. No charge)*, built in 1741 to assemble all the Chinese of Hoi An, stands the **Fujian Congregation Hall****, also called the **Phuc Kien Pagoda** *(46 Tran Phu. Daily 7am-6pm. Entrance charge)*. Built in 1697, it was devoted to the worship of the Goddess of the Sea, **Thien Hau Thanh Mau**, by Chinese mandarins of the Ming dynasty who were forced to flee to Vietnam, following their overthrow by the Manchu in 1644.

A superb pink brick **gate**, restored in 1974, leads onto the shade of a spacious, flowered terrace. On entering the pagoda, notice the two handsome **murals*** on either side of the table where dignitaries would have sat. The one on the left depicts the battle between the Manchu and the Ming, while that on the right features the Goddess of the Sea rescuing a foundering vessel. The first **altar** is devoted to the Goddess of Compassion, while the second is guarded by two strange creatures and is devoted to the Goddess of the Sea, **Thien Ly Nhan** (in green), who can see for over a thousand leagues, and **Thuan Phong Nhi** (in red), who can hear from over a thousand leagues away. To the right of the altar is a **replica** of a Chinese sailing boat similar to that in which the Ming would have fled from China.

An adjacent chamber is devoted to ancestor worship. In the rear courtyard are three magnificent ornately-carved and lacquered wooden altars. The one on the left is devoted to the God of Prosperity, the one in the middle to the six Chinese mandarins from the province of Phuc Kien and the one on the right, to the three Lords of Fertility and to the twelve heavenly mid-wives (one for each month), each of whom teaches the new-born babies different skills.

At 24 Tran Phu, at the crossroads with Nguyen Hue, **Quan Cong Pagoda** (Chua Ong), built in 1653, is the oldest place of worship in Hoi An. Today it is devoted to the Chinese General, Quan Cong, famous for his loyalty, sincerity, integrity and justice. An impressive colourful statue, in a glass case, depicts the general in the company of his adjutant and a civil mandarin who was his adopted son.

A breather in front of Quan Cong Pagoda

B Juge/MICHELIN

A door behind the chapel leads into the courtyard of Quan Am Pagoda, now home to the **Museum of History and Culture*** (*7 Nguyen Hue. Daily 7am-5.30pm. Entrance fee*). A large number of disparate artefacts illustrate the development of Hoi An during the pre- and proto-historic, Champa (7C-15C) and Dai Viet (15C-19C) periods.

On leaving the museum, go down Tran Phu and admire the **Hainan Chinese Congregation Hall**, a handsome building with an elegant carved altar and attractive murals (*10 Tran Phu. No charge. If the heavy wooden doors are closed, go through the little porch to the left*). A short distance away stands the **Chaozhou Chinese Congregation Hall** (Trieu Chau) (*157 Nguyen Duy Hieu. No charge*) whose profusion of ornate wooden carvings is also worth a visit.

Walk down Hoang Dieu towards the river, as far as the junction with Phan Boi Chau, which delineates the **French district***. Intent on setting themselves apart from the Chinese and Japanese, the French built a series of colonial villas along the former Rue Courbet. The yellow façades and blue doors and shutters of these houses make this peaceful, tree-lined street most picturesque. At n° 25, **Tran Duong House*** (*no charge, donations welcome*) is more than worth a pause. Mr Tran greatly enjoys showing visitors around the house and explaining the history of the neighbourhood where he was born. Built in 1887, the house is in its original state and it also boasts a few pieces of early 20C French furniture.

Bach Dang runs alongside the river. The growing clamour in the lane will leave you in no doubt that you aren't far from the **market****, whose bright colours, rich smells and pungent flavours are the heart of this former seaport. Fragrant flowers, heady spices and the odour of dried fish engulf you, while the cries of the market women squatting by their wares attempt to drown out the squawks of chicks and ducklings. Cooks call out to passers-by, vaunting their delicious soup or fresh bread, while in the shade of a parasol or a conical hat, young girls proffer an amazing variety of fresh fish and seafood. Down by the river where the sampans and fishing boats ceaselessly come and go is the best place to get a feel for this town from a bygone era.

Do you want to come to my shop?
Hoi An is the ideal place to replenish your wardrobe on a shoestring budget. The drone of an army of sewing machines echoes throughout the lanes of the old town. Competition is stiff and most tailors employ scouts to entice, but not force, prospective clients into their lair. From a Vietnamese silk "ao dai" or a woollen duffle-coat to a viscose dress or a natty dinner-jacket, just name the style and the fabric and hey presto! Don't hesitate to haggle.

Walk down Nguyen Thai Hoc, at the far end of which stands **Tan Ky House****, one of Hoi An's most prized architectural gems (*101 Nguyen Thai Hoc. Daily 8am-5.30pm. Entrance charge*). Seven generations were born in this late 18C building which was the first Chinese house to be declared a Historic Monument in 1985. Admire the superb wooden columns with poems to the glory of nature written in inlaid mother-of-pearl. The two ornamental columns on the courtyard side are covered in characters formed entirely of birds (50 on each).

Nguyen Thai Hoc takes you into Bach Dang and to the **Japanese Bridge**** (*no charge, but you must show your pass in the pagoda, open from 7am-6pm*). Many different communities settled in Hoi An at the height of its prosperity. The Japanese district developed to the west to the river, the Chinese to the east and the Viet-

Bridge and dragon
According to legend, the bridge-pagoda of Hoi An was built by the Japanese community to overpower a monster so enormous that its body stretched from Japan to India, causing terrible disasters such as droughts, floods and earthquakes. This little edifice was built over the creature's back, thus preventing it from moving and causing such catastrophes.

namese to the north. The task of building a bridge between the communities was finally taken up by the Japanese in 1593. Its construction lasted three years, from the year of the monkey to that of the dog, hence the **statues** at either end of the bridge. In 1719, a Chinese mandarin visiting the town renamed the bridge Lai Vien Kieu, "the bridge built by those from afar". Fifty years later, the Chinese decided to build a **pagoda** in honour of Bac De Tran Vu, a venerated Chinese mandarin. For a time it was a courthouse where conflicts between the different communities were settled.

To the west of the bridge, **Phung Hung House*** *(4 Nguyen Thi Minh Khai. Daily 8am-6pm. Entrance charge)*, built in 1780, was declared a Historic Monument in 1985. Like many of Hoi An's residences, it is a blend of architectural styles. No metal at all was used in the construction of the oak **roof**, which is supported by 80 pillars and held together by wooden dowels and pegs. The rainwater runs off a **four-sided Japanese roof** down gutters and into a concrete basin underneath the house. Upstairs, a Chinese-style vaulted **balcony** is decorated with carp, a symbol of prosperity for the Vietnamese, of good luck for the Chinese and of power for the Japanese. Inside, a hanging altar, devoted to maritime trade, was where sailors came to worship before setting sail. A **trapdoor**, formerly used to bring goods upstairs, is now used to transport the ground-floor furniture to safety every October-November when the districts near the river are flooded.

Turn round and head back the way you came. Fifty metres to the east of the Japanese Bridge, at 176 Tran Phu, is the **Cantonese Chinese Congregation Hall** (Quang Dong) *(Daily 7am-5pm. Entrance charge)*. Created in 1895, it is dedicated to General Quan Cong. Two handsome **carved murals**, depicting the general in the company of his two faithful friends and their wives, can be seen in the first chamber. In the main room, the general is seated with his aides-de-camp, adjutant general and a civil mandarin, his adopted son. Also note the general's famous white and red horses. Two altars on either side are devoted to the Goddess of the Sea (on the left) and the God of Prosperity (on the right).

At the corner of Tran Phu and Nguyen Hue is the **Museum of Sa Huynh Culture** *(149 Tran Phu. Daily 7am-6pm. Entrance charge)*. Very little is known today about this civilisation which existed in the Hoi An region from the 2C BC-5C AD, prior to that of the Cham. Archaeologists and historians are hard at work and over 20 excavation sites, including dwellings and cemeteries, are underway in the area. These have revealed some magnificent **funerary urns**, buried in the sand, which contained the ashes and jewellery of the deceased, together with earthenware, cooking utensils and iron tools.

Around Hoi An

The ideal way to explore and enjoy the nearby countryside is by bicycle.

At the northernmost end of Nguyen Trung To, turn into the sandy track to the right of the Tiger Pagoda and continue down, bearing left all the way. Once at the end of the track, turn left, then right in front of the school (yellow building) not far away.

The maze of raised paths through the lush green rice paddies to the north of the town are perfect for a walk or bicycle ride. In the midst of these vast green meadows stands the forlorn **tomb** of a Japanese merchant who lived in Hoi An in the 17C. *(Cross over the rice paddies to the irrigation canal, then turn left beyond the bridge. Continue as far as a stone-built dike, on the right, where you can leave your bicycle; the tomb is 100m away).*

If you continue along the canal and turn left at the next bridge, you will reach a red dirt track that soon turns into a road. Beyond the Buddhist cemetery, turn right into a path which leads to **Chuc Thanh Pagoda**, set in a quiet spot surrounded by grazing cows. It is said to be Hoi An's oldest pagoda. At the entrance, a trio of towers shelters the tombs of the monastery's monks. A short distance away (*go back onto the path as far as road which you will cross over*), **Phuoc Lam Pagoda** is tucked away in a delightful flowered garden. *Go back the way you came onto the first road near the cemetery. This leads into Nhi Trung, to the north of Hoi An. You can also take the path on the other side of the road which will take you back onto Nguyen Truong To.*

If you leave town on Tran Hung Dao, you will reach Cua Dai Beach, 5km to the east of Hoa Dai. The road, lined with lagoons and coconut trees, is very attractive and the long white sandy beach offers a welcome break from the stifling town (*car park, restaurants and rental of deck chairs*).

Hoi An close up

COMING AND GOING

By bus – The *bus station* is in fact a bus shelter on the corner of Le Hong Phong and Nhi Trung. Departures every 30min to Da Nang (1hr), from 5.20am to 5.50pm. Privately-run companies operate services to other towns and tickets can be bought from hotels or travel agencies. A branch of the *Sinh Café* is at 37 Phan Dinh Phung.

GETTING AROUND HOI AN

Hoi An can only be explored on foot as vehicles are banned from the old city.

By rental bicycle or motorcycle – Enquire in the hotels and travel agencies. Allow 6 000VND per day /for a bicycle.

ADDRESS BOOK

Tourist information – The pass to Hoi An's historical sites can be purchased from the tourist offices located around town (12 Phan Chu Trinh, 37 Tran Phu, 78 Le Loi, 19 Nhi Trung and on Nguyen Thi Minh Khai). Guided tours possible.

Bank / Currency exchange – *Vietcombank*, 4 Hoang Dieu. Monday-Saturday 7.30am-7pm. Travellers' cheques, Visa, MasterCard and American Express accepted. Money transfers by Western Union. Other branches at 78 Le Loi (Monday-Friday 7am-6.30pm) and at 29 Phan Dinh Phung (daily 6am-10pm). *Hoi An Bank for Agriculture*, 92 Tran Phu. Monday-

Saturday 7am-5pm. Visa and MasterCard.

Post office / Telephone – *Buu Dien Hoi An*, corner of Ngo Gia Tu and Tran Hung Dao, ☎ (0510) 86 14 80. Daily 6am-9.30pm. Telephone and Internet.

Internet – Many hotels, restaurants and agencies have an Internet connection. Allow 300VND / min.

Travel agencies – There are dozens of travel agencies in town, all with the same services at the same prices, from bus, boat and air tickets to excursions to My Son, My Lai and the Cham Islands.

Airline companies – *Vietnam Airlines*, 20 Tran Phu, ☎ (0510) 86 32 79.

Medical service – *General Hospital*, 4 Tran Hung Dao, ☎ (0510) 86 12 18.

WHERE TO STAY
Under US$10
Hoi An Trade Union, 50 Phan Dinh Phung, ☎ (0510) 86 23 70, Fax (0510) 86 18 99 – 12rm ⚑ ⊼ A small, spartan establishment but the rooms are clean.

Thanh Binh, 1 Le Loi, ☎ (0510) 86 17 40 / 86 22 64, Fax (0510) 86 41 92 – 15rm ⚑ ⊼ Good value for money for mini-budgets. The rooms are pleasant and well looked-after. Allow US$2 extra for air-conditioning.

Thien Trung, 63 Phan Dinh Phung, ☎ (0510) 86 17 20, Fax (0510) 86 37 99 – 20rm ⚑ ⊼ Similar to the Hoi An Trade Union, this establishment is clean but with no frills.

Between US$10 and US$15

Dong Xanh Hotel, 1C Cua Dai, ☎ (0510) 86 34 84, Fax (0510) 86 31 36 – 20rm ⚑ ⅀ 🅟 📺 ✕ 🆒 Although lacking in charm, the rooms are very good considering the price, and some have a balcony.

Hoai Thanh, 23 Le Hong Phong, ☎ (0510) 86 12 42, Fax (0510) 86 11 35 – 43rm ⚑ 🖿 🅟 📺 Just on the outskirts of the old town, near Hoi An Church, this establishment lacks character but the rooms are clean and comfortable.

Huy Hoang, 73 Phan Boi Chau, near Cam Nam Bridge, ☎ (0510) 86 22 11, Fax (0510) 86 37 22 – 26rm ⚑ ⅀ 🖿 ✕ Near the entrance to the French district, this riverside hotel offers well-kept if somewhat basic rooms. The least expensive are windowless, but the upper categories are more recent and pleasant. Terrace overlooking the river.

Sao Bien, 15 Cua Dai, ☎ (0510) 86 15 89, Fax (0510) 86 13 82 – 15rm ⚑ ⅀ ✕ This hotel is reasonable, but nothing more.

Between US$15 and US$30

🐾 **Cua Dai**, 18A Cua Dai, ☎ (0510) 86 22 31, Fax (0510) 86 22 32, cuadaihotel@dng.vnn.vn – 12rm ⚑ 🖿 🅟 📺 ✕ 🆒 This delightful hotel set in a French colonial-style house provides tastefully decorated, airy, spotless rooms. On the first floor, there is a pleasant terrace. The restaurant is on a nearby veranda. Friendly staff.

Hai Yen, 22A Cua Dai, ☎ (0510) 86 24 45, Fax (0510) 86 24 43, kshaiyen@dng.vnn.vn – 33rm ⚑ ⅀ 🖿 🅟 📺 ✕ 🆒 On the outskirts of town, on the road to Cua Dai Beach. Spacious, attractive, quiet, clean rooms. Some with fan at US$12 and a few suites at US$50.

Pho Hoi 2, Cam Nam, ☎ (0510) 86 26 28, Fax (0510) 86 26 26, phohoiht@dng.vnn.vn – 26rm ⚑ 🖿 🅟 📺 ✕ 🆒 This large three-storey building is on the river-bank, on the other side of Cam Nam Bridge. The spot is quite pretty and the rooms are airy and clean, some overlooking the garden, others the river. A few more basic rooms are available at US$10.

Thanh Binh 2, Nhi Trung, next-door to the Vinh Hung 2, ☎ (0510) 86 37 15 / 86 41 61, Fax (0510) 86 41 92 – 33rm ⚑ ⅀ 🖿 🅟 📺 ✕ Built in the style of a Chinese house, this hotel offers an attractive setting, with bright, well-kept, stylish rooms, particularly the larger ones with sitting-room and balcony.

Vinh Hung 1, 143 Tran Phu, ☎ (0510) 86 16 21 / 86 36 97, Fax (0510) 86 18 93, vinhhung.ha@dng.vnn.vn – 12rm ⚑ 🖿 🅟 📺 🆒 Breakfast included. Right in the heart of the old town; the myriad lanterns strung up around this handsome Chinese house make it easy to spot in the evening. The hotel is welcoming, quiet and pleasant although perhaps not quite as good value as the Vinh Hung 2. The rooms with the most character are in the old section, complete with elegant Chinese furniture and four-poster beds. They are however more expensive (US$40).

🐾 **Vinh Hung 2**, Nhi Trung, ☎ (0510) 86 37 17 / 86 40 74, Fax (0510) 86 40 94, quanghuy.ha@dng.vnn.vn – 31rm ⚑ 🖿 🅟 📺 ✕ ⅏ 🆒 An attractive modern hotel built around a central patio and swimmingpool, which is most welcome during the town's frequent heat waves. The rooms, most of which have a balcony, are spacious, comfortable and tastefully furnished. Those decorated in a Chinese style have the most character. Very friendly, attentive staff.

Between US$30 and US$50

Hoi An Hotel, 6 Tran Hung Dao, ☎ (0510) 86 13 73 / 86 14 45, Fax (0510) 86 16 36, hoianhotel@dng.vnn.vn – 130rm ⚑ 🖿 🅟 📺 ✕ ⅏ ⚘ 🆒 Karaoke, travel agency, shop and beauty parlour, lift. This three-star establishment caters mainly to groups but is rather impersonal. The spacious, comfortable rooms lack character and the high price is in no way justified.

EATING OUT

Make sure you try the regional specialities, such as "cau lau" (rice noodles soaked in water with ashes, covered with marinated pork and served with salad and soya beans), "bong hong trang" or "white rose" (fine, white rice noodles stuffed with crab and shrimp) and "hoanh thanh" or "won-ton" (noodles stuffed with shrimp and fried). Hoi An is also reputed for its fish and seafood, which is served in almost all the restaurants in town and particularly on Bach Dang.

Under 25 000VND

The unbeatable prices of some of the rundown cafés along Le Loi continue to make them popular. Among them are the **Café Bobo**, at n° 18, opposite the Thuy Duong Hotel, and its neighbour, **Dudi Restaurant**.

Between 25 000 and 50 000VND

Dac San Hoi An, 89 Tran Phu, ☎ (0510) 86 15 33 ☂ This establishment has two dining rooms, one of which is upstairs with a balcony overlooking Tran Phu. An à la carte menu features most of Hoi An's specialities and there is also an attractive set menu with four specialities.

Faifoo Restaurant, 104 Tran Phu, ☎ (0510) 86 15 48 ☂ This friendly little establishment gives you a good view of the bustle on Tran Phu. Fish, seafood and Vietnamese dishes, together with a US$3 menu with five regional specialities.

Han Huyen Floating Restaurant, restaurant on stilts next-door to the footbridge linking the peninsula to Hoi An. Pleasantly cool thanks to a refreshing breeze, this restaurant offers a great view of the quay. Vietnamese and Chinese cuisine.

Mermaid Restaurant, 2 Tran Phu, ☎ (0510) 86 15 27 ☂ Although rather unappealing by daylight, come nightfall, dozens of Chinese lanterns and candles entice the passer-by onto the terrace. International and Vietnamese dishes, fish and seafood.

The Thanh Old House Restaurant, 76 Bach Dang, ☎ (0510) 86 13 66. Daily 7am-11pm. Located in an old Chinese house overlooking the river. Vietnamese food, and good choice of fish.

Thanh Thanh Restaurant, 152 Tran Phu, ☎ (0510) 86 13 08 ☂ Good Vietnamese cooking. The establishment's "hot-pot" and barbecued fish are particularly good. Little street terrace.

Yellow River Restaurant, 38 Tran Phu, ☎ (0510) 86 10 53. One of the most delightful restaurants on Tran Phu is located in an old Chinese house. Popular with tourists. Vietnamese and international cooking.

Vinh Hung Restaurant, 147B Tran Phu, ☎ (0510) 86 22 03 ☂ This establishment is peaceful and pleasant, particularly at night-time when the terrace is aglow with dozens of Chinese lanterns. Attractive wood furniture and tablecloths. À la carte Vietnamese menu or set meals of two or three dishes.

Between 50 000 and 100 000VND

Tam Tam Café, 110 Nguyen Thai Hoc, ☎ (0510) 86 22 12, tamtam.ha@dng.vnn.vn ☂ 10am-1am. This tasteful restaurant located in an early 20C colonial residence is run by a Frenchman. Pleasant setting with soft lights and music. International and Vietnamese cooking. Set menus and daily specials. Attentive service.

GOING OUT

Cafés and bars – Tam Tam Café, 110 Nguyen Thai Hoc, ☎ (0510) 86 22 12, tamtam.ha@dng.vnn.vn ☂ 10am-1am. The bar next-door to the restaurant is generally very lively and friendly and is often packed with travellers in the evenings. Wide choice of cocktails, with or without alcohol. Billiards and reading room.

Treat's Café, 158 Tran Phu, ☎ (0510) 86 11 25 ☂ A friendly café with street terrace and a shady inner courtyard with a billiard table. Music. Happy hour from 6-9pm.

Cham Pa Bar, 75 Nguyen Thai Hoc, ☎ (0510) 86 29 74. Traditional dancing and music upstairs every evening. More relaxed downstairs, with billiards and pop music from the 60s up to the present-day.

ZanziBar, 53-54 Nhi Trung, ☎ (0510) 86 44 00. Outside the old town. Cocktails and music. Happy hour from 7-9.30pm.

Shows – The cultural boat moored on the River Thu Bon puts on dance and musical performances every evening (except Sunday) at 7.30pm (20 000VND, groups only). The theatre of the Champa Bar, 75 Nguyen Thai Hoc (40 000VND) also puts on 1hr shows at 9pm.

OTHER THINGS TO DO

Excursions – My Son, promoted by all travel agencies, is very easy to get to from Hoi An (see page 264). Most agencies organise boat trips to the Cham Islands and up the River Hoi An. Little boats moored along the quayside generally charge around 20 000VND for a 1hr-tour of the islands. Allow US$3 for a trip to the potters' village, Thua Thinh and Cua Dai Beach (2-3hr).

Swimming pool – The Hoi An Hotel's swimming pool is open to non-residents (20 000VND).

FEASTS AND FESTIVALS

Fishermen's Festival – Once a year, on the last Sunday of March or first Sunday of April, this festival is held in honour of the spirits and to bring prosperity to the fishing villages. A boat procession of musicians and singers goes up the river.

SHOPPING

Crafts – The **Traditional Craft Shop of Hoi An**, 41 Le Loi, features all the town's different trades, including wood carving, embroidery, basket making, silk spinning and weaving. Upstairs, clothes are made-to-measure. However, all the guided tours come here, and prices are significantly higher than elsewhere.

The town also has a large number of art galleries with paintings and drawings on rice paper.

Clothes – It would be impossible to try and count the number of tailor's shops offering made-to-measure clothes within hours and for next to nothing (see page 268). Shop around and barter. One among many: **Nguyet Thu**, 121 Tran Phu.

Ceramics – You will be lost for choice down by the river, near the market.

THE CHAM ROAD★
FROM HOI AN TO NHA TRANG

Provinces of Quang Nam, Quang Ngai,
Binh Dinh, Phu Yen and Khanh Hoa – Map pages 228-229
510km tour – Allow 2 days

Not to be missed
The My Son site.
Doc Let Beach.

And remember...
This tour is only feasible if you have your own means of transport.
Plan on stopping at Qui Nhon to break up the journey.

From around Da Nang, where the Champa rulers established their first capital, to Phan Thiet, where they resided until the 17C, the narrow coastal plain is dotted with towers built by the Cham. It was along what is now the RN1 that they first expanded and later retreated. The remains of these imposing towers, nestling at the foot of a mountain or proudly perched on a hilltop overlooking the rice fields, bear witness even today to the splendour of the Champa kingdom and the great refinement of its essentially religious art. Depending on how much time you have, it is possible to restrict your visit to just the Da Nang Museum and the temples of My Son, Nha Trang and Phan Rang, which are the best preserved. However those with a vehicle will not regret the opportunity of travelling along this section of the ancient Mandarin Road and exploring sites which are off the beaten track but full of interest.

Carving at My Son

The history of the Cham

As early as the late 2C, Chinese documents mention the existence of an Indianised kingdom called **Lin Yi** along the coast of Annam. It was only to really become the **Champa kingdom** in the 4C, under the reign of King Bhadravarman. From the 8C, the kingdom stretched from the Gate of Annam (Hoanh Son) in the north to the basin of the Dong Nai in the south and consisted of five principalities (Indrapura, Amaravati, Vijaya, Kauthara and Panduranga).

The Cham, who never numbered more than 2.5 million, depended for the most part on agriculture and sea trade, which led them to establish

The Centre

B Brillion/MICHELIN

274

numerous contacts with Arabs, Indians, Chinese, Japanese and Malaysians. For centuries, the kingdom was in a state of conflict with its two powerful neighbours, the Khmer Empire and Dai Viet, before it was finally swallowed up by Vietnam towards the end of the 17C (*see page 22*).

Nowadays the Cham are only one of Vietnam's 54 ethnic minorities and all that remains of this sophisticated civilisation are scattered ruins along the central and southern coast.

Whether setting out from Da Nang or Hoi An, take the RN1 southwards. At Nam Phuoc (36km from Da Nang), turn right towards Hong Son. The road is in poor condition. At Kiem Lam, a signpost indicates My Son to the left (9km). 5km further on, turn left again onto a dirt track which leads to the ticket office.

My Son★★

Set in a lush green valley at the foot of Mt My Son ("Good Mountain") and also known as Hon Quap ("Cat's Tooth"), My Son is without doubt one of the masterpieces of Cham architecture and remains one of the most significant legacies of this civilisation. With over 70 monuments built from the 7C-13C, it comprises one of the richest architectural and religious Champa sites and has justly been compared to other Indian-influenced Southeast Asian cities such as Angkor (Cambodia), Borobudur (Java) and Pagan (Burma).

The Holy Land of the Cham

The foundation of My Son dates back to the 4C and was the work of King **Bhadravarman** who had a temple built here devoted to the worship of the lingam of the God-King Bhadresvara. This wooden structure was burnt to the ground, however, after a great fire in the 6C and it wasn't until the 7C that King **Sambhuvarman** undertook its reconstruction in brick and stone (now B1). Dedicated to the God Sambhudresvara, the temple became the religious centre of the Cham people, and it was here that the kingdom's monarchs withdrew prior to their coronation. They were entrusted with the task of building or restoring a temple at My Son during their reign and of making offerings to the god, hence the site's growing importance over the centuries. Many of the temples were built during the 8C-9C, prior to the emergence of Mahayana Buddhism (also known as the Greater Vehicle). During the brief reign of this Buddhist school in the kingdom of Champa, the position of My Son as religious capital declined in favour of Dong Duong.

However from the early 10C, Hinduism was once more in favour and My Son was returned to its former pre-eminent role in the Cham religion, but it was not until the late 11C that all its prestige was restored thanks to King **Harivarman**. This spell of grandeur was short-lived and the dominance of the Champa kingdom dwindled from the 12C, at the same time as its political centre was transferred to the south. A few temples were built after the 12C, but the Cham religious centre was then focused on the region of Panduranga.

The My Son temples were rediscovered in 1889 by **Camille Paris**, and the scholar **Henri Parmentier** who made a full inventory of the site, numbering the monuments and grouping them together. A team of Polish archaeologists has recently carried out restoration work on these monuments, many of which were seriously damaged during the Vietnam War.

The site

Daily 6.30am-4.30pm. Entrance charge: 50 000VND. Allow 1hr. Park your vehicle near the ticket office and walk across the river to a jeep which will take you to within 500m of the site. From there, you will have to walk. Take the little path which crosses the river and leads to the temples. The tour is not in chronological order, but begins with groups B, C and D which are the best preserved.

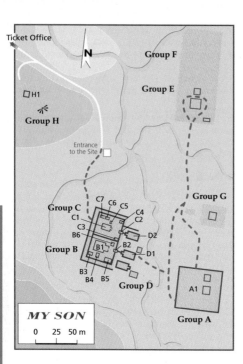

The Centre

Group B✶✶ is the largest group at My Son. It originally consisted of some 15 structures, built for the most part during the 12C-13C, but many were destroyed or damaged by American air raids in 1969. At present, the ground is littered with columns, steles, capitals, lingams and yoni.

Kalan B1 is the main shrine. In its centre the lingam dedicated to the God Sri Ishana Bhadresvara lies on a yoni designed to collect the water from ritual ablutions. The body of the tower has today disappeared and all that can be seen are the sandstone foundations.

To the southwest of the *kalan* stand two edifices devoted to the worship of the sons of Shiva. **Temple B3**, dedicated to Skanda, is typical of Cham towers. It consists of a rectangular tower, decorated with false doors and ornately worked pilasters and is topped by a three-tiered roof.

Its neighbour, **temple B4**, is devoted to Ganesha. Although in worse condition, the main body of the tower and the hall have collapsed, its outer walls and pilasters are an excellent example of the Cham decorative style featuring the distinctive entwined leaf and flower motifs.

To the southeast of B1, **koshagraha B5** is one of the best preserved buildings on the site. It consists of a rectangular chamber with east- and west-facing windows held up by three stone columns and a superb carved roof with barrel vaulting. Notice the delicately carved fresco of the apsaras as well as that of the two elephants over the windows.

To the northeast of the *kalan,* opposite the entrance to the *koshagraha,* **temple B6** contains a small basin used during religious rites. It is in rather poor condition, but is the only known example of this type of edifice.

Finally, to the east of B1, stands the **tower-gate B2**, and the **mandapa D1**. This long chamber today houses a small museum containing some of the best pieces of sculpture found on the site, together with a magnificent bas-relief of Shiva dancing. Several other fine pieces can be seen outside, along the northern wall.

The group was originally surrounded by little **reliquaries** devoted to the *dikpalaka,* gods entrusted with guarding the four cardinal points.

Group C is very similar to Group B, from which it is separated by just a low wall. Restored in the 10C, **kalan C1** nonetheless stands out for its upside down boat-shaped roof, generally reserved for *koshagraha,* and because it housed not a lingam, but a statue of Shiva, today exhibited in Da Nang Museum. Only the altar still remains. The body of the tower and entrance are quite well preserved and the attractive decorative patterns and handsome statues carved directly into the brick and stone-work are typical of Cham architecture.

This group also contains a tower-gate (C2), a storehouse for ritual objects (C3), outhouses (C4) and three other small *kalan* (C5, C6 and C7). Building D2, which is in fact the mandapa of C1, should also be included in this group. Similar to D1, it houses a small museum with a carved mural of Shiva dancing in the company of musicians and dancers, decorative patterns and mythical half-lion, half-elephant creatures.

Now head east and go over the small wooden bridge to Group A.

All that now remains of Group A, almost entirely destroyed by the Americans, are a half-collapsed brick wall, a few stone foundations and piles of rubble. It originally consisted of thirteen structures in different styles, some of them among the oldest at My Son. In particular, the 24m-high **kalan A1** was considered to be a masterpiece of Cham architecture and sculpture (*see the photos in Da Nang Museum*). It was the only shrine with two doors, facing east and west, with in its centre a (*still standing*) finely carved altar. As was the case with Group B, the complex also consisted of little temples devoted to the *dikpalaka*, said to protect the cardinal points (A2 – A7). A8 was a tower-gate, A9 a *mandapa*, A10 a *kalan*, A11 a storehouse for religious objects and A12 and A13 were outbuildings.

A narrow path to the north of Group A leads to **Group G**, but at the time of writing this group was still in a very sorry state and enclosed by a barbed wire fence. Not far away however, near a *kalan* in ruins, is a handsome stele covered in Sanskrit script. By continuing along this path you come to **Groups E and F**, which are also badly damaged but are nonetheless worth seeing because of the bull Nandi, headless statue of Shiva, stele, altar and lingam and other objects scattered among the crumbling buildings.

Go back along the path towards groups B and C and the entrance to the site. On the left of the path which leads to the car park, a little passage through the trees leads up to the top of a hill where **kalan H1** stands. Although all that remains is part of the wall, the spot does provide a lovely view over My Son.

Return onto the RN1 and continue southwards.

Along the Mandarin Road

10km to the north of Tam Ky, beyond kilometre marker 896, the site of Chien Dan lies to the right of the main road.

■ **Chien Dan** consists of three east-facing *kalan* (*so few visitors ever come here, that the monuments are only opened on request. Entrance charge. Allow 15min*). The ravages of time have taken their toll on these 11C and 12C towers and little can still be seen of their original ornamentation, but excavation work carried out in 1989 has unearthed countless remains, such as decorative elements, bas-reliefs and pedestals, which have been preserved in situ or in a small nearby **museum**. Admire, in particular, the superb carved L-shaped **pedestal** at the foot of the middle tower. The eastern façade depicts warriors, dancers and musicians, while the western one features a frieze of graceful dancers. To the north, two elephants graze on lotus flowers. The three *kalan* are partially destroyed and only the middle tower is open to the public.

12km to the south of Chien Dan, 2km beyond Tam Ky, go over the bridge of the same name and take the first turning on the right at a bend in the road. There are no signposts at all. Continue down a stony path for 500m, the towers of Khuong My come into view on the left, amid the vegetation.

■ The three *kalan* of **Khuong My** (*entrance charge. There is no ticket office as such but someone on the site is in charge of selling tickets*) are of similar structure and design and are characteristic of My Son (10C). They have never been the subject of restoration and are now covered in vegetation obscuring the fine detail of their otherwise well-preserved roofs. Specialists consider them to be a masterpiece of Cham art, nonetheless, by virtue of the profusion of decoration on the wall, false doors, pilasters, vaults and corniches, all evidence of the skill of Cham craftsmen in brick sculpture. The **scrolls and motifs** on the main part of the southern *kalan* are particularly well-preserved. Most of the sculpture found on the site is today exhibited in the Cham Museum at Da Nang.

Twenty-eight kilometres further along the RN1 are the remains (airport, gate, memorial) of the American base of **Chu Lai**, whose troops are remembered above all for their part in the massacre of My Lai.

30km from Chu Lai, before the bridge over the River Tra Khuc to Quang Ngai, take the road to the left of the Mitra Hotel (a large pink building) towards Son My. The museum is 12km away.

■ **Son My (My Lai)** – *Daily 7am-5pm. Entrance charge. Guided tours are possible but it is best to book to make sure there is a guide at the site. Allow 30min.*

Today when you see this peaceful site and its little museum, its silence disturbed only by twittering birds and laughing children, it is difficult to imagine that it was the scene of one of the most horrific episodes of the Vietnam War: the **My Lai Massacre**.

On the morning of 16 March 1968, the 11th Infantry Brigade of the American Army, led by Colonel Henderson, received the order to destroy the four hamlets of the sub-district of Son My, suspected of harbouring, or collaborating with, the Viet Cong. The soldiers, based at Chu Lai, were transported at dawn by helicopter and for four hours burnt everything in sight, massacring 504 innocent men, women and children. They met with no resistance and the village was totally destroyed to remove any traces. The American troops emerged unscathed, with the exception of Private Herbert Carter, who shot himself in the foot rather than take part in the butchery. The operation was presented as a successful offensive against a Viet Cong stronghold and was praised by the highest echelons in the army. The soldiers were awarded medals while the surviving villagers were interned in Tra Khuc Camp.

It was a full year later before Private Ronald Ridenhour finally gave in and confessed, followed by others. The affair made front page news, giving rise to protest movements throughout the world. In November 1969 a team of investigators were despatched to Son My to unearth the truth. Countless soldiers were questioned, 25 of them charged, but only Lieutenant William Calley, who was directly in charge of the massacre, was found guilty of 22 murders and condemned to life imprisonment. After three years within the comfortable walls of Fort Benning (Georgia), he was released on parole.

Pictures taken by the American army photographer, Ronald Haeberle, are exhibited in the **museum**, built on the exact spot of the worst-hit hamlet, Xom Lang. They bear witness to the atrocity. One is often at a loss for words to describe such images, particularly that of Lieutenant William Calley raising his fingers in a V for victory... A **memorial** has been erected in memory of the victims in the garden surrounded by a few forlorn tombs.

Return to the RN1 and head for Qui Nhon. Go through the village of Quang Nhai, which is of no particular interest unless you need somewhere to stay.

The highway runs south through a countryside dotted with rice fields. On either side of the road, people can be seen hard at work. Countless figures are busy sowing, stamping on mounds of earth, weeding plantations, reaping, threshing, rolling up stacks of rice, sweeping up the seeds drying in the sun and bagging them before loading them onto rickety bicycles. Eventually, the road and the railway line reach the sea and the first salt marshes come into view.

Field-work alongside the RN1

■ Sixty kilometres from Quang Ngai, the village of **Sa Huynh** is famous for its **beach** lined with coconut palms. Although it makes a pleasant stopping place, the spot is far from heavenly and it is not worth staying overnight. All the more so as the only hotel in the area is run-down and depressing, with very basic rooms and even shabbier bathrooms (*allow between US$12 and US$18*).

Beyond Sa Huynh, the road once more parts company with the sea and the landscape becomes hillier. A few terraced rice paddies come into sight.

88km to the south of Sa Huynh and 13km to the north of Binh Dinh, around kilometre marker 1202, a Cham tower can be seen perched on a hilltop. At kilometre marker 1204, take a dirt track to the right through rice paddies to a cemetery. Park your car here and continue on foot, the tower is 100m away. Make sure you leave nothing of value in the car because hordes of children roam the vicinity, with a tendency to harass the few passing tourists.

■ All that remains today of the citadel of **Cha Ban**, the last bastion of the Cham, is the graceful **Canh Tien Tower**, also known as the "Copper Tower", perched on its hilltop (*no charge*). Built in the early 13C, it is typical of the My Son style and part of its original sandstone ornamentation is still visible, like the four carved pilasters around the main body of the tower, the flame-edged cornice ornaments and the corner turrets. It is a pity that part of the restoration work was carried out with cement.

18km north of Qui Nhon, at the junction with the RN19 towards Plei Ku, a path leads to the towers which can be seen on a hill to the east.

■ **Banh It** (*no charge*) consist of four edifices, in Binh Dinh style, built during the 11C, after the transfer of the Cham capital to the Vijaya region. The **kalan**, also known as the "Silver Tower" is a classical square shape, topped by a three-tiered roof and corner turrets. The tower itself is richly decorated, reinforced with pilasters and graced by finely carved false doors. East of the *kalan*, opposite the door to the temples, stands the **tower-gate**, with the customary two doors, one facing east, the other west. To the southeast stands the **koshagraha**, a long building with a boat-shaped roof. Its edges are decorated with sculptures of Garuda, the bird vehicle of Vishnu. A **Tower Stele** with four arched doors can also be seen, the only one of its kind remaining today.

To get to Qui Nhon, leave the RN1 1km further on, and turn left as signposted. Qui Nhon is 10km away.

■ **Qui Nhon** – The capital of the province of Binh Dinh stands on a little peninsula overlooked by the Ba Hoa and Vung Chua Ranges. Qui Nonh, one of the largest ports of central Vietnam, handles a substantial amount of international trade and considerable funds have been invested here to modernise and develop its facilities. Although not unpleasant as such, the town lacks charm and is unlikely to appeal except as a stopover on the road between Da Nang and Nha Trang.
If you have to stay here, it would be a pity not to visit the site of **Hung Thanh***, also called **Thap Doi** (Twin Towers), and the two splendid Cham towers, all the more interesting because they have been recently restored *(2km to the northwest of the town. Leave town on Tran Hung Dao which leads to the RN1 and at n° 900, turn right into the little street called Thap Doi. The towers are 50m away on your right).* These two late 12C *kalan* are all that remain of a site which originally comprised several buildings. The interest of these two towers lies in their unusual pyramid-shaped roofs, typical of Khmer architecture.
A long **beach** to the south of the town is ideal for a short rest and a swim.

Return onto the RN1 towards Nha Trang.

The road, lined with eucalyptus, coconut and banana trees, takes you through a landscape of rice fields and little thatched-roof mud huts. Twenty-five kilometres out of Qui Nhon it begins to climb up towards the **Deo Cu Mong**, the pass which marks the border between the provinces of Binh Dinh and Phu Yen, before running alongside the sea to the village of **Song Cau** *(60km from Qui Nhon)*. The beach isn't very wide, but the immense bay of Xuan Dai with its cabins on stilts and colourful fishing boats makes a picturesque place to break your journey.
Beyond **Tuy Hoa**, the capital of the province, the coast becomes more built-up and the landscape strewn with great boulders of rock worn smooth by rainwater. Twenty kilometres further on, you will pass the **Deo Ca**, the frontier pass with the province of Khanh Hoa, dominated by a solitary granite peak known as **Hon Vong Phu** (Rock of the Waiting Woman). On the other side of the pass a wonderful view unfolds over the turquoise coastline dotted with islands, which stretches as far as the white sand dunes of the peninsula of **Hon Gom**. **Dai Lanh**, a picturesque fishing village not far away, boasts a beautiful beach tucked away in a vast semicircular bay surrounded by green hills.

37km to the north of Nha Trang, around kilometre marker 1415, take the narrow road to the left towards Cang (11km). Continue for 9km. Beyond a little village and a milestone which reads "Cang 3km", turn right towards Doc Let Beach Resort and continue down the track for 1km.

■ If you fancy a little peace and quiet or a rest from the hawkers of Nha Trang Beach, the idyllic setting of **Doc Let Beach*** is perfect for a few days' rest, far from the madding crowd *(see page 282 for accommodation)*. The long, wide stretch of pristine white sand, the shady coconut trees and the crystal-clear waters of this beach fully justify its reputation as one of the loveliest beaches of Vietnam. Even better, it is off the main bus routes and is, as yet relatively free of tourists and thus blissfully tranquil. Those who choose to stay overnight at Doc Let and who can hoist themselves out of bed at dawn shouldn't miss the chance of visiting the tiny fishing village to the south of the beach. Around 5am every morning, the sight of the fishing boats returning to the harbour with their night's catch is fully worth the effort.

Doc Let Beach

Return to the RN1. 34km north of Nha Trang, near the village of Ninh Hoa, is the junction with the RN26 which heads west towards Buon Ma Thuot (150km) and the province of Dac Lac. 12km further on, beyond Suoi Tre Bridge and kilometre marker 1430, near the Quynh restaurant-café, two stone pillars to the right of the RN1 indicate the way to Ba Ho Falls 3km away. Park your car and walk for 10-15min, following the red arrows.

■ **Ba Ho Falls** (*entrance charge*) are a succession of little rapids and pools, which rise at the summit of Hon Son Mountain and cascade down its flanks over enormous boulders polished by the water. While not exceptional, it is a quiet and peaceful place, where the only noise is the buzz of insects in the nearby jungle. Bathing possible.

Along the roadside you will see countless shrimp beds. 15km north of Nha Trang, at kilometre marker 1438, a signpost indicates the direction of the landing stage for Monkey Island (see page 290). For Nha Trang, don't miss the turning on the left at kilometre marker 1445. Nha Trang is 8km away.

The Centre

COMING AND GOING

By air – The *airport* (Phu Cat Airport) lies 35km to the north of Qui Nhon. Four flights weekly to Hanoi and Ho Chi Minh City (Tuesday, Thursday, Friday, Sunday). Airport tax 10 000VND. Taxis available to and from town.

By train – The Reunification Train stops at *Dieu Tri Railway Station*, 10km from Qui Nhon. Local trains go as far as Qui Nonh, but they are slow and few and far between, and you would do better to catch a taxi or a motorcycle-taxi. While it is in theory possible to buy a ticket at Qui Nhon Railway Station, on Cong Vien Quang Trung Square (☎ (056) 82 20 36), the receptionist speaks no English which makes communication limited. Four trains daily to Hanoi and Ho Chi Minh City.

By bus – Qui Nonh's *bus stations* are in the southwest of the town, on Tay Son. To get there, go down Ly Thong Kiet then Nguyen Thai Hoc, at the far end of which is Tay Son. Turn right for the stations. The first on your left (Ben Xe Lien Linh) has services to the local towns and villages, together with three daily buses at 5am, 6am and 7am, to Hoi An (6hr). The second bus station, a few hundred metres further on, has services to Vietnam's major cities. Daily, very early morning departures to Quang Ngai, Da Nang, Hue, Hanoi, Plei Ku, Nha Trang and Ho Chi Minh City. It is advisable to enquire at the station the day before leaving to confirm times.

GETTING AROUND QUI NHON

By taxi – *Davi Taxi*, ☎ (056) 812 812. *Qui Nhon Taxi*, ☎ (056) 812 666.

Bicycle rentals – Most hotels rent bicycles. Allow 10 000VND / day.

ADDRESS BOOK

Tourist information – *Central Vietnam Tourism*, 122 Le Hong Phong, corner of Hai Ba Trung, ☎ (056) 82 82 82. Daily 7-11.30am / 1.30-5pm. *Binhdinh Tourist Cie Travel Center*, 236 Phan Boi Chau, ☎ (056) 89 23 29, Fax (056) 89 11 62. Closed Sunday.

Bank / Currency exchange – *Vietcombank*, 152 Le Loi, corner of Tran Hung Dao, ☎ (056) 82 14 58. Monday-Friday 7-11am / 1-4.30pm. The *Incombank* also has a branch on the first floor of the Bank Hotel. Monday-Saturday 7-11.30am / 1.30-5pm.

Post office / Telephone – *Buu Dien Qui Nhon*, 197 Phan Boi Chau. Daily 8am-8pm. Postal services, telephone, Internet. Small post office branch at 104 Le Hong Phong, opposite the Vietnam Tourism Agency, and at 1127 Tran Hung Dao, near Tap Doi Street, the main route to the Cham tours.

Airline companies – *Vietnam Airlines*, 2 Ly Thung Kiet, next-door to Thanh Binh Hotel, ☎ (056) 82 31 25. Daily 7-11.30am / 1-4.30pm.

Medical services – *General Hospital*, 104 Nguyen Hue.

WHERE TO STAY, EATING OUT

Under US$10

Anh Thu Mini Hotel, 54(25) Mai Xuan Thuong, ☎ (056) 82 11 68 / 82 30 43, Fax (056) 82 30 43 – 13rm ⁂ 🖳 🖉 📺 ✕ This mini-hotel is right in the centre of town. Basic, clean rooms and good value for money. Friendly staff.

Duong Phong, 60 Mai Xuan Thuong, ☎ (056) 82 29 15 / 82 21 36 – 30rm ⁂ 🌣 🖳 ✕ Although something of a landmark in town, this hotel is relatively basic and the few bathrooms are very uninspiring. Only if the above has no vacancies.

Between US$10 and US$15

Khach San Dien Anh, 296 Phan Boi Chau, ☎ (056) 82 28 76, Fax (056) 82 28 69 – 23rm ⁂ 🖳 🖉 📺 ✕ This hotel is located right in the heart of town, near the square. Although not the quietest of establishments, the rooms are spotless and very reasonable.

Bank Hotel, 259 Le Hong Phong, ☎ (056) 82 35 91 / 82 35 92, Fax (056) 82 10 13 – 20rm ⁂ 🌣 🖳 ✕ Decent hotel in the heart of town.

Between US$15 and US$30

Hai Ha Mini Hotel, 5 Tran Binh Trong, ☎ (056) 89 12 95, Fax (056)

89 23 00 – 14rm ⁣ 📶 🗐 ♟ TV A very pleasant establishment in a quiet street near the beach. The rooms and bathrooms are airy, clean and comfortable. Breakfast is served on a delightful upstairs terrace decorated with potted plants. The staff are very friendly, but only speak faltering English.

Khach San Hai Au, 489 An Duong Vuong, ☎ (056) 84 64 73 / 84 63 77, Fax (056) 84 69 26, ks.haiau@dng.vnn.vn – 56rm 📶 🗐 ♟ TV ✕ ✣ This hotel caters mainly to groups. It rather lacks character, but the least expensive rooms are good value for money, particularly those with a sea view. Much better than Qui Nhon Hotel in the same price category.

Thanh Binh Hotel, 6 Ly Thuong Kiet, ☎ (056) 82 20 41 / 82 23 35, Fax (056) 82 75 69 – 64rm 📶 ⻊ 🗐 ✕ The new wing of this hotel offers decent rooms, but they are rather ordinary for the price. A few more basic (and more gloomy) rooms are available in the old wing at under US$10.

Doc Let close up

WHERE TO STAY, EATING OUT

Doc Let Beach Resort, at Doc Let Beach, ☎ (058) 84 96 63, Fax (058) 84 95 06 – 10rm 📶 ⻊ ♟ TV ✕ Basic, but comfortable bamboo bungalows, facing the sea. A truly peaceful beach complete with palm trees.

B Brillion/MICHELIN

NHA TRANG ★★

Capital of the province of Khanh Hoa – Pop 260 000
445km from Ho Chi Minh City, 215km from Dalat

Not to be missed
Relaxing on the beach.
The Cham towers at Po Nagar.
A boat trip around Nha Trang Bay.

And remember...
Museums and pagodas are best kept for the hottest part of the afternoon.

Although Nha Trang backs onto an impressive range of mountains to the west, this Mediterranean-style seaside resort clearly has its sights set on the sea, making it one of Vietnam's leading tourist centres. Its mild climate and stunningly beautiful bay, dotted with green islets, attract visitors from near and far. With the exception of the Nha Trang Lodge and Saigon Nha Trang Hotels, whose skyscraper outlines dwarf the coconut-lined beach, the town is, as yet, relatively free of the concrete building fever which has blighted other coastlines.

The high midday sun engulfs the town in a sluggish indolence, as the street vendor slowly drops off for forty winks on her deck-chair and an old man yawningly pulls his cap over his eyes as he stretches out in the back seat of his cyclo. The pristine beach is practically deserted at this time of day, save for a "few mad dogs and Englishmen", foolhardy enough to venture out of the shade of the palm trees onto the burning sand. But come 4pm, the town slowly awakens and little by little the promenade along the seafront fills with Vietnamese of all ages. The square next to the Memorial is transformed into an improvised football pitch, squealing motor-cycles transport the town's youth to its favourite haunts and soup merchants materialise on street corners, setting up stalls so tiny they seem to be made for Lilliputians. Nha Trang is a town to relax in, with little to do other than enjoy the pleasures of its spotless beach and turquoise sea.

Alexandre Yersin, the adopted son

To the north of the town, a blue signpost stands at the junction of Pasteur and **Yersin** Streets, whose claim to fame lies in the fact they are the only two thoroughfares still to be named after distinguished French citizens. The first needs no introduction, but the second, while beloved of the Vietnamese, may require more explanation. Nha Trang's adopted son, deemed to be the "revered humanist and benefactor of the Vietnamese people" by the town's fishermen who built a tomb for him on the hill of Suoi Giao, was one of the greatest bacteriologists of the 19C. Sent to China by the French government in 1894 to study **bubonic plague**, Yersin discovered the microbe responsible for this disease when in Hong Kong.

Born in Switzerland in 1863, Alexandre Yersin studied medicine in Paris with Louis Pasteur and Émile Roux, before signing up as ship's doctor aboard a French packet boat operating between Saigon and Manila. This first taste of Asia was to lead him to spend the majority of his life in the Orient. Sailing from place to place along the coast, he explored the Gulf of Tonkin and the mouth of the Red River, before heading inland into the more remote regions of the Highlands and Annam. His observations led him to draw up illustrated reports, maps and plans. It was during this period that he discovered the site of Dalat, which became one of the country's most prized mountain resorts.

This tireless scientist and ever-curious explorer also acquainted himself with the rudiments of astronomy and agronomy, as well as other sciences. At Nha Trang, where he settled in 1895, he introduced and established rubber- and quinine-

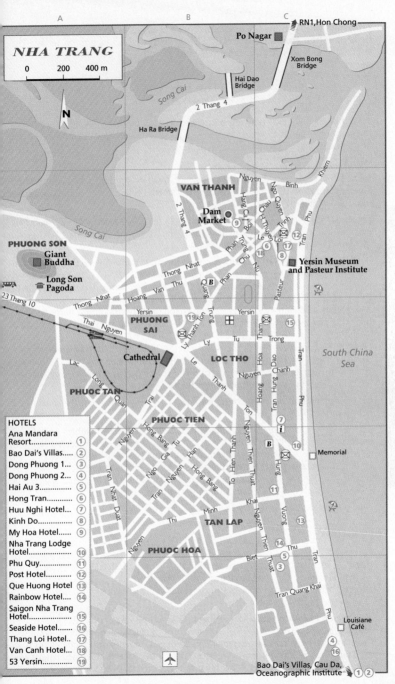

NHA TRANG

0   200   400 m

N

Po Nagar

RN1, Hon Chong

Xom Bong Bridge

Hai Dao Bridge

2 Thang 4

Ha Ra Bridge

Song Cai

VAN THANH

Nguyen

Binh

Khien

Dam Market ⑨

Hang Ca

Bo

H Thuyen

Le Loi

Chau

Ngo Quyen

Trinh

Phu

Tran

⑫

Phan Trung Chu Nu

⑱

⑥

⑰

Yersin Museum and Pasteur Institute

PHUONG SON

Giant Buddha

Long Son Pagoda

Song Cai

23 Thang 10

Thong Nhat

Thong Nhat

Hoang Van Thu

Quang

Phan

Yersin

Pasteur

Yersin

⑲

Thanh Ton

Trung

Thai Nguyen

PHUONG SAI

Ly Thanh Ton

Ly

Tu

Trong

⑮

Lac

Long Quan

Trai

PHUOC TAN

Cathedral

Le

Thanh

LOC THO

Nguyen

Hoa

Tran Hung Dao

Chanh

Tran

Phu

South China Sea

PHUOC TIEN

Nguyen

Hong Bang

Tu

Han

Hong Bang

Ton

Hien To

Nguyen Thien Thuat

Hung

⑦

i

⑩

Memorial

⑪

Tran Nhat Duat

Gia

Tran

Thi

Minh

Khai

TAN LAP

Vuong

⑬

Nguyen Thien Thuat

⑭

Thu

⑤

⑨

PHUOC HOA

Biet

Thuat

③

Tran Quang Khai

④

⑯

Phu

Tran

Louisiane Café

Bao Dai's Villas, Cau Da, Oceanographic Institute ①②

HOTELS

Ana Mandara Resort .... ①
Bao Dai's Villas ..... ②
Dong Phuong 1 ... ③
Dong Phuong 2 ... ④
Hai Au 3 .... ⑤
Hong Tran .... ⑥
Huu Nghi Hotel ... ⑦
Kinh Do .... ⑧
My Hoa Hotel ...... ⑨
Nha Trang Lodge Hotel .... ⑩
Phu Quy .... ⑪
Post Hotel .... ⑫
Que Huong Hotel ⑬
Rainbow Hotel .... ⑭
Saigon Nha Trang Hotel .... ⑮
Seaside Hotel .... ⑯
Thang Loi Hotel .. ⑰
Van Canh Hotel ... ⑱
53 Yersin .... ⑲

producing trees and founded a laboratory to carry on his studies. The latter was to become the **Pasteur Institute** in 1903 and is still functioning today. The adjacent building, where Yersin lived until his death in 1943, now houses the museum to him.

The town
Allow a day

Even though Nha Trang may rely entirely on tourism for its livelihood, if one leaves the wonderful beach to one side, it also possesses a lively town centre with most of the traditional crafts and activities.

The town centre
Right from daybreak, the northern part of town is up and about around the **covered market** (Cho Dam), whose vivid smells, colours and sounds overflow into the neighbouring lanes.

Go down Trung Nu, then turn right into Phan Boi Chau which leads to Thong Nhat. This will take you to n° 23 Thang 10, to the right of which is the entrance to Long Son Pagoda (500m to the west of the railway station).

Built in 1886, **Long Son Pagoda** is one of the most impressive buildings in town (*remember to take your shoes off on entering. Donations welcome*). Its finely carved roof, superb ceramic **mosaics** and recently restored **frescoes** depicting the life of the Buddha, make it well worth a visit. The headquarters of the Buddhist Association of Khanh Hoa province, the pagoda and neighbouring monastery are full of life and monks and novices can often be seen toiling in the garden or playing a high-spirited game of football.

Go up the steps to the rear of the pagoda to the Trai Thuy hilltop where a gigantic **Buddha** (Kim Than Phat To) is seated on a lotus blossom. The view over Nha Trang takes in the surrounding mountains and the sea below. The spot is very touristy and inundated by swarms of pestering children.

On the way back to the town centre, go along Thai Nguyen and past the station to a major crossroads.

Perched on a rocky knoll, Nha Trang's cathedral somewhat resembles a medieval castle with its crenellated walls. It was erected by the French between 1928 and 1934 out of great blocks of grey cement and cannot as such be deemed to be an architectural masterpiece. It nevertheless has some very fine stained-glass windows (*entrance on Nguyen Trai. 2 daily services during the week, at 4.45am and 5pm, and 5 services on Sunday, at 5am, 7am, 3.15pm, 4.45pm and 9.30pm*).

Go down Ly Tu Trong or Le Thanh Ton as far as Tran Phu.

The seafront promenade*
Lined by thick palm trees and dotted with little open-air bars and restaurants, Tran Phu avenue stretches for 7km from the north of town as far as the Cau Da landing stage. A stroll down the breezy promenade is appreciated by foreigners and Vietnamese alike. The long stretch of white **beach*** to the north between Le Loi and Le Thanh Ton is particularly attractive, but you will have to push further south if you want peace and quiet.

The **Yersin Museum*** (Bao Tang Yersin) (☎ *(058) 82 24 06, Fax (058) 82 40 58. Monday-Saturday 8-11am / 2-4.30pm; closed Sundays and national holidays. Entrance charge. Allow 1hr. Explanations in English, French and Vietnamese)* is at 10 Tran Phu, in a handsome residence next to the Pasteur Institute. It tells the story of the scientist's life from his birth in Switzerland in 1863 up until his death

Nha Trang

in Nha Trang in 1943. Founded in 1995 with the help of the Paris Pasteur Institute, the Pasteur Museum and the Medical History Museum of Lausanne, it has numerous items including his laboratory equipment as well as personal documents, effects and furniture. The exhibits are displayed clearly and are well-explained. The library is also open to the public.

The promenade itself does not extend further than the Memorial, so it is best to continue along the seafront by bicycle.

At the southernmost edge of the town, before reaching Cau Da village, one can see **five villas** which Emperor Bao Dai had built in the 1920s. Perched on a headland overlooking the sea and set in lush green parkland, they offer a magnificent view of Nha Trang and Cau Da. Now a hotel, *Bao Dai's Villas* offer spacious rooms at very reasonable rates (see "Nha Trang close up" page 291).

At a bend in the road, just a stone's-throw away, stands a grand French colonial building, home to Nha Trang's **Oceanographic Institute**. Founded in 1923, it was one of Vietnam's earliest scientific research centres and today endeavours to preserve the sea world. The nearby **National Museum of Oceanography** (Bao Tang Hai Duong Hoc) *(daily 7.30am-midday / 1-4.30pm. Entrance charge. Allow 30min)* is however somewhat disappointing. It is little more than a series of old-fashioned and badly cared-for murky aquariums and pools, yellowed jars and mouldy old maps and you will find the aquarium on Mieu Island far more interesting. The museum does boast a fine 18m-long skeleton of a 10t humpback whale found by the farmers of Hai Cuong during irrigation works. The skeleton was buried some 1.2m below the surface and 4km inland.

The road comes to an end at the landing stage of **Cau Da**, a peaceful fishing village whose inhabitants make souvenirs from shells, coral and mother-of-pearl and sell them by the roadside.

Around Nha Trang★★

If a day on the beach doesn't tempt you and you are keen to get out of Nha Trang for a while, why not explore the Cham towers at Po Nagar or go for a walk along the coast and enjoy the wonderful view of the bay?

Po Nagar★★

2km to the north of Nha Trang. Go down Quang Trung then 2 Thang 4 which joins the RN1 in the direction of Hanoi. The towers rise from a little promontory to the left of the road, beyond Xom Bong Bridge which spans the Song Cai. Entrance charge. Remove your shoes before entering the temples. Allow 30min.

The four towers and columns of Po Nagar were formerly part of a much larger complex which would have comprised some dozen or so temples. Originally built out of wood (7C), they were entirely razed by the Javanese in 774 and rebuilt in brick and stone from the 8C-12C. Unless you make it here very early, it is unlikely you will be able to enjoy the place on your own. The site is invariably busy with Vietnamese who come to pray in front of the altar devoted to the **Goddess Po Ino Nagar**, Goddess-mother of the Nation. Young women walk about hand in hand, going from temple to temple laden with offerings, while tactless tourists climb over the ruins to take photos, all under the distant gaze of a few men sitting on a bench.

The octagonal **columns** to the right of the entrance porch used to support the roof of a spacious open *mandapa*, through which the faithful would have walked to reach the temple. A staircase, now no more, linked the two buildings.

The 22.8m-high **kalan**, or North Temple, is a slender square-shaped edifice topped with a three-tiered roof, complete with corner towers and false alcoves. Each façade is embellished with pilasters and a false double-arched door. The well-preserved main door into the vestibule is flanked by two sandstone **door-posts** engraved with 11C-13C Cham inscriptions. Over the door are a gong and a **statue of a dancing Shiva★**, flanked by two musicians and with his foot on the bull Nandi. Two heavy ironwood doors lead into the main chamber whose three altars are the scene of much religious fervour. In a stifling atmosphere heavy with incense, women lay their offerings of

Colourful fishing boats in Nha Trang harbour

fruit in front of the **statue of the Goddess Bhagavati★**, wife of Shiva and identified with the local Goddess Po Ino Nagar. This black stone statue is said to have
been carved in 1050 during the reign of King Jaya Paramesvaravarman. Admire the
ornate carving behind the Goddess's throne.

The more modestly proportioned **Central Temple** has unfortunately been partially
restored with cement and its pyramidal roof is very worn. It is devoted to the worship
of a lingam, a phallic symbol of Shiva.
Further to the left, all that is left of the **South Temple** is a little tower in very bad
condition, within which is an altar devoted to the Buddha.
To the west of the *kalan*, the **Southwest Temple** was used to keep religious objects
(*koshagraha*). Admire the elegant boat-shaped roof of this modest square-shaped
edifice, which dates back to the 10C. Instead of the usual false doors found on towers
of this type, the temple's walls feature three brick sculptures. On the northern side
is a lion, on the western is Indra, "king of the gods" riding an elephant, and on the
southern side Garuda, a mythical half-bird half-human creature which transported
Vishnu.

Before leaving the site, don't miss the wonderful **view★** over Nha Trang and the little
fishing district tucked away in the mouth of the Song Cai. The colourful fishing boats
bobbing up and down on the turquoise water make a very picturesque sight.

Hon Chong
*500m beyond the towers of Po Nagar, go down Nguyen Dinh Chieu to the right of 2 Thang
4, and continue on the road as far as the Bay of Hon Chong. To get to the headland to the
south of the beach, take the little path to the left of a now-closed restaurant and follow the
rocks.*
Although a walk to the headland of Hon Chong makes a moderately pleasant excursion, it is very far from being heaven on earth. The wide crescent-shaped bay and
the transparent waters are inviting enough, but the beach itself leaves a lot to be
desired. The granite headland juts out from a small peninsula to the south of the
beach. Countless little eateries have sprung up all around and deck-chairs can be
rented for a quiet rest while enjoying the view. Work is currently underway to
improve the state of the road and it is expected that the hamlet of Cu Lao will soon
fall prey to property developers.

Nha Trang Bay and its islands★★
Nha Trang Bay is dotted with islands most of which are of little individual interest
but they make a good excuse for a very pleasant boat trip, with countless opportun-
ities for scuba diving and snorkelling (*to organise your cruise, see the "Excursions"
section in "Nha Trang close up" page 295*).

Most boats stop off at **Mieu Island★** (Hon Mieu), which is the closest to Nha Trang
and also the most visited (*crossings by ferry from Cau Da landing stage*). The island is
home to two fishing villages and some 2 000 inhabitants. The village of **Tri Nguyen**
boasts an unusual outdoor **aquarium★** (*entrance charge. Allow 30min*). Although at
first glance the ghost-ship looming on the horizon looks as if it would be more suited
to a fun fair, it is in fact home to a number of fine hawksbill turtles, white sharks
and tiger sharks, together with a wide variety of species of fish and coral. The wonderful view from the top of the ship makes it well worth the climb. From here, walk
to the village and to **Bai Soai**, a pebble beach on the other side of the island.

To the southeast of Mieu Island, the beach of **Tam Island** (Hon Tam) is highly
popular with Vietnamese tourists, and most boat day-trips stop here. Light years away
from a desert island, the spot has been developed with visitors in mind, with everything from bungalows and deck-chairs to bars and restaurants. If you are determined
to enjoy the beach on your own, rent a boat privately and ask to be dropped off first
thing in the morning, as the guided tours generally only arrive in the mid-afternoon.

Birds' nests

One of Nha Trang's culinary specialities is salangane or swifts' nests. The nests are built in the early spring out of salivary secretions and algae. This highly prized and extremely expensive dish is reputed to have medicinal and aphrodisiac virtues but is most difficult to harvest. The swifts build their nests high up on steep cliffs or in caves on the islands, and the men in charge of the harvest often have to perform acrobatics on bamboo or rope ladders to dislodge the nests from the sheer cliff faces.

Further east, **Mot Island** (Hon Mot) and **Ebony Island** (Hon Mun) are famous for their superb sea-beds and most of Nha Trang's scuba divers spend their days here.

To the north of these two islands lies **Bamboo Island** (Hon Tre), which is by far the largest of all (25km²). Its beach, **Bai Tru**, is very pretty, but you will have to hire a private boat to get there.

Monkey Island (Hon Lao) is, at its name suggests, home to a large colony of resident monkeys. Boats can be rented from Cau Da to the island. Although remarkably tame, it should be remembered that monkeys are wild creatures and that they can become aggressive, sometimes biting or scratching, and also demonstrate kleptomaniac tendencies. The island is very touristy, and elephant, monkey and bear shows are staged for the benefit of visitors. *It is cheaper to cross over to the island from the landing stage some 15km to the north of Nha Trang. At kilometre marker 1438, a signpost indicates the landing stage. Boat crossing: 45 000VND return. Regular departures from 7.30am to 5pm.*

An excursion to Doc Let Beach and Ba Ho Falls is also possible from Nha Trang (see page 281).

COMING AND GOING

By air – The *airport* is at 86A Tran Phu, to the south of the town, opposite the Louisiane Café, ☎ (058) 82 11 47. 2 to 3 daily flights to Ho Chi Minh City (1hr), 1 daily flight to Hanoi (2hr-2hr 30min) and 5 weekly flights to Da Nang (75min).

By train – The *railway station* is in the western part of town, at 17 Thai Nguyen, ☎ (058) 82 21 13. Daily 6.30am-10pm. Four daily trains to Hanoi (29-31hr) including one express at 4.18am (25hr), six trains to Ho Chi Minh City (10-11hr) and one express at 9.45pm (7hr).

By bus – The *bus station* is at 58 23 Thang 10 street, west of the railway station, ☎ (058) 82 21 92. Daily 5am-5.30pm. A dozen or so buses leave daily to Ho Chi Minh City (12hr) and Dalat (5hr), and there is one departure, at 5.30am, for Qui Nhon (6hr), Da Nang (14hr) and Hanoi (allow two days). Regular services to Phan Rang (3hr) up until 2pm, after which time catch a bus heading for Ho Chi Minh City which will drop you off on the way.

GETTING AROUND NHA TRANG

By taxi – *Taxi Nha Trang* (☎ (058) 81 81 81), *Nha Trang Taxi* (☎ 82 40 00), *Khanh Hoa Taxi* (☎ (058) 810 810) and *Emasco Taxi* (☎ (058) 81 44 44). All have meters.

By cyclo and motorcycle taxi – Cyclos and motorcycle taxis are often the best way of getting around town if you don't have your own bicycle, and this is particularly true in Nha Trang, which only stretches for 7km from north to south.

Rental vehicles – All the travel agencies in town rent vehicles. Most hotels and travel agencies rent bicycles. Allow US$1 per day for a bicycle.

ADDRESS BOOK

Tourist information office – *Khanh Hoa Tourism*, 1 Tran Hung Dao, corner of Tran Hung Dao and Le Thanh Ton, ☎ (058) 82 27 53, Fax (058) 82 42 06, khtourism@dng.vnn.vn Daily 7-11.30am / 1.30-5pm. Town plans sold, vehicles rented and outings arranged, but mainly for groups.

Bank / Currency exchange – *Vietcombank*, 17 Quang Trung, ☎ (058) 82 39 54. Monday-Friday 7.30-11am / 1.30-4pm. Travellers' cheques accepted and cash withdrawals with a Visa or MasterCard. *Vietnam Bank for Agriculture*, 2 Hung Vuong. Monday-Friday 7-11.30am / 1.30-4.30pm. Visa, Master-Card and JCB cards accepted.

Post office / Telephone – *Buu Dien Nha Trang*, 4 Le Loi, corner of Le Loi and Pasteur. Daily 6.30am-10pm. Express mail by EMS and DHL, telephones, sending and receiving faxes, money transfers. Internet at 2 Le Loi. Daily 7am-midday / 1-9pm. A 24hr post office branch with the same services at 50 Le Thanh Ton. Small branches in Hoang Hoa Tham and Ly Thanh Ton, near the cathedral.

Internet – Getting online is easy. Enquire at travel agencies, restaurants and tourist cafés. Allow 600VND / min.

Medical service – *General Hospital*, 19 Yersin, ☎ (058) 82 21 68.

Travel agencies – Nha Trang has no shortage of travel agencies. All offer the same services at roughly equivalent prices, including tours around Nha Trang, island cruises (US$7), boat trips down the River Ha Ra (US$10), a trip to Monkey Island, Ba Ho Falls and Doc Let Beach (US$15) or a four-day trip to the Highlands (US$35-US$40). You can also book bus tickets and negotiate the rental of a car or a motorcycle. Those with an "Open Tour" ticket can contact the *Sinh Café* at 10 Biet Thu, ☎ (058) 81 19 81 / 81 19 82, sinhcafent@dng.vnn.vn Daily 6am-10.30am.

Airline companies – *Vietnam Airlines*, 12B Hoang Hoa Tham, ☎ (058) 82 37 97 / 82 21 35, Fax (058) 82 37 97. Daily 7-11am / 1.30-4.30pm. National and international reservations and sales.

Safety – *Emergencies*, ☎ 115. *Fire brigade*, ☎ 114. *Police*, ☎ 82 24 85.

WHERE TO STAY

Under US$10

Hai Au 3, 11a Biet Thu, ☎ (058) 81 41 25, triha3@dng.vnn.vn – 10rm ⁿ▯ ▤ ✕ ✍ ⊡ Excellent value for money in its category. On a very busy street where most of the cheap restaurants are located, this hotel offers spotless, practical, airy rooms.

Van Canh Hotel, 5A Phan Chu Trinh, ☎ (058) 82 63 83 – 10rm ⁿ▯ ▤ ✕ This excellent establishment is quite as comfortable as other more expensive ones. The rooms may be a little cramped, but they are clean and very decent. Ask for a window because some only have a fanlight onto the corridor.

My Hoa Hotel, 7 Hang Ca, a stone's throw from the market, ☎ (058) 81 01 11, Fax (058) 82 75 54 – 16rm ⁿ▯ ▤ ✕ This very pleasant hotel provides clean, cheerful rooms with two beds. Ask for one of the rooms at the end of the corridor, which face two ways and have a pretty view, while the others only overlook the corridor. The hotel also has a number of other facilities, including Internet access.

Mini Hotel 53 Yersin, 53 Yersin, ☎ (058) 82 56 45 – 8rm ⁿ▯ ▤ ✕ Breakfast included. Although located on a somewhat noisy street, this small family establishment is most friendly and offers pleasant, spotlessly clean rooms.

Dong Phuong 1, 103 Nguyen Thien Thuat, ☎ (058) 82 59 86 / 82 82 47, Fax (058) 82 59 86, dongphuongnt@dng.vnn.vn – 30rm ⁿ▯ ▤ ✕ ✍ ⊡ ✕ The rooms are spacious, airy and clean and the furniture somewhat tasteless, but this establishment nonetheless offers excellent value for money. The rooms are located in a building with an inner courtyard, off the main street, and are quiet and peaceful.

Between US$10 and US$15

Mini Hotel Kinh Do, 9 Le Loi, junction of Le Loi and Han Thuyen, ☎ (058) 82 45 01 – 10rm ⁿ▯ ▤ ✕ A delightful, very well-kept family establishment which is perfect for shoestring budgets. The hotel is situated in the northern part of town in a quiet neighbourhood near the beach. Double rooms at US$10, but only US$12 for three people.

Khach San Hong Tran, 7 Phan Chu Trinh, ☎ (058) 81 20 70 / 82 67 26 – 23rm ⁿ▯ ▤ ✍ ⊡ ✕ A smart, freshly painted white hotel. The rooms have wooden furniture and the fully tiled bathrooms have a bath. Avoid the darker rooms overlooking the corridor.

Mini Hotel Phu Quy, 54 Hung Vuong, ☎ (058) 81 06 09 / 81 29 54, Fax (058) 81 29 54, phuquyhotel@dng.vnn.vn – 12rm ⁿ▯ ▤ ✕ ⌂ This friendly, pristine establishment boasts a pleasant roof terrace, which is ideal for breakfast, a quiet read, a sunbathe or just to enjoy the view of the town and sea.

Huu Nghi Hotel, 3 Tran Hung Dao, ☎ (058) 82 67 03 / 82 22 46, Fax (058) 82 74 16 – 65rm ⁿ▯ ▤ ✍ ⊡ ✕ Lift. Although this hotel may seem a little off-putting and run-down at first glance, the rooms are pleasant, airy and spotless. It is also one of the few hotels in town with a sea view for US$11!

Ⓐ Dong Phuong 2, 96A 6 / 1 Tran Phu, ☎ (058) 81 45 80 / 81 01 37, Fax (058) 82 59 86, dongphuongnt@dng.vnn.vn – 65rm ⁿ▯ ▤ ✍ ⊡ ✕ The younger brother of the above mentioned Dong Phuong 1, this spick-and-span hotel also offers excellent value for money. The pristine, spacious airy rooms face two ways and overlook the sea. Although the hotel is visible from the road, the path is sandwiched between two buildings.

Between US$15 and US$30

Thang Loi Hotel, 4 Pasteur, ☎ (058) 82 22 41 / 82 25 23, Fax (058) 82 19 05 – 50rm ⁿ▯ ▤ ✍ ⊡ ✕ ⧉ This pleasant hotel near the beach is situated in a peaceful neighbourhood in the northern part of town. The spacious, comfortable rooms are laid out motel-style, on two levels around an inner courtyard. The only drawback is that you have to keep your curtains permanently closed if you value your privacy. Very pleasant restaurant, part of which is open-air.

Khach San Buu Dien – Post Hotel, 2 Le Loi, ☎ (058) 82 12 52 / 82 12 50, Fax (058) 82 42 05, posthotel@dng. vnn.vn – 20rm ⁿ▯ ▤ ✍ ⊡ ✕ ⧉ This handsome seaside hotel lies at the north-ernmost end of the beach. The rooms are pleasant and quiet and the most expensive ones (US$27) have a charming little circular balcony with a lovely view of the sea.

Seaside Hotel, 96B Tran Phu, ☎ (058) 82 11 78 / 82 13 25, Fax (058) 82 80 38 – 15rm 🛏 📺 🎧 📺 A little out of town to the south, this seaside hotel is full of character with its wood panelling, wall hangings and tastefully furnished rooms. The most expensive rooms have a sea view. The prices vary but bargaining is permissible.

☺**Rainbow Hotel**, 10A Biet Thu, next-door to the Sinh Café, ☎ (058) 81 05 01, Fax (058) 81 00 30, rainbowhotel@dng.vnn.vn – 22rm 🛏 📺 🎧 📺 ✕ 🍴 📺 Lift. You can't miss the garish green columns of this hotel. The rooms are pleasant, airy and spotlessly clean and some of the larger ones have a wide bay window opening onto a balcony. The staff are most friendly and helpful. The roof-terrace restaurant overlooks the neighbourhood and affords a lovely view of the sea.

Between US$50 and US$70
Que Huong Hotel, 60 Tran Phu, ☎ (058) 82 50 47 / 82 73 65, Fax (058) 82 53 44, quehuong60@dng.vnn.vn – 58rm 🛏 📺 🎧 📺 ✕ 🍴 📺 Hairdressers, sauna, massages, shop, karaoke, lift. With all the comforts of a regular international hotel, this establishment is also less "factory-like" than the Saigon Nha Trang or the Nha Trang Lodge. The rooms, which overlook the sea or the swimming pool, are very pleasant, but it is a pity that the staff are so stuffy. Six suites at US$100 and a dozen more basic rooms from US$16-US$20.

Bao Dai's Villas, Cau Da, on a headland 6km south of Nha Trang, ☎ (058) 59 01 47 / 59 01 48, Fax (058) 59 01 46 – 48rm 🛏 📺 🎧 📺 ✕ 🍴 The five villas built by Emperor Bao Dai stand on a headland jutting into the bay. Transformed into a hotel, they offer the rustic charm of yesteryear, so do not expect the sophisticated luxury found in other hotels of this category. The spot is peaceful and the setting quite magnificent, if somewhat remote. The immense rooms overlook the sea. Two restaurants, one at the top of the hill and the

other down by the beach. Twenty or so more basic rooms from US$25-US$35.

Between US$70 and US$100
Nha Trang Lodge Hotel, 42 Tran Phu, ☎ (058) 81 05 00 / 81 09 00, Fax (058) 82 88 00, nt-lodge@dng.vnn.vn – 120rm 🛏 📺 🎧 📺 ✕ 🍴 🍴 📺 Conference room, business centre, travel agency, beauty parlour, hairdressers, shop, hammam, sauna, massage, karaoke, nightclub, lift. What a pity this sprawling hotel stands out like such a sore thumb on the coast. Inside, however, refined wood panelling and shades of pastel abound and the muted ambience occasionally borders on the impersonal. The comfortable rooms are tastefully furnished, often enormous, and all overlook the bay. The price of some cheaper rooms at US$50 is explained by their location on the lowest floors.

Saigon Nha Trang Hotel, 18 Tran Phu, ☎ (058) 82 00 90, Fax (058) 82 00 00, sg-nthotel@dng.vnn.vn, www.saigon-tourist.com – 174rm 🛏 📺 🎧 📺 ✕ 🍴 📺 Conference room, fitness centre, jacuzzi, sauna, massage, karaoke, nightclub, lift. One of the other mammoth seaside hotels, with all the luxury you would expect from an international establishment. The rooms are pleasant, airy, tastefully furnished and all have a view of the sea.

Over US$100
☺**Ana Mandara Resort**, Beachside 86 Tran Phu, ☎ (058) 82 98 29, Fax (058) 82 96 29, resvana@dng.vnn.vn, www.soneva-pavilion.com/ana-man-dara – 68rm 🛏 📺 🎧 📺 ✕ 🍴 🎧 ⚗ 🍴 📺 Mini-bar in the rooms, sauna, jacuzzi, massage, nursery, shop. The sophisticated, warm style of Nha Trang's most luxurious establishment blends in wonderfully with the surrounding landscape. Traditionally built villas spread over an immense lush green garden where each bungalow's privacy is guaranteed by a profusion of plants and trees. The whole resort is exquisitely decorated and furnished.

• **In Nha Trang Bay**
Between US$30 and US$50
☺**Whale Island**, on Hon Ong Island, 2hr boat trip from Nha Trang, ☎ and

Fax (058) 84 05 01 – 20rm ⍩ ⌧ ✕ ⌂ ⍟ Full-board accommodation (drinks not included) for US$40 per person (US$45 for a single room). If you've ever dreamt of playing at Robinson Crusoe on a desert island or fancy a few days rest in complete and utter silence, this is the place for you. You will be picked up in Nha Trang and transported to the island. Once you have settled into your bamboo bungalow, relax and stretch out in the shade of the palm trees or sink back into one of the comfortable bar armchairs and enjoy a cocktail while gazing at the turquoise waters. Then, when you've mustered the energy, join in one of the countless activities, including scuba diving, snorkelling, catamaran sailing, wind-surfing, sea canoeing or fun-boarding. The restaurant serves fresh seafood and fish and Vietnamese dishes.

EATING OUT

Under 25 000VND

The tiny eateries along Biet Thu are packed with travellers from dawn until dusk. None is particularly outstanding, and although they all serve decent food for next to nothing, it is more the atmosphere than the cuisine which attracts so many tourists. Just a few among many:

Café des Amis, 13 Biet Thu, ☎ (058) 81 30 09, desamis@dng.vnn.vn Popular with tourists, this friendly establishment serves cheap, simple Vietnamese and international dishes. Ask for Khanh who will be able to help you organise excursions or rentals and also doubles as a guide.

Bombay, 15 Biet Thu, next-door to the above. Quite spicy Indian cooking, very popular among the many tourists who flock here every night.

La Grenouille, 12A Biet Thu, ☎ (058) 81 39 60 ⍟ This pleasant restaurant, located in a shady courtyard off the main street, serves cheap Asian and European fare. A pity the music is so loud.

Between 25 000 and 50 000VND

Thuy Duong, Tran Phu, opposite Nha Trang Lodge, ☎ (058) 82 35 91 ⍟ This pleasant seaside restaurant with a covered terrace serves seafood and Vietnamese dishes.

Coconut Cove Resort, 40 Tran Phu, opposite Nha Trang Lodge, ☎ (058) 82 67 82, Fax (058) 81 01 82 ⍟ A refreshingly breezy, shady spot where lunch is served in straw huts facing the sea. Tropical ambience with bamboo furniture and carved wooden tables. Seafood and Vietnamese dishes.

Dua Xanh – Coco Vert, 23 Le Loi, ☎ (058) 82 36 87 ⍟ 8am-10pm. It may not be wildly special, but the neighbourhood is peaceful and the restaurant has a shady terrace which is most welcome in the heat of the day. Tasty Vietnamese cooking, seafood and an excellent choice of desserts (rare enough to merit a mention), including tarts, icecreams and pancakes.

Louisiane Café, opposite 86A Tran Phu, ☎ (058) 81 29 48, Fax (058) 81 47 22 ⍟ ⌂ Daily 8am-2am. This colourful establishment offers its guests a choice of free facilities, including a swimming pool, private beach, ping-pong table, boules and billiards. It is popular more for its ambience than its food and serves snacks, salads and fish, together with pastries and icecreams. Dancing around the pool every evening. The clientele is mainly foreign during the day and Vietnamese in the evenings.

Thanh The, 3 Phan Chu Trinh, ☎ (058) 82 19 31. An unpretentious establishment serving Vietnamese and vegetarian dishes in a tasteful, spotless setting. Friendly staff.

Hoan Hai, 6 Phan Chu Trinh, ☎ (058) 82 31 33. 8am-10pm. Next to the above, this establishment is just as simple and offers a similar menu, with continental breakfasts, Vietnamese dishes and seafood. Not as friendly though.

Between 50 000 and 100 000VND

Le Prétexte, Tran Phu, opposite the Grand Hotel 44, near the Memorial, ☎ (058) 81 59 64, Fax (058) 81 32 46 ⍟ 8.30am-midnight. If you fancy a change from Vietnamese fare or seafood, you may want to try this attractive French restaurant, which serves duck salad and other authentic French specialities. Polished service. Board games and newspapers available and a next-door shop with an eclectic choice of objects.

La Bella Napoli, Tran Phu, opposite Nha Trang Lodge, ☎ (058) 82 96 21, Fax (058) 82 19 07, labellanapoliviet@hotmail.com 🍴 Nha Trang decidedly has something for everyone. As the name suggests, this establishment serves typically Italian dishes, including the inevitable pizzas, pasta and escalopes milanese.

Nha Trang Sailing Club, 74 Tran Phu, ☎ (058) 82 65 28, Fax (058) 82 19 06, sailingnt@dng.vnn.vn 🍴 🍸 This open-air seaside restaurant under the co-conut palms serves tasty Vietnamese and Japanese fare. The attractive setting is a combination of stone, brick and wood. Deck-chairs for rent on the beach, which is quieter here than around Nha Trang Lodge.

Between 100 000 and 200 000VND

🍴**Ngoc Suong**, 16 Tran Quang Khai, ☎ (058) 82 70 30 🍴 One of Nha Trang's smartest establishments is situated in a quiet side street. Whether dining indoors or on the terrace under a superb arbour of bougainvillaea, you will appreciate the owners' exquisite taste. An extensive menu featuring seafood and Vietnamese cuisine. The efficient service and muted background music make dining here a real pleasure.

GOING OUT

Cafés and bars – Nha Trang has an impressive number of cafés and karaoke joints, which are always packed with young Vietnamese in the evenings. Their strings of fairy lights and deafening music make them easy to spot and also probably explain why so few tourists frequent them, but why not? Among those more popular with tourists are:

Louisiane Café, opposite 86A Tran Phu, ☎ (058) 81 29 48, Fax (058) 81 47 22 🍴 Daily 8am-2am. Wide choice of cocktails. Happy hour every evening from 10pm to 1am and dancing around the pool. Billiards.

Nha Trang Sailing Club, 74 Tran Phu, ☎ (058) 82 65 28, Fax (058) 82 19 06, sailingnt@dng.vnn.vn 🍴 A very pleasant spot for a drink during the day on a sunny terrace or in the evening around the much sought-after billiards table.

Rainbow Bar, 52 Tran Phu, 🍴 A tropical setting with bamboo furniture and blaring music. Billiards. Somewhat overdone and pushy.

Que Huong Club, 60 Tran Phu, 🍴 A performance of Vietnamese music is put on every evening around the swimming pool.

Nightclubs – For those inclined to continue on until the very early hours of the morning, Nha Trang Lodge has a night-club, the **Tropicana Club**.

OTHER THINGS TO DO

Excursions to the islands – Boat trips to the islands are one of Nha Trang's leading attractions. All the travel agencies in town offer day cruises, including a visit to Mun, Mot and Tam Islands and to a little fishing village on Mieu Island. Most programmes revolve around snorkelling, swimming and sunbathing. While seemingly appealing, it is worthwhile knowing that most boats take up to 30 tourists, blast out music at full volume and that the so-called "tour" of the islands is generally too short. If you prefer to get there under your own steam, go directly to the **port of Cau Da**, 6km to the south of Nha Trang (the road ends at the landing stage), from where you can catch a ferry to Mieu Island. Daily departures at 7am from Cau Da, return from Mieu Island at 3pm (US$1.6, allow 15min for the crossing). You can also negotiate a private, personalised boat tour of the islands. The price of the boat is generally divided by the number of occupants (up to 10). Most boats leave around 8am, but it is worthwhile booking the day before at the port.

Scuba diving – Scuba diving is not a sport to be taken lightly and you should choose your travel agency with care, all the more so if you are a beginner.

Blue Diving Club, Tran Phu, opposite the Nha Trang Lodge, ☎ (058) 82 53 90, Fax (058) 81 60 88, bluedivingclub@hotmail.com Authorised PADI, CMAS and FFESSM ANMP centre. Day trips to Mun Island for US$50 (1 dive) and US$90 (2 dives). Daily departures at 8am, return at 3pm. Open Water four-day courses for US$ 320.

Octopus Diving Club, 62 Tran Phu, ☎ (058) 81 06 29, Fax (058) 82 74 36, haison.aaa@dng.vnn.vn A serious club with British, French, Scandinavian and Portuguese diving instructors. Authorised PADI, CMAS, CEDIP, IANMP and SSI centre. One departure per day at 8am, return at 3.30pm. Allow US$40 for 1 dive and US$60 for 2 dives. A beginners' course at US$90 (2 dives). The centre also runs Open Water courses (3-4 days, US$320) and Advanced Diver courses.

Rainbow Divers, 52 Tran Phu, ☎ (058) 82 99 46, Fax (058) 81 12 23, rainbowdivers@divers.com Authorised PADI centre. Daily departures to Mun Island at 7.30am, return mid-afternoon.

Allow US$60 for 2 dives. Night dives of 1hr to 90min for US$40. Beginner dives from US$50 (1 dive) or US$90 (2 dives).

Sports – The **swimming pools** of Vien Dong, Hai Yan and Que Huong Hotels are open to non-residents (from 10 000 to 15 000VND). The Que Huong also has **tennis courts** (30 000VND / hr and 15 000VND to rent a racket).

FESTIVALS

Thap Ba Festival – A major annual festival which takes place from the 20th to the 23rd day of the 3rd lunar month, in honour of the Goddess Po Ino Nagar. The official ceremonies are followed by traditional singing and dancing.

THE SOUTH COAST★★
FROM NHA TRANG TO PHAN THIET

Provinces of Khanh Hoa, Ninh Thuan and Binh Thuan – Map pages 228-229
250km tour – Allow 2 days
Accommodation available at Phan Rang, Phan Thiet and Mui Ne

Not to be missed
The Cham ruins at Po Klong Garai.
A relaxing day at Mui Ne.
And remember...
Stop over at Mui Ne rather than Phan Thiet or Phan Rang.
If you do however stop in Phan Rang, go to Po Klong Garai
in the early morning before the hordes of tourists.

After leaving Nha Trang, the Mandarin Road (RN1) continues southwards towards Ho Chi Minh City and the Mekong Delta through the coastal provinces of Khanh Hoa, Ninh Thuan and Binh Thuan, the area into which the Cham were forced to retreat in the late 16C. It is certainly not the most picturesque section of this part of the country's coastline – the landscape is almost desert-like – but there are a few attractive seaside spots to stop at and there is the opportunity to visit Po Klong Garai, one of Vietnam's best preserved Cham sites.

The road will first take you around the immense bay of **Cam Ranh** (*30km from Nha Trang*). The strategic position and many assets of this natural harbour were a temptation that very few major powers were able to resist and it is still home to a military base (*closed to the public*). Built by the French during the colonial era, it was occupied by the Americans during the Vietnam War and then by the Soviet Union from 1975 to 1990.

Some fifteen kilometres to the north of Phan Rang, it is possible to make out the two *kalan* of **Hoa Lai** (9C), to your left, now in very poor condition.

Joined to the neighbouring town of Thap Cham, **Phan Rang** is the provincial capital of Ninh Thuan, but it is of little interest to tourists, with the exception of those on their way to Dalat or Ho Chi Minh City, who stop here briefly to visit the Cham ruins at Po Klong Garai.

Po Klong Garai is 7km northwest of Phan Rang in the municipality of Thap Cham. To get there, take the RN20 towards Dalat, and take the first turning on the right beyond kilometre marker 268 and Linh Son Pagoda. The towers stand on a hill called Doi Trau some 200m away, in a wilderness of cacti.

■ **Po Klong Garai**★ – *Daily 7am-5pm. Entrance charge.* The complex was built in the late 13C during the reign of King Jaya Simhavarman III. Devoted to King Po Klong Garai (1151-1205), it attracts large numbers of pilgrims, particularly around the time of the Kate Festival, held during the 7th lunar month (around October). During these ceremonies, the Cham commemorate their ancestors and invoke the protection of benefactresses such as the Goddess Po Ino Nagar or the saintly kings Po Rome and Po Klong Garai.

Restored between 1981-86, the Cham temples are laid out in the traditional manner, but their design is characteristic of the Binh Dinh style and marks a decline in Cham architecture from the 12C. The site consists of a *kalan*, a *mandapa*, a *koshagraha* (to store religious objects) and a porch-tower, all surrounded by a low wall. Below the towers, near the path leading to the entrance, it is possible to distinguish a stele which formerly stood in a tower within the site.

13.8m long, 10.7m wide and 20.5m high, the kalan faces east. The God Shiva is worshipped in this main temple. The main door is flanked by two sandstone **door-posts** bearing Cham inscriptions and a list of the offerings made in the temple by King Jaya Simhavarman III. Above it are four arches and a **dancing Shiva**★★ with six arms.

Each of the three other façades of the *kalan*, which is decorated with pilasters and lotus petal carved capitals, has a false door over which is a double arch and a statue of a god in a traditional lotus position with arms crossed. The characteristic three-tiered roof has four corner towers and four false alcoves in which are seated gods in a lotus position with hands clasped as if in prayer.

The vestibule and the main chamber are in extremely good condition. Within the latter a **mukhalinga** rests on a yoni, equipped with a drainage system. The *mukhalinga* bears a carving of one of the five faces of Shiva, depicted as a king with features very similar to those of the local population. In the vestibule is a handsome statue of the bull **Nandi**★, Shiva's mount and symbol of agricultural fertility. The Cham continue to make offerings to Nandi in order to ensure good crops.

All that remains of the four-door **mandapa** opposite the temple is the base. It is however possible to distinguish where the columns supporting the roof used to stand at the four corners.

To the east of the *mandapa*, the **gopura** was the original entrance to the temple, preceded by a steep staircase. It is less well-preserved and of more modest proportions (5.65m high) than the other edifices; although architecturally simpler, it is similar to the *kalan*, with the characteristic false doors, decorative carved flames, alcoves and towers.

The **koshagraha**, also called the Temple of Fire, to the south of the *mandapa*, is where religious objects would have been kept.

Cham towers at Po Klong Garai

R. Mattes/MICHELIN

Return to the RN1 towards Ho Chi Minh City. The road goes through an extremely barren and semi-arid limestone region, dotted only with a few clumps of eucalyptus trees. 32km from Phan Rang, it joins the sea and goes through the village of Ca Na.

■ The peaceful fishing village of **Ca Na** and its magnificent white sandy beach strewn with enormous granite boulders, is a pleasant stop for a break and has a few places to stay, though the nearby highway makes it far from ideal for an overnight stop.

Back on the road to Phan Thiet, you next go through **Vinh Hao**, a little town renowned for its mineral water, which is sold throughout Vietnam. The road now passes through scrubland baking under the sun. The area's pride and joy are its vines, fairly few in number and trained over trellises. The landscape is dotted with tiny hamlets, with primitive bamboo and corrugated iron dwellings and herds of goats and cows. Further south and inland a variety of crops, such as rice and bananas, grow in the better irrigated areas. Near Phan Thiet, where the road joins the coast again, the first orange-coloured dunes come into view.

■ **Phan Thiet** – The capital of the province of Binh Thuan stretches out on either side of the River Ca Ty, where large numbers of little fishing boats are moored. Its role of political, economic and cultural capital of the province has given the town a certain impetus. Essentially a fishing harbour, Phan Thiet is also renowned for its **nuoc-mam** (fish sauce), which is said to be one of the best in Vietnam.

Six kilometres to the northeast of Phan Thiet on the road to Mui Ne, Phu Hai is the site of the three towers of **Poshanu** perched on a hillock to the right of the road. The southernmost of the Cham ruins, they are also the oldest, dating back to the 8C.

The road to Mui Ne goes through a dense coconut grove, whose shade is most welcome when the sun is at its peak. The plantation produces vast quantities of coconuts which can be seen drying in the sun.

■ **Mui Ne★** – This fishing village is famous for the astonishing sight of its exceptionally high dunes of orange-coloured sand overlooking the sea (*to get to them, turn left at the main crossroads and follow the sign to "Hon Rom"*). The village stands on a picturesque bay bathed by the turquoise waters of the South China Sea which break against a long white sandy beach. It is an ideal spot to relax either before or after embarking on a full-scale tour of Vietnam, all the more so because it is off the tourist trail and as yet relatively unspoilt. A host of pleasant resorts have sprung up in the shade of the coconut groves of this little corner of paradise.

Phan Rang close up

COMING AND GOING

By train – Phan Rang *railway station*, where the Reunification train stops, is 7km northwest of the town, not far from the site of Po Klong Garai. The easiest way of getting there is to take a taxi or a motorcycle taxi.

By bus – The *bus station* is 500m to the north of the town centre, on Thong Nhat. Regular departures for Phan Thiet (4hr), Ho Chi Minh City (8hr), Dalat (2hr), Nha Trang (3hr) and Da Nang (5hr), but if you are going north or south, the best plan is to stand at the junction of the RN1 and flag down one of the numerous express buses, because those leaving Phan Rang are extremely slow.

Post office / Telephone – The main post office is on Thong Nhat, just north of the bus station. There is another branch on Le Hong Phong, next-door to the Ninh Thuan Hotel. Daily 6am-9.30pm.

WHERE TO STAY, EATING OUT
Under US$10
Huu Nghi Hotel 1, 354 Thong Nhat, ☎ (068) 82 29 52 – 20rm ✕ This type of establishment is among those one would rather not mention, but it is the only relatively cheap place for those on shoestring budgets. Only as a last resort.

Avoid at all costs the even grottier Huu Nghi 2 Hotel, at 194 Thong Nhat.
Between US$15 and US$30
Ninh Thuan Hotel, 1 Le Hong Phong, ☎ (068) 82 71 00, Fax (068) 82 21 42 – 24rm ♬ 🖪 ✕ 🖉 🖻 ✕ Breakfast included. This hotel opposite a small park may lack appeal, but the rooms are comfortable, spacious and clean. A few rooms with fan at US$22 and one four-person room at US$48. Don't hesitate to haggle over the price.
Between US$30 and US$50
Thong Nhat Hotel, 99 Thong Nhat, ☎ (068) 82 54 06 / 82 72 01, Fax (068) 82 29 43 – 33rm ♬ 🖪 🖉 🖻 ✕ Breakfast included. This recently renovated establishment may lack charm but it is nonetheless the most comfortable in town. Friendly staff. The prices might seem a bit steep, but can be negotiated.

Phan Thiet close up

COMING AND GOING
By train – The *railway station* is at Muong Man, 12km to the west of Phan Thiet.
By bus – The *bus station* is next-door to the 19/4 Hotel, on the corner of Tu Van Tu and Tran Hung Dao, but most buses do a tour of the town to pick up travellers before leaving Phan Thiet. Frequent departures for Ho Chi Minh City (4hr) Nha Trang (7hr) and the North.

ADDRESS BOOK
Post office / Telephone – *Buu Dien Phan Thiet*, Nguyen Tat Thanh. Daily 6am-9pm.

WHERE TO STAY, EATING OUT
As Phan Thiet is of relatively little interest, you will probably only stop off here to break your journey between Ho Chi Minh City and Nha Trang. If you are planning on staying for a few days, try one of the seaside hotels along the road to Mui Ne.

Under US$10
Khach San Suong Hoa, 110 Tran Hung Dao, next to the Phuong Hung Hotel, ☎ (062) 82 82 57 – 17rm ♬ 🖪 ✕ Although the rooms are nothing special, the service is charming and prices are negotiable. Air-conditioned rooms from US$13 and rooms which can sleep up to four people (US$23).
Between US$10 and US$15
Khach San Thanh Cong, 49-51 Tran Hung Dao, opposite the 19/4 Hotel, ☎ (062) 82 50 16, Fax (062) 82 39 05 – 12rm ♬ 🖪 🖻 The orange façade of this hotel makes it very easy to spot. It provides basic but decent rooms, among the cheapest in its category.
Mini Hotel 99A, 99A Tran Hung Dao, opposite the Phuong Hung Hotel, ☎ (062) 82 15 20 – 6rm ♬ 🖪 The establishment may not be as elegant as their card suggests, but the rooms are decent and the staff very helpful.
Nha Nghi 186, 186 Thu Khoa Huan, ☎ (062) 82 70 26 – 5rm ♬ 🖪 A pleas-

ant little family-run establishment with basic, decent, quiet rooms.

Hoang Huu Nhu Mini Hotel, 251 Thu Khoa Huan, ☎ (062) 82 26 15 – 6rm ⚓ 📺 This spotlessly clean family-run mini-hotel offers small, comfortable, pleasant rooms. Charming, non-English speaking staff.

Khach San 19/4, 1 Tu Van Tu, north of town, ☎ (062) 82 17 94 / 82 52 16, Fax (062) 82 51 84 – 84rm ⚓ 📺 ✕ ✗ 📺 ✕ Karaoke, sauna, massage, lift. This grand old Soviet-style establishment is quite well-looked after. It caters mainly to groups of Vietnamese tourists on guided tours, and although its appeal might not extend to more than one night, it is well-situated near the bus station. The hotel has a large restaurant which serves very decent Vietnamese cuisine at reasonable prices. A few very basic rooms for four people at US$7.

Between US$15 and US$30
Phuong Hung Hotel, 112 Tran Hung Dao, ☎ (062) 82 56 19 / 82 56 20, Fax (062) 82 53 00 – 42rm ⚓ 📺 ✗ 📺 ✕ 📺 Mini-bar in the rooms, karaoke, sauna, massages and lift. This comfort-able establishment is situated at the junction of Tran Hung Dao and Thu Khoa Huan, the road to Mui Ne. The rooms are airy and clean and those up-stairs have a pleasant view over the town. Friendly staff.

Over US$100
Novotel Ocean Dunes Resort, 1 Ton Duc Thang, ☎ (062) 82 23 93, Fax (062) 82 33 65, novpht@hcm.vnn.vn, www.hotelweb.fr – 123rm ⚓ 📺 ✗ 📺 ✕ ✗ ♨ ✿ 📺 Mini-bar in the rooms, golf, fitness centre, sauna, massages, nursery, conference room, shop, lift. Built on the edge of an 18-hole golf course in the dunes, this seaside hotel covers an area of 60ha. Although it more than meets the luxury standards of its category, it lacks a personal touch. The clean, comfortable rooms all have a balcony overlooking the golf course or the pool. Two bars and two restaurants, with a choice between set theme or à la carte meals. Wide variety of activities, including golf (18 holes / US$60), volley-ball, foot-ball, badminton and boules. Bicycles and cars rented.

Mui Ne close up

COMING AND GOING

By bus – Regular bus services to Mui Ne leave from Phan Thiet bus station.

By taxi – The easiest way to get to Mui Ne is to take a taxi or a motorcycle taxi (allow between 20 000VND and 30 000VND single by motorcycle).

ADDRESS BOOK

Bicycle rentals – Most hotels have bi-cycles, sometimes motorcycles, for rent by the hour or the day.

WHERE TO STAY, EATING OUT
Numerous resorts have opened up along the road from Phan Thiet to Mui Ne, without affecting the peaceful atmos-phere of the area. The distances indi-cated in the following addresses are given from Phan Thiet, which is 22km from Mui Ne. The choice is wide enough to offer something to meet every taste and every budget.

Under US$10

Huong Bien Mui Ne Resort, kilome-tre marker 18 Ham Tien, ☎ (062) 84 72 58, Fax (062) 84 73 38, ntd_hbmn@hcm.vnn.vn – 20rm ⚓ ✗ ✕ ✿ You can opt either for a Robinson Crusoe-style primitive bamboo bunga-low with shared bathroom (US$7) or a more comfortable room in the little house nearby (US$15 or US$20 with air-conditioning). This lovely spot is quiet, shaded by coconut trees and has direct access to the wonderful sandy beach around the bay.

Between US$10 and US$15

Khu Bai Tam Mui Ne (Coco Beach), kilometre marker 19 Ham Tien, ☎ (062) 84 86 45 / 84 71 53 – 11rm ⚑ 📧 ⍓ ✗ ⌘ This peaceful, shady place is right next-door to the above. The hotel has four bamboo bungalows from US$8 and seven brick bungalows for US$15. The latter are more comfortable, but somewhat gloomy and not at all enhanced by the neon lighting.

Between US$15 and US$30

Small Garden, kilometre marker 11 Ham Tien, ☎ (062) 84 70 12 – 11rm ⚑ ⍓ ✗ ⌘ The peace and quiet of this spot are such that you feel like whispering so as not to disturb the birds singing and cooing in their cage near the entrance. Seven comfortable bamboo bungalows at US$25 and cheaper rooms at US$10 or four dormitory beds at US$7. Walter and Trang, the owners, have lavished much time and care decorating this little haven of peace.

Full Moon Beach, kilometre marker 13 Ham Tien, ☎ (062) 84 70 08, Fax (062) 84 71 60 – 14rm ⚑ ⍓ ✗ ⌘ cc Tucked away in the undergrowth, these prettily decorated bamboo bungalows offer visitors a pleasant, tranquil stay. Camping also possible from US$5.

Paradise Huts – Chez Nina, kilometre marker 13.5 Ham Tien, ☎ (062) 84 71 77 – 8rm ⚑ 📧 ⍓ ✗ ⌘ Yet another of Mui Ne's charming resorts. Two traditionally built bungalows with terrace, bamboo walls and thatched roofs (US$25) and six airy, comfortable rooms available in two neighbouring houses (from US$15-25). The restaurant serves good Vietnamese cooking in a pleasant, seaside setting.

Between US$50 and US$70

Bamboo Village, kilometre marker 11.8 Ham Tien, ☎ (062) 84 70 07, Fax (062) 84 70 95, dephan@netnam².org.vn, www. vietnamtourism.com/muine – 20rm ⚑ 📧 ⍓ 🅿 📺 ✗ ⌘ ♨ ⚜ cc Mini-bar in the rooms, conference room, jacuzzi, nursery. This "village" blends in perfectly with the surrounding landscape, tucked away in the welcome shade of coconut trees. Twenty spacious, airy and tastefully decorated bamboo bungalows. Efficient service and tranquillity guaranteed.

Saigon Mui Ne Resort, kilometre marker 12.2 Ham Tien, ☎ (062) 84 73 03, Fax (062) 84 73 07, saigonmuineresort@hcm.vnn.vn – 50rm ⚑ 📧 🅿 📺 ✗ ⌘ ♨ cc Mini-bar in the rooms, hammam, sauna, massages, karaoke, meeting room, shop. This resort offers comfortable villas and bungalows, which overlook the sea and a pool. Those on a tighter budget can opt for one of the 6- or 8-bed dormitories, with shared bathroom and toilets.

Between US$70 and US$100

Coco Beach Resort, kilometre marker 12.5 Ham Tien, ☎ (062) 84 71 11, Fax (062) 84 71 15, paradise@cocobeach.net, www.cocobeach.net – 22rm ⚑ 📧 🅿 ✗ ⌘ ♨ cc Mini-bar in the rooms, massages. This tastefully decorated resort is set in idyllic surroundings. The traditional wooden bungalows on stilts with thatched roof and a terrace overlooking the sea are dotted around the swimming pool in an impeccably cared-for garden. Three villas, more suited to families, are also available with two rooms, two bathrooms and a spacious living room. Prices vary depending on the season: US$80 (bungalow) and US$160 (villa) from November to April and US$60 and US$130 from April to November.

Over US$100

Victoria Phan Thiet Resort, kilometre marker 9 Ham Tien, ☎ (062) 84 71 70, Fax (062) 84 71 74, victoriapt@hcm. vnn.vn, www.victoriahotel-vietnam. com – 50rm ⚑ 📧 ⍓ ✗ ⌘ ♨ ⚘ ⚜ cc Mini-bar in the rooms. This resort consists of elegant villas set in an immense landscaped garden. Parquet floors, attractive furniture and leather-bound books all contribute to the sophisticated luxury of the villas, whose terraces overlook the garden or the sea. The terrace restaurant serves seafood and Vietnamese cuisine, and simpler fare is served around the pool. Impeccable staff and service.

The countryside around Dalat

THE HIGHLANDS

Far from the muggy Mekong Delta or the sunny coastal regions, the Highlands' sparse population and temperate climate reveal quite another side of Vietnam. Traditionally considered to be hostile and mysterious by lowlanders, wary of its dense forests and the strange customs of its tribes, the region is now attracting the interest of many Vietnamese, some of whom come here as tourists, others as permanent settlers. This interest is no doubt mostly due to efforts made to domesticate both its landscapes and inhabitants, who are now in a minority and well on the way to becoming a sight to be seen in their own lands. At the southern extremity of the Truong Son Cordillera, the Highlands resemble a thick carpet of hilly forests and coffee, tea and rubber plantations where the occasional roar of a remote waterfall can be heard. From Buon Ma Thuot, Plei Ku and Kon Tum, and their unappealing concrete buildings, to Dalat and its tatty, outdated atmosphere, without forgetting the traditional villages of the Ma, Koho, E De, Gia Rai, Ba Na and Mnong, the region revels in paradoxes. Yet for the relatively small number of visitors from abroad, the undeniable highlight of the area is the opportunity it offers of meeting its inhabitants. Their incredibly rich culture, a mixture of animism and Christianity, their traditional way of life, sophisticated architecture, unusual funeral rites and warm welcome never fail to intrigue and delight the curious traveller.

DALAT
Capital of Lam Dong province
300km from Ho Chi Minh City – Pop 130 000
Alt 1500m – Mild, temperate climate

Not to be missed
The French villas and Bao Dai Palace.
Lam Dong Museum and Thien Vuong Pagoda.
The waterfalls in the area.

And remember...
Take a warm sweater.
Hire a bicycle or a motorcycle to explore Dalat.

From the time of the French onwards, Dalat with its elegant colonial villas and hilly landscape of pine trees has been a great favourite with people from Saigon, eager to escape the muggy urban jungle. It is a town of paradoxes, the height of Vietnamese kitsch, home to a number of avant-garde artists and a University Research Centre of Radioactive Medicine surrounded by traditional villages. It was discovered in 1893 by Dr Yersin, who was in fact searching this unknown region for a possible area to grow quinquina. Several years went by before Governor General Paul Doumer decided to establish a mountain resort here, and the project finally got off the ground in 1917. Since then, the surrounding countryside has been extensively developed and the town owes its rich diversity as much to tourism as to its fruit and vegetable crops and horticultural activity. Although Dalat definitely provides a breath of fresh air and some wonderful landscapes, together with the chance to meet the Ma and Koho tribes (the Lat and the Chill), visitors new to Vietnam are sometimes unpleasantly surprised by its lack of exoticism and by the mass tourism it attracts. Yet even if the resort is very popular with Ho Chi Minh City's nouveaux riches, passing Viet Kieu, honeymoon couples and expatriates homesick for Europe, it also offers the chance to catch a glimpse of a sociological pageant full of surprises.

From Ho Chi Minh City to Dalat
300km trip. Map page 317.
Allow one day, including stops.

Leave Ho Chi Minh City on the RN1. 65km further on, at Dau Day, turn left onto the RN20 towards Dalat. Lake Langa is 30km away.

■ Created after the opening of the hydroelectric dam in 1984, **Lake Langa** has no fewer than 200 **floating houses**, all with fish in cages beneath them, as at Chau Doc. Most of the inhabitants are Vietnamese, forced to flee Cambodia at the time of the Khmer Rouge. A memorial near the bridge commemorates the heavy fighting that occured here during the final assault on Saigon in 1975.

■ The road then crosses the unusual plain of Dinh Quan which is dotted with conical, long-since extinct **volcanoes**. Crops of manioc, coffee and corn are grown intensively on the plain's fertile soil. It is possible to climb up some of the volcanoes, but you should ask the farmers' permission first, because they don't always appreciate their crops being trampled underfoot!

A short distance before Ma Da Gui, near the village of Tan Phu (kilometre marker 125), turn left onto a 25km-long dirt track which leads to the Nam Cat Tien National Park.

■ **Nam Cat Tien National Park** (Vuon Quoc Gia Cat Tien) – ☎ *(061) 85 64 49 / 79 12 26, www.blakup.demon.nl/cat_tien Entrance fee. Accommodation possible. For more information; WWF, 85 Tran Quoc Toan, District 3, Ho Chi Minh City, ☎ (08) 932 59 95, Fax (08) 932 59 96.*

The Highlands

Nam Cat Tien, one of the last primeval forests left in the South, is home to rare mammals, such as elephants and Java rhinoceros, and countless birds. As tourists are few and far between, it is best to hire the services of a guide and contact the forest rangers if you want to spend the night locally.

Return to the RN20 and continue on towards Dalat.

The road now heads up to the Di Linh plateau, revealing a number of superb **views★** on the way. The local inhabitants benefit greatly from the **tea plantations** which are being steadily extended. However, the resulting deforestation is causing serious erosion problems with consequent landslides and increase in aridity.

■ The reputation of Bao Loc's silk industry, set in the heart of lush vegetation, is well-established and attracts many visitors, but most also stop to admire the **Dambri Falls★★** *(turn left at the T-junction and continue on for 15km. Entrance charge)*. The deafening torrent can be heard before it can be seen, hidden as it is in a bamboo grove. A **lift** *(fee)* makes the descent effortless, but does rather spoil the view *(there are no shelters at the bottom, so protect your camera from the splashing water)*.

■ Five kilometres before Di Linh, on the way into Lien Dam, a small platform provides a fine view of the **Bo Bla Falls★**, whose 32m-high cascade of water bursts out of the surrounding greenery. A path takes you down *(30min walk)*.

At kilometre marker 191, turn left and continue for 7km through a stretch of moorland.

■ The best is yet to come with the spectacular 30m-high **Pongour Falls★★★** *(entrance fee)*, which form a stunning 150m-long semicircle. A 300m track leads to the foot of the falls, from where the view is quite stunning, particularly in the rainy season.

■ The RN20 continues towards Dalat. **Gougah Falls** *(at kilometre marker 195; easy access)* can be seen from the road, as can the 100m-wide and 15m-high **Lien Khuong Falls★★** *(at kilometre marker 210; the path is slippery)*.

Dalat
Allow 2 days

Dalat, also known as "Little Paris", owes its charming aura of a spa town to **Lake Xuan Huong**, created in 1919 shortly after Dalat's foundation. Located right in the heart of the town and surrounded by hills, the lake is a great favourite with couples

The approach to Dalat

B Juge/MICHELIN

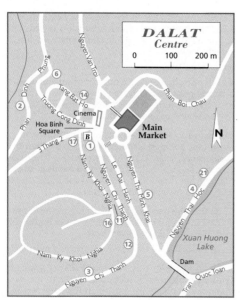

DALAT Centre

0   100   200 m

HOTELS

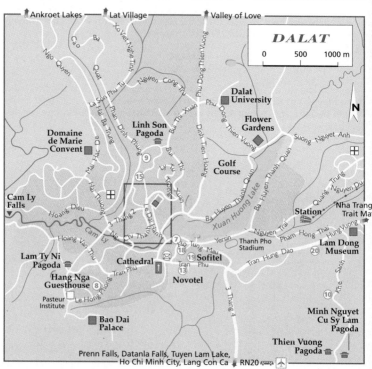

DALAT

0   500   1000 m

and families, all of whom delight in the pleasures of a pedalo on the water or a horse-drawn carriage ride around the shores *(4km)*. The most built-up and the liveliest part of the town lies on the northwestern shore, while the villas and pagodas hidden among the pine trees and orchards on the southern shore offer a more rustic appeal.

The northern shore of the lake

The imposing concrete block at the end of Nguyen Thi Minh Khai Road is the **main market** *(daily 6am-6pm)*. Although totally devoid of elegance, the amazing variety of its locally grown fruit, flowers and vegetables makes it nonetheless well worth a visit.

A flight of stairs takes you down to the cinema on **Hoa Binh Square**, off which run little lanes lined with low buildings, strangely reminiscent of a little provincial town in France frozen in time. From here, venture as far as the **Domaine de Marie Convent** (Nha Tho Lanh Dia Duc Ba) *(6 Mai Hac De)*, which stands on an isolated hill to the northwest of the town. Built in the 1920s, it was extended thanks to the generosity of the wife of Admiral Jean Decoux, who is buried here. A small group of nuns still live within its tranquil walls. Ask them to show you the **garden**, where they grow, among other things, "fairy slippers", a delicate orchid which grows widely in the region of Dalat. The recently renovated parish **church** contains a statue of the Virgin Mary, standing on a globe with a snake at her feet.

Linh Son Pagoda, built on a hilltop in 1942, *(120 Nguyen Van Troi, 800m north of the town centre)* is the oldest in Dalat. It has a tiled roof with raised eaves and is flanked by a handsome **tower**. The orchid garden has sadly gone to seed, but the shrine still houses an enormous 1 250kg bronze **bell**.

An enormous 65ha **golf course**, first created in 1920, reopened in 1994 *(entrance at the top of Phu Dong Thien Vuong)*, and reflects the town's popularity with Ho Chi Minh City's young jet-set. The course faces **Dalat University** which stands in grounds of 40ha. Nearly 2 500 students attend maths, chemistry, history, biology and literature courses. It is the perfect spot to meet the local youth. By the lakeside at the bottom of the street, the **Flower Gardens** (Vuon Hoa Thanh Pho) *(2 Phu Dong Thien Vuong. Daily 7am-6pm. Entrance fee)* have some wonderful orchids.

Perfumes of yesteryear...

At the foot of the impressive telecommunications tower, a distant and somewhat incongruous cousin of the Eiffel Tower, stand two gems of colonial architecture. The **Sofitel Dalat Palace** and the **Novotel**, together with the imposing **Cathedral** (Nha Tho Lon) and its 47m-high **bell tower** *(Tran Phu. Services from Monday-Saturday at 5.30am and 7.15am, Sundays at 5.30am, 7am and 4pm)*. The cathedral was built between 1931 and 1942 and the majority of its 70 **stained-glass windows** were made in Grenoble, France. On a fine day, the sun's rays on the pastel-pink walls give it an almost ethereal look.

The unique **Hang Nga Guesthouse** *(3 Huynh Thuc Khang. Entrance fee)*, also called the "Crazy House", is the fruit of its owner's unbridled imagination and has become one of the sights of Dalat in its own right. The daughter of a leading Vietnamese Communist Party member (successor to Ho Chi Minh), she studied architecture in Moscow before returning to Dalat, building this still-evolving wonderland which is a mixture of spider's web and sand castle.

Lam Ty Ni Pagoda (Quan Am Tu) *(2 Thien My)*, at the end of a short avenue, has been the solitary retreat of the "mad bonze", **Vien Thuc**, since 1968. A painter and poet, he speaks English and French and claims to be a follower of Buddhism while displaying a highly astute flair for business. Visitors flock to the pagoda as much to meet this unusual character as to see his prolific and varied works of art. Vien Thuc, whose rumoured fortune is the subject of much gossip, plans to travel round the world on the proceeds of the sale of his paintings.

Bao Dai Palace** (*Le Hong Pong. Daily 7am-5.30pm. Entrance fee*), perched on a hilltop at the end of a street lined with **French villas***, is a surprising blend of Western and Eastern luxury. Built between 1933-38 by French and Vietnamese architects, it was the last emperor's summer palace until his exile in France in 1955. The residence was then home to South Vietnam's presidents until 1975. The spacious living room and its **period furniture** in the royal colours (red and yellow) seem to have jumped straight out of a museum devoted to interior decoration in the 1940s. The rest of the palace follows suit, from the office with a stuffed deer on the wall (one of the emperor's hunting trophies) to the meeting room with its magnificent table and a superb engraved **glass map** of Vietnam. A little room at the rear with gilt bas-reliefs was apparently where the emperor and his concubines relaxed. While luxurious, the family's private apartments upstairs are not as ostentatious. The sunniest and largest bedroom was the queen's.

On the western outskirts of the town, **Cam Ly Falls** (*Hoang Van Thu. 7am-6pm*), have everything to make them a tourist attraction even though they lack the spectacular quality of some of their neighbours.

Return to the eastern shore of Lake Xuan Huong.

Scattered among the pine groves of the lake's southern and eastern banks, along Tran Hung Dao, Quang Trung and Nguyen Du, countless **villas**, which would look more at home in Normandy or the French Alps, bear witness to the time when Dalat was a favourite holiday resort for the French of Saigon. Some houses have retained their former splendour. In the same spirit, the similarity between the pretty **Dalat Railway Station*** (*1 Quang Trung,* ☎ *(063) 83 44 09. Daily 8am-4pm*) and its distant counterpart in the smart French seaside resort of Deauville is quite striking. Opened in 1933, the railway went as far as Thap Cham, some 100km further on, but services were suspended in the 1960s following Viet Cong attacks. A 7km-long stretch of the line has been reopened as far as **Trai Mat** for the tourists (*30min trip, US$5*), but the journey is aboard a small Russian-built diesel engine, while the steam engine which used to pull the trains remains on the platform.

Go back down Nguyen Trai and onto Pham Hong Thai and Hung Vuong.

Lam Dong Museum** (*4 Hung Vuong. Monday-Friday 8-11am / 1.30-4pm. No entrance charge*), the former Museum of the Highland Tribes, is located in what used to be the home of Nguyen Huu Thi Lan, the wife of Bao Dai. It contains a superb collection of objects found in the province from prehistoric times up until the present day. The first room contains an unusual **lithophone**** (dan da), a strange, almost poetical musical instrument which would play random notes when positioned under a waterfall, as the drops of water moved a stone hanging from a string. The Champa civilisation is represented by an enormous **lingam***, statues, bronze crockery, gold jewellery, a finely carved quartz **yogi**** and a superb silver **bas-relief****, depicting Shiva, all of which date from the 10C-11C.

In the second room are 18C **Chinese vases**, celadon stoneware and **Ming** (14C-15C) and Japanese (17C) chinaware, which bear witness to the breadth of the trade, both in skills and goods, and the depth of relations between the various Highland minorities and their more powerful neighbours over many centuries. A few 15C-16C **bronze bracelets** illustrate the workmanship of the Koho and the Ma, while a third room provides examples of the Ma's skills, including porcelain, funerary vases, jewellery and spears. Upstairs, hunting and fishing implements, textiles, weaving and pottery, together with the **interior of a hut** and a sacrificial **pole** (*klao*) give an idea of the traditional way of life of the Chu Ru and the Ma. Notice the unusual **mouth organ** (bamboo sticks in a marrow plant) used to call the children, each child being summoned by a distinct note.

Go along Khe Sanh to the southeast of the town centre. Thien Vuong Pagoda is 5km away, along a 1km track.

Thien Vuong Pagoda* *(daily 6am-5pm)*, also called **Chua Tau** (Chinese Pagoda) stands on a superb well-wooded hill. Built in 1959, it has three parts. In the first, a jovial Buddha of the Past is seated on a lotus blossom. The second, rather stark building *(remove your shoes)*, contains three enormous 4m-high **sandalwood statues**** weighing one and half tonnes each, which were brought from Hong Kong for the pagoda's inauguration. From left to right are Quan Am, Goddess of Mercy, Amitabha, the Buddha of the Past (or Buddha A Di Da), and the bodhisattva Dai The Chi Bo That who represents the spirit of Amitabha. To preserve the statues' natural fragrance, no incense is burned in this room. The shrine culminates at the hilltop with another statue of the **Buddha**, sitting on a lotus blossom amid pine trees, meditating on the superb **panorama**** stretching out before him.

Peace and quiet reign in the more modestly proportioned **Minh Nguyet Cu Sy Lam Pagoda** *(on the opposite hill, at the end of Khe Sanh)*. The main shrine is built on a platform in the shape of a lotus blossom. It is dedicated to Quan The Am Bo Tat, whose statue stands inside.

Around Dalat

The Valley of Love (Thung Lung Tinh Yeu)
5km north of Dalat along Phu Dong Thien Vuong. Daily 6am-6pm. Entrance fee.
Nestling among pine-covered hills, the Valley of Love contains a small artificial lake whose well-guarded paths and shores are extremely popular with Vietnamese tourists. Swamped by souvenir stalls, it gives the impression of having been designed by a singularly uninspired landscape gardener. However, if you've always nurtured a secret dream of getting dressed up as a cowboy, here's your chance. If posing in full cowboy regalia doesn't appeal, you could always settle for a spin in a pedalo.

Lat and Ankroet Falls
Take Phan Dinh Phung to the village of Lat, some 12km northeast of Dalat. Note that a permit and guide, obtained from Dalat Toserco, are compulsory.

■ The nine hamlets of the village of **Lat** are inhabited by the Ma and above all by the Protestant and Catholic Koho (Lat and Chill), who still live in their traditional stilt houses. The tourist boom does not seem to have done much for the welfare of the villagers who live off crops of sweet potatoes, beans and rice. Lat nestles at the foot of the **Lang Bian****, a 2 163m-high sacred mountain. The walk to the summit is easy if lengthy, but the superb **view**** makes it well worthwhile *(allow 3-4hr one-way along a shady path. Dalat tourist agencies organise walks including the village)*.

■ From Lat, continue on to the **Ankroet Lakes** and **Falls**** *(18km northwest of Dalat; care is required because the last few kilometres are along a track which is practically impassable when it rains)*. The lakes and falls are hidden in a superb, unspoiled spot, where, unfortunately, a tourist complex is planned in the near future.

South of Dalat
Take the RN20 southbound and turn right 5km further on, then continue on for 2km.

■ Tucked away in a thick pine forest, **Tuyen Lam Lake**, built in 1980, is one of the main attractions of Dalat, even if its landscape is, once again, far from unspoiled. Phuong Nam Adventure Tourism organise hikes and elephant rides, but a boat ride or a fishing trip can be just as enjoyable. The impressive **Truc Lam Monastery**, opened in 1994, which dominates the lake's northern shore, is worth a look, if only for its **garden** and lake view.

Back on the RN20, continue along the road for a few hundred metres as far as Datanla Falls.

■ A 400m-long forest path leads down to **Datanla Falls** *(daily 6am-4pm. Entrance fee)*, which cascade down a rocky hillside before entering a narrow canyon. Wooden bungalows built in this refreshing spot illustrate the Vietnamese concept of romanticism.

■ Eight kilometres further on, beyond **Prenn Pass**, the RN20 leads to **Prenn Falls** (*daily 7am-5pm. Entrance fee*), one of the most touristy spots in the region, complete with souvenir stalls selling all sorts of postcards and tacky souvenirs. A path takes you behind the 15m-high falls.

■ Eighteen kilometres from Dalat, **Lang Con Ca**, settled by the French in the early 1950s, is inhabited by the Koho. This impoverished village owes its nickname, "Chicken Village" to an enormous statue, which is said to have been put up by the French to get the villagers used to rising when the cock crowed. This is however only one among a number of rumours in circulation regarding the statue's origins. Lang Con Ca provides an excellent introduction into the culture of these ethnic minorities, and its short distance from Dalat has made it a popular destination with all the travel agencies and tourists are eagerly awaited. During the day, most of the villagers are out tending the sugar cane fields and vegetable crops (tomatoes, beans, carrots and radishes) and only the children and a few women, hard at work at their looms, remain in the village.

Dalat close up

COMING AND GOING

By air – Lien Khuong Airport lies 30km to the south of Dalat, on the RN20 (a bus to and from the town leaves from the Vietnam Airlines office). The airline operates one or two daily flights to Ho Chi Minh City (50min flight).

By bus and mini-bus – Tinh Lam Dong Bus Terminus (3 Thang 4, 2km to the south of the town centre) is open from 6am to midnight. In theory foreigners are not allowed to take these regular buses, but in practice all you need to do is buy a ticket from the driver. Comfort is basic and stops frequent. Several daily departures for Ho Chi Minh City (8hr journey); two buses daily at 5am and 10am to Nha Trang (5hr) and one bus at 5am to Buon Ma Thuot (6-9hr journey depending on the season). For Pleiku, change at Nha Trang.

By tourist bus – Travel agencies in Ho Chi Minh City and Dalat sell "Open Tour" tickets between the two towns (7hr journey), including tourist halts. These buses are more comfortable, leave at fixed times and can pick you up from your hotel. Services to Nha Trang (departure at 8am, 6hr journey), Hoi An and Hue are also possible.

By car – From Ho Chi Minh City, the inland road via Bao Loc is recommended. To rent a vehicle, enquire at local travel agencies.

GETTING AROUND DALAT

By taxi – Dalat Taxi, ☎ (063) 83 08 30. **Thang Loi Taxi**, ☎ (063) 53 59 83. There are plenty of taxi cabs, particularly around Hoa Binh Square. It is also possible to charter a cab to visit the region (around 5 000VND / km).

By motorcycle – This is the ideal way of getting around Dalat and its surrounding hilly countryside. Either rent a motorcycle directly from a private owner (near the terminus), or from your hotel. Allow between US$5-8 depending on the season, and an extra US$10 for a driver.

By bicycle – Those brave enough to choose this mode of transport will appreciate the lack of traffic and mild climate, even if the hilly terrain makes the going hard. Bicycles can be rented from travel agencies and hotels.

ADDRESS BOOK

Bank / Currency exchange – Some hotels change their guests' foreign currency.
Industrial & Commercial Bank, 46 Hoa Binh Square. Monday-Friday 7-11.30am / 1-4.30pm, Saturday 7am-11.30am. Foreign currencies and travellers' cheques (US dollars) exchanged and withdrawals with a credit card for a 3 % commission.
Banque Agricole du Vietnam, 36 Hoa Binh. Monday-Friday 7-11.30am / 1-4.30pm, Saturday 7-11.30am. Foreign

currencies and travellers' cheques (US dollars) exchanged and withdrawals with a credit card for a commission.

Post office / Telephone – *Buu Dien Dalat*, 14 Tran Phu, near the Novotel. Daily 6.30am-9pm. Poste restante and DHL.

Internet – *Viet Hung Internet Cafe*, 7 Nguyen Chi Thanh. Daily 8am-11pm.

Airline companies – *Vietnam Airlines*, 40 Ho Tung Mau, ☎ (063) 82 28 95. Daily 7.30-11.30am / 1.30-4.30pm.

Travel agencies – *Dalat Travel Service (Dalat Toserco)*, 7 3 Thang 2 Street, Hotel Thuy Tien, ☎ (063) 82 21 25, Fax (063) 82 83 30, ttdhhd@hcm.vnn. vn Dalat's official travel agency is highly competent and offers a wide range of services, from rental vehicles and motorcycles to guides and authorisations for Lat village and trips around the region (Lang Bian, Tuyen Lam) and beyond.

Dalat Tourism Service, 9 Le Dai Hanh, ☎ (063) 82 24 79, dltoserco@hcm.vnn. vn The transport branch of Dalat Toserco, agent of the Kim Café in Ho Chi Minh City, sells tickets to Nha Trang and Ho Chi Minh City.

Phuong Nam Adventure Tourism, 6 Ho Tung Mau, ☎ (063) 82 27 81, Fax (063) 83 18 00. This agency specialises in hiking trips and elephant rides around Lake Tuyen Lam, and also offers trips to the Highlands.

Pacific Tour, 9 Bui Thi Xuan, ☎ (063) 82 47 25 / 82 83 03. The local agent of Sinh Café in Ho Chi Minh City organises trips in the region (Lat village, climbs up Lang Bian Mountain, elephant rides and boat trips) and around the rest of the Highlands. Tickets on sale for Nha Trang and Ho Chi Minh City.

Dalat Holidays Ecotours, 73 Truong Cong Dinh, ☎ (063) 82 94 22, langbian@hcm.vnn.vn This agency specialises in outdoor sports (walking, abseiling, canyoning and mountain biking).

WHERE TO STAY

During the peak season from December to February and particularly in January during Tet, many hotels are fully booked and also increase their prices. Most of the mini-hotels are near the cinema and Nam Ky Khoi Nghia, but some don't accept foreigners. It is also possible to rent a villa, mainly on Tran Hung Dao, but this is more expensive.

Under US$10

Trang Anh, 1A Ho Tung Mau, ☎ (063) 82 31 18 – 11rm 📶 📺 This small, family hotel, somewhat far from the centre, is very friendly. 50 % increase during the peak season.

Hoa Binh Hotel – Peace Hotel, 64-67 Truong Cong Dinh, ☎ (063) 82 27 87, Fax (063) 82 24 79 – 17rm 📶 Greatly appreciated by those on shoestring budgets, this establishment is slightly better than the Phu Hoa. Rates go up slightly during the peak season. Bicycle rentals available.

Phu Hoa, 16 Tang Bat Ho, ☎ (063) 82 21 94, Fax (063) 83 39 56 – 35rm 📶 📺 ✗ Well-known among lorry drivers who appreciate its basic but decent amenities, central location and roof-terrace. Small increase in the peak season.

Thanh The, 118 Phan Dinh Phung, ☎ (063) 82 21 80, Fax (063) 83 22 75 – 25rm 📶 ✗ Ideal for mini-budgets. The rooms are basic, but clean and pleasant.

Between US$10 and US$15

Thong Xanh, 33-35 Nam Ky Khoi Nghia, ☎ (063) 82 52 89 – 18rm 📶 🖉 📺 This little family guesthouse, home to four generations, rents out impeccable rooms with a good view. Prices are however somewhat excessive and bargaining is a good idea.

Mimosa Hotel, 170 Phan Dinh Phung, ☎ (063) 82 26 56, Fax (063) 83 22 75 – 30rm 📶 📺 ✗ A pleasant establishment which is basic but quite acceptable. Popular with lorry drivers. 50 % increase during the peak season.

Thuy Tien Hotel, 7 3 Thang 2 Street, at the corner of Nam Ky Khoi Nghia, ☎ (063) 82 21 25, Fax (063) 82 83 30 – 11rm 📶 🖉 📺 This four-storey establishment is centrally located and friendly. The rooms are spotless and spacious (satellite TV), if a little noisy.

Cam Do Hotel, 81 Phan Dinh Phung, ☎ (063) 82 24 82, Fax (063) 83 02 73 – 15rm 📶 📺 ✗ This modern establishment, belonging to Dalat Toserco, has

Dalat close up

well-kept but ordinary rooms. 30 to 50% increase during the peak season.

Hoang Hau Villa, 8A Ho Tung Mau, ☎ (063) 82 14 31, Fax (063) 82 23 33 – 10rm ⚐ ℘ TV Breakfast included. This excellent establishment provides spacious, reasonably-priced rooms (avoid those in the basement). Prices vary depending on the floor and the season.

Nam Ky, 11 Nam Ky Khoi Nghia, ☎ (063) 82 44 93 – 12rm ⚐ TV A pleasant, if ordinary mini-hotel. The least expensive rooms are windowless and those overlooking the street are noisy.

Chau Au – Europa, 76 Nguyen Chi Thanh, ☎ (063) 82 28 70, Fax (063) 82 44 88, europa@hcm.vnn.vn – 15rm ⚐ ℘ TV In a quiet neighbourhood two minutes from the town centre, this fine establishment offers bright, spacious and tastefully-decorated rooms. Internet access and bicycle rentals.

Between US$15 and US$30

Villa Trixaco, 7 Nguyen Thai Hoc, ☎ (063) 82 27 89 – 12rm ⚐ TV This impressive white building overlooking the lake combines old-fashioned charm with friendly, personalised service at reasonable prices. 30% increase during the peak season.

Anh Dao Hotel, 50-52 Hoa Binh Square, ☎ (063) 82 35 77, Fax (063) 82 35 70 – 30rm ⚐ ℘ TV ✗ CC Breakfast included. This quaint old hotel offers light, spacious if dull rooms. 25 to 40% increase during the peak season.

Villa Hotel 28, 28 Tran Hung Dao, ☎ (063) 82 27 64, Fax (063) 83 56 39 – 14rm ⚐ TV Breakfast included. This handsome villa, complete with sitting room and fireplace, is perfect for families or romantic couples (the annexe rooms are more reasonably priced). Friendly staff and pleasant garden.

Minh Tam Villa, 20A Khe Sanh, near Thien Vuong Pagoda, ☎ (063) 82 24 47, Fax (063) 82 44 20 – 22rm ⚐ TV Breakfast included. Ideal for those in search of peace and quiet. Its remoteness makes a car essential. There is a pleasant garden and the rooms are comfortable, if somewhat musty-smelling.

Ngoc Lan Hotel, 42 Nguyen Chi Thanh, ☎ (063) 82 35 22, Fax (063) 82 40 32 – 33rm ⚐ ℘ TV ✗ CC Breakfast included. This prosperous, central establishment provides comfortable, if

uninspired accommodation. The upstairs rooms are the most pleasant.

Between US$30 and US$50

Hang Nga Guesthouse, 3 Huynh Thuc Khang, ☎ (063) 82 20 70, Fax (063) 83 14 80 – 9rm ⚐ CC The "Crazy House" is worth a look, if only for its unusual architecture. The rooms, although quite amazingly decorated, are in fact somewhat basic in terms of comfort.

Between US$ 50 and US$70

Golf 3 Hotel, 4 Nguyen Thi Minh Khai, ☎ (063) 83 05 79, Fax (063) 83 03 96, golf3hot@hcm.vnn.vn – 78rm ⚐ ℘ TV CC Breakfast included. Karaoke, massage. This massive 7-storey hotel cannot be missed. The rooms are impeccable, albeit in rather dubious taste. The bar offers a superb view of Dalat.

☺**Empress Hotel**, 5 Nguyen Thai Hoc, ☎ (063) 83 38 88, Fax (063) 82 93 99 – 19rm ⚐ ℘ TV ✗ CC Breakfast included. This hotel is full of character, providing prettily decorated rooms with wood panelling and tiled floors. Rates can be negotiated. Bar and billiard tables.

Over US$100

Novotel, 7 Tran Phu, ☎ (063) 82 57 77, Fax (063) 82 58 88, novotel@netnam2.org.vn – 144rm ⚐ ℘ TV ✗ ✤ CC Formerly the "Park Hotel", this establishment was built in 1932 and now belongs to the Accor chain of hotels (as does the Sofitel) which has restored it to its former glory. The parquet floors and sophisticated decoration of its rooms cannot however compete with the Sofitel, either in terms of taste or price.

☺**Sofitel Dalat Palace**, 12 Tran Phu, ☎ (063) 82 54 44, Fax (063) 82 56 66, sofitel@netnam2.org.vn – 43rm ⚐ ℘ TV ✗ ✤ CC The former "Dalat Palace" (1922), has been remarkably tastefully renovated and its classical elegance exudes an atmosphere of old-fashioned luxury. Some of the rooms have an open fire and an outstanding view. A gallery with works of the "mad bonze" (see page 309) should soon be opening.

EATING OUT

Known as the garden of Vietnam, the area around Dalat overflows with fruit and vegetables which can be found in all the local markets, with home-made jams, preserved fruit and juices. The majority of tourist restaurants are located around the cinema on Nguyen Thi Minh Khai and Phan Dinh Phung, and close around 10-11pm, at the latest midnight in the peak season. Soup, stews, snails and seafood can all be found ready-cooked at the market, but take care at Le Dai Hanh market which is reputed to be expensive and dishonest.

Under 25 000VND
Vinh Loi, 1 Nam Ky Khoi Nghia. This unpretentious restaurant serves delicious soup and makes a welcome change from the tourist haunts.

Nhu Hai, 40-41 Nguyen Thi Minh Khai. 6am-11pm. In this pleasant, family establishment, tourists mix with the locals (menu in English). Taste the house speciality, "ta pin lu" (fondue of fish, vegetables and meat), the delicious fruit juices and vegetarian dishes (tofu and fresh vegetables).

Hoang Lan, 118 Phan Dinh Phung. 7am-10pm. The large dining room of this neon-lit restaurant is permanently packed with lorry drivers who come for its soups, meat dishes and delicious "ta pin lu" fondue at very modest prices.

Cam Do, Cam Do Hotel. 6am-11pm. This inexpensive little establishment serves very decent vegetarian, Vietnamese and Western cuisine.

Nam Son, 54 Hoa Binh Square. 6am-9pm. Although devoid of charm and complete with neon lights, this restaurant nonetheless serves tasty Vietnamese dishes and excellent vegetable soups.

Between 25 000 and 50 000VND
Dong A Restaurant, 82 Phan Dinh Phung. A wide choice of Vietnamese, Chinese, Western and vegetarian dishes served in a somewhat dreary, if relatively quiet and not too touristy setting.

Huong Tra, 1 Nguyen Thai Hoc. 7am-9pm. Pleasantly located in a pine grove overlooking the lake, this restaurant serves Western dishes but its local speciality is definitely a must.

Thanh Thuy, 2 Nguyen Thai Hoc. 6.30am-11pm. A smart lakeside establishment which serves seafood and Western dishes to the accompaniment of the latest local pop music.

Ngoc Hai, 6 Nguyen Thi Minh Khai. Despite its reputation, the cuisine is tasteless and the bill best checked twice.

Long Hoa Family Restaurant, 6 3 Thang 2 Street, ☎ (063) 82 29 34. This welcoming establishment, and its owner, are most charming. Excellent fried beef, grilled pork and seafood.

Between 50 000 and 100 000VND
Thuy Ta Restaurant, 1 Yersin. 6am-11pm. Formerly the "Grenouillère", this restaurant on stilts by the lakeside is perfectly located, but the food (Western and Vietnamese) is very ordinary. Why not just stop in for a drink?

Thanh Thanh, 4 Tang Bat Hao, ☎ (063) 82 18 36. 11am-10pm. The little bistro-style dining room of one of the best restaurants in Dalat is invariably packed to the seams. Its grilled shrimp in sugar cane, shredded beef and chicken baked in a pot are not to be missed.

Empress, Empress Hotel. 6am-10pm. An elegant restaurant ideal for a romantic dinner for two (seafood, Western and Vietnamese dishes).

Between 100 000 and 200 000VND
Le Café de la Poste, 12 Tran Phu, ☎ (063) 82 54 44. Situated in a handsome colonial decor, the restaurant of the Sofitel and the Novotel serves Vietnamese and simple Western dishes (pizzas, pasta), together with more sophisticated dishes. Prices in US dollars.

GOING OUT

Cafés, bars – A series of almost identical bars has sprung up along Nguyen Chi Thanh, Dalat's liveliest night spot.
Larry's Bar, Sofitel Hotel. 4pm-1am. A somewhat stuffy, if pleasant atmosphere reigns in this Swiss chalet-style pub.

Tea rooms, cake shops – **Café Stop and Go**, 2A Ly Tu Trong. Merry disorder reigns in this gallery-cum-tea room located in a private house.
Hoan Hy Cake Shop, 20 3 Thang 2 Street. Excellent local and French cakes and pastries.

Nightclubs – **PK's Nightclub** (Sofitel Hotel), open at the weekends from 8pm to 1am.

SHOPPING

Crafts – The Highland tribes make dyed woven mats, bamboo rice baskets and clothes which can sometimes be found at Lat.

THE HIGHLANDS
Provinces of Dak Lak, Gia Lai and Kon Tum
46 000km² – Pop 2.3 million
Altitude over 500m – Mild climate

Not to be missed
Dray Sap Falls and Lake Lak.
A ride on an elephant in Yok Don National Park.
The road from Buon Ma Thuot to Plei Ku.
The Gia Rai and Ba Na villages around Kon Tum.

And remember...
The best time to come is during the dry season from November to May.
Make sure you have enough fuel if driving in the Highlands.

For a long time, foreigners were prohibited from visiting the Highlands and even though the region has been open since the early 1990s, it still remains little visited in comparison with the seaside resorts along the coast. It is true that the area has as yet failed to overcome a number of handicaps such as transport and accommodation, but it nonetheless offers some of the most stunning scenery in Vietnam, together with the possibility of getting to know some of the country's most fascinating ethnic minorities. It is still an unspoilt wilderness of impregnable mountains, spectacular waterfalls and thick forests which even the ravages of war and the inexorable spread of tea and coffee plantations have failed to disfigure. While the towns have nothing to recommend a prolonged stay, the villages of the E De, Gia Rai, Ba Na or the M'nong are more than worth the visit. These threatened minorities, who seem to live as if time has stood still, remain deeply attached to their traditions, whose distinguishing characteristics are their architecture, funeral rites and their attachment to matriarchy (with the exception of the M'nong). The troubled events which took place at Plei Ku in February 2001 illustrate how much the rights of these minorities and freedom of worship remain a sensitive subject for Hanoi.

A 220km track, only accessible during the dry season by 4WD vehicle or motorcycle, runs from Dalat to Buon Ma Thuot (enquire about weather conditions before leaving). It takes you through some of the most beautiful landscapes of the Highlands, alternating between thick forests, coffee plantations and M'nong villages.

Buon Ma Thuot and the surrounding area
Capital of the province of Dak Lak. Pop 70 000. Alt 450m.
220km from Dalat, 180km from Nha Trang. Allow 1 day.

Buon Ma Thuot itself is of very little interest to tourists, but it makes an excellent starting point for a trip to the villages of the E De and the M'nong and to Yok Don National Park, where you can go for an elephant ride. All activities are organised by the local tourist office, and a guide and permit are compulsory for the majority of villages. Even though the town may appear to be self-sufficient, this is not the case and the local economy mostly relies on the export of coffee, plantations of which are expanding at an alarming rate to the detriment of the forests. Coffee growing goes back to French colonial times when the tea, rubber and coffee plantations provided settlers with very comfortable revenues.

Before setting out for the villages, have a brief look at the **Ethnographic Museum** (*4 Nguyen Du. Monday-Friday 7-11.30am / 1.30-5pm. Entrance charge*) and get a feel for the craft skills of the E De, M'nong and Gia Rai, which are illustrated by a fine collection of textiles, vases, funerary statues, tools and traditional musical instruments.

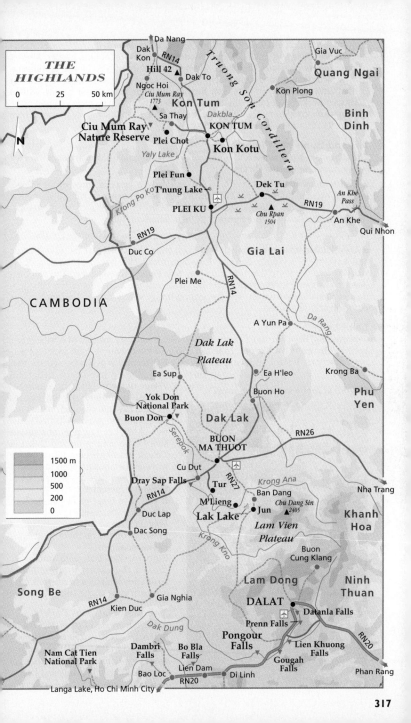

THE HIGHLANDS

0   25   50 km

N

Da Nang
Dak Kon
RN14
Hill 42
Dak To
Ngoc Hoi
Ciu Mum Ray
1773
Kon Tum
Sa Thay
Dakbla
KON TUM
Ciu Mum Ray Nature Reserve
Plei Chot
Kon Kotu
Yaly Lake
Plei Fun
Kröng Po Ko
T'nung Lake
PLEI KU
Dek Tu
RN19
An Khe Pass
Chu Rpan
1504
An Khe
RN19
Qui Nhon
Duc Co
Gia Lai

Gia Vuc
Quang Ngai
Kon Plong
Binh Dinh

Plei Me
RN14
A Yun Pa
Da Rang

CAMBODIA

Dak Lak Plateau
Ea Sup
Ea H'leo
Krong Ba
Phu Yen
Buon Ho
Yok Don National Park
Buon Don
Dak Lak
BUON MA THUOT
RN26
Cu Dut
Dray Sap Falls
RN14
Tur
RN27
Krong Ana
Nha Trang
M'Lieng
Ban Dang
Chu Dang Sin
2405
Duc Lap
Lak Lake
Jun
Khanh Hoa
Dac Song
Krong Kno
Lam Vien Plateau
Buon Cung Klang
Song Be
Gia Nghia
Lam Dong
Ninh Thuan
Kien Duc
RN14
DALAT
Datanla Falls
Dak Dung
Prenn Falls
Lien Khuong Falls
RN20
Nam Cat Tien National Park
Dambri Falls
Bo Bla Falls
Pongour Falls
Gougah Falls
Bao Loc
Lien Dam
Di Linh
RN20
Phan Rang
Langa Lake, Ho Chi Minh City

Truong Son Cordillera

1500 m
1000
500
200
0

Serepok

317

Built by the French in 1931, the prison (*18 Tan Thuat. Monday-Friday 7am-11.30am / 1.30pm-5pm. Donations*) invites you to ponder another aspect of local history. A series of **documents** illustrates the harsh, intransigent nature of the colonial administration, which sentenced a certain Nguyen Xan to seven years imprisonment for "Communist activities" or Chu Van Bien to life imprisonment for having written "seditious works". Ask to see the tiny **cells** where the prisoners were chained up in unimaginable conditions. The photos and, above all, the **paintings** by prisoners help to recreate the atmosphere of this period.

Around Buon Ma Thuot★

Leave Buon Ma Thuot on the RN14 in a southwesterly direction. 13km further on, turn left onto a track near a petrol station.

■ **Tur★**, inhabited by some 400 E De, is clearly a peaceful, prosperous village. Between two and three families live in each of the **longhouses★** on stilts, built around a grassy open space, where coffee and corn are dried. The villagers are Protestant, but in the absence of a church, meet in their homes to pray.

Go back onto the RN14 for 7km. Turn left on leaving Cu Dut and continue for 5km.

■ A few kilometres after meeting up with each other, the Krong Ana and Kno ("female and male rivers") plunge down a 15m-high rocky cliff face over 100m-wide. A stairway leads down to the river and **Dray Sap Falls★★** (*entrance fee*). You will then have to clamber over the rocky river-bed until you reach the foot of the falls (*flip-flops or similar are advisable*). The suspension bridge which leads to the larger falls is unfortunately not in use.

Lake Lak★★★

56km south of Buon Ma Thuot along the RN27. Nestling at the bottom of a wide crater bordered by extinct volcanoes, Lake Lak is one of the province's most beautiful natural attractions. It is in this superb setting, on a tiny peninsula of bamboo groves, that 400 M'nong live in the delightful **village of Jun★★**. Since the "outbreak" of tourism in 1995, the **longhouses** on stilts have not changed, neither has the population given up its traditional way of life, but a number of souvenir shops have sprung up and Dak Lak Tourist has a little branch here which manages two houses open to visitors. In short, the village has become something of a museum.

Funereal sculpture in Buon Don village

G Guérard

If you have time, go for an elephant ride (*relatively expensive; book the day before*) or a boat trip to the **village of M'lieng★** on the northern shore (*permit essential*).

Emperor Bao Dai, who invariably picked the choicest sites, had a **residence** built on a nearby hill, with a superb **view** of the lake.

Yok Don National Park★★

42km northwest of Buon Ma Thuot. Access by bus or motorcycle. Entrance charge. This 58 000ha **nature reserve** is home to over 60 species of mammal (tigers, leopards and bears), nearly 200 species of bird (peacocks and hornbills) and some 46 different types of reptile. The best way of exploring the park is to spend the night here and go down the river by canoe, take an elephant ride or a one- or two-day trek organised by the park rangers (*see page 324*).

Return to the main road. 4km beyond the park, turn left onto a track indicated by a colourful gateway and continue straight on for 3km.

Buon Don*, (*entrance fee*) the capital of Vietnam's elephant breeding industry, is now run by Buon Don Tourist which puts on traditional shows and can arrange accommodation in the village. Although somewhat lacking in character, the village is nonetheless well worth visiting if you take the time to wander about and chat to the villagers. Buon Don is a multi-ethnic conglomeration of hamlets scattered along the Serepok, inhabited by the E De, Lao, Gia Rai and M'nong. They are extremely proud of their ancestral tradition of capturing and rearing elephants and this liveli-hood coexists side by side with agriculture (banana, manioc and papaya). It is however rare to catch a glimpse of these enormous pachyderms who consume vast quantities of grass and thus spend most of their time in remote pastures. On the way into the village, notice the surprising **bamboo bridge** (*charge*) which seems to dis-appear into the boughs of a gigantic tree overhanging the river.

Back on the main road, take the first left, then left again onto a track, at a bend 2km further on.

There are legends galore concerning the exploits of elephant hunters, and in particu-lar those of Y Pui Ne, who is said to have died at the age of 124 after having captured 300 elephants. On the outskirts of the village, his **tomb** lies in the **cemetery*** in the company of the **stupa** of his nephew, another legendary hunter. All around, other burial places decorated with wooden carvings of peacocks and buffalo horns are slowly falling into disrepair.

From Buon Ma Thuot to Plei Ku★★
At midday this road, which passes through a hilly landscape of rubber and coffee plantations and pine groves, is invariably packed with hordes of schoolchildren on foot or bicycle and peasants perched on top of carts pulled by little tractors. Shortly before reaching Plei Ku, the **Ta Grong Pass** (950m) reveals a superb **bird's eye view*** of the town.

Plei Ku and its surroundings
Capital of the province of Gia Lai. Pop 40 000. Alt 785m.
190km from Buan Ma Thuot, 186km from Qui Nhon. Allow 1 day.

If you found yourself indifferent to Buon Ma Thuot's charms, it is most unlikely that you will fall head over heels in love with Plei Ku's ugly concrete architecture. The town developed during the war when American bases were set up here and when villagers from the surrounding countryside fled the bombing. The climate is however pleasant and Plei Ku makes a good starting point for visits to the outlying Gia Rai and Ba Na villages. Once again, bear in mind that such visits are subject to the agree-ment of the local tourist office and while the prospect of a compulsory guide may seem irksome, it does have the advantage of making communication and under-standing a great deal easier.

The **Ethnographic Museum of the Gia Lai** (*28 Quang Trung, ☎ (059) 82 45 20. Opening hours variable. Entrance charge*) is, on the whole, disappointing and it could definitely do with a share of the profits made from the tourist industry to enlarge its collections and renovate its rooms. Apart from a very old **Dong Son drum**, it features costumes, basketwork and Gia Rai gongs, as well as the reproduction of a tomb.

The Highlands

Excursion to a Ba Na village*

East of Plei Ku, the Qui Nhon road (RN19) takes you through the province's "rice bowl". In addition to irrigated rice paddies, which are harvested three times a year, tea, rubber and coffee are also grown on this 10 000ha plain. Higher up though, the dry fields only produce one harvest a year, but of better quality.

On the banks of a fast-flowing stream, the **village of Dek Tu** (*38km from Plei Ku*) possesses a superb thatched roof **communal house★★★**, flanked by the traditional **pole** used during the sacrifice of buffalo. The village's main attraction however is its unusual **cemetery★★**. Ba Na tombs resemble little huts with corrugated iron or bamboo roofs and surrounded by flowers. A ladder enables the deceased to climb up to the land of his ancestors. Among the Ba Na, the largest ethnic minority in the Highlands, maternal lineage remains dominant, but this is beginning to break down and thus the social status of men is advancing. Class divisions are also well defined in this society. Practitioners of slash-and-burn farming techniques, they used to move their village every four or five years in search of more fertile soil. French colonisation and the spread of crops grown in flooded fields however meant that the majority have now settled in one place. Renowned horticulturists, the Ba Na also enjoy a high reputation as singers, dancers and musicians.

Before descending to the coast, the RN19 goes over the An Khe Pass, from where there is a superb panoramic view as far as the sea on a clear day.

Excursion to a Gia Rai village★★

Take the RN14 towards Kon Tum. 8km to the north of Plei Ku, turn right once past the military camp.

Dominated by the imposing outline of the **Truong Son Cordillera**, **T'nung Lake★★** (Bien Ho) (*entrance fee*) lies in the crater of an extinct volcano. Between 30 and 40m deep, the lake is the town's main source of fresh water.

Perched on a little outcrop overlooking a pretty plain of rice fields some 30km to the north of Plei Ku, **Plei Fun★** has retained its traditional dwellings, including the handsome thatched-roof **rong** (communal house). The **cemetery★★** on the outskirts of the village provides a fascinating insight into the Gia Rai's spiritual universe. It houses several collective tombs complete with tiled roofs, railings and vases with food for the deceased. The "abandonment" of a tomb is an important ceremony, extending over several days of feasting and involving the sacrifice of buffalo. During it, objects belonging to the deceased are brought to the tomb together with wooden statues, some of which are most unusual. After the ceremony, the tomb is no longer cared for, because the deceased's soul has left it for the other world.

Kon Tum and its surroundings★★

Capital of the province of Kon Tum. Pop 40 000.
49km from Plei Ku. Alt 530m. Allow 2 days.

Kon Tum is the first town that a visitor to the Highlands might find appealing. It is a fair-sized place, well-located on the banks of the River Dakbla, in the middle of a vast natural amphitheatre and benefits from a particularly mild climate. Peaceful and mysterious, it seems far from the rest of the world, not least because the ancient way of life led in the villages can be felt in the town itself. Those with a little time on their hands will not regret venturing further afield and exploring the more remote parts of this area on foot.

Christian influences

In 1851, the arrival of **Father Dourisboure** in the area was a watershed in the history of Kon Tum, which began to flourish with the setting up of a Catholic mission. During the second half of the 19C, the missionaries reinforced their control with the occasional help of the French army, until the colonial administration officially drew up new frontiers (1905). The Ba Na were converted in order to provide the French with a buffer against the other minorities. Significantly, the Bible was translated and a dictionary created, both of which were greatly instrumental in furthering the cultural inroads made by this new religion. Today the majority of the Ba Na are Christian, with the exception of isolated hamlets along the Cambodian and Laotian borders. There are 650 villages in the province, only 200 of which still have a *rong*. Among the eleven ethnic groups which make up half the total population of 300 000, the most numerous are the Sedang (70 000), the Ba Na (28 000), the

Gia Rai (12 000), the Gie Treng, while the Brau (250) and the Ro Mam (280) are among the country's smallest ethnic minorities.

The **bridge** spanning the Dakbla provides a wonderful view of the sunset at dusk, as the sun turns the mountain peaks a fiery red and bathes the plain in a flood of orange light.

From the bridge, turn right onto Nguyen Hue and continue as far as the corner with Tran Phu where you see **Tan Huong Church**, with its handsome white façade illustrating **St George slaying the dragon**.

Further down the same street, you suddenly catch sight of the high roof of a **traditional house** which stands in front of a **wooden church★★** (*services at 5.30am during the week, and at 8am and 5pm on Sundays*). Built in 1913 in memory of St Cuenot, the first missionary, the church has remained full of character, despite having been partially rebuilt in concrete. The pillars and structure are original, however, as are the superbly carved **door** and the colourful **stained-glass windows** in the nave. Before leaving, take a look at the **orphanage** next door where six nuns care for 200 children.

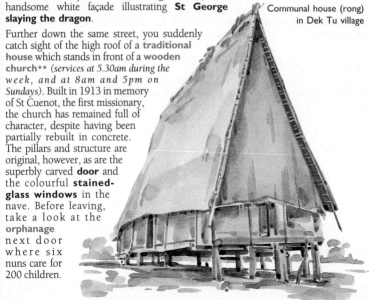

Communal house (rong) in Dek Tu village

G de Benoist/MICHELIN

The surrounding Ba Na villages**

The ancient village of **Plei Tonghia***, near an ugly sugar refinery on the western out-skirts of Kon Tun, is made up of spacious stilt houses with tiled roofs. Its future is however uncertain because the planned construction of Yaly Dam will flood all the sugar cane plantations, thus destroying the village's main source of income.

At **Kon Robang*** (*2km west of Kon Tum*) stands the whitewashed **longhouse*** of the former E De head of all the Highland minority tribes.

In the eastern suburbs of the town, Tran Hung Dao takes you through the villages of Kon Tum Kopong and Kon Tum Konam, and then alongside a river as far as the **Kon Klor suspension bridge** (*3km*), close to which there is a magnificent **rong****. Cross over to the opposite bank, accessible since the bridge was built in the mid-1990s, and go down the track on the left for a few hundred metres to **Kon Jri** (*3km; on foot or by motorcycle*). The village was the scene of one of the most farcical episodes in the history of French colonisation (*see insert*).

Kon Kotu** (*3km*) stands by the riverside in a magnificent wooded setting. It is possible to stay overnight in the *rong* in the middle of the village, a unique opportu-nity to experience the way of life of the Ba Na at close quarters (*information from Kon Tum Tourist*).

Mayréna, the man who wanted to be king

Marie-David de Mayréna (1842-90) may have been a false baron but he was a genuinely unscrupulous adventurer who had to leave France following du-bious stock exchange dealings. He ended up in Saigon in 1888 and, in exchange for exploring the Sedang region, was awarded the concession of any gold mines he discovered. Once on the spot, he made an amazing announcement. After gathering all the tribal leaders together, he had himself crowned King Marie 1st, adopted a constitution, a flag, a national anthem, a Sedang order of merit, and moved into a bamboo palace. A few months later, he paid a visit to the colonial administration and then to the British in Hong Kong, in search of recognition which was refused. Back in Paris, he managed to persuade a Belgian industrialist to finance an expedition, but he was forbidden entry into Indochina and had to seek refuge in the Malaysian island of Tioman, where he died after a hunting accident.

The Sedang region

To the north of Kon Tum, the Dak To Road, which was of major strategic importance during the war, crosses the **Skull Pass**, so dubbed after a Viet Cong attack in 1972. After weeks of heavy fighting, the South Vietnamese army man-aged to regain control of the outpost only to discover that it was full of the rotting corpses of their comrades.

The main square of **Dak To** (*42km from Kon Tum*), with its memorial and two army tanks, is a reminder of the terrible toll of this conflict. In 1966, the South Vietnamese set up an outpost on **Hill 42***, 6km to the north of the town. A runway, today used by the peasants for drying rice, was built by the Americans to cover the infamous Charlie Hill, the key to the region. The capture of this position by the Viet Cong in March 1972 led to the fall of Dak To. In the absence of any memorial, half-buried remnants, such as empty cartridges, barbed wire or fragments of mosquito nets and tents are a poignant reminder of the many lives lost.

A **bamboo suspension bridge*** at the dizzy height of 140m leads to **Dak Ri Jop** (*8km to the east of Dak To*), on the other side of the river. In the centre of the village stands a remarkable **communal house***, which still bears unexpected traces of the war, such as the marks of bombshells or American helmets turned into flower pots. Christianised Animists, the Sedang live in great poverty and only very rarely see tourists, whom they welcome timidly but warmly. From here, it is possible to either walk or drive to **Dak Ri Peng**.

A permit and a guide are required to visit the **village of the Ro Mam** and the **Ho Chi Minh Trail** (*near Ngoc Hoi, 18km from Dak To*).

To the north, the Da Nang road *(318km)* takes you past some of the most stunning scenery in the Highlands, but it is only accessible by jeep or motorcycle.

The Gia Rai villages and the Ciu Mum Ray Nature Reserve**

30km to the west of Kon Tum, beyond Lake Yaly, take the track on the left on the far side of Sa Thay and continue for 5km.

Nestling at the foot of Mt Ciu Mum Ray in the midst of a breathtaking mountain valley, **Plei Chot**** *(435 inhab)* offers an intriguing introduction into the Gia Rai culture, as yet almost untouched by tourism. Their economy is based on hunting, pig and poultry farming and agriculture (rice, sugar cane and cassava), but the Gia Rai are also exceptionally talented weavers and basket makers. As is the case among all the other minority tribes in the area, feasts are major events, and take place, for example, prior to the building of a bamboo and mud house. They involve divinatory rites carried out to determine the ideal position of the house, and the ceremony is concluded by the legendary "passing of the river". This actually refers to a ritual whereby rice alcohol contained in a jar is drunk through a straw until the bamboo stick placed crosswise inside, emerges.

Well-situated on the path to the river and the fields, to ensure that the deceased are never forgotten, the **cemetery***** has numerous wooden statues put in place during the ceremony of the abandonment of the tomb. Among the themes represented are elephant tusks to ward off evil spirits, pregnant women as a sign of fertility or death in childbirth, together with rather strange figures representing French Field Marshal Leclerc or Joan of Arc.

If you would like to climb **Mt Ciu Mum Ray**, which is in the heart of the **forest reserve***** of the same name, enquire at Kon Tum Tourist which organises walks.

Buon Ma Thuot close up

The legislation relating to permits is different in each province, Kon Tum being the most flexible. In practice, it is not very difficult to get to the ethnic minority villages under one's own steam even without this magic card, but what is not so clear is what the penalties are if one is caught without a permit.

COMING AND GOING

By air – The **airport** lies 7km to the south of the town, on the RN27 towards Dalat, ☎ (050) 86 22 48. Vietnam Airlines operate several weekly flights to Ho Chi Minh City (1hr), Da Nang (1hr 10min) and Hanoi (with a change of flights).

By coach and bus – The **terminal** is at 71 Nguyen Tat Thanh, 3km to the north of the town centre, towards Plei Ku. Many regular buses and three express air-conditioned coaches leave between 7am and 9am to Nha Trang (190km, 4hr journey); three coaches leave daily to Plei Ku (198km, 4hr);

three coaches leave daily between 6am and 10am, depending on the state of the road to Dalat (220km, 6hr), otherwise you will have to travel via Nha Trang; three express coaches leave daily between 6am and 3pm to Ho Chi Minh City and Mien Dong terminal.

By car or motorcycle – A jeep, or even better a motorcycle, are the best means of transport to get to and from Dalat along the RN27, but make sure you fill up with petrol before starting out. The roads to Buon Ma Thuot, Nha Trang and Ho Chi Minh City are all in reasonable condition.

GETTING AROUND

By bus – Two buses leave for Lake Lak around 7am (1hr trip), and Buon Don (1hr), at 7am and 2pm, but neither is very comfortable.

Motorcycle rentals – In the absence of an official rental company, it is always easy to rent a motorcycle taxi; allow between US\$5 and US\$8 per day.

ADDRESS BOOK

Tourist information office – Dak Lak Tourist, 3 Phan Chu Trinh, near Thang Loi Hotel, ☎ (050) 85 21 08, Fax (050) 85 28 65. Daily 7am-5pm. The official agency of the province requires a compulsory permit (US$5) and a local guide (US$15) for visits to the Lak, Mlieng and Tur villages. In practice though, such permits are not always checked. The agency also organises elephant rides and canoe outings, but at exorbitant prices. You can also contact the branch in the village of Jun, ☎ (050) 88 61 84, Fax (050) 81 09 26.

Banmeco (Buon Don Tourist), village of Buon Don, ☎ (050) 78 91 19. The agency organises elephant rides and can arrange accommodation in the village.

Yok Don National Park, ☎ (050) 78 91 49, Fax (050) 78 91 22. The park's tourist office organises elephant rides at cheaper rates than Dak Lak Tourist, as well as canoe outings and forest treks with overnight accommodation in a tent or bungalow.

Bank / Currency exchange – A Chau, 60-62 Le Hong Phong. The ASEAN Commercial Bank accepts dollars, travellers' cheques and cash withdrawals with a credit card.

Vietcombank, 121-123 Y Jut. Travellers' cheques and credit cards accepted.

Post office / Telephone – Buu Dien Buan Ma Thuot, 6 Le Duan. Daily 6.30am-9pm. Another branch is also open on Ama Trang Long, near the main square.

Internet – Buu Dien, 6 Le Duan. Daily 7am-8pm. Prices vary depending on the time of day, but remain reasonable.

Airlines – Vietnam Airlines, 67 Nguyen Tat Thanh, ☎ and Fax (050) 85 74 42 / 95 50 55, Fax (050) 86 20 86.

WHERE TO STAY

Book your hotel in advance if you intend to stay during the festival season in March.

Under US$10

Thanh Phat, 41 Ly Thuong Kiet, ☎ (050) 85 48 57, Fax (050) 81 33 66 – 6rm ⌃ ▤ ✈ This recent, reasonably priced establishment is the only one of its category to provide a decent level of comfort. The least expensive rooms don't have a private bathroom. The staff's English is somewhat faltering, so you'll be able to try out your Vietnamese.

Birdnet Chuong Chim, Yok Don Park, ☎ (050) 78 91 49, Fax (050) 78 91 22 – 6rm ⌃ ✈ The park's guesthouse rents comfortable, if basic rooms, in a wooden building on stilts which can get rather stale-smelling. During the dry season, opt for the little bungalows overlooking the river. Bookings necessary, if only to be sure of a meal.

Between US$10 and US$15

Hotel Hong Kong, 35 Hai Ba Trung, ☎ (050) 85 26 30 – 11rm ⌃ ▤ ✈ ✂ TV Even though this hotel's personnel is somewhat depressing and the rooms are noisy and of dubious cleanliness, it remains one of the cheapest places in town. Bargaining permissible.

Hai Ba Trung, 8 Hai Ba Trung, ☎ (050) 85 24 07, Fax (050) 85 31 13 – 21rm ⌃ ▤ ✈ TV ✗ This austere and overrated State-owned hotel has rooms of very varying quality, but rates can be negotiated.

Between US$15 and US$30

Biet Dien, 12 Le Duan, near the post office, ☎ (050) 85 04 87 – 21rm ⌃ ▤ TV Set in a garden near the museum, the rooms of this hotel have definitely seen better days. A pity, because they would be quite stylish otherwise.

Tay Nguyen, 110 Ly Thuong Kiet, ☎ (050) 85 10 09, Fax (050) 85 22 50 – 31rm ⌃ ▤ ✂ TV ✗ Breakfast included. This very comfortable hotel is relatively expensive, but represents quite good value for money for the town. The rooms in the new building are the most attractive, most of the others being windowless.

Agribank Hotel, 111 Le Hong Phong, ☎ (050) 85 78 28, Fax (050) 85 13 38 – 12rm ⌃ ▤ ✈ ✂ TV These stark, tasteless rooms are nothing to write home about, even if they are quite comfortable. The rates are however exorbitant, but you can always try and negotiate.

Between US$30 and US$50

Bach Ma-White Horse, 50-54 Hai Ba Trung, ☎ (050) 85 39 63 / 85 03 79, Fax (050) 85 21 21 – 22rm ◫▤ ♪ ▣ ✕ cc A three-storey hotel whose very commonplace rooms are nonetheless impeccable and comfortable (satellite TV). The roof terrace affords a fine view of the town.

Thang Loi, 1 Phan Chu Trinh, ☎ (050) 85 76 15, Fax (050) 85 76 22 – 40rm ◫▤ ♪ ▣ ✕ ⏚ ⚐ ♨ ✽ ★ cc Breakfast included. A bell-boy in full-scale naval dress welcomes guests and the hotel has spacious, pleasant rooms. The rates vary significantly depending on the floor.

EATING OUT

Under 25 000VND

Tan Lac Vien, 61 Ly Thuong Kiet. This clean, bustling establishment is perfect for breakfast in the company of locals.

Thanh Tram, 22 Ly Thuong Kiet. One of the many restaurants on the street, this one serves simple, but tasty Vietnamese dishes.

Between 25 000 and 50 000VND

White Horse, 50-54 Hai Ba Trung. The large dining room is not very typical, but the restaurant serves good Vietnamese and Western dishes and seafood. Ask for the menu in English with the prices.

GOING OUT

Cafés, tea rooms – Ama Trang Long is the busiest street in town come nightfall and perfect for a drink in the company of the town's lively population.

Banh Mi Ha Noi, 123-125 Le Hong Phong. Wide choice of local cakes and pastries.

OTHER THINGS TO DO

Feasts and festivals – The **Spring Festival** takes place over 2-3 months, from the 10th-11th to the 1st-2nd lunar months, before the harvest. Buffalo are sacrificed in honour of the village spirits and a number of ceremonies relating to the abandoning the tomb ceremony give rise to singing and dancing to the beat of gongs.

Elephant races are organised in the Buon Don village stadium in the 3rd lunar month (early March), during the Minority Festivals.

Motorcycle races – The motorcycle races held on Sundays in the stadium on Le Loi are one of the few attractions of Buon Ma Thuot.

Plei Ku close up

COMING AND GOING

By air – The **airport** lies 7km north of the town, ☎ (059) 82 30 58. Vietnam Airlines operates flights to Ho Chi Minh City (70min), Da Nang (50min) and Hanoi (with a stopover).

By bus – The **bus terminal** is on the eastern outskirts of the town, on the Qui Nhon Road. An express air-conditioned bus leaves at 5pm for Ho Chi Minh City (12hr). Other buses go to Buon Ma Thuot (198km, 5hr) and Qui Nhon (186km, 4hr 30min).

By mini-bus – Mini-buses are generally quicker but not as comfortable. Departures for Buon Ma Thuot (5hr) and Qui Nhon (4hr) leave every 30min, from 6am to 5pm, in front of the terminal and near to Gia Lai Tourist. Frequent services to Kon Tum (1hr) on Le Loi, 100m north of Plei Ku Hotel.

GETTING AROUND

By taxi – **Plei Ku Taxi**, ☎ (059) 99 99 99.

Vehicle rentals – Gia Lai Tourist rents cars with a chauffeur, and some hotels also offer this service (allow US$40 per day for 100km). Motorcycle taxis are readily available (allow US$6 per day).

ADDRESS BOOK

Tourist information – **Gia Lai Tourist Travel Service**, 215 Hung Vuong, ☎ and Fax (059) 82 48 91. Monday-Friday 7.30-11am / 1.30-

4.30pm, Saturday mornings. The province's agency organises trips of between one and several days to the Ba Na villages with excellent English-speaking guides, but they are quite expensive. Individual tourists also have to take a guide (US$12 per day) and a permit for each village (US$ 10).

Bank / Currency exchange – Vietcombank, 12 Tran Hung Dao. Monday-Friday 7.30-11.30am / 1-4.30pm. Travellers' cheques in dollars and credit cards are accepted.

Post office / Telephone – Buu Dien Plei Ku, 87 Hung Vuong, corner of Tran Hung Dao. Daily 6am-10pm.

Internet – Tienviet Computer, 29 Le Lai. Daily 7am-9pm. Allow 350VND / min.

Airline companies – Vietnam Airlines, 55 Quang Trung, near the stadium, ☎ (059) 82 30 58, Fax (059) 82 30 58. Daily 7.30-11am / 1.30-4.30pm.

WHERE TO STAY

Between US$15 and US$30
Than Lich Hotel, 86 Nguyen Van Troi, corner of Phan Boi Chau, ☎ (059) 82 46 74, Fax (059) 82 83 19 – 19rm 📶 🍽 🍴 ♒ 📺 ✗ 🆑 This hotel, which could definitely do with a fresh coat of paint, provides rooms the comfort and price of which vary immensely from one room to the next, from very cheap and basic to clean and cold but expensive.

Vinh Hoi, 39 Tran Phu, ☎ (059) 82 46 44, Fax (059) 87 16 37 – 30rm 📶 🍽 🍴 ♒ 📺 It is difficult to know in which category to put this hotel as the prices of the rooms vary so enormously. The most comfortable rooms are in the new building and those with a private bathroom upstairs offer the best value for money in town.

Hung Vuong Hotel, 215 Hung Vuong, ☎ (059) 82 42 70, Fax (059) 82 71 70 – 31rm 📶 🍽 ♒ 📺 The price of these rooms can double depending on whether you are in the cold, clean, new wing or in the noisy, clean, old one.

Dien Anh-Movie Star Hotel, 6 Vo Thi Sau, ☎ (059) 82 38 55, Fax (059) 82 37 00 – 19rm 📶 🍽 🍴 ♒ 📺 The dreadful linoleum floors and Swiss chalet-style wallpaper are more reminiscent of Soviet austerity than the glitter of Hollywood. The prices are exorbitant given the quality, with the exception of the non air-conditioned rooms.

Yali Hotel, 89 Hung Vuong, ☎ (059) 82 48 43, Fax (059) 82 76 19 – 50rm 📶 🍽 ♒ 📺 This five-storey building provides comfortable rooms the prices of which can double depending on the season (satellite TV).

EATING OUT

Under 25 000VND
My Tam, 3 Quang Trung. 10am-10pm. This basic, very popular restaurant serves the best roast chicken in the area.

GOING OUT

Nightclubs, karaoke – Tre Xanh, 18 Le Lai. Plei Ku is not famous for its nightlife, but you can have a drink in this former cinema complete with fairy lights.

Kon Tum close up

COMING AND GOING

By bus – The **terminal** at the foot of Dakbla2 Hotel is planned to move 2km to the north of the town, on Dak To Road. Buses leave every 30min for Plei Ku (1hr), between 7am and 6pm. Buses to the outlying districts (Sa Thay, Dak To) leave around 5am, followed by other departures between 6am and 7am for longer journeys (Ho Chi Minh City, Hanoi, Buon Ma Thuot, Qui Nhon and Nha Trang).

GETTING AROUND

Bicycle and motorcycle rentals – Ask at Kon Tum Tourist, the hotels or at Dakbla's Restaurant. It is also possible to rent a motorcycle taxi by the hour or the day.

Car rentals – Kon Tum Tourist rents cars, Russian jeeps (US$60 / day) and 4WD vehicles (US$65 / day) with chauffeur. The prices are high, but you can negotiate.

Tourist information – *Kon Tum Tourist*, 2 Phan Dinh Phung, Dakbla Hotel, ☎ (060) 86 16 26, Fax (060) 86 33 36. Monday-Friday 7-11am / 1-5pm, Saturday mornings. The agency does not insist on visitors having permits for the villages around Kon Tum. A guide is however required for the more remote villages, but they are all very pleasant and competent (English-speaking) and definitely enhance the understanding and pleasure of a visit. Trips down the River Dakbla and one- or several-day treks are also organised with the possibility of sleeping in a traditional house. The Brau and Ro Mam villages and Ben Het battlefield are the only places for which a permit is compulsory.

Bank / Currency exchange – *Agriculture Bank*, on the corner of Tran Phu and Phan Chu Trinh. Monday-Friday 7-11am / 1-5pm.

Post office / Telephone – *Buu Dien Kon Tum*, 205 Le Hong Phong. Daily 7am-10pm.

WHERE TO STAY

It is possible to find decent, comfortable hotels at reasonable prices in Kon Tum. If tourism continues to develop and the guesthouses on Le Hong Phong improve a little, it may well become a backpacker's paradise.

Under US$10

Hotel 37, 71 Le Hong Phong, ☎ (060) 86 31 82 – 6rm ✕ This very cheap guesthouse is open to foreigners who are not fussy about their comfort. The rooms are wooden, windowless boxes furnished with a bed and a fan.

Binh Dan, 28B Le Hong Phong, ☎ (060) 86 16 65 – 10rm ✕ Much the same as the above.

Between US$10 and US$15

Dakbla 2, 163 Nguyen Hue, ☎ (060) 86 33 35, Fax (060) 86 33 36 – 15rm ☏ 📺 ✕ 📺 This hotel is situated on the way into town, on the left near the bridge and the bus terminus, which makes for a noisy early-morning start to the day. It enjoys an unparalleled view of the river and is basic, but acceptable.

Between US$15 and US$30

Quang Trung, 168 Ba Trieu, ☎ (060) 86 22 49 – 30rm ☏ 📺 ✕ 🛁 📺 On the northern outskirts of town, this well-equipped establishment provides pleasant, if slightly overrated rooms (with the exception of those with a fan).

Dakbla I, 2 Phan Dinh Phung, ☎ (060) 86 33 33, Fax (060) 86 33 36 – 43rm ☏ 📺 🛁 📺 ✕ This modern building can be found on the way into town, on the right near the bridge. The rooms are rather stark but comfortable and well-kept (satellite TV).

EATING OUT

Between 25 000 and 50 000VND

Hiep Thanh, 129 Nguyen Hue. Soups, seafood and Western dishes served in a pleasant, well-ventilated room. Beware of the menu without prices.

Between 50 000 and 100 000VND

Dakbla's Restaurant, 168 Nguyen Hue. 6am-10pm. The friendliest place in town serves delicious Western and Vietnamese cuisine, as well as excellent breakfasts. Menu in English. The restaurant also sells good quality local crafts.

Dakbla I, 2 Phan Dinh Phung. Located in a rustic cabin with a wonderful view of the river, this restaurant offers a good choice of Western, Vietnamese and seafood dishes. It is also a good place for a drink while watching the sunset.

OTHER THINGS TO DO

Feasts and festivals – Among the Ba Na, the **Earth Ceremony** (Cung Dat Lang) is held at the end of the 2nd lunar month and the beginning of the next, in preparation for the harvest or the moving of the village. To spend **Christmas** and **Easter** among these far-off Christians is also an unforgettable experience. Services are held in the wooden church in Vietnamese, Gia Rai, Ba Na and Sedang. A fine example of ecumenism if ever there was one.

Kon Tum close up

Colours of the Mekong

THE SOUTH

From the vast and fertile rice paddies of the Mekong Delta to the effervescent life on the swarming streets of Ho Chi Minh City, southern Vietnam seems to revel in abundance and extravagance. But Nature's prodigality comes at a price – a pullulating, needy population seeking sustenance from the land or crowding into the towns. Cholon Market, the luxuriant Delta, the beaches of the South China Sea, the faded reminders of French colonial days, all provide the traveller with a wealth of conventional images of the exotic Orient. But with time, the sepia-tinted past gives way to sharper, more up-to-date perceptions of a young country under construction, energetically emerging into the present. In contrast to North Vietnam, steeped in Chinese culture for almost a thousand years, the South grew up with art and religion from the Indianised Kingdom of Funan with further influences from the sophisticated Khmer Kingdoms of Angkor. So strongly have barely three centuries of the Vietnamese presence made themselves felt that this foundation is barely visible. Nevertheless, the South retains its very distinct identity. The all-year-round heat and humidity cannot be held solely responsible for this, any more than the hazards of the country's recent history, which all contributed to Saigon's transformation into a workshop for primitive capitalism while Hanoi chose to practise a particularly hardline version of communism. There seems something irrevocably Latin about the South's ability to wheel and deal, and its traditional defiance of government. On the edge of the Mekong Delta and still Saigon to its inhabitants, Ho Chi Minh City remains an extraordinary hive of activity, a permanent stage for the human drama.

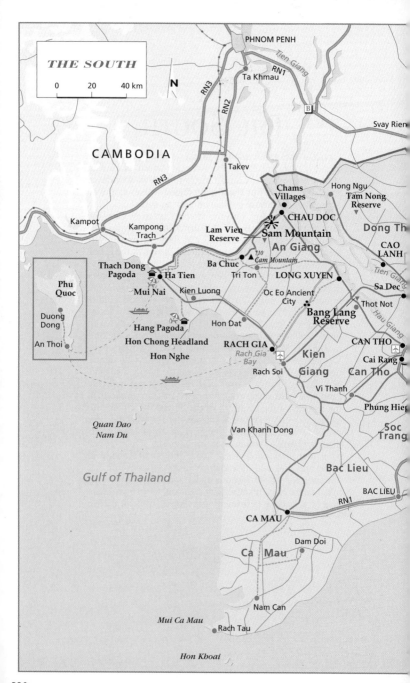

THE SOUTH

0   20   40 km

N

PHNOM PENH

Tien Giang

RN1

Ta Khmau

RN3

RN2

B]

Svay Rien

CAMBODIA

Takev

Chams
Villages

Hong Ngu

Tam Nong
Reserve

CHAU DOC

Dong Th

Kampot

Kampong
Trach

Lam Vien
Reserve

Sam Mountain

An Giang

CAO
LANH

Thach Dong
Pagoda

Ha Tien

Ba Chuc

710
Cam Mountain

Tri Ton

LONG XUYEN

Tien Giang

Sa Dec

Mui Nai

Kien Luong

Oc Eo Ancient
City

Bang Lang
Reserve

Thot Not

Hau Giang

Phu
Quoc

Hon Dat

CAN THO

Can Tho

Duong
Dong

Hang Pagoda
Hon Chong Headland

RACH GIA

Rach Gia
Bay

Kien

Cai Rang

An Thoi

Hon Nghe

Rach Soi

Giang

Vi Thanh

Phung Hiep

Quan Dao
Nam Du

Van Khanh Dong

Soc
Trang

Gulf of Thailand

Bac Lieu

BAC LIEU

RN1

CA MAU

Dam Doi

Ca   Mau

Mui Ca Mau

Nam Can

Rach Tau

Hon Khoai

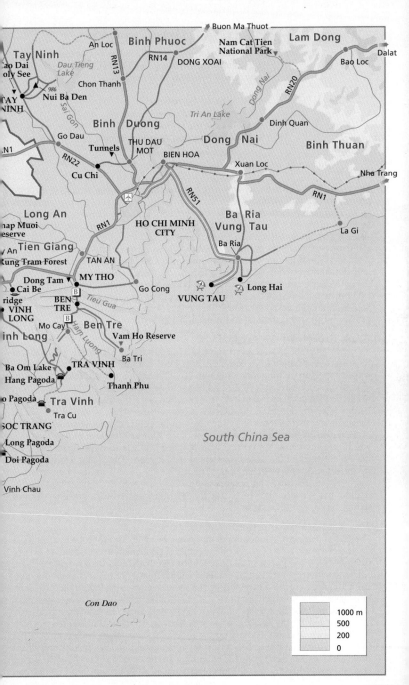

HO CHI MINH CITY ★★

Province of Ho Chi Minh City – Pop 7 million (built-up area)
1 730km from Hanoi – Plans pages 340-341
Rainy season from May to November

Not to be missed
A stroll in the old colonial area,
and a boat trip on the river.
The museums and pagodas. A walk in Cholon.

And remember...
On foot or on a motorcycle, always beware of the anarchic traffic.

The names Ho Chi Minh City and Saigon both conjure up different sides of the split personality of South Vietnam's legendary metropolis. Each facet of the city represents an epochal reality, from the pagodas and temples of timeless Vietnam to the elegant buildings of the French colonial era. Yet for present-day inhabitants, the city is above all a spirited metropolis with an eye to the future, and even if high-rise buildings are still quite rare, wealth is displayed unashamedly in exclusive city-centre stores, light years away from the impoverished suburbs. Ho Chi Minh City reveals itself in all kinds of ways; in the busy markets where all the riches of the Mekong Delta seem to be on display; in the streets filled with buzzing two-wheelers bearing improbable loads or ridden by elegant young ladies in traditional tunics; in its variety shows, billiard halls and karaoke bars, where the people of Saigon can give free rein to their passion for singing, gambling and general joie de vivre.

From Prei Nokor to Angkor

Before history books were even thought of, a thick forest covered the banks of Saigon's river, where a few aboriginal tribes lived from fishing and hunting. In the wake of the **Khmer Kingdom of Funan** (1C), the region of **Prei Nokor** ("Country of the Forest") finally came to life and began to develop thanks to the cultivation of rice in flooded fields and, above all, to its location along the trade routes with China. Earth walls were erected to thwart any Cham attacks. The collapse of the Funan Kingdom and its replacement by the Chen La in the 7C did not upset the stability of the region, in contrast to the emergence of the **Khmer Kingdom of Angkor** (9C), which threw the area into turmoil with repeated conflicts with the Cham and then the Tai. Situated on the eastern borders of the kingdom, Prei Nokor was unaffected by the troubles, and was able to prosper at a steady pace. It had been extended to ward off pirate attacks and comprised 14 villages, but in 1620, after centuries of decline, the Khmers resolved to ask the **Vietnamese** for help, granting them in return the right to settle here.

The Vietnamese and the French

The Vietnamese were the new lords of the manor, in an area they knew as Sai Gon ("forest of kapok"). They gave Chinese refugees permission to set up the market of Cholon (1683) and built a small citadel called **Gia Dinh**. After the Tay Son rebellion, led by two brothers who had controlled the town from 1777 to 1788, the future Emperor Gia Long erected a huge fort on the site of today's cathedral. In the shape of a lotus flower, the building became the administrative centre for the whole of Southern Vietnam. It was demolished and then rebuilt on a smaller scale following the peasant revolt led by the nobleman Le Van Khoi in 1835. On 10 February 1859, 2 000 **French** soldiers advanced up the river in eight warships, took control of the fort in just a few days and then fought off a Vietnamese counter-attack on elephant back. The Vietnamese responded by burning all the city's rice stocks before fleeing en masse, leaving only 25 000 inhabitants out of the previous 200 000. **Saigon**

The South

became the capital of the colony of Cochinchina and was adorned with new buildings (Post Office, Governor's Palace, arsenal, cathedral) hotels and elegant villas, but this "golden age" did little to improve the fortunes of the local population.

A city at war

After the Japanese occupation during the Second World War, the city passed briefly into the hands of the British, who in turn passed it on to the French in September 1945. This marked the beginning of the Indochina War, which ended in 1954 with the division of the country. Saigon became the capital of South Vietnam, and the city saw the

Saigon's final hours

On 29 April 1975, a wave of panic spread throughout Saigon, as their one and only army division awaited imminent attack from 12 North Vietnamese divisions. For several weeks the Americans had been evacuating their nationals as well as the first of 20 000 Vietnamese "at risk", and had been busy destroying official documents. Washington decided to launch Operation "Frequent Wind" with the radio broadcast of the song "White Christmas" giving the signal for the remaining 1 250 Americans to go to their evacuation points. For 18 hours, 70 helicopters shuttled frantically between the ships of the Seventh fleet and the roofs of 13 designated buildings. Almost 6 000 Vietnamese were pulled out amid indescribable chaos, but thousands of others, abandoned by their allies, were left to fend for themselves. Pictures of these tragic moments were shown around the world, a symbol of the collapse of American power. "It was one of the saddest days of my life", declared President Gerald Ford.

arrival of hundreds of thousands of Catholics from the northern part of the country. One of the first moves made by President **Diem** was to bring the powerful militias to heel, notably the Ginh Xuyen gang who controlled racketeering and prostitution. The ensuing devastation was considerable, particularly in Cholon, and repressive measures were extended to all opponents, even including the Buddhists. Diem was

Nguyen Hue Avenue

Eurasia Press/DIAF

HO CHI MINH CITY
Plan 1

0   200   400 m

BINH THANH

DISTRICT 1

DISTRICT 3

National History Museum

Botanical Gardens and Zoo

Hoa Lu Stadium

Jade Emperor Pagoda

Tran Hung Dao Temple

Le Van Tam Park

Van Nghiem Pagoda

British Embassy

American Consulate

Main Post Office

Notre Dame Cathedral

War Museum

N

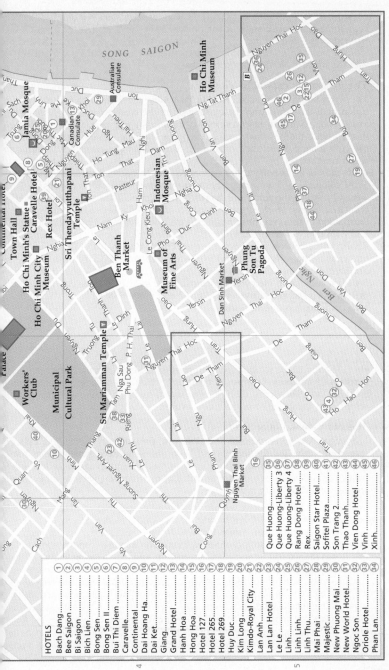

SONG SAIGON

Ho Chi Minh Museum

Australian Consulate

Jamia Mosque

Canadian Consulate

Continental Hotel

Town Hall

Ho Chi Minh's Statue

Caravelle Hotel

Rex Hotel

Sri Thendayyutthapani Temple

Indonesian Mosque

Ben Thanh Market

Museum of Fine Arts

Phung Son Tu Pagoda

Dan Sinh Market

Palace

Workers' Club

Municipal Cultural Park

Sri Mariamman Temple

Nguyen Thai Binh Market

Ben Nghe

B

discarded by the Americans, but afterwards assassinated in 1963. Not only had Saigon become the capital of a country at war, overrun by hundreds of thousands of GI's and by Vietnamese escaping the fighting, but also a stronghold of corruption and vice (56 000 prostitutes). This particular period came to an abrupt end on 30 April 1975 with the arrival of North Vietnamese tanks.

The economic capital of Vietnam

The city of Saigon was renamed **Ho Chi Minh City**, and drifted into practical hibernation until the 1990s with the opening up of the economy and the subsequent tourist boom. Northern functionaries and ambitious young people alike know that this city holds the key to success, and very few leave the area for that reason. The city curls around one of the bends in the Saigon River and comprises 17 districts and 5 rural sectors, but few tourists venture out of the 1st, 3rd and 5th districts, where most of the important sites are located. The 1st district is situated in the heart of the **colonial city** (Plan I), which has kept the name of "Saigon", and spans the Thi Nghe Channel (to the north) and the Ben Nghe Channel (to the south). Several areas of interest include Le Duan to the north, connecting the Botanical Gardens to the Reunification Palace, via the cathedral. Further south, Nguyen Hue and Dong Khoi lead from the river to the main colonial buildings, the theatre and the Town Hall. Finally, at the bottom of Le Loi is the **Ben Thanh Market** (Plan I C4), and a little further on is **Pham Ngu Lao** (Plan I B4), an area for travellers. To the west of Nguyen Thi Minh Khai and Hai Ba Trung, the quiet streets of the 3rd district lined with French houses are an ideal area for a stroll, while southwest of the city, at the end of Tran Hung Dao and Nguyen Thi Minh Khai, **Cholon** (Plan III) covers the 5th district, the Chinese commercial area.

The city centre (Plan I)
Allow 2 days

Ho Chi Minh City has retained several impressive buildings from the French era, and a restrained approach to urban development which is singularly uncommon in Southeast Asia. Wandering through these stylish streets swarming with two-wheel vehicles and losing one's way the little alleyways can be a real treat.

The old colonial quarter**

The **Saigon River**** borders this area to the east, giving the city the image of a place open to the delta and the wider world. From the well-tended gardens along **Ton Duc Thang*** (D3-4), the sight of the constant comings and goings of the frail little sailing craft never ceases to amaze as they dart between the enormous cargo ships arriving from Hong Kong and Taiwan.

Established in the 19C along the line of a filled-in canal, **Nguyen Hue** (formerly Boulevard Charner) (C3-D4) has become the showcase of modern Saigon. It connects the river with the former **Town Hall*** (C3), now headquarters to the People's Committee, and was the subject of heated controversy during its construction (1901-08). It was the symbol of triumphant imperialism, and the "cream-puff" style of the long façade with its pastel yellow belfry decorated with bas-reliefs and Corinthian columns must have seemed fairly unusual at the time. It has since become one of the main emblems of the city. A statue of **Ho Chi Minh** has been erected in the square facing the building.

Built in place of a garage in 1959 on the corner of Le Loi and Nguyen Hue, the **Rex Hotel** (C3) was once a business centre before providing premises for the American News Service and their press conferences. The famous roof-top café boasts a magnificent view.

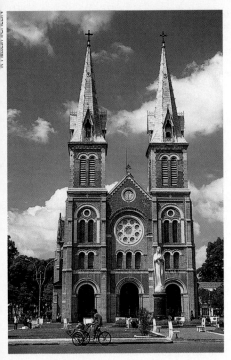
Notre Dame Cathedral

Not far from here, the **Sri Thendayyutthapani Temple*** (C4) *(66 Ton That Thiep. Open daily 6am-7pm)*, built between 1875 and 1880, is further evidence of the city's Indian roots. There are now only 300 Indian families in Vietnam, all descendants of traders who settled here several centuries ago. Green and white tiling is just as prevalent here, but the lively decor (hanging balls and coloured statues surrounded with electric lights) greatly contrasts with the Mosque. Don't leave without admiring the **tower** on the roof, decorated with bas-reliefs displaying an interesting combination of deities of the Hindu pantheon and students dressed in clothes from the 1920s.

Dong Khoi* (C-D3), formerly Rue Catinat, runs parallel to Nguyen Hue from the river to the cathedral. During French colonial times, it was the in-place in Saigon for shopping or for enjoying a Martini on one of the numerous terraces. Under the name of Tu Do ("Freedom"), the street acquired quite a red-light reputation during the American era with the arrival of bars such as Play Boy and Mimi's Bar. All these disappeared, of course, in 1975 and the street was renamed Dong Khoi, "General Uprising", a name a little more in keeping with the atmosphere of the time. Classic names such as Continental, Grand Hotel and Majestic today find themselves linked with shopping centres, bars and fashionable restaurants popular with tourists and ex-patriates.

On the corner of Le Loi and Dong Khoi, the **Town Theatre*** (Nha Hat Thanh Pho) (D3) (1899) appears only slightly more sober than the Town Hall. The building was home to the South Vietnamese Assembly until 1975, but has now reverted to its original role. It is bordered on the right by the tasteful architecture of the **Continental Hotel** (1880), press HQ during the Vietnam War, and to the left is the enormous tower of the recently extended **Caravelle Hotel**.

Nestling at the foot of the Caravelle is **Jamia Mosque** (D3) *(66 Dong Du)*, a peaceful haven incongruously located among such urban confusion. It was built in 1935 by Saigon's Indian community, who nearly all left the country after 1975.

Closing off the view along Dong Khoi is the red brick outline of **Notre Dame Cathedral*** (Nha Tho Chanh Toa Saigon) (C3) (1877-80) *(Open daily 7-11am / 3-4pm. Services at 5.30am and 5pm, and seven daily services on Sundays)* situated on Paris Commune Square *(Cong Xa Paris)*. Its two graceful **spires** are a favourite with newly-weds who insist on being photographed here. The inside lacks interest, with the exception of the **stained-glass windows** and the bilingual **ex-votos** in French and Vietnamese put up in the chapels by devout worshippers.

The façade of the **Main Post Office*** (Buu Dien) (C3) (1886-91), to the right of the cathedral, resembles the architecture of a typical 19C railway station, as does its magnificent arched **metallic roof structure**** designed by Gustave Eiffel. The cool draught of the fans and the slightly archaic atmosphere of the place provide the ideal opportunity to sit back and observe the local people writing their letters on long wooden desks under the watchful eye of Ho Chi Minh, whose portrait adorns the back wall.

Parks and museums**

Le Duan* (C2-3) links the Reunification Palace to the Botanical Gardens via the cathedral, running alongside the new American Consulate (1998) built on the site of the former Embassy.

To the far north of Le Duan, the **Botanical Gardens*** (D2) (*Open daily 7am-8pm. Entrance fee*) provide a welcome break, but a walk round the **zoo** can only incite mixed feelings due to the living conditions of the animals. At the weekend, such a visit becomes more of a sociological study of the habits of the people of Saigon than a lesson in zoology. As for the Vietnamese, they seem even more interested by a rare glimpse of foreign visitors than in that of birds, monkeys or wild animals.

Nearby, the fascinating **National History Museum***** (Bao Tang Lich Su Viet Nam) (D2) (*2 Nguyen Binh Khiem. Open daily 8-11.30am / 1.30-4.30pm, open all day Sunday. Entrance fee*) comprises two sections. The first section concentrates on various eras starting from the Palaeolithic (300 000 years ago) and the Bronze Age (1000 BC), notably the Dong Son civilisation and its **drums****. The period of Chinese domination follows (1C-10C), ending with the Ly Dynasty (11C-13C) and a display of some of its fine **ceramics**. An amazing 19C **mummy** is an interesting exhibit. The Tran Dynasty (13C-14C) is shown through ceramic objects and a scale model of an 11-storey tower, but the section devoted to the Later Le Dynasty (15C-18C) is the most varied, including bronzes, ceramics, weapons, Imperial costumes, furniture and musical instruments. The Tay Son and Nguyen era (18C-20C) conclude this sequence.

The end of the day

After the first room devoted to **Asian ceramics**, the second section of the museum deals with Southern Vietnamese civilisations starting with the people of Funan (1C-6C) and art in the Delta (7C-13C), well highlighted by a 1 500 year-old **wooden Buddha***** and superb **lingams****. Saigon has produced unusual examples of early earthenware jars, but the most exciting items come from Champa. The tour continues with a section devoted to the ethnic minorities of the Central Highlands with basketware, costumes and **funerary statues***. The tour ends with a room given over to Buddhas from different countries of Asia.

Go back along to Le Duan and on to the Reunification Palace and the Municipal Park.

To the south of Le Duan, the **Reunification Palace**** (Dinh Thong Nhat) (B-C3) *(7 Le Duan. Open daily 7.30-11am / 1-4pm. Entrance fee. Guided tours)* was built on the site of the residence of the Governor General of Indochina, destroyed following the attempted assassination of Diem here in 1962. The building is straight out of the modernist movements of the 1960s, and was home to the headquarters of the South Vietnamese Presidency up to 30 April 1975, when tank 879 of the 203rd North Vietnamese Brigade crashed into the entrance gates of the park, marking the end of the war. The palace was then converted into a museum. Time seems to have stood still as you look at the furniture, museum pieces in their own right of 1970s design with just a touch of the East. After visiting the cabinet rooms and the impressive **reception rooms** on the ground floor, head upstairs. A cold elegance pervades the marble galleries leading off to the rooms for the reception of foreign visitors and for the presentation of letters of credit. Take note of the furniture, the very latest design at that time, as well as the huge piece of lacquer-ware hanging on the wall. The third floor is made up of private apartments, notably a projection room fitted out in red velvet and a **waiting room**, where the busy rumblings of the city would never have been more than a muffled echo. Above, the **dance hall** leads directly out onto the roof with its helicopter **landing pad**. The view over Le Duan has remained unchanged. In the basement, the **signals rooms**, covered with numerous campaign maps, paint the picture of a Presidency in dire straits, obsessed with defence. Films about the Vietnam War are shown in the projection room.

Behind the palace, the **Municipal Cultural Park*** (Cong Vien Van Hoa) (B3-4) *(entrance via Nguyen Thi Minh Khai or Huyen Tran Cong Chua)* is the biggest open space in the city centre along with the Botanical Gardens. Enjoy a pleasant walk in the shade of the tall trees, far from the madding crowd. The former **Sports Club** of the French era, now the **Workers' Club** (Nha Van Hoa Lao Dong) (B3), still retains its attractive outside swimming pool, tennis courts and volleyball pitch where the locals come and train.

To the west of the park, the **War Museum*** (Bao Tang Chung Tich Chien Tranh) (B3) *(28 Vo Van Tan, on the corner of Le Quy Don. Open daily 7.30-11.45am / 1.30-4.45pm. Entrance fee)* denounces American aggression and displays **photographs** showing terrible scenes of violence. A display of bombs, tanks and **bombers** in the garden makes an appropriate start to the exhibition. The first part is devoted to the French War, while the second part evokes the many cruel incidents marking the American intervention (the massacre at My Lai, civilian victims of the bombings, a prisoner thrown to his death from a helicopter). After such pictures, the weapons exhibited in the next room take on an even more sinister reality.

To the east of the park, the **Ho Chi Minh City Museum** (Bao Tang Thanh Pho Ho Chi Minh) (C3) *(65 Ly Tu Trong. Open daily 8am-4pm. Entrance fee)*, the former Revolutionary Museum, takes up a huge neo-Classical building (1885-90) that served successively as the Governor's Palace and the Supreme Court. Take a quick look at the **military hardware** on display in the garden (fighter plane, helicopter, tank, ambulance) before going inside. The first room devoted to fishing and the economy presents, among other things, a selection of vacuum flasks, irons, torches and

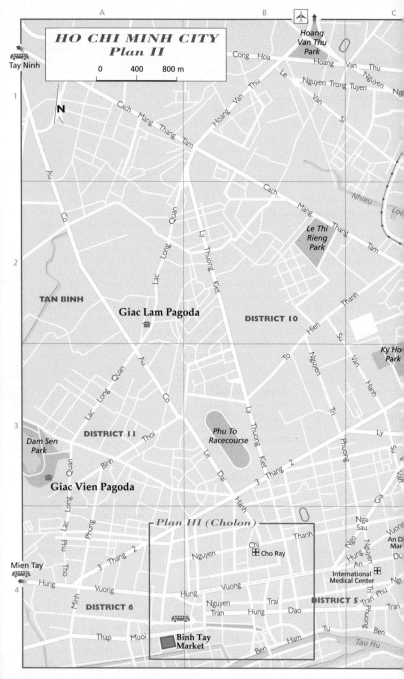

HO CHI MINH CITY
Plan II

0   400   800 m

N

Tay Ninh

Hoang Van Thu Park

Cong Hoa

Hoang Van Thu

Nguyen Trong Tuyen

Le Van Sy

Cach Mang Thang Tam

Hoang Van Thu

Au Co

Quan

Lac Long

Ly Thuong Kiet

Cach Mang Thang Tam

Nhieu Loc

Le Thi Rieng Park

Thanh

TAN BINH

Giac Lam Pagoda

DISTRICT 10

Hien Su

To Nguyen

Van Hanh

Ky Ho Park

Au Co

Lac Long Quan

Thoi

DISTRICT 11

Ly Thuong Kiet

Tri

Ly Su

Van

Phu To Racecourse

Phuong

Dam Sen Park

Binh

Le Dai Hanh

3 Thang 2

Quan

Giac Vien Pagoda

Lac Long Quan

Phung

Phu

Tho

3 Thang 2

─ Plan III (Cholon) ─

Thanh

Nga Sau

Vuon

Mien Tay

Hung

Vuong

Nguyen

Chi

⊞ Cho Ray

Ngo Hung An

Nguyen An

Du

An Di Mar

Minh

DISTRICT 6

Nguyen Tran

Hung

Vuong

Trai

Hung

Dao

⊞ International Medical Center

Tran Phu

DISTRICT 5

Ngi

Tran

Thap

Muoi

Binh Tay Market

Ben

Ham

Tu

Phuong

Ben

Tau Hu

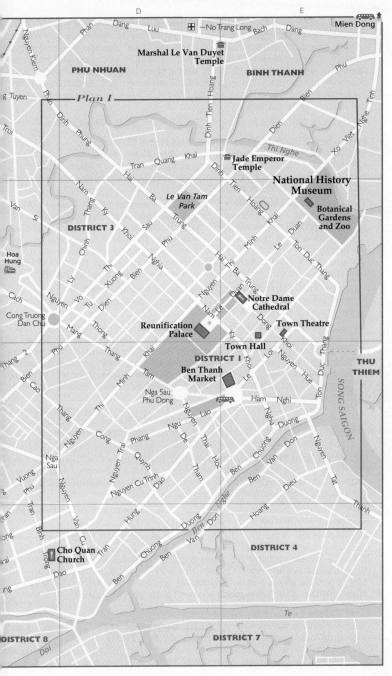

Mien Dong

Dang Luu · No Trang Long · Bach Dang

Phan Dang

Marshal Le Van Duyet Temple

PHU NHUAN

BINH THANH

Phu

Plan 1

Dinh Tien Hoang

Bien

Dien

Xo Viet Nghe Tinh

Thi Nghe

Jade Emperor Temple

Tran Quang Khai

Dinh Tien Hoang

National History Museum

Le Van Tam Park

Botanical Gardens and Zoo

DISTRICT 3

Nam Ky Khoi

Ba Trung

Sau

Phu

Minh

Le Duan

Ton Duc Thang

Hoa Hung

Thi Xuong

Bien Nghia

Nguyen

Nam

Hai Ba Trung

Notre Dame Cathedral

Cong Truong Dan Chu

Cach

Ly

Vo Tu

Dien

Thong

Nguyen

Mang

Khai

Reunification Palace

Dong

Ky

Town Theatre

Ton Duc Thang

THU THIEM

Town Hall

Nguyen Hue

Thang 2

Bien

Cao

Phu

Minh

Thang

Tam

DISTRICT 1

Khoi

Le Loi

Ben Thanh Market

SONG SAIGON

Nga Sau Phu Dong

Thang

Thi

Nga Sau

Nguyen

Cong

Phang

Ngu

De

Lao

Thai Hoc

Ham

Nghi

Nghia

Chuong

Duong

Don

Nguyen Tat Thanh

Nguyen Trai

Quynh

Dao

Tham

Ben

Van

Dieu

Nguyen Cu Trinh

Ben

Hoang

Nguyen Van

Hung

Tran Binh

Chuong

Ben

Duong

Don

Ben Nghe

Cho Quan Church

Trong

Dao

DISTRICT 4

Te

DISTRICT 8

Doi

DISTRICT 7

ceramics. On the first floor, a large **relief map** of Tay Ninh explains the role of this particular region during the war. A large mural and various **contemporary objects** (photos, magazines, printers, heavy weapons, guillotine) illustrate rebel movements from the beginning of the 1930s. Don't miss the small room dealing with traditional fishing and agricultural methods (tools, fishing boats, keep nets, looms) and with the decorative arts (ceramics, furniture with inlaid mother-of-pearl, musical instruments, lacquer-ware). A delightful barouche and a double-bottomed **Viet Cong fishing boat** are on show in the corridor.

Take Nam Ky Khoi Nghia to get back to Le Loi Avenue and Ben Thanh Market.

From Ben Thanh Market to the Ben Nghe Channel

In its vast building topped with a bell tower, **Ben Thanh Market*** (Cho Ben Thanh) (C4) is without doubt one of the liveliest and most interesting markets in the city. A good place to do a little shopping or enjoy a bowl of soup from one of the many stalls serving food at lunchtime.

Two streets further to the west is the **Sri Mariamman Hindu Temple** (B-C4) *(45 Truong Dinh)*, which although it was built in the 19C by the Tamil community, regularly welcomes Vietnamese worshippers. The shrine in the courtyard is dedicated to the goddess Mariamman, weighed down under mounds of flowers and fruit laid as offerings. The walls are riddled with small recesses, home to statues of brightly coloured deities. If restoration work has been completed, make a point of climbing up to the roof, spiked with **sacred towers** decorated with lions and deities.

Cross Ben Thanh Market Square southwards and take Le Cong Kieu, the **antique dealers' street**, as far as the small **Indonesian Mosque** (C4) *(45 Nam Ky Khoi Nghia)*, where you can take a short break.

Not far from here is the **Museum of Fine Arts*** (Bao Tang My Phuat) (C4) *(97A Pho Duc Chinh. Open Tuesday-Sunday 9am-5pm; closed Mondays. Entrance fee)* housed in the Art Deco residence which once belonged to a wealthy Chinese. It offers an interesting insight into contemporary **Vietnamese painting*** with an inspiring section of **children's drawings***. The first floor shows **watercolours** of the war as well as recent works of art (lacquer-ware, ceramics, statues), while the second floor presents local **decorative art** from the 18C to the 20C (bronzes, furniture with inlaid mother-of-pearl, wooden statues or painted ceramics). The most interesting section is devoted to the **Champa**** (7C-13C), as well as **art from Oc Eo**** and from later civilisations, including a wooden Buddha, worn with age, but quite beautiful (4C-6C), and a stone Vishnu with traces of chrome (7C-10C).

Carry on as far as **Phung Son Tu Pagoda** (C5) *(338 Nguyen Cong Tru)*, a charming little brick building with porthole-like windows under a roof topped with dragons. Inside, a few ageless elders stop for a meditative break enveloped in clouds of fragrant incense. Brightly-coloured frescoes line the walls.

Time permitting, extend your tour of this lively shopping area to the **Ben Nghe Channel**, where **market** stalls overflow with seafood and other fare.

On the other side of the canal, the **Ho Chi Minh Museum** (D4) *(1 Nguyen Tat Thanh. Open daily from 7.30-11.30am / 1.30-4.30pm. Entrance fee)* is in the former Customs House. It is from here that the young Nguyen Tat Thanh (Ho Chi Minh) left for Europe in 1911. The museum houses a number of photos and several of Ho Chi Minh's personal effects, notably his watering can and his famous radio. The quality of the graphics of the **propaganda posters*** is an interesting detail.

Thu Thiem

There is no better way than an organised boat trip on the Saigon River to get a closer look at the busy harbour traffic, and especially **Thu Thiem**, the eastern bank that has remained surprisingly rural *(take the boat to Ton Duc Thang or negotiate the rental of a motorboat for 1 or 2 hours. Allow US$5 / hour)*. For the moment, only a few little houses on stilts continue to cling to the river banks, in the shadow of enormous bill-boards advertising products far beyond the reach of their inhabitants. It is still possible to navigate along the **floodwater channels**, but this will change in the near future, since the construction of a modern shopping centre has been planned, with access through a tunnel from the town centre.

Pagodas to the north of the city centre
Allow 3hr

Go back up Hai Ba Trung as far as Dien Bien Phu, turn right and then carry on for a further 600m. Turn left into Mai Thi Luu, just beyond the junction with Dinh Tien Hoang.

The **Jade Emperor Pagoda**, (Phuoc Hai Tu / Chua Ngoc Hoang) (Plan I C1) *(73 Mai Thi Luu. Open daily 6am-6pm)*, built by the Cantonese community at the beginning of the 20C, is one of the most interesting pagodas in the city. Hidden behind a decorative-dragon façade at the back of a small courtyard planted with banyan trees is a maze of ochre-coloured rooms perfumed with incense. The Taoist divinity called the **Jade Emperor** sits enthroned in the main shrine flanked by his guards, the four Big Diamonds, so named because they are said to be as hard as diamonds. A group of colourful **statues★★** surrounds them, representing different gods and heroes, among them two generals holding down a dragon and a tiger with their feet. **Thanh Hoang**, the Master of Hell, stands in a room to the left of the altar, next to his red horse. On the walls, the sculpted **wooden panels** depict the torments awaiting impure souls in each of the Ten Regions of Hell. Finally, in a small adjacent room, outstanding **ceramic figures★★** exemplify certain human characteristics, good or bad, while the room to the right is a shrine dedicated to ancestor worship.

Next is the **Tran Hung Dao Temple** (Plan I B1) *(36 Vo Thi Sau)* dedicated to the hero who thwarted the Mongol invasion led by Kublai Khan in 1287. Taxidermists should be in their element here with enormous elephant tusks and fine examples of a tiger and a panther stopped in their tracks in front of the altar, among others.

Go back to the northernmost tip of Dinh Tien Hoang.

The **Marshal Le Van Duyet Temple** (Plan II D-E1) *(126 Dinh Tien Hoang. Open daily from 6am-6pm)* is situated in the middle of a garden which is popular with the older members of the community, who come here in their pyjamas for their daily gymnastic sessions. The eunuch Le Van Duyet (1763-1832) was a friend of the French and a faithful ally to Gia Long but, because he refused to restrain the Catholics, he was disgraced by Emperor Minh Mang, who tried him posthumously and, in an outrageous act of profanity, desecrated his grave. Ten years later, his tomb was restored and Le Van Duyet now rests in peace beside his wife, in the shelter of a small wall. He was considered a national hero in the South, but his involvement with the French made him unpopular with nationalists. The temple itself is of no particular interest, but the two fine, carved wooden doors are worthy of note. The interior is decked out with red fabric embroidered with pearls, and houses wooden sculptures of horses and wading birds on tortoises, together with spears engraved with ideograms. Costumed plays are performed here on the 1st and 8th days of the lunar month.

Go back down Vo Thi Sau, then turn right into Nam Ky Khoi Nghia.

Vinh Nghiem Pagoda (Plan I A1) *(399 Nam Ky Khoi Nghia. Open daily 7.30-11.30am / 2-6pm. Take your shoes off before entering)* is easily visible due to its seven storeys. This huge building was constructed in 1971 with the help of the Japanese-Vietnamese Friendship Association. Novices have lessons in a room on the ground floor under the vast sanctuary containing a **golden Buddha** accompanied by two bodhisattvas. The most remarkable aspect of the pagoda is without doubt the **funerary tower** located at the back. It serves as a repository for hundreds of ceramic urns containing various people's ashes with their respective photos.

Cholon★ (Plan III)
Allow half a day

"Cholon is a Chinese enclave on Vietnamese soil, an ever-present reminder of the country's great neighbour. It works faster, sells cheaper, and remains utterly unfathomable", in the words of the French writer, Didier Lauras. When the "Great Market" was founded in the 17C by the Chinese, it was 5km away from Saigon, but today it is an integral part of Ho Chi Minh City and one of the most important cogs in the machinery of the nation's economic capital. It has been able to preserve its character, however, which explains the presence of 500 000 Sino-Vietnamese or Hoa. Rice from the Mekong and electronic goods from Taiwan all converge here before filling the shelves of the city's shops. It's a sort of theatre of illusions, a buzzing hive of day-long activity revealing nothing of its innermost mysteries, a unique district where the two most sacred places are pagodas and markets.

Ever since the founding of Cholon, the Chinese have formed influential congregations according to their regional origin, each under the protection of a revered tutelary deity in a temple or pagoda. Half-way between a medieval merchants' guild and an American syndicate, each group has control over a particular economic sector (retailing for those from Canton, catering for those from Fukien, weaving and leather work for the Hakka). The difficult period at the end of the 1970s which provoked the mass exodus of the Sino-Vietnamese in the face of oppression (*see insert page 32*) has faded from memory, and the economy is now booming. The grey economy, not included in official statistics, has been estimated at 40%, and includes girlie bars, clandestine gambling joints, illegal sweatshops or secret financial transactions. The congregations are powerful self-help groups with a social regulatory function responsible for financing schools, hospitals and temples.

Arriving in Cholon along Avenue Nguyen Thi Minh Khai, go past the enormous Nga Sau roundabout, along Hung Vuong and then left into Tran Binh Trong and continue for 500m.

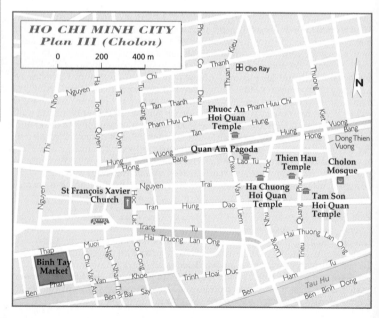

On the way to Cholon, stop off at **Cho Quan Church** (Plan II C4) *(133 Tran Binh Trong. Open daily from 4-7am / 3-6pm, Sundays 4-9am / 1.30-6pm)*, and admire its pastel-yellow façade and bell tower. The original structure (18C) was rebuilt several times before finally attaining its present-day form at the beginning of the 20C. Nearby is a convent, as well as a primary school and a hospital, which before 1975 were all linked to the church.

Take Nguyen Trai back to the centre of Cholon.

The **Cholon Mosque** *(641 Nguyen Trai. Important prayer meeting on Fridays at 12.30pm)* was built in 1923 by the Tamils and is today used by the Cham from Chau Doc. The interior is quite sparse in contrast with the pagodas.

One street further on is **Tam Son Hoi Quan Temple** *(118 Trieu Quang Phuc, at 370 Tran Hung Dao)*, built by the Fujian Congregation in the 19C. The architecture is of no special interest, but it has retained its original decoration. People come here to worship General **Quan Cong**, who is flanked by General Chau Xuong to the left and the mandarin Quan Binh to the right, but the temple is officially dedicated to **Me Sanh**, the Goddess of Fertility. She can be found at the back of the pagoda next to her daughters, in the company of Thien Hau and Ong Bon.

Thien Hau Temple** *(710 Nguyen Trai. Open daily from 6am-5.30pm)* is one of the most important temples in Cholon, built by the Cantonese Congregation at the beginning of the 19C. It is dedicated to the **Goddess of the Sea**, who offers protection to sailors and to whom travellers should traditionally pay homage before or after a long journey. This was indeed the case with the boat people in the 1980s, and the custom is maintained today by Sino-Vietnamese expatriates returning to the country. The temple is deservedly the most popular among tourists. It comprises three interconnecting buildings separated by interior courtyards. In the first building, where incense and imitation money are burned, note the extraordinary **ceramic figurines**** inspired by the legend of the Three Kingdoms which dance atop the roof. The three statues of **Thien Hau Thanh Mau** standing behind the altar are paraded through the city during the festivities on the 23rd day of the third lunar month.

The attractive **Ha Chuong Hoi Quan Temple*** *(802 Nguyen Trai. Open daily from 7am-6pm)*, built by the Chinese from Fujian, is also dedicated to Thien Hau and probably dates back to the end of the 18C. Inside, the temple has four stone **pillars** in the shape of dragons and is decorated with outstanding painted **bas-reliefs****, all caught up in the bewitching fragrance of wispy joss stick smoke.

The influence of the Fujian Congregation is also noticeable in the numerous **ideograms** that ornament the walls and pillars of the **Quan Am Pagoda*** *(12 Lao Tu, near to Chau Van Liem. Open daily from 6am-5pm)*, as well as in the ceramic trimmings on the rooftop depicting Chinese legends. Magnificent **stone dragons**** guard the entrance and the front doors are delicately sculpted with **gold panels***.

Chinese-style credit

The Hoa operate a traditional, highly unorthodox, credit system which has so far enabled them to ward off any attempts at infiltration from Western banks. Tontines are informal groups of private borrowers, and meetings are held either at one of the member's homes or in the back of a shop. After the initial contributions of equal amounts, each member then notes on paper the maximum rate of interest he is willing to pay for a loan. The winner is the one who suggests the highest rate. This primitive form of financial market, which operates quite informally over a meal washed down with a certain amount of alcohol and interspersed with numerous negotiations, leaves no written proof. It is entirely a matter of confidence. Some wealthy savers take part in several tontines, which can lead to a tangled web of infinite complexity. Financial involvement may sometimes reach astronomical proportions, and from time to time, as happened in 1993, the insolvency of one of the borrowers can cause financial collapse.

The temple is an important place of worship and is dedicated to Quan Am, the Goddess of Mercy, whose statue stands under a glass case near the main altar, next to the Sakyamuni Buddha and a laughing Ameda, and opposite a gold figure of Thien Hau. The Goddess, dressed in white robes, can also be found in the room at the back, again opposite Thien Hau.

Phuoc An Hoi Quan Temple✶✶ (*184 Hung Vuong, on the corner of Thuan Kieu. Open daily from 7am-5pm*) was built at the beginning of the 20C on the site of a communal house and is one of the most beautifully ornamented pagodas in Cholon. By a subtle trick of the light, the sun's rays enter and fade in a small area cloaked in incense smoke. Note the **wooden panels**✶✶ decorating the pillars and the columns, and the celebrated **ceramic horse**✶ belonging to Quan Cong to the left of the entrance. Behind a huge earthenware jar flanked by two ceramic cranes stands the **statue** of the general, easily recognisable by his crimson face.

From the crossroads, go along Chau Van Liem and turn left 300m further on.

Weary of temples? Walk up **Hai Thuong Lan Ong**✶, a street specialising in Chinese pharmacopoeia. When you recover from the shock of seeing the selection of stuffed cats, shark's teeth, tortoise shells, crocodile skin, and tiger's testicles, to name but a few of the strange items on display, it is important to realise that most of these are endangered species precisely because of this sort of trade. However, such a threat in no way affects the thousand and one spices spilling out of the sacks.

The elegant, bright shape of **St François Xavier Church** (Cha Tam) (*25 Hoc Lac. Open daily from 7-11am / 1.30-4.30pm*) appears at the end of Tran Hung Dao, a very lively avenue. The pastel-yellow façade is extremely attractive, but this is not the reason for the church's notoriety. It is in fact the place where President Diem and his brother were captured during the coup d'état on November 1 1963, before being executed on the way to Saigon. The church has two schools, Vietnamese to the right and Chinese to the left.

The general hustle and bustle and the sheer numbers of people increase significantly as you approach **Binh Tay Market**✶✶ (*Thap Muoi*), a vast ochre-coloured building with a tiled roof designed by a French architect and financed by Quach Cam, a rich Chinese businessman. Once over this temple of trade, the visitor is immediately swallowed up in a stream of stallholders, customers and porters obstructing the alleys lined with all manner of stands.

To the north of Cholon
Go west along Hung Vuong and then turn right into Phu Tho, which becomes Lac Long Quan. 100m beyond the entrance to Dam Sen Park, go down a dirt track off to the left and carry on for another 200m.

Giac Vien Pagoda✶✶✶ (Plan II A3) (1744) is tucked away at the end of a winding track which runs through a lively quarter on the edge of the countryside. The atmosphere is one of intense calm and it is said that Emperor Gia Long often came here for a moment of private prayer. The ochre-coloured façade, covered with a tiled roof which emerges suddenly from beneath the trees, is typical of the traditional style of the building. About twenty bonze live in the adjoining buildings.

Once in the sanctuary, note the **golden Buddha** sitting on a lotus flower, and the altars containing tablets and photographs of the deceased. The three statues on display are those of **Hai Tinh Giac Viena**, the founder of the pagoda, carrying a horsehair fly-swat, and his successors. They face the Goddess **Chuan De** with her eighteen arms, one of the likenesses of Quan Am. In another room (take your shoes off), an **A Di Da Buddha** sitting in front of an electric mandorla takes pride of place in the middle of a whole host of statues.

A Cholon pagoda

Go back up Lac Long Quan for 1km and then turn left after Au Co.

Giac Lam Pagoda*** (Plan II A2) (*118 Lac Long Quan*) was built in the 18C and is one of the oldest and most interesting pagodas in Ho Chi Minh City. A large seven-storey **tower** heralds the approach to the sanctuary, located near a **cemetery** dominated by a number of large tombs. The pagoda has three ground level sections, the main sanctuary, the meeting room and the bonze room. Inside, the hundred or so **wooden pillars** supporting the bulky roof structure are covered with Vietnamese (and not Chinese) ideograms. Dusty candelabras, worn ceramic tiles, well-polished tables and ageless monks – it's a place where time seems to have stood still. The pagoda contains 113 red and gold **statues** in breadfruit-tree wood, as well as 500 **tablets** of nine generations of bonze from Hue. In the centre, a ray of light high-lights **Chuan De** with her eighteen arms. At the back of the sanctuary to the left (*take off your shoes*), numerous statues cover the altar, including an **A Di Da Buddha** accompanied by the disciples Kasaype to the right and Ananda to the left. A **Thich Ca Buddha** and a Buddha child stand just in front. From among all the other characters, note a plump, jolly-looking **Ameda** surrounded by children, and to his left, the **Jade Emperor**. Faithful worshippers come to hang their prayers on a wooden structure similar to a Christmas tree before lighting one of the 49 oil lamps.

Ho Chi Minh City close up

COMING AND GOING

By plane – *Tan Son Nhat* inter-national airport is located at the end of Truong Son, 7km northwest of the city centre (Plan II B1), ☎ (08) 884 31 79. The easiest way to get there is by taxi (US$6, 20min) or by one of the airport buses operated by travel agents (US$4). Don't forget to include the airport tax for domestic (25 000VND) or international flights (US$12). There are regular flights to major European and Asian cities, as well as to the main Vietnamese cities.

By train – *Hoa Hung*, the Ho Chi Minh City station is at the end of Nguyen Thong, 3km northwest of the city centre (Plan II C2). Tickets are avail-able at the counter reserved for foreign visitors ☎ (08) 843 65 27 / 844 02 18. Open daily from 7.30-11.30am / 1.30-4.30pm. Otherwise you can book at a travel agency (several days in advance for an air-conditioned sleeper), or at the ***Saigon Railways Tourist Service Company***, 275C Pham Ngu Lao, ☎ (08) 836 76 40, Fax (08) 843 88 30. Monday-Friday 7.30-11.30am / 1.30-4pm. The line serves the coast as far as Hanoi (for times see page 102).

By bus and minibus – For local buses, go straight to the terminal and buy your ticket just before departure. However, you can book at a travel agency for the express minibus services. Seating from 12 to 24 passengers, these vehicles are sometimes air-conditioned and are gen-erally faster since they are not supposed to pick up passengers along the way. The Van Thanh terminal was closed in 1998 and buses now leave from Mien Dong (see below). The terminal at Cholon may very well go the same way in the not so distant future. Apart from the terminals, note that minibuses for Vung Tau leave from Ham Nghi, near the Que Huong 2 Hotel (20 000-30 000VND). Certain agencies also pro-vide a service for Phnom Penh.

Ben Xe Tay Ninh (Xe Khach Lien Tinh or An Suong Station): from Ben Thanh Market, go up Cach Mang Thang Tam as far as Le Dai Hanh (8km west of the centre) (Plan II A1). Regular departures from 5am-5pm (or 7pm depending on the season) for Cu Chi (90min, then take a motorcycle taxi for the last 25km to the tunnels) and Tay Ninh (2hr).

Ben Xe Cholon, near Binh Tay Market (Plan III). Reached by bus from Ben Thanh. The terminal serves the whole of the Mekong Delta, with departures from 4.30am to 6-7pm. There are hourly de-

The South

partures for My Tho (2hr), Ben Tre (about 3hr), Vinh Long (3hr) and Can Tho (4hr) and departures every two hours for Cao Lanh (about 3hr 30min) and Soc Trang (6hr).There are six to seven daily buses for Long Xuyen (6-7hr) but it is better to change at Can Tho, five daily buses for Chau Doc (7hr) and three or four for Tra Vinh (5hr, but it is better to take the Vinh Long bus and change there), Rach Gia (7hr) and Ha Tien (9hr).

Ben Xe Mien Tay, in An Lac, in the Binh Chanh district, 10km west of the city centre (Plan II A4). Although it is located beyond Cholon, this terminal is more practical because it is open almost all the time, and there are more frequent departures and more express minibuses (some air-conditioned). The terminal is accessible by bus from the Ben Thanh station and it serves all the towns in the Mekong Delta with departures every 30min for some of the larger towns (My Tho, Can Tho, Long Xuyen, Chau Doc, Cao Lanh).

Ben Xe Mien Dong, 227/6 RN13, 5km north of the city centre, via Nguyen Thi Minh Khai, then Xo Viet Nghe Tinh (Plan II E1). Open daily from 4.30am-5.30pm. It serves the Central Highlands and the coast to the north of Ho Chi Minh City. Hourly departures from 5am-6pm for Dalat (7-8hr or 6hr express), and departures every two hours for Buon Ma Thuot via Highway 14 (7-8hr or 6hr express). Four or five daily buses for Plei Ku (11-12hr or 9hr express) and Kon Tum (12-13hr or 10hr express).

An air-conditioned bus leaves every half hour for Vung Tau (2hr 30min), with hourly departures for Phan Thiet (4hr or 3hr 30min express) and Nha Trang (9hr-10hr or 8hr express), three daily departures for Da Nang (27hr or 24hr express) and Hue (29hr or 26hr express), and two or three daily departures for Hanoi (2 days and 1 night).

"Open Tour" – Fiditourist, Sinh Café, Kim Travel and Saigon Tourist / Kim Café offer "Open Tour" tickets to Dalat, Phan Thiet, Mui Ne, Nha Trang, Hoi An, Hue and Hanoi. Services and rates vary very little from one agency to another. They operate air-conditioned buses which pick you up from your hotel (except in Ho Chi Minh City) and stop off at popular tourist sites. Although practical, this service offers no contact with the local population.

By chauffeur-driven car – See below under "Travel agencies".

By boat – See "Making the most of the Mekong Delta" page 391.

By hydrofoil – Ideal for Vung Tau and the Mekong Delta. See pages 369 and 391.

GETTING AROUND

On foot – The short distances that need to be covered around the city centre and as far as Pham Ngu Lao make walking the ideal way to see Ho Chi Minh City, but a certain amount of experience is required before venturing across any avenue or negotiating any intersection in the face of on-coming two-wheelers.

By bus – You will hardly ever need to use a city bus, except perhaps to get to Cholon or to the terminals on the outskirts of the city. The main bus station is opposite Ben Thanh Market.

By taxi – The fleet of cars has been updated and air-conditioned Japanese vehicles fitted with a meter have replaced the French ones, now almost a thing of the past. Taxis are easy to find in front of big hotels and at Phan Ngu Lao. There is no need to worry about prices or the routes taken, since drivers are generally fairly honest and a number of taxis have radio-links with their central office; **Airport Taxi**, ☎ (08) 844 66 66. **Festival Taxi**, ☎ (08) 845 45 45. **Vina Taxi**, ☎ (08) 811 08 88 / 811 11 11.

By motorcycle taxi – Very practical, and "xe om" or "Honda" can be found parked at nearly every crossroads. Negotiate the price of the trip beforehand.

By cyclo – Almost 50 000 "xi lo dap" or cyclos operate around Ho Chi Minh City, so you shouldn't have any trouble finding one, and more often than not, they will find you first. This particular profession seems to have become the major source of new employment for the former soldiers of the South-Vietnamese army, which explains in part why a lot of the drivers speak English. Negotiate the price of the journey in advance, and note that there are certain city centre streets where cyclos are prohibited, so a certain number of detours are inevitable. It is quite useful to bring along the visiting card of the place you are travelling to, especially that of your hotel.

Motorcycle rental – This is an ideal way of getting around the city, but do please check the state of your vehicle first, and be particularly careful, since the traffic is absolutely chaotic. Crash helmets are not compulsory, but it is advisable to wear one. There are countless hire companies, especially on Pham Ngu Lao. The price varies according to the size of the engine, from 50cc (about US$5 / day) to 250cc (about US$15 / day). Negotiate a reduction in price if you are renting a vehicle for several days and check the excess payable in case of theft. The vehicles are not insured.

Bicycle rental – Again an excellent way to join the crowd, following the same rules of caution as for motorcycles. For further information, contact the local hotels and cafés, especially around Pham Ngu Lao. The average price is around US$1 / day.

ADDRESS BOOK

Tourist Office – Saigon Tourist, 49 Le Thanh Ton, ☎ (08) 829 89 14, Fax (08) 822 49 87, sgtvn@hcmc.net-nam.vn **Vietnam Tourism Ho Chi Minh City**, 234 Nam Ky Khoi Nghia, ☎ (08) 932 67 76, Fax (08) 932 67 75, vnthcm@hcm.vnn.vn

Bank / Currency exchange – ANZ, 11 Me Linh. Monday-Friday 8.30am-4pm. Automatic cash dispenser.
HSBC, New World Hotel, 75 Pham Hong Thai. Monday-Thursday 8.30am-4.30pm, Friday 8.30am-5pm. Withdrawals in dollars with a credit card. Cash dispenser.
Sacombank, 211 Nguyen Thai Hoc, on the corner of Pham Ngu Lao. Monday-Saturday 7.30am-7.30pm, withdrawals at the counter with a credit card. **Western Union**, 104-106 Nguyen Hue. Monday-Friday 8am-12noon / 1.30-6pm, Saturdays 8am-12noon. Foreign money transfers (commission).

Post Office – GPO, 2 Cong Xa Paris, near the cathedral (Plan I C3). Open

daily 6am-10pm. Poste restante. Other offices at 125 Cong Quynh, near Nguyen Cu Trinh (6am-9pm) and 14 Bui Vien (7am-10pm).
For packages or urgent letters contact: **VN Cargo**, GPO, ☎ (08) 823 75 56, Fax (08) 823 44 10. Airmail. **FedEx**, 146 Pasteur, ☎ (08) 829 09 95, Fax (08) 823 68 41. Monday-Friday 7am-8pm, Saturdays 7-11.30am. **Airborne Express**, 80C Nguyen Du, ☎ (08) 829 43 10; 2E Tien Giang, ☎ (08) 848 56 73. **DHL**, 4 Pham Thuc Duyen, near the airport, ☎ (08) 844 62 03, Fax (08) 845 68 41. Monday-Friday 7.30am-12noon / 1-5pm.

Telephone – International calls can be made from most Post Offices or private agencies located in the tourist areas. For local calls, the normal rate is 1 200VND for the first three minutes.

Internet – Numerous cyber cafés along Pham Ngu Lao provide Internet connections at unbeatable prices. The ones in the city centre are a little more expensive. Most of the cafés have a printer and sometimes a scanner.

Medical service – The Emergency Centre, 125 Le Loi, District 1, ☎ (08) 829 2071, open 24hr a day with English-speaking doctors. **Cho Ray Hospital**, 291 Nguyen Chi Thanh, Cholon (Plan III), ☎ (08) 855 41 37. This Vietnamese hospital has an emergency service, as well as a service for foreign visitors at very reasonable rates. **International Medical Center**, 520 Nguyen Tri Phuong (Plan II C4), ☎ (08) 865 40 25/26. Consultations at reasonable prices. **Columbia Asia**, 1 No Trang Long, ☎ (08) 803 06 78. A very expensive international clinic (consultations from 7am-midnight). **The Medical Consultancy Service,** 243 Hoang Van Thu, Tan Binh District, ☎ (08) 865 1586 ext 221, Fax (08) 844 3442, open 24hr a day, 7 days a week, and has doctors who speak various languages including English. **Oscat-AEA**, 65 Nguyen Du (Plan I C2-3), ☎ (08) 829 85 20. This international clinic is run by former members of the Samu, a French emergency service, providing a 24hr outpatient service, as well as home calls, a dental service and repatriation arrangements. Rates are very high.

Pharmacies – Situated on De Tham, and a little further out on Cao Thang. *Dong Khoi*, 197-199 Dong Khoi, ☎ (08) 829 05 77. A big chemist's, the staff speak English. Monday-Saturday 8-11.30am / 1.30-5.30pm. *Kim Dinh*, 205 Hai Ba Trung. 7am-12noon / 2-9pm. *My Chau*, 389 Hai Ba Trung, ☎ (08) 822 22 66.

Embassies and Consulates – See "Practical Information" page 96.

Immigration Police – *Phong Quan Ly Nguoi Nuoc Ngoai*, 254-258 Nguyen Trai, on the corner of Nguyen Cu Trinh (Plan II D3), ☎ (08) 839 22 21. Monday-Friday 8-11am / 1.30-4.30pm. Allow 5 to 7 days for a visa extension, but it is probably better to contact a travel agency.

Airlines – *Aeroflot*, 4H Le Loi, ☎ (08) 829 34 89, Fax (08) 829 00 76. *Air France*, 130 Dong Khoi, ☎ (08) 829 09 81/82, Fax (08) 822 05 37. *British Airways*, 58 Dong Khoi, ☎ (08) 829 12 88, Fax (08) 823 00 30. *Cathay Pacific*, 58 Dong Khoi, ☎ (08) 822 32 03, Fax (08) 825 82 76. *Garuda*, 132-134 Dong Khoi, ☎ (08) 829 36 44. *KLM*, 2A-4A Ton Duc Thang, ☎ (08) 823 19 90/91, Fax (08) 823 19 89. *Lao Aviation*, 93 Pasteur, ☎ and Fax (08) 822 69 90. *Lufthansa*, 132-134 Dong Khoi, ☎ (08) 829 25 29/49, Fax (08) 829 85 37. *Malaysia*, 132-134 Dong Khoi, ☎ (08) 829 25 29, Fax (08) 824 28 84. *Qantas*, Saigon Center, 65 Le Loi, ☎ (08) 821 46 60, Fax (08) 821 46 69. *Royal Air Cambodge*, 11 Dong Khoi, ☎ (08) 829 93 63, Fax (08) 829 58 32. *Singapore Airlines*, 29 Le Duan, ☎ (08) 823 15 88, Fax (08) 823 15 54. *Thai*, 65 Nguyen Du, ☎ (08) 822 33 65 / 829 28 10, Fax (08) 822 34 65. *United Airlines*, 58 Dong Khoi, ☎ (08) 823 47 55, Fax (08) 823 00 30. *Vietnam Airlines*, 116 Nguyen Hue, ☎ (08) 832 03 20 / 829 21 18, Fax (08) 823 02 73; 20 Tran Hung Dao, ☎ (08) 836 07 89.

Travel agencies – You may opt for an all-inclusive tour or else hire a chauffeur-driven car for a more personalised programme, but in that case negotiate the price beforehand and check the route and the services provided (food and lodging for the driver, entrance fees to sites, type of car and air-conditioning). Most of the agencies work with individual guides and offer the same sort of tours (including the Mekong Delta, Cu Chi and Tay Ninh) and services (including visa extensions, car and motorcycle rental, and bus and plane reservations). Others also organise "Open Tour" trips. Compare prices, but keep in mind that tried and tested agencies generally guarantee the quality of the services.

Along Pham Ngu Lao (Plan I B4), competition is strong, and prices are low: *Fiditourist*, 195 Pham Ngu Lao, ☎ (08) 836 80 18, Fax (08) 836 19 22. An efficient team with reasonable rates. *Kim Café*, 268 De Tham, ☎ (08) 836 81 22, sgnkimcafe@hotmail.com This cheap agency is one of the oldest in the area, and has a good reputation. *Kim Travel*, 270 De Tham, ☎ and Fax (08) 835 98 59, cafekim@hcm.vnn. vn A more recent agency, (the usual tours and services), vying for customers by creating some confusion over their name, which is very similar to their neighbours. *Saigon Tourist*, 187A Pham Ngu Lao, ☎ (08) 836 85 42, Fax (08) 836 75 35, sgnkimcafe@hotmail.com A large, private organisation in partnership with Kim Café offering every guarantee, but at higher prices. A wide choice of tours and services. *Sinh Café*, 246-248 De Tham, ☎ (08) 836 73 38, Fax (08) 836 93 22, sinhcafevietnam@hcm.vnn.vn The most famous name in the area with an experienced team and some of the lowest prices. They work in partnership with a number of agencies in the country, which means they are able to offer original and varied services (a possible option of renting a motorcycle from here and then dropping it off in another town). There is a minibus service available as far as Moc Bai, and then bus or boat to Phnom Penh.

Other agencies further up the range include *Ann Tours*, 58 Ton That Tung, ☎ (08) 833 2564, Fax (08) 832 3866. *Atlas Tours*, 164 Nguyen Van Thu, ☎ (08) 822 4122, Fax (08) 829 8604.

Cholon Tourist, 192-194 Su Van Hanh, ☎ (08) 835 9090, Fax (08) 835 5375. **Global Holidays**, 71-73 Dong Khoi, ☎ (08) 822 8453, Fax (08) 822 8454. **Hung Vi/Superb Travel**, ☎ (08) 822 5111, Fax (08) 824 2405. **Mai Linh Co**, 64 Hai Ba Trung, ☎ (08) 825 8888, Fax (08) 822 4496. **Star Tours**, 166 Nam Ky Khoi Nghia, ☎ (08) 824 4673, Fax (08) 824 4675. **Vietnam Tourism**, 69-71 Nam Ky Khoi Nghia, ☎ (08) 829 1276, Fax (08) 829 0775. **Vita Tours**, ☎ (08) 823 0767, Fax (08) 824 3524. **Youth Tourist**, 292 Dien Bien Phu, ☎ (08) 829 4580.

Specialised agencies include **Mekong Star**, 58 Mac Dinh Chi, ☎ (08) 823 63 79, Fax (08) 829 75 26. Cruises across the Mekong Delta. **SinhBalo Adventures**, 43 Bui Vien, ☎ and Fax (08) 836 76 82, sinhbalo@hcm. vnn.vn A private organisation created by the founder of the Sinh Café runs tours in the Mekong Delta and the Central Highlands at reasonable prices. **Découvrir**, 236 Nguyen Trong Tuyen on the way to the airport, ☎ (08) 845 80 96, Fax (08) 844 02 05, decouvrir@fmail. vnn.vn This agency is run by a Frenchman offering sampan cruises down the Mekong and unique Highland treks with experienced guides. Rates are high.

Some agencies operate with groups and expatriates, such as **Exotissimo**, 37 Ton Duc Thang, ☎ (08) 825 17 23, Fax (08) 829 58 00.

WHERE TO STAY

• In the city centre (Plan I)

Cheap accommodation is rare on Dong Khoi and Le Loi which boast several legendary palaces to which have been added a number of other luxury international hotels.

Between US$15 and US$30

Kim Long, 58 Mac Thi Buoi, ☎ (08) 822 85 58, Fax (08) 822 50 24 – 15rm 🍽 🗎 🥂 TV CC Satellite TV, lift. Quite unusually, this modern residential block offers decent accommodation in small, reasonably-priced rooms.

Linh, 16 Mac Thi Buoi, ☎ (08) 824 39 54, Fax (08) 824 39 49, annamtour@hcm.vnn.vn – 10rm 🍽 🗎 🥂 TV CC Satellite TV. A pleasant hotel with large rooms at modest prices for the area. The 5th floor is the cheapest.

Between US$30 and US$50

Bach Dang, 33 Mac Thi Buoi, ☎ (08) 825 15 01, Fax (08) 823 05 87 – 16rm 🍽 🗎 🥂 TV ✕ CC Lift. Breakfast included. A rather plain hotel, but quite respectable with spotless rooms and good value for money.

Bong Sen II, 61-63 Hai Ba Trung, ☎ (08) 823 58 18, Fax (08) 823 58 16, bongsen2@hcm.vnn.vn – 57rm 🍽 🗎 🥂 TV CC Satellite TV, lift. Breakfast included. An address worth knowing, with tastefully decorated, pleasant little rooms. Prices vary according to the view.

Bong Sen, 117-123 Dong Khoi, ☎ (08) 829 15 16, Fax (08) 829 80 76, bongsen@hcm.vnn.vn – 165rm 🍽 🗎 🥂 CC Bar with a view, massage, satellite TV, lift. A reasonably-priced luxury hotel. The rooms are comfortable but lack character.

🏩 **Grand Hotel**, 8 Dong Khoi, ☎ (08) 823 01 63, Fax (08) 823 57 81, grand-hotel@fmail.vnn.vn – 107rm 🍽 🗎 🥂 TV ✕ ⍓ CC Bar, souvenir shops, massages, sauna, satellite TV. A magnificent 1920s building with exceptionally large, sunny rooms and a delightful swimming pool on the 1st floor of the inside courtyard.

Between US$70 and US$100

Rex, 141 Nguyen Hue, ☎ (08) 829 21 85, Fax (08) 829 65 36, rexhotel@sg-tourist.com.vn – 227rm 🍽 🗎 🥂 TV ✕ ⍓ ✾ CC Satellite TV, nightclub, sauna. Another city-centre institution offering attractive, carpeted rooms, as well as a suite in a rather over-ornate Chinese style. Fabulous roof terrace with swimming pool and tennis courts.

Over US$100

Continental, 132-134 Dong Khoi, ☎ (08) 829 92 01, Fax (08) 829 09 36, continental@hcm.vnn.vn – 83rm 🍽 🗎 🥂 TV ✕ CC Bar, satellite TV, massage, fitness centre. The impressive façade of this legendary hotel (1880) is one of the city-centre gems, though the rather outmoded luxury rooms could do with a facelift.

Kimdo – Royal City, 133 Nguyen Hue, ☎ (08) 822 59 14, Fax (08) 822 59 13, kimdohotel@fmail.vnn.vn – 135rm 🍽 🗎 🥂 TV CC Satellite TV. A luxury hotel run by Saigon Tourist with a lovely view over the city. Prices are high, but promotional offers are available. The bar-restaurant terrace on the 4th floor is very pleasant.

Majestic, 1 Dong Khoi, ☎ (08) 829 55 14, Fax (08) 829 55 10, hotel-majestic@sgtourist.com.vn – 122rm ⛫ ▤ ℗ TV ✕ ☲ CC This 1920s Art Deco pearl has preserved all its former glory with extremely luxurious rooms with parquet flooring. The cheaper rooms, however, only have one window looking out onto the corridor. The roof-terrace bar with a view over the river is well worth a visit.

Sofitel Plaza, 17 Le Duan, ☎ (08) 824 15 55, Fax (08) 824 16 66, sofitelsgn@hcmc.netnam.vn – 290rm ⛫ ▤ ℗ TV ✕ ☲ CC Bar, patisserie, souvenir shop, satellite TV. A recently-constructed luxury hotel with an impressive lobby and an amazing terrace swimming pool (18th floor). The rooms and service are impeccable and the buffet is one of the best in town (European or Asian cuisine).

Caravelle, 19 place Lam Son, ☎ (08) 823 49 99, Fax (08) 824 39 99, hotel@caravellehotel.vnn.vn – 335rm ⛫ ▤ ℗ TV ✕ ☲ CC Boutique, sauna, satellite TV. The old Caravelle is flanked by a glass tower housing a very elegant, luxury hotel. The rates are such that you may want to stick to a drink in the 10th floor bar (superb view).

• **Along Pham Ngu Lao** (Plan I)
Cheap hotels abound between the streets of Pham Ngu Lao, Bui Vien and De Tham, where numerous services are available, along with aggravating street sellers.

Under US$10
Ngoc Son, 178/32 Co Giang, ☎ (08) 836 47 17 – 5rm ⛫ ▤ ✕ Breakfast included. A new, very clean little boarding house tucked away in a back street to the south of Pham Ngu Lao, for those looking for a real Vietnamese atmosphere.

Que Huong – Liberty 3, 187 Pham Ngu Lao, ☎ (08) 836 95 22, Fax (08) 836 45 57, qhuong@libertyhotel.vnn.vn – 56rm ⛫ ▤ ✕ TV ✕ CC One of the oldest hotels in the area and was cer-

tainly ready for a spot of renovation. Prices will probably reflect the changes.
Bich Lien, 171/16 Co Bac, ☎ (08) 836 06 41 – 18rm ⛫ ▤ ✕ TV Breakfast included. This huge, brand-new building is out of all proportion to this back street near Ngoc Son, but it provides clean, spacious accommodation at good value for money.

Hotel 269, 269 Pham Ngu Lao, ☎ (08) 836 73 45, Fax (08) 836 81 71 – 46rm ⛫ ▤ ✕ ℗ TV Lift. The rooms are excellent value for money, if noisy.

Linh Thu Guesthouse, 72 Bui Vien, ☎ (08) 836 84 21, linhthu72@yahoo.com – 7rm ⛫ ▤ ✕ An address worth remembering. A family atmosphere with cheap, clean, pleasant rooms.

Giang Guesthouse, 40/26 Bui Vien, ☎ (08) 837 11 83, Fax (08) 836 95 59, pqgiang@yahoo.com – 13rm ⛫ ▤ ✕ TV Clean, simple rooms, and excellent value for money.

Between US$10 and US$15
Mini Hotel Xinh, 185/14 Pham Ngu Lao, ☎ (08) 837 18 81, Fax (08) 836 73 39 – 10rm ⛫ ▤ ✕ ℗ CC A quiet little hotel with clean, spacious rooms at interesting rates that vary considerably according to the floor and availability of air-conditioning.

Hotel 265, 265 De Tham, ☎ (08) 836 75 12, Fax (08) 836 18 83, hotel-duy@hotmail.com – 13rm ⛫ ▤ ✕ ℗ TV CC A warm welcome (English spoken), with clean, quiet rooms, good value for money.

Linh Linh, 175/14 Pham Ngu Lao, ☎ (08) 837 30 04, Fax (08) 836 18 51 – 12rm ⛫ ▤ ✕ ℗ TV Satellite TV. Choose the rooms overlooking the courtyard that are a little more expensive, but bright and spacious. Allow extra for air-conditioning.

Lan Anh, 252 De Tham, ☎ (08) 836 51 97, Fax (08) 836 51 96, lan-anh-hotel@hcm.cnn.vn – 22rm ⛫ ▤ ✕ ℗ TV CC Satellite TV. Breakfast included. A pleasant hotel offering the choice between bright, noisy rooms on the street, or dark, quiet rooms to the back. Choose a room with a balcony.

Phan Lan, 70 Bui Vien, ☎ / Fax (08) 836 95 69, phanlan@hcm. vnn.vn – 9rm ⛫ ▤ ✕ TV Satellite TV. A charming little place where you can dine with the family. An adjoining building in a quiet area at 100/23 Tran Hung Dao provides accommodation for long-stay foreign visitors.

Vinh, formerly Le Le 2, 289 De Tham, ☎ (08) 836 85 85, Fax (08) 836 87 87, lelehotel@hcm.fpt.vn – 9rm ⊶ ▤ 🛒 🔎 🖵 ✗ ᴄᴄ No character, but comfortable, offering a choice of accommodation with prices set according to the size and brightness of the room. Quite a decent hotel in its category.

Hotel 127, 127 Cong Quynh, ☎ (08) 836 87 61, Fax (08) 836 06 58, guesthouse127@bdvn.vnd.net – 15rm ⊶ ▤ 🛒 🖵 Satellite TV, breakfast included. No-fuss, spotless rooms, and a pleasant welcome make this hotel popular with backpackers.

Hong Hoa, 185-28 Pham Ngu Lao, ☎ (08) 836 18 15, honhoarr@hcm.vnn.vn – 7rm ⊶ ▤ 🔎 🖵 ᴄᴄ A pleasant little hotel, very clean, with a free 2hr Internet connection for each guest. The rooms on the street are bigger, brighter, and more expensive.

Que Huong, 28/10 Bui Vien, ☎ (08) 837 42 08 – 13rm ⊶ ▤ 🔎 🖵 Satellite TV. A respectable establishment with the usual range of accommodation for the area with a choice between dark, quiet rooms over the courtyard and bright, noisy rooms onto the street.

Huy Duc, 74 Bui Vien, ☎ (08) 837 05 38, Fax (08) 836 95 91, huyduchotel@hcm.fpt.vn – 20rm ⊶ ▤ 🛒 🔎 🖵 ᴄᴄ Satellite TV, lift. This seven-storey building enjoys an outstanding view over the area. The rooms are very comfortable but rather small.

Between US$15 and US$30

Thao Thanh, 58 Ho Hao Hon, ☎ (08) 836 55 66, Fax (08) 836 53 22 – 10rm ⊶ ▤ 🔎 🖵 ᴄᴄ Satellite TV. Located in a quiet street set back from Pham Ngu Lao. This rather attractive, hacienda-style hotel provides spacious rooms. It has a pleasant little bar backing onto an interior courtyard.

☺**Bee Saigon**, 185/16 Pham Ngu Lao, ☎ (08) 836 06 78, Fax (08) 836 79 47, bisaigon@saigonnet.vn – 6rm ⊶ ▤ 🔎 🖵 ᴄᴄ Satellite TV. Modest, comfortable rooms and pleasant staff make this establishment one of the best value for money in the area, like its twin, the Bi Saigon, next door.

Le Le Hotel, 171 Pham Ngu Lao, ☎ (08) 836 86 86, Fax (08) 836 87 87 – 31rm ⊶ ▤ 🛒 🔎 🖵 ✗ ᴄᴄ Satellite TV, lift. Twinned with its neighbour, the Giant Dragon, this hotel provides flawless service. Prices vary greatly.

Mai Phai Hotel, 209 Pham Ngu Lao, ☎ (08) 836 58 68, Fax (08) 837 15 15, maiphaihotel@saigonnet.vn – 27rm ⊶ ▤ 🛒 🔎 🖵 ✗ Satellite TV, lift. Decent accommodation. Pity that the rooms are rather small and noisy.

☺**Bi Saigon**, 185/26 Pham Ngu Lao, ☎ (08) 836 06 78, Fax (08) 836 79 47, bisaigon@saigonnet.vn – 9rm ⊶ ▤ 🛒 🔎 ᴄᴄ Satellite TV. A safe bet for the area, providing quiet, comfortable accommodation with an efficient English-speaking staff. It is a little more expensive than the Bee Saigon, with bright rooms giving onto the street and dark terrace rooms to the back of the building.

Hanh Hoa, 237 Pham Ngu Lao, ☎ (08) 836 02 45, Fax (08) 836 14 82 – 14rm ⊶ ▤ 🛒 🔎 🖵 ✗ Satellite TV, lift, breakfast included. A warm welcome, a high standard of comfort, but a little expensive for its particular category. The rooms overlooking the street are very light, but a little noisy.

Between US$30 and US$50

Que Huong-Liberty 4, 265 Pham Ngu Lao, ☎ (08) 836 45 56, Fax (08) 836 54 35, qhuong4@libertyhotel.vnn.vn – 71rm ⊶ ▤ 🔎 🖵 ✗ ᴄᴄ Karaoke, bar, massage, satellite TV, lift. Quite an ordinary building, but the rooms have all the necessary amenities with a number of different services, and a 9th floor restaurant with a marvellous view.

Vien Dong Hotel, 275A Pham Ngu Lao, ☎ (08) 836 89 41, Fax (08) 836 88 12, viendonghotel@hcm.fpt.vn – 109rm ⊶ ▤ 🔎 🖵 ✗ ᴄᴄ Lift. Flawless comfort and very professional staff. The hotel also has a bar with a fountain on the 1st floor, as well as a massage parlour and a panoramic restaurant.

• Near the Reunification Palace (Plan I)

Between US$10 and US$15

Bui Thi Diem, 17 Tu Xuong, to the north of Reunification Palace, ☎ (08)

932 58 19 – 3rm 🛏🍴 This attractive, colonial house situated in a residential area provides rooms with all the necessary facilities, but unfortunately the decor is not in keeping with the rest of the building.

Dai Ket, 15 Tu Xuong, ☎ (08) 932 56 42, Fax (08) 932 50 71 – 20rm 🛏▤🍴 This boarding house run by a Catholic association provides simple, tidy rooms, although a little expensive. Inviting terrace on the 1st floor.

Between US$15 and US$30

Son Trang 2, 39 Bui Thi Xuan, ☎ (08) 925 32 37, Fax (08) 839 34 74 – 30rm 🛏▤ ✎ TV CC Satellite TV, lift, breakfast included. This new, seven-storey hotel has chosen a flashy, rather pretentious decor that will delight certain punters.

Lan Lan Hotel, 42 Bui Thi Xuan, ☎ (08) 925 25 57, Fax (08) 833 48 92 – 21rm 🛏▤ ✎ TV CC Satellite TV, lift, breakfast included. This quiet, tree-lined street near the centre is perfect for those wishing to avoid backpackers. Slightly more modest than the Son Trang 2, but prices and facilities are very similar.

New Phuong Mai, 413 Nguyen Dinh Chieu, ☎ (08) 833 26 03 – 17rm 🛏▤ 🍴 ✎ TV This family hotel with a pleasant owner is made up of two buildings, one facing the street and the other facing an alleyway. Prices vary according to the different floors. The climb up to the 5th floor is rather arduous, but it is worth it for the view.

Oriole Hotel, 74 Le Thi Rieng, ☎ (08) 832 34 94, Fax (08) 839 59 19, oriolehotel@saigonnet.vn – 14rm 🛏▤ ✎ TV CC Satellite TV. The hotel is near the centre, but the area is not particularly tourist-orientated. The rooms are spotless and prices decrease on the higher floors. The staff are very welcoming and always ready to help out.

Dai Hoang Ha, 214 Nguyen Thi Minh Khai, ☎ (08) 930 55 25 – 30rm 🛏▤ ✎ TV CC Satellite TV, lift. An address to remember. The rooms have every facility, but are rather expensive.

Between US$30 and US$50

Rang Dong Hotel, 81-83 Cach Mang Thang Tam, ☎ (08) 839 82 64, Fax (08) 839 33 18 – 114rm 🛏▤ ✎ TV 🍴 CC

Satellite TV, lift, breakfast included. This enormous, white building has something of the atmosphere of a swimming pool, but exudes comfortable, old-world charm. Apart from the prices, that is, which are changeable and rather high for this category.

Saigon Star Hotel, 204 Nguyen Thi Minh Khai, ☎ (08) 930 62 90, Fax (08) 930 63 00, saigonstarhotel@hcm. vnn.vn – 72rm 🛏▤ ✎ TV 🍴 CC Massage, sauna, satellite TV, lift, breakfast included. Pleasant, no-fuss luxury. The prices of the most expensive rooms hardly seem justified. The bar-restaurant with terrace enjoys a very pleasant view.

Over US$100

New World Hotel, 76 Le Lai, ☎ (08) 822 88 88, Fax (08) 823 07 10, nwhs@hcm.vnn.vn – 498rm 🛏▤ ✎ TV 🍴 ⟁ ✿ CC Gymnasium, bookshop. In November 2000, President Clinton stayed in this luxurious palace which boasts a terrace bar with a magnificent view over the city. The rooms and service are, of course, impeccable, but only to be expected at these prices.

WHERE TO EAT

Ho Chi Minh City is a culinary paradise with something for everyone. More and more luxury hotels are offering tempting buffets, but the city is more renowned for its cheap eating places, where you can try the simple delights of the local cuisine while enjoying watching the activities on the lively streets. The choice is vast, but bear in mind the specialities offered in the following areas: Nguyen Du for "pho ga" (chicken noodle soup), Pasteur for "pho bo" (beef noodle soup), Pham Van Hai for "bun cha" (a bowl of rice noodles with grilled pork, salad, herbs and spices), Vo Van Tan for "hu tieu" (a type of "pho bo" with a sweet and sour sauce), Dinh Tien Hoang for "banh cuon" (spring rolls with meat and seasoned chicken). There are also little snacks available in most markets, such as Ben Thanh and Ton That Dam. Try the sandwiches made with a French baguette filled with cheese or pâté, cucumber and soya sauce.

• **In the city centre** (Plan I)

Under 25 000VND

Quan Banh Xeo, 49A Dinh Cong Trang, the small backstreet opposite the church on Hai Ba Trung (B2). A lively, cheap eating place with delicious savoury pancakes and grilled meat.

Le An, 2 Binh Khiem (D2). A small, simple restaurant at the entrance to the park, ideal for a snack after the museum.

Indian restaurant, 66 Dong Du (D3). Inside the mosque itself, this is without doubt one of the most original and economic eating places in the area.

Between 25 000 and 50 000VND

Pho Hoa, 260C Pasteur (C3-4). A very busy restaurant serving some of the best soup in the city. A lot of Vietnamese customers, always a good sign.

Between 50 000 and 100 000VND

Mango, 15C4-C8 Thi Sach (D3). Just a stone's throw from the Idecaf, this street is alive with busy terraces where Vietnamese and foreign visitors alike tuck into delicious seafood.

Hoang Yen, 7 Ngo Duc Ke (D4). [CC] Not as well known as its neighbour Restaurant 13, but nevertheless serves tempting Vietnamese cuisine (pork in coconut milk, chicken in ginger). Air-conditioned, menu in English. Another dining room at 148 Hai Ba Trung.

Ciao Restaurant, 71 Nguyen Hue / 21-23 Nguyen Thi Minh Khai. This trendy, air-conditioned bar-restaurant is a perfect place for lunch (sandwiches, pizzas, steaks, pasta) or ice cream and cakes.

3T Restaurant, 29-31 Ton That Thiep (C-D4), above the Temple Club. A new and unusual restaurant where you can dine on the roof of a small building overlooking a busy street scene. Seafood and grilled meats.

Sama, 35 Dong Du (D3). Closed on Sundays. Quiet and very pleasant, popular with expatriates, and also doubles as a grocery store. Ideal for lunch, with a selection of cheeses, cold meats, sandwiches and French style salads, the only touch of exoticism in these parts.

Givral, 169 Dong Khoi (D3-4). [CC] This esteemed institution has lost a lot of its charm since renovation (air-conditioning). The cakes, fruit juices, ice cream and sandwiches are worth a try nonetheless, but the dishes are nothing to write home about (Vietnamese or Western).

TIB, 187 Hai Ba Trung. [CC] Trinh Cong Son specialises in the Imperial cuisine of Hue (rice with lotus flower seeds, chicken in a lotus leaf), and has an air-conditioned dining room and a small courtyard.

Lemon Grass, 4 Nguyen Thiep (D3). Serves Vietnamese cuisine adapted to the Western palate, with rather a bland result.

Chao Thai, 16 Thai Van Lung. Serves some of the best Thai cuisine in town, in a superb decor.

Floating Restaurants, Ton Duc Thang (D4). Departure at 8pm for a romantic dinner on a two-hour boat trip. Opt for the smaller boat with a more intimate atmosphere.

Between 100 000 and 200 000VND

Why Not?, 24 Thai Van Lung (D3). A cheerful little restaurant, and quite central, run by French nationals serving delicious French cuisine.

La Bibliothèque, 84A Nguyen Du (C3). ☎ (08) 823 14 38 (advance booking recommended). A discreet sign points to La Bibliothèque (library) belonging to Mme Dai, a former lawyer and Vice-President of the South-Vietnamese Senate. The restaurant serves adequate French and Vietnamese cuisine in a pleasant atmosphere, surrounded by old law books.

Temple Club, 29 Ton Tat Thiep (C-D4), 1st floor, ☎ (08) 829 92 44. This new restaurant with well-worn brick walls, located in a former boarding house for pilgrims visiting the neighbouring Hindu temple, serves original Vietnamese cuisine. It also doubles as antiques showroom. Enjoy a drink on the balcony overlooking the street.

La Fourchette, 9 Ngo Duc Ke (D4), ☎ (08) 829 81 43. [CC] The recreation of a true French bistro. Typically French menu with reasonable prices and tasty dishes (salads, lamb chops, quiche lorraine). An informal meal French style.

Angkor Encore, 5 Nguyen Thiep (D3), ☎ (08) 822 62 78. A new, sophisticated Khmer restaurant (steamed fish with coconut, prawns with caramel). Air-conditioned dining room.

Chez Bibi, 8A/8D2 Thai Van Lung (D3). [CC] Closed Sunday lunchtime. Whether they trade in wine, coffee or generators, the city's entire expatriate contingent come here to enjoy its delicious Mediterranean dishes.

La Marine, 17A 4 Le Thanh Ton, ☎ (08) 829 22 49. [cc] Closed Sunday lunchtime. An intimate seafaring atmosphere, where they serve appetizing Vietnamese and French dishes (seafood, traditionally-cooked pizzas), notably stuffed clams and Grand Marnier soufflé.

La Villa, 11 Thai Van Lung (D3), ☎ (08) 822 32 40. 🍴 [cc] Closed Sunday lunchtimes. An elegant colonial-style restaurant. Delectable but expensive Thai, Western and vegetarian dishes. Try the exquisite seafood ravioli.

Mandarin, 11A Ngo Van Dam (D3), ☎ (08) 822 97 83. [cc] White tablecloths and high-quality service. This large restaurant is popular with expatriates, but be careful of the prices. To the gentle tones of a piano and a violin, enjoy prawn ravioli, peppered duck, sea food and chocolate mousse.

Augustin, 10 Nguyen Thiep (D3). [cc] This was once the best French restaurant in town with a very tempting menu (pork filet with mustard sauce, duck à l'orange), but its moment of glory has passed.

Over 200 000VND

La Camargue, 16 Cao Ba Quat, ☎ (08) 824 31 48. [cc] (advanced booking recommended). One of the best restaurants in town on the first floor of a tastefully-restored, colonial house. French and international cuisine.

• Around Pham Ngu Lao (Plan I B4)
Under 25 000VND

Thu Thuy, 26 Cach Mang Thanh Tam. This modest eating place does not look anything special, but serves simple, delicious, Vietnamese food (spring rolls, soup, seafood, noodles with sausages).

Giac Du, 98-100 Le Thi Rieng, near the Hotel Oriole. A small restaurant serving Vietnamese, Taiwanese and vegetarian food, popular with the locals.

Zen, 185/30 Pham Ngu Lao. A restaurant catering for every taste with a choice of vegetarian, Indian, Vietnamese, Italian and Mexican cuisine. The fruit juices are excellent.

Bodhi Tree, 175/6 Pham Ngu Lao. A good choice of cheap, vegetarian cuisine (tofu, spinach, salads, soups) with no less than 121 different dishes, including Mexican and Italian specialities.

Between 25 000 and 50 000VND

Saigon Tomorrow Cafe, 40/27 Bui Vien. This little bar-restaurant, open until midnight, serves breakfast and an interesting choice of Vietnamese and Western dishes. An ideal opportunity to relax in front of a video.

Saigon Café, 196 Pham Ngu Lao. 🍴 One of the many cheap eating places on the street serving decent Vietnamese and Western dishes.

Café 333, 201 De Tham. 🍴 Restaurant, bar, boarding house, travel agency, Internet – you name it, they provide it. One of the best street restaurants for breakfast or lunch (Vietnamese or Western). The prawn salad is delicious.

Sinh Café, 248 De Tham. 🍴 A well-known establishment that is a travel agency, bar and restaurant all rolled into one (Vietnamese and Western cuisine, breakfast).

Kim Café, 272 De Tham. Another street institution modelled on the Sinh Café.

Margherita, 175/1 Pham Ngu Lao. This small, inexpensive and very pleasant Italian restaurant serves quite respectable pizzas, lasagne, and pasta.

Between 50 000 and 100 000VND

Good Morning Vietnam, 197 De Tham. Salads, sandwiches, pasta, meat and pizza served in a delightful bamboo decor. An air-conditioned room on the first floor.

Song Ngu, 70 Suong Nguyet Anh. [cc] This large, elegantly-decorated residence is popular with the jet-set of Saigon, who come here to enjoy seafood dishes. The first floor is even cosier.

Thanh Binh, 142 Le Thanh Ton. This excellent Vietnamese restaurant, a stone's throw from Ben Thanh market, specialises in soup and seafood and attracts the local population.

• Outside the city centre
Between 25 000 and 50 000VND

Tri Ky Restaurant, 478 Nguyen Kiem (Plan II C1). A garden of Eden for the more adventurous. Among other unusual items, try their snake, tortoise, monkey and bat dishes.

Between 50 000 and 100 000VND

😊**Com Nieu Saigon**, 6C Tu Xuong (Plan I A3). This lively eating area, a meeting place for Saigon's middle classes, offers a succulent choice of Vietnamese or Thai dishes, as well as seafood. Don't miss the house special, which is rice cooked in an earthenware pot, which is then broken with a hammer and tossed across the room to one of the waiters.

Phuong Nam Quan, 110-112 Vo Van Tan (Plan I A4). 🍴 An enormous tree-lined terrace facing a colonial building, serving seafood, Vietnamese fondue and prawns in beer.

Over 200 000VND

Le Bordeaux, F 7-8 Road D2, north of the city centre towards Vung Tau, ☎ (08) 899 98 31. Closed Sunday lunchtime. This restaurant is located in an elegant, classic-style house with the reputation of serving the best French dishes in town.

GOING OUT

Cafés, cake shops, ice cream parlours – Kem Bach Dang, 26-28 Le Loi; 68 Hai Ba Trung. Open daily 8am-11pm. Supposedly the best ice cream in Vietnam, but try the cakes as well. **Pat'a Chou**, 65 Hai Ba Trung. Bread, croissants and pastries. **Dong Du Café**, 31 Dong Du. A chic, Italian café serving espressos and home-made ice cream. **Paris Deli**, 31 Dong Khoi. This Parisian bistro-style café serves pastries, croissants and sandwiches. **Fanny**, 29-31 Ton That Thiep. French ice creams. **Bo Gia**, 20 Ho Huan Nghiep. A bookshop converted into a café serving ice creams. **Chi Lang Cafe**, Chi Lang Park, Dong Khoi. An ideal place to watch the world go by. Art gallery next door.

Bars, pubs – Bars generally close at 1am (2am at the weekend) and almost all of them have a billiard table. For the rest, the atmospheres are highly varied. The "bia hoi" are modest drinking places with cheap beer. Among them: **Nguyen Chat**, 159 Pham Ngu Lao, **Thanh Ha**, 6 Hai Ba Trung.

The bars along Pham Ngu Lao are mostly popular with backpackers.

😊**Long Phi**, 163 Pham Ngu Lao. A relaxed atmosphere and top marks for the music, a far cry from the usual sentimental stuff.

Allez Boo, Pham Ngu Lao, on the corner of De Tham. The liveliest place in the area, and an ideal place for get-togethers, but don't expect a good chat, considering the level of noise.

Guns & Roses Bar, 207 Pham Ngu Lao. A quieter atmosphere.

Bars in the city centre which tend to attract expatriates:

😊**Vasco's**, 16 Cao Ba Quat. The Camargue bar, with its courtyard decorated with palm trees, is one of the most attractive in the city. The Friday-night rock group guarantees an exciting evening.

O' Brien's Factory, 74A2 Hai Ba Trung. Closed Sunday lunchtime. A very attractive pub with well-worn brick walls.

Underground, 69 Dong Khoi. THE new place in Ho Chi Minh City.

5 Ly Tu Trong, a bar just recently set up in a stylish French villa.

For a more intimate, even slightly formal atmosphere, try the hotel bars.

Rooftop Garden, a terrace on three levels on the 5th floor of the Rex Hotel. An amazing view of the city.

Saigon Saigon, on the 10th floor of the Caravelle. Smart and tasteful, with an equally exceptional view, and a live group every evening.

Breeze Sky, on the 6th floor of the Majestic. Open 24hr a day. The panoramic terrace on three levels is an ideal place for a nightcap.

Panorama, 37 Ton Duc Thang, on the 33rd floor of the Saigon Trade Centre. Its only claim to fame is being the highest point in the city.

Nightclubs – Again, the choice is extremely varied. **Apocalypse Now**, 2B Thi Sach. This techno temple is a wicked place for Vietnamese and Westerners of all ages to meet up.

Vietnamese nightclubs are slightly more conventional, but just as eventful. **Gossip**, Mercury Hotel, 79 Trang Hung Dao. One of the more famous clubs with live music every evening. **Mua Rung**, 5-15 Ho Huan Nghiep. This new club, fitted out with the latest sound and lighting systems, organises dance shows. *KTV* (formerly called Orient), 104 Hai Ba Trung. A Vietnamese-style nightclub where dance and techno music blare out until 2 in the morning. *Club Monaco*, 651 Tran Hung Dao. A huge dance floor, with video screen and laser lighting.

Dance halls, although rather outdated, seem to help maintain that traditional female activity considered long gone, that of hostess. *Queen Bee*, 104-106 Nguyen Hue. This cult establishment survived 1975 and is still very popular among Saigon yuppies. *Dancing at the Rex*, 141 Nguyen Hue. A Saturday night hot-spot, where punters of all ages come to listen to local popsters.

Shows – "The Guide" is a good source of information for all cultural events. At the weekend, you are more than likely to come across one of those variety shows that draws crowds to the parks in the evenings.

Municipal theatre, 7 Lam Song Square on Dong Khoi, ☎ (08) 825 15 63. Open every day from 8pm. A very varied programme of traditional theatre, ballet and variety shows. *Nha Hat Hoa Binh*, 14 3 Thang 2 Street, ☎ (08) 865 52 15. The "Theatre of Peace" has several rooms (maximum 2 400 places) where traditional plays, circus performances, variety concerts and Western pop music are scheduled. *Nha Hat Ben Thanh*, 6 Mac Dinh Chi, ☎ (08) 823 16 52. Open every day at 8pm. Concerts, fashion shows. *Kich Sai Gon*, 59 Pasteur. A local theatre showing Vietnamese light comedy. *Water puppet shows*, The History Museum of Vietnam, 2 Nguyen Binh Khiem, Botanical Gardens. Daily performances at 9am, 10am, 11am, 2pm, 3pm, 4pm. Allow US$1.

Academy of Music, 112 Nguyen Du, ☎ (08) 839 66 46. Classical Western and traditional Vietnamese music (Mondays and Fridays at 7.30pm, from March to May and from October to December).

Cinema – *CLB Phim Tu Lieu*, 212 Ly Chinh Thang, ☎ (08) 822 23 24. Films in English subtitled in Vietnamese. *Rex Cinema*, 141 Nguyen Hue and *Vinh Quang*, 59 Pasteur show Vietnamese films. *Rap Dong Khoi*, 163 Dong Khoi. *Tan Son Nhat Cinema*, 186 Nguyen Van Troi, ☎ (08) 842 16 13.

OTHER THINGS TO DO

Outdoor pusuits – Consult "The Guide" for the different activities available in the city (bowling, golf, swimming, tennis). Most of the pools in the luxury hotels are open to non-residents for a small fee. Popular with expatriates are the *International Club*, 285B Cach Mang Thang Tam, 342 Tran Binh Trong, ☎ (08) 835 80 28 (pool), and the *Lan Anh Country Club*, 291 Cach Mang Thang Tam, ☎ (08) 862 71 44 (tennis), with excellent facilities. *The Workers' Club*, 55B Nguyen Thi Minh Khai, Van Hoa Park. This former Sports Club has preserved all its facilities from the colonial era, notably the tennis courts and the large open-air swimming pool.

Massage – *Municipal Association for the Blind*, 185 Cong Quynh, ☎ (08) 839 66 97. Open daily from 9am-8.30pm. Their reputation is well-established and any money collected by the association goes to the school for the blind next door. The bigger hotels normally have a massage parlour. You can also try a facial massage, an unforgettable experience, at the Thuy hairdressing salon, 32 Bui Thi Xuan.

Horse racing – *Phu To Stadium*, 2 Le Dai Hanh, Cholon. Betting opens Saturday and Sunday afternoon.

SHOPPING

Markets – There are two markets in the city centre. *Ben Thanh* (below Le Loi) is a huge covered building where you can find food and clothing, while *Cho Cu* (Ton That Dam and Ton That Thiep) specialises in electronic goods, food and miscellaneous products. The *Dan Sinh* army surplus store (on the corner of Yersin and Nguyen Cong Tru) is not as popular as before. *Cau Ong Lanh* is one of the most colourful and the most sweet-smelling fresh produce markets in the town (Nguyen Thai Hoc and the Ben Chuong Duong quaysides). *Nguyen Thai Binh* (west of Pham Ngu Lao) overflows with fresh produce, while *An Dong* (at the intersection of Tran Phu and An Duong Vuong) is spread over four floors. But the most famous and the most vibrant of all markets is of course **Binh Tay**, in Cholon (see page 346).

Antiques, arts and crafts – The choice of handicrafts and antiques in Ho Chi Minh City is far more limited than in Hanoi and the prices are much higher. Le Cong Kieu, the antiques street, is lined with stalls selling ceramics, clocks, statues, lacquer-ware, paintings, furniture, Zippo lighters, to name but a few, in an atmosphere of friendly confusion. Bargaining is essential, but most of the so-called antiques are imitation. The same goes for the stamps and coins offered by street vendors, especially as you can buy better quality stamps at the main Post Office. The shops along Dong Khoi also sell complete series of stamps from the French period, at rather high prices. Prices along Pham Ngu Lao are more reasonable.

Craft Home, 39A Ngo Duc Ke. Attractive ethnic goods (bags, baskets, clothes). **Heritage**, 53 Dong Khoi. An expensive shop which sells superb baskets, lacquer-ware and decorative or everyday objects based on traditional designs. **Loan Anh**, 26B Le Loi. Compasses, watches, and infrared binoculars, old or new. **Sapa**, 29 Ngo Duc Ke, 223 De Tham. Laquer-ware, traditional fabrics or copies from North Vietnam, and genuine basketware. **Nguyen frères**, 2A Le Duan. Excellent choice of furniture and decorative items (antique or reproduction). **Quoc Dung Co**, 36 Dong Khoi. Wooden furniture.

Art galleries – Ho Chi Minh City offers a wide range of lacquerware and paintings on silk, canvas or rice paper, but there is almost too much choice considering the number of galleries, particularly along Dong Khoi. As far as paintings are concerned, have a look at the works in the Museum of Fine Arts and adjacent galleries before making up your mind.

Ancient Gallery, 50 Mac Thi Buoi. A stylish gallery with a wide choice of contemporary paintings. **Hoang Hac**, 73 Ly Tu Trung. One of the more exclusive galleries in the city. **Tu Do Gallery**, 142 Dong Khoi, ☎ (08) 823 17 85. Watercolours on silk, lacquer-ware and canvas, and wooden sculptures. **Vinh Loi Gallery**, 41 Ba Huyen Thanh Quan, ☎ (08) 822 20 06. A reputable art gallery.

Clothes – The area around Pham Ngu Lao is crammed with boutiques selling printed T-shirts, waterproofs, backpacks and silk sleeping bags. Ben Thanh Market and the adjacent streets (Le Thanh Ton and Ly Tu Trong) is an equally good area for off-the-peg clothes and shoes. The shops along Dong Khoi are more expensive. If you want a garment made up, then it is best to bring along your own design as an example.

Wine – **La Cave**, 54 Le Thanh Ton, ☎ (08) 824 42 51. This is well-stocked with French wine on the initiative of the expert in this field, Youri Korsakoff.

Bookshops – The unscrupulous photocopying of books is still rampant, and you will find a number of guides, essays and novels in English about Vietnam. The city also has some proper bookshops. **Bookazine**, 28 Dong Khoi. Novels and magazines in English, as well as maps and old books. **The Cat Book**, 243 De Tham. Novels, guides and essays in English, as well as postcards and old books. **Xuan Thu Bookshop**, 185 Dong Khoi. A wide selection of guides, novels, maps and magazines.

B Pérousse/MICHELIN

Around Ho Chi Minh City★★
Cu Chi – Tay Ninh
Ho Chi Minh and Tay Ninh Provinces – Map pages 330-331
115km from Ho Chi Minh City
Allow one day – Accommodation available in Tay Ninh

No to be missed
The Cu Chi Tunnels.
The Cao Dai Temple in Tay Ninh.
And remember...
Visit both sites together, either by motorcycle or rented car.
Start with Cu Chi,
and attend the big midday service at Tay Ninh.

Tay Ninh Province, located on the Cambodian border, suffered particularly badly during the Vietnam War. One of the most poignant war pictures was taken along Highway 22 in Trang Bang, showing a little girl running down the road, screaming with pain, her body burnt by napalm. The girl in question, Phan Thi Kim Phuc, later emigrated to Canada where she married and was appointed ambassador to Unesco in 1997. There are two main sites to be visited in one day from Ho Chi Minh City; firstly the Cu Chi Tunnels, a symbol of the Viet Cong's struggle against the Americans and a real insight into the sheer hell of the Vietnam War, and secondly Tay Ninh, the capital of this small border province and the centre of Cao Dai.

■ The Cu Chi Tunnels★★
Allow 1hr

45km northwest of Ho Chi Minh City. Take Highway 22 as far as the village of Cu Chi (35km), and then turn right. Carry on for about 10km to Ben Dinh. Open daily from 6am-6pm. Entrance fee, 65 000VND. Guided tours only.

The Cu Chi Tunnels were of major importance during the Vietnam War. They are a striking testimony to the resourcefulness and determination of the Vietnamese in the face of the extraordinary military power deployed by the Americans in the area. Thirty years later the weapons are silent, but tourists come in droves to visit this small part of the underground network that is a reminder of the tragedy.

The "Iron Triangle"
The first tunnels at Cu Chi, 40km long, were built by the Viet Minh on 1948 on a rubber tree plantation, first to hide their arms, and then to hide themselves. From 1960 onwards, the Viet Cong set about repairing and enlarging the network, which finally extended for 250km and was intended to link pockets of resistance and provide backup for hit-and-run attacks on Saigon. Cu Chi had the added advantage of being close to the southern end of the Ho Chi Minh Trail, above the level of the river, thereby minimising the risk of flooding. The **clay soil** was difficult to dig, but fortunately provided sufficient resistance against passing tanks and air-raids. The tunnel diggers' main problem was the disposal of the soil collected, which was generally tipped into the river under cover of darkness. Large areas of the forest were systematically razed to the ground, and when the wood used for the tunnel supports became a rare commodity, the fighters would steal necessary materials from enemy bases. The tunnel shafts measured 80cm x 80cm and spread over several levels with interconnecting **rooms** (dormitories, latrines, kitchens, meeting rooms, field hospitals). Small trapdoors led into the tunnels and some openings were hidden underwater, with numerous other false entrances set up by the Viet Cong. Pepper

was put down around the trapdoors to distract the American sniffer dogs and the Viet Cong went as far as wearing captured American uniforms and washing with stolen American soap to confuse the dogs even further. Finally, an ingenious system allowed smoke to escape through termites' nests and thickets some metres away. Overcrowding, stifling heat, lack of hygiene and oxygen, constant dim light, smells, rats, snakes, and scorpions were all part of the atrocious living conditions of the Viet Cong, reduced to living like animals. Moreover the fighters generally had to make do with tapioca, leaves and roots as their staple diet.

The Americans were desperate to take control of this **strategic zone** near the capital, and used all possible means to destroy the tunnel network. At the beginning of 1963, the villages were relocated into "strategic hamlets" in an attempt to cut the fighters off from the local population, but the plan failed and some of the hamlets even found themselves directly linked to the underground passages. From 1965, the Americans dotted the area with military bases, but even one of these was unknowingly set up directly above one of the tunnels. The area was then cleared with defoliant, napalm, petrol and bulldozers, and replanted with highly inflammable grasses. Finally, to immobilise the tunnels, special units were sent in, consisting of American nationals at first, and then enlisted Mexican soldiers (they were smaller), followed by South Vietnamese. Caught in booby-trapped bottlenecks spiked with bamboo stakes or filled with snakes, these "tunnel rats" suffered huge losses. After the Tet Offensive of 1968, the Americans carpet-bombed the entire area of Cu Chi, and infiltrated the Viet Cong network (Operation Phoenix). But the tunnels had already fulfilled their mission at the cost of the lives of 12 000 fighters and countless civilians.

Visiting the tunnels

Two of the tunnel sites are open to the public. **Ben Dinh** attracts few tourists and is made up of a section of underground passages as well as a visitor centre which includes maps of the tunnel system. The main site of **Ben Duoc★★** is several kilometres further on, just beyond the war cemetery where 10 000 victims were laid to rest, and is actually a reconstruction of one of the tunnels, widened slightly to accommodate Westerners. Creeping down into these narrow, damp passageways, with only a torch to light the way can be quite an experience. The tour begins with a film which pays tribute to the Viet Cong fighters using material recorded at the time, and then continues with a guided tour through the undergrowth.

Go back to the village of Cu Chi and take Highway 22 in the direction of Tay Ninh (64km).

■ Tay Ninh★★
Allow 1hr

This province is situated on the outer edges of Vietnam along the Cambodian border, and serves as the headquarters of one of the country's most interesting religions, founded in the 1920s by a petty government official of the colonial administration, Ngo Van Chieu *(see page 63)*. Under the control of his successor, Pham Cong Tac, **Cao Dai** played a significant political role and throughout its history has shown an amazing ability to champion the loser (Japanese, French, American). Accused of nationalism, the movement was first quashed by the French in 1937 and its leader forced into exile for 6 years. During the Second World War, its followers brought together a 20 000-strong military force backed by the Japanese, and then took up the fight with the French against the Viet Minh. After the division of Vietnam, they strengthened their control over Tay Ninh Province, effectively forming an independent state, and entered into conflict with President Diem, but American intervention led them to deploy their forces against the Viet Cong. After 1975, the movement's anti-Communist antecedents led to its suppression, its leaders were sent to rehabilitation camps and their assets confiscated. The Cao Dai movement was legalised again in 1985 and has since recovered its places of worship and over two million followers.

Ceremony at the Cao Dai Temple in Tay Ninh

Cao Dai Holy See★★

The Holy See is situated 5km west of Tay Ninh. During the ceremonies (6am, noon, 6pm and midnight), wear respectful attire. The rest of the time you may visit the church quite freely. Cameras are allowed but the use of flash is forbidden and it is only polite to ask permission before taking a picture.

The monastery has been the headquarters of the Cao Dai religion since 1927, and comprises a number of buildings including dormitories, administrative buildings, a refectory, a printing room and electrical installations. All these facilities are spread out over a 1km² park in the middle of which stands the **Cao Dai Grand Temple★★** (Thanh That Cao Dai), built in 1933. The temple is a pagoda, cathedral and Taoist place of worship all rolled into one. Its rather garish, Baroque architecture perfectly reflects the syncretic philosophy of the Cao Dai religion, and the vast 107m-high Sino-Vietnamese-style edifice is definitely disconcerting. Two **towers** flank the main façade, which is decorated with statues of the spirits of Good (to the left) and Evil (to the right), and with bas-reliefs representing Le Van Trung (Ly Thai Bach) to the right, the first Cao Dai pope, and Lam Huong to the left, the first woman cardinal. On the sides, floral sculptures with ornamental apertures surround a triangle containing a "divine eye". A **mural★** in the large entrance hall depicts the three divine missionaries sent as spiritual guides for humanity in the creation of the Third Alliance. They are Sun Yat-sen, founder of the Chinese Republic, Nguyen Binh Khiem, the great Vietnamese poet, and, more surprisingly, Victor Hugo, the reincarnation of Nguyen Du. Bathed in light, the **nave★★★**, features enormous dragons twisted around the columns, seemingly on their way down from the star-studded heavens. The nave extends over nine levels, representing the nine steps to heaven. On the seventh level stands the **throne of Gia Tong** (pope), empty since the founder's death, as well as those of the advisors and cardinals. On the ninth level, hidden behind some curtains, a perpetual flame burns inside a giant **blue globe★★** ornamented with stars and the Master's "divine eye", a perfect symbol of universal religion. The Cao Dai pantheon is represented above the altar by the Goddess Quan Am, Lao-tzu, the Sakyamuni Buddha, Confucius, the Chinese God of War Quan Cong, Ly Thai Bach, Jesus Christ and the Chinese spirit Khuong Thai Cong (Khuong Tu Nha).

The ritual – A daily stream of tourists come to witness the important midday prayer session *(30min)*. After entering the church by one of the side doors, visitors are led to the galleries above the nave. The general commotion does not seem to disturb the meditation of the faithful dressed in white sitting in line on the floor, ladies to the left, men to the right. The first rows contain dignitaries dressed in yellow (Buddhism), blue (Taoism) or red (Christianity). Following an unchanged ritual, a small group of musicians in the gallery above the entrance charm the congregation with their beguiling music, while the faithful chant monotonously. The ceremony has no sermon, but offerings of flowers, tea, alcohol and incense are presented to the Supreme Being. Almost one million faithful congregate at Tay Ninh during the festivities of 9 January and mid-August.

Go in a northeasterly direction to Nui Ba Den (15km from Tay Ninh).

■ Black Lady Mountain★ (Nui Ba Den)

Nui Ba Den seems to rise up from nowhere. It is the highest mountain in the south of the country (986m), often shrouded in mist, and was the scene of fierce fighting during the war. In 1962, the Americans established a summit base here, which included a landing strip and a telecommunications aerial.

The climb to the top may attract the more energetic visitor *(entrance fee. Allow 6hr round trip)*, otherwise enjoy a trip to the **Ba Pagoda** either on foot *(90min round trip)* or by cable car *(35 000VND)*. A statue of the Goddess of Mercy stands in front of the sanctuary entrance (1995), while inside sit the **statues** of the 18 repentant bandits of Eastern mythology, as well as the Goddess with 18 arms. There is a remarkable **panoramic view★★** over the rice paddies from the summit. The mountain has been revered since time immemorial by the Vietnamese, the Cham and the Khmer, and attracts about one million pilgrims during the festivities held in the middle of January.

———— Tay Ninh close up ————

COMING AND GOING

By bus – In Ho Chi Minh City, buses for Tay Ninh leave from the **Ben Xe Tay Ninh** terminal which is accessible by motorcycle taxi. Departures every 20min from 5am-6pm (5hr journey), but you are strongly advised to take one of the express buses to Tay Ninh that leave on the hour from 7am-4pm (3hr). To get to the Cu Chi tunnels, take a bus from Tay Ninh, get off in Cu Chi, then travel the remaining 15km by motorcycle taxi. Good luck!

By motorcycle – To rent a motorcycle, see page 350.

By car – Undoubtedly the best way to visit the two sites in the same day, especially if several travellers can share expenses. For further information on the agencies, see page 351.

ADDRESS BOOK

Bank / Currency exchange – Incombank, 30 Thang 4, near the Anh Dao Hotel. Monday-Friday 7.30-11am. Visa and MasterCard accepted.

WHERE TO STAY

Between US$15 and US$30
Hoa Binh Hotel, 210 30 Thang 4 Street, ☎ (066) 82 13 15, Fax (066) 82 23 45 – 150rm ⚓ 🍽 ☒ 🛁 ♪ 📺 ✗ Breakfast included. A large Soviet-style building with all the necessary facilities offering a wide range of rooms, some with satellite TV.

Anh Dao Hotel, 30 Thang 4, ☎ (066) 82 73 06, Fax (066) 82 21 26 – 18rm ⚓ 🍽 ♪ 📺 ✗ A rather tacky, old-fashioned hotel, but quite respectable. The Hoa Binh is better value-for-money.

EATING OUT

Between 25 000 and 50 000VND
Hoa Don, 30 Thang 4, near the Anh Dao Hotel. 🍴 A small, simple restaurant somewhat lacking in excitement, but only to be expected in Tay Ninh.

Vung Tau★

Capital of Ba Ria-Vung Tau Province
Pop 100 000 – 125km from Ho Chi Minh City

Not to be missed
A tour of the coast and the beach at Bai Sau.
A climb up to the Giant Jesus.
The Long Hai resort.

And remember...
Avoid visiting Vung Tau at the weekends,
when the hotels are fully booked and increase their prices.

The favourite seaside resort of the people of Saigon, Vung Tau is no longer the Riviera-like place it was in colonial times. Devoted to mass tourism, the town is now home to huge hotels, karaoke-bars and beaches of varying degrees of cleanliness, which could deter any honest holiday-maker. However, the wonderful setting, the prospect of a dip in the sea and an encounter with the lively, fun-loving and boisterous, although sometimes a little flashy locals, make the journey well worthwhile. Apart from the beaches, coastal strolls, nightlife and a climb up to the Giant Jesus constitute the main attractions of Vung Tau. To the northeast, the resort of Long Hai is ideal for those looking for a little peace and quiet.

Oil and golden beaches...

Portuguese sailors are supposed to have moored their vessels here as early as the 15C, naming the place after their patron saint, St James. But it was not until the end of the 19C that it became the favourite seaside resort of the Saigon French under the name of **Cap St Jacques** (St James' Point). During the Vietnam War, it enticed American GIs looking for some fun, and then after 1975, Soviet experts working on the oil rigs. At the end of the 1970s, Cap-St-Jacques also became one of the main departure points for the boat people trying to flee the country (*see page 133*). The course of history has since changed, and the flood of Vietnamese pouring onto the beaches every weekend is no longer in search of other distant shores. As for the industrial side of Vung Tau, represented by the offshore petroleum exploration company VietsovPetro, it seems to be marking time.

Vung Tau, the epitome of beach resorts
Allow 2 days

Vung Tau occupies the tip of a rocky spur that juts out into the South China Sea. The main part of the town extends between two hills, Bai Truoc Beach (Front Beach) and the airport, while most of the hotels are situated along the strips of sand that skirt the peninsula. Backing onto the town centre, **Bai Truoc** (Coconut Palm Beach) (B4) is the least enticing and most polluted beach in the whole of Vung Tau. However, you can still enjoy a morning stroll watching the colourful fishing boats come in, or sit down in the evening at one of the little seafood places along Quang Trung, a wide avenue planted with coconut palms.

Small Mountain★ (Nui Nho)

To the south of the bay stands a massive hill, 197m high, with forest-covered slopes, at the bottom of which winds the coastal road, the former **Route de la Petite Corniche** (*6km*), with wonderful panoramic views. A **lighthouse** was built on top of the Small Mountain in 1910 to guide boats into the port (*after the post office, follow the coastal road for 200m, and then take the little path to the left and turn right after 500m. Allow 1hr round trip*). The **view★★** is spectacular, but for some obscure security reasons, photography is not permitted from the top of the lighthouse.

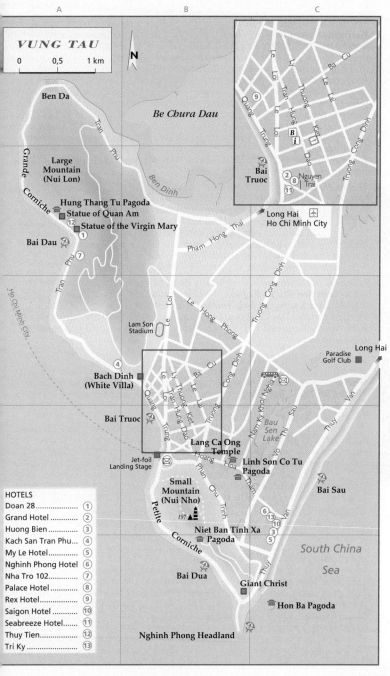

VUNG TAU

0   0,5   1 km

N

Ben Da

Be Chura Dau

Grande Corniche

Large Mountain (Nui Lon)

Tran Phu

Ben Dinh

Hung Thang Tu Pagoda
Statue of Quan Am
⑫ Statue of the Virgin Mary
①

Bai Dau

Tran Phu

⑦

Pham Hong Thai

Long Hai
Ho Chi Minh City

Le Loi

Ly Thuong

Le Lai

Ba Cu

Quang Trung

⑨

Tran Hung Dao

B
i

②
⑧
⑪

Bai Truoc

Nguyen Trai

Truong Cong Dinh

Ho Chi Minh City

Lam Son Stadium

Le Loi

Le Hong Phong

Truong Cong Dinh

Paradise Golf Club

Long Hai

Bach Dinh (White Villa)

Quang Trung

Le Loi

Ly Thuong Kiet

Tran Hung Dao

Ba Cu

Cong Dinh

Truong

Nam Ky Khoi Nghia

Bau Sen Lake

Vo Thi Sau

Thuy Van

Bai Truoc

④

Lang Ca Ong Temple

Hoang Hoa

Phan Chu Trinh

Linh Son Co Tu Pagoda

Bai Sau

Jet-foil Landing Stage

Small Mountain (Nui Nho)

197

Niet Ban Tinh Xa Pagoda

⑥
⑬
⑩
③
⑤

Thuy Van

Petite Corniche

Bai Dua

Giant Christ

South China Sea

Hon Ba Pagoda

Nghinh Phong Headland

Several hundred metres from the post office, a road leads off to the **Niet Ban Tinh Xa Pagoda** *(open daily from 7am-5pm)*, a modern structure famous for its 5-tonne **bronze bell** and its 12m-long reclining **Buddha**. Below stretches Bai Dua (Pineapple Beach), known as "Roches Noires Beach" (Black Rock) from colonial days, in fact a thin strip of sand reached along a small path.

Restaurants, hotels and pavilions are increasingly scarce as you approach the tip of the peninsula. Suddenly, jutting out over the road, the enormous figure of the **Giant Jesus*** (Thanh Gioc) appears, his arms open seawards *(a path leads to it)*. This 28m-high statue was built in 1971 and clearly echoes the one in Rio de Janeiro. Inside the statue, steps lead to the top and the breathtaking **view****. There is a small beach at the bottom of the **Nghinh Phong Headland**, "ideal for anglers and adventure-lovers", according to the Tourist Office leaflet. Whatever your interests, admire the view over Bai Sau and the unusual **Hon Ba Pagoda***, perched on a small rock 200m from the shore, accessible on foot at low tide.

The road then leads down to **Bai Sau***, a vast stretch of sand 8km long, where trees have long since been replaced by unsightly hotels and restaurants. Apart from swimming, the beach is also an invitation to a total sociological immersion, with its display of bathers in flowery attire, proud builders of sand castles, large families, and elegant ladies in high heels, to name but a few. The atmosphere is friendly, despite the beginner jet-skiers merrily weaving in and out of the swimmers. As you relax on a sun-bed *(for hire)* shaded by a parasol, you may as well give in to one of the jolly crab sellers pestering you to buy some of their delicious seafood.

A little off the beaten track along Hoang Hoa Tham towards Bai Sau and Bai Truoc, stands **Linh Son Co Tu Pagoda**, the oldest around Vung Tau (19C). On the other side of the road, **Lang Ca Ong Temple** is dedicated to the worship of whales. There are some preserved skeletons, and every year, on the 16th day of the 8th lunar month, a ceremony interspersed with various offerings and chants is held in honour of this noble cetacean.

Large Mountain* (Nui Lon)

Another 10km tour to the north of Vung Tau follows the coastal road, the former **Grande Corniche,** around Large Mountain (520m). Several hundred metres to the north of Bai Truoc, **Bach Dinh*** (White Villa) stands out amid the vegetation *(entrance at 12 Tran Phu. Open daily from 7am-5pm. Entrance fee 5 000VND)*. The Governor General of Indochina, Paul Doumer, who appreciated the better things in life, chose this area for his holiday home (1898). Emperor Thanh Thai was kept here under house arrest in 1906 before being deported to the French island of Réunion, and Emperor Bao Dai and President Nguyen Van Thieu often stayed here. The mansion itself is very stylish, sporting a highly decorative Art Deco frieze at the front. Inside, the cool, large, high-ceilinged rooms have furnishings that once belonged to the Emperor (elephant tusks, vases), and **ceramics** salvaged from a 17C wreck discovered near Con Dao Island. The **view**** from the first floor is outstanding.

Buildings become sparse as you leave Bai Truoc, and the **view**** is once again quite remarkable. At twilight, the fiery glow of the setting sun fades across the South China Sea, a romantic backdrop for lovers. The four-lane road suddenly narrows to two just before the approach to **Bai Dau** (Mulberry Beach). A rather ordinary beach, but a peaceful area for tourists attracted to the charm of the small boarding houses and private villas that have blossomed in the area, so unlike the cold large-scale developments around Vung Tau. A series of bars and restaurants on stilts lines the seafront, and new hotels are being built. Nearby, an enormous **statue of the Virgin Mary** carrying the infant Jesus stands at the foot of the hill, a symbol to triumphant Catholicism, cocking a snook at Buddhism. Next to it, backing on to the **Hung Thang Tu Pagoda**, is the **statue of Quan Am**, a lot smaller, but probably from the same workshop. *From here, you can either turn round or carry on along a narrow, bumpy road which leads through the fishing village of Ben Da, before returning to Vung Tau.*

Long Hai

46km northwest of Vung Tau. Access is possible by bus via Ba Ria. With its fine, sandy beach, parasols, sun-beds and crab sellers, Long Hai offers the same sort of amenities as Vung Tau, except that the village is much smaller and there is only a handful of hotels. The area will attract those looking for a little peace and quiet, so avoid the weekends when everything is in full swing. Alongside the Huong Bien Hotel, groups of delightful little **boats** with their pennants flapping in the wind are a reminder that the villagers' main livelihood is fishing.

Vung Tau close up

COMING AND GOING

By bus – The **terminal** is situated at 192 Nam Ky Khoi Nghia, to the north of the town. It serves mainly Ho Chi Minh City (2hr) and Long Hai (1hr). In Saigon, the buses leave from the Mien Dong terminal.

By minibus – From Saigon, minibuses for Vung Tau (2hr) leave from Ham Nghi as soon as they are full (this departure point is likely to change, so contact your hotel for further information), and drop passengers off on Tran Hung Dao, near the cathedral. From Vung Tau, the minibuses wait near the Seabreeze Hotel. There are frequent departures up until 9am and you can easily negotiate the price of the trip (about 30 000VND); after that, departures are every 30min. The journey is tiring.

By hydrofoil – The easiest and the most comfortable way to get to Vung Tau (75min). Two companies operate between Ho Chi Minh City and Vung Tau, with identical facilities (allow US$10). In Ho Chi Minh City, the **landing stage** is on Ton Duc Thang, at the end of Ham Nghi. In Vung Tau, it is situated at the end of Bai Truoc, at the beginning of the Petit Corniche coastal road.

Greenlines - Vina Express, Vung Tau, landing stage ☎ (064) 85 65 30, Ho Chi Minh City, 8A Nguyen Tat Thanh, ☎ (08) 826 32 01, Fax (08) 940 29 49. Departures every two hours both from Vung Tau and Ho Chi Minh City from 6.30am-4.30pm.

Petro Express, Vung Tau, 20 Truong Cong Dinh, ☎ (064) 81 63 08, Fax (064) 81 63 07. Tickets are available at the landing stage, ☎ (064) 81 06 25, Fax (064) 59 01 37. The office in Ho Chi Minh City is on the Bach Dang Quay,

☎ (08) 821 06 53, Fax (08) 821 06 50. Departures from Ho Chi Minh City and Vung Tau at 8am, 10am, 2pm and 4pm.

GETTING AROUND

By taxi – *Gili Taxi*, 247 Truong Cong Dinh, ☎ (064) 85 85 85. ***Petro Taxi***, ☎ (064) 85 18 51 / 81 81 81. ***Vung Tau Taxi***, ☎ (064) 84 84 84, in front of the Palace Hotel.

By bicycle – A pleasant way to travel, but watch out for the distances. Contact the hotels and restaurants.

By motorcycle – The best way to get around Vung Tau. A number of hotels rent out motorcycles.

By rental car – *Vicarrent*, 54 Tran Hung Dao, ☎ (064) 85 24 00 / 85 69 55. Further information from the big hotels.

By cyclo – As always, the "xi lo dap" is ideal for short distances.

ADDRESS BOOK

Tourist information – *Ba Ria - Vung Tau Tourist Corporation*, 29 Tran Hung Dao, ☎ (064) 85 64 46, Fax (064) 85 64 44. Monday-Saturday 7am-5pm, closed at lunchtime. Tours, car rental and hotel reservations.

Bank / Currency exchange – *Vietcombank*, 27-29 Tran Hung Dao. Monday-Friday 7.30-11.30am / 1.30-4pm.

Post Office / Telephone – 4 Ha Long, to the far south of Bai Truoc. Open daily from 6.30am-8pm.

Internet – Some hotels provide this service (see "Where to stay").

Airline companies – *Vietnam Airlines*, 29 Tran Hung Dao, next to Vung Tau Tourist, ☎ (064) 85 60 99. Monday-Saturday 7.30-noon / 2-6pm, Sundays 8-11.30am.

The South

• Bai Truoc Beach

Between US$15 and US$30

Grand Hotel, 28 Quang Trung, at the corner of Nguyen Trai, ☎ (064) 85 64 69, Fax (064) 85 60 88 – 76rm ⏁ 🍽 ✕ ✗ ⌁ ✗ c Breakfast included. Massage, karaoké. This big, town-centre hotel provides spacious, comfortable rooms, although perhaps a little run down. Some have air-conditioning, a balcony facing the sea and satellite TV. The service is a little slow, but the staff speak English.

Between US$30 and US$50

Seabreeze Hotel, 2 Nguyen Trai, ☎ (064) 85 63 92, Fax (064) 85 68 56 – ⏁ 🍽 ✕ ✗ 📺 ✗ ⌁ CC The decorative taste of the enormous rooms is questionable and the hotel could be better value for money.

Palace Hotel, 1 Nguyen Trai, ☎ (064) 85 64 11, Fax (064) 85 68 78 – 120rm ⏁ 🍽 ✗ 📺 ✗ ⌁ ✗ CC Breakfast included, Internet access. This luxury hotel has a pleasant swimming pool (a charge for non-residents) and bar with comfortable accommodation. The rates are the same during the week as at the weekend, but try and negotiate.

Rex Hotel, 1 Duy Tan, ☎ (064) 85 21 35, Fax (064) 85 98 62 – 78rm ⏁ 🍽 ✗ 📺 ✗ ⌁ ✗ CC Breakfast included. Bicycles for hire, Internet access, satellite TV, bar, karaoke. The hotel was built in 1972 for American officers on leave and still preserves a certain elegance from that period, despite more recent renovation work. The rooms are comfortable, but rather expensive (rates for the better equipped rooms are twice as high). The staff speak English.

• Bai Sau Beach

Under US$10

Tri Ky, 180 Hoang Hoa Tham, ☎ (064) 85 91 98 – 16rm ⏁ 🍽 ✕ 📺 This simple, very clean hotel with all the necessary facilities represents excellent value for money for its category (rates are 20% lower in the week).

Between US$10 and US$15

Saigon Hotel, 85 Thuy Van, ☎ (064) 85 23 17, Fax (064) 85 42 24 – 121rm ⏁ 🍽 ✕ ✗ 📺 ✗ A wide range of prices. The rooms in the old building are rather outdated (ventilator), but those in the new building should meet all your requirements (satellite TV, hot water, breakfast included), but the decor is a bit tacky. The staff are quite professional and speak English. Motorcycles for hire.

Huong Bien, 59 Thuy Van, ☎ (064) 52 20 50, Fax (064) 85 31 77 – 30rm ⏁ 🍽 ✕ Popular with the local people, this pleasant hotel provides accommodation in small chalets looking out over a garden, but the facilities are rather basic and the rooms quite small. Prices can double according to the level of comfort and are higher at the weekend.

Between US$30 and US$50

Nghinh Phong Hotel, 172 Hoang Hoa Tham, main entrance on Thuy Van, ☎ (064) 85 24 78, Fax (064) 85 22 85 – 52rm ⏁ 🍽 ✗ 📺 ✗ A vast entrance hall sets the tone of this comfortable establishment, but the atmosphere is rather cold. Impeccable facilities and spotless rooms, but the weekend rates are really too high.

Between US$50 and US$70

My Le Hotel, 100-102 Thuy Van, ☎ (064) 85 21 77, Fax (064) 85 31 77 – 100rm ⏁ 🍽 ✕ ✗ 📺 ✗ ✗ CC Although the facilities are perfect, this huge modern deluxe hotel offers a somewhat icy welcome. Numerous services including satellite TV, sauna, massages, discotheque, Internet access and vehicles for rent, with the addition of a swimming pool in the near future.

• The Grande Corniche and Bai Dau Beach

Under US$10

Nha Tro 102, 102 Tran Phu, on the coastal road, ☎ (064) 83 61 05 – 12rm ⏁ A small hotel with basic facilities, ideal for backpackers not too fussy about their home comforts.

Doan 28, 106 Tran Phu, in front of the statue of Mary, ☎ (064) 83 32 59 – 16rm ⏁ ✕ ✗ A simple, decent little boarding house overlooking a rather dirty beach. A friendly area, very popular with the Vietnamese.

Between US$10 and US$15

Thuy Tien, 84 Tran Phu, ☎ and Fax (064) 83 52 20 – 30rm 🛏️📺 ⚡ 📺 ✗ Breakfast included. A new hotel with perfect rooms with views over the sea, in a quiet, pleasant spot.

Khach San Tran Phu, 42 Tran Phu, after the White Palace, ☎ (064) 85 24 89 – 14rm 🛏️📺 ✗📺 ✗ A simple, clean hotel with all the necessary facilities situated along the coastal road boasting magnificent views over the sea. A friendly welcome, but only basic English.

● **Long Hai**

On reaching the village, take the road to the left to the beach and the hotels.

Under US$10

Palace Hotel, ☎ (064) 86 83 64 – 18rm 🛏️📺 ✗✗☼〰️ The building has retained some of its 1970s luxury, but with a rather inappropriate name. A charm to be savoured if you can ignore the dust and lack of facilities.

Rang Dong, ☎ (064) 86 83 56 – 18rm 🛏️📺 ✗📺 Very dated, as a last resort.

Doan an Duong 298, ☎ (064) 86 83 16, Fax (064) 86 86 48 – 32rm 🛏️📺 ✗✗☼ Very pleasant, basic rooms, reasonable rates and situated in a lovely shaded spot along the beach.

Huong Bien, ☎ (064) 86 83 56 – 10rm 🛏️📺 ✗✗☼ Opposite Rang Dong, next to the beach. The hotel offers accommodation in concrete bungalows dotted along the beach. Basic facilities, but charming surroundings.

Over US$100

🦀**Anoasis Beach Hotel**, ☎ (064) 86 82 27, Fax (064) 86 82 29, anoasisresort@ hcm.vnn.vn – 18rm 🛏️📺 ✗ ⚡ 📺 ✗ ⚓☼ This luxurious complex, 2km north on the coast, offers charming rooms in spacious bungalows.

EATING OUT

● **Bai Truoc Beach**

Vung Tau has a wide range of restaurants, specialising particularly in seafood, but prices can be rather high and most restaurants close at 9pm. A better idea would be to try the eating places along Quang Trung, opposite the Grand Hotel.

● **Bai Sau Beach**

Between 25 000 and 50 000VND

Thu Trang, 95 Thuy Van, opposite the Saigon Hotel. 🍴 A modest seafront establishment serving fish, prawns and crab. The room has strip-lighting, but the terrace on the first floor is an ideal place for a drink looking out over the sea.

● **Bai Dau Beach**

Between 50 000 and 100 000VND

🦀**69 Cay Bang**, 69 Tran Phu. 9am-9pm. Popular with local people, this restaurant on stilts serves delicious seafood, but the strip-lighting and the tiled walls are more reminiscent of a fishmongers. The menu is in English.

Quan Tre, 7 Tran Phu. 🍴 9am-9pm. Situated on the seafront, with the swish of the waves for gentle background music. The restaurant offers an excellent choice of seafood (fish farm).

● **Long Hai**

Under 25 000VND

Nha Hang Ling Tien, 🍴 7am-10pm. This seafood restaurant situated on the seafront serves plain seafood dishes at very reasonable prices.

Between 50 000 and 100 000VND

Anoasis Beach Hotel, 🍴 Very pleasant, facing the sea, serving seafood as well as Vietnamese and Western dishes.

GOING OUT

Bars, nightclubs – The nights are hot in more ways than one at the weekend in Vung Tau, and Karaoke and techno fans will be in their element. For a more romantic atmosphere, try the terrace bars on the coastal roads.

OTHER THINGS TO DO

Excursions – Poulo Con Dao is likely to be a popular future destination in South Vietnam, but for the moment, these islands attract few tourists. They are accessible from Vung Tau by helicopter (contact the Vietnamese Airlines for further information) or by boat: Con Dao Transportation, 35 Truong Cong Dinh, ☎ (064) 85 90 89.

Sports – Paradise Golf Club, 1 Thuy Van, ☎ (064) 85 64 45..Jet-skis are available for rent along the beaches of Bai Sau and Long Hai.

THE MEKONG DELTA★★★

Allow a minimum of 3 to 5 days – Map pages 330-331
Pop 16 000 000 – Sub-equatorial climate

Not to be missed

A boat trip along the waterways of My Tho, Vinh Long or Can Tho.
The bird sanctuaries at Cao Lanh and Long Xuyen.
The Khmer pagodas at Tra Vinh and Soc Trang.
The floating market at Cai Rang and the floating houses at Chau Doc.
A climb up Sam Mountain and a rest on the beaches of the Gulf of Thailand.

And remember...

Avoid visiting the Delta in September when there is a risk of floods.
Bring along a pair of binoculars for the bird sanctuaries.

"Along my way, if I find some ducks, I'll grab them, if I find a charming young lady, I'll marry her, if I see a pagoda, I'll become a monk" (a South Vietnamese saying).

Life in the Mekong Delta flows to the rhythm of work in the fields and the constant comings and goings of the peasants, on foot, on bicycle, on the back of buffaloes, by bus, but most of all by boat. The delta is a startling combination of land and water, an area in permanent limbo between liquid and solid. The crane, which spends its time in the watery fields of the rice paddies elegantly foraging for its offspring, has become the symbol of the delta. The River Mekong flows into Vietnam from Cambodia via two main branches, the Tien Gang (Upper Mekong) and the Hau Giang (Bassac River), which empty into the South China Sea through nine separate branches, the famous Cuu Long (Nine Dragons) of eastern mythology. A glorious carpet of paddy fields furrowed with channels rich in silt and teeming with fish stretches far into the distance. The region is, however, prone to catastrophic flooding, as in October 2000, when more than 300 lives were claimed and 350 000 people were made homeless. This verdant countryside provides a harmonious backdrop for the close-knit network of towns where most of the region's religious and commercial activities are centred. To explore the Mekong properly, take a boat trip along one of the watercourses or a casual stroll around an orchard, but also try and visit a busy market or enter one of the many temples, pagodas and churches, guardians of the Delta's mysterious spirit.

My Tho, the "sweet and fragrant maiden"

Capital of Tien Giang province. Pop 150 000.
Allow half a day.

My Tho is an industrious and prosperous city that has retained some attractive riverbank houses from the French colonial period, as well as an appealing Chinese quarter. Above all, the city is the starting point for a very pleasant trip to the island fruit orchards, a first taste of the lavish landscapes of the delta that attract an ever-increasing number of tourists.

The city

Go over the bridge at the end of Thu Khoa Huan, then turn right into Phan Thanh Gian. The **Chinese Quarter** is nothing more than one lively street lined with little shops in traditional one-storey buildings with tiled roofs. The Chinese, who came from Formosa by sea and founded the city in the 17C, had an instinctive flair for commerce that has never failed them since. Traders from Ho Chi Minh City come here by boat to buy fruit wholesale which they sell in the great metropolis.

To get to the Vinh Trang Pagoda, about 1km to the east of the centre at 60A Nguyen Trung Truc, go along Dinh Bo linh.

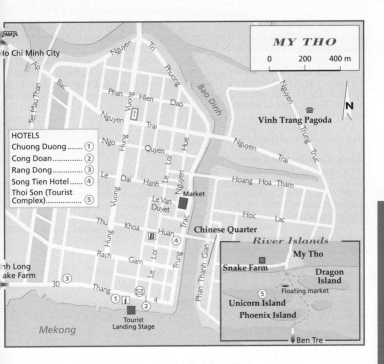

Dedicated to the Greater Vehicle of Buddhism, **Vinh Trang Pagoda** (1849) stands in a coconut grove. The building is an odd collection of architectural styles, with Chinese ceramics and carved murals mingled with Vietnamese lotus flowers and the ochre tones of the Khmer. In the darkest part of the sanctuary, made even more sombre by coatings of incense, gilded carvings give off a dull sheen. The prevailing silence is broken only by the passing novices and during prayer times, when the bonzes chant their orisons to the rhythm of a beating drum

The river islands

A few hours aboard a boat on the river and along the channels with a visit to one of the main islands, should be enough to satisfy your curiosity (*contact the agency near the landing stage. See "My Tho close up"*).

A few hundred metres from the quayside on the other side of a small channel, lush **Dragon Island** (Con Tan Long) can be reached by boat (*allow 5min*), whereas visits to the other islands must be arranged through the local agency.

The river is 15m deep in some places and fishing nets are strategically placed to catch tench, catfish, carp, *tai tuong* ("fish with elephant's ears"), eels and freshwater snakes. Just before reaching **Unicorn Island**★ (Con Thoi Son) (*30min journey*), the boat goes past a **floating market**, open for business only at high tide. Nature is generous with her bounty; palm leaves are used for roofing, mangrove roots as floats. But the strength of the current means that the farmers have to strengthen the river-banks with wood and stones. The boat will probably draw alongside a restaurant in the middle of an **orchard** (*see "My Tho close up"*). A guided tour of the island can be delightful on a quiet day. It includes exotic fruit tasting, a demonstration of traditional music and a boat trip along one of the luxuriantly vegetated **channels**.

373

Phoenix Island (Con Phung) (*25min crossing, also accessible from Ben Tre*), also known as the "Coconut Monk Island" (Ong Dao Dua), owes its nickname to Nguyen Thanh Nam (1909-91), a visionary who claimed to have meditated for three years surviving only on coconuts. He founded the Dao Sect, an unusual mixture of Buddhism and Christianity with a following of over 2 000 disciples. Repeatedly arrested, both under the Diem regime and then by the Communists, he finally died during one of his stays in prison and his followers were dispersed. The sanctuary is more like a big tropical fun-fair than a place of meditation, and always attracts crowds of Vietnamese visitors. The island has several **orchards**, but no watercourses. During the war, the area was much favoured by Western war correspondents in search of peace and quiet after the furious fighting.

Dong Tam Snake Farm

10km from My Tho on the road to Vinh Long. Open daily from 6am-6pm. Entrance fee. Allow 40 min. Reptile enthusiasts should make a point of visiting this farm where some of the pythons weigh more than 70kg! The bite of the king cobra is fatal and death can occur in only two minutes, just enough time to get hold of some of the antivenom serum produced at the farm. Other creatures exhibited here include crocodiles, monitors, wild cats, otters, monkeys, birds, and a strange, yellow aquatic animal resembling a turtle, but belonging to the rat family. Don't leave without tasting one of the snake dishes served at the restaurant.

Ben Tre, "the bamboo corner"
Capital of Ben Tre province. Allow half a day.

A group of allegorical statues dedicated to revolutionary heroes stands at the entrance to Ben Tre, where foreign visitors are quite a novelty. This country town and its little **Truc Giang Lake** are nonetheless charming.

Not far from the river, the former French Prefecture now houses the **Revolution Museum** (*on Cach Mang Thang Tam. Open Monday-Friday 7-11am / 1.30-5pm. Free entrance*), an elegant 19C **colonial building★** surrounded by gardens. The building has more to offer architecturally than its actual collections, which include photographs, crude weaponry and a scale model of a Viet Cong tunnel.

Vien Minh Pagoda (*open daily from 7.30-11.30am / 1.30-9pm*) stands on Nguyen Dinh Chieu, opposite the market. A large **statue** of the Goddess of Mercy is situated in front of this elegant 19C building covered with a two-tiered square roof.

Vam Ho Bird Sanctuary★ (San Chim Vam Ho)

35km southeast of Ben Tre. If you do not have your own vehicle, take the bus to Ba Tri and continue by motorcycle taxi (one bus per day). Be careful over the last few kilometres of the track, which is impassable in wet periods. Boats also ply between the sanctuary and Ben Tre (allow 4hr round trip). You can also contact the official agency (2hr round trip by hydrofoil). Entrance fee. Allow 45min for a tour of the sanctuary.

The road from Ba Tri leading to the riverside sanctuary soon dwindles to a simple track. A colony of bitterns, herons and cranes has taken up residence here, right in the middle of a small jungle of bamboo and high trees. The best time to come is either at dawn or around 5pm when the birds are returning to their nests.

Vinh Long
Capital of Vinh Long province. Pop 180 000.
Allow one day.

Opened in June 2000, a 1.5km-long **suspension bridge★**, spans the Mekong River and provides an alternative to the Cai Be ferry for getting to Vinh Long. The bridge was financed by the Australians and has already become a tourist attraction thanks to the superb **view★★★** over the delta. Vinh Long is a lively city, but not worth an extended stay, and most visitors are satisfied with just a boat trip down the waterways on Binh Hoa Phuoc.

On the river-bank, **Van Thanh Mieu Temple** (*on Tran Phu, 1km to the south on the road to Tra Vinh*), is the only Temple of Literature and one of the rare Confucian shrines in South Vietnam. In the courtyard to the left stands a wonderful little square building covered with a tiled two-tiered roof. With a bit of luck, the caretaker will take you up to the **old library** on the first floor, where the revolutionary leaders used to hide during the colonial period. At the end of the avenue, the **shrine** contains a portrait of Confucius flanked by a strangely earless wooden horse and by cranes perched on top of turtles' backs.

Binh Hoa Phuoc Island★

The Cuu Long Tourist agency offers several different trips of 3hr or 5hr, but remember that the waterways are often impassable during the dry season (see "Vinh Long close up" page 394). Just beyond a small **floating market**, the boat lands at the island which is crossed by a wide **canal** dug by hand at the beginning of the 20C in order to shorten the journey between Vinh Long and Cai Be. Boats of all shapes and sizes are in constant motion, their motors making an ear-splitting racket. A cheerful atmosphere prevails. Boatmen exchange greetings, and foreign visitors may find themselves treated to a selection of local fruit. The boat turns left by a church into a narrow channel through a **mangrove swamp**. Typical of the Delta, such mangrove swamps are rich in fish and are particularly valuable in protecting the gardens from erosion and storms. Over the last 15 years, the local farmers have earned their livelihood from the lush orchards (6 000ha) planted in place of the old rice paddies.

There are several things to see during the tour, starting with the **house of Nguyen Thanh Giao★** (*30min journey*), set in a charming **bonsai garden**. In the main room, souvenir plates of the Eiffel Tower and Notre Dame take pride of place on the family altar. Don't leave without trying the famous "elephant-ear fish".

Further on stands a **colonial building** of 1860 that used to house a French garrison. The annexe reserved for Vietnamese soldiers is now used to welcome tourists for a tea-tasting ceremony and a demonstration of traditional music (*camp beds are available for the night*). The owner, Mr Hai Hoang, also manages one of the **orchards**. The boat then runs alongside a row of **stilt houses** to the **orchard of Mr Pham Van Lan**, (*accommodation available*).

At the end of the channel, the boat emerges into the Mekong River, 1 200m wide and 20m deep at this point. **Cai Be floating market** is held on the opposite bank, where you will see boats piled high with longans, pineapples, sweet potatoes, rice and carrots, and in the background, the incongruous spire of a **Catholic church** (1931). The many new sights and sounds of this trip definitely make it well worthwhile, despite the tiring drone of the engines.

Tra Vinh

Capital of Tra Vinh Province.
Allow half a day.

The sleepy town of Tra Vinh stands on one of the secondary branches of the Mekong River, exuding a certain melancholy charm that can probably be explained by the presence of the large Khmer community. The 140 pagodas dotted around the area provide an enthralling insight into these people and their culture.

Ong Met Pagoda (*on Ngo Quyen, behind the post office*) still retains its nickname of "Bat Pagoda", even though the creatures fled after the American bombings in 1968. The building miraculously survived along with the surrounding line of **sculpted heads** with four faces. Inside, a **Buddha** sits enthroned between statues of two disciples who rather unusually face him. The eye-catching inlaid ceramics of the flooring, the murals and the ornate pillars make this attractive pagoda well worth a visit.

The Khmers of the delta

Up until the 18C the delta belonged to Cambodia, so it is hardly surprising that almost 900 000 Khmers still reside along the border, as well as in Tra Vinh and Soc Trang. Although now well integrated into the rest of the population, they still retain a number of their own characteristics, notably their stilt houses built by the water or atop low mounds. They are outstanding farmers and produce no less than 140 different varieties of rice, which supplement their staple diet of fish. Yet the main distinguishing feature of this society is its support for the Buddhist school of the Lesser Vehicle (Theravada), observed in monasteries where the Khmer language is taught. The bonzes subsist on offerings from their followers, a practice banned for a long time by the Vietnamese authorities. The Water Festival encourages large gatherings organised around regattas and buffalo races.

The sacred lake*

7km north of Tra Vinh on the road to Vinh Long. Take the road to the left and carry on for a further 1km. **Ba Om Lake***, a delightful square-shaped lake surrounded by magnificent mango trees, is a spiritual site for the Khmers, but also an area popular with young couples. In the middle of a group of palm trees to the south of the lake stands the imposing **Vat Angkor Icha Borei Pagoda*** (Chua Samrong Ek) that dates back to the 10C. Inside, colourful **murals*** illustrate the life of the Buddha, and the rafters and pillars are delicately decorated with gilt. Those with time to spare could pop into the **Museum of Khmer Culture** *(Wednesday-Sunday, 7-11am / 1-5pm. Entrance free)*.

The Khmer Pagodas*

Go by car or motorcycle taxi. There is also a bus service. This beautiful **road**** is dotted with bamboo houses, flame, eucalyptus, palm and coconut trees, in a rural setting of rice paddies and canals. The pagodas are hidden by small groups of trees, since part of the Lesser Vehicle Buddhist tradition commits each follower to the planting of one or several trees during the course of his life, which will then be cut down at his death and used for the cremation.

■ A strange, lopsided portico precedes the **Hang Pagoda*** (The Cave Pagoda) *(5km south of Tra Vinh),* a delicately attractive, white building *(under repair)*.
The novices are housed in little cells built on stilts in the shade of the hundred-year-old coconut and mango trees that surround the pagoda. The sanctuary was completely destroyed in 1968, and only the **statue of the Buddha** was spared. Various photos bear witness to these tragic yet distant events, and a certain restful tranquillity pervades the life of the monastery today.

■ About 45km further on, an elegant avenue of eucalyptus trees leads off to the left towards **Co Pagoda**** (Stork Pagoda), so named because of the colonies of storks, ibises, cranes and herons around the nearby pond *(the birds return to their nests around 5pm)*. In the centre of the monastery, the 19C **pagoda** is topped with a tiled tiered roof with bird-shaped eaves. The rather naïve murals depict hell, the Buddhist pantheon and various other naturalistic subjects, all under the watchful eye of an enormous sitting **Buddha**.

Phung Hiep floating market

Sa Dec

Dong Thap Province.
Allow half a day.

Sa Dec gained fame as the setting of the film based on the book *The Lover* by **Marguerite Duras**, and is undeniably popular with admirers of this French novelist who spent her childhood here. Other visitors will find no particular points of interest in the town, which is otherwise known for its nurseries of flowers and bonsai trees.

In search of "The Lover"

On arrival from Vinh Long after crossing the River Sadec, turn right into Tran Hung Dao. The **Confucian Pagoda of Kien An Cung*** (Chua Ong Quach), former home of the Mandarin Quach *(on Phan Choi Boi, south of the channel)*, is easy to spot with its old gabled walls, the raised eaves of its tiled roof and its numerous decorative features. Delicately-carved gilded **woodwork** and intricate **murals** flank the altar that faces on to a small open **courtyard** called the "heavenly well", where incense is burned to facilitate contact with the deities.

Beyond the canal, just a few steps from the landing stage *(Nguyen Hue)* on Tran Hung Dao stands a high building topped with a spire. It could very well be a church, but the nearby traders in their conical hats enthroned among chickens, ducks, fish and spices, prove otherwise; it is in fact the old **covered market***.

On Nguyen Hue is the **house of the Mandarin Huynh Thuan**, or "The Blue House", the old residence in "The Lover". It has since been converted into a police station and so visitors have to make do with just an outside impression *(no photos)*. The quaysides used to be the centre of the Chinese quarter, and, until recently, a big market area, which has since been transferred to a large, modern building a few streets away. Luckily, a series of colourful shops selling all sorts of provisions and utensils still guarantees a lively atmosphere. On the other side of the river, several **colonial houses**, the last remains of the **French quarter**, emerge out of the luxuriant vegetation.

Go back up Tran Hung Dao as far as Tran Phu and turn left. **Trung Vuong Primary School** with its faded yellow walls was where Marguerite Duras went to school. Ask to see the book containing records of the establishment since its opening in 1902. It includes photographs of the novelist and her mother, Mme Donnadieu, headmistress at the school from 1918 to 1930.

As is common in the delta towns, the presence of Taoist, Catholic and Protestant sanctuaries, as well as temples dedicated to ancestor worship, is proof of the amazing religious eclecticism of the Vietnamese. **Buu Quang Pagoda** *(on the corner of Hung Vuong and Tran Phu)* is not very interesting, but stands next to **Tu Hung Pagoda**, a communal house built by "The Lover". His photo can be seen among the others on the altar dedicated to ancestors.

Cao Lanh

Capital of Dong Thap Province.
Allow one day.

An ostentatious **war memorial** in Socialist Realist style welcomes visitors to this modern but rather sleepy city situated on the northern edge of the delta. Interesting tours to the former Viet Cong base in the Rung Tram Forest and to the bird sanctuaries of the area leave from here, but the city does not attract very many foreign visitors.

Go along Pham Huu Lau which forms the continuation of Nguyen Hue towards Chau Doc, and turn left just after the second bridge.

Situated in the middle of a pleasant little park planted with frangipani is the **Nguyen Sinh Sac Grave Site** (*open daily from 7.30-11am / 1.30-5pm*). It honours Ho Chi Minh's father (1862-1929), with a reconstruction of the native home of this hero of Independence.

Thap Muoi Nature Reserve**

36km northeast of Cao Lanh. When travelling to the Reserve by car, it is better to take a guide since the journey is rather complicated. Take the road to Cai Be, and then 13km further on turn left along a small tarmacked road as far as Thap Muoi (21km). At the crossroads, turn left towards the village of My An, where you cross the river by boat. You can also reach Thap Muoi by bus, finishing the journey by motorcycle taxi, or else take the boat trip organised by the Cao Lanh Tourist Office (see " Cao Lanh close up" page 396). Free entrance.

Lined with palm and eucalyptus trees, this delightful road wends its way through rice paddies and canals as far as the Vuon Co Thap Muoi Reserve. On the edge of a small hamlet of wooden houses and bamboo huts is a little pond, whose shimmering green waters are very popular with a multitude of local wading birds. The graceful movements of the storks and the red-headed herons flying high above the tall bamboo is a sight to behold.

Rung Tram Forest**

26km southeast of Cao Lanh. Take the road to Cai Be and 20km further on, turn off onto a dirt track to the left of the road. The forest is another 6km. It is also accessible by boat from Cao Lanh (90min). For further information, contact the Tourist Office (see "Cao Lanh close up" page 396).

The former **Xeo Quit Viet Cong Base**, tucked away in the heart of the Rung Tram Forest, is both a fascinating and moving testimony to the bitter fighting of the Vietnam War (*open daily from 7.30am-4pm. Entrance fee. Wear boots because of the ants, and mosquito repellent could prove useful*). The area was a vast swamp before becoming the main Viet Cong base for the province between 1960 and 1975. Helped by the local people, the fighters dug a network of underground tunnels and planted trees to make the forest impenetrable. No fewer than ten American camps were positioned around the base, one of which was just 1km away! The Americans, however, were never able to destroy the base, despite repeated attacks and bombings.

Today, the clamour of war has long since faded away and the forest is nothing more than a tangled mass of eucalyptus trees etched with the passage of numerous streams dotted with clumps of graceful reeds. The area is nonetheless riddled with signs of the violence of the past fighting, such as the innumerable craters left by falling bombs that now form little ponds. To attack the base, the Americans had to zigzag through a minefield avoiding Viet Cong fire from the edge of the forest. In the face of their approach, the Viet Cong fighters hid underwater or in tiny traps where they could only breathe through narrow bamboo sticks. These resourceful fighters also spread pepper around to put off the American tracker dogs. The Vietnamese were forced to adapt to this particularly hostile environment, and slept in tents or hammocks during the day and then kept watch during the night, surrounded by snakes and mosquitoes. Visitors can today go down into one of the **underground hideouts** and look round the **group of huts** built after the Paris Accords in 1973. The site also includes a rather small, uninspiring **museum**, as well as a shaded restaurant on stilts.

Tam Nong Bird Sanctuary (Tram Chim Tam Nong)

45km north of Cao Lanh. Access is quite complicated, so ask for information at the Dong Thap Tourist Agency. The best time to visit is in Spring, from 4-5am and from 4-5pm.

This sanctuary is home to more than 200 species of birds, notably **storks** and rare **red-headed herons**. Unfortunately, the forest was devastated by fire, and so it will take several years for the local ecological community to re-establish itself.

Can Tho★

Capital of Can Tho Province. Pop 165 000.
Allow one day.

"Can Tho, white rice and beautifully clear waters. Once you're here, you won't want to leave" (popular song).

Can Tho is the main administrative centre of the region and a university town, which owes its flourishing economy to the port and the constant comings and goings of the cargo boats arriving from Hong Kong. They arrive laden with all sorts of manufactured goods, and then go back overflowing with rice, fruit and prawns. It's also a crossroads town, a focal point for travellers, whom it will not disappoint, since the insignificance of the modern architecture is more than compensated for by the attraction of its lively streets, the crisp order of its wide avenues and its riverside promenade. Beyond the city gates, the remarkable network of canals threading the countryside reveals some of the most fascinating facets of the delta.

After watching the sunset from the shade of the gardens laid out along the banks of the Mekong River parallel to Hai Ba Trung, take a deep breath and venture into the **covered market** near the statue of **Ho Chi Minh**. The market is nothing short of an Ali Baba's cave, attracting farmers from the surrounding area who come here to sell their produce up until 10pm. Young beggar children, outcasts of the growing economy, roam the streets until late at night.

Resembling a multi-coloured cake shop crammed with good things, the **Khmer Munirangsyaram Pagoda★** (*36 Hoa Binh*) stands incongruously in the middle of this urban setting. Although architecturally uninteresting, the structure has a certain elegance. The complex includes various different buildings with a shrine situated on the first floor.

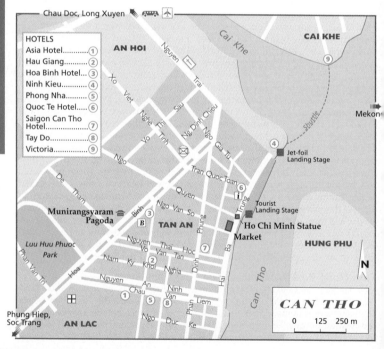

The orchards and floating markets**

There are several ways to enjoy a trip on the Upper Mekong and a visit to the floating markets. The least expensive would be to charter a motorboat, preferably covered, at the main landing stage (see "Can Tho close up" page 397). The price is negotiable, but allow a minimum of US$2 per hour. The travel agencies also organise guided tours, but at higher prices. Whatever you opt for, leave very early to be at the market from between 6 and 8am. Allow 3hr.

This boat trip is one of the most exotic in the delta, combining urban landscapes, floating markets, orchards and waterways. The makeshift houses of **Xom Chai**, the village opposite Can Tho, perch precariously on stilts, in incongruous contrast to the enormous billboards proclaiming the merits of international consumer goods. Further on, opposite the port of Can Tho, the boat passes under a recently-opened bridge that should encourage industrial development on the other side of the river. Spare a thought for these lush riverbanks free from construction which may soon be taken over by warehouses and towers. **Cai Rang Floating Market**** *(also accessible by road)* has recently been moved several hundred metres upstream to ease the boat traffic. The market is an extraordinary sight, with countless little boats laying siege to craft filled to capacity with bananas, rice, mangoes, pineapples and potatoes, all at unbeatable prices. To return to Can Tho, take the second branch of the river, stopping off at the **My Khanh Orchard** or the **Muoi Day Orchard** to try a selection of the local exotic fruits. If the waterlevel is sufficient, the tour ends with a trip up the narrow **channels****, their banks eaten away by coconut palms.

At the junction of seven different channels, **Phung Hiep Market** *(25km from Can Tho, on the road to Soc Trang)* was once the biggest in the delta, but is now in decline. From the bridge, enjoy the spectacular **view**** over the different branches of water, the scene of dense river traffic. Take a look at the "land" market too, where live snakes, turtles and monitors can still be bought, despite the ban on this particular trade.

Soc Trang, "the golden village"*
Capital of Soc Trang Province. Pop 165 000.
Allow half a day.

This sleepy village with its elegant pagodas lies a little off the tourist trail, but makes a good day's outing from Can Tho. It is home to large Chinese and Khmer communities (one third of the population), and the mystic peacefulness of the area is quite striking. Don't leave without sampling the local speciality of bat!

The post office, which appears to be the village's main attraction, is situated next door to the high telecommunications aerial, at the foot of which a theme park is planned.

Go back up Mau Than 68, a continuation of Hai Ba Trung, as far as the intersection with Nguyen Chi Thanh.

Kh'leng Pagoda, or "Golden Pagoda" is a huge, concrete complex built in 1905 to replace the original bamboo structure that dated back to 1533. This colourful **sanctuary**, surrounded by palm trees, is typical of Khmer architecture with the extended eaves of its tiled roof raised up in the shape of a bird. The gilt doors, however, are reminiscent of the Balinese style.

On the other side of Nguyen Chi Thanh, the **Khmer Musem** *(Open Monday-Friday 7-10.30am / 1-5pm. No charge. There are occasional traditional performances)* is well worth a look, even if the collection of costumes, musical instruments and unusual traditional masks made of papier-mâché are of rather poor quality.

Continue along Mau Than 68 to the outskirts of the village.

In contrast to the Khmer pagodas, the **Clay Pagoda**★ (Chua Dat Set), also known as Buu Son Tu, is of no particular architectural interest, although it is something of a curiosity. It was decorated by a Chinese monk who devoted his life to the creation of the sanctuary's hundreds of **terracotta Buddhas and animals** in a naïve style. Two giant **candles** have been burning here since the artist died in 1970.

Pagodas around Soc Trang★★

Large colonies of **bats** hanging from the trees, the tombs of sacred **pigs** with five toes... a strange atmosphere surrounds **Doi Pagoda**★★ (*on the road to Ca Mau. 2km from Soc Trang, take the left fork and carry on for a further 1km. The pagoda is difficult to find*). The building, well-known for its architectural sophistication, is tucked away deep in the peaceful countryside. Some of the bats that have mysteriously taken up residence here weigh up to 2kg with a wing span of about 1.5m. The best time to come is at the end of the afternoon, when hundreds of the creatures swoop out of the trees. Two rows of decorative columns delicately sculpted with floral motifs, divide the sanctuary into traditional proportions. The long, colourful **pirogue** (25m) lying in the garden is used during the Water Festival (Ok Om Bok) which attracts all the local Khmer.

Xa Long Pagoda (*8km southwest of Soc Trang on the road to Ca Mau*), dating back to the 18C, was rebuilt in 1923 with subsequent extensions. Known as the "Ceramic Pagoda", it too is typically Khmer, though with obvious Vietnamese influences, notably the **plates** embedded in the walls. As is often the case, the spirits of Good and Evil keep watch over the entrance.

Long Xuyen

Capital of An Giang Province. Pop 100 000.
Allow half a day.

Long Xuyen is the smuggling hub of South Vietnam and the surrounding countries and seems proud of its flourishing economy. This busy, well-organised city with large Chinese and Khmer communities, claims to want no part in any illicit dealings or prostitution, and yet plans for tourist development are not really forthcoming. The city's ideal facilities, however, make it a perfect place to stop off on the way to Chau Doc should you be a little short of time after visiting Sin Chin Bang Lang.

Hai Ba Trung and Doan Van Phoi, the two wide, impressive avenues running through the city centre, are the only lively spots in the evening, along with Nguyen Trai.

Heading up Hung Vuong, you will come face to face with **St Teresa's Church**★, a tall, concrete structure (50m) not entirely without charm. It was built in the 1960s and its immense nave can seat up to 1 000 worshippers.

The An Giang Museum★ (*Le Minh Ngu On. Open Tuesday and Thursday 7.30-10.30am, Saturday and Sunday 7.30-10.30am / 2-4.30pm*) comprises four rooms devoted to the War, the development of the region since 1975, the Vietnamese, Chinese, Khmer and Cham cultures in the area (handicrafts, clothing) and to the Hinduized kingdom of Funan. The museum mainly displays artefacts from the 5C and 6C from the ancient site of Oc Eo (*see page 390*), notably lingams, yoni, pottery, statuettes and a slightly damaged, but quite magnificent **wooden statue of the Buddha**★★. The museum is soon to move to a different site with new exhibits planned.

Bang Lang Bird Sanctuary★★★

Make for Thot Not, 12km from Long Xuyen on the road to Can Tho, where you can take a boat (30min) or hire a motorcycle taxi. Entrance fee. Allow 1hr. This sanctuary is definitely one of the most spectacular in the Delta. The boat trip on the canal from the village of Thot Not passes villages, rice paddies and bamboo hedges and marks the start of a wonderful visit. On arrival at the sanctuary, a 6m-high pontoon affords an

Mekong wading birds

overall view of the site (13 000m) where thousands of herons, sacred ibises, bitterns, common cranes and cormorants all come to nest. The wading birds of the delta, threatened by changes to the environment, have all found a safe haven here. Geese have also been introduced into the sanctuary, since their droppings are supposed to keep away snakes, the birds' main predator. The males, who make up 80 % of the colony, are away during the day foraging for food, returning at the end of the afternoon. The best time to visit the sanctuary is between September and December when storks are also part of this big happy family, and when the owners of the site reserve a special attraction for visitors at 5pm sharp!

Chau Doc★★
An Giang Province. Pop 60 000.
Allow 2 days.

Chau Doc backs on to the Cambodian border and its undistinguished appearance is in stark contrast to the prosperity of Long Xuyen. Cham, Vietnamese, Chinese and Khmer, in fact most religions seem to be gathered here, in a motley muddle of huts and shacks.

Around the **main market**, the little shopping streets stretch as far as the water's edge with its precarious jumble of **stilt houses**. The **view**★★★ over the Hau Giang (Bassac) River at the meeting-point of several waterways, where wooden boats of all sizes can be seen drifting along, seems to distil the very essence of the timeless delta.

The mosques of the Mekong
A guide is recommended for this fascinating trip through the Cham villages (see "Chau Doc close up" page 400). Allow 2hr. You can also hire a boat at the general landing stage. Try and visit the mosques on a Friday at the end of the morning, but wait outside until the end of the service so as not to disturb the worshippers.

383

The Muslim Cham, a forgotten minority

Every Friday at the Jamiul Azhar Mosque, crowds of men dressed in a sarong and the traditional white cap gather at prayer time. In a land of Taoism and Buddhism, such a sight confirms that the delta is a true melting pot of religions. Unlike their cousins in central Vietnam, the Cham from the Mekong are followers of the Prophet. Islam was most probably introduced by Arab, Indian or Malaysian traders at the beginning of the 10C and developed further during the 15C when the Champa kingdom was wiped out. Islam as understood by the Cham today is far removed from the orthodox canons. They pray only once a week instead of five times a day. They fast for only three days instead of the traditional one month during Ramadan, they don't make pilgrimages to Mecca, they are allowed to drink alcohol and, above all, they still continue to worship the ancient spirits of Vietnam, on Sam Mountain in particular.

First on the journey upstream is an amazing **floating village**★★. The owners of these solid wooden houses with flower-decked balconies enjoy all the home comforts (television in particular), and each house has its own stock of live fish, both for family consumption or for sale in markets throughout Vietnam. Just lift up the trap door and help yourself!

The boat then approaches a small **Cham village**★ with typical **stilt houses**. The spotless white **Ehsan Mosque** (*also accessible by ferry*) was built recently.

Along a secondary branch of the river on the other side at Chau Phong is **Jamiul Azhar Mosque**★, a graceful, neo-colonial structure with a minaret topped with a silver dome (*the mosque is also accessible via Chau Doc. Take the ferry for Chau Giang at the landing stage to the south of the Victoria Hotel, and then take a motorcycle taxi, or else it is a 15min walk to the left*). Have a look at the **cemetery** lined with simple Islamic steles. The nearby **Moubarak Mosque** (1km) is home to a Koranic school.

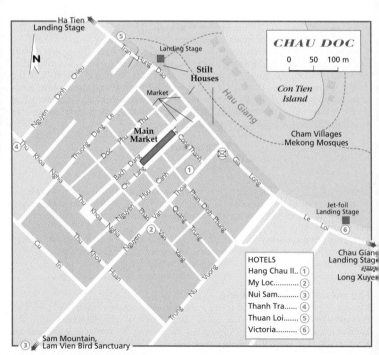

CHAU DOC

0   50   100 m

HOTELS
Hang Chau II.. (1)
My Loc............ (2)
Nui Sam.......... (3)
Thanh Tra...... (4)
Thuan Loi....... (5)
Victoria.......... (6)

Sam Mountain*** (Nui Sam)

7km southwest of Chau Doc. If you do not have a vehicle, the best plan is to hire a motorcycle taxi the day before (allow 20min and from 15 000 to 20 000VND). You can walk up the path that starts off from the Thoai Ngoc Hau Mausoleum (40min) or carry on up the road by motorcycle taxi. It is advisable to visit Sam Mountain at sunrise, around 5.30am.

The path leading directly to the foot of **Nui Sam** from Chau Doc is choked with hundreds of thousands of worshippers during the pilgrimage season. "Crab Mountain" is aptly named since, from the air, it resembles a small crab. The imposing outline of this 230m-high mountain stands out rather incongruously against the delta. It is one of the most sacred sites in Vietnam and affords one of the most beautiful views in the area. Before reaching the top, try to resist the enticing invitation to rest in one of the shady hammocks in the eating places along the way and keep a look-out for the countless little **sanctuaries** which appear from behind the stones, obscured by the traditional clouds of incense smoke. The **panorama***** from the summit is outstanding. The utterly flat landscape of shimmering rice paddies unrolls as far as the eye can see. **Mt Cam** (710m) can be seen far to the south while the border with Cambodia is only 3km to the west. The Vietnamese rather chauvinistically insist that the rice paddies are always a lot greener on their side of the border.

On the way from Chau Doc, turn right at the foot of the mountain and continue for another hundred metres or so as far as the **Temple of the Goddess Chua Xu*** (Mieu Ba Chua Xu), the region's patron saint. The original sanctuary of 1825 was made of bamboo, but was replaced at the beginning of the 1970s by a huge, rather tacky structure topped with a triple-tiered roof with green tiles. Inside, a painted **statue** of the goddess, adorned with an electric, multicoloured halo, is greatly revered. Offerings of whole roast pig, complete with carving knife, often lie at her feet. In an adjacent glass case, the goddess's heavy, elaborately-embroidered tunic is changed every day according to the dictates of tradition. The area at the back of the temple has been set aside for the pilgrims during the festivities. The **adjoining buildings** include a dormitory and the goddess's private dressing room containing several hundred tunics offered by her devoted worshippers.

On the other side of the road, a black and white elephant watch over the **Tay An Pagoda**. One of the elephants has six tusks, since it is said that before giving birth to Siddharta, his mother dreamt about such an animal. The sanctuary, built in the 19C and then rebuilt in 1958, is a colourful structure incorporating an amazing combination of Hindu, Muslim and Vietnamese styles. Figures of lions and tigers decorate the roof, and on the inside stand hundreds of painted **statues** of the Buddha and Lohan - the 18 protectors of the Buddhist faith. Multicoloured bonze **tombs** are dotted around the building.

A little further to the west is the **Tomb of Thoai Ngoc Hau**, a valiant knight of the Nguyen dynasty (1761-1829) who devoted his life to the protection of the province. He also built the great Vinh Te Canal which marks the border with Cambodia, thereby improving the yields of local crops. Inside, the tomb is flanked by those of his two wives and is crowned with his **copper bust**.

For the next 2km follow the road that goes westwards around the hill heading towards the Cavern Pagoda.

Also known as Chua Hang, the **Cavern Pagoda** (Chua Phuoc Dien) is on the other side of the hill. A long flight of stairs leads to the sanctuary containing

Divine Intercession

According to legend, the statue of the Goddess Chua Xu, the region's patron saint, was carried off by Siamese invaders. The statue, however, became too heavy and cumbersome to bear and they were forced to abandon it a little further on. Following an announcement from the Goddess, virgins from the village moved the statue and placed it at the bottom of the hill where a temple was then constructed.

statues of the Buddha. At the back is the opening to a natural cave where the female bonze Le Thi Tho was one day interrupted in her meditation by a white and a green snake. It is said that the two reptiles never left her side from that moment on, vanishing only after her death. A shrine dedicated to Quan Am, the Goddess of Mercy, has been erected in the cave.

Lam Vien Bird Sanctuary★★

17km to the south of Chau Doc, between Sam Mountain and Mt Cam. Take the track on the left and continue for a further 5km. The best time to come is at dusk. Contact the Victoria Hotel for further information.

With the potential to become a major tourist attraction, the Lam Vien Bird Sanctuary is sited in a mangrove swamp. A rather wobbly boat is the only suitable means of transport along the narrow channels if there is to be any hope of spotting the resident wading birds before they fly off. The best viewpoint is however at the top of a purpose-built wooden tower in the middle of the swamp.

Along the Cambodian border★

This rather sleepy road from Chau Doc to Ha Tien (*95km, muddy in the rainy season*), little known to tourists, is a traditional thoroughfare for Cambodian contraband. The bloody incursions of the Khmer Rouge, then in power in Phnom Penh, remain a grisly memory for the local inhabitants, particularly in the village of **Ba Chuc** (*40km from Chau Doc*). These attacks were one of the main reasons cited by the Vietnamese in justifying their invasion of Cambodia and the overthrow of Pol Pot in 1979. Morbid and moving at the same time, the **Skull Pagoda** houses the skulls of 1 500 victims of the Khmer Rouge. It was erected on the site of another pagoda that was destroyed in the April 1978 attack which caused the death of almost 4 000 people. Photographs of the massacre are displayed in an adjoining building.

Ha Tien★★

An Giang Province. Pop 80 000.
Allow one day.

Ha Tien is a large, peaceful town with very few tarmacked roads, located at the end of a cul-de-sac at the southwestern tip of Vietnam, 8km from Cambodia. It boasts a fairy-tale setting, on the edge of the Gulf of Thailand at the foothills marking the entrance to a saltwater lake. In addition to the temples, the nearby beaches make up the area's main attraction. Yet things were not always quite so peaceful, particularly at the end of the 1970s, when Khmer Rouge raids forced the inhabitants to flee. Today, the economy thrives on the production of black pepper, brine, fish and particularly prawns, which are put out to dry in front of the houses, creating a rather pungent aroma.

The floating bridge spanning the **Dong Ho** ("East Lake") sea inlet provides the only access to Ha Tien. To its left, next to the **market**, is the liveliest quarter of the city.

Go up Phuong Thanh as far as the intersection with Mac Thien Tich.

A large **statue** of the Goddess of Mercy standing under palm trees heralds the approach to the **Sac Tu Tam Bao Tu Pagoda** (*open daily from 7am-7pm*) dedicated to Mahayana Buddhism. It was founded in the 18C by Mac Cuu and houses another **statue of Quan Am** with a thousand arms and a thousand eyes, symbols of her omnipresent power. This Bodhisattva of Mercy, capable of taking on any form as the saviour of humans, is represented here with female features, as is often the case. A small **bonsai garden**, with some of the trees trimmed in the shape of animals, has been created behind the pagoda.

On the other side of the street, in an enthusiastic surge of ecumenism, stands the tall, crisp outline of a **Catholic Church**.

Head up Phuong Thanh and turn left as far as **Binh Son Hill**. **Phu Dung Pagoda** (Pagoda of the Pink Hibiscus) is named after the wife of Mac Thien Tich, the former governor of the province. In the 18C, he had the pagoda erected in honour of his beloved wife who had vowed to spend the rest of her life in contemplation and meditation. A **statue of Phu Dung** stands inside, accompanied by two phoenixes, symbols of beatitude.

A little further south, at the foot of the hill, is the **Mac Cuu Sanctuary**, a pretty little building with a tiled roof completed in 1902. The family **tombs**, lavishly decorated with multicoloured mythological animals, are scattered over Nui Lang Hill ("the Hill of Tombs"). The tomb of Mac Cuu himself is particularly revered. From the top of the hill, enjoy the superb **panorama★★** which extends over the town and the east coast.

A fiercely contested piece of land

At the beginning of the 18C, Ha Tien was a Cambodian possession under the rule of Mac Cuu, a Cantonese immigrant who had escaped from China with his followers in 1644 when the Ming were expelled by the Manchu. In the face of attacks by the Siamese, he turned to the Vietnamese for protection in 1708, but to no avail, and the enemy took the town. Their victory was, however, short-lived, since Mac Cuu and his Vietnamese allies were soon able to drive them out. He was succeeded as ruler by his son Mac Thien Tich in 1736, who had to face more Siamese raids and the Tay Son rebellion. With help from the Nguyen lords, he emerged victorious. The unification of Ha Lien with Vietnam in 1798 was in theory definitive, but the Cambodians have never really accepted its annexation.

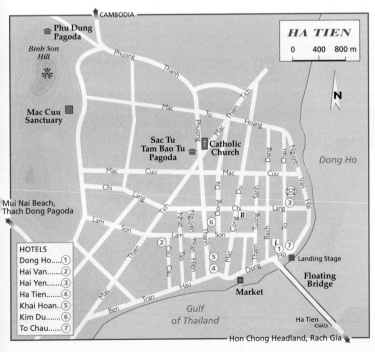

To the west of Ha Tien

3.5km from the city, on the road to Mui Nai. If you do not have a vehicle, you can always rent a motorcycle taxi. **Thach Dong Pagoda**★★ ("Cave Pagoda") is an astonishing, colourful building nestling at the bottom of a hollowed-out limestone cliff. It contains a **statue of Ngoc Hoang**, the Jade Emperor in the Taoist religion, as well as a **statue of Quan Am**. A gentle, refreshing wind blowing through the passageways creates some enchanting melodies. At the entrance, a small **stele** commemorates the massacre of 130 civilians by the Khmer Rouge on 14 March 1978.

Just 5km from Cambodia, **Mui Nai Beach**★ *(entrance fee)*, nestling in a small cove surrounded by wooded hills stretching down into the sea, is the centre of the local tourist industry. Numerous families come here for a paddle or to try the local seafood under the shade of the pine trees. To the right is a **lighthouse** lost in the middle of some trees, and just off the coast are small, rocky islets. On a clear day, you can see as far as Phu Quoc. Don't even consider camping rough though, because at night the area is apparently rife with smugglers.

Between Ha Tien and the Hon Chong Headland, the road crosses beautiful countryside dotted with **limestone hills** which seem to rise up from the depths of the earth. Unfortunately, enormous cement factories are gradually eating up these unique landscape features of the delta.

Hon Chong Headland★★ (Binh Anh)

Hon Chong Beach★ is a delightful stretch of sand shaded by coconut trees with several little eating places made of bamboo serving mouth-watering fresh fish. Despite the area's obvious charm, regulars of the beaches of Thailand or Indonesia are hardly likely to be impressed. In the distance, **Nghe Island** is apparently home to some superb beaches *(it is possible to charter a boat from one of the eating places along the beach. Allow 1hr one way)*.

At the end of the road, 2km from Hon Chong, **Hai Son Tu Pagoda** *(entrance fee)* backs on to a hill. It conceals the opening to a vast chamber where a strong aroma of incense and bat droppings fills the air. This houses **Hang Pagoda**★★, an extraordinary shrine hidden in the half-light and containing a **statue of Quan Am**.

Prawn fishing on Ha Tien Beach

F Soreau/MICHELIN

At the end of this labyrinth is **Duong Beach★★**, tucked away in a small cove surrounded by crystal-clear waters and two rocky islets known as **Hon Phu Tu** ("Father and Son Isle") *(there is a boat trip around the isle)*. They serve as a sanctuary for colonies of swifts whose nests are a very sought-after item in Vietnamese cuisine. There are dozens of eating places and food stalls all along the beach, a favourite with hordes of local people looking to let off steam. It is a very pleasant atmosphere, but unfortunately such popularity has taken its toll on the cleanliness of the beach. At the end of the day, as the last merry-makers head for home, an impressive sunset often lights up the bay.

The simplest way to leave Hon Chong is to go to Ba Hon (17km) by motorcycle taxi and then stop one of the buses which run between Ha Tien (20km) and Rach Gia (64km).

Rach Gia
Capital of Kien Giang Province. Pop 150 000.
Allow one day.

Rach Gia is an unsophisticated, lively, thriving city and an important stop-off for tourists on their way to Phu Quoc. Although traditionally focused on fishing and agriculture, and even contraband, the town aims to challenge Can Tho as the centre of the delta's economy with a new port now under construction. Its position on the edge of the Gulf of Thailand and on the outlet of the canal leading to Long Xuyen is one of its major assets. Rach Gia is home to Chinese and Khmer minority groups and almost all the different religions (Confucianism, Buddhism, Cao Dai, Christianity and ancestor worship), each with their own sanctuaries.

Getting around Rach Gia is quite simple; Nguyen Trung Truc runs north to south through the city centre and converges on a small island in the middle of the canal. Start by a visit to the **port** *(on Nguyen Cong Tru)* where colourful boats crowd together in anticipation of an imminent departure. On the other side of the canal, old and elegant **Chinese gabled houses**, which have known better days, still play an important role in local trade.

A few hundred metres from the landing stage is **Nguyen Trung Truc Temple** dedicated to the local hero famous for his part in the struggle against the French occupying forces around 1860. This is a perfect illustration of the way in which the Vietnamese can create a cult around a particular historical character and associate it with a religion, in this case Confucianism. The **portrait** of Nguyen Trung Truc hangs above the altar, and in the main room, two coloured **carved murals** relate his two major feats, the burning of the Governor's Palace and of the ship **Espérance**. After years of hiding, he was forced to give himself up to the French who had taken his wife hostage. He was then executed.

You can stop off for a refreshing drink at the small **theme park** nearby, where the local youth and photographers enjoy an iced coffee together.

Several sanctuaries are dotted along Quang Trung to the north of the city. In the **Confucian Pagoda of Ong Bin** (Chua Ong Bin), with its attractive colourful frontage, the traditional **inner courtyard** is equipped with a well, intended to receive the "heavenly light". Note the colourful, naïve **mural** depicting a tiger.

Ignore Phat Quang Pagoda further up the street and go directly to **Phat Lon Pagoda** (18C) which stands in the middle of a clump of trees. This is the biggest Khmer Theravada pagoda in the delta and its distinctive style is immediately recognisable. Inside the sanctuary, elaborately decorated with murals, is a statue of the **Buddha** sitting in front of a circle of flashing lights. Behind the pagoda is an interesting **cemetery** dotted with stupas.

Go back down towards the city centre.

Apart from the inevitable section devoted to the Vietnam War, the **Rach Gia Museum*** *(21 Nguyen Van Troi. Open daily from 7.30-11am / 1.30-5pm. Entrance fee. Allow 20min)* has an interesting collection of **Hindu artefacts** from the archaeological excavations at Oc Eo (1C-6C), notably pottery, lingams, yonis and jewellery.

If you find yourself with time to kill in Rach Gia before boarding the boat to Phu Quoc, complete the tour of the city with a visit to **Tam Bao Pagoda** *(go down Nguyen Trung Truc and turn left into Thich Thien An)* and its decorative gardens with trees in the shape of animals. Further south, at the intersection of Nguyen Trung Truc and Nguyen An Minh, there is also a **Cao Dai Temple**.

There is very little to see, however, at the **Ancient City of Oc Eo** *(11km from Rach Gia, near the village of Vong The; contact Kien Giang Tourist for further information)* and it is not really worth visiting.

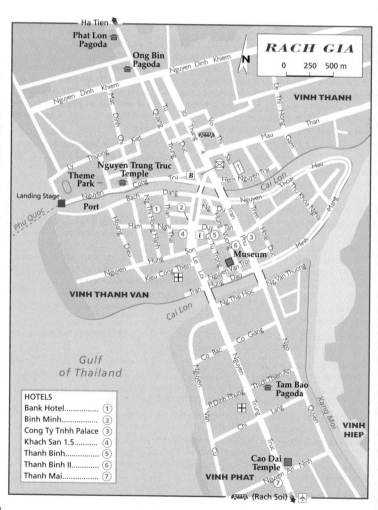

RACH GIA

HOTELS
Bank Hotel..............①
Binh Minh...............②
Cong Ty Tnhh Palace...③
Khach San 1.5...........④
Thanh Binh.............⑤
Thanh Binh II..........⑥
Thanh Mai.............⑦

The Mekong Delta close up

COMING AND GOING

Road conditions in the Delta are fairly satisfactory on the whole, and, apart from a few exceptions (notably between Chau Doc and Ha Tien), roads between the major cities are all tarmacked. Journey times to the south of the Delta have been considerably reduced with the opening of the Vinh Long bridge. Ferries are very efficiently run and remain a vital part of the Delta's economy and infrastructure. However, in the high season, there may be a long wait before boarding the boat. Bear in mind that express buses have priority.

Distances by road between the major cities in the Mekong Delta

	(1)	(2)	(3)	(4)	(5)	(6)	(7)	(8)	(9)	(10)	(11)	(12)	(13)
(1) HCM	–	72	86	136	202	143	171	169	231	190	245	338	248
(2) My Tho	72	–	14	73	140	80	108	106	170	127	184	275	185
(3) Ben Tre	86	14	–	63	155	98	116	125	186	127	189	292	203
(4) Vinh Long	136	73	63	–	66	25	52	34	97	73	127	220	130
(5) Tra Vinh	202	140	155	66	–	91	121	100	163	139	193	286	196
(6) Sa Dec	143	72	98	25	91	–	28	58	119	48	102	195	123
(7) Cao Lanh	171	108	116	52	121	28	–	86	147	75	130	223	133
(8) Can Tho	169	106	125	34	100	58	86	–	62	62	116	205	113
(9) Soc Trang	231	170	186	97	163	119	147	62	–	124	178	267	177
(10) Long Xuyen	190	127	127	73	139	48	75	62	124	–	54	185	75
(11) Chau Doc	245	184	189	127	193	102	130	116	178	54	–	218	129
(12) Ha Tien	338	275	292	220	286	195	223	205	267	185	218	–	90
(13) Rach Gia	248	185	203	130	196	123	133	113	177	75	129	90	–

By bus and minibus – _Mien Tay Terminal_ (3am-midnight), 10km west of Ho Chi Minh City serves the whole Delta. **_Cholon Terminal_** (4.30am-6.30pm) serves the same area, but departures are less frequent and there are fewer express buses.

Hourly departures for My Tho (2hr journey), Ben Tre (about 3hr depending on the wait at the ferry), Vinh Long (3hr) and Can Tho (4hr), every two hours for Cao Lanh (3hr 30min) and Soc Trang (6hr), every three hours for Long Xuyen (about 6hr), but it is probably easier to change at Can Tho. Three or four departures per day for Tra Vinh (5hr), but it is better to change at Vinh Long, for Rach Gia (7hr) and for Ha Tien (9hr). Five departures per day for Chau Doc (about 6hr 30min).

By car – Budget permitting, or if there are several of you travelling, the best way to visit the Delta is to hire a chauffeur-driven car (see "Ho Chi Minh City close up" page 351).

By boat – Travelling by ferry in the Delta requires a lot of time and the facilities are very basic, but an interesting experience is guaranteed (take your own provisions). In Ho Chi Minh City, the **landing stage** for the ferries for My Tho (6hr) is on the quayside at the end of Dai Lo Ham Nghi, ☎ (08) 829 78 92. There are hourly departures for Ben Tre (8hr) from 4am-10pm from **Ben Pha Rach Mieu**, 1km west of the city centre.

Some agencies in Ho Chi Minh City (see "Ho Chi Minh City close up" page 351) also organise cruises over several days in specially equipped sampans .Yet another way to see the Delta.

By hydrofoil – _Greenlines_, 8A Nguyen Tat Thanh, Q4, ☎ (08) 821 56 09 / 940 06 21, Fax (08) 940 29 49. Services depart from Ho Chi Minh City every Tuesday, Thursday and Saturday at 8am stopping off at My Tho at 9.55am (US$12) and arriving in Vinh Long at 10.55am (US$16). In the other direction, departures from Vinh Long every Wednesday, Friday and Sunday at 10.30am stopping off at My Tho at 11.30am and arriving at Ho Chi Minh City at 1.30pm. Services to Chau Doc seem to be temporarily suspended.

Another hydrofoil leaves from Ho Chi Minh City at 7.30am stopping off at My Tho at 9.30am and arriving in Can Tho at 11.30am. In the other direction, it leaves from Can Tho at 1.30pm stopping off at My Tho at 3.30pm and arriving in Ho Chi Minh City at 5.30pm.

GETTING AROUND

Considering the limited size of the cities in the Delta, in most cases the best way to sightsee is invariably on foot. Otherwise there is always the option of taking a cyclo, a motorcycle taxi, a bicycle taxi or even a small cart pulled by a motorcycle, as in Chau Doc. It is more difficult to find ordinary taxis, though there are some in Can Tho.

WHEN TO VISIT THE MEKONG DELTA

Travel by boat can be very difficult during the rainy season from May to October, particularly during the September floods which often prove catastrophic. There is torrential rain practically every day, but the rest of the time the heat is not so intense (26°C on average) and the light is ideal for would-be photographers. The dry season lasts from November to April when the average temperature is 28°C, reaching highs of 38°C in February and March. Watch out for the Tet festival and other local festivities since hotels in most towns are fully booked at this time.

My Tho close up

COMING AND GOING

By bus – In addition to Ho Chi Minh City, My Tho **terminal** also operates services to Vinh Long (2hr) and Can Tho (4hr). For Chau Doc (6hr), change buses after the new bridge at Vinh Long.

By hydrofoil – Greenlines, ☎ (073) 82 93 72. **Tourist landing stage**, 30 Thang 4, opposite the Post Office. For times, see "The Mekong Delta close up".

Renting a car – Contact the hotels, especially the Cong Doan.

ADDRESS BOOK

Tourist information – Tien Giang Tourist, 8 30 Thang 4 Street, by the boat landing, ☎ (073) 87 31 84, Fax (073) 87 35 78. This government agency has a monopoly over all the island excursions. Rates are high and non-negotiable but vary according to the number of people, so try and join up with other tourists. Tours include the boat trip to one island (US$23.50) or two islands (US$34), running commentary from one of the guides, a musical interlude and fruit tasting.

Bank / Currency exchange – V Bard Tien Giang Bank, corner of Thu Khoa Huan and Le Loi. Open Monday-Friday 7.30-11am / 1.30-4pm. Dollars changed.

Bureau de change, 5 Le Van Duyet. Open Monday-Friday 7.15-11.15am / 1.30-4.30pm. Withdrawals over the counter with Visa or MasterCard.

Post Office / Telephone – 30 Thang 4, opposite the landing stage. Open daily from 6am-9pm. 24hr telephone service.

Internet – Cau lac bo tin hoc thanh nien, 7 Hung Vuong, on the corner of Ngo Quyen. Open daily from 7am-9pm.

WHERE TO STAY

Under US$10

Cong Doan, 61 30 Thang 4 Street, ☎ (073) 87 43 24, Fax (073) 87 88 57 – 12rm ⌂ ▤ ✕ ✗ TV This government-run hotel is part of a huge building opposite the Chuong Duong Hotel offering rather cheerless, large tiled rooms (some with hot running water and air-conditioning), but there is a friendly welcome and the staff speak English.

Rang Dong, 25 30 Thang 4 Street, ☎ (073) 87 44 00 – 22rm ⌂ ▤ ✗ TV As a last resort, since less value for money than the Cong Doan (hot water).

Between US$10 and US$15

Song Tien Hotel, 101 Trung Trac, ☎ (073) 87 20 09 – 40rm ⌂ ▤ ✕ Very lacklustre, only the prices seem to be have been brought up to date.

Between US$15 and US$30

Chuong Duong, 10 30 Thang 4 Street, ☎ (073) 87 08 75 – 26rm ⌂ ▤ ✿ TV ✕ A luxury hotel with cable television and faultless facilities. Some rooms have a balcony overlooking the river.

The Thoi Son Tourist Complex, Thoi Son Island, ☎ (073) 87 73 71 – 6rm ⌂ ▤ ⤬ ✿ TV ✕ Very pleasant facilities surrounded by orchards for those less pushed for time looking for a little peace and quiet (the island comes alive with each new morning arrival of tourists). Respectable bungalow accommodation.

EATING OUT

For tasty, traditional dishes, try the series of small restaurants along the quayside on Trung Trac.

Between 50 000 and 100 000VND

Chuong Duong, near the hotel of the same name. ☂ A delightful, covered terrace on the riverside serving frogs, soup, seafood and their special "fish with elephant's ears".

Ngoc Gia Thrang, 196A Ap Bac. ☂ Located on the outskirts of the city, set back from the road. Boasts a very peaceful, tree-lined garden with a covered terrace along a small canal. The varied, high quality menu includes seafood, grilled meat, soup, fruit and "Fish with elephant's ears".

Trung Luong, at the Trung Luong intersection on the outskirts of the city, near the bus terminal. ☂ The largest state-run restaurant in the Mekong, tends to cater mainly for groups. The atmosphere suffers a little as a result, but the food is well prepared and the tree-lined garden dotted with little gullies is very appealing.

The Thoi Son Tourist Complex, Thoi Son Island. ☂ A must for those visiting the islands. The restaurant is part of a huge, wooden, traditional residence offering a mouth-watering selection of fruit from the local orchards.

SHOPPING

Markets – The new market and shopping area can be found on Nguyen Hue and the adjacent streets.

Ben Tre close up

COMING AND GOING

By boat – The Ben Tre **landing stage** is on the western edge of My Tho. After the crossing (30min), take the bus for Ben Tre (8km).

ADDRESS BOOK

Tourist information – Ben Tre Tourist, 65 Dong Khoi, ☎ (075) 82 96 18. 7.30-11am / 1.30-5pm. This official agency organises speed-boat trips to the bird sanctuary. They sell cards and brochures.

Post Office / Telephone – 3 Cach Mang Thang, near the main beach.

WHERE TO STAY

The town has a wide choice of hotels, but don't expect luxury.

Under US$10

Nha Nghi 99, 73 Phan Ngoc Tong, ☎ (075) 83 12 34 – 17rm ⌂ ▤ ⤬ ✿ TV ✕ A boarding house in a two-storey building with spotless, white rooms. The atmosphere is rather cold, but the place is good value for money.

Khach San Du Lich Cong Doan, 36 Hai Ba Trung, ☎ (075) 82 50 82 – 11rm ⌂ ▤ ⤬ ✿ ✕ A cooperative hotel with rather dreary rooms, but clean with all the necessary facilities (hot water). Prices double if you opt for air-conditioning, television and breakfast.

Ben Tre Hotel, 8/2 Tran Quoc Tuan, ☎ (075) 82 22 23 – 19rm ⌂ ▤ ⤬ ✿ TV ✕ This establishment is located on the large square on the outskirts of the city offering basic accommodation, but clean and well looked after. The rooms over the street are rather noisy.

Hung Vuong Hotel, 177 Hung Vuong, ☎ (075) 82 24 08 – 19rm ⌂ ▤ ⤬ Supposedly plush rooms, but very poorly maintained. Only the upstairs rooms with air-conditioning are acceptable.

Between US$15 and US$30

Dong Khoi, 16 Hai Ba Trung, ☎ (075) 82 22 40, Fax (075) 82 24 40 – 25rm ⌂ ▤ ✿ TV ✕ The best and also the biggest hotel in the city, located on the main square opposite the lake. Clean, respectable rooms, but nothing more. Try and negotiate the price, because rates are rather high.

EATING OUT

Eating out is nothing special in Ben Tre. The choice is between cheap market eating places or expensive, but rather uninspiring restaurants.

Between 25 000 and 50 000VND

Don Khoi, 16 Hai Ba Trung. The hotel restaurant is in a large, open dining room, but the food is rather tasteless and the staff don't speak much English. Try the frog's legs.

Nha Hang Ben Tre, A "floating restaurant" moored near to the footbridge to the city centre. 🚉 It is open late (10pm) and has a lovely view over the river, but the menu is the same as at Don Khoi and the food is equally bland. Make do with just a drink.

Vinh Long close up

COMING AND GOING

By bus – The **terminal** is at 3 Thang 2, near the post office. Journey times from Ho Chi Minh City (3hr) and My Tho (90min) have been reduced since the opening of the bridge.

By hydrofoil – The **landing stage** is at 1 Thang 5. For times, see "The Mekong Delta close up".

Renting a car – Contact Hotel Cuu Long B.

ADDRESS BOOK

Tourist information – Cuu Long Tourist, 1 Thang 5, ☎ (070) 82 36 16, Fax (070) 82 33 57. "Your faithful companion around the Mekong Delta" according to the brochure, and the government agency in Vinh Long is, in fact, quite efficient. They have a monopoly on boat trips along the waterways and offer tours of the Delta over several days.

Post Office / Telephone – Hoang Thai Hieu. Open daily 7-11am / 1.30-5pm.

Internet – Delta, 2G Hung Vuong Phuong.

WHERE TO STAY

Under US$10

Long Chau, 1 Thang 5, near the landing stage, ☎ (070) 82 24 94 – 10rm ⚄ ⊞ ⤬ TV A grotty little hotel that should only be used as a last resort, but it does have a pleasant view over the river. The upstairs rooms with a fan are better value for money.

The Pham Van Lan Residence, Binh Hoa Phuoc Island, ☎ (070) 85 99 92 – 2rm. A warm welcome, with well-ventilated, rustic-style rooms and a lush orchard. What more could you ask for? There will be a commission to pay if you go through the official agency.

Between US$15 and US$30

An Binh, 3 Hoang Thai Hieu, opposite the Post Office, ☎ (070) 82 31 90, Fax (070) 82 23 31 – 36rm ⚄ ⊞ ⤬ TV ⤬ A wide choice of rooms from the most basic (upstairs with bathrooms), to the most luxurious (with air-conditioning, satellite TV, bath and hot running water). The staff could be more welcoming.

Cuu Long A, 1 Thang 5, near the landing stage, ☎ (070) 82 24 94, Fax (070) 82 38 48 – 15rm ⚄ ⊞ ℘ TV ⤬ Breakfast included. This rather old-fashioned hotel, owned by the Tourist Office, offers tidy, comfortable rooms (satellite TV), although a little expensive for their category. Some have a balcony with a magnificent view over the Mekong.

Between US$30 and US$50

Cuu Long B, Hung Vuong, near the landing stage, ☎ (070) 82 24 94, Fax (070) 82 38 48 – 34rm ⚄ ⊞ ℘ TV ⤬ ✻ Breakfast included. A luxury hotel with perfect facilities (hot water and satellite TV). Worthy of any stately home.

EATING OUT

There is not much choice in Vinh Long, but, as always, you can tuck into a bowl of soup at the market.

Between 50 000 and 100 000VND
Phuong Thuy Restaurant, 1 Thang 5, near the landing stage. The best restaurant in town, in partnership with the Cuu Long Hotels, is wonderfully situated on a covered pontoon that was once a helicopter landing pad for the Americans during the war. Vietnamese and tourists alike enjoy Western and Vietnamese cuisine.

Tra Vinh close up

COMING AND GOING

By bus – The **bus station** is on the outskirts of the town.

ADDRESS BOOK

Tourist information – Tra Vinh Tourist, 64-66 Le Loi, ☎ (074) 86 25 59, Fax (074) 86 67 68. Go up Pham Thai Buong, turn left at the market and then right. This official agency organises visits to the Khmer Pagodas, as well as boat trips to the fishing villages at My Tho and the oyster island at Con Ngheu.

Bank / Currency exchange – Ngan hang, on Pham Thai Buong, near the post office. Open Monday-Friday from 7-11am / 1-5pm. Only American dollars are accepted.

Post Office / Telephone – At the end of Pham Thai Buong. Open Monday-Friday from 7am-9pm.

Internet – 1 Dien Bien Phu. 7-11am / 1-5pm. Only one computer.

WHERE TO STAY

The town has very few hotels, all with quite basic facilities. The situation should improve shortly with the re-opening of the Cuu Long Hotel, currently closed for renovation work.

Under US$10
Thanh Tra Hotel, 1 Pham Thai Buong, opposite the post office, ☎ (074) 86 36 21, Fax (074) 86 37 69 – 39rm ⚐ 🍽 ✗ A luxury hotel with quite basic rooms and cleaning is kept to a minimum. Price differences between the cheapest and the most exclusive rooms (air-conditioning, telephone, TV, hot water and bath) may be threefold.

Thanh Binh, 1 bis Le Thanh Ton, ☎ (074) 86 61 70 – 15rm ⚐ 🍽 ✗ A moderate, spacious hotel, but unfortunately could be cleaner. Price differences between the basic rooms (fan) and the better equipped (air-conditioning, TV, hot water) may be double.

Phuong Hoang, 1 Le Thanh Ton, ☎ (074) 86 22 70 – 33rm ⚐ 🍽 TV A respectable, private hotel with slightly better facilities than the Thanh Binh Hotel for a similar price.

EATING OUT

Cheap eating places along the main street and around the market which serve Chinese food in the evenings.

Under 25 000VND
Huy Huong, 8 Dien Bien Phu. A small, inexpensive restaurant on the square serving excellent Vietnamese food.

Between 25 000 and 50 000VND
Viet Hoa, 80 Tran Phu. 8am-8pm. The rather dreary decor of this family restaurant inside the garage of a private house is more than made up for by the quality of the Chinese and Vietnamese food, which includes chicken, beef, eel, crab, fish and even fruit charlotte.

Quan Hai Yen, 74-76 Le Loi. An unsophisticated, pleasant little restaurant with an upstairs room overlooking the street. Teams of attractive waitresses serve Vietnamese specialities, but good luck with the menu written in the local dialect.

GOING OUT

Bars – Nightlife is non-existent in Tra Vinh, but to get the feel of the place have a drink on the terrace of one of the bars along Pham Thai Buong (up to 10pm).

OTHER THINGS TO DO

Festivals – The **Khmer New Year** (April) is a time for numerous ceremonies and festivities, notably the Dua ghe Ngo, an exciting pirogue race.

Sa Dec close up

COMING AND GOING

By bus – Sa Dec can be reached by bus from Vinh Long. The **terminal** is 300m southeast of the town centre.

ADDRESS BOOK

Post Office / Telephone – The main office is on the corner of Quoc Lo and Hung Vuong. Internet access available.

WHERE TO STAY, EATING OUT

Between US$15 and US$30
Khach San Sa Dec, 108/5A Hung Vuong, ☎ (067) 86 14 30, Fax (067)

627 30 – 40rm ☏ 📧 🍴 🎱 📺 ✕ This two-storey, modern building provides respectable, basic accommodation, although slightly over the top with decorative, satin bed covers. The staff are very welcoming and the restaurant serves local specialities at reasonable prices. Stay clear of the private, air-conditioned function rooms though, they are just too gloomy and run-down.

Cao Lanh close up

COMING AND GOING

By bus – The **bus station** is in the city centre on Thap Moi, next to the market. Direct bus service for Vinh Long (90min), Chau Doc, via Hong Ngu (5-6hr) and Ho Chi Minh City (3hr 30min).

ADDRESS BOOK

Tourist information – **Dong Thap Tourist**, Nguyen Hue, opposite Doc Binh Kieu, ☎ (067) 85 13 43.

Post Office / Telephone – On the main square on the corner of Nguyen Hue and Ly Thuong Kiet.

Internet – **IPC Service**, 218 Nguyen Hue, ☎ (067) 85 54 65. Open daily from 7am-10pm except for Wednesdays, Fridays and Sundays (7am-7pm).

WHERE TO STAY

Under US$10
Binh Minh, 147 Hung Vuong, ☎ (067) 85 34 23 – 11rm ☏ 🎱 📺 An ideal central hotel for backpackers looking for good deals and who are not too bothered about their home comforts or the size of their room. The manager speaks English.

Between US$10 and US$15
Thien An, 177 Quoc Io 30, ☎ (067) 85 30 41 – 23rm ☏ 📧 🎱 🔨 📺 A straightforward, respectable hotel with clean, basic facilities (hot water).

Between US$15 and US$30
Xuan Mai, 2 Le Quy Dong, ☎ (067) 85 28 52, Fax (067) 85 30 58 – 18rm ☏ 📧 🎱 📺 ✕ A private hotel with comfortable accommodation, but rather high rates compared to the state-run equivalents… negotiation possible.
Hoa Binh, Highway 30, on the outskirts of the city, just before the bridge, ☎ (067) 85 14 69, Fax (067) 85 12 18 – 39rm ☏ 📧 🎱 📺 This modern, state-run hotel provides perfect facilities (satellite TV, lift, hot water in the luxury rooms), but the cleaning isn't quite up to scratch. It is still good value for money.
Song Tra, 178 Nguyen Hue, ☎ (067) 85 26 24, Fax (067) 85 26 23 – 47rm ☏ 📧 🎱 📺 ✕ This recent, state-run, three-storey building with no lift offers clean and tidy accommodation with perfect facilities, although the prices are high.

EATING OUT

There is a cluster of different restaurants at the end of Nguyen Hue.

Under 25 000VND
Quan Tranh, Pham Huu Lau, just before the bridge. 🛖 The restaurant's specialities include soup with seafood or pumpkin flower, as well as prawns, grilled chicken and a superb steamed tuna, all served in small straw huts in the middle of a garden.

Can Tho close up

COMING AND GOING

By air – The military **airport** of Tra Noc, 7km north of the city, was opened up to commercial traffic in 1998. Buses leave from the Post Office.

By bus – The **bus station** is at the end of Nguyen Trai, 1km from the city centre. The ferry crossing between Cai Von and Can Tho lasts about 10 min. There are services from Can Tho to almost all the other towns in the Delta, including Vinh Long, Chau Doc, Rach Gia, Long Xuyen and Soc Trang. Buses for Ho Chi Minh City run between 5am and 3pm (4hr journey).

By boat – The local **landing stage** is on Hai Ba Trung, near the market, and the special one for tourists is a little higher up, opposite the Lodge Hotel.

By hydrofoil – The **landing stage** is at the northernmost point of Hai Ba Trung, near to the Ninh Kieu Hotel. For times, see "The Mekong Delta close up".

GETTING AROUND

By taxi – **Mailinh**, 1B Nguyen Trai, ☎ (071) 82 82 82.

ADDRESS BOOK

Tourist information – **Can Tho Tourist**, 20 Hai Ba Trung, ☎ (071) 82 18 52, Fax (071) 82 27 19. This government agency organises various tours in the surrounding area with English-speaking guides. Chauffeur-driven car or minibus rentals from here.

Travel agencies – **Sacatours**, 55 Phan Dinh Phung, in the Saigon-Cantho Hotel, ☎ (071) 81 24 19, Fax (071) 82 32 88. This is a joint-venture between Saigon Tourist and Can Tho Tourist offering tours in the Mekong and throughout Vietnam. A professional, English-speaking team providing cars and boats for hire.

Victoria, Cai Khe Ward. The hotel offers an original choice of boat trips to the floating market at Cai Rang, but also to Soc Trang, the Bang Lang Bird Sanctuary or into the mangrove swamps. The prices are, however, rather high.

Bank / Currency exchange – Can Tho has a number of banks where you can change different currencies and withdraw money on a credit card. **Vietincombank**, 7 Hoa Binh, opposite the Munirangsyaram Pagoda. Open Monday-Friday 7.30-10.45am / 1-4.30pm.

Post Office / Telephone – 2 Hoa Binh, Open daily from 6am-8pm.

Internet – Some hotels offer Internet access, as does the Nam Bo restaurant.

WHERE TO STAY

To the delight of all travellers, Can Tho provides the best choice of hotels in the Delta, and a new luxury hotel called The Lodge is being built on Hai Ba Trung.

Under US$10

Hotel 31, 31 Ngo Duc Ke, ☎ (071) 82 52 87 – 10rm ⌖ 🍽 ☲ A·respectable hotel with good facilities for its particular category. The two rooms overlooking the street are slightly noisier.

Between US$10 and US$15

Hau Giang, 34 Nam Ky Khoi Nghia, ☎ (071) 81 18 51, Fax (071) 82 18 06 – 35rm ⌖ 🍽 ☲ ♪ 📺 Breakfast included. A pleasant hotel, but not much character. Double rates for the more exclusive rooms, and those with fans are the best value for money.

Between US$15 and US$30

Asia Hotel (Achau), 91 Chau Van Liem, ☎ (071) 81 28 00, Fax (071) 81 28 08 – 22rm ⌖ 🍽 ♪ 📺 ✕ 🆑 Internet access at reception. Breakfast included. A modern hotel with a marble lobby offering flawless accommodation at very reasonable prices (satellite TV).

Between US$30 and US$50

Ninh Kieu, 2 Hai Ba Trung, to the far north of the quayside, ☎ (071) 82 11 71, Fax (071) 82 45 83 – 40rm ⌖ 🍽 ♪ 📺 ✕ Situated in a quiet part of the town, a stone's throw from the town centre, this well-equipped hotel, although somewhat old-fashioned, provides rooms whose prices vary according to the size and the quality of the view.

Tay Do, 61 Chau Van Liem, ☎ (071) 82 70 09, Fax (071) 82 70 08 – 31rm ⌖ 🍽 ♪ 📺 ✕ 🆑 Good facilities and very clean rooms, but the whole atmosphere is rather depressing and offers less value for money than the Asia Hotel. The cheapest rooms don't have windows. Try and negotiate the price.

Hoa Binh Hotel, 5 Hoa Binh, ☎ (071) 82 00 59, Fax (071) 81 02 17 – 50rm ⌖

📇 ✒ TV ✗ CC Breakfast included. Another luxury residence with beautiful, carpeted rooms whose prices are solely dependent on size (satellite TV). Strangely enough, the most expensive rooms have just one window overlooking a courtyard.

Saigon-Can Tho Hotel, 55 Phan Ding Phung, ☎ (071) 82 58 31, Fax (071) 82 32 88 – 45rm ⌁ 📇 ✒ TV ✗ CC Sauna, travel agency, Internet access. Breakfast included. The hotel is situated near the market and boasts a very professional service. The rooms are pleasant enough, but expensive for their category, especially the ones without windows (satellite TV).

Quoc Te Hotel, 12 Hai Ba Trung, on the quayside, ☎ (071) 82 20 79, Fax (071) 82 10 39 – 42rm ⌁ 📇 ✒ TV ✗ CC Breakfast included. The marble hall impresses any visitor to this elegant, but slightly tacky hotel. The best rooms have a balcony with a superb view over the Mekong, but prices reflect the available facilities and those on a more limited budget will have to be satisfied with a windowless room.

Over US$100

☞**Victoria**, Cai Khe Ward, north of the city centre, ☎ (071) 81 01 11, Fax (071) 82 92 59 – 92rm ⌁ 📇 ✒ TV ✗ ⛱ ⚒ CC Travel agency, shop, Internet access. Situated on the banks of the Mekong River in fairy tale surroundings, this elegant, neo-classical building in true colo-nial style provides a professional service worthy of any luxury hotel. The restaurant overlooks a garden and boasts an excellent wine list, but you can also enjoy an informal pool-side drink.

EATING OUT

Under 25 000VND

Ca phe Thuan Loi, 30 Nam Ky Khoi Nghia. This popular eating place, situated on a busy intersection lined with shops, provides the ideal opportunity for a bite to eat while watching the world go by.

Ngoc Mai, 131 street 3 Thang 2, the road to Soc Trang, 2km south of the city centre, 300m to the left beyond Rach Ranh. A superior transport café serving excellent Vietnamese cuisine, fried or steamed (prawns, fish, eels, octopus, pork, beef). The menu is in English.

Between 25 000 and 50 000VND

Mekong, 38 Hai Ba Trung. ⛲ This small restaurant opens out onto the street opposite the Mekong and serves simple food, perfect for backpackers craving for Western cooking (soup, chicken) or a more traditional breakfast.

☞**Nam Bo**, 50 Hai Ba Trung, on the corner of Ngo Quyen. Delicious French and Vietnamese cuisine. A friendly welcome and the upstairs balcony affords a wonderful view over the busy street below. Bar and Internet access.

Song Hau, Hai Ba Trung. An original way to dine cruising down the river between 8 and 9pm.

Soc Trang close up

COMING AND GOING

By bus – The *bus station* is on Nguyen Chi Thanh, north of the city centre. There is a bus for Ho Chi Minh City (5-6hr), via Can Tho and My Tho.

ADDRESS BOOK

Post Office / Telephone – At the end of Hai Ba Trung. Daily from 6am-9pm.

WHERE TO STAY

Accommodation is nothing to write home about in Soc Trang, where hotels are few and far between, expensive and with poor facilities. They are, however, fully booked during Ok Om Bok.

Under US$10

Don Tien, ☎ (079) 82 10 27, Fax (079) 82 00 99 – 55rm ⌁ 📇 ⚒ The dubious room service and basic facilities make this a last resort stop-over.

Between US$10 and US$15

Cong Doan, ☎ (079) 82 56 14 – 25rm ⌁ 📇 ⚒ ✒ TV A rather dreary, state-run hotel, but decent nonetheless.

Between US$15 and US$30

Khanh Hung, ☎ (079) 82 18 88 – 37rm ⌁ 📇 ⚒ ✒ TV ✗ Breakfast included. The best hotel in town (although this is not much of a reference in Soc Trang), located in a modern building offering decent accommodation (hot water) where prices double for the better equipped rooms.

EATING OUT

On Hai Ba Trung and the adjacent streets are a number of stalls serving Chinese, Vietnamese and Khmer specialities.

Between 25 000 and 50 000VND

Quan Thuan 2, 10A Tran Hung Dao. This roomy restaurant, more like an over-lit village hall, serves good, varied food (noodles, steak, eel). The menu is in English and the prices are very reasonable (closes at 9pm).

GOING OUT

Cafés – Hai Ba Trung boasts several terrace cafés where you can enjoy a beer.

OTHER THINGS TO DO

Festivals – The **Khmer New Year** (Ok Om Bok), on the 15th day of the 10th month of the lunar calendar, is sometimes known as **Bon Sam Peak Preah**, when offerings are made to the moon. The sticky-rice crop is also celebrated and offerings are made for future harvests. Teams from the pagodas of the area come together for spectacular boat races using pirogues designed for dozens of oarsmen.

———— Long Xuyen close up ————

COMING AND GOING

By bus – The **bus station** is on Tran Hung Dao in the southern part of town. Buses go to Ho Chi Minh City, Can Tho, Chau Doc, Ha Tien and Rach Gia. For Cao Lanh and Sa Dec, catch the bus from the An Hoa landing stage on Ly Thai To, southeast of the city.

By boat – A boat leaves for Sa Dec, Chau Doc and Rach Gia near the bridge over the Thi Nieu, next to the Ong Bon Pagoda.

ADDRESS BOOK

Tourist information – An Giang Tourmoundimex, 17 Nguyen Van Cung, ☎ (076) 84 16 35, Fax (076) 84 16 48. 7-11am / 1-5pm. Don't expect much from this tourist agency which organises boat trips along the canals and to Cho Moi.

Post Office / Telephone – 42 Ngo Gia Tu. Open daily from 6am-10pm.

Internet – The Hung, 81 Nguyen Hue B, on the corner of Luong Van Cu. Open daily from 7.30am-9.30pm.

WHERE TO STAY

Under US$10

An Long, 281 Tran Hung Dao, on the southern outskirts of the city, ☎ (076) 84 32 98 – 26rm 🛏 📺 ⤬ ℘ A simple, friendly little hotel run by a Chinese. Good value for money.

Long Xuyen Hotel, 19 Nguyen Van Cung, ☎ (076) 84 19 27, Fax (076) 84 24 83 – 35rm 🛏 📺 ⤬ ℘ 📺 ✕ Breakfast included. A welcoming, bright pink hotel, perfectly clean and tidy with flawless facilities. It is located in a modern 4-storey building.

Between US$10 and US$15

An Giang, 40 Hai Ba Trung, ☎ (076) 84 12 97 – 16rm 🛏 📺 ⤬ ℘ 📺 A very central, friendly little hotel, but a little noisy. There are rooms to suit every budget and prices vary fourfold between the different standards of rooms.

Thoai Chau 2, 238A Tran Hung Dao, ☎ (076) 84 38 82, Fax (076) 84 32 20 – 12rm 🛏 📺 ⤬ ℘ 📺 This four-storey establishment with no lift, next to the An Long Hotel, offers small, but clean and functional rooms (most of them have hot running water).

Thai Binh 2, 4 Nguyen Hue, ☎ (076) 84 18 59 – 40rm 🛏 📺 ⤬ ℘ 📺 A four-storey hotel with no lift, but a huge tiled lobby. The rooms are ordinary, but clean and good value for money.

Cuu Long, 21 Nguyen Van Cung, ☎ (076) 84 13 65, Fax (076) 84 31 76 – 20rm 🛏 📺 ℘ 📺 ✕ Breakfast included. The hotel is just opposite the Long Xuyen, but for practically the same facilities, prices are a little higher. Pity about the rather unfriendly staff.

Chau Doc close up

COMING AND GOING

By bus – The **terminal** is 2km south-east of town, on the road to Long Xuyen. There are buses to Ho Chi Minh City, Can Tho, Vinh Long, Rach Gia and other towns, but they are full during holidays.

By car – If you have your own vehicle, go straight to Ha Tien on the track along the Cambodian border (96km).

By boat – To get to the **landing stage** for Ha Tien, go 400m northwards from the Thuan Loi Hotel along Tran Hung Dao as far as No 86A. Apparently, Ha Tien can now be reached by boat along a river canal running alongside the Cambodian border (2 departures per week. Allow 10hr). An unusual way to see life through the eyes of a local boatman while admiring the scenery. Ask for further information on-the-spot and bring something to eat and drink.

The ferry for Con Tien Island leaves from near the market place and the Thuan Loi Hotel, at the end of Thuong Dang Le. The **landing stage** for Chau Giang is at the end of Duong Le Loi, south of the city.

By hydrofoil – The landing stage is at the Victoria Hotel. For times, see "The Mekong Delta close up".

ADDRESS BOOK

Post Office / Telephone – On the quayside, on the corner of Nguyen Van Thoai. Open daily from 6am-10pm.

Internet – **Internet Quoc Thai**, 16/2 Nui Sam, on the road to Sam Mountain, 1km from the city centre. 7.30-10.30pm. Connection time is expensive, but not as much as the excessive rates at the Victoria Hotel.

WHERE TO STAY

Don't count on finding accommodation during festival times if you have not booked in advance. The chain of Victoria

Hotels belongs to a French group which are currently building another residence on Sam Mountain.

Under US$10
Mini Hotel My Loc, 51B Nguyen Van Thoai, 300m from the market on the road to Sam Mountain, ☎ (076) 86 64 55 – 26rm 🛏 📧 🍴 A three-storey building with basic facilities, only to be considered as a last resort.

Thanh Tra, 77 Thu Khoa Nghia, ☎ (076) 86 67 88, Fax (076) 86 68 45 – 27rm 🛏 📧 🍴 Cheap, standard accommodation with a dormitory or rooms with TV, air-conditioning and hot water.

Between US$10 and US$15
🛏**Thuan Loi**, 18 Tran Hung Dao, ☎ (076) 86 61 34, Fax (076) 86 53 80 – 26rm 🛏 📧 🍴 ♂ 📺 Decent accommodation at reasonable prices in a mini-hotel on stilts with a wonderful view over the Mekong (ask for an upstairs room). In the restaurant, for some strange reason, the staff seem to begrudge serving single travellers.

Hang Chau 2, 10 Nguyen Van Thoai, ☎ (076) 86 88 91, Fax (076) 86 51 40 – 14rm 🛏 📧 ♂ 📺 An ordinary, three-storey hotel, but the rooms are very clean, the facilities are ideal and the price is right (hot water, satellite TV).

Between US$15 and US$30
Nui Sam, at the foot of Sam Mountain, to the left when approaching the city from Chau Doc, ☎ (076) 86 16 66, Fax (076) 86 16 00 – 21rm 🛏 📧 ♂ 📺 ✕ Breakfast included. A comfortable, two-storey hotel with perfect facilities (satellite TV), but despite the price and noise, it is often fully-booked.

Between US$70 and US$100
🛏**Victoria**, 33 Le Loi, ☎ (076) 86 50 10, Fax (076) 86 50 20 – 90rm 🛏 📧 ♂ 📺 ✕ 🏊 CC Shop, sauna. Breakfast included. Finding such a luxurious hotel

The South

in this rather remote area is quite a surprise. It affords marvellous views of this exceptional site at the confluence of two waterways. The sophisticated, neoclassical architecture is at one with the quality of the services provided. Prices are high, but you can always opt for the small, reasonably-priced family room.

EATING OUT

Tasty, local dishes are not at all difficult to find in the small streets near the market and along the quayside.

Under 25 000VND

Lam Hung Ky, 71 Chi Lang. Lunchtime and evening meals. Chinese and Vietnamese cuisine, and excellent seafood.

My Quang, 25 Doc Phu Thu. A cheap and cheerful restaurant, popular with backpackers, serving Western and Vietnamese dishes.

Between 100 000 and 200 000VND

Victoria, 33 Le Loi. ☂ The hotel restaurant offers a sophisticated choice of Western and Vietnamese specialities with an impressive wine list in luxurious surroundings. Prices are higher than anywhere else, but nonetheless affordable.

GOING OUT

Bars – Retire to the heavenly peace and quiet of the Victoria's bar and swimming pool (admission fee).

OTHER THINGS TO DO

Excursions – The Thuan Loi Hotel organises a 2hr covered-boat trip to the Cham villages and the floating markets (allow 50 000VND per hour).

Festivals – The great **Goddess Chua Xu festival** takes place on Sam Mountain on the 23rd and 25th day of the 4th lunar calendar month, after the Tet Festival in May.

In the Khmer community, the **Chol-Chnam-Thmay**, the Theravada Buddhist New Year, is celebrated on 12 and 13 April, and spectacular buffalo races are organised during the **Dol-ta**, on the 29th day of the 8th lunar month.

The Muslim Cham celebrate a number of festivals, particularly the **Romadol**, which lasts throughout the month of May, and the **Hazi** which is held on the first two days of the 6th lunar month.

Ha Tien close up

COMING AND GOING

By bus – The **terminal** can be found just before the floating bridge. Regular departures for Rach Gia (4-5hr), but also for Ho Chi Minh City (9hr) and Can Tho.

By boat – Phu Quoc is apparently accessible by boat from Ha Tien. Ask for further information at the local hotels or at Kien Giang Tourist.

ADDRESS BOOK

Tourist information – Kien Giang Tourist, Dong Ho Chi Minh City Hotel. This regional branch sells local maps.

Bank / Currency exchange – Bank for Investment & Development of Vietnam, on the corner of Chi Lang and Mac Cong Du. Monday-Friday 7-11am / 1-5pm. Dollars only.

Post Office / Telephone – From the boat landing, go 150m along To Chau. Open daily from 6.30-8.30pm.

WHERE TO STAY

The city offers a wide choice of accommodation at very reasonable prices.

● **Ha Tien**

Under US$10

Ha Tien, 36 Tran Hau, ☎ (077) 85 15 63 – 10rm ☂ A large, colonial building with slightly shabby rooms, although with a certain charm. The bigger ones with air-conditioning and bathrooms are good value for money.

To Chau, 55 Dong Ho, facing the port, opposite the bridge, ☎ (077) 85 21 48, Fax (077) 85 21 41 – 11rm ⌗ ☰ ☂ Pleasant, airy rooms with basic facilities, but unfortunately the hotel is a little noisy. The rooms with TV, hot water and air-conditioning are twice as expensive and some have a balcony.

Dong Ho, Tran Hau, opposite the landing stage, ☎ and Fax (077) 85 21 41 – 20rm ⌗ ☰ ☂ ✐ 📺 A large building with simple, high-ceilinged rooms. A wide choice ranging from the most basic with no bathroom to the more luxurious with hot water, air-conditioning, TV, mini-bar and telephone.

Between US$10 and US$15

Hai Yen, 15 To Chau, ☎ (077) 85 15 80, Fax (077) 85 18 89 – 24rm ⌂ 🍽 ☂ ℘ TV Clean, comfortable accommodation, but the modern, four-storey building has very little character. The rooms have hot running water.

Kim Du, 14 Phuong Thanh, ☎ (077) 85 19 29, Fax (077) 85 21 19 – 40rm ⌂ 🍽 ℘ TV ✗ This five-storey hotel (with lift) offers perfect rooms representing excellent value for money (satellite TV). Hopefully they won't increase their prices when they become better established. The larger rooms have hot running water and a balcony with a wonderful view over the bay. The staff speak English.

Hai Van, 646A Lam Son, on the corner of Cau Cau, ☎ (077) 85 28 72 – 25rm ⌂ 🍽 ☂ ℘ TV ✗ The rooms on the ground floor are cheap but rather gloomy, but the other more comfortable rooms are good value for money.

Khai Hoan, 4 Phuong Thanh, ☎ (077) 85 22 54 – 15rm ⌂ 🍽 ☂ ℘ TV This small establishment charges similar rates to its neighbour, the Kim Du, but for an inferior category of hotel. The rooms are basic, but pleasant.

• **Hon Chong**

Under US$10

Phung Tao, Binh An, ☎ (077) 85 43 57 – 15rm ⌂ ☂ ✗ ☼ Use this hotel only as a last resort, since the rooms, located either in little wooden huts or in the main building, have seen better days.

Between US$10 and US$15

Du Lich Cong Doan, Binh An, ☎ (077) 85 46 06 – 38rm ⌂ 🍽 ☂ TV ✗ ☼ This large hotel, a stone's throw from the beach, comprises two different buildings: the older of the two buildings has passed its sell-by date, but is cheap, while the other one offers spacious rooms with all the necessary facilities. The staff speak English.

Hon Trem, Binh An, ☎ and Fax (077) 85 43 31 – 17rm ⌂ 🍽 ℘ TV ✗ ☼ Quaint little wooden or brick-built bungalows scattered among the coconut trees on the edge of the beach. Basic, decent facilities and rates are very reasonable (satellite TV). English speaking staff. In short, a heavenly spot.

My Lan, Binh An, ☎ (077) 75 90 44, Fax (077) 75 90 40 – 18rm ⌂ 🍽 ☂ ℘ TV ✗ ☼ A new, private hotel quite close to the beach offering clean, faultless facilities (hot water, satellite TV). The rooms are identical, but prices increase if you use the air-conditioning. They speak English.

EATING OUT

Ha Tien boasts a wide choice of food, and caters for both seafood enthusiasts and lovers of Vietnamese cuisine. Try the local eating places near the market.

Between 25 000 and 50 000VND

Xuan Thanh, 20 Ben Tran Hau, opposite the covered market. This restaurant offers an interesting selection of seafood and local Vietnamese dishes. The menu is in English.

Between 50 000 and 100 000VND

Thuy Tien, aboard a boat moored on the river beyond the floating bridge on the way to town. ☲ 6am-10pm. Delightful restaurant with first-rate seafood.

COMING AND GOING

By plane –Rach Soi *airport*, 8km south of the city, serves Ho Chi Minh City (2hr 40min), via Phu Quoc (40min). Departures at 9.30am every Tuesday, Thursday, Friday and Sunday.

By bus – Ben Xe Rach Gia terminal, 30 Thang 4, not far from the post office, serves Ha Tien (4-5hr), and, in the evening, minibuses go to Ho Chi Minh City (5-6hr). The other terminal, **Ben Xe Rach Soi**, 8km on from Nguyen Trung Truc, near the airport, provides regular services to Ho Chi Minh City (6-7hr), Long Xuyen and Cantho (4hr).

By boat – See "Phu Quoc close up" page 406.

ADDRESS BOOK

Tourist information – Kien Giang Tourist, 12 Ly Tu Trong, ☎ (077) 86 20 81, Fax (077) 86 21 11. The English-speaking staff are very friendly and supply lots of information about the city and the different ways to get to Phu Quoc, but unfortunately provide very few services, except for the rental of chauffeur-driven cars.

Bank / Currency exchange – Vietcombank, 1 Huynh Man Dat, near the post office. Open Monday-Friday 7-11am / 1-4pm. Cash, travellers' cheques and Visa cards.

Post Office / Telephone – You can't miss this modern main post office building on Tu Duc, just after the bridge leading to the small island in the city centre. Open daily from 6.30am-10pm.

Airlines – Vietnam Airlines, 180 Nguyen Trung Truc, ☎ (077) 86 18 48. 7-11am / 1-5pm.

WHERE TO STAY

Under US$10

Thanh Binh, 11 Ly Tu Trong, ☎ (077) 86 30 53, Fax (077) 86 21 11 – 14rm ⌐ 🗙 ℘ A very cheap, no-fuss boarding house in a neo-colonial building just opposite the Tourist Office, a short walk from the city centre.

Thanh Binh II, 37 Hung Vuong, ☎ (077) 86 19 21 – 19rm ⌐ 🗏 Basic facilities and the toilets are upstairs, but who minds at this price.

Khach San 1.5, 16 Le Loi, ☎ (077) 86 37 18, Fax (077) 86 21 11 – 17rm ⌐ 🗏 🗙 ℘ 📺 🗙 The "1 May Hotel" offers undeniably tacky accommodation, but the rooms are nonetheless comfortable, although a little expensive for this category. Some have no windows.

Binh Minh, 44 Pham Hong Thai, ☎ (077) 86 21 54 – 19rm ⌐ 🗏 🗙 ℘ This four-storey hotel on the main square (rather noisy) offers no more than the basic facilities, but rates are very reasonable, especially for the rooms with air-conditioning and television.

Between US$10 and US$15

Thanh Mai, 260 Nguyen Trung Truc, ☎ (077) 86 38 57, Fax (077) 87 19 17 – 10rm ⌐ 🗏 🗙 ℘ 📺 Brand new, this is the best hotel in town, offering perfect accommodation and excellent value for money. Hopefully the prices won't increase too much (hot water, satellite TV to come).

Between US$15 and US$30

Cong Ty Tnhh Palace, 41 Tran Phu, ☎ (077) 86 30 49 – 20rm ⌐ 🗏 🗙 ℘ 📺 Clean, decent accommodation, but tasteless decor and quite expensive for this category.

Bank Hotel, 3 Nguyen Thi Hong Hanh, ☎ (077) 86 22 14, Fax (077) 86 72 04 – 27rm ⌐ 🗏 ℘ 📺 A friendly hotel with all the necessary facilities, but the downside is the big difference in rates charged for Vietnamese or foreign guests. Most rooms have hot water and satellite TV.

EATING OUT

Under 25 000VND

Ao Dai Moi, 26 Ly Tu Trong. A small, first-rate Vietnamese restaurant run by a Chinese. Breakfast is available, but sadly, it is closed in the evenings.

Hung Phat, 7 Nguyen Du, near the main square. 10am-9.30pm. This restaurant serves stylish, sophisticated, Vietnamese cuisine (frogs' legs, fish, hummingbird). Another restaurant has just opened at 357 Lam Quang Ky.

Between 50 000 and 100 000VND

Hai Au, 2 Nguyen Trung Truc. 🕭 A perfect riverside location just beyond the bridge with a delightful view. The menu is in English and includes delectable seafood dishes.

PHU QUOC ★★

Kien Giang Province
48km from Ha Tien and 120km from Rach Gia
Pop 55 000 – Sub-equatorial climate

Not to be missed
The beaches of Bai Truong and Bai Khem.
The northern forests.

And remember...
It is forbidden to take pictures on the northern beaches
near the Cambodian border.
Contact the hotels to find out which beaches need special authorisation.
From November to April, don't forget to book hotels in advance.

Anchored a few hundred metres off the Cambodian coast in the Gulf of Thailand is Phu Quoc, Vietnam's largest island (585km²), a miraculously well-preserved little Garden of Eden. It stretches for 45km from north to south, covered with wooded hills rising to 603m. The island's tremendous tourist potential of superb beaches and untouched forests has yet to be exploited despite local airport facilities and the construction of several hotels. Consequently, road communications are practically non-existent, except for a few tracks just about suitable for cars. Moreover, the large number of military bases in the area encourage little development in this direction. Poverty is widespread, particularly in the remote villages in the north where the surprise appearance of the odd tourist still arouses great curiosity. It is thus more than likely that this island will continue to rely more on fishing and the production of black pepper and nuoc-mam for its staple source of income than it will on tourism.

A refuge and a prison
Known as Kho Tral, the island belonged to the Khmer right up to the 18C, and Cambodia has never accepted Vietnam's appropriation of the island, a mere 15km from its coast. Phu Quoc's rather isolated location has often played an important role in the making of Vietnamese history. Indeed, it was here that Prince Nguyen Anh found refuge when he fled from the Tay Son uprising in the 1770s. His meeting with the French missionary Pigneau de Béhaine turned out to be crucial, since the latter strongly supported the Prince in his efforts to reclaim the throne, thus enabling the French to gain a foothold in Vietnam (*see page 23*). In the 1860s, Phu Quoc served as a refuge for the rebel Nguyen Trung Truc (*see "Rach Gia" page 389*), and later the island was useful to the Americans as a prison for captured Viet Cong during the Vietnam War.

A visit to Phu Quoc
Allow 2 days

For most visitors, the island's appeal lies less in its historical background than in its glorious sands and the soothing sound of the waves as you laze in the shade of its palm trees.

The West Coast★★
The island's biggest and most beautiful beach is accessible by boat from An Thoi and then along the track leading to Duong Dong. **Bai Truong★★★** is a spectacular expanse of white sand lined with coconut palms stretching for more than 30km. It is one of the only beaches in Vietnam where you can see the sun set over the sea. A handful of hotels have been built in the area, grouped together in the northern part near Duong Dong. It's a safe bet that the area won't resist the greedy appetites of property developers, who will soon find a way to convince the local fisherman to move.

Duong Dong is a large market town crisscrossed by streets of beaten earth. It is attractively situated astride the estuary of a small river forming a loop blocked by a sand-bank. At sunset, admire the fairy-tale image of the fleet of multicoloured **fishing boats** against a background of coconut palms and bamboo huts.

On the way into town from the south, turn left into Bach Dang towards the **Thien Hau Temple** dedicated to the Goddess of the Sea (not very interesting), and carry on to the end of the road. Standing on the top of a rocky promontory is a small **lighthouse** flanked by a temple affording a clear **view★** of the port. A tour around the rest of the town includes a trip to the **market** (*turn left after the bridge across the river*), where you may find yourself the centre of attention. If you don't like strong smells, don't bother with the town's other main attractions, its **nuoc-mam factories**, the most important of which, Hung Thanh, is on the outskirts.

The north of the island★

In theory, special authorisation is needed to enjoy these beaches, but ask at your hotel for further information. Jump on your moped and take the road heading north that soon becomes just a track disappearing into a magnificent **virgin forest★** of high trees echoing with birdsong. The road stops at **Ganh Dau★** (*40km*), a small fishing village nestling in a delightful **bay** at the northwestern tip of the island, where a string of colourful boats are moored. Out to sea is a series of little islands, seemingly within easy reach but in fact inaccessible because they are in Cambodia (*photography is strictly prohibited, at the risk of having your film confiscated*). Quench your thirst with a fresh coconut at the drinks stand at the end of the track, on the edge of a white, sandy **beach★★**. The obvious poverty of the local villagers contrasts sadly with this otherwise idyllic scene.

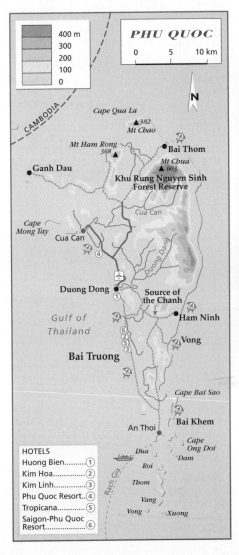

PHU QUOC

400 m
300
200
100
0

0   5   10 km

N

CAMBODIA

Cape Qua La

▲382
Mt Chao

Mt Ham Rong
368 ▲   ● Bai Thom

Ganh Dau   Mt Chua
▲603

Khu Rung Nguyen Sinh
Forest Reserve

Cua Can

Cape
Mong Tay
Cua Can   ④

Duong Dang

Duong Dong   Source of
①   the Chanh

Gulf of   ● Ham Ninh
Thailand

⑥   ● Vong
⑤
③

Bai Truong

Cape Bai Sao

Bai Khem

An Thoi   Cape
Ong Doi
Dua   Dam

HOTELS
Roi
Huong Bien..........①
Kim Hoa..............②   Thom
Kim Linh.............③
Phu Quoc Resort..④   Vang
Tropicana............⑤
Saigon-Phu Quoc   Vong   Xuong
Resort...................⑥

Rach Gia

The track leading to **Bai Thom** in the north of the island runs through the impressive **Khu Rung Nguyen Sinh Forest Reserve★**.

To the east

On arriving in Duong Dong from the south, take the first street to the right. After 1km, on the bend just before the bridge, take the track leading off to the right, and then continue for another 10km. Tucked away in the middle of the forest, the **source of the Chanh** is a delightful, shady torrent where young people and lovers come for a swim *(refreshments available and parking charge; don't forget your mosquito repellent)*. The track continues as far as the undeveloped but not particularly attractive **Ham Ninh** beach. Take the road leading southwards instead *(road surfacing in progress)*. Several paths lead to the beaches on the east coast. Try the beach at **Vong** if you're looking for somewhere really quiet. Further south, just before An Thoi, is **Bai Khem★★**, a beautiful white sandy beach open to visitors, despite being part of a military base.

Phu Quoc close up

COMING AND GOING

By air – The *airport* is situated to the north, on the outskirts of Duong Dong, ☎ (077) 84 60 86. Open daily from 7.30-11am / 2-4.30pm. Vietnam Airlines operates in both directions between Phu Quoc and Ho Chi Minh City every morning except for Saturday, as well as flying to Rach Gia every Tuesday, Thursday, Friday and Sunday. Book your seats as soon as possible, and don't forget the airport tax (10 000VND).

By boat – From Rach Gia, the *ferry* for An Thoi (8hr) leaves every morning at 9am from the landing stage situated at the end of Nguyen Cong Tru. Buy your ticket at the landing stage (58 500VND), if possible the day before, and check in 30min before departure. The crossing can be quite gruelling in rough seas (take along something to eat), but not half as gruelling as the actual disembarkation onto a rickety wooden pontoon. The whole town seems to be waiting to greet the arriving visitors, all doing their best to get a foot on solid ground. The boat leaves at 10am in the other direction. Foreigners are now able to take the ferry from Ha Tien to Ham Ninh, on the east coast of the island, but ask your hotel for further details.

By hydrofoil – The opening of a hydrofoil service with the mainland is supposedly imminent. Ask on the spot for further details.

GETTING AROUND

By minibus – A minibus service between An Thoi and Duong Dong operates in conjunction with the arrival of the ferry. It will stop at your hotel on request.

By motorcycle – An ideal way to visit the island. You will be plagued with motorcycle taxis in An Thoi. The ride down the track leading to Duong Dong and Bai Truong (45min) with a pack on your back might just be the final straw, especially after such a gruelling boat trip, but it's worth it for the breathtaking countryside! Motorcycles can easily be rented at the hotels.

ADDRESS BOOK

Bank / Currency exchange – The bank at Duong Dong accepts foreign currency, but the Tropicana Hotel will also change money. It is advisable, however, to bring some dongs with you, since exchange rates are not as advantageous as on the mainland.

Post Office / Telephone – *Buu Dien Duong Dong*, on 30 Thang 4, near the bank, left at the crossroads on the way from Bai Truong.

WHERE TO STAY, EATING OUT
Between US$10 and US$15
Kim Hoa, Bai Truong, 7km south of Duong Dong, ☎ (077) 84 70 39, Fax (077) 84 61 44 – 17rm 🖼 🖭 🌂 📺 ✕ 🐾 Tucked away by the beach, this hotel has very ordinary rooms and chalets, but the facilities are quite decent with good value for money. The service is a little overpowering, but try and negotiate a reduction during low season. The staff speak English.
Kim Linh, 7km south of Duong Dong, ☎ (077) 84 66 11 🖼 🖭 🌂 🐾 ✕ 🌂 The forerunner of all the hotels in Bai Truong is now in need of a fresh coat of paint. It is still a good place for those on a tight budget.

Huong Bien, Duong Dong, on the beach, 200m south of the lighthouse, ☎ (077) 84 61 13, Fax (077) 84 70 65 – 60rm ⌂ 🗏 ⌗ ✕ 🛱 This huge, state-run hotel attracts a Vietnamese clientele, tends to be noisy, and the beach is not as enticing as at Bai Truong. The better-equipped rooms with air-conditioning, hot running water and satellite TV are twice the price of the more basic rooms located in the annex.

Phu Quoc Resort, Thang Loi, 6km north of Duong Dong along the coastal road, ☎ (091) 919 891, Fax (077) 84 61 44 – 20rm ⌂ ✕ 🛱 Very pleasant little bamboo chalets on the beach.

Between US$15 and US$30

🅰**Tropicana**, Bai Truong, 7km south of Duong Dong, ☎ (077) 84 71 27, Fax (077) 84 71 28 – 15rm ⌂ 🗏 ⌗ ✕ 🛱 cc A warm welcome in heavenly surroundings. This hotel offers the most attractive accommodation on the island in comfortable chalets next to the beach. The better equipped rooms are double the basic price, but ask for a reduction during the low season. The restaurant overlooks the sea and serves succulent seafood dishes specially prepared by the proprietor. Mopeds and snorkels are available for hire.

Between US$30 and US$50

Saigon-Phu Quoc Resort, Bai Truong, 6km south of Duong Dong, ☎ (077) 84 69 99, Fax (077) 84 71 63 – 30rm ⌂ 🗏 ♪ tv ✕ ⌗ 🛱 cc Perfect chalet accommodation (hot water, satellite TV), but lacking in character. Prices vary considerably according to the view. The English-speaking staff offer a variety of different services (island tours, trips out to sea, cars, mopeds and snorkels for hire). The restaurant serves excellent seafood.

OTHER THINGS TO DO

Excursions – The most economical way to tour the tiny An Thoi Islands is to charter a boat from the landing stage. A simpler solution, although more expensive, would be to go through the Tropicana Hotel or the Saigon-Phu Quoc Resort, who both organise fishing or diving excursions.

SHOPPING

Pearls – Phu Quoc Pearls, Bai Truong, in between Duong Dong and An Thoi, ☎ (091) 99 32 02. This Australian-Vietnamese joint-venture sells cultured pearls at very reasonable prices.

Phu Quoc close up

Sea, sand and sun...

G Guérard

INDEX

Hanoi: curiosity, site with description
Ho Chi Minh: person
Buddhism: term, practical information with description

o Chi Minh City Bus Station

S. Favre/MICHELIN

Maps and Plans

Manufacture Française des Pneumatiques Michelin

Société en commandite par actions au capital de 304 000 000 EUR
Place des Carmes-Déchaux – 63000 Clermont-Ferrand (France)
R.C.S. Clermont-Fd B 855 200 507

© Michelin et Cie, Propriétaires-éditeurs, 2002
Dépôt légal février 2002 – ISBN 2-06-100060-6– ISSN 0763-1383
No part of this publication may be reproduced in any form without
the prior permission of the publisher.

Printed in France 02/02/1.1
Typesetting: Nord Compo – Villeneuve d'Ascq
Printing: IME – Baume-les-Dames

Cover photography:
Working in the rice paddies (B. Brillion/MICHELIN)
Young girl (B. Pérousse/MICHELIN)
Thien Hau Pagoda, Cholon (J. Brun/EXPLORER-HOA QUI)

Please send us your comments and suggestions to help us improve this guide.

Michelin Travel Publications   or   **Michelin Travel Publications**
Hannay House   PO Box 19008
39 Clarendon Road   Greenville
Watford, WD17 1JA   SC 29302-9008
UK   USA

neos@uk.michelin.com

Tell us of your experiences. You may have come across a restaurant or hotel that we haven't mentioned, or a pretty village that we haven't pointed out. Please let us know. Please also indicate any out-of-date information.

■ **Have you bought any other NEOS guides?**

   Yes ☐   No ☐

■ **If so, which title(s)?**

_____

_____

■ **What made you choose this guide?**

	(1 = not important)		*(4 = very important)*	
Cover and layout	☐ 1	☐ 2	☐ 3	☐ 4
Practical information	☐ 1	☐ 2	☐ 3	☐ 4
Information on culture	☐ 1	☐ 2	☐ 3	☐ 4
Contact details for hotels and restaurants	☐ 1	☐ 2	☐ 3	☐ 4
Maps and plans	☐ 1	☐ 2	☐ 3	☐ 4
The Michelin brand	☐ 1	☐ 2	☐ 3	☐ 4
Brand loyalty	☐ 1	☐ 2	☐ 3	☐ 4

■ **How would you rate the following aspects of your NEOS guide?**

	(1 = poor)		*(4 = excellent)*	
Cover design	☐ 1	☐ 2	☐ 3	☐ 4
Illustrations	☐ 1	☐ 2	☐ 3	☐ 4
Information on culture	☐ 1	☐ 2	☐ 3	☐ 4
The "Meeting the people" chapter	☐ 1	☐ 2	☐ 3	☐ 4
The choice of places covered	☐ 1	☐ 2	☐ 3	☐ 4
Touring programmes	☐ 1	☐ 2	☐ 3	☐ 4
Site descriptions (eg style, length, descriptions)	☐ 1	☐ 2	☐ 3	☐ 4
Practical information (eg transport, useful addresses)	☐ 1	☐ 2	☐ 3	☐ 4
Accommodation suggestions	☐ 1	☐ 2	☐ 3	☐ 4
Maps and plans	☐ 1	☐ 2	☐ 3	☐ 4

Comments _____

_____

_____

■ **How often did you use the following chapters?**

	(1 = never)		*(4 = often)*	
Setting the scene (red border)	☐ 1	☐ 2	☐ 3	☐ 4
Meeting the people (green border)	☐ 1	☐ 2	☐ 3	☐ 4
Practical information (orange border)	☐ 1	☐ 2	☐ 3	☐ 4
Exploring… (blue border)	☐ 1	☐ 2	☐ 3	☐ 4

Comments _____

_____

_____

■ **Were there enough contact addresses?**

	Not enough	*Enough*	*Too many*
Hotels	☐	☐	☐
Restaurants	☐	☐	☐

Comments _____

_____

_____

■ **How many marks out of 10 would you give your NEOS guide?**
(1 = poor; 10 = excellent)
_____/10

■ **Which other destinations would you like to see covered by the NEOS collection?**

_____

_____

_____

■ **Personal details**

Male ☐   Female ☐

Age: under 24 ☐   25-34 ☐   35-49 ☐   50-64 ☐   over 65 ☐

Name: _____

Address: _____

_____

_____

This information is for the sole use of Michelin Travel Publications.

416